Exploring the Northeast States through Literature

Exploring the United States through Literature Series

Kathy Howard Latrobe, Series Editor

Exploring the Northeast States through Literature
Edited by P. Diane Frey

Exploring the Southeast States through Literature
Edited by Linda Veltze

Exploring the Great Lakes States through Literature
Edited by Kathy Howard Latrobe

Exploring the Plains States through Literature
Edited by Carolyn S. Brodie

Exploring the Southwest States through Literature
Edited by Pat Tipton Sharp

Exploring the Mountain States through Literature
Edited by Sharyl G. Smith

Exploring the Pacific States through Literature
Edited by Carol A. Doll

Exploring the Northeast States through Literature

Edited by P. Diane Frey

State Editors
Judith W. Whitcomb, Connecticut
Sharon Brubaker, Delaware
Bester Bonner, District of Columbia
Gene Moll, Maine
Paula Montgomery, Maryland
Richard A. Neubauer, Massachusetts
Linda Mack, New Hampshire
Amy G. Job, New Jersey
Mary R. Lenart, New York
Margaret Jetter, Pennsylvania
Gloria Schmidt, Rhode Island
Helene W. Lang, Vermont

Exploring the United States through Literature Series
Kathy Howard Latrobe, Series Editor

Oryx Press
1994

The rare Arabian Oryx is believed to have inspired the myth of the unicorn. This desert antelope became virtually extinct in the early 1960s. At that time several groups of international conservationists arranged to have 9 animals sent to the Phoenix Zoo to be the nucleus of a captive breeding herd. Today the Oryx population is over 800 and nearly 400 have been returned to reserves in the Middle East.

© 1994 by The Oryx Press
4041 North Central at Indian School Road
Phoenix, Arizona 85012-3397

All rights reserved. No part of this publication may be reproduced or transmitted in any form or by any means, electronic or mechanical, including photocopying, recording, or by any information storage and retrieval system, without permission in writing from The Oryx Press.

Published simultaneously in Canada
Printed and Bound in the United States of America

The paper used in this publication meets the minimum requirements of American National Standard for Information Science—Permanence of Paper for Printed Library Materials, ANSI Z39.48, 1984.

Library of Congress Cataloging-in-Publication Data

Exploring the Northeast states through literature / edited by P. Diane Frey: state editors, Judith W. Whitcomb, Connecticut . . . [et al.].
   p. cm. — (Exploring the United States through literature series)
Includes bibliographical references and indexes.
ISBN 0-89774-779-8
   1. Northeastern States—Juvenile literature—Bibliography.
I. Frey, P. Diane. II. Series.
Z1251.N67E97 1994
[F4.3]
016.974—dc20   94-28270
                                                                                     CIP

Contents

Series Statement vii

Preface ix

Contributors xiii

Connecticut 1
    by Judith W. Whitcomb

Delaware 19
    by Sharon Brubaker

District of Columbia 26
    by Bester Bonner

Maine 49
    by Gene Moll

Maryland 66
    by Paula Montgomery

Massachusetts 84
    by Richard A. Neubauer

New Hampshire 100
    by Linda Mack

New Jersey 114
    by Amy G. Job

New York 132
    by Mary R. Lenart

Pennsylvania 154
    by Margaret Jetter

Rhode Island 184
    by Gloria Schmidt

Vermont 200
    by Helene W. Lang

Directory of Publishers and Vendors 215

Author Index 231

Title Index 237

Subject Index 251

Series Statement

The *Exploring the United States through Literature Series* comprises seven annotated regional resource guides to selected print and nonprint materials for grades K-8. Each regional resource is divided into state sections identifying materials that relate to the history, culture, geography, resources, industries, literature and lore, and famous figures of the states in the region. The seven volumes cover the following regions and states:

- *Exploring the Northeast States through Literature:* Connecticut, Delaware, District of Columbia, Maine, Maryland, Massachusetts, New Hampshire, New Jersey, New York, Pennsylvania, Rhode Island, Vermont
- *Exploring the Southeast States through Literature:* Alabama, Arkansas, Florida, Georgia, Kentucky, Louisiana, Mississippi, North Carolina, South Carolina, Tennessee, Virginia, West Virginia
- *Exploring the Great Lakes States through Literature:* Illinois, Indiana, Michigan, Minnesota, Ohio, Wisconsin
- *Exploring the Plains States through Literature:* Iowa, Kansas, Missouri, Nebraska, North Dakota, South Dakota
- *Exploring the Southwest States through Literature:* Arizona, New Mexico, Oklahoma, Texas
- *Exploring the Mountain States through Literature:* Colorado, Idaho, Montana, Nevada, Utah, Wyoming
- *Exploring the Pacific States through Literature:* Alaska, California, Hawaii, Oregon, Washington

The materials included in these resource guides were selected because they can be used by teachers and librarians to enrich young people's understanding of the histories and contemporary cultures of the 50 states, and because they are suitable for use with young people from any of the regional or ethnic groups of the contemporary United States. Each annotation includes a brief description of the particular work and at least one learning activity compatible with the identified interest level of the resource.

Purpose

The *Exploring the United States through Literature Series* offers teachers, school library media specialists, and public librarians valuable assistance in resource selection and user guidance. The suggested activities demonstrate each title's potential for involving young people in creative thinking and problem-solving and for inspiring teachers and librarians to invent other imaginative uses for the title. The series can also be used effectively by school library media specialists and teachers as they work together to develop curricular units and plan learning experiences about the geographic regions of the United States or about specific states. Reading, language arts, and social studies teachers will find the series particularly useful.

The series addresses needs created by the following recent and important educational trends:

1. The whole language approach to learning, especially the integration of literature, the arts, and social studies curricula
2. Rapidly changing social environments that demand flexible curricula and multiple learning resources
3. Multicultural education with an emphasis on multicultural diversity and a recognition of the importance of encouraging young people to accept and appreciate diversity
4. The position of the Curriculum Task Force of the National Commission on Social Studies (NCSS) that the social studies curriculum should include both breadth and depth

The NCSS emphasizes the discovery approach to learning and maintains that young people should develop an overview as well as immerse themselves in the details of history and social studies.

Scope

Each regional editor coordinated the contributions of state editors who brought to the series a familiarity with and understanding of the notable and special features of their states and regions. The state editors used their own judgment in selecting materials that could most effectively assist young people in learning and understanding the many dimensions of each state. The editors' goal was not to include a predetermined number of entries, but rather to select pertinent items of merit. Because there are similarities across the regions, a few titles appear in more than one state bibliography. These duplicate entries serve to reinforce students' experiences with the region or to take the title in a new direction with a different activity. Also, some books listed under only one state may be appropriate for other states as well.

Each state editor valued diversity—in subject matter, in time period, and in media. The editors sought to capture the past and present of each state by including not only books, but also such items as periodicals, computer programs, sound recordings, and videocassettes. A major goal of the series is to bring alive to young people each state's sights, sounds, tastes, music, stories and legends, natural environment, and people.

Activities

The state editors, who are professionally involved either directly or indirectly with the education of young people, have devised learning activities that can appropriately extend the work being described. Denoted by a diamond (♦) in each entry, the activities are designed to enhance young people's understanding of each state and to encourage further exploration of the topic at hand. The activities relate the work to young people themselves, to specific geographic areas, to associated disciplines and subjects, or to broader concepts within social studies.

Sources of Materials

Because of the diversity and regional or state focus of materials, no single jobber can deliver all the included items upon request. Therefore, a "Directory of Publishers and Vendors," including specialized sources for state and regional materials, has been included in each volume. The agencies and departments of state and local governments, state and local historical societies, and other state and local organizations are also excellent sources of informational materials.

Organization

Each volume is organized first by the states within the region (arranged alphabetically). Each state section is then subdivided into Nonfiction (by Dewey Classification), Biography (collective biography, then individual biography, alphabetically by subject), Periodicals, and Professional Materials (by Dewey Classification). Reference works listed in the Nonfiction section are identified immediately following the Dewey number.

Most bibliographic entries identify Dewey Classification number, author, title, publisher or producer, ISBN or ISSN, date of publication or release, number of pages, black-and-white or color illustrations, cost of nonprint materials, any special purchasing information, and running time and format specifications for nonprint items. No ISBNs were available for some out-of-print and older titles. Each entry also includes an interest level designation and relevant subject headings, which have been based on the *Sears List of Subject Headings* and the Library of Congress Subject Headings.

Three indexes provide access by author, title, and subject. The state-by-state division within the book allows teachers and librarians to access materials by state, and the Subject Index provides access to materials appropriate to more than one state and to topics with regional significance.

The Dewey Decimal Classification numbers, while appropriate for each volume's organization, are not offered as recommendations for cataloging/classification purposes. Many items are open to classification in more than one area.

—Kathy Howard Latrobe
Series Editor

Preface

Exploring the Northeast States through Literature is one of seven regional annotated bibliographies of print and nonprint materials for young people in grades K-8. The resources included in this volume give young people a better understanding of the history, development, and contemporary cultures of Connecticut, Delaware, District of Columbia, Maine, Maryland, Massachusetts, New Hampshire, New Jersey, New York, Pennsylvania, Rhode Island, and Vermont. This volume can function as a selection tool, a resource for teachers and media specialists who are preparing literature-based curricular units, and a guide for young people who are studying and researching geographic regions or specific states.

A recurring theme throughout the literature of the Northeast states is their rich history. Many of these states were part of the 13 original colonies and contributed heavily to the development of the United States. From Paul Revere's famous ride to the Liberty Bell to the Statue of Liberty to the battlefields of Gettysburg, these states have many historical attractions.

Connecticut

American history is deeply rooted in Connecticut, one of the oldest of the 50 states, and the many Connecticut entries reflect these historical roots. Known as the Constitution State because of its adoption of what is thought to be the first written constitution, Connecticut provides a blend of the very old and the very new.

Connecticut also claims many famous persons in American history, including Mark Twain, Noah Webster, Eli Whitney, and Harriet Beecher Stowe. Biographical entries focus on their contributions to American life.

Also emphasized in the Connecticut section are natural resources. Materials focus on nature hikes, marine life, plants and animals, and natural disasters.

Delaware

Delaware is the second smallest state in the United States but the first state to approve the U.S. Constitution. Historical entries describe Delaware from its colonial period to contemporary times. Many entries focus on the Lenape, the first inhabitants of Delaware.

Delaware lies along the Atlantic coastline, and the Delaware River plays a major role in the state's economy. Other topics covered in the Delaware section are scenic Delaware, transportation, and the Cape May-Lewes Ferry.

District of Columbia

The District of Columbia, which lies on the northern bank of the Potomac River, is one of the few national capitals founded solely to serve as a nation's seat of government. The government is by far Washington's biggest industry and dominates the economic and social life of the city.

Tourism, also an important part of Washington's economy, is virtually a year-round activity. People come to see the splendor of the cherry blossoms in the spring; the extraordinary art treasures; the Lincoln, Washington, and Jefferson Memorials; the Vietnam Veterans Memorial; and the Smithsonian Institution. Washington, DC, is truly a repository of America's cultural and historical heritage.

People of every ethnic background and national origin live in Washington, providing rich and varied cultural experiences. This cultural diversity is well represented in the Washington materials.

Maine

Maine, largest of the New England states, is best known for its beautiful shoreline, lighthouses, sandy beaches, and quiet fishing villages.

Maine's scenic, rugged shoreline and natural resources attract thousands of visitors each year.

Entries describe important Maine industries, such as the fishing industry, including lobstering, and the logging industry. Other entries focus on Maine's history, from colonial times through the Revolutionary War, statehood, economic growth, and Civil War to modern times.

Two very popular authors, Barbara Cooney and Robert McCloskey, also hail from the state of Maine.

Maryland

The Chesapeake Bay is a major focus of the Maryland entries, because the bay provides jobs, food, and recreation to thousands of people. Entries cover the natural resources, ecology, weather, flora and fauna, and marine life of the bay, as well as the fishing industry. The Assateague Island National Seashore is also described, with special emphasis on the ponies of Assateague.

Baltimore, one of Maryland's major cities and one of the world's largest port cities, is the subject of many entries in the Maryland section. Baltimore has a major impact on Maryland's economy and supports a national baseball team. Babe Ruth grew up in Baltimore.

Historical entries describe the development of Maryland from colonial times to the present. The story of the "Star Spangled Banner"; the city of Annapolis and its role in the history of Maryland; and famous historical and contemporary figures of Maryland, including Clara Barton, Frederick Douglass, Harriet Tubman, John Paul Jones, Thurgood Marshall, and Jim Henson, are some of the topics covered.

Massachusetts

Massachusetts was the scene of more famous historical events than any other state in the nation. Readers get a sense of the historical significance of Massachusetts as the entries take them from famous battles of the American Revolution to Paul Revere's ride, the Boston Tea Party, Lexington and Concord, and the first Thanksgiving. Biographical entries share the lives of famous historical figures such as Anne Hutchinson, John Adams, Pocahontas, John Hancock, and John F. Kennedy.

Boston plays a prominent role in these historical events. Several entries reference resources that explore the city of Boston, describing its history, present-day neighborhoods and attractions, and culture.

Other entries encourage readers to explore the entire state of Massachusetts—mountains, coasts, farms, cities, and towns—all the areas that make Massachusetts unique.

New Hampshire

Through the New Hampshire entries, readers can trace the history of the state, including Native American settlements, colonization, and statehood. Materials referenced present a complete and informative account of the people, places, and events that have influenced the state's development.

The unique character and spirit of the people of New Hampshire, including the Shakers, are also reflected. Robert Frost, one of New Hampshire's well-known poets; Tasha Tudor, a beloved illustrator of children's books; and Christa McAuliffe, the first teacher in space, are just three examples of the character of New Hampshire's people.

The famous White Mountains of New Hampshire, covered bridges, museums, and historic houses are some of the other topics explored in this section.

New Jersey

New Jersey lies between the Hudson and Delaware Rivers and between New York City and Philadelphia—a location that gives it great economic importance. New Jersey also played an important role in U.S. history. Both of these characteristics are reflected in the literature of the state. Entries introduce the geography, history, government, economy, culture, and historic attractions of New Jersey and paint a portrait of the richness and diversity of its land and people.

Famous people of New Jersey are highlighted, including Thomas Alva Edison, Grover Cleveland, Alexander Hamilton, Aaron Burr, Henry Hudson, Woodrow Wilson, Dorothea Dix, Samuel Morse, and Bruce Springsteen.

New York

Approximately one-third of all the battles of the Revolutionary War were fought in New York, a fact well represented in the historical literature.

Materials in the New York section also document the history of New York from its beginning as an Indian territory to statehood.

Entries also focus on contemporary New York City, the largest city in the United States and a leading center of banking, communications, and finance. The materials provide a comprehensive guide to museums, collections, exhibitions, and places of interest for kids.

Pennsylvania

Pennsylvania is ranked as one of the nation's most historic states, and this history is reflected in the rich and varied literature on the state. Entries illustrate the key role Pennsylvania played in the development of our country, which earned it the nickname the Keystone State. Historical tourist attractions covered in this section include the battlefields of Gettysburg, Valley Forge, Benjamin Franklin's birthplace, Betsy Ross's house, and the Liberty Bell.

In addition, Pennsylvania is well known for its peoples, including the Pennsylvania Dutch, Amish, and Mennonite populations. The literature presents a history of these peoples, along with an overview of their traditions, principles, and culture, including their lifestyles, ceremonies, community, and family life. Biographical materials introduce many well-known personalities from Pennsylvania, such as Andrew Wyeth, Bill Cosby, and Milton Hershey.

Some other Pennsylvania highlights covered in this bibliography are the steel and oil industries; "Falling Water," a house designed by Frank Lloyd Wright; and the world's largest chocolate and confectionery factory, located in Hershey, Pennsylvania.

Rhode Island

Rhode Island, the smallest state in the United States, lies on the beautiful Narragansett Bay. The history and ecology of the bay, as well as its recreational uses, are topics covered in this section.

Many materials focus on the cultural diversity of present-day Rhode Island. Entries include resources that describe Rhode Island's Native American heritage, as well as the Italians, French, Portuguese, Irish, Jews, and Southeast Asians in the state.

Rhode Island's natural resources, such as its beaches and coastal regions and hiking and walking trails, are emphasized. The 24 current lighthouses in the state are also described in several materials.

Vermont

Nature is a recurring theme in the Vermont section. Entries describe the famous Green Mountains, which run the entire length of central Vermont; animal tracks and tracking; special animal locations; and famous hiking trails.

A second theme in this section is country life and country ways. The passing of family farms from generation to generation is emphasized, along with the lifestyle, traditions, and cultural heritage of Vermonters.

Contributors

Regional Editor

P. Diane Frey is program coordinator for Technology and Library Media Services for the School District of Lancaster in Pennsylvania. She is the author of various journal articles and a contributing author to *Multicultural Aspects of Library Media Programs*. Dr. Frey has given presentations at various workshops and conferences and works as a consultant to school districts.

State Editors

Bester Bonner is director of the Library and Media Services Unit of the District of Columbia Public Schools in Washington, DC. She is a contributing author to *The Developing Black Family*.

Sharon Brubaker is a freelance writer and a school and community college librarian in Newark, Delaware, and North East, Maryland.

Margaret Jetter is an associate professor in the Department of Library Science at Clarion University of Pennsylvania. Dr. Jetter teaches courses at the undergraduate and graduate levels in children's and young adult literature.

Amy G. Job is a librarian and instructor at William Paterson College in Wayne, New Jersey. Dr. Job is the coauthor of *From Cape to Point: New Jersey—A Selected Bibliography* and the forthcoming *Reference Work in School Library Media Centers*.

Helene W. Lang is an associate professor at the University of Vermont. Dr. Lang has served as a visiting professor in Scotland, England, and Canada and has provided consulting services and presentations to various institutions and organizations.

Mary R. Lenart is a junior-senior high school library media specialist at Clymer Central School, Clymer, New York.

Linda Mack, who was a classroom teacher for 15 years, now serves as media generalist at the primary level for the Goffstown, New Hampshire, school district. She provides library and audiovisual services to staff members and students in preschool through grade three at Bartlett Elementary School and Maple Avenue School.

Gene Moll, a reading consultant at the Presumpscot Elementary School in Portland, Maine, has also been a special education teacher and an elementary school principal. A specialist in children's literature, Ms. Moll is a coauthor of the revised language arts and reading handbook and of the new spelling handbook for the Portland schools, grades K-8.

Paula Montgomery is publisher of *School Library Media Activities Monthly;* author of *Approaches to Literature through Theme* (Oryx, 1992) and *Approaches to Literature through Subject* (Oryx, 1993); and former chief, School Library Media Services, Maryland State Department of Education, Baltimore, Maryland.

Richard A. Neubauer is a library science educator and coordinator of the Library Media Program at Bridgewater State College in Bridgewater, Massachusetts.

Gloria Schmidt is a library media specialist in Portsmouth, Rhode Island. Her longtime interest in Rhode Island history was sparked by a research project on colonial Newport while she was pursuing a Master of Arts in Teaching Social Studies degree from Brown University.

Judith W. Whitcomb is a library media specialist and a former public school administrator and faculty member of Southern Connecticut State University. Presently, she is an educational consultant and serves on a number of Connecticut state educational committees.

Connecticut

by Judith W. Whitcomb

Nonfiction

133.4
Taylor, John. *The Witchcraft Delusion in Colonial Connecticut, 1640-1747.* Corner House Publishers (287928-053-0), 1974. 172p. B/W illus. (Interest level: grade 7-adult).

Originally published in 1908 and retaining the language and spelling of colonial times, Taylor's work cites some Connecticut witchcraft trials and includes grounds for examination of a witch. New Haven, along with Salem, Massachusetts, had its share of witchcraft trials and the actual accounts are fascinating, if difficult, reading.
♦ With the teacher's help, students may read the grounds for examination of a witch. A trial reenactment may be followed by a discussion of how and why witch trials happened.
1. Connecticut—History   2. Witchcraft.

353.9 (Reference)
Connecticut State Register and Manual. Secretary of the State (No ISBN), 1993. 892p. B/W and Color illus. (Interest level: grade 6-adult).

Every year the secretary of the state publishes the register, which is mandated by the general statutes. Historical documents, biographies with photos, lists of committee members, local government and political information, and the organization of the judicial system are included.
♦ Using the manual, young people may find the names of their representatives in local, state, and federal government. They may then write to a politician on the appropriate committee to express their views on a controversial subject.
1. Connecticut—Directories   2. Connecticut—Registers   3. Connecticut—Politics and government.

359.96
Stephen, R. J. *Picture Book of Submarines.* Franklin Watts (0-531-14011-3), 1990. 29p. Color photos. (Interest level: 3-7).

Primarily a collection of photos, Stephen's book has clear explanations and a short history of submarines, including the first submarine, which was built in Connecticut, and the nuclear submarines still built there. Large and clear pictures are complemented by a glossary and a fact page.
♦ Readers may compare and contrast size, cost, use, and construction of David Bushnell's first submarine with submarines in use today.
1. Submarine boats   2. Submarine warfare.

361.9746 (Reference)
A Changing Connecticut. United Way of Connecticut (No ISBN), 1992. 71p. B/W illus. (Interest level: grade 4-adult).

The rapidity of change in the United States and the world has affected Connecticut in many social and economic ways. The United Way has produced this environmental scan, which includes statistics and charts as well as an excellent summary of trends, as a guide to institutions. The book will also serve admirably as a current affairs awareness manual for a wider audience.
♦ Students may choose one of the current problems discussed and make a scrapbook of related articles from newspapers and periodicals.
1. Connecticut—Politics and government   2. Social services—Connecticut.

363.69 (Reference)
Cunningham, Janice. *Historic Preservation in Connecticut.* Connecticut Historical Commission (No ISBN), 1992. 58p. B/W photos and maps. (Interest level: grade 6-adult).

Because Connecticut is one of the oldest settled areas in the United States, the Connecticut Historical Commission is publishing by geographic area six planning documents to help the state preserve its historic resources. This volume, the first in the series, contains a historical and architectural overview and a management guide listing the criteria for historic places.
♦ If students live in an area for which a guide has been published, they may investigate the places listed as historic for their town. If not, using the management matrix, readers can list the requirements to select sites they think should be historic. They may forward their choices and rationale to the commission.
1. Connecticut—History.

363.7289 (Reference)
Low-Level Radioactive Waste Management Plan, 1993. Connecticut Waste Management Service (No ISBN), 1993. 56p. B/W illus. (Interest level: grade 7-adult).

Connecticut is embroiled in dispute over transportation of radioactive wastes and waste disposal sites. Although the plan is technical and unreadable in its entirety by seventh and eighth graders, they would understand enough parts to form a basic understanding that they could enhance with further investigations.
♦ After perusing the plan and defining in class what the federal government considers low-level radioactive wastes and what the federal restrictions are, young people may pursue newspaper reports on hearings on disposal sites. They might choose sites of their own and defend their choices.
1. Radioactive waste disposal—Connecticut 2. Radioactive waste sites—Connecticut.

381.109
VanRynbach, Iris. *Everything from a Nail to a Coffin.* Orchard Books (0-531-05941-3), 1991. Unpaginated. Color illus. (Interest level: K-adult).

As the author traces the history from 1874 to the present of one building on Main Street in Glastonbury, Connecticut, she also traces the life of the town and its people. The full-page, sometimes double-page, watercolor illustrations are packed with interesting details, which help make this unusual book appeal to every age group.
♦ Children may do some historical digging in their own towns to trace the history of an old commercial building.
1. Stores—Retail—Connecticut—Glastonbury—History 2. Glastonbury (Conn.)—Social life and customs.

385.09
Turner, Gregg M. and **Jacobus, Melanchthon W.** *Connecticut Railroads: An Illustrated History.* Connecticut Historical Society (0-940748-89-4), 1986. 317p. B/W photos and maps. (Interest level: grade 4-adult).

This fascinating pictorial history of the heyday of the New York New Haven and Hartford Railroad, the Air Line, and a multitude of reproductions of smaller railroads is well done. Included are timetables, reproductions of disasters, railway maps, rail distances, and reprints of posters.
♦ Young people could devise an advertisement to attract riders from Hartford to New York in 1890. They also might compare the facilities available, train frequency, and commuting times from New Haven to Hartford now and in the past.
1. Railroads—History 2. Connecticut—Transportation—History.

398.2
Beck, Horace. *Folklore and the Sea.* Mystic Seaport Museum (0-913372-36-6), 1973. 463p. B/W illus. (Interest level: grade 7-adult).

The true and apocryphal stories included here are short and often humorous. Those stories specific to Connecticut can be identified through the index. Sea shanties are included with music as well as words.
♦ Teacher guidance is suggested as there is some rather salty language included. Students could learn some of the sea shanties and perform them for the class.
1. Ocean—Folklore 2. Seafaring life—Folklore.

398.2
Philips, David E. *Legendary Connecticut.* Curbstone Press (1-880684-05-5), 1992. 302p. B/W illus. (Interest level: grade 4-adult).

Divided into personal, local, supernatural, and colonial legends about Native Americans, this hefty volume recounts many old stories about specific places in Connecticut. The legends, which are short in most cases, are simply told by a gifted storyteller and will hold the interest of readers of all ages.
♦ Readers may find legends about a particular part of their state, pinpoint the location on the map, and retell them to classmates in a storytelling time.
1. Legends—Connecticut 2. Tales—Connecticut.

398.208
Martin, Rafe. *The Rough-Face Girl.* Illus. by David Shannon. Putnam (0-399-21859-9), 1992. Unpaginated. Color illus. (Interest level: grade 2-adult).

This beautifully illustrated story of the burn-scarred maiden who alone sees the Invisible One and so can marry him is the Algonquin version of Cinderella. Although the story takes place on the shore of Lake Ontario, the Algonquins also inhabited Connecticut; the story relates to the heritage of the Connecticut Algonquins as well.

♦ Younger students may discuss why the Invisible One thought the rough-faced girl was beautiful. Older students may develop theories regarding why so many different cultures produce similar legends.
1. Algonquin Indians—Legends   2. Native Americans—Legends.

550.916
Bell, Michael. *The Face of Connecticut: The People, Geology and the Land.* State Geological and Natural History Survey of Connecticut (No ISBN), 1985. 196p. B/W and Color photos. (Interest level: grade 6-adult).

Divided into two sections, landscapes and geology, the book explores the connection between Connecticut's people and its bedrock, soil, water, and landscape. The first part concentrates on the history of the land and how lives are affected by land resources today. The second part recounts Connecticut's geologic history and how it was pieced together.
♦ Using the public library historical collection, young people can research how the land in their town was used by previous generations and compare how the same land is used today.
1. Geology—Connecticut   2. Connecticut—Geology.

551.46
Kingsley, Gretchen H. *Links of Life: The Housatonic and You.* Schooner (No ISBN), 1992. 53p. B/W illus. (Interest level: 5-8).

This handy little paperback is a discovery curriculum divided into two sections: physical resources and energy for life. The history and the physical and biological aspects of Long Island Sound are examined in experiments loosely constructed to encourage individualized exploration by students.
♦ Children may investigate the sewage disposal of their own town or a nearby shore town and how the sewage treatment plant impacts the Sound.
1. Aquatic biology   2. Ecology—Connecticut—Long Island Sound.

551.46
McArdie, Dana. *Project Soundwise.* Schooner (No ISBN), 1992. 60p. B/W illus. (Interest level: K-4).

McArdie's curriculum guide to 26 projects for teachers and students covers physical oceanography, ecology, and the biology of the Long Island Sound. The sections on human issues in Long Island Sound and the follow-up projects are particularly useful.
♦ All 26 projects are activities. An interesting one that might appeal to a whole school is the trash analysis project.

1. Aquatic biology   2. Ecology—Connecticut—Long Island Sound.

551.46 (Reference)
Weiss, Howard M. and Dorsey, Michael W. *Investigating the Marine Environment: A Sourcebook. Vol. 1: Field Studies.* Project Oceanology (No ISBN), 1979. 318p. B/W illus. and photos. (Interest level: grade 3-adult).

Weiss and Dorsey's soft-covered manual contains field-oriented studies and procedures for studying the natural marine environment, fisheries, resources, pollution, and history of the waters off Connecticut. The detailed guide teaches exactly how to get started on a field study. A teacher's manual is also available (*see* p. 17).
♦ Students may create a classroom mural of the kinds of instruments used to make ocean observations, with a short narrative to accompany each instrument pictured. Students in Connecticut may also take an instructive trip on the classroom boat out of Avery Point during the school year with a professional instructor.
1. Aquatic biology   2. Ecology—Connecticut—Long Island Sound   3. Seashore biology.

551.46 (Reference)
Weiss, Howard M. and Dorsey, Michael W. *Investigating the Marine Environment: A Sourcebook. Vol. 2: Lab Studies.* Project Oceanology (No ISBN), 1979. 611p. B/W diagrams, photos, and charts. (Interest level: grade 3-adult).

With its step-by-step instructions for lab studies, this second manual is similar to the first (*see* preceding entry). Hermit crab shell selection and marine plant collections are two of the subjects clearly explained with many pictures. Teachers will also be interested in volume 3, a teacher's manual (*see* p. 17).
♦ Class members may set up and maintain a sea aquarium following directions given in the sourcebook.
1. Aquatic biology   2. Ecology—Connecticut—Long Island Sound.

551.552
The Great Hurricane of 1938. (Sound filmstrip). American People's Historical Society, 1979. (Great Events and People in Connecticut Series). (15 min.). $34.95. (Interest level: 4-6).

September 21, 1938, wind, flood, and fire in the form of a hurricane struck Connecticut, possibly the worst disaster to ever hit the state. Reproductions of actual photos from private files and newspapers allow students to witness the awful devastation of places with which they may be familiar.
♦ Children may interview grandparents and older acquaintances about the storms they have experienced and report their stories.

1. Connecticut—History 2. Hurricanes—New England 3. Hurricanes—Connecticut.

574.5263
Wetland Protection in Connecticut. (Videocassette). Connecticut Department of Environmental Protection, 1990. 1 videocassette, VHS, Color, (14:10 min.). $25.00. (Interest level: grade 4-adult).

After major destruction occurred with increased development, Connecticut enacted legislation to protect wetlands. The terms "marsh," "swamp," "bog," and "flood plain" used in the legislation are explained and beautifully illustrated. The necessity of their continued existence and regulations are discussed.
♦ Students may consult the Environmental Protection Agency or Zoning Commission to locate areas in their community that are protected. Then they may make a map locating and describing the type of area and protection.
1. Wetlands—Connecticut.

574.92
Atkin, John. *The Soundbook.* Illus. by Donna Kern. Long Island Soundkeepers Fund (No ISBN), 1992. 64p. B/W illus. and photos. (Interest level: 3-6).

The Long Island Soundkeepers Fund has published this book to show interested citizens how they can help preserve the Sound. The book provides a history of the Sound and charts of the drainage basin and discusses the impact of development including sewage. Half of the book is devoted to what readers can do to lessen the impact of development on the Sound.
♦ Young people can list the ways they can help in their own homes to protect the environment. They may log their accomplishments on a monthly chart.
1. Ecology—Long Island Sound (N.Y. and Conn.)
2. Long Island Sound (N.Y. and Conn.).

574.92
Taylor, Sally L. and **Villalard-Bohnsack, Martine.** *Plants and Animals of the Estuary.* Connecticut Arboretum Bulletin No. 24. Illus. by Sybil Hausman. Connecticut College Arboretum (No ISBN), 1978. 43p. B/W illus. (Interest level: grade 6-adult).

In addition to a good description of an estuary, this well-illustrated guide gives information useful for identification of species of crustaceans, bivalves, snails, and mollusca, and where to find them. Included is a map of Connecticut with the habitats and distribution of each species.
♦ Using the guide for identification, students may make and mount a collection of estuary plants and animals.
1. Ecology—Connecticut—Long Island Sound
2. Seashore biology—Connecticut 3. Estuarine biology—Connecticut.

574.92
Wahle, Lisa. *Plants and Animals of the Long Island Sound.* Illus. by Susan Stone. Connecticut Sea Grant College Program (No ISBN), 1991. 34p. B/W illus. (Interest level: grade 5-adult).

This free paperback is a gold mine of information on the life forms found in the Sound, how and why each lives there, and how they all are interrelated. The language is fairly simple for a complex subject, the drawings and charts are excellent, and an index and bibliography add to the book's usefulness.
♦ Young people may draw a nutrient and energy cycle naming specific species of carnivores, herbivores, producers, and decomposers.
1. Animals—Connecticut—Long Island Sound
2. Plants—Connecticut—Long Island Sound
3. Long Island Sound (N.Y. and Conn.).

581.5
Niering, William and **Goodwin, Richard H.** *Inland Wetland Plants of Connecticut.* Illus. by Richard M. Brown. Connecticut Arboretum Bulletin No. 19. Connecticut College Arboretum (No ISBN), 1973. 24p. B/W illus. (Interest level: grade 7-adult).

Types of inland wetland plants are described here along with their ecological roles. Although scholarly, the good descriptions of habitat and illustrations may be useful for fifth and sixth graders as a means of identification.
♦ The class may consult the town zoning agency to find a designated wetlands nearby. After a field trip with an identification checklist, class members can speculate on the value of keeping the wetlands undeveloped.
1. Ecology—Connecticut 2. Plants—Connecticut.

581.5
Niering, William A. and **Warren, R. Scott.** *Salt Marsh Plants of Connecticut.* Connecticut Arboretum Bulletin No. 25. Illus. by Christine Ameele. Connecticut College Arboretum (No ISBN), 1980. 32p. B/W illus. (Interest level: grade 7-adult).

This well-illustrated bulletin explores the role of 22 tidal marsh plants found in Connecticut. The good coverage given each plant includes a full-page description with environmental impact and a facing-page illustration.
♦ Students may collect, dry, and mount an exhibit of marsh plants.
1. Ecology—Connecticut 2. Plants—Connecticut.

589.22
Cooke, John C. *Common Mushrooms of New England.* Connecticut Arboretum Bulletin No. 29. Connecticut College Arboretum (No ISBN), 1984. 47p. B/W illus. (Interest level: grade 7-adult).

Cooke's guide is arranged according to mushroom structure, and each mushroom name is followed by pectoral groups, illustrations, and descriptions for identification. The illustrations are clear and the descriptions point out important identifying features.
♦ Readers may search for and identify mushrooms, look up further resources on mushrooms, and prepare a historical display of their uses and legends.
1. Mushrooms—New England—Identification.

589.3
Taylor, Sally L. and **Villalard, Martine**. *Seaweeds of the Connecticut Shore: A Wader's Guide*. Connecticut Arboretum Bulletin No. 18. Connecticut College Arboretum (No ISBN), 1985. (Interest level: grade 4-adult).
Connecticut shores abound with seaweed. Taylor and Villalard's guide identifies 60 of the most frequently encountered kinds of brown, green, and red algae.
♦ Following the directions in the bulletin, students may construct an herbarium after a seaweed-collecting trip.
1. Marine algae 2. Marine flora 3. Algae.

597.6
Klemens, Michael W. *Checklist of the Amphibians and Reptiles of Connecticut*. Connecticut Department of Environmental Protection (0-942085-01-9), 1991. 24p. Color illus. (Interest level: grade 3-adult).
Connecticut has several amphibians and reptiles that are feared or are never seen because they are night creatures. More than a checklist with distribution information, this guide has strikingly beautiful color plates with full descriptions of the more uncommon species.
♦ Young people may make a list of diurnal and nocturnal species, investigate their habits, and make a checklist of observations.
1. Amphibians—Connecticut 2. Reptiles—Connecticut.

598.2
Askins, Robert A. *Birds of the Connecticut College Arboretum*. Connecticut Arboretum Bulletin No. 31. Connecticut College Arboretum (No ISBN), 1990. 43p. B/W illus. and charts. (Interest level: grade 4-adult).
Intended as a guide to birds sighted in the Connecticut College Arboretum, this checklist of seasonal appearances is applicable to similar habitats throughout coastal Connecticut.
♦ The class may start a seasonal checklist of birds sighted, recording where, when, and how many times a species is sighted.
1. Birds—Connecticut.

598.2
Stone, James. *Birds of Connecticut Salt Marshes*. Connecticut Arboretum Bulletin No. 27. Illus. by J. Susan Cole-Stone. Connecticut College Arboretum (No ISBN), 1981. 48p. B/W illus. (Interest level: grade 5-adult).
Stone's clearly written paperback explores the habitats and feeding habits of 20 birds found in Connecticut salt marshes. The seasonal checklist and list of birding places, along with full-page descriptions and illustrations, make this book invaluable.
♦ A field trip to one of the listed birding spots would allow students to develop their own salt marsh birding log. Certain species should be targeted for sighting before embarking.
1. Birds—Connecticut.

598.91
Billings, Gene. *Birds of Prey in Connecticut*. Illus. by Julie Zickefoose. Rainbow Press (No ISBN), 1990. 461p. B/W illus. (Interest level: grade 4-adult).
Hawks, eagles, vultures, and owls live in Connecticut, and this guide has information about where and when each species can best be seen. Basic information about characteristics, behavior, and preferred habitats is included for each species, but there are no color pictures or identification hints.
♦ Since this is not an identification guide, students may read up on species likely to be seen on their bird walk and use another guide for identification.
1. Birds of prey—Connecticut.

623.2
Clouette, Bruce and **Roth, Matthew**. *Connecticut's Historic Highway Bridges*. Connecticut Department of Transportation (No ISBN), 1991. 101p. B/W photos. (Interest level: grade 4-adult).
There are many Connecticut highway bridges listed on the National Register of Historic Places. This glossy paperback not only has photos, history, and statistics for each bridge, but also five case studies of how deteriorating bridges were restored and a diagrammatic glossary of terms.
♦ Since bridge repair is a continual problem in Connecticut on both town and state highways, children may investigate a bridge near them that is under repair and question why it needs repair and how it is being repaired. Then they may determine whether it is of historical importance by researching in town records.
1. Historical bridges—Connecticut.

641.59
Apicerno, William, ed. *250th Anniversary Cookbook and Recipe Collection: Cooking from a Connecticut Farm*. Lyman Orchards (No ISBN), 1991. 88p. (Interest level: grade 4-adult).

For 250 years the Lymans have been part of Connecticut history as farmers and politicians. Two collections of recipes are included in the book: one from the Lyman Orchards restaurant and one of old family favorites. Both give students a good idea of the fruits and vegetables grown commercially in Connecticut.
♦ Students might enjoy preparing some of these recipes for a class Connecticut food festival.
1. Cookery, American—New England style.

641.5973
Kerr, Mary Brandt. *America: A Regional Cookbook.* Chartwell Books (No ISBN), 1986. 208p. Color photos. (Interest level: grade 6-adult).

Although only 29 pages of Kerr's cookbook are devoted to New England cooking, the first two are an excellent overview of how and why New England cookery developed. Recipes are fun and typical of the Connecticut area. (The Joe Frogger cookies are an example.)
♦ Young people may use the recipes to plan their own Connecticut dinner. They might compare the amounts of ingredients in the same recipes used in their homes for similar food.
1. Cookery, American.

641.5973
Simmons, Amelia. *American Cooking.* Silverleaf Press (0-915591-00-60), 1984. 155p. B/W illus. (Interest level: grade 4-adult).

This reissue of the first cookbook written and published in Connecticut and America retains the early American flavor, although the type has been reset and annotations and illustrations have been added. One of the three remaining original copies resides in the Connecticut Historical Society, but this is a good substitute for classroom use as it teaches an interesting lesson on the important foods in colonial New England.
♦ Students may write a letter describing a meal at which they were entertained in Connecticut. Using the glossary in the book will help students use authentic terms.
1. Cookery, American—Early works to 1800.

641.5973
Stern, Jane and **Stern, Michael.** *A Taste of America.* Andrews and McMeel (0-8362-2125-7), 1988. 274p. (Interest level: grade 6-adult).

The Sterns list restaurants in 11 towns in Connecticut that they consider to be among the best in the United States along with a few recipes from each restaurant. Especially interesting are the sidenotes, which are full of local history and color.
♦ Using the description of the Noah Webster birthday party, the class can celebrate his birthday by having a similar party with the appropriate foods.
1. Cookery, American.

720.9 (Reference)
Inshaw, Norman. *Early Connecticut Houses.* Dover Publications (0-486-26374-6), 1990. 303p. B/W illus. (Interest level: grade 8-adult).

This reprint of a 1900 edition contains architectural information too technical for most students, but the 115 illustrations are worth studying. Students would probably read sections on particular houses in which they are interested.
♦ Using the town index, the class may locate an early house nearby and plan a visit. Students outside of Connecticut may research and visit a historic house in their area.
1. Architecture, Domestic—Connecticut 2. Historic buildings—Connecticut.

720.9
Peterson, William N. and **Coope, Peter M.** *Historic Buildings at Mystic Seaport Museum.* Mystic Seaport Museum (0-913372-35-8), 1985. 136p. B/W and Color illus. (Interest level: grade 6-adult).

Twenty-one historic structures are pictured and discussed, including a schoolhouse, a bank, and a mill. Although all the buildings did not originally stand in Connecticut, they are typical of what would be found in an eighteenth- or nineteenth-century whaling town in Connecticut.
♦ Young people may build a replica of a whaling village, copying some of the buildings in the book. Mystic Museum also has reduced price student tours.
1. Historic buildings—Mystic Seaport—Conservation and restoration.

917.3 (Reference)
Clements, John. *Connecticut Facts/Rhode Island Facts.* Clements Research II (ISSN 1050-4613), 1990. 117p. B/W and Color illus. (Interest level: grade 5-adult).

A compendium of facts, charts, and data on Connecticut and Rhode Island, this book contains a chronological history, county data, major market and business regulations, climate information, and natural resources. Up-to-date facts and the full text of the Connecticut State Constitution make this exceptionally valuable.
♦ Readers may locate their counties and find the zip code for an unincorporated community. They might also make a list of recreation areas within 25 miles of their homes and explain why a certain site appeals to them.
1. Connecticut 2. Rhode Island.

917.404
Lewis, Cynthia C. and **Lewis, Thomas J.** *Best Hikes with Children in Connecticut, Massachusetts, & Rhode Island.* Mountaineers Books (0-89886-265-5), 1991. (Best Hikes with Children Series).

256p. B/W maps and photos. (Interest level: grade 4-adult).

The Lewises present 120 pages on Connecticut describing 29 sites, including types of hikes, degree of difficulty, distance, elevation, approximate hiking time, best time of year to hike, sights to look for, picnicking spots, hours trails are open, and admission fees. Each entry also includes information that is fun to read even if the reader doesn't plan to hike the trail, including how some Connecticut parks, such as the Devil's Hopyard, got their odd names.
♦ Students may choose a short hike near them and plan a field trip for the class with a checksheet for observations. Or, they can write a journal entry describing an imaginary hike along a Connecticut trail.
1. Hiking—New England—Guidebooks 2. Family recreation—New England—Guidebooks 3. New England—Description and travel—Guidebooks.

917.46
Connecticut: A Picture Book to Remember Her By. Outlet Book Company (0-517-47787-4), 1991. Unpaginated. Color photos. (Interest level: 3-8).

This photographic essay of typical and special houses, scenic panoramas, public buildings, churches, town centers, and industries includes concise captions. The beautiful photographs convey a real Connecticut flavor.
♦ Further investigation of some of the buildings may encourage students to make models, floor plans, or reproductions of the structures and some of the furnishings used, as well as to speculate on why some of them were built as they were.
1. Connecticut.

917.46
Connecticut's First. (Online database). Links to Learning. SNET Connet. Free. (Interest level: grade 3-adult).

This database gives brief information from out-of-print books on "firsts" in Connecticut, such as a first-time event or a first achievement for a Connecticut resident.
♦ Students can browse through this online database and choose an event or person for further research.
1. Connecticut—Miscellanea.

917.46
Grant, Marion Hepburn, ed. *In and about Hartford: Its People and Places.* Connecticut Historical Society (0-940748-97-5), 1989. 393p. B/W photos. (Interest level: grade 7-adult).

Intended as a tourist guide, this well-indexed paperback gives the history and background of sights in and around Connecticut's capital city. The concise history for each subject is well-documented and the extensive index makes this a handy reference.
♦ Young people may draw a map of Hartford, mark the location of famous buildings, and create models.
1. Connecticut—Description and travel—Guidebooks.

917.46
Kent, Deborah. *Connecticut.* Childrens Press (0-516-00453-0), 1990. (America the Beautiful Series). 143p. Color photos. (Interest level: 5-8).

The climate, industry, culture, geography, and history of Connecticut are all treated in this overview, from the state's colonial origins to the present. Excellent photos, a time line, a list of important people with photographs, a variety of maps, and an index make this a useful, if not exciting, starting point.
♦ Using the list of famous people, children may choose one about whom to write and perform a skit demonstrating why that person is or was important to Connecticut.
1. Connecticut—History.

917.46
Marsh, Carole. *Connecticut Jeopardy.* Gallopade (0-7933-4098-5), 1991. 36p. B/W illus. (Interest level: 3-8).

Similar in format to other Marsh books, this contains questions on Connecticut geography, people, events, institutions, history, and vocabulary. Answers to the questions are listed, but since no references or explanations are given, this is fun but of limited value.
♦ A Jeopardy game using the book's questions might be a culminating activity for a unit on Connecticut.
1. Connecticut—History—Miscellanea 2. Connecticut—Miscellanea.

917.46 (Reference)
Marsh, Carole. *The Connecticut Media Book: A Surprising Guide to the Amazing Print, Broadcast, and Online Media of Our State for Students, Teachers, Writers, and Publishers.* Gallopade (07933-3180-3), 1991. 36p. B/W illus. (Interest level: grade 4-adult).

Marsh's book, divided into sections for print, radio, and television, lists the towns in which the media are located. Here again, incomplete data in the entries limit the usefulness, although it is handy to have even this much information in one place.
♦ The class may visit a nearby television studio, radio station, or publisher. Students may write arguments for which medium they think is the most effective in disseminating information and/or persuading an audience.

1. Mass media—Connecticut 2. Periodicals—Connecticut—Bibliography.

917.46
Marsh, Carole. *Connecticut's Most (Devastating) Disasters and Most (Calamitous) Calamities.* Gallopade (0-79330-211-0), 1992. 36p. B/W illus. (Interest level: 3-8).

Hard-to-find accounts of disasters such as the 1938 hurricane, the Hartford circus fire, the 1955 flood, and the 1984 blizzard are here, along with simple explanations of some of their causes. This is the best of the Marsh books, although it is padded with events such as the 1920s stock market crash and the sinking of the *Titanic,* which are really not Connecticut disasters.
♦ Young people can make a chart of kinds of disasters and how to prevent them or lessen their impact.
1. Disasters—Connecticut—Miscellanea 2. Natural disasters—Connecticut—Miscellanea 3. Connecticut—Miscellanea.

917.46
Marsh, Carole. *The Hard-to-Believe-but-True! Book of Connecticut History, Mystery, Trivia, Legend, Lore, Humor, & More.* Gallopade (0-7933-0229-3), 1990. 35p. B/W illus. (Interest level: grade 3-adult).

Some little-known facts and legends about Connecticut that are hard to find elsewhere are briefly recounted here in a humorous fashion and in large print. Although superficial and padded with some anecdotes not specific to Connecticut, the book's easy reading level and unintimidating format will entice reluctant students.
♦ As a language arts activity, readers may invent further adventures for the legendary figures introduced in the book.
1. Curiosities and wonders—Connecticut 2. Connecticut—Miscellanea 3. Trivia—Connecticut.

917.46
Ritchie, David and **Ritchie, Deborah.** *Connecticut off the Beaten Path.* Globe Pequot Press (0-87106-240-2), 1992. 160p. B/W illus. (Interest level: grade 6-adult).

Divided into five regions and then into towns, the Ritchies' guidebook provides information on all kinds of places to visit, from a maple sugar farm to an Indian archaeological museum, and includes each place's address and telephone number. This entertaining and useful book has great ideas for class trips.
♦ Young people could test their knowledge with such questions as: "What do a copper mine and a prison have in common?" or "Where can you make casts of dinosaur tracks?" A follow-up visit to one of the many places listed might follow.
1. Connecticut—Description and travel—Guidebooks.

974
Tuckerman, Stephen, ed. *Appalachian Mountain Club River Guide.* 2nd ed. Appalachian Mountain Club Books (1-87823-900-7), 1990. 240p. (Interest level: grade 7-adult).

The Housatonic River, the Connecticut River, the Thames River, and the Merrimack River are the four major drainage basins in southern New England and offer canoeing on the main stem and the tributaries. The rivers are listed by state boundaries and rated by difficulty in season.
♦ Students may map a canoe trip for a specific time of year and write diary entries describing the imagined trip.
1. Canoes and canoeing—Connecticut—Guidebooks 2. Connecticut—Description and travel.

974.004
Calloway, Colin G. *Indians of the Northeast.* Facts on File (0-8160-2389-1), 1991. (First American Series). 96p. B/W and Color photos. (Interest level: 4-8).

Calloway locates on a map the tribes of the Northeast, organized into language families, and traces their histories from early times to the present. An extremely attractive format, many unusual and nonstereotypical pictures, and excellent organization make this a "can't-put-down" book.
♦ The class can locate early Connecticut tribes on a large map and, using other references, especially daily newspapers, locate tribes today.
1. Native Americans—Northeastern states.

974.6
Between Boston and New York. (Videocassette). Connecticut Humanities Council, n.d. VHS, Color, (60 min.). $10.00. (Interest level: grade 6-adult).

Connecticut is sandwiched between New York and Massachusetts and has parts of both in its culture. This video explores the state's movie image, tourist industry image, and ethnic makeup, historical and economic, in an enjoyable effort to clarify Connecticut's identity.
♦ Young people may write their own view of Connecticut at the beginning of a unit on the state. At the end of the unit, they may write another essay on the same subject and compare the two.
1. Connecticut—Social life and customs.

974.6
Connecticut: The Early Years. (Sound filmstrip). American People's Historical Society, 1979. (Great Events and People in Connecticut Series). (18 min.). $34.95. (Interest level: 4-8).

A brief history of the Pequot Wars and King Philip's War and the legend of the Charter Oak are given in words and excellent pictures. Although there are a few grammatical errors in the script, the film is worth viewing.
♦ Students may write a newspaper story about the Charter Oak.
1. Connecticut—History—Colonial period, 1600-1775.

974.6
Connecticut in the Civil War. (Sound filmstrip). American People's Historical Society, 1979. (Great Events and People in Connecticut History Series). (12 min.). $34.95. (Interest level: 4-8).

Because the filmstrip uses original print reproductions featuring John Brown, Eli Whitney, the Amistad, Prudence Crandall, and the Underground Railroad, it has an air of authenticity, which is furthered by appropriate music and sound effects. Although the presentation is uneven, it shows effectively how Connecticut people contributed to the outcome of the Civil War.
♦ Students may further investigate the Underground Railroad and the people associated with it, such as Harriet Tubman, and then, if possible, create a classroom map of the Underground Railroad. They might also visit homes in their locale that were part of the Underground Railroad. Local historical societies can help identify these places.
1. Connecticut—History—Civil War, 1861-1865.

974.6
Connecticut in the Revolution. (Sound filmstrip). American People's Historical Society, 1979. (Great Events and People in Connecticut Series). (9 min.). $34.95. (Interest level: 4-8).

Along with clear and brief explanations of the Coercive Acts, the Stamp Act, and the tea tax, this filmstrip shows the roles of Israel Putnam, Nathan Hale, and Benedict Arnold in the American Revolution. Good sound effects, well-chosen prints, and a simple script add to the production.
♦ Class members could stage a debate on whether the colonists were justified in refusing to pay the stamp tax.
1. Connecticut—History—Colonial period, ca 1600-1775 2. Connecticut—History—Revolution, 1775-1783.

974.6
Dreyer, Glenn D. *Connecticut's Notable Trees.* 2nd ed. Memoirs of the Connecticut Botanical Society (No ISBN), 1990. 94p. B/W illus. (Interest level: grade 6-adult).

Historic trees, biggest trees, a list of tree locations, and numerous appendixes on specific types, numbers, and measurements make this little book a find. A useful index will help Connecticut readers locate large and historic trees near home.
♦ Young people may search their neighborhoods for large trees, measure them as described in the book, and compile a list of their own.
1. Trees—Connecticut.

974.6
Faude, Wilson H. and **Friedland, Joan W.** *Connecticut Firsts.* Peregrine Press (0-933614-26-8), 1985. 106p. B/W illus. (Interest level: grade 4-adult).

Under topics such as architecture, religion, science, and education, students will find contributions to society that came first from Connecticut. The book, which is fun, should not be taken too seriously but certainly will be approached with the same student fervor that the Guinness Records books engender.
♦ Young readers may pick a few "firsts" and write about how their own lives are affected by them.
1. Connecticut—Civilization 2. Connecticut—History—Miscellanea.

974.6
Fradin, Dennis B. *The Connecticut Colony.* Childrens Press (0-516-00393-3), 1990. 160p. B/W photos, illus., and maps. (Interest level: 4-8).

Fradin offers pictures, maps, charts, and a time line to give a cursory history of Connecticut. The book also includes the history of the founding of Yale College and short biographies of important men of Revolutionary Connecticut. Large print, pictures, and details of home life in early times will hold student interest.
♦ The five largest Connecticut towns in 1756 are listed in the book. Students may locate them on the map, identify the five largest today, and explain why any changes occurred.
1. Connecticut—History—Colonial period, ca 1600-1775 2. Connecticut—History—Revolution, 1775-1783.

974.6
Gelman, Amy. *Connecticut.* Lerner (0-8225-2709-X), 1991. 77p. Color illus. (Interest level: 3-6).

A brief history, followed by facts about Connecticut's industrial development and present-day occupations, includes an excellent section on Connecticut's environmental policy and recycling efforts. Good up-to-date pictures, a section of Connecticut biographies, and a time line add to the book's usefulness.
♦ Children may investigate what their own town is doing to further environmental protection and how they might help in recycling.
1. Connecticut 2. Connecticut—History.

974.6
Keyarts, Eugene. *Sixty Selected Nature Walks in Connecticut*. 2nd ed. Globe Pequot Press (087106-723-4), 1988. 180p. B/W maps. (Interest level: grade 7-adult).

Five hundred miles of cleared and marked trails, known as "blue trails," are open to walkers in Connecticut. This concise guide is arranged by county first and then by season, with approximate distances and interesting sights.

♦ After choosing a trail they would like to walk, students can make a list of what they would look for and compare sightings. Children should always know the purpose of a nature walk before starting.

1. Hiking—Connecticut—Guidebooks 2. Connecticut—Description and travel.

974.6
Once upon a Time in Connecticut: How the Early Settlers Lived, 1635-1800. Connecticut Heritage (No ISBN), 1990. 50p. (Interest level: 4-8).

Stories of daily living in the 1600s and 1700s in Connecticut give details on what early settlers ate, their clothing, daily activities, and their relationships with the Indians. The true stories in this collection have been reprinted from a variety of out-of-print sources.

♦ Imagining that they are early settlers, young people may keep diaries for a week.

1. Connecticut—History.

974.6
Scherer, Thomas E. *The Connecticut Atlas*. Kinderatlas (No ISBN), 1990. B/W maps. (Interest level: 4-8).

Divided into sections—Physical Connecticut, History and Settlement, People and Culture, and Transportation and Economy—this spiral-bound book of maps is comprehensive, clear, and lies flat for tracing. The only thing lacking in Scherer's extremely useful collection is an index, but the format encourages browsing.

♦ Students may compare the location of major cities in 1860 with those of major cities today. They should support their conclusions with information from other maps on economy, population, and transportation.

1. Connecticut—Geography 2. Connecticut—Demography 3. Connecticut—Economy 4. Connecticut—History 5. Connecticut—Statistics 6. Connecticut—Maps.

974.6
Weibust, Patricia. *The Italians in Their Homeland, in America, in Connecticut*. World Education Project (0-685-05455-1), 1975. (Peoples of Connecticut Multicultural Ethnic Heritage Series). 121p. B/W photos. (Interest level: 7-8).

A short history of Italy as a country is followed by a readable regional history of Italian immigration to Connecticut since colonial times. Occupations, religion, festivals, the padrone system, folk beliefs, and social organizations are treated separately. Although this book is almost 20 years old, it includes interesting history, especially for Hartford and New Haven.

♦ Readers may investigate ethnic neighborhoods near them using interview techniques and oral history recording with old residents or new immigrants.

1. Italians in the United States—Connecticut.

974.602
Fennelly, Catherine. *Connecticut Women in the Revolutionary Era*. Globe Pequot Press (0-87106-064-7), 1975. (Connecticut Bicentennial Series). 60p. B/W illus. (Interest level: grade 8-adult).

Fennelly's small but complete book details everyday life in the home during the Revolutionary War, including typical meals, dress, social life, education, and legal status of women. Because the book is intended for an adult audience, students will need help interpreting some passages, but the invaluable information is worth the added effort.

♦ Students may prepare a meal with foods common in Revolutionary-era Connecticut or host a sewing bee or another social event of the era.

1. Women—Connecticut—History—Colonial period, ca 1600-1775 2. Connecticut—History—Colonial period, ca 1600-1775.

974.603
Callahan, North. *Connecticut Revolutionary War Leaders*. Globe Pequot Press (0-87106-120-1), 1973. (Connecticut Bicentennial Series). 52p. B/W illus. (Interest level: grade 8-adult).

Short biographies of Ethan Allen, Israel Putnam, Rufus Putnam, David Wooster, Benedict Arnold, and others are included in this well-researched work. Intended for adults, the biographies are short but give an idea of each person's contribution to the Revolution.

♦ Young people may check city street maps of Connecticut to locate areas, streets, and institutions named for some of the famous figures of the Revolution.

1. Connecticut—Biography 2. Connecticut—History—Revolution, 1775-1783.

974.603
Trecker, Janice Law. *Preachers, Rebels, and Traders—Connecticut, 1818-1865*. Globe Pequot Press (0-87106-130-9), 1975. (Connecticut Bicentennial Series). 95p. B/W illus. (Interest level: grade 8-adult).

This publication of the American Revolution Bicentennial Commission of Connecticut is well

researched and well documented. Although much of it is too dry for elementary school students, the chapter on African Americans, abolition, and slavery gives concise accounts of Prudence Crandall's school and the *Amistad* case, which are hard to find in books for younger students.
♦ Students may re-create the court scene from the *Amistad* case after further research.
1. Connecticut—History, 1818-1865.

974.603
Tucker, Louis Leonard. *Connecticut's Seminary of Sedition: Yale College.* Globe Pequot Press (0-87106-148-1), 1974. (Connecticut Bicentennial Series). 78p. B/W illus. (Interest level: grade 8-adult).

As one of the nine colleges in colonial America, Yale, with its 200 students, became a powerful influence for rebellion against England. This adult study of Yale will appeal to those interested in Ezra Stiles or Yale University itself.
♦ Readers may research the other eight colleges in the colonies and compare the reasons for their establishment. They might also compile a list of famous Yale graduates using biographies listed here and other biographical sources.
1. Connecticut—History 2. Yale University.

974.603
White, David O. *Connecticut's Black Soldiers.* Globe Pequot Press (0-87106-119-8), 1973. (Connecticut Bicentennial Series). 71p. B/W illus. (Interest level: grade 8-adult).

The list of Connecticut's black soldiers and the reproduction of documents such as a pay voucher and an employment advertisement, as well as the explanation of how a slave could earn freedom and the laws governing blacks, are eye-openers for many Connecticut students. Although this book is intended for adults, it is written in an anecdotal style that will appeal to older students.
♦ Young people could write a few pages in a diary from an African American soldier's perspective during the Revolution.
1. Connecticut—History 2. African Americans—Connecticut—History.

974.68
Cutler, Carl C. *Mystic: The Story of a Small New England Seaport.* Mystic Seaport Museum (0-913372-14-5), 1980. 56p. B/W illus. and map. (Interest level: grade 7-adult).

This is an updated reissue of a 1945 edition written by the founder of the Mystic Museum. A history of shipbuilding and marine commerce is enhanced by a new map of the shipbuilding sites on the Mystic River.
♦ After browsing through the book, students may propose theories about why so many shipyards existed at Mystic and why the industry has declined.
1. Mystic (Conn.)—History.

974.6814
Decker, Robert Owen. *The Whaling City: A History of New London.* Globe Pequot Press (0-87106-053-1), 1976. 415p. B/W photos. (Interest level: grade 7-adult).

Decker presents a scholarly history of New London, from colonial times to the present. This book would be useful mainly for the 150 excellent photos of everyday life, business, and industry.
♦ In the chapter on business and industry, newspaper help-wanted ads are reproduced, listing wages and requirements. Students may compare types of employment, costs, wages, and labor laws in the 1800s and now.
1. New London (Conn.)—History.

Biography

920
Black American Heroes. (Online database). Links to Learning. SNET. Free. (Interest level: grade 4-adult).

The database contains short biographies of 16 African Americans who are important in Connecticut history. Some of the people are little known outside Connecticut, especially the contemporary heroes, and their biographies are not easy to find.
♦ Young people may discuss what qualities a hero has and write a short biography of someone they know and consider to be a hero.
1. African Americans—Connecticut—Biography.

920
Colby, Barnard. *Whaling Captains of New London County, Connecticut: For Oil and Buggy Whips.* Mystic Seaport Museum (0-913372-54-4), 1990. 224p. B/W illus. (Interest level: grade 8-adult).

New London was second only to New Bedford as a whaling port, and the 23 biographical sketches of its whaling captains make colorful and fascinating reading. Copies of original documents, as well as lists of vessels, their masters, and their voyages, are included.
♦ Students may write a log for a week as captains of a whaling vessel.
1. New London (Conn.)—History 2. Whaling—Connecticut—History 3. Whalers—Connecticut—Biography.

920
Connecticut Originals. (Videocassette). SNET, 1986. VHS, Color, (100 min.). Free on loan from SNET Ed. Dept. (Interest level: grade 4-adult).

Produced by the telephone company in conjunction with the New Haven Historical Society and the commerical television station, this collection of biographies is divided into 25-minute segments as they were shown on television. Well-known historians, competent actors, and actual on-site photography make the subjects come alive.

♦ Using some of the other biographies as sources and following the same format as the SNET film, class members may produce their own video biographies of famous Connecticut people not in the SNET production.

1. Arnold, Benedict, 1741-1801   2. Colt, Samuel, 1814-1862   3. Hale, Nathan, 1755-1776   4. Stowe, Harriet Beecher, 1811-1896   5. Twain, Mark, 1835-1910   6. Connecticut—Biography.

920

Great Leaders from Connecticut. (Sound filmstrip). American People's Historical Society, 1979. (Great Events and People in Connecticut Series). (16 min.). $34.95. (Interest level: 4-8).

Short pictorial biographies of Nathan Hale, Eli Whitney, John Brown, Mark Twain, and Jackie Robinson focus primarily on their contributions to society. For the most part, the script and frames are well done.

♦ Students may read a biography of one of the people shown in the filmstrip.

1. Connecticut—Biography.

920

Marsh, Carole. *Connecticut State Greats.* Gallopade (1-55609-547-3), 1991. 36p. B/W illus. (Interest level: 3-6).

Along with biographies of well-known people, this book includes short biographies of Amos Alonzo Stagg, Limes Yale, Abell Buell, and other lesser-known Connecticut natives. The book explains what a biography is and gives guidelines for students in writing biographies.

♦ Children may discuss the important facts to be included in a biography and the difference between an authorized and unauthorized biography. After reading two different accounts of the life of the person of their choice, they can discuss why there are discrepancies between two biographies of the same person.

1. Connecticut—Biography.

92 Bushnell, David

Swanson, June. *David Bushnell and His Turtle: The Story of America's First Submarine.* Illus. by Mike Eagle. Atheneum (0-689-31628-3), 1991. 40p. B/W and Color illus. (Interest level: grade 6-adult).

Just before the American Revolution, Saybrook's David Bushnell entered Yale and started experiments that eventually led to his invention of a working submarine. Good illustrations add to the exciting tale of an accomplishment that led to a major Connecticut industry.

♦ Young people may construct models of Bushnell's underwater mine and submarine or construct a submarine of their own design using his principles.

1. Bushnell, David, 1742?-1824   2. Naval architects—United States—Biography   3. Submarine boats—History   4. Inventors—United States—Biography   5. United States—Revolution, 1775-1783—Naval operations—Submarine.

92 Gaullaudet, Thomas Hopkins

Neimark, Anne E. *A Deaf Child Listened.* William Morrow (0-688-01719-3), 1983. 116p. (Interest level: 4-8).

Thomas Gallaudet, a descendant of the founders of Hartford, Connecticut, was so frail and puny that he was denied his rightful place as valedictorian of his class at Yale. This book about how he developed the American Sign Language method for the deaf after meeting nine-year-old Alice Cogswell is sensitive without being sentimental.

♦ Class members may study a book on American Sign Language and learn some conversational phrases.

1. Gallaudet, Thomas Hopkins, 1787–1851   2. Deaf education   3. Teachers of the deaf—United States—Biography.

92 Philip, Sachem of the Wampanoags

Fradin, Dennis B. *King Philip: Indian Leader.* Enslow (0-89490-231-8), 1990. (Colonial Profiles Series). 48p. B/W illus. and maps. (Interest level: 3-6).

Most of this biography focuses on how King Philip became the leader of the Wampanoags and the history of Massasoit and Metacomet with less emphasis on King Philip's War than other books. Although the book does give brief information about the war, the details of the massacre are not as graphic as in other accounts.

♦ Children may construct a family tree for King Philip and show relationships with the colonists.

1. Philip, Sachem of the Wampanoags, 1639?-1676   2. Native Americans—Biography   3. King Philip's War, 1675-1676.

92 Philip, Sachem of the Wampanoags

Roman, Joseph. *King Philip.* Chelsea House (0-7910-1704-4), 1992. (North American Indians of Achievement Series). 112p. B/W illus. (Interest level: 6-8).

Although the Wampanoags lived primarily in Rhode Island, King Philip's War involved Massachusetts and Connecticut as well. Reproductions of early paintings, charts, maps, and diagrams help clarify this complicated war.

♦ Young people may create a map noting the various tribes involved in the war and their locations and identify the towns that were sites of battles.
1. Philip, Sachem of the Wampanoags, 1639?-1676 2. Wampanoag Indians—Biography 3. King Philip's War, 1675-1676.

92 Stowe, Harriet Beecher
Harriet Beecher Stowe. (Sound filmstrip). American People's Historical Society, 1979. (Great Events and People in Connecticut Series). (9 min.). $34.95. (Interest level: 4-8).

Clear narration and a fast-moving script give an emotional account of Stowe's life and a condensation of the storyline of *Uncle Tom's Cabin.* The production is well done for the most part.
♦ Students may read about some of the other abolitionists mentioned in the filmstrip and make a class booklet of their quotations.
1. Stowe, Harriet Beecher, 1811-1896 2. Authors, American—19th century—Biography 3. Abolitionists—United States—Biography.

92 Stowe, Harriet Beecher
Jakoubek, Robert E. *Harriet Beecher Stowe.* Chelsea House (1-55546-680-X), 1989. (American Women of Achievement Series). 111p. B/W photos. (Interest level: 6-8).

The writer of *Uncle Tom's Cabin,* born in Litchfield, Connecticut, lived a tumultuous life: she had a huge family, financial disasters, and a son who disappeared. Jakoubek emphasizes Stowe's influence in the abolitionist movement but does not gloss over her problems or the controversies about her.
♦ Together, class members may read *Uncle Tom's Cabin* and dramatize a scene from the book.
1. Stowe, Harriet Beecher, 1811-1896—Biography 2. Authors, American—19th century—Biography 3. Abolitionists—United States—Biography

92 Twain, Mark
Greene, Carol. *Mark Twain: Author of Tom Sawyer.* Childrens Press (0-516-04228-9), 1992. 47p. B/W photos. (Interest level: 2-4).

Using Halley's comet as the framework for the beginning and ending of Mark Twain's life, the author concentrates more on that than Twain's work. Very short sentences, large print, and many pictures make this more suitable for a younger reader than most biographies.
♦ Since Mark Twain was a wonderful storyteller and told stories from his own experiences, young people may create and tell stories based on their own experiences.

1. Twain, Mark, 1835-1910 2. Authors, American—Biography.

92 Webster, Noah
Ferris, Jean. *What Do You Mean? A Story about Noah Webster.* Illus. by Steve Michaels. Carolrhoda (0-876-14330-3), 1988. 63p. B/W illus. (Interest level: 3-7).

Noah Webster went from his home town of West Haven, Connecticut, to New Haven to study at Yale, to Glastonbury to teach, to Hartford to study and practice law, and to Sharon to open a school before he wrote his schoolbooks and finally his dictionary. The fast-moving story of a true scholar is set against a vibrant background of Revolutionary times, events, and people.
♦ The class may visit a local historical society or library that has copies or reproductions of Noah Webster's blue-backed speller and his dictionary. Students might compare these to the spellers and dictionaries in use now.
1. Webster, Noah, 1758-1843 2. Lexicographers—United States—Biography 3. Teachers.

92 Whitney, Eli
Alter, Judith. *Eli Whitney.* Franklin Watts (0-531-10875-90), 1990. 63p. Color illus. (Interest level: 3-7).

A no-nonsense biography of Whitney, this text concentrates on his inventions and his business problems in the period after the Revolutionary War. Excellent pictures and diagrams, as well as a bibliography, glossary, and index, add to the book's usefulness.
♦ Students may investigate the copyright law, how it has changed, and how students today are affected by it.
1. Whitney, Eli, 1765-1825 2. Inventors—United States—Biography.

92 Whitney, Eli
Latham, Jean. *Eli Whitney: Great Inventor.* Illus. by Louis F. Cary. Chelsea House (0-791-01453-3), 1991. 80p. Color illus. (Interest level: 3-5).

Lathan's fictionalized biography of New Haven's Eli Whitney has an easy-to-read, storylike format that highlights his personality as well as his inventions. Large print, easily recognizable facts, and numerous conversations make this worthwhile and enjoyable reading.
♦ Children may locate where Eli Whitney and other Connecticut inventors lived and worked using symbolic logos on the map.
1. Whitney, Eli, 1765-1825 2. Inventors—United States—Biography.

Fiction

Avi. *Windcatcher.* Avon Books (0-380-71805-7), 1991. 120p. B/W illus. (Interest level: 4-6).

Tony searches for sunken treasure among the Thimble Islands in Long Island Sound off Guilford, Connecticut, in this sailing adventure story. The excitement of small boat sailing in rocky Long Island Sound and the activities of a small shore town are accurately portrayed.
♦ Children may draw a map of the real Thimble Islands (the book takes geographical liberties), locating reefs and shoals where ships might have gone aground. Students also may research actual shipwrecks and read about legendary ones in other sources.
1. Connecticut—Fiction   2. Sailing—Fiction.

Boehm, Bruce. *Connecticut Law.* Houghton Mifflin (0-39-5291518-1), 1980 (out of print). 113p. B/W illus. (Interest level: 4-7).

A 14-year-old boy who feels he is a disappointment to his family proves himself by his heroics during a great flood of the Connecticut River Valley. This story is especially pertinent as the last few years have seen many disastrous floods in the state.
♦ After reading the book and viewing a filmstrip on the 1952 floods, students may compile a list of what to do and what not to do when flooding is imminent.
1. Floods—Fiction   2. Connecticut—Fiction.

Burchard, Peter. *Whaleboat Raid.* Coward (0-69-820412-3), 1977 (out of print). 91p. B/W illus. (Interest level: 4-6).

Based on a real incident, this 1777 adventure story of revolutionists rowing and sailing across Long Island Sound to raid the British at Sag Harbor is seen through the eyes of a young boy. Burchard shares with readers the exciting history of the Connecticut shoreline.
♦ Students can draw a map of the Connecticut shoreline and Long Island Sound and trace the journey from shore to shore.
1. Connecticut—History—Fiction.

Collier, James Lincoln and **Collier, Christopher.** *The Bloody Country.* Scholastic (0-685-10091-1), 1976. 180p. (Interest level: grade 7-adult).

In the late 1700s, when Connecticut tried to enforce an old land grant that gave it ownership of the Wyoming Valley in Pennsylvania, Benjamin and his family moved to Wilkes Barre. The exciting and emotionally wrenching story makes history come alive and emphasizes the call for economic, political, and racial freedom.
♦ Readers may research original Connecticut land grants and investigate in particular the land claims of Connecticut Paugussett Indians at this time, using newspaper stories.
1. Frontier and pioneer life—Fiction   2. Pennsylvania—Fiction.

Collier, James Lincoln and **Collier, Christopher.** *The Clock.* Illus. by Kelly Maddox. Doubleday (0-385-30037-9), 1992. 101p. B/W illus. (Interest level: grade 6-adult).

In 1810 Connecticut, 15-year-old Annie slaves in a textile mill with a cruel overseer to help pay her father's debt, all the while plotting revenge. Written by Connecticut's official state historian and James Lincoln Collier, the book gives an accurate and exciting view of a less-than-glorious and often ignored part of the state's past.
♦ Students may investigate the passage of child labor laws, how they were viewed at the time, and debate the pros and cons.
1. Mills and mill work—Fiction   2. Work—Fiction.

Collier, James Lincoln and **Collier, Christopher.** *My Brother Sam Is Dead.* Bantam Doubleday (1-557-36038-3), 1988. (Interest level: 6-8).

Connecticut was a hotbed of rebellion during the American Revolution, but many people supported England and some took neither side. The Meeker family of Redding, Connecticut, is torn apart as one son joins the rebels while the rest of the family stays neutral in this well-researched and exciting book.
♦ Students can write letters as neutrals or Tories to convince a friend to side with them.
1. United States—History—Revolution, 1775-1783—Fiction.

Collier, James Lincoln and **Collier, Christopher.** *My Brother Sam Is Dead.* (Sound filmstrip). Miller Brody, 1981. Color, (48 min.). $71.00. (Interest level: 6-8).

This filmstrip captures the highlights of the story. The narration is clear and the illustrations are bright and suitable.
♦ After reading the book, young people may watch and listen to the audiovisual version. They can contrast the two versions and give the advantages of each.
1. United States—History—Revolution, 1775-1783—Fiction.

Dalgliesh, Alice. *The Courage of Sarah Noble.* Illus. by Leonard Weisgard. Aladdin Books (0-689-71540-4), 1954. 64p. (Interest level: 1-3).

In this Newbery Award–winning book, eight-year-old Sarah travels with her father from Massachusetts to New Milford, Connecticut, to settle land. The recounting of Sarah's time living with a Native American family is gentle, easy to read, and introduces Native American family life without warpaint

and feathers. This story is also available in sound-filmstrip format from Miller-Brody.
♦ Students might locate New Milford on the map and figure how Sarah and her father had to travel to get there from Massachusetts. A discussion of how fast they could travel and why would encourage further research.
1. Indians of North America—Fiction.

Eager, Edward. *Magic or Not?* Illus. by Katie T. Treherne and N. M. Bodecker. Harcourt Brace & Company (0-15-251160-1), 1989. 197p. B/W illus. (Interest level: 3-7).

In this story children who move from the city to a small town in Connecticut discover what seems to be a wishing well. Their first wish is granted, and they are sure they will have an unusual summer. This is a rather tame and outdated book, but it gives one view of small-town Connecticut life.
♦ Students can write a story contrasting city life with small-town life.
1. Magic—Fiction   2. Connecticut—Fiction.

Estes, Eleanor. *Ginger Pye.* Harcourt Brace Jovanovich (0-152-30930-6), 1951. 250p. B/W illus. (Interest level: 3-5).

Cranbury, a fictional town outside New Haven, Connecticut, is halfway between Boston and New York; trains connect it to both. Although this warm family story about the lost puppy, Ginger, is a very old Newbery winner, it is just as poignant today. The Pyes search West Rock, East Rock, Sleeping Giant, and Judge's Cave for the missing puppy.
♦ Since the places mentioned are not fictional, readers may locate them on a map and possibly take a field trip to one of the places.
1. Connecticut—Fiction.

Estes, Eleanor. *The Moffat Museum.* Harcourt Brace Jovanovich (0-15-255086-9), 1983. 262p. B/W illus. (Interest level: 3-5).

Small towns in Connecticut have a flavor all their own as they exist next to and between giant cities. The Moffat children of Cranbury, Connecticut (modeled after the author's home town of West Haven), establish a museum with some unusual exhibits.
♦ Class members may assemble a museum of their own and invite other classes to visit.
1. Connecticut—Fiction.

Herzig, Alison. *The Ten Speed Babysitter.* Dutton (9-99-127050-7), 1991. 144p. (Interest level: 4-6).

Tony finds baby-sitting is not as easy as he thought in this short, humorous novel, which describes a summer experience in a Connecticut seashore town. Although not great literature, this story of life at the shore is funny.

♦ Ask students to write a short story about something that could happen to them during a summer stay at the shore.
1. Babysitters—Fiction   2. Connecticut—Fiction.

Konigsburg, E. L. *From the Mixed-Up Files of Mrs. Basil E. Frankweiler.* Dell (0-44-43180-8), 1993. 161p. B/W illus. (Interest level: 6-8).

Claudia and her brother run away from home and hide out in the Metropolitan Museum of Art in New York. In trying to solve a mystery, they end up at the estate of Mrs. Frankweiler in Farmington. Although Connecticut appears only incidentally in this book, Farmington, a Hartford suburban community in which estates are not uncommon, is discussed.
♦ If possible, students may plan a trip to New York and the Metropolitan Museum of Art, or they may send to the museum for a schedule and any free materials.
1. New York (N.Y.)—Metropolitan Museum of Art—Fiction 2. Runaways—Fiction.

Maestro, Betsy. *Ferryboat.* Illus. by Giulio Maestro. Crowell (0-690-04520-4), 1986. Unpaginated. Color illus. (Interest level: K-2).

This story about the second oldest ferry in Connecticut, the Chester-Hadlyme ferry, is beautifully illustrated in pastel watercolors. Although the story is meant for very young children, it is also appropriate for elementary school-age children, and the historical note on the last page, which gives an interesting and concise history of the ferry, is suitable for older students.
♦ Using a map of Connecticut to locate the ferries, students may write to the department of transportation to find out how they may get schedules and seasons for the ferries. They can then make a chart of seasons and times for all the ferries still running in Connecticut.
1. Ferries—Connecticut.

Murray, Michele. *Crystal Nights.* Dell (0-44-093355-2), 1975 (out of print). 310p. (Interest level: 7-8).

Set on a farm in Connecticut during the hard times of 1938, this story depicts two families learning to survive together. Murray provides an interesting view of Connecticut in a time often neglected.
♦ Students may investigate their own family history during the thirties and write a family memoir of that time.
1. Family—Fiction.

Roche, A. K. *The Pumpkin Heads.* Prentice-Hall, 1971 (out of print). Unpaginated. Color illus. (Interest level: K-3).

The story of how New Haveners came to be known as Pumpkin Heads when a half pumpkin was used to shape their haircuts is retold from an anec-

dote that appeared in the *General History of Connecticut* by the Rev. Samuel Peters in early 1781. This is a funny and unusual book.
♦ Students may draw pictures of themselves or their families with haircuts like early New Haven settlers.
1. Connecticut—Fiction.

Speare, Elizabeth George. *The Witch of Blackbird Pond.* Bantam Doubleday (1-55736-138-X), 1958. 280p. B/W illus. (Interest level: 4-7).

When Kit, coming from Barbados, goes to live in colonial Wethersfield, Connecticut, with an aunt, she becomes involved in a witch hunt. The story is exciting and the writing is smooth in this book, which won a Newbery Award in 1959.
♦ Young people could read more about the Society of Friends and also the witch trials in Connecticut.
1. Connecticut—History—Fiction 2. Witchcraft—Fiction.

Twain, Mark. *A Connecticut Yankee in King Arthur's Court.* Bantam (0-533-21143-9), 1983. 208p. (Interest level: grade 8-adult).

A Hartford native, an arms maker by trade, is knocked out and awakens in Camelot, which he mistakes for Bridgeport. His adventures poke satirical fun at America, Europe, and the church in a clash of times and cultures. The story goes much beyond Connecticut, but the state is used as a measuring stick in many allusions.
♦ Students may view one of the many available videotapes of this story and compare the plots, especially the endings.
1. King Arthur—Fiction.

Underwood, Betty. *The Tamarack Tree.* Houghton Mifflin (0-39-512761-0), 1971. 230p. (Interest level: 6-8).

This novel is based on the trials Prudence Crandall faced when she established her school for "young ladies of color" in Canterbury, Connecticut, in 1833. The book brings to life an important event in Connecticut state history.
♦ Students in Connecticut may plan and undertake a visit to the Prudence Crandall house, which is open for school visitors. Other students may investigate the role of women in society—past and present.
1. Women—Education—Fiction 2. Prejudices—Connecticut—Fiction.

Voigt, Cynthia. *Homecoming.* Atheneum (0-689-30833-7), 1981. 312p. (Interest level: 5-8).

Thirteen-year-old Dicey and her brothers, after being abandoned by their mother in a parking lot, walk the length of Connecticut on Route 1 along the shoreline. The many difficulties of their trip make an exciting and different geography lesson. This is also available on audiocassette from Recorded Books (1992).
♦ Students can make a map and trace Dicey's journey. As a class, discuss what alternatives are available to children in your town should such an event occur.
1. Survival—Fiction 2. Family life—Fiction.

Whitney, Phyllis A. *Mystery of the Angry Idol.* Dell (0-45-109617-7), 1981 (out of print). 224p. (Interest level: 5-7).

A young girl on vacation in Mystic is determined to solve the hidden mystery of a Chinese idol that is in the house she is staying in. The idol is stolen, and the story reaches an exciting climax on the last of the whaling ships, the *Charles W. Morgan*, which is still in Mystic Seaport Museum.
♦ Students in Connecticut may visit the *Charles W. Morgan* and walk through the ship themselves. A cutaway view of the *Charles W. Morgan* could be drawn after visiting the ship. Other students could create a model of the *Charles W. Morgan* to display.
1. Whaling—Fiction 2. Mystery—Fiction.

Periodicals

598
Connecticut Audubon News. Connecticut Audubon Society (No ISSN). Quarterly. (Interest level: grade 4-adult).

Regular features include a calendar of events with trips listed as well as projects and shows; notes from Birdcraft, the society's museum and sanctuary in Fairfield; and tips for bird watching. This pamphlet is excellent for learning about upcoming bird-watching events and increasing and decreasing bird populations.
♦ Students may take a class trip to the society's museum and sanctuary. Other children may plan a bird-watching trip of their own to a nearby park.
1. Birds—Connecticut 2. Connecticut—Periodicals.

639
Connecticut Wildlife. Connecticut Department of Environmental Protection, Bureau of Natural Resources (No ISSN). (Interest level: grade 4-adult).

Short articles concentrate on endangered wildlife in Connecticut, including recent news, special projects, and tips. Often instructions tell how to get further and more specific information on endangered species additions and projects.
♦ Students may take part in one of the many surveys the bureau conducts and send for all the fact sheets on Connecticut endangered species.
1. Wildlife—Connecticut 2. Connecticut—Periodicals.

974.6
Connecticut Magazine. Communications International (ISSN 0889-7670). B/W and Color illus. Monthly. (Interest level: grade 6-adult).

This magazine features a restaurant and travel guide, regular columns on gardening and politics, and articles on controversial subjects, giving a somewhat sophisticated view of Connecticut. The magazine could be useful when certain sections of the state are featured or legislative acts discussed.
♦ Students may read a feature on a controversial subject, read further in local newspapers, and debate the issues.
1. Connecticut—Miscellanea 2. Connecticut—Periodicals.

Professional Materials

326.0973
Sawyer, Kate. *Free Men: The Amistad Revolt and the American Anti-Slavery Movement.* Connecticut Historical Society Education Department (No ISBN), n.d. 88p. B/W photos and maps. (Interest level: Professional).

Written by teachers for teachers at a Yale institute, this book prepares the classroom teacher to present a well-documented unit on an important part of Connecticut history. The curriculum unit outline contains background information, classroom discussions and activities, handouts, and student worksheets.
♦ The suggested activities include math, language arts, and social studies projects that could easily be adapted for grades 4 through 8.
1. Amistad (Schooner)—United States—Connecticut 2. Cinque, Joseph 3. Slavery—United States—Insurrections.

551.46
Weiss, Howard M. and **Dorsey, Michael.** *Investigating the Marine Environment: A Sourcebook. Vol. 3: Teacher Manual.* Project Oceanology (No ISBN), 1979. 435p. B/W illus. and photos. (Interest level: Professional).

The third manual in this series was prepared by Project O to help teachers plan and set up the field and lab studies described in the first two manuals. Everything the teacher needs to know to help students study Connecticut waters in field or lab studies is explained in the same step-by-step manner as in the other manuals (*see* p. 3).
♦ Teachers could help students locate and set up equipment necessary for projects chosen in the first two volumes.
1. Aquatic biology 2. Ecology—Connecticut—Long Island Sound.

917.46
Collier, Christopher and **Collier, Bonnie B.** *The Literature of Connecticut History.* Connecticut Humanities Council (No ISBN), 1983. 376p. (Interest level: Professional).

This scholarly, yet readable, bibliography was prepared by Christopher Collier, Connecticut's official historian, and Bonnie Collier specifically for teachers and students. The annotations are evaluative, often witty, and organized by subject for easy use.
♦ Teachers can find subjects, lists of famous people, and historical events with suggested sources for students to research.
1. Connecticut—History—Bibliography.

917.46
Roth, David M., ed. *Connecticut History and Culture: An Historical Overview and Resource Guide for Teachers.* Connecticut Historical Commission (No ISBN), 1985. 555p. B/W illus. (Interest level: Professional).

Divided into six parts—general information and statistics, period surveys of persons and events, topical surveys, resources, the teaching of Connecticut history, and a time line—this should be an invaluable resource to teachers at all levels. All the sections are useful, but professionals will be greatly helped by the section on teaching Connecticut history.
♦ Teachers might refer to the section on teaching as a starting point for their own units and use resources listed as part of those units.
1. Connecticut—History.

917.46
Tobin, Michael F., ed. *Connecticut Field Trip Guide Book.* EMSPAC (No ISBN), 1986. 22p. B/W illus. (Interest level: Professional).

Tobin's manual, which lists state parks, museums, theaters, early homes, and historical societies in Connecticut suitable for class visits, will need to be updated regularly as it is so useful. The manual includes telephone numbers to call for reservations, information, addresses, and hours.
♦ Students in Connecticut may find four sites within their area that relate to their social studies class, decide in class discussion which would be the most beneficial, and make plans to visit that place. Other students could write to some of the sites for more information.
1. Field trips—Educational 2. Connecticut—Description and travel—Guidebooks.

974.6
Stave, Bruce and **Sutherland, John F.** *Talking about Connecticut: Oral History in the Nutmeg State.* Connecticut Humanities Council (No ISBN), 1985. 118p. B/W illus. (Interest level: Professional).

Oral history is a way of preserving the memories of our citizens that would never be recorded in a book or printed in a periodical. This practical manual gives the mechanics of making oral history tapes with forms and checklists, some especially formulated for schools, as well as some interesting samples.

♦ Using the forms provided in the manual and the directions for creating oral history, the teacher can help children select a subject and put together an oral history of their own.

1. Connecticut—History.

Delaware

by Sharon Brubaker

Nonfiction

386.6
Miller, William J., Jr. *A Ferry Tale, Crossing the Delaware on the Cape May-Lewes Ferry.* Delapeake Publishing (0-911293-03-5), 1984. 110p. B/W photos. (Interest level: grade 6-adult).

Miller presents a complete history of the Cape May-Lewes Ferry, from its conception to its completion and successful business operation. Many interesting anecdotes of ferry history are included, along with useful graphs, maps, and appendixes. This book could supplement a unit on transportation or inland water transport.
♦ Students can build a model of the ferry or create a map of ferries in Delaware from historical times to the present.
1. Cape May-Lewes Ferry   2. Inland water transport—New Jersey   3. Inland water transport—Delaware   4. Delaware.

398
To Market! To Market! Illus. by Peter Spier. Doubleday (0-385-05352-5), 1967. Unpaginated. Color illus. (Interest level: K-adult).

Traditional nursery rhymes highlight the wordless picture story of a farmer and his family going to market in Old New Castle. The brief two-page history of New Castle that appears at the end of the book would be useful on a walking tour of Old New Castle.
♦ The class could create a market day and invite other students in the school.
1. Nursery rhymes.

398.2
Greene, Ellin. *The Legend of the Cranberry.* Simon & Schuster (0-671-75975-2), 1993. 32p. Color illus. (Interest level: K-adult).

Greene offers a retelling of the Delaware Indian legend of the great battle between the early Native Americans and animals against the mastodons. The legend explains that the cranberry is a symbol given by the Great Spirit to represent peace and remind people of the battle.
♦ Young people might enjoy making and tasting various cranberry concoctions such as cranberry juice, cranberry relish, or cranberry bread.
1. Delaware Indians—Legends   2. Mastodons—Folklore   3. Cranberries—Folklore   4. Woolly mammoths—Folklore   5. Mammoths—Folklore   6. Indians of North America—Folkore.

574.9
Amsel, Sheri. *A Wetland Walk.* Millbrook Press (1-56294-213-1), 1993. 32p. Color illus. (Interest level: K-3).

A child's discovery of a marsh is the subject of this rhyming story. An informational page on wetlands is found at the end of the book.
♦ Readers can use the book to assist in identifying plants and animals in wetland areas.
1. Marsh animals   2. Marsh plants   3. Wetland ecology   4. Ecology.

574.974
Hansen, Judith. *Seashells in My Pocket.* Appalachian Mountain Club Books (0-910146-72-1), 1988. 125p. B/W illus. (Interest level: 3-8).

This superb guidebook to seashells also contains a checklist of plants and animals found along the Atlantic Coast. A "sea searchers award" is included in the back of the guide. Readers can use the ruler that is printed inside the back cover to measure finds.
♦ Using this guide, students can create scavenger hunts for one another for a field trip.
1. Seashore biology—Atlantic Coast (U.S.)   2. Shells—Atlantic Coast (U.S.)—Identification.

591.92
Epstein, Sam and Epstein, Beryl. *What's for Lunch? The Eating Habits of Seashore Creatures.* Macmillan (0-02-733500-3), 1985. 48p. B/W illus. (Interest level: 3-6).

The Epsteins describe how various shore creatures such as gulls, crabs, and jellyfish seek and find their food. Though brief, the comprehensive and well-written descriptions will hold the interest of young readers. Detailed black-and-white line drawings clearly illustrate the animal reports.
♦ After researching one of the animals listed in the text, children can create a restaurant menu for that creature.
1. Seashore biology   2. Animals—Food habits.

592.092
Wyler, Rose. *Seashore Surprises.* Messner (0-671-691165-1), 1991. 32p. Color illus. (Interest level: 2-4).

Along with descriptions of plant and animal life, Wyler's book includes explanations of how waves and sand form at the shore. Activities and experiments are suggested.
♦ Children can perform one or more of the activities or experiments suggested in the book, such as trying to make a smooth sea pebble by rubbing a stone against sandpaper, observing a seahopper in the sand and in the water, or counting the ridges on a scallop shell to tell its age.
1. Seashore biology   2. Marine animals   3. Seashore   4. Biology.

598
MacPherson, Mary. *BirdWatch.* Summerhill Press (0-920197-57-4), 1988. 136p. B/W illus. (Interest level: 4-8).

Young bird-watchers will find this a comprehensive, informative guide. MacPherson suggests projects and ideas.
♦ Readers may research, track, and map the species of birds spotted near their school or home.
1. Bird watching   2. Birds.

599
Dingwall, Laima. *Nature's Children—Muskrats.* Grolier (0-7172-1921-6), 1986. 48p. Color photos. (Interest level: 2-5).

Pictorial and factual information on muskrat lifestyle and habitats is gathered here. Dingwall's discussion of muskrat habitats—how muskrats live, where they live, and what they eat—is accompanied by color photos.
♦ Young people can research the muskrat industry of Delaware.
1. Muskrats.

599.32
Arnosky, Jim. *Come Out, Muskrats.* Illus. by author. Lothrop, Lee & Shepard Books (0-688-05458-6), 1989. Unpaginated. Color illus. (Interest level: K-3).

Using a poem-like format, the author creates an exquisite good night book, which follows muskrat activities during the late afternoon and into the twilight. Arnosky's watercolors provide a perfect backdrop as readers step into a peaceful evening with the muskrats.
♦ Students could create a collage of muskrat habitats and activities.
1. Muskrats.

917.49
Lord, Beman. *On the Banks of the Delaware, a View of Its History and Folklore.* Henry Z. Walck (0-8098-2074-9), 1971. 64p. B/W illus. (Interest level: 8).

Folklore and history of the people and places along the banks of the Delaware River are combined in this book. A ghostly tale of the former Delaware governor Johann Printz, who was dared to stay overnight in a haunted house, will interest readers.
♦ The class can collect folklore and tales of their own community by doing research, talking with parents and relatives, or visiting with senior citizens. Students can then compile their own folklore book.
1. Delaware—History   2. Folklore—United States.

917.51
Beautiful Delaware. Beautiful American Publishing (0-89802-208-8), 1981. 69p. Color illus. (Interest level: 4-8).

Here is a county-by-county compilation of photographs of scenic Delaware. Brief explanations of stellar sites and historical figures are given for each county.
♦ Young people can compile a photographic essay of the beauty that represents their own community.
1. Delaware—Description and travel.

917.51
Carpenter, Allan. *Enchantment of America—Delaware from Its Glorious Past to the Present.* (Enchantment of America). Childrens Press (0-516-04108-8), 1979. 95p. Color photos. (Interest level: grade 4-adult).

This work provides an easy-to-read, comprehensive history of Delaware. Students may be familiar with the "Enchantment of America" series. Carpenter writes brief, yet informative passages on the geography, history, Native Americans and settlers, natural and human resources, and industries of

Delaware. Color photographs show various points of interest in the state.
♦ Students can choose a particular time in Delaware history, research it thoroughly, and create a descriptive news program.
1. Delaware—Description and travel.

917.51
Comegys, Fred. *Delaware, Close to Home*. Photos by author. Jared Company Publishers (0-89802-520-6), 1988. 184p. B/W photos. (Interest level: K-adult).

Comegys has compiled a "coffee table" book of photographs of Delaware. The pictures capture images of Delaware and its contemporary history.
♦ Students may write a story about what occurred before, during, or after one or more of the photographs in the book.
1. Delaware—Description and travel.

917.51
Fradin, Dennis. *Delaware in Words and Pictures*. Childrens Press (0-516-03908-3), 1980. 48p. Color photos. (Interest level: 3-6).

"Where were the first log cabins in America built?" "Where did they make the space suits that astronauts wore on the moon?" Fradin proceeds to answer these and other questions about Delaware, covering the history, geography, industries, tourist attractions, and famous Delawareans in an easy-to-read style. A pronunciation guide is incorporated into the text for difficult words, and an appendix listing "facts about Delaware" is included.
♦ Children could write to the Delaware Department of Tourism, requesting travel brochures on Delaware. After discussing the components of these brochures, students could create their own.
1. Delaware—Description and travel.

970.1
The Afton Portfolio of Indians of the Forest. (Posters). Afton Publishing, 1975. 6 posters. (Interest level: K-adult).

This illustrated poster series is designed so that each poster can be used as a unit. Instructional information appears on the back of each.
♦ Readers might conduct further research into the Indians described in this poster series.
1. Indians of North America—Delaware 2. Indians of North America—New Jersey.

970.1
Bock, William Sauts Netamuxwe. *A Coloring Book of the First Americans, Lenape Indian Drawings*. Middle Atlantic Press (0-912608-04-8), 1974. Unpaginated. B/W illus. (Interest level: K-4).

Excellent black-and-white line drawings illustrate Lenape life (including Lenape houses, fishing, food gathering), face paint patterns, and tools. Brief, yet informative notes accompany the illustrations, so that the coloring book pages can be used in a worksheet fashion. These pages are an excellent supplement to other information on Lenape life.
♦ Young people can re-create Lenape face paint patterns as they paint each other's faces.
1. Indians of North America—Delaware 2. Indians of North America—New Jersey.

970.1
Bock, William Sauts Netamuxwe. *The First Americans, Lenape Indian Drawings*. (Kit). Middle Atlantic Press (0-912608-07-2), 1978. Teacher's guide; 22 drawings; 2 full-size posters. (Interest level: 3-6).

Bock's excellent teaching kit on the Lenape Indians of the Mid-Atlantic states includes the history of the Lenape Indians, crafts, tools, games, and recipes.
♦ Children can try one of the recipes or re-create messages from the "Walam Olum," or Lenape picture writing.
1. Indians of North America—Delaware 2. Indians of North America—New Jersey.

970.1
Ewin, Gail. *Lenape Lore—Clothing, Shelter, Crafts, Weapons, Tools, Specialties*. (Kit). Middle Atlantic Press (0-912608-09-9), 1979. Teacher's guide; 16 pages of illus. teaching charts; treasure hunt. (Interest level: 3-6).

The teacher's guide of this kit includes a bulletin board activity, a learning center, whole class lessons, and instructions on how to mount and preserve and make realia.
♦ Students could create some Lenape musical instruments, such as a box turtle rattle or a drum. They could then listen to Native American chants and re-create these chants with their own instruments.
1. Indians of North America—Delaware 2. Indians of North America—New Jersey.

970.1
Ewin, Gail. *Lenape Lore—Foods and Medicines*. (Kit). Middle Atlantic Press (0-912608-08-0), 1978. Teacher's guide; 16 pages of illus. teaching charts; medicine treasure hunt. (Interest level: 3-6).

Ewin's kit includes a teacher's guide, which describes a bulletin board activity, a learning center, lesson plans, and how to turn the classroom into an Indian museum with student curators.
♦ After studying the plant lore and legends of the Delaware area using the kit, young people could go on a nature walk to locate some of the plants listed in the guide. Invite a guest speaker to the classroom to discuss natural foods and medicines. Or, students could create an illustrated chart of

Lenape food and plants that can be found in their community.
1. Indians of North America—Delaware 2. Indians of North America—New Jersey.

970.1
Fenimore, Harvey Curtis, Jr. *Mike and Marnie Learn about Delaware's Indians.* Dover Post Company (No ISBN), 1990. 50p. Illus. (Interest level: 3-6).

Via a somewhat contrived story line, Grandpa tells the factual history of Delaware's Indians to his grandchildren, Mike and Marnie. The information presented is excellent, and the material is broken down into short chapters for easy reading.
♦ Using sticks and small pieces of brushwood and rush or bamboo place mats, children can create their own wickiup or other Indian dwelling.
1. Indians of North America—Delaware 2. Delaware—History.

970.1
Penn, William. *William Penn's Own Account of the Lenni Lenape or Delaware Indians.* Edited by Albert Cook Myers. Middle Atlantic Press (0-912608-13-7), 1970. 96p. B/W photos. (Interest level: 6-8).

William Penn's personal impressions of the Lenape Indians in 1683 are contained in this book. Portions can be read aloud or excerpted for use with younger children.
♦ After reading the colorful descriptions of the Lenni Lenape, young people can create illustrations for the diaries, either in the form of a book or a bulletin board.
1. Indians of North America—Delaware.

975.1
Fenimore, Harvey Curtis, Jr. *Mike and Marnie Learn about Delaware's Symbols, Slogan, Name, and Nicknames.* Dover Post Company (No ISBN), 1990. 136p. B/W illus. (Interest level: 3-6).

Mike and Marnie learn about Delaware from their storytelling grandfather. Fennimore presents a useful book that conveys factual information via a story format.
♦ After reading the book, students can create a Delaware trivia or a Delaware Jeopardy game.
1. Delaware—History.

975.1
Hoffecker, Carol E. *Brandywine Village, the Story of a Milling Community.* Old Brandywine Village (No ISBN), 1974. 111p. B/W photos. (Interest level: 7-8).

Hoffecker provides a historical account of Brandywine Village in Wilmington, Delaware. An excellent photographic history is interspersed throughout the book.
♦ Readers in Delaware can take a ride on the Wilmington-Western Railroad to view the mill area along the Brandywine. Others can make a model of the mill.
1. Wilmington (Del.)—History.

975.1
Kent, Deborah. *America the Beautiful. Delaware.* Childrens Press (0-516-00454-9), 1991. 144p. Color photos and illus. (Interest level: 4-8).

Kent summarizes the geography, history, industry, and people of Delaware. Excellent appendixes list important dates and notables with thumbnail biographies
♦ Children can create their own mini-tour of Delaware in pamphlet form or illustrate a large map with information and drawings.
1. Delaware.

975.1
Lunt, Dudley Cammett. *Taylor's Gut.* Middle Atlantic Press (0-912608-30-7), 1968. 303p. (Interest level: 6-8).

This book provides a naturalist's look at Taylor's Gut, a lovely natural area in Delaware. The prose, some of which appears in diary format, is exquisite. A map of the area is included.
♦ Students in Delaware can read this book before visiting Taylor's Gut. Compare the text with the naturalist writings of Henry David Thoreau, Edwin Way Teale, and Hal Borland.
1. Delaware.

975.1
Lyman, Nancy A. *The Colony of Delaware.* Franklin Watts (0-531-00829-0), 1975. 88p. B/W illus. (Interest level: 4-8).

The author concentrates on Delaware's various political activities and leaders and the state's active role in America's fight for freedom. Lyman provides a comprehensive history of early Delaware before the ratification of the Constitution.
♦ Readers can take on the roles of Tories and Sons of Liberty and debate whether or not America should become independent.
1. Delaware—History—Colonial period, ca 1660-1775 2. Delaware—History—Revolution, 1775-1783.

975.1
Pyle, Katharine. *Once upon a Time in Delaware.* Colonial Dames of America (No ISBN), 1911 (out of print). 164p. B/W illus. (Interest level: 4-6).

Pyle writes stories of significant events in Delaware history, such as the arrival of the Dutch in Zwannendael, the building of Fort Christina, William Penn's landing in New Castle, Caesar Rodney's ride for freedom, and George Washington's and Lafayette's visits to Delaware. The historical

events are described in an interesting story format, excellent for reading aloud.
♦ Young people might choose an important historical event, write a story about it, and then share the stories aloud with classmates.
1. Delaware—History.

975.1
Reed, Clay. *Delaware Colony*. Crowell-Collier (No ISBN), 1970. 131p. (Interest level: 3-8).
Clay paints a vivid portrait of Delaware history from the colonial period to the American Revolution. An excellent addendum lists places to visit in Delaware.
♦ Students can create colorful time lines of Delaware history from the colonial period to the American Revolution.
1. Delaware—History—Colonial period—ca 1600-1775.

975.1
Thompson, Kathleen. *Delaware*. Raintree Publishers (0-86514-450-8), 1987. 48p. Color photos; B/W map. (Portrait of America Series). (Interest level: 3-6).
Delaware history, economics, and culture are covered in this brief overview. Useful appendixes and a black-line map of Delaware's counties are included.
♦ Using the black-line map, students can chart information they have gleaned from the book. Children could also make a salt dough or clay relief map.
1. Delaware.

975.1
Weslager, C. A. *A Man and His Ship: Peter Minuit and the Kalmar Nyckel*. Kalmar Nyckel Foundation (0-9625563-1-9), 1989. 225p. B/W photos and maps. (Interest level: grade 8-adult).
Biographical as well as historical, this book describes the historical events surrounding Peter Minuit and his business—sailing from Europe to the colonies. These trips led to the founding of the first permanent European settlement in Delaware.
♦ If possible, students can visit Fort Christina Park in Wilmington, Delaware. Or, they could map the voyages of the *Kalmar Nyckel*.
1. Delaware—History.

975.1
Weslager, C. A. *New Sweden on the Delaware: 1638-1655*. Illus. by Nancy Sawin. Middle Atlantic Press (0-912608-65-X), 1988. 219p. B/W illus. (Interest level: grade 8-adult).
Weslager documents the voyages and settlements of Swedish immigrants in Delaware from 1638 to 1655 and relates how the Swedes settled the Delaware colony, traded with the Native Americans, and interacted with the Dutch. This is an interesting and vivid portrait of the life of early Delawareans.
♦ Students can construct a model of an early Swedish-Finn homestead.
1. Delaware—History.

975.1
Wilson, W. Emerson. *Fort Delaware*. University of Delaware (No ISBN), 1986. 32p. B/W photos. (Interest level: 6-8).
Wilson provides a brief history of Fort Delaware and its importance as a prison during the Civil War. Additional information on how the fort was modernized and later became a state park is also included.
♦ Teachers might use this work before or after a visit to the historical site or with a unit on the Civil War and Delaware's role during the war. As a follow-up, children can pretend they are Civil War prisoners and write accounts of life in a Civil War prison.
1. United States—History—Civil War, 1861-1865—Prisoners and prisons 2. Fort Delaware (Del.)—History.

975.102
Christensen, Gardell Dano and Burney, Eugenia. *Delaware*. Thomas Nelson (0-8047-7118-5), 1974. 156p. B/W photos. (Interest level: 6-8).
The authors summarize the history of Delaware, from its discovery and first settlement to the ratification of the Constitution.
♦ Working with partners, young people can imagine they are time travelers and write, illustrate, and explain which of Delaware's historical figures they would choose to bring to the present and why.
1. Delaware—History—Colonial period, ca 1600-1775. 2. Delaware—History—Revolution, 1775-1778.

975.11
Sawin, Nancy. *Up the Spine and Down the Creek, a Pictorial History from Queen Christina to William Penn*. North Light Studio (No ISBN), 1982. 97p. B/W illus. (Interest level: K-adult).
Sites of northern Delaware and southeastern Pennsylvania are the focus of this pictorial history. Anecdotes and useful illustrations of early tools of the settlers are provided.
♦ Students might design and create their own sketchbooks of various Delaware sites.
1. Historic sites—Delaware 2. Delaware—History—Pictorial works.

975.11
Sawin, Nancy and McEwing, Barbara. *North from Wilmington by Oulde Roades and Turnpikes, including Brandywine and Christina Hundreds, Dela-

ware; and Adjacent Areas of Pennsbury and Bethel Townships, Pennsylvania. North Light Studio (No ISBN), 1992. 138p. Illus. (Interest level: K-adult).

This work is primarily a sketchbook of historical homes and sites of northern Delaware and southeastern Pennsylvania.
♦ Young people could research the history of roads and transportation in the Delaware area, focusing particularly on the route of Old Baltimore Pike and/or the New Castle Frenchtown Railroad.
1. Delaware—History.

Biography

92 Bradford, Phoebe George
Wilson, W. Emerson, ed. *Diaries of Phoebe George Bradford, 1832-1839*. Historical Society of Delaware, 1976. 84p. (Interest level: 7-8).

Fascinating diaries of a Wilmington woman provide insight into society life. The diaries focus on day-to-day events and include brief passages of Phoebe's encounters with other noted Delawareans, her duty to her church and society, her thoughts on political issues, and events both city- and nationwide.
♦ Students in Delaware can take a walking tour of Phoebe's world, noting changes in the architecture and in the city of Wilmington. Other students can compare and contrast Phoebe's life events to those of Catharine in Joan Blos's *A Gathering of Days* (Aladdin, 1990).
1. Bradford, Phoebe George—Biography 2. Delaware—History 3. Wilmington (Del.)—History.

92 Rodney, Caesar
Frank, William P. *Caesar Rodney Patriot, Delaware's Hero for All Times and All Seasons*. Illus. by Ann N. Wyeth. Delaware American Revolution Bicentennial Commission (No ISBN), 1975 (out of print). 32p. Illus. (Interest level: 7-8).

Frank's brief biographical pamphlet delineates Caesar Rodney's various accomplishments, including his famous ride to Philadelphia to sign the Declaration of Independence.
♦ If possible, the class can take a field trip to downtown Wilmington, Delaware, to view the statue of Caesar Rodney in Rodney Square. Or, students can map out Rodney's ride to Philadelphia to sign the Declaration of Independence.
1. Rodney, Caesar, 1728-1784—Biography 2. Delaware—History.

Fiction

Albert, Burton. *Where Does the Trail Lead?* Illus. by Brian Pinkney. Simon & Schuster (0-671-73409-1), 1991. 32p. Color illus. (Interest level: All ages).

Albert's story of a boy's exploration of an island evokes the feelings familiar to many Delawareans about marsh, bay, and sea areas. Pinkney's scratchboard illustrations add to the magic of the boy's discoveries.
♦ Using paint, crayons, or scratchboard paper, children can make their own scratchboard pictures.
1. Seashore—Fiction.

Coatsworth, Elizabeth. *The Big Green Umbrella*. Grossett and Dunlap (No ISBN), 1944 (out of print). Unpaginated. B/W illus. (Interest level: 2-6).

Coatsworth tells the story of the biggest, greenest silk umbrella in New Castle, Delaware, which flies from the hands of Mr. Thomas and is rescued by a ship's captain in the Delaware River. The umbrella travels from Delaware to China and back again.
♦ Students can map the umbrella's travels. A replica of the big green umbrella can be seen at the Amstel House in Old New Castle, Delaware.
1. Delaware—Fiction.

Curran, Polly. *Pea Patch Island*. Illus. by Ronald Himler. Golden Press (0-307-15693-1), 1975 (out of print). 32p. B/W illus. (Interest level: K-4).

This humorous folktale tells how Pea Patch Island was created in the midst of the Delaware River. After a colonial ship runs aground on a sandbar in the Delaware River, dumping a load of peas, an island of peas begins to grow in the middle of the river.
♦ As a science project, young people can grow peas in individual cups to create their own Pea Patch Islands.
1. Folklore—United States.

De Angeli, Marguerite. *Elin's Amerika*. Doubleday (No ISBN), 1941 (out of print). 96p. B/W illus. (Interest level: 3-6).

The story of young Elin of Sweden and her family as they pioneer in young America mirrors the lives of Swedish settlers in northern Delaware and southeastern Pennsylvania. This is an excellent read-aloud.
♦ Students in Delaware can visit the site of the Old Swedes Church in Wilmington. Children might also enjoy re-creating the Swedish holiday custom of St. Lucia.
1. Pioneers—Fiction 2. Family life—Fiction.

Meg, Elizabeth. *Packet Alley, a Magic Story of Now and Long Ago*. G. P. Putnam's Sons (No ISBN), 1951 (out of print). 182p. B/W illus. (Interest level: 4-8).

A wonderful read-aloud, this is the story of two children who are granted the use of magic glasses from a "little dutchman." The glasses take them back in time to visit important New Castle, Delaware, historical events.

♦ As the book is read aloud, children can make a list of dignitaries who pass through Packet Alley. Then they can research each of these people further. If possible, students can also visit Packet Alley in Old New Castle.
1. Delaware—Fiction.

Mitchell, Barbara. *Cornstalks and Cannonballs*. Dell Young Yearling (0-440-40533-5), 1980. 46p. Illus. (Interest level: 1-4).

Mitchell tells how the people of Lewes, Delaware, tricked the English navy into thinking they had a much larger army guarding the town during the War of 1812. As a result, the English retreated.
♦ Students can compare and contrast this tale of trickery with other folklore tales of tricksters.
1. Lewes (Del.)—History—War of 1812 2. United States—History—War of 1812—Naval operations.

Professional Materials

917.49
O'Brien, Alice Rowan. *Places to Go with Children in the Delaware Valley*. Chronicle Books (0-87701-581-3), 1989. 139p. B/W photos. (Interest level: Professional).

A listing of area museums and attractions in the Delaware Valley, which includes Pennsylvania, Delaware, and New Jersey, is provided in this book.
♦ Gathering information from the book and from informational tourist pamphlets, students can plan a real or imaginary trip to one of the sites using maps and gauging travel time and distance from home or school.
1. Delaware River Valley (Penn., Del., and N.J.)—Description and travel—Guidebooks 2. Family recreation—Delaware River Valley (Penn., Del., and N.J.)—Guidebooks.

District of Columbia

by Bester Bonner

Nonfiction

328.7
Our Federal Government: The Legislative Branch. (Videocassette). Rainbow Educational Video, 1991. (Our Federal Government Series). Color, (22 min.). $99.00. (Interest level: 5-8).

Decisions made by government leaders in Washington, DC, affect the lives of people throughout the United States. From this video, students will learn requirements for becoming a member of Congress and pertinent information on how the legislative branch interacts with other branches of government in the nation's capital. Live action, historical prints, graphics, and documentary footage help tell the story.
♦ After viewing the video, young people can list the requirements for becoming a member of Congress and discuss the validity of each.
1. United States—Congress.

347
Our Federal Government: The Supreme Court. (Videocassette). Rainbow Educational Video, (1-56701-0253), 1991. (Our Federal Government Series). Color, (22 min.). $99.00. (Interest level: 5-8).

Washington, DC, is a city where federal legislation is initiated, enforced, and interpreted. This video, which is relatively easy to follow and understand, describes the origins of the judicial branch of the federal government, including the Supreme Court, and explains how the balance of power works among the three branches of government. Librarians and teachers will find this resource a useful addition for social studies and government classes.
♦ Children can conduct research on the Supreme Court Building in Washington, DC, and identify the composition of the Supreme Court. Class members could conduct a mock Supreme Court session.
1. United States—Supreme Court.

353.03
Our Federal Government: The Presidency. (Videocassette). Rainbow Educational Video (1-56701-024-5), 1991. (Our Federal Government Series). Color, (22 min.). $99.00. (Interest level: 5-8).

This video explores how the Constitution established the executive branch of the federal government and provided for the separation of powers. Viewers will also learn how the executive branch relates to the legislative and judicial branches of the federal government.
♦ Using information in the video series and other sources in the library, students can chart how a bill becomes a law.
1. Executive power—United States.

362.7
Hubbard, Jim. *Shooting Back: A Photographic View of Life by Homeless Children.* Chronicle Books (08118-0019-9), 1991. 115p. B/W illus. (Interest level: 1-8).

In response to the worsening plight of the homeless comes this moving collection of black-and-white photographs taken by homeless children in Washington, DC. Shooting Back, an education and media center founded by photographer Jim Hubbard in 1989, brings together volunteer photographers and homeless and other at-risk children. This vital program gives the children the basic skills needed to convey their vision of the world through the medium of photography.
♦ Children can organize a pen-pal photography club and communicate through photography.
1. Homeless children—Washington (D.C.)—Pictorial works   2. Inner cities—Washington (D.C.)—Pictorial works.

641.5
The Washington Cookbook: A Tasteful Tour of the Nation's Capital. Illus. by Lily Spandorf. Washington Opera/John F. Kennedy Center for Performing

Arts (0-9610542-0-4), 1982. 200p. (Interest level: grade 8-adult).

This cookbook to benefit the Washington Opera contains over 500 recipes, including appetizers, breads, and pasta. Line drawings of Washington sights have cleverly been placed in the book. Recipes are listed by categories at the beginning and completely indexed at the end.
♦ Students can prepare recipes from this cookbook when studying various units in history/social studies.
1. Cookery—Washington (D.C.).

784.5
National Gallery of Art. *An Illustrated Treasury of Songs.* Rizzoli (0-84781376-2), 1991. 128p. (Interest level: grade 1-adult).

With old-fashioned appeal, this book combines traditional songs with quality prints of paintings selected from the National Gallery of Art in Washington, DC. For each print, the title, artist's name, and date are given, supplemented by more information at the end of the book. More than 50 songs, ranging from nursery rhymes to old favorites, are included.
♦ Young people can plan a concert and perform the songs in this book for other children in the school.
1. Music, Popular 2. Songs, American.

917.3
Aikman, Lonnelle. *We the People, the Story of the United States Capitol.* United States Historical Society (0-916-20001-9), 1967. 143p. Color photos; B/W illus. (Interest level: 6-8).

Aikman takes a historical look at one of Washington's most famous and respected landmarks, the Capitol building. The congressional meeting hall is featured with a chronology of its development and vivid interior and exterior photos and illustrations. Although this is an earlier work on the United States Capitol, it has exceptionally good photographs and the text has been carefully researched.
♦ This will provide an excellent reference tool for students as they research the Capitol building.
1. Historic buildings—Washington (D.C.)—Description.

917.5
Berman, Eleanor. *Reflections of Washington, D.C.* Photos by Robert Llewellyn. Gallery Books/Wilt Smith (0-8317-9311-2), 1991. 175p. Color photos. (Interest level: 6-8).

Washington, DC, is a showcase for everything that is best about the United States, and its splendor is captured in glorious color by one of Washington's most noted photographers, Robert Llewellyn. Berman presents a human chronicle of the city's development from swamp-ridden backwater to world center. All of Washington's drama, excitement, and beauty is captured in over 200 brilliant photographs and a fascinating account of the city's past and present.
♦ In groups, students can select photographs of various buildings, find and read books about the buildings, and stage a guided tour.
1. Washington (D.C.) in art 2. Washington (D.C.)—History—Pictorial works.

917.5
Brown, Ellen, et al. *The Best of Washington, D.C.* Prentice Hall (0-1306-8230-6), 1990. 389p. (Interest level: grade 8-adult).

Readers will find a variety of discriminating information on restaurants, cafes, delis, hotels, and shopping bests, as well as tips on how to get around and enjoy the very best of Washington, DC. Alcohol advertisements might require adult guidance if contents are used for teaching activities with young people.
♦ For a unit involving Washington, DC, young people can select specific sections from one of the guides to the city. After they have completed their books, they can lead a class discussion comparing and contrasting the contents of the different guides.
1. Washington (D.C.)—Description—Guidebooks.

917.5
Choukas-Bradley, Melanie and **Alexander, Polly.** *City of Trees: The Complete Field Guide to the Trees of Washington, D.C.* Acropolis Books (0-8018-3320-5), 1987. 354p. B/W and Color photos and illus. (Interest level: 1-8).

Each spring, thousands converge on the shores of the Potomac hoping to get a glimpse of Washington, DC's famous cherry trees in bloom. In this stunning and complete botanical and historical guide to trees in DC, the authors identify over 300 species from all over the world. Informative narrative is complemented by brilliant color photos of trees and line drawings of various leaves.
♦ Children can take a nature walk in their community and collect leaves. Using this book and others, they can identify and then mount and display the leaves.
1. Trees in cities—Washington (D.C.) 2. Trees—Washington (D.C.) 3. Washington (D.C.)—Description.

917.5
Churchman, Deborah and **Oman, Anne H.** *Saturday's Child: Family Activities in Metropolitan Washington.* Illus. by Becky Heavner. Washington Book Trading Company (0-9151-6811-1), 1987. 209p. B/W illus. (Interest level: grade 4-adult).

In writing this book, the authors combined their roles as parents and journalists. They took their children to attractions all around the region and took

notes, focusing on opportunities that are not well known. This guide will be helpful in planning outings for any day of the week.
♦ Young people may identify places they have visited in Washington, DC, or a place they would like to visit. They can then make a book of places to visit, either in Washington, DC, or other places, such as their own community, and place it in the library for others to use.
1. Washington (D.C.)—Description—Guidebooks 2. Children—Travel—Washington (D.C.)—Guidebooks 3. Family recreation—Washington (D.C.)—Guidebooks.

917.5
Clark, Diane. *A Kid's Guide to Washington, D.C.* Harcourt Brace Jovanovich (0-15-200459-9), 1989. 153p. B/W illus. (Interest level: 1-4).

Clark's guide contains everything that a traveling kid needs for the perfect vacation in the nation's capital, including what the weather is like, where to go, how to go, and what to do once you're there. A travel diary, puzzles, and calendar of events add to the appeal of the book.
♦ After reviewing this book, students can put together their own guide to their community.
1. Washington (D.C.)—Description—Guidebooks 2. Children—Travel—Washington (D.C.)—Guidebooks.

917.5
Climo, Shirley. *City! Washington, D.C.* Illus. by George Ancona. Macmillan Child Group (0-12-719036-6), 1991. 64p. Color illus. (Interest level: 3-7).

In a delightful, beautifully illustrated book on Washington, DC, Climo skillfully intertwines heritage and ongoing history, taking the reader on a grand tour of the city. The text is brief but informative; the illustrations are superb; and a two-page map of the city and an index are included. This is one of the more recently published books on Washington, DC, for this interest level.
♦ Students can use this book as a model as they prepare a similar guide to their own community or state.
1. Washington (D.C.)—Description—Guidebooks.

917.5
Colbert, Judy. *Places to Go with Children in Washington, D.C.* Chronicle Books (0-87701-818-9), 1991. (Places to Go Series). 157p. (Interest level: 3-8).

A recently published work on Washington, DC, this book features a wide range of attractions for children and teenagers, from the best-known and most often visited places to such surprising sites of interest as the catacombs under the Lincoln Memorial and the fiberglass triceratops on the Washington Mall. A number of backstairs tours are listed for those who love to see how things work. Visitors and residents alike will find this to be a useful travel and planning guide to activities and points of interest in the nation's capital, and libraries may want to purchase the book to supplement some of their older titles.
♦ Readers can choose one of the points of interest listed in this book to research more fully and report to the class. They might also use this resource to plan a trip to Washington, DC, real or imaginary.
1. Washington (D.C.)—Description—Guidebooks 2. Children—Travel—Washington (D.C.)—Guidebooks 3. Family recreation—Washington (D.C.)—Guidebooks.

917.5
Douglas, Evelyn E. and **Dickerson, Paul**. *On This Spot: Pinpointing the Past in Washington, D.C.* Farragut (0-918535-14-X), 1991. 266p. B/W photos and illus. (Interest level: grade 6-adult).

This historical guidebook to Washington, DC, carries the reader back in time and locates the sites where important (or just plain fascinating) events took place and where figures from American history lived, worked, and died. The user will want to read this work in bits and pieces. The text, along with more than 125 black-and-white photos and line drawings, highlights the sites.
♦ Class members can create a slide/tape show of historic places in Washington, DC.
1. Washington (D.C.)—Description—Guidebooks 2. Historic sites—Washington (D.C.)—Guidebooks 3. Washington (D.C.)—History.

917.5
Duffield, Judy; **Kramer, William**; and **Sheppard, Cynthia**. *Washington, D.C.: The Complete Guide.* Random House (0-394-71030-4), 1982. 360p. B/W illus. (Interest level: grade 5-adult).

Readers follow the authors from the state rooms of the White House to the Houses of Congress as they depict the beauty of the capital city in this complete guide to historic and tourist sights. This guide, like many others, contains a wealth of information on the nation's capital, both past and present.
♦ Students can browse through different guidebooks on Washington, DC, and explain what they like or dislike about particular ones. They can then use this information as they create their own guidebook to their community or state capital.
1. Washington (D.C.)—Description—Guidebooks.

917.5
Fitzpatrick, Sandra and **Goodwin, Maria R.** *The Guide to Black Washington: Places and Events of Historical and Cultural Significance in the Nation's Capital.* Hippocrene Books (0-87052-832-7), 1989.

289p. B/W photos and illus. (Interest level: grade 6-adult).

Fitzpatrick and Goodwin provide a guide to many of the people and places of historical significance within the black community in Washington, DC. Residences, churches, auditoriums, schools, and people are highlighted.

♦ To encourage an appreciation of cultural diversity and have students experience a greater understanding of African American culture, have students locate books by and about blacks in Washington, DC, read them, and share the books with the class.

1. Washington (D.C.)—Description—Tours 2. African Americans—Homes and haunts—Washington (D.C.)—Guidebooks 3. Historic buildings—Washington (D.C.).

917.5
Fradin, Dennis B. *Washington, D.C.* Childrens Press (0-516-03851-6), 1992. (From Sea to Shining Sea Series). 64p. Color photos. (Interest level: 2-4).

Fradin's introduction to the nation's capital city, its people, and sites of interest recounts the city's history. The book highlights not only many famous landmarks, but also some of the other things that the District of Columbia is known for, such as giant pandas, the Washington Redskins, and famous personalities. Readers will find the "Gallery of Famous Washingtonians" fascinating. A historical chronology, map key, and glossary give added appeal to this title.

♦ Children may select one of the people listed in the "Gallery of Famous Washingtonians" and read a biography on that person. Then, each student can role-play the person he or she has selected, while class members try to identify the person portrayed.

1. Washington (D.C.).

917.5
Frommer's Family Travel Guide: Washington, D.C. with Kids. Prentice Hall (0-13-333360-4), 1992. (Frommer's Family Travel Guide Series). 253p. (Interest level: grade 4-adult).

Enjoy the best Washington, DC, family vacations and other visits with this comprehensive, easy-to-use guide. The book has the following features: a calendar of events, what to plan for or avoid, suggested itineraries for every age group, easy-to-read maps, city and area sights, and hotel and restaurant locations—all referred to in or keyed to the text. All the essentials are provided at a glance: business hours, currency, embassies, emergency services, and more.

♦ Students can borrow other guidebooks on Washington, DC, from the school library and plan an imaginary trip for the class to Washington, DC.

1. Washington (D.C.)—Description and travel—Guidebooks.

917.5
Going Places with Children in Washington, D.C. Green Acres School (0-9608998-2-0), 1989. 260p. B/W illus. (Interest level: grade 4-adult).

Readers will be instantly drawn to this guide. Families visiting Washington, DC, often find this guide more valuable than the conventional guidebooks because parents have actually explored and evaluated the places listed. Included are main sights and museums in DC and other areas, day trips outside the city, nature, shopping, entertainment, and more.

♦ Based on the evaluations given in the book, children can choose specific sites to visit and explain their choices.

1. Washington (D.C.)—Description—Guidebooks 2. Washington region—Description and travel—Guidebooks 3. Family recreation—Washington (D.C.) 4. Family recreation—Washington region.

917.5
Gottlief, Steven. *Washington: Portraits of a City.* Acropolis Books (0-87491-771-9), 1991. 140p. Color photos. (Interest level: grade 4-adult).

A magnificent work in an oversized format, this album of 94 remarkable full-color photographs captures every aspect of the nation's capital, from the familiar monuments to the less familiar sculptures, quiet churches, and small parks. These fresh and luminous images, along with Washington art critic Frank Getlein's words, create a truly memorable portrait of a great city. Students will find the photographer's notes and technical data for each photograph useful and informative.

♦ Students could create a photo essay of their own community, capturing the essence of the area. Appropriate captions should accompany the photographs. A descriptive introduction could explain why certain photographs were included.

1. Washington (D.C.)—Description—Views.

917.5
Kane, Robert S. *Washington, D.C. at Its Best.* Passport Books (0-8442-9584-1), 1991. 221p. (Interest level: grade 8-adult).

This fully indexed guide to Washington attractions, written by one of America's top travel writers, includes parks, museums, embassies, churches, residences, restaurants, famous buildings, and hotels that may interest travelers or sightseers. The arrangement of this book, alphabetic by headings, makes it easy to locate information.

♦ Readers could choose a specific church, park, or restaurant to research further to find out its history and how and why it became famous.

1. Washington (D.C.)—Description—Guidebooks.

917.5
Krementz, Jill. *A Visit to Washington, D.C.* Scholastic (0-590-40583-7), 1987. 48p. Color illus. (Interest level: K-2).

Six-year-old Matt and his family visit usual and unusual points of interest in Washington, DC. A good introductory guide for children, this book takes readers on a tour of famous landmarks in the nation's capital through large color photographs and brief text. Endpapers provide maps that clearly indicate all sites mentioned in the text. A reference list of places to visit, with addresses, telephone numbers, and visiting times, is included.
♦ This is another source for children to consult as they prepare their own guidebook.
1. Washington (D.C.)—Description—Guidebooks.

917.5
Llewellyn, Robert. *Washington: The District and Beyond.* Howell Press (0-943231-10-8), 1991. 123p. Color photos. (Interest level: 6-8).

Llewellyn takes readers on an aerial sight-seeing tour of the nation's capital, with spectacular portraits of historic neighborhoods, renowned universities, and noted cultural centers. From high above the District of Columbia and its environs, he captures with great artistry the area's sprawling beauty and diversity. Readers will discover that the text and the full range of flawless color photos create a breathtaking panorama of the Washington region.
♦ Guide students in activities that will give them greater appreciation for their own communities. Children could take photographs and write accompanying descriptions that capture a specific aspect of their community—such as beauty, diversity, or history.
1. Washington (D.C.)—Description—Views.

917.5
Price, Robert L., comp. and ed. *The Washington Post Guide to Washington.* McGraw (0-07-68394-8), 1989. 430p. (Interest level: grade 8-adult).

The authors of this book are Washington reporters, men and women who have walked the streets of Washington reporting the gigantic events and the little happenings in this vitally important place. In addition to intriguing accounts of suspense and drama, the authors provide the reader with comprehensive information on places to see in Washington, DC. The appendix, index, floor plans, and maps add to the value of this delightful guide to Washington.
♦ Arrange a visit to a newsroom to get firsthand information on the job of a reporter. Students can then produce a newsletter about their own community based on the contents of this book.
1. Washington (D.C.)—Description—Guidebooks.

917.5
Reps, John William. *Washington on View: The Nation's Capital since 1790.* University of South Carolina Press (0-807-19488-4), 1991. 297p. Color and B/W photos. (Interest level: grade 6-adult).

History and modern life come together in this pictorial history, which includes more than 100 views of the nation's capital from 1790 through the present, most in full color. The photographs in this oversized book, combined with appropriate text, can effectively support history, art, and communication arts classes. Bibliographical references and an exhaustive index enhance its usefulness.
♦ Young people can use this resource as they research the historical background of the city. They could then create a model or several models of how the city appeared in its early days of development.
1. Washington (D.C.)—Description—Views
2. Washington (D.C.)—History—Pictorial works
3. Washington (D.C.) in art.

917.5
Ross, Betty. *A Museum Guide to Washington, D.C.* Americana Press (0-9616144-0-4), 1986. 242p. B/W photos. (Interest level: grade 6-adult).

Ross's carefully researched book, designed for residents and tourists, young and old, art lovers and history buffs, tells readers what to see in 50 DC museums, historic houses, libraries, and special places open to the public. Included are biographies and historical backgrounds, anecdotes, in-depth reports on museum collections, information on hours, restaurants, and much more.
♦ Each student can choose a painting, sculpture, or artifact to research in-depth. This source would be an excellent starting point.
1. Museums—Washington (D.C.)—Guidebooks
2. Historic buildings—Washington (D.C.)—Guidebooks 3. Washington (D.C.)—Description—Guidebooks.

917.5
Sasek, Mirosla. *This Is Washington, D.C.* Macmillan (0-0204-5180-6), 1969. (This Is . . . Series). 60p. Color illus. (Interest level: 2-4).

In this delightful book on Washington, DC, Sasek takes the young reader on an adventurous tour of a number of historic places—the Bureau of Engraving and Printing, the Corcoran Gallery of Art, the Washington Memorial, and the Supreme Court Building, to name a few. Lovely color drawings enhance the text. Though not as current as some of the other books on the city, this book merits continued inclusion in library collections because the author's treatment gives the young reader a good, yet brief introduction to Washington, DC.
♦ Students can use this resource to create a slide/tape show about what to see and do in the

District of Columbia. They may wish to make one tape for younger children and one for adults. They should indicate why they chose specific places.
1. Washington (D.C.)—Description and travel—Guidebooks.

917.5
Shaw, Ray. *Washington for Children.* Charles Scribner's Sons (0-684-14016-0), 1974. 196p. (Interest level: grade 6-adult).

Over 300 things to do are presented in this comprehensive guide to the unusual, offbeat, and exciting in and around Washington, DC, for young people, families, and teachers. Shaw outlines the attractions in eight chapters, covering topics from technology and modern life to gardens and nature. Entries give pertinent information on sites, and an index and a listing of annual events are included.
◆ Young people could create a similar guidebook for their own community featuring unusual and offbeat places to visit and things to do.
1. Washington (D.C.)—Description and travel—Guidebooks.

917.5
Turck, Mary. *Washington, D.C.* Crestwood House/Macmillan (0-89686-470-7), 1989. (See the USA Series). 48p. Color photos. (Interest level: 3-7).

Stimulate interest in Washington, DC, with this guide to attractions. Exciting places to explore include the Smithsonian Institution, the White House, and Arlington National Cemetery. A brief history, an index of people and places, city maps, and weather tips further add to the value of this title.
◆ Ask each student to submit two questions on Washington, DC. Then, divide students into teams and give each team an equal number of questions. Using guidebooks in the library, teams will locate answers to the questions. Upon completion, young people can share answers in a "share and tell"session.
1. Washington (D.C.)—Description—Guidebooks
2. Washington region—Description and travel—Guidebooks.

917.5
Washington, D.C.: A Picture Book to Remember Her By. Crescent Books (0-517263017), 1987. 64p. Color photos. (Interest level: 3-8).

Photographs, taken all over Washington, DC, of monuments and tourist attractions, both daylight and nighttime views, make up this beautiful book. The text, which has been kept to a minimum, consists of one- or two-paragraph descriptions of each monument photographed.
◆ Students can compare historical dates to architectural forms of monuments in the resources and then write reports telling how historical events impact art forms.
1. Washington (D.C.)—Description—Views
2. Washington (D.C.)—History.

917.5
Washington, DC: A Traveler's Guide to the District of Columbia and Nearby Attractions. Official National Park Guidebook. National Park Service (0-912627-36-0), 1989. 175p. (Interest level: grade 8-adult).

Washington, DC, is the home of many of the nation's monuments and memorials, which are often run by the National Park Service. This guide is designed to promote understanding and enjoyment of the park and to serve as informative reading and a useful guide before, during, and after a park visit. Colorful photographs of people and places, basic information on places to visit, and a comprehensive index are included.
◆ Readers may use maps of their states to locate state and national parks in their region. They could then plan a trip to a national or state park and create a guidebook of things they wish to see and do.
1. Washington (D.C.)—Description and travel—Guidebooks.

917.5
Washington, D.C., Fancy Free. (Videocassette or 16mm film). National Audiovisual Center, 1976. Color, (22 min.). $110.00 for video; $235.00 for 16mm film. (Interest level: 3-8).

This photomontage illustrates the wide variety of opportunities for visitors to Washington. Viewers get geographical coverage of Washington, DC, as well as a glimpse of history, government, and recreational aspects of the nation's capital. The production quality of this work is high and the supporting visuals are strong.
◆ Young people could choose one of the photographs to use as the setting in a creative writing assignment.
1. Washington (D.C.)—Description.

917.5
Wood, James Playsted. *Washington, D.C.* Illus. by Joseph Papin. Seabury Press (No ISBN), 1966. 126p. B/W illus. (Interest level: 6-8).

Wood discusses Washington's past and present, the daily activities of its public and private citizens, and its tourist attractions. Although published in 1966, this book is included here because of the prominent line drawings that enhance the text and candidly portray the history of the city. Large print and uncluttered pages make the book readable.
◆ Readers can identify people and places that should be added to the drawings. Following the

format of this work, young people can update DC history to the present.
1. Washington (D.C.)—Description—Views 2. Washington (D.C.)—History.

923.1
Bourne, Miriam. *White House Children.* Illus. by Gloria Kamen. Random House (0-394-940996), 1979. B/W illus. (Interest level: 1-4).

Children are intrigued by the enormous house at 1600 Pennsylvania Avenue in Washington, DC, called the White House, the home of the president. Bourne attempts to remove some of the mystery by describing the lives of the children and grandchildren of presidents who have lived in the White House. Young readers learn that these children's lives are much like their own.
♦ Children could discuss how their lives might change if their parent were president of the United States.
1. Presidents—United States—Children—Biography 2. Presidents—Children 3. Washington (D.C.)—White House.

959.7
Ashabranner, Brent K. *Always to Remember: The Story of the Vietnam Veterans Memorial.* Photos by Jennifer Ashabranner. Dodd (0-396-09089-3), 1988. 100p. B/W photos. (Interest level: 4-8).

Ashabranner tells the story of Jan C. Serapp, a Vietnam veteran who was determined that American men and women who died in Vietnam should have a fitting memorial in Washington, DC. Young readers will learn how the Vietnam Veteran Memorial has helped to bring a divided nation together, and teachers will find this work a useful commentary on American social history and complex social issues.
♦ After viewing the PBS videotape *Vietnam Memorial* (see p. 38), young people can compare and contrast the way controversies surrounding the memorial are addressed by the writers of the book and the producers of the video.
1. Vietnam Veterans Memorial (Washington, D.C.) 2. National monuments—United States 3. Washington (D.C.)—Buildings, structures, etc.

973.5
Ayer, Eleanor. *Our National Monuments.* Millbrook Press (1-56294-078-3), 1992. (I Know America Series). 48p. Color photos. (Interest level: 1-4).

Washington, DC, is home to more of the United States' famous monuments than any other city in the nation, although Ayer covers monuments throughout the country. The famous monuments cited will be of particular interest to young children in introducing them to the history, creation, and symbolism of our national monuments. Bibliographical references and color photos supplement the text.
♦ Children can discuss what they think makes a national monument. They can then design a monument that reflects their own community.
1. National monuments—United States 2. Washington (D.C.)—Buildings, structures, etc.

973.9
The Watergate Scandal: People, Power, and Politics. (Sound filmstrip). Random House (0-537-69285-1 Part 1; 0-537-69288-6 Part 2), 1984. (Turning Points Series). 2 filmstrips, 2 cassettes, B/W and Color, (Part 1: 16:30 minutes; Part 2: 15:35 min.). $94.00. (Interest level: 6-8).

Two filmstrips chronicle the Watergate affair in Washington, DC, from the initial burglary at the Democratic National Headquarters in the Watergate building, through the investigations, cover-up, testimonies, and impeachment proceedings against Richard Nixon, to the final resignation of the president. Actual voices and photographs of the main participants enliven the filmstrips.
♦ Students can conduct additional research on the Watergate scandal and follow up on the people involved.
1. Watergate affair, 1972-1974.

975.2
Potomac: American Reflections. (Videocassette). Robert Cole Films (0-7936-0492-3), 1986. Color, (60 min.). $49.95. (Interest level: 7-8).

For most Americans, the Potomac River is simply the geopolitical site of the nation's capital. This beautiful and introspective video surveys the Potomac's splendor and recalls its place in U.S. history. Personal interviews with various persons who live along the Potomac, including a Piscataway tribal member, complement an already beautiful, well-documented graphic presentation.
♦ This resource can be used effectively for teaching across the curriculum in American studies, history, folklore, fresh water ecology, and more. A Native American with knowledge of the Piscataway tribe might also be invited to speak to the class.
1. Potomac River.

975.2
Reber, James Q. *Potomac Portrait.* Liveright (0-87140-585-7), 1974. 95p. B/W photos. (Interest level: 5-8).

Potomac Portrait is a celebration of the beautiful Potomac River, which flows past our nation's capital. A majority of the 61 stunning photographs are double-page spreads that extend the full length of the pages. A section called "Photographic Notes" briefly describes techniques involved in the photography, including vantage points for shooting and the type of equipment used. Photography buffs, as well as those who simply love the beauty of outdoors,

will enjoy viewing these marvelous photographs of the mighty Potomac.
♦ Involve students in photographing their own community and designing a photographic essay about it. Students could also compare the still photography in Reber's book with the video graphics in *Potomac: American Reflections* (see p. 32).
1. Potomac River.

975.3
Bigler, Philip. *Washington in Focus*. Vandamere Press (0-918339-07-3), 1988. 144p. B/W photos. (Interest level: grade 8-adult).

Bigler combines over 100 historical photographs with a fast-paced and entertaining narrative to bring to the reader not only the history of Washington, DC, but the drive and spirit behind that history. The text discusses sights that are familiar to visitors and residents, including the Capitol, the White House, and the Lincoln Memorial. Crisp black-and-white photos of both the familiar and unfamiliar take the reader through time and space from 1789 to the Vietnam Memorial in 1982. A bibliography and index are included.
♦ Young people may use this resource as a guide in preparing a history of their own community. They may wish to write a historical drama of their town and give a public performance.
1. Washington (D.C.)—History—Pictorial works 2. Washington (D.C.)—Description—Views 3. Washington (D.C.)—History.

975.3
Black Georgetown Remembered. (Videocassette). Georgetown University Learning Resource Center, 1988. Color, (40 min.). $100.00. (Interest level: grade 6-adult).

Through recollections of members of the Georgetown black community, some of whom still reside in Georgetown, the documentary pays tribute to a community that thrived amidst Jim Crow laws, slavery, and economic inequity. The video features remembrances of the decades from the 1930s to the 1950s, when the population of Georgetown changed markedly. A book of the same title is available (*see* p. 35).
♦ Teachers, librarians, and other adults can use this video to develop intergenerational activities. Students could conduct interviews with parents, grandparents, and senior citizens to create an oral history of their community.
1. Georgetown (Washington, D.C.)—History 2. African Americans—Washington (D.C.)—History 3. Washington (D.C.)—History.

975.3
Bruce, Preston, et al. *From the Door of the White House*. Lothrop, Lee, and Shepard (0-688-00883-6), 1984. 76p. B/W illus. (Interest level: 6-8).

Bruce, a doorman at the White House for almost 20 years, shares his experiences, reflecting upon his work during the Eisenhower, Kennedy, Johnson, Nixon, and Ford administrations. Readers will experience life in the White House from a different perspective.
♦ Readers can compile a list of interview questions that they could ask someone who works or has worked at the White House. Then, young people may role-play the interview.
1. White House (Washington, D.C.) 2. Presidents—United States.

975.3
Carpenter, Allan. *District of Columbia: From Its Glorious Past to the Present*. Illus. by Tom Dunnington. Childrens Press (0-5160-4151-7), 1979. (New Enchantment of America Series). 96p. Color illus. (Interest level: 4-8).

Carpenter's description of the capital of the United States, its history, prominent people, and places of interest covers a variety of attractions, including museums, parks, libraries, and recreational areas. The reader will find such aids as an "Annual Events in D.C." section, an index, and instant facts useful.
♦ Students may write about Washington, DC, using any form to express their ideas: poetry, essays, drawings, cartoons, etc. Combine these to create a special edition newspaper to send to their parents.
1. Washington, D.C.

975.3
City out of Wilderness: Washington. (Videocassette). Filmic Archives (0-7800-0712-3), 1975. Color, (30 min.). $19.95. (Interest level: 6-8).

This graphic presentation tells the story of Washington, DC, simply, clearly, and dramatically with archival and contemporary materials, providing unusual documentation of the growth of a city and a nation. The producer skillfully draws on early drawings and diagrams, documents, daguerreotypes and photographs by Mathew Brady, and spectacular shots from a helicopter to create a definitive history of the development of the nation's capital.
♦ Young people could document the growth and development of their own community by researching original documents, visiting museums, and talking with local historians.
1. Cities and towns—United States—Photography.

975.3
Cleere, Gail S. *The House on Observatory Hill: Home of the Vice President of the United States*. U.S. Government Printing Office, n.d. 73p. B/W and Color photos. (Interest level: 8).

Everyone talks about the White House in Washington, DC, but seldom is attention focused on the

house occupied by the vice president. Cleere's historic overview of the vice president's house includes a description of its early settling and neighborhood and a brief summary of the history, organizational relationship, and scientific work of the U.S. Naval Observatory. Photographs complement the text, including colorful, vivid White House photographs of President Bush, Vice President Quayle, and their families in a variety of engaging poses. A bibliography, architectural drawings, and a pocket map of the U.S. Naval Observatory supplement the text.
♦ Students can conduct further research on the residence of the vice president and then discuss other possible locations for the vice president's house.
1. Historic sites—Washington (D.C.) 2. Vice presidents—United States.

975.3
Epstein, Sam and **Epstein, Beryl**. *Washington, DC: The Nation's Capital*. Franklin Watts (0-531-04253-7), 1981. 80p. B/W photos. (Interest level: 4-8).

The Epsteins introduce Washington, DC, its history, day-to-day life, and points of interest, providing ample detail on the city's many attractions, which draw people from all over the world. This title holds wide appeal and gives broad coverage on a range of topics related to the nation's capital.
♦ Students can read other books on Washington, DC, and write an updated version of the Epsteins' narrative on "Washington Today."
1. Washington, D.C.

975.3
Fisher, Leonard. *The White House*. Holiday House (0-8234-0774-8), 1989. 96p. B/W photos. (Interest level: 4-8).

Fisher presents a fresh, captivating commentary on the conception and evolution of the White House. Through anecdotal prose and historical photos, he removes some of the mystery surrounding the prestigious monument by showing it to be a home, complete with its foibles, quirks, and inconveniences.
♦ Children can construct a layout of their house. They also might discuss the White House as home to the president and what home improvements should be made.
1. White House (Washington, D.C.).

975.3
Fogle, Jeanne. *Two Hundred Years: Stories of the Nation's Capital*. Illus. by Edward Fogle. Vandamere (0-918-339-16-2), 1991. 188p. (Interest level: 8).

The author re-creates the lives and works of a select group of Washingtonians who shared their money, talents, and aspirations to build a real city that could truly serve as the nation's capital. Readers will meet a host of politicians, civil servants, speculators, and businessmen who have contributed to the growth of the nation's capital.
♦ Readers may write letters to the author recommending people they think should have been included in this work, supporting their choices by citing worthwhile contributions made to Washington, DC.
1. Washington (D.C.)—History.

975.3
Francek, Thomas, ed. *The City of Washington: An Illustrated History*. Knopf (0-394-40812-8), 1977. 383p. B/W photos. (Interest level: 8).

In this tribute to the capital of the United States and its citizens, nearly 700 illustrations depict the city, from wilderness days through the 350 years of Washington's colorful and vibrant history. Although written in the late 1970s, the memoirs and newspaper reports in this book make history come alive.
♦ Young people may conduct further research on the individual(s) who created the layout of the city, those who designed the various memorials, and those who have had a major impact on the history and development of Washington, DC.
1. Washington (D.C.)—History 2. Washington (D.C.)—Description.

975.3
A History of Washington, D.C. (Sound filmstrip). Society for Visual Education, 1982. (Our Nation's Capital Series). 39 frames, (10 min.). $39.00. (Interest level: 4-6).

The history of Washington, DC, from its planning to the present, is featured in this filmstrip. Personalities who played a key role in the development of the capital are included.
♦ Students may use the format of the filmstrip to create their own slide show about Washington, DC, or the development of their town.
1. Washington (D.C.)—History 2. Washington (D.C.)—Description.

975.3
Hoig, Stan. *A Capital for the Nation*. Cobblestone Books/Dutton (0-525-65034-2), 1990. 132p. B/W photos. (Interest level: 4-7).

Readers of this book will vicariously live the history and construction of Washington, DC. Majestic memorials, edifices, statues, commemorative parks, and other representations of the nation's past are described in text and illustrated with various photographs and old prints.
♦ Each student may select one person listed in Hoig's book, conduct research, and then role-play a scene from that person's life. Students may also write letters describing Washington, DC, from the perspective of a person from DC history.
1. Washington (D.C.) 2. United States—Capital.

975.3
Junior League of Washington. *The City of Washington.* Knopf (0-349-40812-8), 1977. 384p. B/W photos and illus. (Interest level: 8).

This is a vivid portrayal of the nation's capital, from the wilderness days through the 350 years of Washington's history. Photos, drawings, paintings, and documents give life to historical perspectives.
♦ Students may write research papers on any topics contained in the book and find or create additional visuals to illustrate their papers.
1. Washington (D.C.)—History 2. Washington (D.C.)—Description.

975.3
Katakis, Michael. *The Vietnam Veterans Memorial.* Photos by author. Crown (0-1575-7019-X), 1988. 76p. B/W photos. (Interest level: 8).

Katakis skillfully combines quotes from Vietnam veterans and relatives and friends of soldiers killed in action with many black-and-white photographs of visitors to the Vietnam Veterans Memorial in Washington, DC. Photographs show survivors seeking out and touching names, praying, grieving, placing personal mementos on the memorial, and making connections with loved ones and friends lost in the Vietnam War.
♦ Young people may interview veterans of World War II and the Vietnam conflict and compare the issues and feelings involved. A panel discussion might be an excellent forum.
1. Vietnam Veterans Memorial (Washington, D.C.)—Pictorial works 2. National monuments—United States 3. Washington (D.C.)—Buildings, structures, etc.

975.3
Kent, Deborah. *Washington, D.C.* Childrens Press (0-516-00497-2), 1991. (America the Beautiful Series). 142p. Color photos, maps, and illus. (Interest level: 4-6).

One of a series of books about the states and the District of Columbia, this volume presents a good overview of history, events, people, and sites associated with the U.S. capital. The text is well organized and has colorful illustrations, including photographs, maps, charts, drawings, and lists.
♦ Readers may locate another book in the series and compare the history of that state with Washington, DC. What are the similarities and differences?
1. Washington (D.C.).

975.3
Landmarks and Legends. (Videocassette). WETA (0-7936-0458-3), 1989. Color, (30 min.). $49.95. (Interest level: 6-8).

The District of Columbia is bursting with historical landmarks and remarkable legends. Host Robert Rash highlights the living museum that characterizes our nation's capital.
♦ Young people may write short narratives describing the contents of this video to share with the class.
1. Washington (D.C.)—Buildings, structures, etc.—Pictorial works.

975.3
Lesko, Kathleen; Bass, Valerie; and Gibbs, Carroll R. *Black Georgetown Remembered: A History of Its Black Community from the Founding of the Town of George in 1751 to the Present Day.* Georgetown University Press (0-87840-525-7), 1991. 210p. B/W photos. (Interest level: grade 6-adult).

Readers will share a series of recollections by members of the Georgetown black community that demonstrate how black residents managed to emerge with dignity and strength despite slavery, economic inequity, and Jim Crow laws. The book was inspired by the documentary video produced for Georgetown University for its Bicentennial Celebration in 1989 (*see* p. 33).
♦ Class members may interview an older person in their community and create a documentary on the creation of their town.
1. Georgetown (Washington, D.C.)—History 2. African Americans—Washington (D.C.)—History 3. Washington (D.C.)—History.

975.3
Lewis, David L. *District of Columbia: A Bicentennial History.* Norton (0-3930-5601-5), 1976. (The States and Nations Series). 208p. B/W photos. (Interest level: grade 8-adult).

Lewis gives a comprehensive history of Washington, DC, but his writings far exceed the historical perspective and cover the city's art, journalism, and internal politics as well, along with the changing nature of its many distinct neighborhoods. He also considers the special meaning of the city historically for black Americans who are now its racial majority.
♦ Students can develop a time line of Washington, DC's development, highlighting historical and social events.
1. Washington (D.C.)—History 2. Washington (D.C.)—Description.

975.3
Loewen, Nancy. *Washington, D.C.* Rourke (0-865-92-5445), 1989. (Great Cities of the USA Series). 47p. Color illus. (Interest level: 3-6).

Loewen presents a general overview of Washington, DC's history, from a muddy rural settlement to a powerful capital city, through text and beautiful color illustrations. Strong emphasis is placed on activities and attractions. A glossary, lists, and a map are included.

♦ Children may create a photographic overview of the historic sites in their own community to share with classmates.
1. Washington (D.C.)—Description 2. Washington (D.C.).

975.3
Lumley, Catherine Wentzel. *District of Columbia in Words and Pictures.* Illus. by Richard Willie. Childrens Press (0-516-03951-2), 1981. 47p. Color illus. (Interest level: 2-4).

Facts about the District of Columbia are given in this beautifully illustrated book. Included are the capital city's history, people, natural resources, important sites, and much more. Children will find the beautiful pictures appealing. Maps, pronunciation guides, historical dates, and an index stimulate interest and support the text.
♦ Young people may draw their own pictures with supporting text and display them on a bulletin board identified for that purpose.
1. Washington (D.C.).

975.3
McGraw, Ryder. *New Columbia: State of the Union.* (Videocassette). D.C. Statehood Commission, 1989. Color, (15 min.). No price available. (Interest level: 6-8).

The term "taxation without representation" is relevant to citizens of the District of Columbia, as they have no voting representatives in Congress. The video explains why and how the DC statehood commission and other agencies are pushing to create "New Columbia," the stay state. Interest in making the District of Columbia a state is voiced by various citizens in on-the-spot interviews.
♦ Students may be participants on a mock talk show. Divide students into groups of three—one host and two panelists. The panelists may debate the pros and cons of statehood for the District of Columbia.
1. Washington (D.C.)—Politics and government.

975.3
Miers, Earl Schenck. *The Capitol and Our Lawmakers.* Grosset & Dunlop (No ISBN), 1965. 48p. Color photos. (Interest level: 3-6).

Several people shaped the nation's capital, its buildings, and the governmental bodies they house. This retrospective look at those people features a pictorial chronology of the Capitol's development and several portraits of notable individuals. Although this is an earlier work, it is still useful for its historical perspective.
♦ Children may conduct further research on the individuals who had a significant impact on the development of Washington, DC, and present their findings orally to the class.
1. Washington (D.C.)—History.

975.3
Miers, Earl Schenck. *The White House and the Presidency.* Grosset & Dunlap (No ISBN), 1965. 48p. B/W and Color photos. (Interest level: 3-6).

Miers tells the story of the White House as it has been used by presidents, including those events and people that affected the structure or interior features of the great mansion, including Benjamin Latrobe and Pierre-Charles L'Enfant. Although an early work, this book still provides a vibrant history and introduction to the White House.
♦ Readers can locate and read biographies about people who created the plan for the layout of Washington and the White House and dramatize or illustrate important events in their lives.
1. White House (Washington, D.C.).

975.3
Munro, Roxie. *The Inside-Outside Book of Washington, D.C.* Illus. by author. Dutton (0-525-44298-7), 1987. Unpaginated. Color illus. (Interest level: 2-4).

Munro captures the feeling of the nation's capital and tours familiar, and some less familiar, landmarks and historic sites. The author's prizewinning line drawings enhance this book of few words, depicting the often ponderous lavishness of federal buildings with careful attention to architectural motifs and just a touch of humor. Written detail about each location completes the work.
♦ Young people may collect pictures of Washington's landmarks and historic sites in preparation for a mural of the city. The mural can be displayed in an area that is accessible to the entire school.
1. Washington (D.C.)—Buildings, structures, etc.—Pictorial works.

975.3
Of Monuments and Myths. (Videocassette). WETA (0-7936-0489-3), 1988. Color, (30 min.). $49.95. (Interest level: 7-8).

Intriguing and often humorous stories of the famous and not-so-famous landmarks in Washington, DC, are related in this informative and entertaining video. Viewers take a special tour of monuments, from the top of the Capitol to the catacombs beneath the Lincoln Memorial. Robert Rash enthusiastically recounts the history surrounding the structures that celebrate the events and people of our nation.
♦ Using a similar format, students may create a video about their own community.
1. Washington (D.C.)—Buildings, structures, etc.
2. National monuments—United States.

975.3
Pitch, Anthony S. *Exclusively Washington Trivia.* Mino Publications (0-931719-00-3), 1984. 172p. (Interest level: 2-8).

Pitch provides little-known trivia about the history, politics, scandals, sports, and more of Washington, DC. Readers can check their skills as they flip the pages, since the answers are right at their fingertips.
♦ Children could become roving reporters and gather news about Washington, DC, from newspapers, radio, or television. They could then develop their own current trivia questions and create a Washington trivia show.
1. Washington (D.C.)—History.

975.3
Reef, Catherine. *Washington, D.C.* Macmillan/Child (0-87518-411-1), 1989. (Downtown America Series). 60p. Color illus. Newsprint pages. (Interest level: K-6).
In a beautifully illustrated book that will delight children of all ages, Reef describes the past and present neighborhoods, historic sites, attractions, and festivals of Washington, DC. This excellent book for introducing younger children to the city includes a list of places to visit, a historical time line covering the years 1789-1989, a list of presidents of the United States, U.S. maps pinpointing the city, a key map designating points of interest with an accompanying legend, and an index.
♦ Children could write about or videotape neighborhoods, festivals, and other attractions and activities that reflect their community.
1. Washington (D.C.)—History 2. Washington (D.C.)—Description.

975.3
Reflections on the Wall, the Vietnam Veterans Memorial. Stackpole Books (0-8117-1846-8), 1987. 160p. B/W photos. (Interest level: 4-8).
The Vietnam Veterans Memorial has become one of Washington's most visited sites since its dedication in November 1982. During the five days of the national salute to Vietnam Veterans, a team of Smithsonian photographers worked from dawn until long into the night recording hundreds of images. The historic photos are accompanied with an introduction and narration by Edward Clinton and a foreword by several others.
♦ Students may research the background of the Vietnam Veterans memorial, discussing the social issues involved. Or, they may select five photographs from the book and write an appropriate caption for each, taking into account the sentiments expressed in the pictures.
1. Vietnam Veterans Memorial (Washington, D.C.)—Pictorial works.

975.3
St. George, Judith. *The White House: Cornerstone of a Nation.* Putnam (0-399-22186-7), 1990. 160p. B/W photos and map. (Interest level: 4-8).

Award winner Judith St. George highlights the White House from the beginning of construction in 1792 to the impact of twentieth-century television coverage, referencing every president who has lived in the White House through George Bush. The narrative is smooth, solid research gives substance to the work, and 75 fascinating black-and-white photos enhance the text. An extensive bibliography and a listing of presidents through George Bush are included.
♦ Young people can write poems about the White House, which can be compiled in an anthology and placed in the school library for others to read and enjoy.
1. White House (Washington, D.C.) 2. Presidents—United States—History 3. Washington (D.C.)—Buildings, structures, etc.

975.3
Saures, J. C. *Washington, D.C.* Photos by Bill Harris. Harry N. Abrams (0-8109-1787-4), 1987. 223p. Color photos. (Interest level: grade 3-adult).
An artistically remarkable work that presents the District of Columbia in all its splendor, this oversized resource contains 160 illustrations, including 136 plates in full, vivid color. The introductory text to the 13 chapters and extensive captions help the reader understand both the purpose and function of this work.
♦ After reviewing this book, students could write questions to answer with further research, conduct their research, and share their findings with the class.
1. Washington (D.C.)—Description—Views.

975.3
Smith, Catherine Schneider, ed. *Washington at Home: An Illustrated History.* Illus. by Bill Rice. Windsor (0-89781-205-0), 1988. 367p. B/W and Color illus. (Interest level: 8).
Smith's informative work, based on hundreds of interviews in various communities, focuses on the District of Columbia as a typical community made up of homes, schools, small businesses, and religious institutions; reflects the city's people; and captures the true spirit of the city's diverse communities. A map of the neighborhoods is included. This guide is useful for increasing awareness and appreciation for cultural diversity.
♦ Class members may analyze demographics in their community. Discuss sensitivity, prejudice, discrimination, and ways to break down racial and cultural barriers.
1. Washington (D.C.)—History 2. Washington (D.C.)—Description 3. Washington (D.C.)—Social life and customs.

975.3
Stein, R. Conrad. *The Story of the Burning of Washington.* Illus. by Richard Willie. Childrens

Press (0-516-04678-0), 1984. (Cornerstones of Freedom Series). 31p. Color illus. (Interest level: 3-6).

Stein describes the events of the British invasion of Washington, DC, in 1814. The color illustrations are dramatic, and the layout and design are superb.
♦ Students can research the effects of the burning of Washington on the War of 1812 and how the city was rebuilt. Students could also read Esther Brady's *A Wish on Capitol Hill* (*see* p. 45) and hold a book discussion comparing the epilogue in Brady's book with Stein's account.
1. Washington (D.C.)—History—Capture by the British, 1814 2. United States—History—War of 1812.

975.3
Sullivan, George. *How the White House Really Works*. Dutton (0-525-67266-4), 1988. 117p. B/W photos. (Interest level: 5-8).

Sullivan provides a behind-the-scenes look at life in the official residence of the president of the United States, describing how staff and facilities affect the president's daily life. A chapter on the president's Secret Service protection is included. Sports and leisure-time activities enjoyed by various presidents add a bit of spice to this White House account.
♦ Children can discuss the staff needed by the president. Can staff be reduced?
1. White House (Washington, D.C.) 2. Presidents—United States.

975.3
Vietnam Memorial. (Videocassette). PBS (0-7936-0617-9), 1991. Color, (52 min.). $19.95. (Interest level: 8).

In November 1982, 150,000 people celebrated the national salute to Vietnam veterans in Washington, DC. This video offers in-depth analysis of U.S. and world history, government, politics, and social issues and captures the emotion of the five-day tribute, which included a parade honoring the returning veterans and the dedication of the Vietnam Memorial. Interviews with veterans, those who stayed home, and those who were too young to remember the Vietnam War are featured.
♦ After viewing this video, students may write a narrative expressing their feelings about the Vietnam Veterans Memorial.
1. Vietnam Veterans Memorial (Washington, D.C.) 2. Washington (D.C.)—Buildings, structures, etc. 3. National monuments—United States.

975.3
Walton, William and **Hofer, Evelyn**. *The Evidence of Washington*. Harper & Row (No ISBN), 1966. 132p. B/W and Color photos. (Interest level: 6-8).

Washington, DC, is a city with a rich and powerful history. Evidence of this history and history in the making is shown in this fully narrated pictorial. Clear, vivid photographs complement the rich text. The book includes an index and a key to portraits.
♦ Students can illustrate their own feelings about Washington, DC, through a variety of media, including pen and ink, chalk, and watercolor. Then display the illustrations for all to see.
1. Washington (D.C.)—Description—Views
2. Washington (D.C.)—History.

975.3
Washington, D.C. 2nd ed. (Videocassette). Encyclopaedia Britannica Educational Corporation, 1984. Color, (23 min.). $99.00. (Interest level: 2-8).

This informational film explores Washington shrines, monuments, and vast complexes that house the various functions of the federal government, focusing on the city's unique qualities as an international cultural hub and the nucleus of U.S. government. Some of the political personalities have changed but this in no way negates the film's historical significance.
♦ Children could discuss the characteristics and qualities that are important for a national capital city and compare these qualities to Washington, DC.
1. Washington (D.C.)—Description.

975.3
Washington, D.C. (Videocassette). National Geographic Society, 1983. Color, (20 min.). $70.00. (Interest level: 6-8).

Use this video to take an exciting tour of the United States capital, a truly international community where many different cultures thrive. The District of Columbia's early history is reenacted through a brief historical sequence, and L'Enfant's original plan for the city and modifications to it are examined.
♦ Young people can write and produce a play dramatizing important aspects of the nation's history.
1. Washington (D.C.)—History 2. Washington (D.C.)—Description.

975.3
Washington, D.C.: A Capital Adventure. (Videocassette). International Video Network (0-681-60748-3), 1988. Color, (50 min.). $24.95. (Interest level: 6-8).

With dramatic flair, this video simply and clearly examines and explains the historical significance of the District of Columbia and introduces prominent people who led its development. Original music complements the narration. This video would be best shown in segments rather than in one sitting.

♦ Viewers could research the people who played a prominent role in the founding and development of their own community. They may want to dramatize the founding and film it.
1. Washington (D.C.)—Description 2. Washington (D.C.)—History.

975.3
Washington, D.C.: The Nation's Capital. (Sound filmstrip). Eye Gate Media, 1982. (American Cities Series). One filmstrip with cassette, Color, (14 min.). $44.00. (Interest level: 2-8).

Unlike most cities in the United States, Washington was designed before construction began on the first buildings. This filmstrip, with accompanying cassette, introduces viewers to one of the most beautiful of the world's centers of government and power, its history, its great buildings and monuments, its people and their work. A wealth of information is condensed into a single filmstrip that teachers can effectively utilize in encouraging further exploration of the nation's capital.
♦ Children can choose one aspect of Washington, DC, presented in this filmstrip to research further and present their findings to the class.
1. Washington (D.C.) 2. Washington (D.C.)—History.

975.3
Washington, D.C. Today. (Sound filmstrip). Society for Visual Education, 1982. (Our Nation's Capital Series). 39 frames, (10 min.). $39.00. (Interest level: 4-6).

This filmstrip describes the branches of government, important government buildings, and famous landmarks.
♦ Children could document the government of their town and compare it to the organization and functioning of our national government.
1. Washington (D.C.)—History 2. Washington (D.C.)—Description.

975.3
Washington Monuments. (Videocassette). Atlas Video Library (0-945716-02-8), 1987. Color, (30 min.). $14.95. (Interest level: 6-8).

The history and beauty of the capital's major landmarks are captured in a presentation that is informative, picturesque, and entertaining. Featured sites include the U.S. Capitol, the Smithsonian museums, the White House, the Jefferson Memorial, and more.
♦ Students could choose a national monument or a monument in their own community to research. They could create a model and prepare a short presentation for the class.
1. Washington (D.C.)—Buildings, structures, etc. 2. National monuments—United States.

975.3
Waters, Kate. *The Story of the White House.* Scholastic (0-590-43335-0), 1991. 40p. Color photos. (Interest level: 3-8).

Forty-one famous families have lived in the White House, and the text and photographs of this work depict history and trivia of the White House and its tenants. Readers see portraits of presidents and their spouses or relatives who served as official White House hosts and learn "Fun Facts to Know about the White House Residents." A selective bibliography and index are included.
♦ After reading this book and other resources on the White House, young people can write an editorial to be published in the newspaper. In preparation, they should read newspaper editorials for journalistic style.
1. White House (Washington, D.C.) 2. Presidents—United States.

975.3
Wilroy, Mary Edith and Prinz, Lucie. *Inside Blair House.* Doubleday (0-385-157870), 1982. 299p. (Interest level: 8).

There is a hotel in Washington, DC, so exclusive that one cannot get in without a White House invitation. It is Blair House, the president's guest house. Wilroy entertains and enlightens the reader with memoirs of her 15 years as Blair House manager. Through this warm-hearted account, readers share for a time the excitement of state visits and the pomp and pleasure of a stay at the house reserved for America's most special guests.
♦ Students can discuss the importance of having a place such as Blair House and what amenities should be offered guests of the president.
1. Blair House (Washington, D.C.) 2. Washington (D.C.)—Social life and customs.

975.5
Washington, D.C. (Videocassette). Finley Holiday, 1986. (American Adventure Series). Color, (30 min.). $24.95. (Interest level: 8).

Washington's rich heritage, magnificent architecture, historical treasures, and honored memorials and monuments are the focus of this video.
♦ Young people could study the architecture in their own community. They may want to share their findings with the community through a public presentation.
1. Washington (D.C.)—Buildings, structures, etc.

Biography

920
Applegate, Katherine. *The Story of Two American Generals, Benjamin O. Davis, Jr. and Colin L. Powell.* Dell (0-440-40595-5), 1992. (Dell Yearling Bi-

ography Series). 107p. B/W photos. (Interest level: 3-4).

Applegate provides readers with an outstanding introduction to the lives of Benjamin O. Davis, Jr., born in Washington, DC, and Colin L. Powell, of Harlem, New York, both of whom served as military leaders during critical periods in our nation's history. The carefully researched text, based on authentic autobiographies, writings, and commentaries, is illustrated with photographs. Davis's perseverance and his record as the first black U.S. officer to become a major general in the U.S. Air Force and Powell's ascendancy as national security advisor and chairman of the Joint Chiefs of Staff will serve as examples for all young readers.
♦ Children could write essays comparing the two men's lives and careers.
1. Davis, Benjamin O., Jr. (Benjamin Oliver), 1912-   2. Powell, Colin, 1937-   3. Generals—United States   4. African Americans—Biography.

920
Haskins, James. *The March on Washington*. Harper Children's Books (0-06-021290-X), 1993. 128p. B/W photos. (Interest level: 7-8).

A detailed account of the great nonviolent march on Washington that took place on August 28, 1963, this compelling book also gives the history of the civil rights movement and chronicles the lives of six renowned men who devoted their lives to it: Martin Luther King, Jr.; James Farmer; Roy Wilkins; Whitney Young, Jr.; John Lewis; and A. Philip Randolph. The text also relates information on Bayard Rustin, who planned the historic march, and includes a bibliography and a time line. For readers unfamiliar with the historical details of the march, the photos, parts of speeches, and pertinent comments will be enlightening.
♦ Students can conduct interviews with people in their community who remember the march on Washington and compile an oral history. They could then compare their account with Haskins's account.
1. March on Washington for Jobs and Freedom (Washington, D.C.), 1963   2. Civil Rights demonstrations—Washington, D.C.—History—20th Century   3. African Americans—Civil Rights.

920
Haskins, Jim. *One More River to Cross*. Scholastic (0-590-42896-9), 1992. 160p. Color illus. (Interest level: 7-8).

Haskins brings us brilliantly moving biographies of 12 African Americans who courageously fought against racism to become leaders in their fields, including prominent Washington, DC, physician Charles Richard Drew. The author has taken great pains to include African Americans in a variety of occupations, representing the fields of science, the arts, business, politics, and sports. The collection features photos of each subject, including Crispus Attucks, Madame C. J. Walker, Matthew Henson, Ralph Bunche, Shirley Chisolm, and Ronald McNair, a bibliography, and an index. Recommended for school and public libraries, this straightforward book not only provides valuable information but also leaves the reader with positive images of African Americans.
♦ Each student can select a person from the book, conduct further research, and then construct a time line of the life of that person and/or role-play an important historical moment in his or her life.
1. African Americans—Biography.

920
Igus, Toyomi, et al. *Great Women in the Struggle, an Introduction for Young Readers*. Vol. 2. Just Us Books (0-9409-7527-0), 1991. (Books of Black Heroes Series). 96p. B/W photos. (Interest level: 4-8).

Two Washington-born notables, Fannie Jackson Coppin, for whom Coppin State College in Baltimore, Maryland, is named, and Eleanor Holmes Norton, a representative to Congress for the District of Columbia and a civil rights activist and lawyer, are among the 80 historical and contemporary black women profiled in this brief, timely collective biography. Subjects range from politicians to entrepreneurs such as Maxine Waters and Oprah Winfrey. This book is noteworthy for its inclusion of amazing women who have received little or no recognition for significant contributions they have made. A chronology from the 1500s to 1990, a selective bibliography, source notes, and an index are included.
♦ Readers could research how the role of women has changed in our society over the years, what brought about those changes, and contributions women have made to our society.
1. African American women—Biography   2. Coppin, Fannie Jackson, 1837-1913   3. Norton, Eleanor Holmes, 1937-.

920
Morey, Janet Nomuira and **Dunn, Wendy**. *Famous Asian Americans*. Cobblehill Books (0-525-650-80-6), 1992. 170p. B/W photos. (Interest level: grade 5-adult).

Morey and Dunn share the childhoods, goals, setbacks, and accomplishments of 14 outstanding Asian Americans including Connie Chung, highly acclaimed broadcast journalist, who was born in Washington, DC. Overall, this is a good personal and professional introduction, but it should be supplemented by more comprehensive readings. Of special note is the bibliography on each subject. A foreword by Dr. Harry H. L. Kitano, professor of Social Welfare and Sociology, University of California; well-chosen black-and-white photographs; a

preface; and an index enhance the worth of a book that brings remarkable Asian American personalities to the attention of readers of all ethnicities.
♦ Children can research further the achievements and contributions of Asian Americans in our society, as well as obstacles they have encountered and how they overcame them.
1. Asian Americans—Biography 2. Chung, Connie, 1946-.

92 Banneker, Benjamin
Conley, Kevin. *Benjamin Banneker*. Chelsea House (1-55546-573-0), 1989. (Black Americans of Achievement Series). 108p. B/W photos. (Interest level: grade 5-adult).
Conley gives readers an interesting and lively account of the life, struggles, and achievements of "America's first black man of science" Benjamin Banneker. This eighteenth-century tobacco farmer, who taught himself mathematics, astronomy, and clock making, became famous for his almanacs and is credited with assisting Andrew Ellicott in the original survey of Washington, DC. Written in a colorful, straightforward style, this work is handsomely complemented with photographs, artwork, and documents and includes an introductory essay by Coretta Scott King, a handy short chronology of Banneker's life, and a list of further reading.
♦ Readers can make models of Banneker's tools or inventions, for example, clocks or survey instruments. Art, history, science, and math teachers could also develop interdisciplinary projects for students based on ideas in the biography.
1. Banneker, Benjamin, 1731-1806 2. Astronomers—United States 3. African Americans—Biography.

92 Bell, Alexander Graham
Pelta, Kathy. *Alexander Graham Bell*. Silver Burdett (0-382-09529-4), 1989. (Pioneers in Change Series). 137p. B/W photos. (Interest level: 5-7).
Bell was born in Edinburgh, Scotland, but lived for more than 40 of his 75 years in Washington, DC. Pelta's fine biography presents an all-encompassing view of Bell's life and times, including his personal and professional growth and creative genius. High-interest photographs illustrate important stages of Bell's life. The book includes an extensive bibliography.
♦ This is an excellent opportunity for teachers to design a thematic interdisciplinary learning activity around the use of technology in communicating globally. Students can plan and develop projects demonstrating changes in telecommunications today. They may want to research computer technology, interactive television, teleconferencing, or fiber optics.
1. Bell, Alexander Graham, 1847-1922 2. Inventors—United States—Biography.

92 Davis, Benjamin O., Jr.
Reef, Catherine. *Benjamin Davis, Jr.* Twenty-first Century Books (0-8050-2137-X), 1992. (An African-American Soldiers Book Series). 80p. B/W photos. (Interest level: 3-7).
Reef examines the life of Benjamin O. Davis, Jr., the famed commander of the Tuskegee Airmen, America's first unit of black combat pilots, and the first black to graduate from West Point in the twentieth century, who was born in Washington, DC. With candor, Reef portrays Davis's perseverance and eventual triumph in his military career. Young readers will find the "Chronology on African Americans in the Armed Services," the bibliographical references, and the index valuable resources for acquiring information on African Americans who served their country with distinction. Photos have been carefully chosen to complement the clear and easy-to-read text.
♦ Imagining they are members of the Tuskegee Airmen, young people can write a letter to a friend at home describing their experiences.
1. Davis, Benjamin O., Jr. (Benjamin Oliver), 1912- 2. Generals—United States 3. African Americans—Biography.

92 Davis, Benjamin O., Sr.
Fletcher, Marvin E. *America's First Black General: Benjamin O. Davis, Sr., 1880-1970*. University Press of Kansas (0-7006-0381-6), 1989. 226p. (Interest level: grade 8-adult).
Not only a tribute to America's first black general, Benjamin O. Davis, Sr., this book is also an account of a youngster growing up in a segregated Washington, DC, in the late 1880s and early 1900s. Davis's story proves that determination and diplomacy can overcome many barriers raised by racial bigotry. A foreword by Benjamin O. Davis, Jr., source notes, and an extensive bibliography supplement the book. This resource is written for more mature audiences and is a good professional reference.
♦ Students can analyze the effects of political, social, economic, and environmental factors on the lives of both father and son. How are these same factors affecting our lives today?
1. Davis, Benjamin O., Sr., 1880-1970 2. African Americans—Biography.

92 Drew, Charles
Mahone-Lonesome, Robyn. *Charles Drew*. Chelsea House (1-55546-581-1), 1990. (Black Americans of Achievement Series). 108p. B/W photos. (Interest level: grade 5-adult).
Mahone-Lonesome chronicles the life of the famous surgeon Charles Richard Drew, who was born and grew up in Washington, DC. Drew pioneered research on the properties and preservation of blood plasma and spearheaded the first comprehensive

blood banking program. Students will find the book well written and easy to read, with black-and-white photographs illustrating the text. An index, a complete chronology of Drew's life, and an introduction by Coretta Scott King are also included.
♦ Young people can conduct further research on the blood bank program as it exists today. Invite a speaker from the local blood bank to speak to the class.
1. Drew, Charles Richard, 1904-1950 2. Surgeons—United States—Biography 3. African Americans—Biography.

92 Drew, Charles
Wolfe, Rinna Evelyn. *Charles Richard Drew, M.D.* Watts (0-531-20021-3), 1991. 64p. Color photos. (Interest level: 4-6).

Wolfe describes clearly and concisely the life of the noted physician, Charles Richard Drew, focusing on his discovery of methods for separating plasma from blood. The bold, bright pictures will appeal to readers, as will the large and inviting format. A handy glossary provides a "ready reference" to meanings of some words used in the text, and bibliographical references and an index enhance the usefulness of this source.
♦ Discuss the significance of Drew's discovery and how it has impacted modern medicine.
1. Drew, Charles Richard, 1904-1950 2. Surgeons—United States—Biography 3. African Americans—Biography.

92 Ellington, Duke
Collier, James Lincoln. *Duke Ellington.* Oxford University Press (0-19-503770-7), 1986. 340p. B/W photos. (Interest level: grade 8-adult).

This definitive biography covers the story of Duke Ellington from childhood as a "pampered son of a middle class" Washington, DC, black family, to his death in 1974. Collier claims that Ellington ranked among the giants in the history of jazz; not all may agree with Collier's assessment, but jazz buffs and anyone who is interested in jazz will want to read this biography. The section on "Discographical Notes" reflects the enormity of Ellington's musical output and recordings in print throughout the world. Included also are extensive notes and an index.
♦ Guide students in broadening their perspective on various types of music by developing an interdisciplinary thematic unit with music, art, and language arts. Students can create commercials or other types of videos using some of Ellington's music.
1. Ellington, Duke, 1899-1974 2. Jazz—Musicians—United States—Biography.

92 Ellington, Duke
Frankl, Ron. *Duke Ellington.* Chelsea House (1-55546-584-6), 1988. (Black Americans of Achievement Series). 112p. B/W photos and illus. (Interest level: grade 5-adult).

Frankl chronicles the life of Washington's internationally acclaimed jazz musician, Edward Kennedy "Duke" Ellington from the Harlem Renaissance through later years. This volume would enhance a biography collection, because there are few biographies for young readers on Ellington, who is considered one of the great jazz geniuses of the twentieth century. A bibliography, an index, and a chronology of Ellington's life are provided.
♦ Class members can make a video depicting Duke Ellington's musical career and including other performers of the era.
1. Ellington, Duke, 1899-1974 2. Jazz—Musicians—United States—Biography.

92 Gallaudet, Thomas Hopkins
DeGering, Etta. *Gallaudet: Friend of the Deaf.* Gallaudet University Press (0-913580-84), 1987. 184p. B/W illus. (Interest level: grade 7-adult).

Thomas Hopkins Gallaudet is a native of Connecticut, but because of the importance of Gallaudet University in Washington, DC, and the nation, this book is included here. Gallaudet founded the first school for the deaf in America in 1817, and his son, Edward, is credited with founding Gallaudet University, the first institution of higher learning for the deaf in the United States.
♦ If possible, students can visit Gallaudet University or invite a representative from the university to speak to the class. Or, contact the local deaf association about information and speakers. Young people may also want to learn sign language.
1. Gallaudet, Thomas Hopkins, 1787-1851 2. Deaf education 3. Teachers of the deaf—United States—Biography.

92 Gallaudet, Thomas Hopkins
Neimark, Anne E. *A Deaf Child Listened.* William Morrow (0-688-01719-3), 1983. 116p. (Interest level: 4-8).

In the summer of 1814, when Gallaudet met a nine-year-old deaf girl named Alice Cogswell, he found his vocation. Drawing on letters and diaries of Gallaudet, this story illuminates the man whose work and foresight opened doors of opportunity to many with physical limitations. Neimark's well-written book contains a wealth of information, including a directory of national service organizations and centers for the deaf, and should be promoted for its timeliness in addressing the issues of diversity and respect for individual differences.

♦ Invite a representative from the local deaf association to speak to the class, preferably one who will be accompanied by a translator who will use sign language to interpret students' questions. Students can prepare a list of questions before the visit.
1. Gallaudet, Thomas Hopkins, 1787-1851 2. Deaf education 3. Teachers of the deaf—United States—Biography.

92 Hayes, Helen
Kittredge, Mary. *Helen Hayes*. Chelsea House (1-55546-656-7), 1988. (American Women of Achievement Series). 111p. B/W photos. (Interest level: K-8).

This splendid pictorial biography covers the life of the celebrated actress Helen Hayes, from her childhood in Washington, DC, through her 80 dazzling years as a stage and screen actress. The richly illustrated biography will appeal to readers and provides a balanced portrayal of Hayes, who helped shape the course of American theater.
♦ After preparing a list of movies or plays in which Helen Hayes starred, young people can dramatize scenes from some of them.
1. Hayes, Helen, 1900-1993   2. Actors—United States—Biography.

92 Jackson, Jesse
Haskins, James. *I Am Somebody: A Biography of Jesse Jackson*. Enslow Publishers (0-8949-0240-7), 1992. 112p. (Interest level: grade 6-adult).

Haskins presents the life, accomplishments, and goals of the civil rights activist and politician Jesse Jackson, from his childhood in North Carolina through his years in Chicago and Washington, DC. Young readers will enjoy this book, which will be quite useful as part of a unit on African American history, social studies, or government.
♦ Readers can make a time line of the events in Jackson's life, beginning with his graduation from high school to the present day.
1. Jackson, Jesse, 1941-   2. African Americans—Biography.

92 Jackson, Jesse
Jakoubek, Robert. *Jesse Jackson*. Chelsea House (0-7190-1130-5), 1991. (Black Americans of Achievement Series). 127p. B/W photos. (Interest level: grade 5-adult).

Jakoubek examines the life and political career of Jesse Jackson, the charismatic civil rights leader, who now maintains a residence in Washington, DC. Readers are given a lively and complex look at Jackson, beginning with his bid for the presidency, then going back to his youth, the challenges he faced, and his achievements as a controversial civil rights activist and political leader. The insightful introduction by Coretta Scott King, splendid photographs, a chronology, and a bibliography add appeal to this work.
♦ Class members can dramatize events from Jackson's life.
1. Jackson, Jesse, 1941-   2. African Americans—Biography 3. Civil Rights workers—United States—Biography.

92 Jackson, Jesse
Jesse Jackson: Civil Rights Leader and Politician. (Videocassette). Schlessinger Video Productions (1-8791-5114-6), 1992. (Black Americans of Achievement Series). Color, (30 min.). $39.95. (Interest level: grade 5-adult).

The life and times of Jesse Jackson, Washington, DC's "shadow senator," are the focus of this video, adapted from the biography of Jesse Jackson by Robyn Mahone-Lonesome. In addition to presenting basic biographical information, the video explores inspirational and motivational factors in Jackson's life, analyzes the significance of the biography in society today, and examines with candor critical issues discussed in classrooms today. The Schlessinger videos are bound to stimulate discussion, healthy controversy, and thinking among viewers.
♦ Students can discuss factors and turning points in Jackson's life that led him to become what he is today. They might also examine the lives of other leaders in today's society for similar traits or factors.
1. Jackson, Jesse, 1941-   2. African Americans—Biography.

92 Jackson, Jesse
Wilkinson, Brenda. *Jesse Jackson: Still Fighting for the Dream*. Silver Burdett (0-382-09926-5), 1990. 130p. B/W photos. (Interest level: grade 5-adult).

This book, divided into five manageable chapters, follows the life and career of Jesse Jackson, who sought the Democratic presidential nomination and continues to fight for civil rights for all. A chronology of events in the civil rights movement, a timetable highlighting events in the life of Jesse Jackson, an introduction by Andrew Young, suggested additional reading, and maps tracing the routes of the Freedom Riders' protest demonstrations in the South add to the value of this source.
♦ Students can discuss how Jesse Jackson's civil rights quest has changed over the years.
1. Jackson, Jesse, 1941-   2. African Americans—Biography 3. African Americans—Civil Rights.

92 Sousa, John Philip
Greene, Carol. *John Philip Sousa: The March King*. Childrens Press (0-516-04226-2), 1992. (A Rookie Biography Series). 47p. B/W photos. (Interest level: K-3).

Young readers will be thrilled by this simple, colorful biography of the "March King," John Philip Sousa, born in Washington, DC, who composed more than 100 marches, including "Semper Fidelis" and the "Washington Post March." During his lifetime he led both the Marine and Navy bands; organized the Sousa band, which played all over the United States; and helped school bands and orchestras. An "Important Dates" section and an index are provided.
♦ Children can read this biography and others, and then listen to some of Sousa's marches. They could then create models of musical instruments found in bands that play his music. This activity could be done in conjunction with the art and music teachers.
1. Sousa, John Philip, 1854-1932   2. Composers—United States—Biography.

92 Washington, George
Adler, David. *A Picture Book of George Washington.* Holiday House (0-8234-0732-0), 1989. (A Picture Book Biography Series). Unpaginated. Color illus. (Interest level: K-3).

This readable but brief account of the life of George Washington captures the attention of readers from start to finish, and the good-sized, brilliantly colored illustrations augment the text. A listing of important dates in the life of George Washington is also included. Adler's delightful picture book will be useful in any juvenile collection and can be effectively utilized for cooperative learning activities by language arts, art, and art history teachers.
♦ Young people can retell the story of George Washington by "reading" the pictures. Others might choose one of the pictures to describe in writing.
1. Washington, George, 1732-1799   2. Presidents—United States—Biography.

92 Washington, George
Adler, David A. *George Washington: Father of Our Country.* Holiday House (0-8234-0717-9), 1988. (A First Biography Series). 48p. B/W illus. (Interest level: 2-5).

Writing in a clear and easy-to-follow style, Adler presents a detailed introduction to the commander of the Continental Army and first president of the United States. Adler begins with George Washington's childhood and discusses his family, his work as a surveyor, and other events that led to his being named the "Father of our Country." Readers will appreciate the attractive, well-placed illustrations that complement the text. Important dates and an index are included.
♦ Imagining that George Washington will be visiting their town, young people can plan a press conference for his arrival.

1. Washington, George, 1732-1799—Biography
2. Presidents—United States—Biography.

92 Washington, George
Giblin, James Cross. *George Washington: A Picture Book Biography.* Illus. by Michael Dooling. Scholastic (0-590-42550-1), 1992. 48p. Color illus. (Interest level: K-8).

Giblin's well-written, well-researched story, combined with Michael Dooling's expressive oil paintings, brings young readers a fresh understanding of George Washington. This is a portrait of a gentle, fair-minded man who became a strong leader in the American Revolution and helped shape the democracy we enjoy today.
♦ Students could create picture books of other presidents or of local community officials who have had an impact on their town.
1. Washington, George, 1732-1799   2. Presidents—United States—Biography.

92 Washington, George
Meltzer, Milton. *George Washington and the Birth of Our Nation.* Franklin Watts (0-5311-0253-X), 1986. 188p. B/W photos and maps. (Interest level: grade 7-adult).

Meltzer's biography of George Washington, which covers his childhood in Virginia to his death at Mount Vernon, brings to life the extraordinary man behind the monuments and memorials, whose leadership had a profound effect upon his country's destiny. This work clearly portrays what Washington was really like—ambitious, energetic, vulnerable, and courageous—and how his character was formed by the turbulent times in which he lived. Photographs and maps are included.
♦ Young people can write essays describing how they think George Washington influenced the development of the United States and share these essays with the class.
1. Washington, George, 1732-1799 2. Presidents—United States—Biography   3. United States—History—Revolution, 1775-1783.

92 Washington, George
Quackenbush, Robert. *I Did It with My Hatchet.* Pippin (0-945912-04-8), 1989. 36p. Color illus. (Interest level: 2-6).

The author's humorous rendition of George Washington's life, which includes both famous and little-known cartoonlike anecdotes and full-page drawings, blends facts and comedy into an engaging whole. This is an excellent example of a biography for young readers with both visual and human appeal.
♦ Students can create their own humorous biographies of other presidents.

1. Washington, George, 1732-1799—Anecdotes
2. Washington, George, 1732-1799—Legends
3. Presidents—United States—Biography.

Fiction

Blair, Anne Denton. *Arthur, the White House Mouse.* Illus. by Lily Spandorf. Media/America (No ISBN), 1975 (out of print). 25p. Color and B/W illus. (Interest level: 2-4).

Skillfully weaving White House history into an interesting story that children will find pleasing and memorable, Blair describes life past and present in the White House through the eyes of one of its residents, a mouse. Readers learn about the executive mansion and its families, St. John's Church, and Lafayette Square as they navigate through this delightful story, the first piece of fiction about the White House published for children. The book is out of print but still on the shelves of many public and school libraries.
♦ Children can share how they would change the story if they were the author, or they could make puppets of the characters and retell the story in a puppet show.
1. White House (Washington, D.C.)—Fiction.

Blair, Anne Denton. *Where's Rachel?* Illus. by Carol Watson. Acropolis Books (0-87491-264-4), 1978 (out of print). 45p. B/W illus. (Interest level: 2-4).

Blair offers another adventure of Arthur, the White House mouse, when Arthur's cousin Rachel, of the St. John's Church mice, runs away to see the White House for herself, Arthur and Rachel's brother, Thomas, search for her, facing dangers cleverly and bravely. This book abounds in authentic details, in both text and illustrations, and the black-and-white drawings with touches of color will have special appeal to children. Although this book is out of print, it can be found in school and public libraries.
♦ Students could write a sequel to this book or another adventure for Arthur.
1. White House (Washington, D.C.)—Fiction.

Brady, Esther W. *A Wish on Capitol Hill.* Crown (0-517-572-53-2), 1988. 139p. (Interest level: 3-6).

Eleven-year-old Dorsey's woes begin when her new stepbrother from Philadelphia slaps her in the face with a dead fish. Just as she's wishing that something would happen to make her stepmother and stepbrother go back to Philadelphia, the family is caught in the path of the British Army advancing on Washington, DC, in the summer of 1812. As they brave the danger, they come to understand each other better. The epilogue puts into perspective the historical significance and setting for the story.

♦ Young people may write essays describing how they would have reacted to a new family and the dangers encountered by this family. They may also write essays about wishes they have made and relate them to Dorsey's experiences.
1. Washington (D.C.)—History—Capture by the British, 1814 2. Family life—Fiction.

Bunting, Eve. *The Wall.* Illus. by Ronald Himler. Clarion Books (0-395-51588-2), 1990. 32p. Color illus. (Interest level: 6-8).

In this touching story, a boy and his father go to the Vietnam Veterans Memorial in Washington, DC, to locate the name of the boy's grandfather, who was killed in the Vietnam conflict. Bunting has skillfully woven poignant illustrations and text into a captivating story that young readers will read or listen to from cover to cover. This is a good introduction to the significance of the Vietnam conflict for this age group.
♦ Students can interview Vietnam veterans in their community and create a documentary or oral history.
1. Vietnam Veterans Memorial (Washington, D.C.)—Fiction.

Lindbergh, Anne. *The Hunky-Dory Dairy.* Illus. by Julie Brinkloe. Harcourt Brace Jovanovich (0-15-237449-3), 1986. 147p. B/W illus. (Interest level: 4-6).

Eleven-year-old Zannah McFee lives in Washington, DC. Zannah's old-fashioned horse-and-buggy dairy wagon magically transports her to a small nineteenth-century town, removed by witchcraft, where she befriends a girl named Utopia Graybel. This tale of fantasy, which will delight readers, tells how Zannah copes while traveling through time, becoming an important part of Hunky-Dory Dairy, and dealing with her own life.
♦ Children may write a fantasy of their own about life in a different time period.
1. Washington (D.C.)—Fiction 2. Friendship—Fiction 3. Space and time—Fiction 4. Magic—Fiction.

Lindbergh, Anne. *People in Pineapple Place.* Harcourt Brace Jovanovich (0-15-260517-7), 1982. 153p. (Interest level: 4-6).

Ten-year-old August is unhappy when his mother moves from Vermont to Georgetown until, in an alley labeled "Pineapple Place," he meets seven children of various ages who take him back to an earlier time where he has many interesting experiences. No sooner does August decide he likes Georgetown than the "people in Pineapple Place" move again, but April, one of the children, has thoughtfully arranged for August to find a substitute friend after their departure. This story will require careful presentation as it involves some sensitive areas.

♦ Students can write their own stories about traveling in space to a different time period and their experiences with the people they meet.
1. Moving, Household—Fiction   2. Washington (D.C.)—Fiction   3. Space and time—Fiction.

Periodicals

070
City Paper. (Newspaper). Weekly. (Interest level: 8).

City Paper is a general-interest tabloid emphasizing urban issues and politics, particularly the pros and cons of life in the nation's capital from the perspective of insiders. Diverse issues ranging from homelessness to ecology to race relations in the District of Columbia are covered.
♦ Young people could choose a social issue in their own community on which to conduct a public opinion poll, checking past and current issues of the local newspaper for articles or editorials. They may wish to publicize their results.
1. Newspapers—Washington (D.C.).

070
The Washington Capital Spotlight. (Newspaper). Weekly. (Interest level: grade 1-adult).

One of Washington's oldest black-owned newspapers, published since 1952, this paper serves Washington's business, civic, political, and social communities, with special emphasis on working with District of Columbia Government Advisory Neighborhood Commissions.
♦ Teachers and other adults who work with young people may use this resource to complement more widely circulated newspapers for positive views on the Washington, DC, black community. Students may wish to work with the local newspaper and submit articles or editorials on issues within the school and community.
1. Newspapers—Washington (D.C.).

070
The Washington Monthly. (Periodical). 10 issues per year. (Interest level: grade 6-adult).

Established in 1969, this nationally circulated political opinion magazine provides editorials on local, national, and international events, particularly as they relate to Capitol Hill. The periodical is noted for containing controversial political cartoons.
♦ The magazine may be used for analyzing political and social issues.
1. Periodicals—Washington (D.C.).

Professional Materials

016.7
Washingtoniana Photographs: Collections in the Prints and Photographs Division of the Library of Congress. Library of Congress (0-8444-0588-4), 1989. 310p. B/W illus. (Interest level: Professional).

Through a generous grant from the Morris and Gwendolyn Cafritz Foundation, the Print and Photographs Division at Library of Congress was able to employ a staff to physically process and arrange its photographs, film negatives, and original glass negatives of Washington, DC. More than 750,000 photographs that had been in storage and unavailable to researchers are now accessible. Entries are arranged by collection name, subject, date, photographer, publisher, physical description, and source.
♦ These photographs are powerful teaching tools that visually depict historical, cultural, political, and social events that affected the lives of people in our capital city.
1. Washington (D.C.)—History—Pictorial works—Catalogs   2. Photograph collections—Washington (D.C.)—Catalogs   3. Library of Congress—Prints and Photographs Division—Catalogs.

306.2
United States National Planning Commission.
Worthy of the Nation: The History of Planning for the National Capital. Smithsonian Institution Press (0-87474496-2), 1977. (National Planning Commission Historical Studies Series). 415p. B/W illus. (Interest level: Professional).

Two hundred and seventy-five illustrations tell the story of Washington—where the city has been, where it is now, and where it might go in the future. Bibliographic essays are keyed to the text by chapter and section, and the epilogue addresses the new Washington and makes assertions about its future growth. The book's technical quality and format are outstanding.
♦ Teachers, library media specialists, and others who are responsible for educational planning should place the work on their required reading list.
1. Washington (D.C.)—City planning—History
2. City planning—Washington metropolitan area.

352
INDICES: A Statistical Index to District of Columbia Services. Offices of Policy and Program Evaluation (ISSN 09895-027X), 1992. 412p. (Interest level: Professional).

INDICES, a comprehensive statistical index published by the District of Columbia government, provides current and historical data about people, neighborhoods, the local economy, and the District of Columbia government. The useful reference book is divided into eight chapters, covering such

topics as government finance, housing and education, and economic development.
♦ Students could create a District of Columbia trivia game and use this book as a source for gathering interesting facts.
1. Washington (D.C.)—History 2. Municipal government—Washington (D.C.).

708.1
Arden, Lorraine, et al. *Washington Art: A Guide to Galleries, Art Consultants, and Museums*. Art Calendar (0-945388-00-4), 1988. 176p. B/W illus. (Interest level: Professional).

A comprehensive guide to Washington art, this book contains detailed profiles of 135 commercial galleries, 58 art centers and alternative spaces, 23 museums, and 23 art consultants. The art collector, artist, and visitor will all find Arden's informative guide useful.
♦ This is an excellent source for art teachers seeking ideas for field trips.
1. Washington (D.C.)—Description—Guidebooks 2. Museums—Washington (D.C.)—Guidebooks.

708.1
Kopper, Philip. *America's National Gallery: A Gift to the Nation*. Harry N. Abrams (0-89468-159-1), 1991. 338p. Color and B/W photos and illus. (Interest level: Professional).

This volume highlights the incomparable drama that led to the founding of the National Gallery of Art and the gallery's masterpieces of painting, sculpture, and graphic and decorative arts. Archival photographs never before published introduce the user to the rich, powerful, and generous men and women whose shared dream gave the United States its National Gallery of Art.
♦ Teachers may use this resource to develop integrated learning activities in English/language arts, history, and the arts.
1. National Gallery of Art (U.S.).

917.5
Butler, Brian. *D.C. for Free: Hundreds of Free Things to Do in Washington, D.C.* Mustang Publishing (0-914457-34-9), 1990. 95p. (Interest level: Professional).

Washington, DC, is renowned for its marble monuments, great museums, and celebrated sights, but few of the 18 million annual visitors to the nation's capital know that hundreds of the best attractions and events are free. This guide will help users discover priceless works of art, national shrines, exciting zoos, concerts, and much more that they can visit for free. Pertinent information is provided on the sites, including admission days and hours, addresses, and phone numbers.

♦ Butler's succinct and easily readable guide is a great source for teachers and those who direct children's activities.
1. Washington (D.C.)—Description—Guidebooks 2. Washington region—Description and travel—Guidebooks.

917.5
Frommer's Budget Travel Guide: Washington, D.C. '92-'93 on $40 a Day. Prentice Hall (0-133-334939-X), 1992. (Frommer's $ A-Day Guides Series). 325p. (Interest level: Professional).

Budget travelers will find this an invaluable guide to travel planning, reliable accommodations, and meals in the metropolitan Washington, DC, area. The guide offers thorough reports on sights and activities, cultural attractions, and special events, along with a special "Cool for Kids" section. A detailed map, keyed to the text, suggested itineraries, and a wealth of money-saving information are included.
♦ Teachers may use this travel guide creatively in math, economics, social studies, and other curricular areas to achieve integrated learning activities.
1. Washington (D.C.)—Description—Guidebooks.

917.5
White House Historical Association. *The White House: An Historic Guide*. Grossett & Dunlop (0-9123-0843-5), 1962. 144p. Color photos and illus. (Interest level: Professional).

The White House Historical Association gives a detailed account of the history of this enshrined mansion, which has been the residence of all presidents since John Adams. The text, enhanced with color photographs and line drawings, takes readers on a guided tour of the house and gives them a history of its development. This is an older work, but it depicts the historical significance of the White House.
♦ History and social studies teachers will find this resource useful for background information in preparing units on the White House.
1. White House (Washington, D.C.).

975.3
Russell, John, ed. *Washington, '91. A Comprehensive Directory of the Key Institutions and Leaders of the National Capital Area*. Columbia Books (0-91041619-5), 1991. 1102p. (Interest level: Professional).

This annual publication is a guide to significant public and private institutions in the Washington metropolitan area and the national government, local governments, labor unions, medicine and health, community affairs, and more. Additional features include a map identifying the counties served and

an alphabetical index of organizations and individuals showing multiple affiliations.
♦ This is a good source for identifying human and physical resources to expand learning experiences for students.
1. Washington (D.C.)—Directories 2. Washington metropolitan area—Directories 3. United States—Executive department—Directories.

975.3
Seale, William. *The President's House: A History.* 2 vol. White House Historical Association (0-912308-28-1), 1986. 1222p. B/W illus. (Interest level: Professional).

In this brilliant, lucidly organized, and gracefully written work, Seale examines the lives of the presidents in the White House from Washington to Truman. The epilogue speaks to the current status of the White House. Seale uses hundreds of remarkable sources to document this book, including unpublished manuscripts and personal papers of presidents, their families, associates, and friends. Bibliographical notes, an index, and a list of illustrations are included.

♦ This is a book that serious researchers on life in the White House must consult.
1. White House (Washington, D.C.) 2. Presidents—United States.

975.3
Washington Information Directory, 1991-92. Congressional Quarterly (0-87187-585-3), 1992. 1118p. (Interest level: Professional).

An invaluable source for getting information on the federal government as well as the private and public sectors, this directory covers 17 areas, including communication and media, science and space, health and education, and culture. Names, addresses, and telephone numbers of state officials, members of Congress, U.S. ambassadors, and foreign diplomats stationed in this country are provided. This user-friendly resource can put readers in touch with human resources for expanding young people's knowledge of Washington, DC.
♦ This is highly recommended for all libraries as a reference source for professionals.
1. Washington (D.C.)—Directories 2. Washington metropolitan area—Directories 3. United States—Executive department—Directories.

Maine

by Gene Moll

Nonfiction

398.2
Bruchac, Joseph, ed. *The Faithful Hunter: Abenaki Stories*. Illus. by Kahionhes. Greenfield Review Press (0-912678-75-5), 1988. 61p. B/W illus. (Interest level: 4-8).

Bruchac's collection of stories from the Western Abenaki Indians includes tales of animal tricksters, human heroes, and ordinary people. Besides seven stories of Gluskabe, the great Abenaki god-man, there is also a map of where the Wabanaki lived.
♦ African tales are also often tales of tricksters. Students may compare a tale of Anansi the spider from African literature with a tale of Azeban the raccoon, the Wabanaki trickster.
1. Indians of North America—Folklore.

398.2
Crompton, Anne. *The Winter Wife: An Abenaki Tale*. Illus. by Robert Andrew Parker. Little Brown (0-316-16143-8), 1975. 47p. Color illus. (Interest level: 2-4).

A lonely hunter finds his wishes for a companion and a successful hunting season coming true, until he disobeys the command of his mysterious winter wife and takes a summer wife too. Parker's paintings enhance the mystery of this Abenaki legend.
♦ Many folktales are told to teach a lesson. What lesson can be found in this tale? Children can find other stories that teach lessons.
1. Indians of North America—Legends.

398.2
Mitchell, Lewis. *Passamaquoddi Legends: When Koluskap Left the Earth*. Illus. by Lee Suta. Wabanaki Bilingual Education Program (No ISBN), 1976. B/W illus. (Interest level: K-8).

When Koluskap can't make the Indians live better lives, he leaves them, but three Indians find him and he grants each one a desired wish. In a split-page format, the Abenaki legends are told both in the Passamaquoddy language and in English.
♦ Young people may write several sentences and translate them into the Passamaquoddy language.
1. Indians of North America—Folklore.

597
Gibbons, Gail. *Sharks*. Illus. by author. Holiday House (0-8234-0960-0), 1992. Unpaginated. Color illus. (Interest level: K-8).

From the dwarf shark to the great white shark, this book describes physical characteristics of sharks, how they differ from other fish, and how they survive in their environment. Illustrations complement the science-oriented text.
♦ Sharks live in many waters besides those of Maine. Each student can choose a type of shark to research and describe its physical characteristics, habits, and environment.
1. Sharks.

599.5
McMillan, Bruce. *Going on a Whale Watch*. Photos and illus. by author. Scholastic (0-590-45768-3), 1992. 40p. Color photos and illus. (Interest level: K-6).

Two six-year-olds on a whale-watching expedition off Kennebunk, Maine, see different kinds of whales. McMillan captures their excitement in color photos.
♦ Children can create photo essays of their own pets or of animals with which they are familiar.
1. Whale watching   2. Whales.

623.1
Bardwell, John D. *Maine Forts, the Eastern Frontier*. (Videocassette). Bardwell/Thompson, 1991. VHS, Color, (30 min.). $19.95. (Interest level: K-8).

This video takes viewers on a tour of 22 forts, from Fort McClary in Kittery to Fort Sullivan in Eastport, which were built to guard the Maine coast

from the French, the Indians, the British, and other potential enemies. The long coastline of Maine was a disadvantage during historic times of trouble.
♦ All parts of the United States have forts. Students can visit a fort in their area and research its history.
1. Fortification   2. Maine—History.

623.89
Bardwell, John D. and **Thompson, William O.** *Maine Lighthouses, the Last Watch.* (Videocassette). Bardwell/Thompson, 1991. VHS, Color, (30 min.). $19.95. (Interest level: K-8).

Narrator John Bardwell takes the viewer on a tour of 20 of Maine's most beautiful and famous lighthouses and tells about shipwrecks, lighthouse keepers and their families, and even ghosts! Marine paintings by Kennebunkport artist Ron Goyette complement the narration.
♦ Viewers may draw pictures of lighthouses and write accounts of what it would have been like to run a lighthouse in the 1850s.
1. Lighthouses.

624
Bardwell, John D. *Maine Historic Bridges, a Vanishing Treasure.* (Videocassette). Bardwell/Thompson, 1992. VHS, Color, (30 min.). $19.95. (Interest level: K-8).

Scenic shots of 15 of Maine's historic bridges are combined with historic information about these structures. Computer graphics are used to explain construction details, and a map shows where the bridges are located.
♦ Young people may research covered bridges in New England or other types of bridges in their own area.
1. Bridges—Maine.

630.1
Kimber, Robert. *UpCountry: Reflections from a Rural Life.* Lyons and Burford (1-55821-121-7), 1991. 166p. (Interest level: grade 5-adult).

Kimber writes realistically about what it is like to live in up-country Maine: blackflies, wood stoves, early frosts, fiddleheads in May, and "making do." These essays reflect a love for Maine as well as the realities of a hard existence.
♦ After conducting interviews and research, students may write essays about life in their area.
1. Maine   2. Country life.

674
Nevison, Henry. *From Stump to Ship, a 1930 Logging Film.* (Videocassette). Sheldon Weiss Productions, 1985. VHS, B/W, (28 min.). $19.95. (Interest level: K-8).

Tim Sample, a Maine humorist, narrates this 1930 film of the long log drive, the spring journey down icy streams and rivers moving logs from the forest to the mill for sawing into boards, laths, and clapboards. This film survives as the best, most complete film record of the logging business.
♦ Children may interview senior citizens in their community about the jobs they held in the 1930s.
1. Lumber and lumbering.

674
Woodsmen and River Drivers, Another Day, Another Era. (Videocassette). Northeast Archives of Folklore and Oral History, 1989. VHS, B/W, (30 min.). $19.95. (Interest level: 4-8).

This 1930s film footage from the Machias Lumber Company takes viewers back to winter life in rough lumber camps: raging spring rivers, frozen boots, and life-threatening logjams. Viewers will get a sense of the pride of these people, whose survival took ingenuity, raw muscle, and skill.
♦ Imagining that they are loggers from the 1930s, young people can write narratives describing life in a lumber camp.
1. Lumber and lumbering.

680
Wilbur, C. Keith. *Indian Handcrafts: How to Craft Dozens of Practical Objects Using Traditional Indian Techniques.* Illus. by author. Globe Pequot Press (0-87106-496-0), 1990. 144p. B/W illus. (Interest level: grade 2-adult).

Wilbur describes and gives instructions for making many traditional Indian tools, clothing, toys, and homes. This well-researched volume will be an invaluable resource for students studying Northeast Indians.
♦ Readers can make a fire stick, a woven belt, or an animal snare using the directions found in this book.
1. Indians of North America—Industries   2. Handicraft—North America.

709.741
Skolnick, Arnold, ed. *Paintings of Maine.* Clarkson Potter (0-517-58229-5), 1991. 428p. Color photos. (Interest level: K-adult).

From archival paintings of ships foundering in the mouth of the Kennebec River to samples of the work of N. C. Wyeth, Andrew Wyeth, and Jamie Wyeth to modern portraits of Maine, this volume contains more than 80 landscapes and seascapes and shows Maine painting at its dramatic best. Quotes from Maine authors enhance the paintings.
♦ After reading and viewing this book, students may want to paint scenes that reflect their area.
1. Maine—Painting   2. Painting, American.

796.54
Kuller, Alison Murray. *An Outward Bound School.* Photos by Tom Stewart. Troll (0-8167-1732-X),

1990. (Let's Take a Trip Series). 32p. Color photos. (Interest level: 5-8).

Text and photographs highlight the activities at the Hurricane Island Outward Bound School in Rockland, Maine, as students face the challenges of nature, discover personal strengths, and learn the value of teamwork. Outstanding action photos show exactly what Outward Bound students do.
♦ Many programs promote physical fitness and self-reliance. Students may investigate such programs in their area and write for guides.
1. Physical fitness.

808.83
Holmes, Edward M. *A Part of the Main: Short Stories of the Maine Coast*. Illus. by Arlene K. Thomson. University of Maine Press (0-89101-031-9), 1973. 177p. B/W illus. (Interest level: grade 6-adult).

The author, Ted Holmes, has been a seaman, lobster trucker, and organizer of fisherman's cooperatives. These classic stories grew out of his experiences working on the coast of Maine.
♦ After reading one of these stories, children can write a letter or journal entry as a character from the story.
1. Short stories—Maine.

911
Morris, Gerald E., ed. *The Maine Bicentennial Atlas, an Historical Survey*. Maine Historical Society (No ISBN), n.d. 20p. B/W maps. (Interest level: grade 5-adult).

This volume of maps of the state of Maine includes historic maps from explorers and land grants, population growth maps, and modern maps of counties, towns, geology, and industry. The atlas is an invaluable tool for anyone studying the state of Maine.
♦ Referring to maps, students can describe their local area or another area in Maine.
1. Atlases   2. Maine—Maps.

917
Frost, Ed and **Frost, Roon**. *Just for Kids, the New England Guide and Activity Book*. Illus. by Carol Leach. Glove Compartment Books (0-9618806-2-7), 1989. 142p. B/W illus. (Interest level: 2-6).

Maine is one of six New England states covered in this travel guide for young people. Valuable information about places to see and things to do is included.
♦ Readers can create a similar travel guide for their area.
1. New England—Description and travel   2. Maine—Description and travel.

917.41
Calvert, Mary. *Maine, Captured in Color*. Photos by author. Twin City Printery (0-9609914-1-7), 1980. Unpaginated. Color photos. (Interest level: 4-8).

Calvert's comprehensive photo collection, with limited text, covers Maine woodlands, architecture, industry, recreational activities, and waterways. It gives an excellent cross section of Maine scenes.
♦ After viewing the photos in this book, students can write a journal entry describing a real or imagined stay in Maine.
1. Maine—Description and travel.

917.41
Gibbons, Gail. *Surrounded by Sea, Life on a New England Fishing Island*. Illus. by author. Little Brown (0-316-30961-3), 1991. Unpaginated. Color illus. (Interest level: K-3).

Beginning with spring, the author tells what happens on a Maine fishing island throughout the seasons. The work of the lobstermen, clearly illustrated with drawings of lobster traps, is described, along with the tourists, cottage caretakers, clammers, and other fisherfolk.
♦ Young children may want to make a big book describing what happens in each season where they live.
1. Fishing villages—Maine   2. Fishing—Maine   3. Atlantic Coast (Me.)—Social life and customs.

917.41
Grierson, Ruth Gortner. *Nature Diary of Mt. Desert Island*. Illus. by Eileen Buzzanco. Windswept House (0-932-433-98-7), 1993. 132p. B/W illus. (Interest level: 4-8).

Grierson presents a month-by-month chronicle of the animals, birds, fields, and forests of the 107-square-mile island that houses Acadia National Park. Each section has a "Highlights" list at the end, which details events such as the birth of seal pups and the migration of cormorants.
♦ Young people may collect or draw pictures of local flora and fauna, do further research on these species, and write short, informative descriptions to accompany their pictures.
1. National parks and reserves   2. Acadia National Park.

917.41
King, B. A. *My Maine Thing*. Photos by author. Black Ice Publishers (0-939250-00-4), 1981. Unpaginated. (Interest level: 6-8).

The stark photos and limited text reveal the author's affection for the southern coast of Maine and its way of life. From a small boy dragging a piece of kelp across a vast beach to fishermen loading lobster bait, the photos reveal a nostalgia for the coast of Maine.

♦ Students may create photo essays of places that have special significance for them.
1. Maine—Description.

917.41
Morgan, Patricia Griffith. *A Mountain Adventure.* Photos by Michael Plunkett and Tom Herde. Troll (0-8167-1174-7), 1988. (Let's Take a Trip Series). 32p. Color photos. (Interest level: 5-8).

Morgan's story follows a group of hikers as they climb Mount Katahdin, the highest peak in Maine, and observe the flora, fauna, and interesting sights along the way. Clear explanations of mountain-climbing terms help the reader through the text.
♦ Readers can make a dictionary of specialized terms for a favorite sport or activity.
1. Hiking—Maine 2. Mountains—Maine.

917.41
Morgan, Patricia Griffith. *A River Adventure.* Photos by Michael Plunkett. Troll (0-8167-1172-0), 1988. (Let's Take a Trip Series). 32p. Color photos. (Interest level: 5-8).

This story follows a group of canoeists as they explore and enjoy 92 miles of waterway along the Allagash River in northern Maine. Outstanding photos of flora and fauna, plus pictures of camping, paddling, and portaging, bring this adventure to life.
♦ Students may want to interview canoeists in their area or invite them to speak to the class.
1. Canoes and canoeing—Maine—Allagash River 2. Allagash River.

917.41
Rich, Louise Dickinson. *State O'Maine.* Illus. by Aldren A. Watson. Harper & Row (No ISBN), 1974. 302p. B/W illus. (Interest level: grade 7-adult).

Rich's classic book covers Maine history from the state's geologic formation to the 1960s. This volume is particularly good in its coverage of the French and Indian Wars and the early days of statehood.
♦ Students can choose one aspect of Maine history, such as the historic hunting-trapping relationship of the French with Native Americans, on which to conduct further research.
1. Maine—History.

917.41
Scheid, Margaret. *Discovering Acadia, a Guide for Young Naturalists.* Illus. by author. Acadia Press (0-934745-04-8), 1987. 80p. Color illus. (Interest level: 2-6).

Starting with a pledge for children to sign, "I promise not to destroy nature while I enjoy nature," this guide takes children through Acadia's trees, tide pools, animals, and treasures. The visually stimulating book, with a wealth of nature information for young readers, includes quizzes and crossword puzzles to reinforce information.
♦ Class members can create their own guides to state or national parks in their area.
1. National parks and reserves 2. Acadia National Park.

917.41
Trueworthy, Nance. *Maine in Four Seasons.* Photos by author. Down East Books (0-89272-262-2), 1988 (out of print). Unpaginated. Color photos. (Interest level: 6-8).

Trueworthy's collection of exquisite color photographs reinforces the fact that the geography and topography of an area are inseparable from its way of life. The book, divided into four seasons of photographs, consists primarily of water views but also includes some inland shots of Aroostook County farming and many shots of Portland, Maine.
♦ Students can take photographs of their area and compile a seasonal scrapbook.
1. Seasons 2. Maine—Description.

917.41
Unl, Michael. *Exploring Maine on Country Roads and Byways.* Clarkson Potter (0-517-57455-1), 1991. 262p. Maps. (Interest level: grade 5-adult).

A travelogue of a 10,000-mile journey from Kittery, in the south, to the Canadian border, this book takes the reader off the beaten track to see farm country, forests, and the sea. The text also provides standard information about information centers, lodgings, camping facilities, and restaurants.
♦ Young people could design an audio and/or video travelogue of their town.
1. Maine—Description and travel.

917.412
Villani, Robert. *Forever Wild, Maine's Magnificent Baxter State Park.* Photos by author. Down East Books (0-89272-306-8), 1991. 112p. Color photos. (Interest level: grade 4-adult).

Divided into three main parts—alpine zones, ponds, and forests—this book describes in text and photos the topography, flora and fauna, and beauty of Baxter State Park. A large amount of scientific information, such as Latin names of plants and animals, is included, along with facts about the 170 trails that lace the park.
♦ Students can describe their area or a nearby state or national park using Latin names for plants and animals. Children also could plan a day at a local community or state park.
1. Parks—Maine 2. Baxter State Park.

917.44
Nyiri, Alan. *Exploring the Maine Coast.* Photos by author. Down East Books (0-89272-256-8), 1989. 122p. Color photos. (Interest level: 6-8).

Maine's scenic rocky shore is the subject of this collection of outstanding photographs. The details and fine color separation of these photos aid in depicting the ever variable coastline.
♦ Children can design a postcard collection illustrating whatever region they are studying.
1. Maine—Description—Pictorial works.

970.1
Day, Michael. *Berry Ripe Moon.* Illus. by Carol Whitmore. Tide Grass Press (No ISBN), n.d. 54p. B/W illus. (Interest level: 3-8).

A young Indian boy, Dragonfly, from the village of Panawampskik, the largest Penobscot community (now Old Town, Maine), spends the Berry Ripe Moon (the month of July) in the seaside summer campgrounds where the Penobscot gather food for winter. This book, in story form, is actually a factual account of Indian life in the 1700s, illustrated with excellent drawings of Indian life.
♦ Imagining they are members of the same Indian tribe as Dragonfly, students can write journal entries describing life in the tribe.
1. Indians of North America—Social life and customs.

971.5
Whitehead, Ruth Holmes and **McGee, Harold.** *The Micmac, How Their Ancestors Lived Five Hundred Years Ago.* Illus. by Kathy Kaulbad. Nimbus (0-920852-21-1), 1983. 60p. B/W illus. (Interest level: 2-8).

The Micmac Indian environment and culture is captured in this comprehensive view of the clothing, shelter, transportation, trade, crafts, and medicines of these early residents of northern Maine. Detailed drawings combine with text to reveal the daily lives of the Micmac.
♦ Young people can research Indian tribes of their own region and present their findings orally to the class.
1. Micmac Indians   2. Indians of North America—Atlantic provinces.

973.7
Kallgren, Beverly H. and **Crouthamel, James L.**, eds. *"Dear Friend, Anna": The Civil War Letters of a Common Soldier from Maine.* University of Maine Press (0-89101-079-3), 1992. 161p. B/W photos. (Interest level: 6-8).

Abial Edwards, an 18-year-old textile mill worker from Lewiston, Maine, served in the 10th and 29th Maine regiments during the Civil War, from 1861 to 1866. Edwards wrote regularly about the dangers, sicknesses, and violence of war to his friend Anna Conant of Portland, Maine.
♦ Pretending they are serving with Abial Edwards, students can write letters home to friends or family members describing life in the regiment.

1. Edwards, Abial Hall   2. U.S. Army, Maine infantry regiments.

974
Aylesworth, Thomas G. and **Aylesworth, Virginia L.** *Northern New England: Maine, New Hampshire, Vermont.* Chelsea House (1-55546-551-X), 1988. 64p. Color photos, illus., and maps. (Interest level: 3-6).

This volume discusses the geographical, historical, and cultural aspects of Maine, Vermont, and New Hampshire. With maps, illustrated facts, and a heavy emphasis on history, the authors highlight the land, history, and people of each state.
♦ Children could research one activity, such as lumbering or maple sugaring, that takes place in all three states.
1. New England   2. Maine   3. Vermont   4. New Hampshire.

974.1
Balano, James W. *The Log of the Skipper's Wife.* Down East Books (0-89272-062-X), 1979. B/W photos. (Interest level: grade 6-adult).

Dorothea Moulton Balano spent 20 years as a skipper's wife aboard various Maine windjammers, sailing around the world and raising her family on board. This diary, compiled and edited by her son, describes in daily installments what life was like from 1908 until 1927, living aboard a sailing and later steam vessel.
♦ After doing some research, students can write essays describing present-day life aboard a ship.
1. Seafaring life.

974.1
Banks, Ronald R. *Maine Becomes a State.* New Hampshire Publishing Company/Maine Historical Society (0-912274-35-2), 1973. 266p. B/W photos and illus. (Interest level: grade 6-adult).

Maine was a part of the province of Massachusetts until 1820. Banks describes the events leading to statehood, including the politicians, parties, and views of the people.
♦ Readers can conduct research on the statehood of their state.
1. Maine—History.

974.1
Bennett, Dean B. *Maine Dirigo, "I Lead."* Down East Books (0-89272-103-0), 1980. 300p. B/W photos, maps, and illus. (Interest level: 5-8).

History, geography, native peoples, occupations, and wars are detailed in this comprehensive volume, which was originally intended as a text for Maine schoolchildren. One fascinating chapter reproduces the diaries of a 16-year-old Maine farm boy in 1809 in Turner, Maine, and a 16-year-old classics student at Berwick Academy, South Berwick, Maine, along

with the diaries of three other Maine young people. The dates of the diaries range from 10 years after the American Revolution to the beginning of the twentieth century.
♦ Using the five diaries reproduced in this volume, students can compare the influence of religion and the church on children of the past and on children today.
1. Maine—History 2. Religion.

974.1
Carpenter, Allan. *The New Enchantment of America: Maine.* Childrens Press (0-516-04119-3), 1979. 96p. Color photos. (Interest level: 3-8).

This presentation of the Pine Tree State includes its history, geography, resources, Indian tribes, famous citizens, and places of interest.
♦ Students can present a persuasive speech to classmates on why they should visit the state of Maine. They could also create a travelogue on the state of Maine, designing a kid-oriented trip from Kittery in the south to Madawaska in the north.
1. Maine.

974.1
Church, Thomas. *The History of Philip's War, 1675-1676.* Facsimile reprint by Heritage Books (1-55613-179-8), 1989. 360p. (Interest level: grade 8-adult).

The French and Indian Wars dominated Maine history in the 1600s. This classic volume gives a clear account of the earliest of these wars. The account was written by Thomas Church, based on the papers of his father, Colonel Benjamin Church, who was involved in the wars.
♦ Young people can use this volume as they research the French and Indian Wars.
1. United States—History—French and Indian Wars.

974.1
Day, Michael and **Whitmore, Carol.** *Maine Folk History in Story, Legend and Myth.* Tide Grass Press (No ISBN), 1978. 48p. B/W illus. (Interest level: 3-8).

Divided into sections ("Gluskap's People," "Along the Coast of Land and Water," and "Curses and Cures"), this book explains Maine folk history from the harvest of salt hay to the invention of earmuffs by Chester Greenwood in Farmington. These 45 illustrated stories, legends, and myths shed light on some of the lesser-known facts and myths of Maine.
♦ Students can research myths and legends of their town and share them orally with the class.
1. Maine—History 2. Maine—Legends.

974.1
Dibner, Martin, ed. *Portland.* 2nd ed. Greater Portland Landmarks (0-939761-00-9), 1986, 1972. 229p. B/W photos, illus., and maps. (Interest level: grade 5-adult).

Dibner's history of Portland, Maine's major city, emphasizes the city's architectural history. The book, which covers the years 1628 to the early 1900s, includes excellent archival photographs, drawings, and maps.
♦ Readers can study the architecture of their own town, since many towns contain an interesting mix of Federal, Greek Revival, Italianate, and Victorian buildings.
1. Portland (Me.)—Description.

974.1
Engfer, LeeAnne. *Maine.* Lerner (0-8225-2701-4), 1991. (Hello USA Series). 72p. Color photos. (Interest level: 3-8).

Engfer introduces the geography, history, industries, people, and other highlights of Maine. An extensive collection of color photographs reinforces the readable text.
♦ After reviewing the appendix of Maine famous people, students can compile a similar list of famous people in their state or community.
1. Maine.

974.1
Fendler, Donn and **Egan, Joseph B.** *Lost on a Mountain in Maine.* Beech Tree (0-688-11573-X), 1978. 109p. B/W photos. (Interest level: 4-8).

A 12-year-old boy describes his nine-day struggle to survive on Mount Katahdin, in north central Maine, after being separated from his companions. Bears, blackflies, cold temperatures, and injuries contributed to his tribulations, along with a futile search for food and water.
♦ Class members can dramatize a talk show with the 12-year-old boy as the guest.
1. Katahdin, Mount (Me.) 2. Survival.

974.1
Fradin, Dennis B. *Maine in Words and Pictures.* Illus. by Richard Wahl; maps by Len W. Meents. Childrens Press (0-516-03919-9), 1980. 48p. Color photos, illus., and maps. (Interest level: 3-6).

Fradin presents a brief history and description of the Pine Tree State. A list of 35 facts about the state of Maine is included.
♦ Using headings from the book, students can list similar facts about their own state, such as area, borders, state flower, state mineral, and capital.
1. Maine.

974.1
Freeman, Melville and **Perry, Estelle H.** *The Story of Maine for Young Readers.* Bond Wheelwright

(No ISBN), 1962. B/W photos and illus. (Interest level: 2-6).

The history and geography sections of this easy-access guide to Maine for young readers are still current. The book has many interesting photos and drawings.

♦ Young people can create a trivia game about the state of Maine or another state they are studying.

1. Maine—History.

974.1
Graff, Nancy Price. *The Call of the Running Tide, a Portrait of an Island Family*. Photos by Richard Howard. Little Brown (0-316-32278-4), 1992. 80p. B/W photos. (Interest level: 2-8).

In text and photos, Graff chronicles the Joyce family, who harvest the bounty of the sea from Swans Island, five miles off the coast of Maine. Many varied photos and the personalized text give the reader an accurate picture of the life of a lobsterman and his family.

♦ Students can write to the Swans Island Consolidated School, Swans Island, ME 04685, for a pen pal or for information about Swans Island from a student's perspective.

1. Swans Island (Me.) 2. Fishing, Maine.

974.1
Harrington, Ty. *Maine*. Childrens Press (0-516-00465-4), 1989. (America the Beautiful Series). 144p. Color photos. (Interest level: 3-8).

Harrington introduces all aspects of the state of Maine, including history, landforms, government, industry, and culture. Modern and historical photographs augment the clear text.

♦ Readers may research any aspect of the state of Maine, such as agriculture, products, or recreation, and compare it to their own state.

1. Maine.

974.1
Martin, Kenneth R. and **Lipfert, Nathan R.** *Lobstering and the Maine Coast*. Maine Maritime Museum (0-937410-04-7), 1985. 143p. B/W photos and illus. (Interest level: grade 5-adult).

The authors tell the history of Maine lobstering, including its economic, political, social, and technological dimensions. The book is richly illustrated with archival materials, historic photographs, and expert drawings.

♦ Students may trace the development of the lobster trap or the lobster boat from its beginnings to its present-day form. They may want to make a model.

1. Lobster fisheries—Maine.

974.1
Rich, Louise Dickinson. *The Kennebec River*. Illus. by Lili Rethi. Holt, Rinehart & Winston (No ISBN), 1967. 125p. B/W illus. (Interest level: 5-8).

This is a history of the greatest river in Maine, from the European explorers' first encounter with the Abenaki Indians to the days after the Civil War, when shrewd Mainers filled their empty ships with Kennebec ice to market around the world. Rich was one of the first writers to direct a history of Maine at children.

♦ Children can research the Kennebec River today since major shipbuilding still occurs there.

1. Rivers—Maine 2. Kennebec River 3. History—Maine.

974.1
Rolde, Neil. *Maine, a Narrative History*. Tilbury House (0-88448-069-0), 1990. 368p. B/W photos. (Interest level: grade 6-adult).

From prehistoric people to the French and Indian Wars, English settlement, Revolutionary War, statehood, economic growth, Civil War, and modern Maine, this volume tells it all in a clear, readable style. The text is enhanced by an extensive bibliography.

♦ Students may create a time line, showing the historic and economic development of Maine or another state they are studying.

1. Maine—History.

974.1
Rowe, William Hutchinson. *The Maritime History of Maine: Three Centuries of Shipbuilding and Seafaring*. Harpswell Press (0-88448-063-1), 1989. 333p. B/W photos. (Interest level: grade 6-adult).

Beginning with the first winter fishing stations of 1614, this book covers the great shipbuilders, ports, shipyards, and sailors who established Maine as the most important maritime region in the country. Although originally published in 1948, this book is still the most substantive account of Maine maritime history.

♦ Young people can research present-day maritime activities in Maine, such as building ships for the U.S. Navy, building tugboats, or building pleasure yachts.

1. Shipbuilding 2. Seafaring life 3. Maine.

974.1
Sanger, David. *Discovering Maine's Archeological Heritage*. Maine Historic Preservation Commission (No ISBN), 1979. 156p. B/W photos. (Interest level: grade 5-adult).

The purpose of this book is to make available to the layman information about the archaeology of Maine from earliest times to the present. In Maine, the prehistoric record for man begins about 11,000

years ago. This book includes sites, methods, tools, and archaeological artifacts.
♦ Readers may investigate archaeology and the contributions archaeologists have made to society.
1. Archaeology—Maine.

974.1
Searles, James W., ed. *Immigrants from the North: Franco Americans Recall the Settlement of their Canadian Families in the Mill Towns of New England.* Pen Mor Printers (0-9607904-0-3), 1982. 63p. (Interest level: grade 6-adult).

From 1880 to 1920, hundreds of thousands of French Canadians streamed into Maine to fill jobs created by rapidly expanding factories. This remarkable history, backed by grants from the U.S. Department of Health, Education, and Welfare and others, and put together by faculty and students of Hyde School in Bath, Maine, is a testimony to what student research can create.
♦ Using this book as a model, students can create a history of the ethnic groups that make up their community.
1. New England—History 2. Immigration and emigration.

Biography

920
Agger, Lee. *Women of Maine.* Guy Gannett (0-930096-21-5), 1982. 237p. B/W photos. (Interest level: grade 6-adult).

These mini-biographies of Maine women cover the earliest days, when Mary Patten piloted the square rigger *Neptune's Car* around the Horn to San Francisco when her captain husband fell ill, to modern events in the lives of people like Olympia Snow, Lewiston congresswoman. More than 100 outstanding Maine women are discussed.
♦ Students may wish to compile biographies of famous women in their town or geographic area.
1. Maine—Biography 2. Women—Biography.

920
Niss, Bob. *Faces of Maine.* Guy Gannett (0-930096-20-7), 1981. 214p. B/W illus. (Interest level: grade 6-adult).

From Henry Wadsworth Longfellow and Robert Peary of North Pole fame to Edna St. Vincent Millay and L. L. Bean, this book takes the reader through mini-profiles of the people who have shaped Maine. Readers will be amazed at the number of leaders, national and international, who call Maine their home.
♦ Children can research famous people from their state and put together a similar book.
1. Maine—Biography 2. Maine—History.

920
Pohl, William L. *The Voice of Maine, Interviews with 31 Outspoken Maine People.* Photos by Abbie Sewall. Thorndike Press (0-89621-075-8), 1983. 201p. B/W photos. (Interest level: grade 6-adult).

Pohl presents a volume of contemporary photographs of, and interviews with, 26 Maine people who are linked mainly by their independence and lifestyle. This book would be valuable to young adults who are struggling to establish their personal identities.
♦ Students can compile their own oral histories of people in their community.
1. Maine—Biography.

920
Shain, Charles and **Shain, Samuella**, eds. *Growing Up in Maine, Recollections of Childhood from the 1780's to the 1920's.* Down East Books (0-89272-312-2), 1991. 264p. B/W photos and map. (Interest level: grade 6-adult).

In this book, 92 people recount memories of their Maine childhoods. A map in the beginning pinpoints the locations of the homes of the young people who are the subjects of the autobiographies.
♦ Young people can interview senior citizens in their town and compile oral histories.
1. Maine—Biography.

92 Burgess, Abbie
Abbie Burgess, Lighthouse Heroine. Down East Books (No ISBN), 1969. 190p. (Interest level: 3-8).

Abbie Burgess was only 14 when she became a lighthouse keeper's daughter on Mafinicus Rock, off the coast of Maine, in 1853. When her father was forced to sail to the mainland for supplies, Abbie tended the two lights alone for several weeks while violent storms raged around the lighthouse.
♦ Lighthouses were an essential part of navigational safety for more than 100 years. Students may research lighthouses on the Atlantic Coast and write about the people who ran them.
1. Burgess, Abbie 2. Lighthouses.

92 Burgess, Abbie
Roop, Peter and **Roop, Connie**. *Keep the Lights Burning, Abbie.* Illus. by Peter E. Hanson. Carolrhoda Books (0-87614-275-7), 1985. 40p. B/W and Color illus. (Interest level: 1-4).

In the winter of 1856, a storm delayed the lighthouse keeper's return to an island off the coast of Maine, and his daughter, Abbie, had to keep the lights burning by herself. Strong watercolor illustrations enhance this story of bravery.
♦ Students can write about or share orally a time when they were brave.
1. Burgess, Abbie 2. Lighthouses.

92 Haley, John West
Silliker, Ruth L., ed. *The Rebel Yell and the Yankee Hurrah, the Civil War Journal of a Maine Volunteer*. Down East Books (0-89272-186-3), 1985. 310p. B/W photos. (Interest level: grade 5-adult).

John West Haley served in Company I, 17th Maine Volunteer Regiment, from August 7, 1862, the day the regiment was formed, to June 10, 1865, the date it was mustered out, when he was suffering the sicknesses, fear, and starvation of a Civil War soldier. This remarkable journal of his three-year service makes the Civil War come to life.
♦ After researching a particular Civil War battle, young people may write letters home describing the battle and life in the regiment.
1. Haley, John West 2. United States—History—1861-1865.

92 Jewett, Sarah Orne
Keyworth, Cynthia. *Master Smart Woman: A Portrait of Sarah Orne Jewett*. North Country Press (0945980-02-7), 1988. 179p. B/W photos. (Interest level: 6-8).

Keyworth's portrait of Sarah Orne Jewett includes period photographs and text sprinkled with quotes from Jewett's writing. The pictures are an outstanding accompaniment to the strong characters and places Jewett wrote about and to her affirmative view of country society.
♦ Students who read this book may want to assemble a collection of photographs from local magazines and newspapers about a well-known local person. They may also want to invite a local author to speak to their class.
1. Jewett, Sarah Orne, 1849-1909 2. Authors, American—19th century.

92 Jewett, Sarah Orne
Sargent, Ruth. *Always Nine Years Old: Sarah Orne Jewett's Childhood*. Graphics Communications (No ISBN), 1985. 51p. (Interest level: 6-8).

Sarah Orne Jewett, one of Maine's most famous authors, published books about Maine from 1877 until 1901. Ruth Sargent tells of one year of Jewett's childhood when she was hampered by illness but nonetheless tried to piece together her family's history and have a normal childhood.
♦ Young people can share some of their most vivid childhood memories with the class.
1. Jewett, Sarah Orne, 1849-1909 2. Authors, American—19th century.

92 Langlais, Bernard
Reef, Pat Davidson. *Bernard Langlais, Sculptor*. Kennebec River Press (0-933858-06-X), 1985. (Maine Art Series for Young Readers). 46p. B/W photos. (Interest level: 3-8).

A 65-foot statue of an American Indian stands in Skowhegan, Maine, created by Bernard Langlais to honor the first peoples of Maine. This book, simply written, traces the development of Langlais as a sculptor in a Maine setting. Langlais's large wooden sculptures enhance college campuses and museums in Maine and elsewhere.
♦ Young people can try to make animals or birds of wood in the style of Bernard Langlais.
1. Sculpture, American 2. Langlais, Bernard.

92 Perry, Rae
Perry, Rae. *Wild Friends: A True Story of Life with Animal Orphans*. Gannett Books (0-930096-82-7), 1987. 107p. B/W photos. (Interest level: K-8).

This is the story of Rae Perry, who from age seven, when she acquired a young fawn, has nursed orphaned Maine animals back to health. Personal snapshots of animals, from flying squirrels to baby raccoons, are combined with anecdotes about animals and a chronicle of Perry's nursing adventures.
♦ Invite a veterinarian to speak to the class about wildlife rehabilitation.
1. Perry, Rae.

Fiction

Aldridge, Josephine. *A Penny and a Periwinkle*. Illus. by Ruth Robbins. Parnassus Press (No ISBN), 1961. Unpaginated. Color illus. (Interest level: K-2).

Sy, the old Maine fisherman, needs only a penny and a periwinkle to conduct his peaceful Maine coast life: the penny for a sharp new fish hook and the periwinkle for bait. The rest will come from the sea.
♦ Children can discuss ways in which we can simplify our modern life and make lists of things we can do without.
1. Fishing—Fiction.

Ardizzone, Edward. *Tim to the Lighthouse*. Illus. by author. Oxford University Press (0-19-272107-0), 1987. 48p. Color illus. (Interest level: K-3).

Little Tim awakens in the middle of a stormy night and realizes the light from the lighthouse is not shining. When he and his friend old Captain McFee investigate, they find wreckers have been there.
♦ Young people can share with the class orally or in writing a time they were brave. The class could also discuss what it means to be brave.
1. Lighthouses—Fiction.

Baker, Marybeth. *The Adventures of Maynard . . . a Maine Moose*. Illus. by author. Gannett Books (0-930096-60-6), 1985. 44p. Color illus. (Interest level: K-3).

Maynard is unhappy as a moose because he is so big and clumsy, but when all the animals choose him to be the symbol of the Maine woods, Maynard feels

very special. Maynard's friends are all the typical Maine forest creatures: deer, bear, skunk, raccoon, turtle, chipmunk, squirrel, and eagle.
♦ Young people can write about a time they were not happy with themselves and what they did about it. How did they make themselves feel better?
1. Moose—Fiction 2. Animals—Fiction.

Baker, Marybeth. *Maynard's Allagash Friends.* Illus. by author. Gannett Books (0-929906-25-X), 1989. Unpaginated. Color illus. (Interest level: K-3).

Whittle, the rhyming woodpecker, guides Maynard the Moose to the Allagash wilderness, where Maynard meets the Allagash animals and sees new plants. This charming story will introduce students to the Allagash flora and fauna.
♦ Children can write about a time they visited a new place.
1. Animals—Fiction.

Baldwin, Sidney. *Marjorie of Monhegan, a Year in a Girl's Life on a Maine Coast Island.* Illus. by Ann Watson. J. B. Day (No ISBN), 1973, 1930. 300p. B/W illus. (Interest level: 6-8).

Marjorie, a city girl, spends a year on Monhegan Island, where she grows to love the moods of the sea and the fog and the winter winds, as well as the strong-minded people. This classic story has been read by young people in Maine for over 60 years.
♦ Students can make a culture map of Monhegan Island, describing food, clothing, shelter, and occupants.
1. Ocean—Fiction 2. Maine—Fiction.

Bernier, Evariste. *Baxter Bear and Moses Moose.* Illus. by Dawn Peterson. Down East Books (0-89272-287-8), 1990. Unpaginated. Color illus. (Interest level: K-3).

Baxter Bear wants to find a moose who will give up his antlers to house Baxter's hat collection, and Moses Moose wants a bear who will sleep on his floor in winter to keep his feet warm. This charming Maine tale is basically a story of friendship.
♦ Children can brainstorm ways they have found friends; then they can put together a classroom big book showing themselves and their friends.
1. Moose—Fiction 2. Bears—Fiction 3. Friendship—Fiction.

Carpenter, Mimi Gregoire. *Mermaid in a Tidal Pool.* Illus. by author. Beachcomber Press (0-9614628-0-9), 1985. Unpaginated. Color illus. (Interest level: K-3).

Carpenter tells the story of Tessa, an imaginative eight-year-old who conjures up a look-alike mermaid to play with. The author's exquisitely detailed illustrations of tidal pool and beach sea life greatly enhance the story.
♦ Students can write and illustrate stories about imaginary friends.
1. Mermaid—Fiction 2. Imaginary playmates—Fiction.

Carpenter, Mimi Gregoire. *What the Sea Left Behind.* Illus. by author. Down East Books (0-89272-123-5), 1981. 30p. Color illus. (Interest level: K-5).

Tessa tells the story of the beach and the tide pool treasures she finds, pointing out the beauty of color, shape, and design from a young artist's perspective.
♦ In the story, Tessa encourages students to draw, paint, or make collages or clay forms of the things they find in the natural world. Children can make a collection of natural objects, such as leaves, stones, or insects, and depict them in any art form they choose.
1. Beaches—Fiction 2. Art.

Clifford, Harold. *Clear Sailing: How an Augusta Boy Becomes a Monhegan Fisherman.* Grey Gull Publications (0-9614592-2-0), 1987. 143p. B/W photos and illus. (Interest level: 6-8).

Young Walter Davis is taken in by a Monhegan Island fishing family after his father dies in a Civil War battle. This historic piece tells what life was like on Monhegan Island during the Civil War.
♦ Readers may want to research further the effect the Civil War had on their own state or community.
1. United States—History—Civil War, 1861-1865—Fiction 2. Maine—History—Fiction.

Clifford, Harold B. *Sea Horse.* Illus. by Alta Ashley. Grey Gull Publications (0-9614592-3-9), 1987. 66p. B/W illus. and photos. (Interest level: 3-8).

Charlie Reed finds a Shetland pony that has swum to Monhegan Island from a Barnum and Bailey Circus steamship that was sunk in a storm. This actually took place in 1885.
♦ Students can write more adventures for Charlie and his pony.
1. Ponies—Fiction.

Cooney, Barbara. *Island Boy.* Illus. by author. Trumpet Club (0-440-84039-2), 1988. Unpaginated. Color illus. (Interest level: K-6).

Matthais Tibbetts was the youngest of 12 children who grew up in the early 1800s on Tibbetts Island, off Green Harbor, Maine, and went to sea as a young boy on his uncle's schooner. In his old age, Matthais came back to Tibbets Island to live with his widowed daughter Annie and his grandson, little Matthais. This intergenerational tale is beautifully illustrated by the author.

♦ After reading this book, young people may trace their own family histories and find out what their grandfathers did for a living and where they grew up.
1. Family life—Fiction.

Cooney, Barbara. *Miss Rumphius.* Illus. by author. Puffin Books (0-14-050539-3), 1982. Unpaginated. Color illus. (Interest level: K-4).

After traveling to exotic places in her youth, Miss Rumphius settles down in a seaside cottage in Maine, where she spends her days scattering the seeds of blue and purple lupines along the highways and down the country lanes. Barbara Cooney's elegant illustrations enhance the story line.
♦ Students can study wild flowers in their area. Or, a comparison literature study could be made between Johnny Appleseed and Miss Rumphius.
1. Aunts—Fiction 2. Wildflowers—Fiction.

Davis, Marion. *Sam Predicts a Storm.* Illus. by Anne Johnston. Starboard Cove Publishing (0-9622221-1-9), 1991. 36p. B/W illus. (Interest level: 1-3).

Sam, the wise old sea cat, warns his fisherman master that a nor'easter is on the way. Gray tones in the black-and-white drawings help readers predict the impending storm.
♦ Class members can attempt to identify the clues of the impending storm.
1. Storms—Fiction 2. Cats—Fiction.

Deans, Sis Boulas. *Blazing Bear.* Illus. by Nantz Comyns. Downeast Graphics and Printing (0-932433-94-4), 1992. Unpaginated. Color illus. (Interest level: 5-8).

Blazing Bear was a Norridgewock Indian, a skilled hunter and fisherman who lived on the banks of Maine's largest river, the Kennebec. This tale of his bravery in defending his baby sister from a marauding bear, using a log from the fire, is designed to teach as well as entertain.
♦ Students can read other Indian tales and plan a storytelling hour with another class.
1. Indians of North America—Fiction.

Dietz, Lew. *Andre.* Illus. by Stell Shevis. Down East Books (0-89272-052-2), 1979. 83p. B/W illus. (Interest level: 2-6).

Dietz tells the story of Toni Goodridge, who grew up with Andre, the harbor seal who came as a baby to live with Toni's family in Rockport, Maine. This tale is full of adventure and human interest, as well as scientific information about seals.
♦ Children can research seals and present an oral report to the class. They could also write about their own experiences in training animals.
1. Seals—Fiction.

Dodd, Anne Wescott. *Footprints and Shadows.* Illus. by Henri Sorenson. Simon & Schuster (0-671-78716-0), 1992. Unpaginated. Color illus. (Interest level: K-5).

In this poetic text, illustrated with soft, glowing paintings, the author attempts to capture the fleeting quality of footprints and shadows. The paintings are all Maine scenes, from a dog following a man and boy down a woodland path to a Maine pasture with cows sleeping in the night.
♦ Students can connect this book with their study of the sun, light and dark, and shadows by taking photos or making drawings of shadows in their community.
1. Shades and shadows—Fiction.

Emerson, Kathy Lynn. *The Mystery of Illiard's Castle.* Down East Books (0-89272-213-4), 1985. 160p. (Interest level: 5-8).

Kerry and Lyle Odell are uprooted from their New York State home and deposited in a remote Maine town, where their family rents a haunted old mansion. Kerry's school project in genealogy leads her to conclude that she and Lyle are in real danger and could be killed like her father and grandparents were.
♦ Young people can research their own family histories.
1. Mystery and detective stories—Fiction 2. Castles—Fiction.

Field, Rachel. *Calico Bush.* Illus. by Allen Lewis. Macmillan (0-440-40368-5), 1931. 201p. B/W illus. (Interest level: 4-8).

Young Marguerite, a French orphan, is "bound out" to a family that goes to Maine to pioneer in 1743, when Indian raids, cold, and hunger are part of daily life. The struggles, both physical and emotional, of making a home in the wilderness are graphically portrayed in this story.
♦ Readers can make a map of Sargent's land claim, Sunday Island, and the surrounding forests, marking where significant events took place.
1. Frontier and pioneer life—Fiction.

Gjelfriend, George E. *High Island Treasure.* Illus. by Pam DeVito. Windswept House Publishers (0-932433-84-7), 1992. 119p. (Interest level: 6-8).

In this mystery, set on an island off the coast of Maine, 12-year-olds Jennifer and Jeremy search for a hidden treasure. Some interesting characters, a smart cat, and lots of twists and turns keep the reader interested.
♦ Young people can write their own mysteries using a local setting.
1. Mystery and detective stories 2. Buried treasure—Fiction.

Gore, Doris. *Miracle at Egg Rock, a Puffin's Story.* Illus. by Bonnie Bishop. Down East Books (0-89272-205-3), 1985. 48p. B/W illus. (Interest level: 4-8).

Puffin #Q7 is a pioneer chick, taken from her nest in Canada by Audubon Society scientists to start a new puffin colony on Egg Rock, off the coast of Maine. This story of learning to fly, swim, catch fish, and avoid the dangers of life is told from the point of view of the young puffin.
♦ In many areas, scientists are attempting to preserve endangered species. Students may investigate what scientists in their area are doing to protect wildlife.
1. Wildlife conservation—Fiction.

Goudey, Alice. *Houses from the Sea.* Illus. by Adrienne Adams. Charles Scribner's Sons (0-684-12458-0), 1959. Unpaginated. Color illus. (Interest level: K-4).

This is the story of two children who are beachcombing and collecting shells. Along with the ethereal illustrations, this book has a shell identification chart in the back and a brief article on how shells are formed.
♦ Students can bring their collections to school to share with the class.
1. Shells—Fiction.

Harriman, Edward. *Leroy the Lobster and Crabby Crab.* Illus. by author. Down East Books (0-89272-000-X), 1967. Unpaginated. Color illus. (Interest level: K-2).

Leroy Lobster and Crabby Crab find a sunken treasure, but escaping with their lives and part of the haul is the problem. The humorous illustrations will amuse a younger audience.
♦ Children can imagine what it would be like to find a sunken treasure and then illustrate the type of sunken treasure they would like to find.
1. Lobsters—Fiction   2. Buried treasure—Fiction.

Haskell, Bess C. *The Hunky Dory.* Illus. by Ann M. Poole. Coastwise Press (0-9626857-2-0), 1992. 41p. B/W illus. (Interest level: 2-6).

This book is the second in a six-volume series about two children who are learning the proper handling of a watercraft. Through a series of misadventures, Muffin and Dan, turn-of-the-century children of Tenants Harbor, Maine, learn to row the dory and catch fish.
♦ Class members can share their own experiences of learning new skills.
1. Sailing—Fiction.

Haskell, Bess C. *The Raft.* Illus. by Ingrid Fetz. Kennebec River Press (0-933858-26-4), 1988. Unpaginated. B/W illus. (Interest level: 2-6).

Muffin and Dan, turn-of-the-century Maine coast children, help their Pa make a raft to float cordwood down to the sawmill and accidentally launch the raft with themselves, their dog, and their cat aboard. Realistic line drawings of Maine scenes enhance this story.
♦ Students can write their own adventure story, imagining they are living at the turn of the century and have to use a raft on a river or lake near their home.
1. Adventure and adventurers—Fiction.

Hassett, John and **Hassett, Ann.** *Moose on the Loose.* Illus. by authors. Down East Books (0-89272-245-2), 1987. Unpaginated. Color illus. (Interest level: K-3).

In his quest to find out what people are like, Max, the backwoods moose, ends up on the roof of a multistory city building. This is a silly adventure story that contrasts Maine backwoods with city life.
♦ Young people could write more adventures for Max.
1. Moose—Fiction.

Ipcar, Dahlov. *Brown Cow Farm.* Illus. by author. Doubleday (0-385-07856-0), 1959. Unpaginated. Color illus. (Interest level: K-2).

Starting with one brown horse and two brown hound dogs, Ipcar progresses to 10 brown cows, standing in their stalls, giving milk. The twist to this counting book is that in the spring, the 10 brown cows each have a little brown calf, making 10 brown calves, and the two brown hounds each have 10 puppies, making 20 puppies. This progresses, and the challenge at the end is to count all the animals on the farm.
♦ Students can create their own counting book.
1. Counting—Fiction   2. Farm life—Fiction.

Jane, Mary Childs. *Mystery at Pemaquid Point.* Illus. by Raymond Abel. Down East Books (0-89272-050-6), 1957. 126p. (Interest level: 3-6).

Someone has been setting fires and breaking into cottages at Pemaquid Point, and Elisabeth, the "girl from away," and Henry, her new friend, are determined to find out who it is. This exciting tale is set in one of Maine's most rugged and beautiful rocky coastal points.
♦ Readers can draw postcards that show the setting of the story.
1. Mystery and detective stories—Fiction.

Jane, Mary Childs. *Mystery in Longfellow Square.* Illus. by Raymond Abel. Down East Books (0-89272-048-4), 1964. 128p. B/W illus. (Interest level: 3-6).

Linda, Phil, and Howie solve two mysteries by poking around the old buildings and abandoned church in Longfellow Square, in Portland, Maine.

This is a typical Mary C. Jane mystery, with the kids as heroes.
♦ Children can discuss the characteristics of a good mystery story and then write one of their own.
1. Mystery and detective stories—Fiction.

Jewett, Sarah Orne. *The Country of the Pointed Firs.* Illus. by Douglas Alvord. David R. Godine (0-87923-894-1), 1991, 1896. 197p. B/W illus. (Interest level: 7-8).

Set in the small coastal town of Tenant's Harbor, Maine, this 1896 collection of stories and sketches describes rugged Maine people coping with their harsh coastal environment after the Civil War. The women characters are the most vivid in this book, which reflects the fact that men had migrated to cities to earn their living.
♦ Students can research famous women or women of importance in their own community.
1. Women—Fiction 2. Maine—Fiction 3. Quality of life—Fiction.

Jewett, Sarah Orne. *A White Heron.* Illus. by Douglas Alvord. Tilbury House (0-88448-082-8), 1990, 1886. Unpaginated. B/W illus. (Interest level: 6-8).

Jewett tells the story of a young girl who keeps the nesting place of a white heron a secret. Alvord's pen-and-ink drawings highlight the unique spirit and strength of Maine characters as well as the beauty of Maine's scenery.
♦ This book sounds more like poetry than the prose we are accustomed to. Students can analyze the language and tell how it is different from the way it would be written today.
1. Birds—Fiction 2. Maine—Fiction.

Ladd, Elizabeth. *Meg of Heron's Neck.* Illus. by Mary Stevens. William Morrow (No ISBN), 1961. 191p. B/W illus. (Interest level: 3-6).

Meg Elwell and her brother Allen are orphans who live aboard the *Sea Mouse,* a small lobster boat, and value their independence more than life's comforts. This classic Maine story has been enjoyed by Maine children for over 30 years, because it reflects the spirit of Maine people.
♦ Pretending they are the Elwells today, students could write about how they would survive in their community.
1. Maine—Fiction 2. Quality of life—Fiction.

Langley, Virginia. *Babes in the Woods.* Illus. by Patrick Davis. Gannett Books (0-930096-82-7), 1987. Unpaginated. Color illus.; B/W photos. (Interest level: 2-5).

Peter's summer adventure with his grandfather is a hike through the woods near Eagle Lake, Maine, to see baby animals. This charming story is enhanced with line drawings and black-and-white photos of Maine baby animals such as moose, loons, deer, foxes, and raccoons.
♦ Young people can observe and draw or photograph animals in their area and conduct research on each of the animals they find.
1. Animals—Fiction 2. Grandfathers—Fiction.

Langley, Virginia. *Hurray for Christopher! The Story of a Maine Coon Cat.* Illus. by Patrick Davis. Gannett Books (0-930096-71-1), 1986. Unpaginated. Color illus. (Interest level: K-8).

Young Christopher Kitten feels inferior to his feline friends who have pedigrees until his great granduncle, Captain Tom, tells him he is probably descended from Viking Norwegian skagcats, Marie Antoinette's abandoned royal cats, and early American seafaring cats. The moral of the story is that pedigree isn't everything.
♦ Students may want to make a family tree of their ancestors, identifying countries of origin.
1. Cats—Fiction.

Langley, Virginia. *Thar She Blows, a Whale of a Vacation Surprise.* Illus. by Patrick Davis. Gannett Books (0-930096-87-8), 1986. Unpaginated. Color and B/W illus. (Interest level: 2-4).

During his summer vacation in Maine, Peter looks forward each year to a special surprise his grandfather plans for him. This story, well illustrated with action drawings, shows the whale watch Peter and his grandfather participate in one summer.
♦ Children can write about or draw what they look forward to doing during summer vacation.
1. Whale watching—Fiction 2. Grandfathers—Fiction.

Lapp, Eleanor. *Blueberry Bears.* Illus. by Margot Apple. Albert Whitman (0-8075-0976-2), 1983. Unpaginated. B/W illus. (Interest level: K-2).

Hungry bears invade Bessie Allen's cabin after she picks clean the blueberry patch in the woods and stockpiles the berries in her kitchen. This is a cute story about the necessity of sharing.
♦ Students can discuss sharing and ways in which they share with their classmates and with family members. Compare this book with *Blueberries for Sal* (*see* p. 62) by Robert McCloskey.
1. Bears—Fiction.

Larkin, Alice True. *Zachary Goes Groundfishing on the Trawler Lucille B.* Illus. by Abbey Williams. Down East Books (0-89272-084-0), 1982. 52p. B/W illus. and map. (Interest level: 3-6).

Ten-year-old Zachary spends the day on a trawler watching the crew locate fish, tow the trawl net, clean and sort the fish, and finally mend the nets. Illustrations of different types of fish and the mechanics of the trawl net, along with a map of Seguin Island, enhance the text.

♦ Young people can create more adventures for Zachary aboard the trawler.
1. Fishing—Fiction.

Lasky, Kathryn. *Jem's Island.* Illus. by Ronald Himler. Charles Scribner's Sons (0-684-17624-6), 1982. 56p. B/W illus. (Interest level: 4-8).

Jem goes on his first overnight kayak trip with his father to an island in Penobscot Bay. This book presents a nice portrait of a father-and-son relationship.
♦ Readers can write about adventures that Jem and his father might have on another kayak trip.
1. Kayaks and kayaking—Fiction 2. Fathers and sons—Fiction 3. Camping—Fiction 4. Islands—Fiction 5. Maine—Fiction.

Lasky, Kathryn. *My Island Grandma.* Illus. by Emily McCully. Frederick Warne (0-7232-6159-8), 1979. Unpaginated. Color illus. (Interest level: 1-4).

Abbey travels with her parents to their summer cottage on an island off the coast of Maine, where she spends her time with her rugged and resourceful grandmother. The ink-and-wash drawings capture the island's beauty and the loving relationship between Abbey and her grandmother.
♦ Students can interview senior citizens and ask them to describe their childhood experiences.
1. Grandmothers—Fiction.

Levin, Betty. *Brother Moose.* Greenwillow Books (0-688-09266-7), 1990. 213p. (Interest level: 6-8).

In the late nineteenth century, during a fierce winter, Joe, an American Indian, leads two orphans on a dangerous trip through northern Maine to a foster family. The story of Nell and Louisa is a dramatic tale of tradition and survival, prejudice and cruelty, loyalty and love.
♦ Have a class discussion on prejudice, and ask students how prejudice affects society.
1. Orphans—Fiction 2. Frontier and pioneer life—Fiction 3. Indians of North America—Fiction 4. Maine—Fiction.

McCloskey, Robert. *Blueberries for Sal.* Illus. by author. Viking Press (0-670-17591-9), 1948. 55p. B/W illus. (Interest level: K-3).

Little Sal and her mother are picking blueberries to can for the winter, while mother bear and her cub are eating berries to store fat for the winter. When both the bear cub and the little girl wander off, each encounters the wrong mother.
♦ Students can describe how they would react to meeting a bear or some other animal. This would be a good opportunity to discuss the dangers of interacting with wild animals.
1. Bears—Fiction.

McCloskey, Robert. *Burt Dow, Deep Water Man.* Illus. by author. Viking Press (0-670-19748-3), 1963. 63p. Color illus. (Interest level: K-3).

Burt Dow, a retired deep-water man who lives on the Maine coast with his impatient sister Leela, spends most of his time repairing his old boat, the *Tidely Idely*. One day, while out fishing for cod, Burt inadvertently hooks a whale's tail and puts a peppermint-striped Band-Aid on it for solace. After being swallowed and regurgitated by that whale, Burt finds himself in the middle of a school of whales, all of whom want Band-Aids.
♦ Students can discuss why the whales wanted Band-Aids and how people feel about being alike and different.
1. Whales—Fiction.

McCloskey, Robert. *One Morning in Maine.* Illus. by author. Viking Press (0-670-52627-4), 1952. 64p. B/W illus. (Interest level: K-3).

The morning Sal is supposed to row to Buck's Harbor with her Dad and little sister Jane from their island home, she discovers she has her first loose tooth. Sal plans to put the tooth under her pillow and wish for a chocolate ice-cream cone. But, when she finds her Dad, who is digging clams on the shore, the tooth drops into the muddy clam hole and is lost. Sal decides to wish on a seagull feather instead, and her wish is granted by the kindly storekeeper in Buck's Harbor.
♦ Children can write about, illustrate, or tell about the loss of their first tooth. This activity could be combined with a dental health lesson.
1. Wishes—Fiction 2. Teeth—Fiction.

McCloskey, Robert. *Time of Wonder.* Illus. by author. Viking Press (0-670-71512-3), 1957. 63p. Color illus. (Interest level: K-4).

In a poetic rendition, McCloskey recounts the passing of a summer on the coast of Maine. The preparations for an early fall hurricane are detailed, as are the feelings of the family waiting out the hurricane, singing songs and playing games. At the end of the story, McCloskey describes how the family returns to its winter home with regret and anticipation.
♦ Children may write about a storm they experienced, how they prepared for it, and what damage it did. This could be combined with a science study of weather.
1. Seasons—Fiction 2. Weather—Fiction 3. Storms—Fiction.

MacDonald, Amy. *Little Beaver and the Echo.* Illus. by Sarah Fox-Davies. G. P. Putnam's Sons (0-399-22203-0), 1990. Unpaginated. Color illus. (Interest level: K-2).

Unaware that the voice from across the pond telling him he is lonely is his echo, a little beaver sets out to make a friend of that voice. Along the way, he encounters real Maine animal friends.
♦ Children can discuss friendship and share how they have met their friends.
1. Friendship—Fiction 2. Beavers—Fiction 3. Animals—Fiction.

McMillan, Bruce. *Finestkind O'Day, Lobstering in Maine.* Photos by author. Down East Books (0-89272-185-5), 1977. 48p. B/W photos. (Interest level: K-6).

Brett, a young boy in Port Clyde, Maine, learns the meaning of the fisherman's expression "Finestkind," when he is a sternman on a lobster boat.
♦ Invite a variety of individuals into the class to speak about their professions. Students could then put together a description of each profession, indicating skills needed for the job, training, and a contact in the area.
1. Lobster fisheries—Fiction 2. Jobs—Fiction.

Martin, Charles. *Island Winter.* Illus. by author. Greenwillow Books (0-688-02590-0), 1984. Unpaginated. Color illus. (Interest level: K-3).

Heather must stay behind on Monhegan Island after the summer people have left, and she wonders what to do. Funny illustrations give a very accurate picture of life on Monhegan Island.
♦ Young people can draw pictures showing what they would do during the off season if they lived on Monhegan Island.
1. Islands—Fiction.

Martin, Charles E. *Island Rescue.* Illus. by author. Greenwillow Books (0-688-04258-9), 1985. Unpaginated. Color illus. (Interest level: K-3).

After a summer picnic, Mae wanders off and breaks her leg. She is taken by the Coast Guard from Monhegan Island to the mainland for medical care. The humorous illustrations convey Mae's feelings throughout the story.
♦ Students can visit the children's ward of a local hospital or ask a representative from the children's ward to visit their class.
1. Hospitals—Fiction 2. Medical care—Fiction 3. Maine—Fiction.

Moulton, Deborah. *Summer Girl.* Dial Books (0-8037-1153-0), 1992. 133p. (Interest level: 6-8).

Because her mother is dying, Tommy is sent to Maine to live with her estranged father. She gradually comes to understand him and the death of the woman they both love. Coastal Ellsworth is the setting of this father-daughter story of resentment, misunderstanding, and finally forgiveness and love.
♦ Young people may write about their own family experiences.

1. Death—Fiction 2. Family life—Fiction 3. Fathers and daughters—Fiction.

Oatway, Pete. *The Hunting Camp.* Illus. by Dick Smith. Bowerbook Publishers (No ISBN), 1992. 59p. B/W illus. (Interest level: 6-8).

Pete Oatway, who spent the bulk of his hunting experience at a deep woods camp near Guilford, Maine, based these short stories on the diary he kept during 25 years at the camp. Humorous adventures and misadventures are shared.
♦ Invite a hunter into the classroom to talk about his/her experiences and safe hunting tips. Class members may also wish to debate the pros and cons of hunting.
1. Hunting—Fiction.

Parnall, Peter. *Winter Barn.* Illus. by author. Macmillan (0-02-770170-0), 1986. Unpaginated. B/W illus. (Interest level: K-3).

The centuries-old Maine barn is a winter refuge for all creatures from the ribbon snake in the massive stone foundation, to the horses and sheep, to the sleeping bats in the rafters. The exquisite illustrations attest to the fact that Peter Parnall is first of all an award-winning artist.
♦ Imagining that they are creatures that live in the old barn, students can write or dramatize a day in their life in the barn.
1. Winter—Fiction 2. Animals—Fiction.

Robert McCloskey Library (Videocassette). Children's Circle, 1992. Distributed by Weston Woods. B/W and Color, (58 min.). $195.00. (Interest level: K-3).

This video library contains: *Lentil, Make Way for Ducklings* (see p. 98), *Blueberries for Sal* (see p. 62), *Time of Wonder* (see p. 62), *Burt Dow, Deep Water Man* (see p. 62), and *Getting to Know Robert McCloskey* (documentary).
♦ Invite a local author or illustrator into the classroom to speak to the class. The class could also choose an author and create a "Getting to Know" video.
1. McCloskey, Robert 2. Children's literature—Fiction.

Robinson, Jane W. *The Whale in Lowell's Cove.* Illus. by author. Down East Books (0-89272-308-4), 1992. Unpaginated. Color illus. (Interest level: 1-4).

In the summer of 1990, a young humpback whale really did swim into Lowell's Cove in the tiny seaside town of Harpswell, Maine. Local residents and fishermen spent many hours studying the habits of the whale and trying to figure out how to get her back out to sea.
♦ Children can write about the whale's experience from the whale's perspective. What was she thinking? How did she feel?
1. Whales—Fiction.

Rowinski, Kate. *L.L. Bear's Island Adventure.* Illus. by Dawn Peterson. Down East Books (0-89272-320-3), 1992. Unpaginated. Color illus. (Interest level: 1-4).

L. L. Bear paddles his kayak to Blueberry Island for one last autumn picnic with his friends: the seals, a puffin, and a fox. But little Sam, the baby seal, has disappeared. This charmingly illustrated tale gets its suspense from the lost-and-found theme.
♦ Young people can write about Sam's experience from Sam's point of view.
1. Bears—Fiction   2. Animals—Fiction.

Sargent, Ruth S. *The Littlest Lighthouse.* Illus. by Marion C. Litchfield. Down East Books (0-89272-119-7), 1981. 28p. B/W illus. (Interest level: 2-3).

The littlest lighthouse has a jolly time watching the lobster boats, sailboats, and tankers until one day, when a "pea soup" fog settles in, he realizes what his job is really all about. This book is a nice introduction for children to the functions of a lighthouse.
♦ Students can write stories about the seagull and the lighthouse, comparing and contrasting their lifestyles. They could then illustrate their stories.
1. Lighthouses—Fiction.

Scott, Donnie Porter. *New ABC's of Maine.* Illus. by Patrick Davis. Gannett Books (0-930096-96-7), 1987. Unpaginated. Color illus. (Interest level: K-3).

In each alphabet page of this book, Tikitum, a lady bear, points out the alphabetized objects. Tikitum takes the young reader from the apple orchard "A" to the "Z" of a bear snoozing in hibernation.
♦ Children can create alphabet books using illustrations from their own geographical area.
1. Alphabet—Fiction.

Smith, Harry W. *ABC's of Maine.* Illus. by author. Down East Books (0-89272-070-0), 1980. Unpaginated. Color illus. (Interest level: K-4).

For each letter of the alphabet, Smith highlights natural features and animals of Maine. Each entry includes an adjective/noun descriptor and a watercolor painting. An appendix gives more information on the entries.
♦ Students can create an alphabet book with an appendix about their own state. They can work cooperatively to decide what the most important features of their state are.
1. Alphabet—Fiction.

Smith, Harry W. *Michael and the Mary Day.* Illus. by author. Down East Books (0-89272-046-8), 1979. 59p. B/W and Color illus. (Interest level: K-3).

Michael has always wanted to cruise Penobscot Bay aboard a windjammer, and today is the day his dream comes true. This old favorite is the story of a child's hopes realized.
♦ Children can share one of their dreams either orally in class or in writing.
1. Sailing ships—Fiction   2. Maine—Fiction.

Speare, Elizabeth George. *The Sign of the Beaver.* Dell (0-440-47900-2), 1983. 135p. (Interest level: 4-8).

Twelve-year-old Matt only survives in the 1700s Maine wilderness because of his tenuous friendship with a Native American boy, Atlean. This friendship story gives an accurate picture of Maine wilderness life in Milo in the 1700s.
♦ Young people can illustrate the story or assemble a collection of artifacts connected to the story.
1. Frontier and pioneer life—Fiction   2. Indians of North America—Fiction.

Stapler, Sarah. *Spruce the Moose Cuts Loose.* Illus. by author. G. P. Putnam's Sons (0-399-21861-0), 1992. Unpaginated. Color illus. (Interest level: K-3).

Spruce the Moose's enormous antlers cause him all sorts of problems in his daily life. The bright caricatures of Spruce and his forest friends enhance this imaginative story in a Maine setting.
♦ Students can write and illustrate a story about an animal whose physical characteristics get in the way.
1. Moose—Fiction   2. Animals—Fiction.

Thurston, Doris. *Beloved Brick House.* Illus. by author. Oxford Hills Press (No ISBN), n.d. 75p. B/W illus. (Interest level: 6-8).

Reminiscences of life on a farm at the turn of the century, from the visit of the ragman, to evenings filled with harmonica and piano music, to the constant arrival of new litters of kittens, fill this small book. This is not really a story, but rather a series of vignettes of life in a rural Maine setting.
♦ Based on information in this book, young people may do a cultural profile of rural Maine farm life and compare it with Maine farm life today.
1. Farm life—Fiction.

Titherington, Jeanne. *Pumpkin Pumpkin.* Illus. by author. Greenwillow Books (0-688-05695-4), 1986. 24p. Color illus. (Interest level: K-2).

Jamie plants a pumpkin seed, and, after watching it grow, carves the pumpkin for Halloween and saves some of the seeds to plant in the spring. Beautiful colored pencil drawings depict the sequence of plant development and the reactions of young Jamie.
♦ Students may plant seeds in class and watch them grow, recording their observations.
1. Gardening—Fiction   2. Pumpkins—Fiction.

Verrier, Suzy. *Titus Tidewater.* Illus. by author. Down East Books (0-89272-289-4), 1970. Unpaginated. Color illus. (Interest level: K-3).

Titus Tidewater, a Maine lobster, is caught in a trap and later purchased by two children who want him as a pet. Scientifically accurate information about lobster habits is woven into this simple tale.
♦ Children can research the different kinds of environments that animals need.
1. Lobsters—Fiction.

White, Sylvia. *Home Is Best.* Illus. by Pam DeVito. Windswept House Publishers (0-932443-48-0), 1988. 44p. B/W illus. (Interest level: K-2).

Wenda, Hector, and Sophie, three Maine farm geese, are chased by a black dog out onto an ice floe, which takes them five miles from home and forces them to fend for themselves until they accidentally find their way home again. The black-and-white line drawings enhance the Maine setting of this story.
♦ Students can tape record further adventures of the three geese before they reach home.
1. Geese—Fiction.

Professional Materials

970.1
The Wabanakis of Maine and the Maritimes: A Resource Book about Penobscot, Passamaquoddy, Maliseet, Micmac and Abenaki Indians. American Friends Service Committee (No ISBN), 1989. 547p. B/W illus. (Interest level: Professional).

This teaching guide for grades 4-8, compiled by teachers for teachers, leads the reader through the history of the tribes, legends, and modern life. The guide's purpose is to dispel stereotyping through an in-depth study of the culture and history of the Wabanaki.
♦ Students can research place-names in their area that derive from American Indian words.
1. Indians of North America—History 2. Indians of North America—Social life and customs 3. Indians of North America—Legends.

Maryland

by Paula Montgomery

Nonfiction

317.3752 (Reference)
Hagerstown Town and Country Almanack. Gruber Almanack Company. B/W illus. (Interest level: 6-8).
This fascinating annual, which has been published since 1797 in Hagerstown, Maryland, will appeal to students who have not looked at a local or regional almanac. Black-and-white woodcuts portray early farm scenes from Maryland. Students will find this useful both as a reference book and as a document for understanding agriculture needs.
♦ Readers may compare information in this almanac with that in a more general almanac and look at the types of predictions and accounts that are given for local interests.
1. Almanacs   2. Hagerstown (Md.)—Almanacs.

333.91 (Reference)
United States Department of the Interior. *Atlas of National Wetlands Inventory Maps of the Chesapeake Bay.* United States Department of the Interior (No ISBN), 1986. B/W maps. (Interest level: grade 6-adult).
Official maps refer to the inventory of national wetlands within the state. The details and information may be used in a variety of ways as students engage in social studies and environmental and science activities.
♦ Young people may examine some of the maps near their own locality and discuss their understanding of a wetland. What kinds of life do wetlands support? Can students see such life in these areas?
1. Chesapeake Bay—Maps   2. Chesapeake Bay—Ecology   3. Marshes.

333.95 (Reference)
Lippson, Alice Jane. *The Chesapeake Bay in Maryland: An Atlas of Natural Resources.* Illus. by author. Johns Hopkins University Press (0-8018-1467-7; 0-8018-1468-5 pbk), 1973. 64p. (Interest level: 4-8).
Lippson offers complete guide to the natural resources in the state.
♦ Young people can use this as a reference as they conduct research for oral and written reports, including in their reports what resources are in their community.
1. Chesapeake Bay—Atlases   2. Maryland—Atlases   3. Natural resources—Maryland.

353.9752 (Reference)
Carr, Lois Green and **Papenfuse, Edward.** *A Declaration of Maryland.* Maryland State Archives Publications (0-942370-16-3), 1984. 62p. B/W illus. (Interest level:7-8).
Jesuit Father Andrew White wrote a promotional tract for Maryland in 1633 to attract investors and settlers to the new colony. An introduction describes the promotion and its impact on the history of the colony.
♦ Young people may compare White's promotion with what might be promoted today and discuss what is appealing to investors now as compared to the 1700s.
1. Maryland—History—Colonial Period, ca 1600-1775.

353.9752 (Reference)
The Charter of Maryland. Maryland State Archives Publications (0-942370-27-9), 1990. 32p. B/W illus. (Interest level: 7-8).
Seekers of primary materials find here a facsimile of the original charter that granted the colony of Maryland to Cecil Calvert in 1632. The introduction provides historical information supplied by Edward Papenfuse, the state archivist. Illustrations accompany the commentary.
♦ Students may examine the facsimile of the charter and discuss its contents. They might then write their own version of a charter for their school.

1. Maryland—Charter 2. Maryland—History—Colonial period, ca 1600-1775.

353.9752
Rollo, Vera Foster. *Maryland's Government.* Maryland Historical Press (0-917882-18-0), 1985. 300p. B/W illus. (Interest level: 6-8).

Rollo explains Maryland's governments at the town, city, county, and state levels in a simple black-and-white illustrated format. A description of the U.S. government is also given for comparison. Documents relevant to the state include the constitution of Maryland, the Maryland charter, the Declaration of Independence, and the U.S. Constitution. An 88-page teacher's guide and glossary of terms are of value.

♦ Students may use a city, county, and state approach to identify how an individual in a particular place might be subject to different governing situations. Students may list the differences in rulings among each jurisdiction.

1. Maryland—Government.

355.3
United States Naval Academy. (Sound filmstrip). Enjoy Communicating, 1981. Color, (10 min.); teacher's guide. $35.00. (Interest level: 4-7).

Viewers will learn the history of the U.S. Naval Academy and see the campus and events during the course of the year that prepare the midshipmen for military life. The filmstrip might be used for social studies units on government agencies, career development, and history.

♦ Students might supplement their knowledge of the academy by locating current periodical articles that show what has happened at the academy with social change. What effects have the women's movement and the end of the cold war had on the academy?

1. United States Naval Academy.

384.7
Airports: A Community Need. (Sound filmstrip). Enjoy Communicating, 1992. Color, (10 min.); teacher's guide. $35.00. (Interest level: 2-6).

Outlining the three major and four minor types of airports, this sound filmstrip focuses on the role of airplanes as transportation. The Baltimore-Washington International Airport is one of the major airports featured in the filmstrip. Other smaller airports show the role of the airplane in moving goods, delivering mail, and providing services. Although specific to the Baltimore-Washington area, the filmstrip might be used to show how different combinations of air services help provide services in large metropolitan areas.

♦ Viewers might research airport transportation and design their own version of what they think an airport would be. They could combine services and prepare layouts to show where the services would be provided.

1. Airports—Maryland 2. Transportation—Maryland.

387.2
Snediker, Quentin and **Jensen, Ann.** *Chesapeake Bay Schooners.* Tidewater Publishers (0-87033-435-2), 1992. 256p. Illus. (Interest level: 7-8).

The Chesapeake Bay schooner was perfected in the United States, where it became known for its beauty and speed. With the development of the ship came stories of captains and sailors. This work chronicles the history and eventual demise of the ships on the Chesapeake Bay. The photographs, figures, and maps add to the research value of the volume for social studies and transportation units.

♦ As students examine the schooners, they may look at the role of the ships in Maryland and U.S. history. Students can make time lines to show their development.

1. Ships—Maryland 2. Schooners—Chesapeake Bay.

394.2
Maryland Day, March 25th. (Videocassette). Enjoy Communicating, 1992. VHS, Color, (13 min.); teacher's guide. $65.00. (Interest level: 4-7).

On March 25, 1634, the first colonists arrived safely on St. Clements Island. The date is celebrated as a holiday in Maryland as a way of honoring the beginning of the state. This videotape gives a history of the event and information about the symbols of the state using pictures and photographs.

♦ Children may use this and other information to produce their own re-enactments of the arrival of the colonists on St. Clements Island.

1. Holidays—Maryland 2. Maryland—History.

398.2
Carey, George, G. *Maryland Folklore.* Tidewater Publishers (0-87033-396-8), 1989. 163p. B/W illus. and maps. (Interest level: 6-8).

A former Maryland state folklorist fascinates readers with many types of folklore, from legends and tall tales to rhymes and herb remedies. Stories might be selected for short read-alouds or used during the study of a particular geographic area. Readable and entertaining, these stories will give readers a view of Maryland culture.

♦ Young people may read about some of the local characters and their deeds, identify individuals in their own neighborhood who qualify as local heroes, and determine qualities that make a local or folk hero.

1. Maryland—Folklore.

398.2
Gallagher, Trish. *Ghosts and Haunted Houses of Maryland.* Tidewater Publishers (0-87033-382-8), 1988. 96p. B/W illus. (Interest level: 6-8).

Ghostly tales include 25 stories about figures such as Patty Cannon, Samuel Mudd, and the slave kidnapper. Many of these characters are historical figures. The stories might be used for a scary read-aloud or in a unit on short stories.
♦ Readers might select a story about a real figure and compare the ghost story with biographical materials. The class could discuss how ghost stories originate.
1. Maryland—Folklore.

551.6 (Reference)
Jacoby, Mark E. *Bayside Guide to Weather on the Chesapeake.* Maryland Sea Grant Publications (0-943676-19-3), 1984. 52p. B/W illus. (Interest level: 4-8).

The processes involved in the makeup of the Chesapeake Bay weather are summarized with information about how to guard against hazards. This work is useful to all who live and work near the bay and will be especially suitable for geography units in identifying weather patterns and general expectations.
♦ Provide students with a list of different types of jobs related to the bay, such as oystermen, farmers, or shopkeepers, and ask them to identify the information in the book that would help these workers prepare for their jobs.
1. Weather   2. Chesapeake Bay—Weather.

574.5
Ecology of the Bay. (Sound filmstrip). Enjoy Communicating, 1982. Color, (11:41 min.); teacher's guide. $35.00.(Interest level: 3-6).

The Chesapeake Bay provides jobs, food, and recreation to thousands of people in Maryland. This filmstrip uses the Chesapeake Bay as an example of the interrelationships of people and the environment.
♦ Children can speculate about what would happen to people in Maryland if the Chesapeake Bay became completely polluted. Following the filmstrip, young people may revise their speculations and discuss how Maryland citizens have a relationship with the bay.
1. Ecology—Maryland   2. Marine life—Maryland.

574.5 (Reference)
White, Christopher P. *Chesapeake Bay: Nature of the Estuary, a Field Guide.* Illus. by Karen Teramura. Tidewater Publishers (0-87033-351-8), 1989. 212p. B/W illus. (Interest level: 5-8).

The Chesapeake Bay's habitats are arranged according to the nine major habitats, such as wetlands and marshes. Flora and fauna for each habitat are described here, and over 500 species are recorded in 350 pen-and-ink drawings. This book will become handy for identifying species while on walks or other nature activities.
♦ Students may set up nine illustrated habitats to show the flora and fauna of each, using the text to locate the appropriate species in each area.
1. Chesapeake Bay—Biology   2. Ecology—Chesapeake Bay—Maryland.

595.3
Coldrey, Jennifer. *The World of Crabs.* Photos by Oxford Scientific Films. Gareth Stevens (1-55532-063-5), 1986. (Where Animals Live). 32p. Color photos and illus. (Interest level: 2-4).

Written with a controlled vocabulary, this guide to crabs includes color photographs that support the concepts of crab behavior presented. Line drawings show the animals in the context of the food chain and provide insight into the crab's known life cycle. The work is also available in audiocassette format as a read-along for young readers.
♦ Students may prepare food chain mobiles, using paper figures, string, and straws, with the crab in its likely place in the food chain. Students must read and think about the animals mentioned in the book to decide where the crab belongs in the food chain.
1. Maryland—Biology   2. Crabs   3. Marine animals.

595.3
Johnson, Sylvia A. *Crabs.* Photos by Kazunari Kawashima. Lerner (0-8225-1471-0), 1982. (Lerner Natural Science Book). 48p. Color photos. (Interest level: 4-6).

Body parts, life stages of the crab, and the molting process are included in this photographic work. The combination of text and photographs makes this work of special interest to children who want to learn about animals.
♦ Children may prepare a life cycle ring showing the various stages of development of the crab. When are crabs most vulnerable?
1. Maryland—Biology   2. Crabs   3. Marine animals.

598.297
Meanley, Brooke. *Birds and Marshes of the Chesapeake Bay Country.* Tidewater Publishers (0870033-207-4), 1975. 157p. (Interest level: 6-8).

The Chesapeake Bay supports a diverse bird population that is both indigenous and migratory. Meanley's guidebook helps bird watchers identify the various environments of bird populations, from the cattails to the cordgrass. The index and appendix make this even more useful for bird identification.

♦ Locate pictures or photographs of various birds of the Chesapeake and ask students to find the names of the birds and their chosen habitat.
1. Birds—Chesapeake Bay 2. Chesapeake Bay—Maryland—Birds.

598.297
Taylor, John W. *Birds of the Chesapeake Bay.* Johns Hopkins University Press (0-8018-4380-4), 1992. 96p. Color illus. (Interest level: 7-8).

Taylor's beautiful book includes 40 of the artist's paintings of many of the region's best-loved birds, including the Canada goose, laughing gull, osprey, snowy egret, sora rail, and peregrine falcon, in their habitat. The text and natural histories demonstrate an awareness of the bay as something to be conserved and valued for its natural beauty.
♦ Readers may review the birds that the author selected and research one of the birds in more detail to learn more about its habitats and needs.
1. Chesapeake Bay—Maryland—Birds 2. Birds—Chesapeake Bay.

636.1
Keiper, Ronald P. *The Assateague Ponies.* Tidewater Publishers (0-87033-330-5), 1985. 102p. B/W photos. (Interest level: 7-8).

Twenty-one ponies were released on the north island in the Assateague Island National Seashore. Slowly the number of ponies has grown. Keiper, an animal behavior specialist, writes about the free-roaming ponies, describing how they forage and survive on the island. His treatment is scientific and supplies a great deal of data on the ponies.
♦ Students may compare this scientific treatment with books about the ponies that take a narrative point of view and describe the ponies in stories.
1. Horses—Assateague (Md.) 2. Assateague (Md.)—Ponies.

639
Watermen and Lighthouses of the Chesapeake Bay. (Sound filmstrip). Enjoy Communicating, 1981. Color, (13 min.); teacher's guide. $35.00. (Interest level: 3-7).

As a look at the fishing industry, the filmstrip provides a view of the ecology of the Chesapeake Bay; marine life such as oysters, clams, crabs, and bluefish; and the role of lighthouses in the bay. Viewers will learn how the watermen try to make a living within the federal and state laws.
♦ Young people may collect statistics on the amount of different bay products harvested during the past 50 to 100 years. How has the ecology of the bay changed?
1. Ecology 2. Lighthouses—Maryland.

639.544
Warner, William W. *Beautiful Swimmers: Watermen, Crabs and the Chesapeake Bay.* Illus. by Consuelo Hanks. Penguin (0-1400-4405-1), 1987. 304p. (Interest level: 7-8).

In this narrative Warner skillfully reveals how Atlantic blue crabs mate and form part of a way of life for many watermen and dinner for people in the state. The crab stories and the colorful, frank people who work along the water make this a flavorful portrayal of the bay. For the more advanced reader, this book has become a classic in environmental literature.
♦ Young adults may compare sections of this narrative with examples of expository writing about the crab and discuss the differences.
1. Chesapeake Bay 2. Blue crabs.

728.752
Dowell, Susan Stiles. *Great Houses of Maryland.* Photos by Marion E. Warren. Tidewater Publishers (0-87033-384-4), 1988. 179p. Color photos. (Interest level: 6-8).

Dowell and Warren have carefully researched the famous houses of Maryland. The descriptions of the homes and over 160 color photographs tell the history of the people in the great houses. The homes document the changes in architectural style over 350 years in Maryland.
♦ Students might select a home in one of the photographs and find out more about the people who built it and why they chose a particular style. They might also compare styles shown in the book with styles of homes in their community.
1. Homes—Maryland 2. Houses—History 3. Architecture—Maryland.

728.752
Swann, Don. *Colonial and Historic Homes of Maryland.* Johns Hopkins University Press (0-801-84244-76), 1975. 224p. B/W illus. (Interest level: 7-8).

This reprint of the original 1939 edition includes over 100 etchings by the author. The homes pictured will give insight into what was considered of historic interest at that time. Teachers will find this a good source for illustrating the setting of various events in the state's history.
♦ Students may select one of the homes or mansions pictured in the book and develop a more detailed report about the people or events that were connected with the building.
1. Homes—Maryland 2. Houses—History 3. Architecture—Maryland.

784.7
Key, Francis Scott. *Star-Spangled Banner.* Illus. by Peter Spier. Doubleday (0-385-09458-2), 1973. Un-

paginated. Color illus. and map. (Interest level: K-6).

Spier has illustrated the first four stanzas of the national anthem, showing the verses, score, and the history of the War of 1812. Endpapers show the history of the U.S. flag. Though most children know the first verse, they may find the other verses a surprise. Compare the pictures in this version with other illustrations of the anthem.
♦ Children may select one stanza and produce their own illustrations. The art teacher may suggest other art media for preparing the illustrations.
1. Star-Spangled Banner   2. United States—History—War of 1812   3. Flags   4. Patriotism—Music.

789.2
Miller, Natalie. *The Story of the Star Spangled Banner.* Illus. by G. Wilde. Childrens Press (0-516-04636-5), 1965. (Cornerstones of Freedom). 32p. Color and B/W illus. (Interest level: 3-6).

The national anthem is presented chronologically as it developed from a poem to a musical score. The historical approach will be useful for providing background information to students during the study of nationalism and pride in U.S. symbols.
♦ After young people learn about the history of the national anthem, they may compare it with other patriotic songs. They may also try to write their own patriotic song.
1. Star-Spangled Banner   2. Patriotism—Music   3. United States—History—War of 1812   4. Flags.

796.357
Rambeck, Richard. *Baltimore Orioles.* Creative Education (0-88682-451-6), n.d. (Baseball: The Great American Game). 32p. Color photos. (Interest level: 3-6).

The history of the Orioles and the names of the players who helped make the team great are captured in this color photograph album. Students will learn about both past and present players in the context of the team history. This book will be appropriate for free reading at a variety of levels.
♦ Students may use this book to help them develop their own Baltimore Oriole Hall of Fame. After deciding on the great players, games, and events during the course of the team's history, students may create their own team with logo, uniform designs, players, and managers.
1. Baseball—History.

912.752 (Reference)
Morrison, Russell and **Hansen, Robert.** *Charting the Chesapeake.* Maryland State Archives Publications (0-942370-31-7), 1990. 167p. B/W maps. (Interest level: 6-8).

Early maps, such as that completed by Robert Tindall in 1607, to present-day sophisticated maps completed by the U.S. Coast and Geodetic Survey and National Ocean Service are included in this one-volume collection. The maps provide an understanding of how people have come to learn about the Chesapeake Bay region.
♦ Young people may select a map representing a given view for a period of time. They can research the uses of the bay at that period of time and speculate as to what would have been important to the users of that particular map.
1. Chesapeake Bay—Maps   2. Maryland—Maps.

917.52
Anderson, Elizabeth B. *Annapolis: A Walk through History.* Tidewater Publishers (0-87033-311-9), 1984. 152p. Maps. (Interest level: 6-8).

Readers of this guide will tour the old and new Annapolis, which represents colonial, Georgian, federal, Gothic, revival, Victorian, and modern architecture. Though this is a tourist guide, it also provides historical material on a city that has played an integral part in U.S. history.
♦ Readers may select one area or building they found especially interesting. They may decide which architectural style had the most significant impact on that building and the influence of history on its design.
1. Annapolis (Md.)—Description and travel   2. Annapolis (Md.)—History.

917.52
Annapolis and Maryland State Symbols. (Sound filmstrip). Enjoy Communicating, 1978. Color, (10:20 min.); teacher's guide. $35.00. (Interest level: 3-6).

This filmstrip introduces students to the city of Annapolis, which was at one time the U.S. capital, and the major role it has played in the history of Maryland. The presentation includes the legislature, important events, people, and state symbols. The comprehensive nature of the filmstrip provides visual reinforcement for social studies units.
♦ Viewers may use the filmstrip as an introduction to finding facts about the state. When finished, they may supplement what they have heard using almanacs and encyclopedias to add details about symbols and events.
1. Maryland—History   2. Annapolis (Md.)—History.

917.52
Baltimore Harbor and Skyline. (Sound filmstrip). Enjoy Communicating, 1982. Color, (6:20 min.); teacher's guide. $35.00. (Interest level: 4-6).

Photographs and narration explain changes in the revitalized skyline and harbor, such as the commercial vessels that use the harbor facilities for import and export and have an impact on the economy of Maryland. The filmstrip demonstrates how

the third largest port on the east coast serves in the transport of goods throughout the country.
♦ Children may prepare collage versions of the Baltimore harbor, showing how the skyline has changed. They may also want to research the procedures for a ship's entering and leaving the harbor.
1. Baltimore (Md.) 2. Transportation 3. Harbors—Maryland.

917.52 (Reference)
Goldstein, Louis L. *Goldstein's Maryland*. Illus. by Don Swann. Maryland State Archives Publications (0-942370-17-1), 1985. 156p. B/W illus. (Interest level 4-8).
  Goldstein, the state comptroller of the treasury since 1959, covers each of the 23 counties, as well as Baltimore City, Charter Day, and Maryland Day. Based on a series of radio talks for the state's 350th anniversary, this lively and interesting guide will be a useful source on history and development of the counties of Maryland.
♦ Students may select one of the counties and decide what makes that particular county special.
1. Maryland—Counties—Government 2. Maryland—History.

917.52 (Reference)
Kaminkow, Marion J. *Maryland A to Z: A Topographical Dictionary*. Maryland Historical Press (0-910946-26-4), 1985. 402p. B/W illus. and maps. (Interest level: 7-8).
  Towns and various locations in Maryland are listed in alphabetical order with descriptions from local history collections. There are 65 black-and-white illustrations and 23 maps. The collection includes lakes, rivers, collective areas, ghost towns, counties, mountains, airports, parks, railroads, dams, hills, and institutions. A selective bibliography and index enhance this reference guide to the geographical features of the state.
♦ The class could create a Maryland Jeopardy game, using geographical information from this dictionary, then divide into groups or teams and play it.
1. Maryland—Dictionaries 2. Maryland—Description and travel.

917.52
Kent, Deborah. *Maryland*. Childrens Press (0-516-00466-2), 1990. (America the Beautiful Series). 144p. Color photos and maps. (Interest level: 4-7).
  Kent's emphasis is on the geography, history, government, economy, arts, and recreation of the state. The book is designed for current research on the state and includes specific facts, important dates, significant people, political and topographical maps, and an excellent index. A teacher's guide, prepared by Social Science Educational Consortium, outlines numerous ways to use the work in concert with a regional study.
♦ Children may use this as a starting point in researching the state in preparation for an oral, written, or multimedia report.
1. Maryland—Geography.

917.52 (Reference)
Maryland Manual. Maryland State Archives Publications (0-942370-30-9), 1991. 800p. B/W photos. (Interest level: 3-8).
  All the state agencies related to the running of the three branches of the government are described here. For each agency, there are listings for the key personnel, addresses, and telephone numbers. Pictures of the constitutional officers, legislators, and principal judges are provided, along with brief biographies.
♦ Students may use this guide to find the names of agencies and officials that have a direct relationship to their community.
1. Maryland—Government 2. Maryland—Biography.

917.52
Reef, Catherine. *Baltimore*. Dillon Press (0-87518-427-8), 1991. (Downtown America Series). 60p. Color photos. (Interest level 4-7).
  Photographs and text provide a concise view of places to visit and the history of Baltimore. Maps and a time line help give children a perspective on the city.
♦ The teacher can suggest that a visitor to the city has only three hours to see the most important sites. After looking at the book, students must plan an itinerary for their visitor with a rationale for their selections.
1. Baltimore (Md.)—Description and travel 2. Maryland—Description and travel.

917.52
Rollo, Vera Foster. *A Geography of Maryland: Ask Me! (about Maryland)*. Maryland Historical Press (0-917882-10-5), 1982. 188p. B/W photos and illus. (Interest level: 2-5).
  Twelve sections related to physical geography, counties, environment, population, animals and plants, economy, education, energy, transportation, and labor are included in easy-to-read language. Black-and-white photographs and illustrations supplement the text, and puzzles, exercises, and activities appear at the end of each section. A teacher's guide is available that will make this useful as a text for an entire class.
♦ Students might focus on the section on water and determine how the population of Maryland gets most of its water. Maps and other information in the text should help students figure out the major drainage basins and the flow of water from the

rivers. Young people might also create their own "Ask Me" book about Maryland or about their own community.
1. Maryland—Geography.

917.52
Wroten, William. *Assateague.* Tidewater Publishers (0-87033-168-X), 1972. 58p. Color photos. (Interest level: 6-8).

Assateague is the northernmost island in a chain that extends from Delaware's boundary to the mouth of the Chesapeake Bay. The author covers the island's discovery, inhabitants, recreational activities, natural bounty, and ponies. Older readers will find more than ponies to pique their interest.
♦ Children may enjoy speculating on the origin of the ponies, based on the information and materials suggested in the book. The niche occupied by the ponies could be discussed in relation to the other plant and animal inhabitants.
1. Assateague—Ecology 2. Maryland—Description and travel.

920.752 (Reference)
An Historical List of Public Officials of Maryland: Governors, Legislators, and Other Principal Officers of Government, 1632 to 1990. Maryland State Archives Publications (0-942370-26-0), 1990. 542p. (Interest level: 4-8).

The first comprehensive listing of public officials from 1632 to 1990, this volume includes colonial and state government officials; members of the Senate and House of Representatives; members of the Constitutional Convention; selected local officials, such as the mayors of Baltimore and Annapolis; members of the U.S. Congress; and major federal officeholders. Names of the offices and officeholders as well as incumbents are included in part one, and an index of all names is provided in part two.
♦ Children may use the index to find names of individuals who have held more than one office and trace how they served their government over a period of time. Then young people may look for information about those time periods and find out what kinds of issues these individuals confronted.
1. Maryland—Government—Biography.

970.1
Piscataway Indians of Maryland. (Sound filmstrip). Enjoy Communicating, 1978. Color, (12 min.); teacher's guide. $35.00. (Interest level: 3-6).

This filmstrip focuses on the known history of the Piscataway Indians and their contributions in crafts, music, and dance. Students may identify the Indian heritage through clothing, artifacts, and crafts. The material is specific to Maryland but might be useful in units on multicultural heritage in the early colonies.
♦ After watching the filmstrip, each student may imagine him- or herself as a Piscataway Indian and illustrate how he or she might have dressed, lived, eaten, played, and survived.
1. Indians of North America—Maryland 2. Piscataway Indians.

973.5
Bosco, Peter I. *The War of 1812.* Millbrook Press (1-56294-004-X), 1991. 128p. Color and B/W illus. (Interest level: 7-8).

The events surrounding the War of 1812 are the subject of this history. The confrontation with England was a national event, but war activity centered around Maryland at Fort McHenry. Bosco discusses the causes of the war, people involved in the battles, and events in the war.
♦ Students may prepare a time line of the events that occurred during the War of 1812.
1. United States—History—War of 1812.

973.5
Marrin, Albert. *1812: The War Nobody Won.* Atheneum (0-689-31075-7), 1985. 175p. B/W illus. and maps. (Interest level: 5-8).

Marrin investigates the causes of the War of 1812 and major sites where the war was fought, including Fort McHenry. Many interesting details and anecdotes make this an excellent reference. Diagrams, engravings, and maps will provide students with a visual perspective on the war.
♦ Ask class members to explain why nobody won the war and to clarify the issues and propose ideas for what might have constituted a victory for either side.
1. United States—History—War of 1812.

974.232
Peffer, Randall S. *Watermen.* Johns Hopkins University Press (0-8018-2177-0), 1979. 195p. (Interest level: 7-8).

For over 300 years Tilghman islanders have harvested oysters. The islanders are considered watermen and are a part of the history of the bay. Their sometimes rough language and life are portrayed in this narrative about the author's search for his own roots. The work provides insight into the lifestyle of the watermen and their families.
♦ Use this work with other fiction works about watermen or people living on the eastern shore of the bay. As more advanced readers compare the stories, they may locate newspaper articles about the effect that changes in economics and lower catches have had on the watermen.
1. Oysters—Maryland 2. Fishermen—Maryland—Tilghman Island 3. Tilghman Island (Md.).

975.004
Ruskin, Thelma G. *Indians of the Tidewater Country of Maryland, Virginia, North Carolina, and*

Delaware. Illus. by Yvonne P. Patton. Maryland Historical Press (0-317-46003-X), 1986. 132p. B/W illus. (Interest level: 2-6).

Basing her text on historic research on the Tidewater Indians, Ruskin writes about the past in an easy-to-read style. Evidence of how the native peoples lived, hunted and gathered food, and communicated are examined. The network of tribes and peoples with trading systems is suggested and connections these people had throughout the region are explained.

♦ Children may use information in the book to prepare a mock-up of an occupied area of native people. They should think about what would have been present besides the homes. These mock-ups can be made from natural materials and built to scale.

1. Indians of North America—Maryland.

975.2
Boyce-Ballweber, Hettie. *The First People of Maryland*. Maryland Historical Press (0-917882-245), 1987. 110p. B/W illus. (Interest level: 3-6).

Complete with many line drawings and simple illustrations, the book introduces the native people present when the area now known as Maryland was discovered and colonized. Much of what is known about these people has been gained from archaeological digs, and the author, an archaeologist, reports how such information is gathered. Colonists are also pictured in their encounters and efforts to survive. The book includes puzzles and games and is indexed with teacher information and a glossary.

♦ Children may use the information provided to make a model reconstruction of a village or scene showing the first people of Maryland.

1. Maryland—History.

975.2
Carpenter, John Allan. *Maryland*. Rev. ed. Childrens Press (0-516-04120-7), 1978. (New Enchantment of America State Books). 96p. Color photos. (Interest level: 4-7).

Carpenter's overview of the state is similar to an encyclopedia article, with much more detail. Photographs and illustrations provide general coverage of the history, physical geography, economy, culture, and development of Maryland.

♦ Students may use this book as they research the state in preparation for a multimedia presentation.

1. Maryland—Description and travel 2. Maryland—History.

975.2
Carr, Lois Green; Menard, Russell R.; and Peddicord, Louis. *Maryland . . . At the Beginning*. Maryland State Archives Publications (0-942370-18-X), 1984. 37p. B/W illus. and maps. (Interest level: 4-8).

In a concentrated format, this book deals with the first 20 years of the Maryland colony. The authors look at the voyage from England, the first settlement of St. Mary's City, the growth of the colony, and the frontier as seen during that early period. The black-and-white illustrations and maps help students understand the first people who settled in the colony.

♦ Young people may pretend that they are settlers who came over to the new Maryland colony. What would have been their major concerns? What would they have had to do to survive? What would the essential tools have been for their survival?

1. Maryland—History—Colonial period, ca 1600-1775.

975.2
Fradin, Dennis B. *Maryland: In Words and Pictures*. Illus. by Richard Wahl; maps by Len W. Meents. Childrens Press (0-516-03920-2), 1980. (Young People's Stories of Our States Series). 48p. Color photos, illus., and maps. (Interest level: 3-6).

Combine readable text with color photographs, maps, and historical prints and the main focus of this historical perspective of the state is clear. This overview of the history of Maryland covers first visitors to current events. Fact sheets and time lines will help students understand the events that made the state what it is today.

♦ Children might select two different time periods for research and comparison. They can use the facts represented in the text as well as the illustrations to form ideas about the relationships.

1. Maryland—History.

975.2
Fradin, Dennis Brindell. *The Maryland Colony*. Childrens Press (0-516-00394-1), 1990. (The Thirteen Colonies Series). 160p. B/W photos and maps. (Interest level: 4-7).

The colonists learned slowly how to care for themselves in the new wilderness, and this book looks at the first two centuries of Maryland colonial life and the individuals who helped make the country their own. The methods for survival are shown along with the manner in which the colonists learned to govern themselves. The colonists in early St. Mary's City and other locations are discussed in terms of their relationships with local native peoples and the British in England.

♦ Children may select one period or aspect of colonial Maryland life and illustrate it with pen and ink or dark pencils.

1. Maryland—History 2. United States—History—Colonial period, ca 1600-1775.

975.2
Hall, Clayton Colman. *Narratives of Early Maryland, 1633-1684*. Reprint Services (0-7812-6281-X), 1991, 1910. 460p. Map. (Interest level: 6-8).

A reprint of the 1910 version, this book is a valuable source of documents for accounts of early Maryland history. For example, Lord Baltimore's instructions to the colonists are included. Father Andrew White's account of the voyage to the colony, George Alsop's discussion of the character of the province of Maryland, Augustine Herrman's journal of the Dutch Embassy to Maryland, and a letter of Governor Leonard Calvert to Lord Baltimore provide primary materials for students.
♦ As students study the actual accounts of the early explorers and settlers, they may develop their own account of the individuals' motives for going to the colony.
1. Maryland—History—Colonial period, ca 1600-1775.

975.2
Here and There in Maryland: Field Trips. (Videocassette). Maryland Instructional Television, 1982. 17 videocassettes, VHS, (10 min. each); teacher's guide. Prices will vary depending on how materials are obtained. (Interest level: 4-8).

This series of programs highlights various locations of historical, environmental, or economical importance in the state of Maryland. Originally aired on public television, the programs reinforce visiting sites, learning from the past, and researching the events and views at various sites. Locations include: Antietam National Battlefield, Assateague Island, Baltimore and Ohio Railroad Museum, Baltimore Museum of Art, Baltimore-Washington International Airport, Blackwater National Wildlife Refuge, Calvert Marine Museum, Carroll County Farm Museum, Chesapeake and Ohio Canal, Fort Frederick State Park, Johns Hopkins Hospital, Lexington Market, Maryland Science Center, NASA-Goddard Space Flight Center, National Aquarium in Baltimore, Sotterley, and Wye Oak.
♦ Students may examine large road or state maps and locate the various places on those maps. A short narrative can be written about each site and placed on a large map of the state drawn by students.
1. Maryland—Description and travel.

975.2
Kaessman, Beta Ennis; Randall, Harold; and **Wheeler, Joseph L.** *My Maryland: Her Story for Boys and Girls.* Maryland Historical Society (No ISBN), 1971. 446p. B/W illus. (Interest level: 4-6).

This volume served as a text of Mayland history from the first edition in 1939. Although older, the information on the colonial period will be helpful to students.
♦ Young people may select one particular time period for more in-depth study.
1. Maryland—History.

975.2
Manakee, Harold. *Indians of Early Maryland: A Book on Maryland Life.* Maryland Historical Society (No ISBN), 1981. 47p. Illus. (Interest level: 3-6).

Originally published in 1959, this simple text provides information on native peoples in the state. Manakee gives general information about the early Native Americans who occupied the region. This will be helpful for introducing students to some of the early customs.
♦ Children can discuss what the lives of Native Americans would have been like had the colonists not come to Maryland in comparison to the lives of the Europeans who came to settle.
1. Indians of North America—Maryland.

975.2
Maryland: A Regional Study. (Sound filmstrip). Enjoy Communicating, 1980. 8 sound filmstrips, (15 min. each); teacher's guides. $65.00 for each regional set; $230.00 for complete set. (Interest level: 4-7).

Designed to provide both history and geographical description, the eight sound filmstrips are divided into four subsets for four main regions: southern Maryland, central Maryland, eastern shore, and western Maryland. Each sound filmstrip deals with the historical sites, environment, and folk culture of the particular area. The regional sets may be ordered separately.
♦ Viewers can select two different regions and compare and contrast them based on several characteristics such as land forms, economy, and history.
1. Maryland—History 2. Maryland—Geography.

975.2
Portrait of America: Maryland. (Videocassette). Turner Broadcasting System, 1985. Color, VHS, (49 min.). $166.00. (Interest level: 6-8).

Primarily a travel program, the videotape shows the history of the state and identifies its many immigrants. Topics such as residents' incomes, fishing, services, and heavy industry are discussed in terms of history and future problems. Views of Annapolis, Baltimore, and Cumberland are featured.
♦ Students may show segments of the videotape in their oral presentations about the state of Maryland.
1. Maryland—Description and travel 2. Maryland—History.

975.2
Radoff, Morris, ed. *The Old Line State—A History of Maryland.* Maryland State Archives Publications (0-942370-07-4), 1971. 498p. B/W illus. (Interest level: 7-8).

Radoff collected several important essays about the history of Maryland completed by renowned historians: Aubrey C. Land informs readers on the

colonial period of the state, Henry Chandlee Forman discusses the state's diverse architecture, and Marion V. Brewington reviews the history of shipbuilding. This compilation will be useful for the study of the state by older students and will serve as background information for the teacher.
♦ Young people may select one aspect of the state history and use the essay as an introduction to changes that have occurred.
1. Maryland—History.

975.2
Rollo, Vera Foster. *Your Maryland.* Maryland Historical Press (0-917-88235-0), 1985. 414p. (Interest level: 7-8).
The author presents a history of Maryland from 1630 to the 1980s, including commentary on the growth and changes in Maryland as they parallel those in the United States.
♦ Students may prepare two parallel time lines showing Maryland and U.S. history and draw some conclusions on the effects that U.S. development had on the development of Maryland.
1. Maryland—History.

975.2
Schaun, George and **Schaun, Virginia.** *Everyday Life in Colonial Maryland.* Maryland Historical Press (0-917882-11-3), 1982, 1959. 130p. B/W illus. (Interest level: 3-8).
Originally published in 1959, this reprinted bound document provides many details and facts about the life of early Maryland colonists. Everything from basic food gathering to the ways in which individuals made a living is covered. The chapters and pen-and-ink drawings help the reader understand facets of colonists' lives including their food, drink, heating, lighting, homes, furnishings, clothing, money, product manufacturing, mail, printing, medicine, and transportation.
♦ Children may select one specific area and use the many details in this book to try to reconstruct that aspect of life for a colonist.
1. Maryland—Social life and customs—Colonial period, ca 1600-1775.

975.2
Thompson, Kathleen. *Maryland.* Raintree (0-8174-434-6), 1991. (Portrait of America Library). 48p. Color illus. and photos. (Interest level: 4-7).
Thompson's overview includes a history of Maryland, unique economic aspects, almanacs, special places to visit, maps, and projections for the future of the state. The table of contents and index help students use this source for research.
♦ Readers can create their own almanac for the state of Maryland and compare important events in U.S. history with events in Maryland.

1. Maryland—History 2. Maryland—Description and travel.

975.2
Titus, Charles. *The Old Line State: Her Heritage.* Illus. by Thomas E. Jones. Tidewater Publishers (0-87033-159-0). 1971. 86p. B/W illus. (Interest level: 7-8).
Titus groups 24 stories about points of interest in four geographic sections including western Maryland, southern Maryland, Baltimore, and the eastern shore. The stories and text are illustrated with pen-and-ink drawings. A bibliography makes this useful for further research.
♦ Young people may create their own stories about points of interest in their own community.
1. Maryland—Description and travel 2. Maryland—History.

975.2
Williams, Harold A. *Baltimore Afire.* Schneidereith and Sons (0-960-23041-6), 1991. B/W illus. (Interest level: 7-8).
This reprint was done on the 50th anniversary of the fire. Old photographs of the devastation are most compelling. The teacher will find multiple uses for this volume showing the aftermath of a fire, the work that must be done to rebuild, and the problems at the turn of the century with which city dwellers had to contend.
♦ Students might compare the photographs and information in this book with pictures and information of disasters in other cities and discuss what fire disaster means in terms of destruction to people and buildings.
1. Baltimore (Md.) 2. Fires—History.

975.2
Wilson, Richard and **Bridner, E. L., Jr.** *Maryland: Its Past and Present.* 4th ed. Maryland Historical Press (0-917882-13-X), 1992. 234p. (Interest level: 4-6).
Designed and written as a geography and history textbook, this work functions as a basic overview of Maryland, focusing on history, geography, economics, and cultural development. The text, written at a fourth-grade level, may serve as an outline for the study of Maryland as well as a focus for study of an early colonial area.
♦ Children may use the book to help them determine Maryland's most valuable asset by developing a list of events, products, people, and sites.
1. Maryland—History.

975.256
Burdett, Harold. *Yesteryear in Annapolis.* Illus. by Eric Smith. Tidewater Publishers (0-87033-197-3), 1974. 90p. (Interest level: 7-8).

Using a series of vignettes, Burdett presents the city of Annapolis as seen by visitors at various times in the past. Because the city has not changed much in some areas, it is easy for readers to visualize some of the stories. The vignettes might be useful as read-alouds for a class studying the state.
♦ Students might role-play the vignettes before an audience of other classes.
1. Annapolis (Md.)—History.

975.518
Tilp, Fay and **Tilp, Fred**. *Chesapeake: Fact, Fiction and Fun: Pungoteague, St. Clement, Patapsco.* . . . Heritage Books, 1988. (Interest level: 7-8).

Words, jokes, and other trivia special to the people of Maryland are arranged in alphabetical order. Definitions and specific local terms that show the character of the people of the state are gathered here.
♦ Children may want to collect words, jokes, and other trivia used in their community and publish it for others to read. They may then compare what they have found in their own community with what is found in this book.
1. Chesapeake Bay—History.

Biography

92 Banneker, Benjamin
Ferris, Jeri. *What Are You Figuring Now? A Story of Benjamin Banneker*. Illus. by Amy Johnson. Carolrhoda (0-87614-331-1), 1988. 64p. B/W illus. (Interest level: 4-6).

Focusing on Benjamin Banneker's love of numbers, the author introduces students to an eighteenth-century astronomer, surveyor of Washington, D.C., and almanac compiler. Banneker farmed for a living as a free black man.
♦ Children may collect interesting facts related to the time in which Banneker lived and discuss how the time may have influenced Banneker.
1. Banneker, Benjamin, 1731-1806   2. African Americans—Biography   3. Maryland—Biography.

92 Barton, Clara
Dubowski, Cathy East. *Clara Barton: Healing the Wounds*. Silver Burdett (0-382-09940-0), 1991. 122p. B/W and Color photos and illus. (Interest level: 6-8).

Clara Barton spent 18 years as a teacher and founder of a school. Her life as a healer, which followed this career, is the focal point of the book. Barton worked and nursed during the Civil War to save lives and led the effort to found the American Red Cross.
♦ Students may use this book to find out what contributions Barton made to the Red Cross.
1. Barton, Clara, 1821-1912   2. Nurses—Biography   3. American Red Cross   4. Maryland—Biography.

92 Douglass, Frederick
Davidson, Margaret. *Frederick Douglass Fights for Freedom*. Scholastic (0-590-42218-9), 1968. 80p. B/W illus. (Interest level: 2-5).

Frederick Douglass, who educated himself, ran away when he was 23 to freedom in the North. He later returned as an abolitionist and spent the rest of his life fighting for the freedom of African Americans through speeches and help on the Underground Railroad.
♦ Students may research Douglass's impact on the abolition movement.
1. Douglass, Frederick, 1817-1895   2. African Americans—Biography   3. Abolitionists—Biography   4. Maryland—Biography.

92 Douglass, Frederick
Frederick Douglass: An American Life. (Videocassette). National Park Service/National Audiovisual Center, 1985. VHS, Color, (32 min.). No price available. (Interest level: 4-6).

Dramatizing his speeches and writings, this video shows how Frederick Douglass recalled his past as a slave and his life as a free man.
♦ After young people view the tape about Douglass, they may discuss Douglass as a slave and as a free man and what changes in his life influenced him.
1. Douglass, Frederick, 1817-1895   2. African Americans—Biography   3. Abolitionists—Biography   4. Maryland—Biography.

92 Douglass, Frederick
McKissack, Patricia and **McKissack, Frederick**. *Frederick Douglass: Leader against Slavery*. Enslow (0-89490-306-3), 1991. (Great Americans). 32p. B/W illus. (Interest level: 2-5).

The authors include anecdotes about Frederick Douglass's work as an abolitionist and civil rights worker. His persuasiveness in working toward equal rights for freed slaves is dramatized in many ways.
♦ Children may use this book in their research on abolitionists and create a time line of these famous people.
1. Douglass, Frederick, 1817-1895   2. African Americans—Biography   3. Abolitionists—Biography   4. Maryland—Biography.

92 Douglass, Frederick
Miller, Douglas. *Frederick Douglass and the Fight for Freedom*. Facts on File (0-8160-1617-8), 1988. 152p. B/W illus. (Makers of America). (Interest level: 6-8).

Miller traces the early life of Frederick Douglass through his success as an orator and covers the conflicts between slaves and slave owners, whites

and blacks, and North and South. The teacher may find this book useful for explaining a number of issues involved in the struggle during the Civil War.
♦ Readers may identify what events caused Douglass to change his name. They could also discuss the issues involved in slavery.
1. Douglass, Frederick, 1817-1895   2. African Americans—Biography   3. Abolitionist—Biography   4. Maryland—Biography.

92 Harford, Henry
Rollo, Vera Foster. *Henry Harford: Last Proprietor of Maryland.* Maryland Historical Press (0-917882-06-7), 1976. 236p. (Interest level: 5-8).

Henry Harford was the last proprietor of colonial Maryland. The foreword by Morris L. Radoff explains proprietorship and its purpose. Harford was somewhat mysterious, and the book provides some insights that will help students learn about the man and the job that he did.
♦ Students may research the subject of proprietorship, the people who held that position in Maryland, and why it ended.
1. Harford, Henry   2. Maryland—Biography.

92 Henrietta, Maria
Sticles, Frances Copeland. *A Crown for Henrietta Maria: Maryland's Namesake Queen.* Maryland Historical Press (0-917882-27-X), 1988. 100p. B/W illus. (Interest level: 3-7).

Henrietta Maria, queen of England's Charles I and princess of France, married in 1625. Because of the war, she spent time in France, England, and Holland. This biography of Henrietta Maria is illustrated with portraits and drawings from the seventeenth century.
♦ Children may write a biographical sketch about Henrietta Maria.
1. Henrietta Maria, Queen, Consort of Charles I, King of England, 1609-1669   2. Great Britain—Queens—Biography.

92 Henson, Jim
Aaseng, Nathan. *Jim Henson: Muppet Master.* Lerner (0-8225-1615-2), 1988. 40p. Color illus. (Interest level: 5-7).

Jim Henson made Kermit from his mother's old green coat, and so began the world of the Muppets as we know them today. This book focuses on the life of the puppeteer as an artist and humanitarian.
♦ Students may watch several of the puppet movie features and then re-create a short puppet script of their own.
1. Henson, Jim   2. Television producers and directors—Biography   3. Maryland—Biography

92 Henson, Matthew
Ferris, Jeri. *Arctic Explorer: The Story of Matthew Henson.* Carolrhoda Books (0-87614-370-2), 1989. 80p. B/W photos and maps. (Interest level: 4-6).

Matthew Henson, the African American explorer who accompanied Robert Peary on six expeditions to the North Pole, is portrayed as determined and courageous in overcoming the obstacles encountered on those trips.
♦ Young people might write a narrative on what it would be like to lead an exploration into an unknown territory.
1. Henson, Matthew   2. Explorers—Biography
3. African Americans—Biography   4. North Pole
5. Maryland—Biography.

92 Jones, John Paul
Brandt, Keith. *John Paul Jones: Hero of the Seas.* Illus. by Susan Swan. Troll (0-89375-849-3), 1983. 48p. B/W illus. (Interest level: 4-6).

The son of a Scottish gardener, Jones worked his way up through the ranks in the merchant shipping business. This biography discusses his contribution to the fledging United States.
♦ Students may use this work to locate other facts that would help them understand why Jones is so important in the history of the U.S. Navy.
1. Jones, John Paul, 1747-1792   2. United States—Navy—Biography   3. United States—History—Revolution, 1775-1783—Biography.

92 Marshall, Thurgood
Aldred, Lisa. *Thurgood Marshall.* Chelsea House (1-55546-601-X), 1990. 112p. Color illus. (Interest level: 7-8).

The strength of this volume lies in its portrayal of Thurgood Marshall as a strong figure in the fight for civil rights and justice for all people. An introduction by Coretta Scott King also adds insight into the importance of Marshall. Aldred has written a valuable study of the civil rights movement and of U.S. government.
♦ Young people might prepare an outline showing key events in Marshall's life.
1. Marshall, Thurgood, 1908-1993   2. United States Supreme Court—Justices—Biography   3. African Americans—Biography   4. Maryland—Biography.

92 Marshall, Thurgood
Greene, Carol. *Thurgood Marshall: First Black Supreme Court Justice.* Illus. by Steven Dobson. Childrens Press (0-516-04225-4), 1991. (Rookie Biographies). 48p. Color and B/W illus. and photos. (Interest level: K-3).

Easy-to-read text introduces children to the first African American to sit on the bench of the highest court of the United States. Readers will learn about Thurgood Marshall's law practice and background, his work for civil rights, and his importance as a Supreme Court justice.
♦ Readers may list what a Supreme Court justice does and what made Marshall special as a justice.

1. Marshall, Thurgood, 1908-1993 2. United States Supreme Court—Justices—Biography 3. African Americans—Biography 4. Maryland—Biography.

92 Ruth, Babe
Eisenberg, Lisa. *Story of Babe Ruth: Baseball's Greatest Legend.* Dell (0-440-40274-3), 1990. (Dell Yearling Biography). 92p. B/W photos. (Interest level: 4-6).

Babe Ruth grew up in Baltimore and was a rough-and-tumble player. Eisenberg presents a balanced portrayal of his physical strength and his excesses. His records and skill in baseball are contrasted with the events of his personal life.
♦ Class members may create a Hall of Fame with a picture of Ruth along with the records he holds and the famous plays he made.
1. Ruth, Babe, 1895-1948 2. Baseball players—Biography 3. Maryland—Biography.

92 Tubman, Harriet
Epstein, Sam. *Harriet Tubman: Guide to Freedom.* Illus. by Paul Frame. Garrard (0-8116-4550-9), 1968. 96p. Color illus. (Interest level: 3-6).

An easy-to-read version of the life of Harriet Tubman, this book looks at the events that propelled her to work to free slaves. After the Civil War Tubman lectured about the needs of the newly freed slaves.
♦ After reading about the events and activities in Tubman's life, students may use her life to define the term "abolitionist."
1. Tubman, Harriet, ca 1820-1913 2. African Americans—Biography 3. Abolitionists—Biography 4. Maryland—Biography.

92 Tubman, Harriet
Ferris, Jeri. *Go Free or Die: A Story about Harriet Tubman.* Illus. by Karen Ritz. Carolrhoda Books (0-87614-317-6), 1988. 63p. Color illus. (Interest level: 3-6).

Harriet Tubman made 19 trips between 1850 and 1861 to bring over 300 slaves to freedom. Ferris concentrates on Tubman's perseverance in maneuvering the Underground Railroad and in fighting for equal rights.
♦ Children can write about what would be most frightening during a trip along the Underground Railroad. They may keep a journal of a period of time in Tubman's life.
1. Tubman, Harriet, ca 1820-1913 2. African Americans—Biography 3. Abolitionists—Biography 4. Maryland—Biography.

Fiction

Cummings, Priscilla. *Chadwick and the Garplegrungen.* Illus. by A. R. Cohen. Tidewater Publishers (0-87033-377-1), 1987. 30p. Color illus. (Interest level: K-4).

Chadwick and his friends Orville the Oyster, Belly Jeans the Flounder, Dr. Mallard the Duck, and Baron Von Heron wonder about the green and purple gunk that is bubbling up from the water in the Chesapeake Bay. They set out to get rid of it. How they do this will delight young readers.
♦ The book might be used during an environmental unit of study. As a creative-writing assignment, students might write a descriptive story about the green and purple gunk and how they might rid the water of it.
1. Water—Pollution—Fiction 2. Crabs—Fiction 3. Chesapeake Bay—Fiction 4. Maryland—Fiction.

Cummings, Priscilla. *Chadwick the Crab.* Illus. by A. R. Cohen. Tidewater Publishers (0-87033-347-X), 1986. 30p. Color illus. (Interest level: K-3).

Chadwick, a Chesapeake blue crab, desires adventure and wants to be a star in the Baltimore aquarium. Children are introduced to his friends, animals who live in the Chesapeake Bay, as the little crab realizes his dream.
♦ Students can identify what types of things happen to crabs and use these ideas to write other adventures for Chadwick.
1. Crabs—Fiction 2. Chesapeake Bay—Fiction 3. Maryland—Fiction.

Cummings, Priscilla. *Chadwick's Wedding.* Illus. by A. R. Cohen. Tidewater Publishers (0-87033-390-9), 1989. 30p. Color illus. (Interest level: K-4).

Chadwick the crab is marrying Esmerelda, and Baron Von Heron is officiating. The animals in the Chesapeake Bay are involved in the plans for the event. At first Chadwick wonders whether or not he is ready, but quickly decides when Esmerelda disappears.
♦ Children can make puppets based on the characters in the book and act out the story.
1. Crabs—Fiction 2. Chesapeake Bay—Fiction 3. Weddings—Fiction 4. Maryland—Fiction.

Cummings, Priscilla. *Oswald and the Timberdoodles.* Illus. by A. R. Cohen. Tidewater Publishers (0-87033-411-5), 1990. 30p. Color illus. (Interest level: K-3).

Oswald is a great blue heron who can't straighten his neck. During his turn at guard, he can't see over the tall grass, so he reads a book. While he is reading, a fox almost grabs his cousin Ophelia, and Oswald is banished until the birds recognize that he has another talent.
♦ Students may list the talents of other students in their class and discuss the importance of accept-

ing people for who they are and realizing that people have different skills.
1. Birds—Fiction 2. Herons—Fiction.

Cummings, Priscilla. *Sid and Sal's Famous Channel Marker Diner.* Illus. by A. R. Cohen. Tidewater Publishers (0-87033-423-9), 1991. 30p. Color illus. (Interest level: K-3).

Two ospreys, Sid and Sal, live on a dead pine in a cove until the pine tree is knocked down for a condominium. They find a new home on a channel marker at the mouth of Shady Creek and decide to open a diner because of the spaciousness of their new location. But another disaster strikes!
♦ Children may find out more about ospreys and what they might serve at an imaginary diner.
1. Ospreys—Fiction 2. Chesapeake Bay—Fiction 3. Environment—Fiction.

Eichelberger, Rosa Kohler. *Big Fire in Baltimore.* Illus. by Rex Schneider. Stemmer House (0-916144-37-2), 1979. 204p. Color illus. and maps. (Interest level: 5-8).

Tod Morton and his family fight for two days to save the family shoe business during the great Baltimore fire in 1904, when over 1,500 buildings were destroyed. The tension rises when Tod tries to find his dog. Eichelberger insightfully introduces the life, street cars, horse-drawn fire wagons, and other elements of this period.
♦ Using the information gathered from this story, children may discuss how they might have reacted in a similar catastrophic situation.
1. Baltimore (Md.)—Fire, 1904—Fiction 2. Maryland—History—Fiction 3. Fires—Fiction 4. Family life—Fiction.

Fradin, Morris. *Hey-Ey-Ey, Lock: Adventures on the Chesapeake and Ohio Canal.* Illus. by Carol Stuart Watson. Tidewater Publishers (0-87033-244-9), 1977. 112p. B/W illus. (Interest level: 4-7).

A captain takes an English boy for a summer's work on a barge that travels the C & O Canal. The story provides rich detail about the life of people during the early days of the canal; each detail plays an integral part in the plot of the story.
♦ Students may collect nonfiction material about the canal and compare the story with pictures and facts. They might also write their own versions of what they might have done if they worked for a summer along the canal.
1. Chesapeake and Ohio Canal—Fiction.

Hahn, Mary Downing. *Jelly Fish Season.* Clarion Books (0-89919-344-7), 1987. 192p. (Interest level: 5-8).

Two families must live together for economic reasons and the situation starts to wear on everyone involved. Kathleen's cousin gets her involved in a plot, her father begins drinking, and family tempers flair. The summer at the beach becomes a time of conflict.
♦ Class members could discuss how to resolve conflict and how to avoid conflict in stressful situations.
1. Maryland—Fiction 2. Family life—Fiction.

Hahn, Mary Downing. *Tallahassee Higgins.* Clarion Books (0-89919-495-8), 1987. 192p. (Interest level: 4-6).

Tally's immature and thoughtless mother places Tally with a relative and goes off to pursue her own dreams. Tally, who is both lonely and gutsy, is always getting into trouble. As she extricates herself from her troubles, she gradually learns to understand her mother.
♦ Young people might use this story to gain insight into dealing with family difficulties.
1. Mothers and daughters—Fiction 2. Maryland—Fiction.

Howard, Elizabeth Fitzgerald. *Aunt Flossie's Hats (and Crab Cakes Later).* Illus. by James Ransome. Clarion Books (0-395-54682-6), 1991. Unpaginated. Color illus. (Interest level: K-3).

Every Sunday, two sisters visit great-aunt Flossie and play with her hats, each of which has a story that Aunt Flossie shares. The oil paintings reflect the continuity and history passed on to the girls as they learn about the great Baltimore fire, the dog who saved the hat, and the parade following the great war.
♦ Prepare a trunk of hats and have students write a creative story about them.
1. Hats—Fiction 2. Great-aunts—Fiction 3. Maryland—Fiction 4. Baltimore (Md.)—Fiction.

Howard, Elizabeth Fitzgerald. *Chita's Christmas Tree.* Illus. by Floyd Cooper. Bradbury (0-02744621-2), 1989. Unpaginated. Color illus. (Interest level: 1-4).

The annual excursion to find a Christmas tree takes Chita and her father, a doctor, outside the city of Baltimore at the turn of the century. In illustrating Chita and her father choosing and later decorating the tree, Cooper portrays the Baltimore setting and a professional African American family during that time period.
♦ The illustrations in this book could spur children to imagine how they might have decorated a tree during this time. Children may share their favorite Christmas reminiscences.
1. Christmas—Fiction 2. Christmas tree—Fiction 3. Maryland—Fiction 4. Baltimore (Md.)—Fiction.

Howard, Elizabeth Fitzgerald. *Train to Lulu's.* Illus. by Robert Casilla. Bradbury (0-02-744620-4), 1988. Unpaginated. Color illus. (Interest level: K-4).

Two young sisters, Beppy and Babs, take a train trip alone from Boston to Baltimore and follow their mother's instructions for eating, bathroom trips, and listening to the conductor. The descriptions of the train and the watercolor illustrations vividly portray the sisters' travel to Aunt Lulu.
- After reading the story, students may review the events that happened and use them as a model for playing "I'm going on a trip," in which they think of something that they would do on a trip.

1. Railroads—Fiction 2. Sisters—Fiction.

Jones, Rebecca C. *The Biggest (and Best) Flag That Ever Flew.* Illus. by Charles Geer. Tidewater Publishers (0-87033-381-X), 1988. 32p. Color illus. (Interest level: 2-4).

Caroline Pickersgill helps her mother, Mary, cut out the pieces for the largest flag in the world, which will fly over Fort McHenry during the War of 1812 and inspire Francis Scott Key to write the poem that becomes the national anthem.
- Children can make their own flag and write poems describing it.

1. United States—History—War of 1812—Fiction 2. Star-Spangled Banner—Fiction 3. Flags—Fiction.

Levinson, Nancy Smiler. *Clara and the Bookwagon.* Illus. by Carolyn Croll. HarperCollins (0-06-023838-0), 1988. 64p. Color illus. (Interest level: 1-4).

A Maryland farm girl, Clara, works hard and helps her family with the chores on their farm, but she longs to know about the rest of the world. There are no books or schools for children to learn how to read where she lives. One day a black book wagon, driven by Mary Titcomb, comes down the road, Clara is introduced to the library on wheels, and checks out her first book. Maryland was the first state to develop bookmobiles.
- Students may decide what types of books should be in a bookmobile and how it should function in the community.

1. Libraries, Traveling—Maryland—Fiction 2. Farm life—Maryland—Fiction 3. Books and reading—Maryland—Fiction.

Lockhart, Barbara and **Lockhart, Lynne.** *Once a Pony Time at Chincoteague.* Illus. by Lynne Lockhart. Tidewater Publishers (0-87033-436-0), 1992. 30p. Color illus. (Interest level: 1-4).

Mr. and Mrs. Emory's picnic lunch on Assateague Island is interrupted by a small herd of ponies, and a stallion eats part of their lunch before a lifeguard helps them. Later in the week they attend the Chincoteague Pony Penning and hope to win a foal in the raffle for their grandchildren.
- Young people might write about what it must be like to be surrounded by wild ponies. What would be the best way to deal with such an episode? What would they do if they won a pony?

1. Assateague Island—Fiction 2. Horses—Fiction.

Lockhart, Lynne and **Lockhart, Barbara M.** *Rambling Raft.* Illus. by Lynne N. Lockhart. Tidewater Publishers (0-87033-392-5), 1989. 30p. Color illus. (Interest level: 1-4).

A raft intended for a waterman's son is a part of several adventures along the Chesapeake Bay. The raft gets loose and initiates a number of episodes, from children playing pirates to ducklings swimming in it.
- In a creative writing assignment, children may write additional adventures for the raft.

1. Adventure—Fiction 2. Rafts—Fiction 3. Chesapeake Bay—Fiction.

Meacham, Margaret. *The Secret of Heron Creek.* Illus. by Lynne N. Lockhart. Tidewater Publishers (0-87033-414-X), 1991. 136p. (Interest level: 4-7).

While out rowing, William Constable sees a sea monster named Chessie who lives in Heron Creek. William introduces his buddy, Tommy, to the sea monster and they become playmates, but in the process, Chessie is spied by a greedy man who plans to catch the monster. William and Tommy plan a night rescue of the Chessie.
- Students may design their own sea monster and act out adventures they write themselves.

1. Sea monsters—Fiction 2. Chesapeake Bay—Fiction.

Paterson, Katherine. *Jacob Have I Loved.* Crowell (0-690-04078-4), 1980. 228p. (Interest level: 5-8).

This narrative of twins growing up on Eastern Shore Rass Island in the Chesapeake Bay during the 1940s is told by competent and practical Sara Louise, who is jealous of her beautiful talented twin Caroline. Sara Louise takes up with her friend Call, who changes throughout the book as much as does Sara Louise. Paterson won the Newbery Medal in 1981 for this book on sibling rivalry.
- Readers may collect other examples of twins from myths, legends, and fiction and read to find out how the twins in these stories get along with each other. After discussing the idea of sibling rivalry, young people may find other stories of brothers and sisters who exhibit this behavior.

1. Chesapeake Bay—Fiction 2. Maryland—Fiction 3. Twins—Fiction.

Paterson, Katherine. *Jacob Have I Loved.* (Audiocassette). Miller-Brody (0-394-07690-7), n.d. $14.00. (Interest level: 5-8).

This audiocassette dramatizes the print version of the same title.
♦ Students may dramatize a favorite story of their own.
1. Chesapeake Bay—Fiction 2. Maryland—Fiction 3. Twins—Fiction.

Paterson, Katherine. *Jacob Have I Loved.* (Videocassette; Sound filmstrip). American School Publishers, 1988. VHS; 2 sound filmstrips, (55 min. each). $66.00. (Interest level: 5-8).

The enhanced video, using color illustrations and sound effects, focuses on the obstacles that Sara Louise must face.
♦ Children may select a feeling that the main character experiences and illustrate it with colored tissue collage and drawing pencils.
1. Chesapeake Bay—Fiction 2. Maryland—Fiction 3. Twins—Fiction.

Rodowsky, Colby. *H. My Name Is Henley.* Farrar, Straus & Giroux (0-374-32831-5), 1982. 183p. (Interest level: 4-7).

Henley is transported by her mother from city to city in search of a job and friends. When Henley finds happiness and security on the Maryland shore, she decides to stay when her mother leaves. The story examines a family structure that does not provide the stability that young Henley desires and needs.
♦ Young people might write a poem about the feelings that Henley might have experienced.
1. Family life—Fiction 2. Mothers and daughters—Fiction 3. Maryland—Fiction.

Rodowsky, Colby. *Lucy Peale.* Farrar, Straus & Giroux (0-374-36381-1), 1992. 208p. (Interest level: 7-8).

Lucy Peal's father is a fundamentalist preacher who sees the world in terms of black and white. When Lucy gets pregnant, he refuses to accept that she was raped, so Lucy runs away to Ocean City where she meets Jake. The theme is self-reliance and can be used at a number of levels.
♦ This book might be grouped with other examples of realistic fiction for students to use in a book discussion group. Students may be asked to consider various characters who run away or have difficult family backgrounds and discuss how each character gets out of the situation or deals with the problem.
1. Ocean City (Md.)—Fiction 2. Self-reliance—Fiction.

Seabrook, Brenda. *Boy Who Saved the Town.* Tidewater Publishers (0-87033-405-0), 1990. 30p. Color illus. (Interest level: 2-5).

When young Barnaby Sharp practices climbing trees to become a ship's captain, he has an idea of how to outwit the British. This story, which takes place in Maryland, one of the major sites during the War of 1812, shows that age does not limit smart thinking.
♦ Children might read about the war and try to visualize themselves during this period. They may identify types of problems and write about them.
1. United States—History—War of 1812—Fiction.

Seabrook, Brenda. *The Chester Town Tea Party.* Illus. by Nancy C. Smith. Tidewater Publishers (0-87033-422-0), 1991. 30p. Color illus. (Interest level: 1-4).

In May 1774, the people of Chester Town, Maryland, voted to boycott all tea in support of Boston. Amanda Wetherby is a nine-year-old who wants to participate in the tea party just like her brother.
♦ Seabrook's version of another tea party might be used as part of a read-aloud during the study of this period of U.S. history. Students might identify where tea parties took place and what these events were meant to symbolize.
1. United States—History—Revolution, 1775-1883—Causes—Fiction 2. Maryland—History—Fiction.

Sharpe, Susan. *Waterman's Boy.* Bradbury (0-02-782351-2), 1990. 170p. (Interest level: 5-7).

Ben is determined to discover who is responsible for the pollution that is killing the sea life and his father's, a waterman's, catch. As he gets closer to the people involved, Ben is in danger.
♦ The story is useful for discussion of issues related to environmentalism. Class members might discuss how they could participate in the move to clean up the bay.
1. Environmental protection—Fiction 2. Chesapeake Bay—Fiction.

Townsend, George Alfred. *Katy of Catoctin: Or Chair Breakers.* Tidewater Publishers (0-87033-037-3), 1959. 567p. (Interest level: 7-8).

Originally written in 1886, this reprint tells of a romance in the Catoctin Mountain region. The author, a Civil War correspondent and nationally syndicated newspaper columnist, includes the Civil War, John Brown, Lincoln's assassination, and the trial of the conspirators.
♦ As students read this historical novel, they may find some of the views slightly different from their own. They may identify what the author

considered important and show how an author's point of view affects a story.
1. United States—History—Civil War, 1861-1865 2. Maryland—History—Fiction.

Voigt, Cynthia. *Dicey's Song.* Atheneum (0-689-30944-9), 1982. 196p. (Interest level: 5-8).

This book, which won the Newbery Award in 1983, is an excellent introduction to the eastern shore of Maryland. Four children live with their grandmother on the eastern shore because their mother is in a mental hospital. Dicey, who is the oldest, must deal with the old problems of the family as well as the new, and getting to know Gram is one of the challenges.
♦ Children may investigate and discuss the purpose of mental hospitals and the problems that might arise from having a family member in need of such services.
1. Brothers and sisters—Fiction 2. Family life—Fiction.

Voigt, Cynthia. *Homecoming.* Atheneum (0-689-30833-7), 1981. 312p. (Interest level: 5-8).

When Dicey's mother abandons them in a parking lot in Connecticut, Dicey leads the children to their rich aunt's house in Bridgeport, but Aunt Cilla has died. So begins the long trek to an unknown grandma's house on the eastern shore of Maryland. This journey changes Dicey and her siblings.
♦ Readers may trace the trip that Dicey and her brothers and sisters made to get to Gram's. Use road maps and identify specific routes that might have been taken. This would be an excellent way to reinforce map reading skills.
1. Survival—Fiction 2. Family life—Fiction.

Professional Materials

015.752
Reynolds, Michael M. *Maryland: A Guide to Information and Reference Sources.* Research and Reference Publications (0-917698-00-2) (out of print). (Guide to State Information and Reference Sources, Number 7). 151p. (Interest level: Professional).

Although old and out of print, this document provides bibliographic access to historic publications that may be of use. Teachers interested in locating past materials for more intensive study of the state will find this guide helpful.
♦ Use this guide to identify materials that might be obtained through interlibrary loan.
1. Maryland—Bibliography.

016.752
A Guide to Government Records at the Maryland State Archives: A Comprehensive List by Agency and Record Sites. Maryland State Archives Publications (0-942370-32-5), 1991. 409p. (Interest level: Professional).

The information in this book is divided into two sections—record series and government agencies—both of which are indexed. The records listed have been identified from sources kept since 1634. The text identifies the location of the records and the types of records available for various agencies.
♦ This volume will be of assistance to the teacher interested in more in-depth research.
1. Maryland—Archives.

574.5
Decision Making, the Chesapeake Bay: An Interdisciplinary Environmental Education Curriculum Unit. Maryland Sea Grant Publications (ISSN UM-SG-ES-85-01), 1985. B/W illus. (Interest level: Professional).

This unit includes a teacher's guide, scripts of slide/tape and videotape programs, a Chesapeake Bay data bank, seven specific activities, and 11 optional activities. Student materials are included.
♦ Although written for teachers of senior high school students, this may be useful for others in identifying areas of study concerning the Chesapeake Bay and its environs.
1. Marine ecology—Chesapeake Bay 2. Chesapeake Bay—Research 3. Chesapeake Bay—Environmental aspects.

574.5
Greer, Jack. *Food Webs in an Estuary (A Marine Science Education Workbook).* Maryland Sea Grant Publications (UM-SG-ES-79-02), 1979. 26p. B/W illus. (Interest level: Professional).

The teacher's narrative, activities, and bibliographies introduce and reinforce an understanding of the food chains in the Chesapeake Bay. The program coordinates the activities with various middle and junior high school textbooks.
♦ Although designed for the Chesapeake Bay, the activities may be adapted to similar estuarine environments.
1. Environment 2. Maryland—Biology.

594
Greer, Jack. *The American Oyster.* Maryland Sea Grant Publications (UM-SG-ES-79-03), 1979. (A Marine Science Education Workbook). 57p. B/W illus. (Interest level: Professional).

Aimed at the middle or junior high school student, this workbook examines the oyster as an important food source for the state. Teacher materials, student resources, and bibliographies are included.
♦ The guide includes a number of charts and graphs that might be adapted for study in class.
1. Oysters 2. Marine animals 3. Maryland—Biology.

917.52
The Eastern Shore of Maryland: An Annotated Bibliography. Queene Anne Press (No ISBN), 1980. 233p. B/W illus. (Interest level: Professional).

Detailed annotations and bibliographic data are arranged for browsing the materials available on the history of the eastern shore. Edited under the auspices of the Enoch Pratt Free Library, the book includes materials and sources covering description and travel, economics, cultural life, religion, personalities, history, and imaginative literature.
♦ Use this guide to identify resource materials.
1. Maryland—Bibliographies   2. Eastern Shore—Bibliographies.

975.2
Czarra, Fred, comp. *Maryland History Resource Guide.* Maryland State Archives Publications (0-942370-19-8), 1988. 76p. B/W illus. (Interest level: Professional).

The compiler provides six chapters, which are organized to present students of all ages with information about the history of the state. Specific areas include museums, historic sites, sources of information, speakers, audiovisual resources, and a bibliography.
♦ This guide will prove to be invaluable for teachers developing a section on state history.
1. Maryland—History.

Massachusetts

by Richard A. Neubauer

Nonfiction

031 (Reference)
Meltzer, Ida, ed. *People Who Made America Pictorial Encyclopedia.* 21 vol. U.S. History Society (No ISBN), 1975 (out of print). Color illus. (Interest level: grade 3-adult).

This encyclopedia is an excellent resource for children studying Massachusetts biographies. An easy-to-use index and a teacher activity volume, which offers numerous lesson plans, add to the value of this set.
♦ Children can create and play a famous people of Massachusetts bingo game.
1. Inventors—Massachusetts 2. Authors—Massachusetts 3. Poets—Massachusetts.

069
Old Sturbridge Village. (Videocassette). Video Tours, 1989. VHS, (30 min.). $39.95. (Interest level: 4-8).

Life in a nineteenth-century New England village, including a barn raising and the crafts of printers, potters, and blacksmiths, is illustrated in this video.
♦ As a class, re-create a colonial village. Students may choose occupations to research and re-enact.
1. Massachusetts—Galleries and museums 2. Sturbridge (Mass.)—History.

069
Plimoth Plantation. (Videocassette). Video Tours, 1989. VHS, (30 min.). $39.95. (Interest level: 4-8).

Plimoth Plantation describes what life was like in the 1627 colony and how the "living museum" is staffed.
♦ Students can assume the roles of museum guides, speaking as if they were actually living in the old Plimoth Colony and describing their work.

1. Massachusetts—Galleries and museums 2. Pilgrims (New England colonists)—Social life and customs.

133.4
Starkey, Marion. *The Visionary Girls: Witchcraft in Salem Village.* Little, Brown (0-316-81087-8), 1973. 176p. (Interest level: 5-8).

Starkey tells the story of the madness that rooted itself in Salem, Massachusetts, in 1692, when young girls held an entire community hostage with their accusations of witchcraft.
♦ Young people can re-enact a courtroom scene from the witchcraft trials.
1. Witchcraft—Salem (Mass.).

331.48
Selden, Bernice. *The Mill Girls: Lucy Larcom, Harriet Hanson Robinson, Sarah G. Bagley.* Atheneum (0-689-31005-6), 1983. 191p. B/W illus. (Interest level: 6-8).

Three women—a teacher and poet, a writer and suffragette, and a journalist and labor organizer—who at one time all worked in the textile mills of Lowell, Massachusetts, are the subjects of Selden's text.
♦ Using scenes from the book, children can develop a floor plan of the mill and act out a day in the life of a mill worker.
1. Women textile workers 2. Lowell (Mass.)—History 3. Larcom, Lucy 4. Robinson, Harriet Hanson 5. Bagley, Sarah G.

377.44
Hornor, Edith R., ed. *Massachusetts Municipal Profiles, 1990-91.* Information Publications (0-931845-20-31), 1990. 385p. (Interest level: grade 5-adult).

Massachusetts Municipal Profiles was designed to provide concise yet comprehensive profiles for every city and town in Massachusetts. Included are

those facts that have the greatest interest for the broadest cross section of readers.
♦ Students can research information about their own community or town and then prepare charts and graphs of the information.
1. Massachusetts—Statistics.

639
Audubon Wildlife Adventure: Whales. (Microcomputer program). Top Ten Software, 1990. (Audubon Wildlife Adventure Series). 4, 5 1/4" floppy disks for Apple IIe computers. (Interest level: 4-8).

This simulation program combines the study of whales with four different games, including solving the mystery of a New Bedford whaling captain's mansion and photographing whales on a whale-watching trip.
♦ Children can compare the skills used in modern whale watching with old-time whale-hunting skills. They could then discuss why people today are more interested in watching whales than hunting them.
1. Whaling 2. New Bedford (Mass.).

745.5
D'Amato, Janet and **D'Amato, Alex**. *Colonial Crafts for You to Make*. Messner (0-671-327054), 1975. 64p. Color illus. (Interest level: K-4).
D'Amato, Janet and **D'Amato, Alex**. *More Colonial Crafts for You to Make*. Messner (0-671328-417), 1977. Color illus. (Interest level: K-4).

These companion volumes introduce various crafts that flourished during the colonial period and give instructions for making replicas of many representative items. The first book covers items found in a typical home, and the second covers education, draftsmen, private instruction, ladies' amusements, and toys. Easy-to-follow directions are accompanied by clear diagrams and scale drawings.
♦ Students could make one or several of the items described in these books, such as a corn husk doll or a dancing man on a stick.
1. Handicraft 2. United States—Social life and customs—Colonial period, ca 1600–1776.

903.44
Massachusetts Gazetteer. American Historical Publications, 1985. 204p. (Interest level: grade 5-adult).

A gazetteer is a dictionary of places, and the primary function of this historical gazetteer is to give detailed information on events that have occurred in Massachusetts and the people who participated in them.
♦ Students in Massachusetts can choose a town or city in the state and write a paragraph describing what they imagine that place's history to be. Then they can refer to the gazetteer to learn the town or city's true history. Students outside of Massachusetts can find a town or city in their state that has the same name as a town or city in Massachusetts. They can compare the history of both to see whether there is a relationship between the two and write a paragraph explaining their findings.
1. Massachusetts—History.

912.44
Wilkie, Richard W. and **Tager, Jack**. *The Historical Atlas of Massachusetts*. University of Massachusetts Press (0-87023-697-0), 1991. 160p. Color illus. and maps. (Interest level: 5-8).

The authors weave the past with the present, describing Massachusetts history and political and economic development. This book shows the forces of change that shaped not only the state of Massachusetts but the nation as a whole.
♦ Young people may select a town or city and write an essay discussing the topographical, historical, and social changes that have occurred through the years.
1. Massachusetts—Maps 2. Massachusetts—History 3. Massachusetts—Social conditions—Maps.

917.3
Cape Cod: Sands of Time. (Videocassette). Media Basics Video, 1984. VHS, (48 min.). $29.95. (Interest level: 4-8).

This videocassette provides a description of the Cape Cod National Seashore, its history, attractions, and the danger it faces from erosion and civilization.
♦ Viewers can compare this national seashore to a national park in their community and discuss the need for national parks and what characteristics most national parks have.
1. Cape Cod (Mass.)—Description and travel.

917.4
New England. (Videocassette). National Geographic Society, 1983. (United States Geography Series). VHS, (23 min.). $80.00. (Interest level: 4-8).

Viewers of this videocassette tour Boston, Plymouth, and other sites in Massachusetts as well as other New England states.
♦ Using a map of New England, students can locate the sites explored in the video.
1. New England—Description and travel.

917.44
Chesler, Bernice. *In and out of Boston with (or without) Children*. 4th ed. Globe Pequot Press (0-87106-968-7), 1982. 327p. (Interest level: grade 5-adult).

Chesler's book is like an encyclopedia of Boston as well as a guide to exploring the city's cultural areas and recreational sites, well-known historical places, and intriguing distractions. Ideas in the book

will appeal to all ages, grandparents as well as three-year-olds.
♦ Readers can choose five places that they would like to visit in Massachusetts and write a paragraph describing the things they would see or do while visiting the places they have chosen.
1. Boston (Mass.)—Description and travel—Guidebooks 2. Boston (Mass.)—Suburbs and environs 3. Guidebooks.

917.44
Gleason, David King. *Over Boston*. Photos by author. Louisiana State University (0-8071-1283-6), 1985. 134p. Color photos. (Interest level: 5-8).

Gleason presents 130 spectacular photographs of Boston with captions that place the pictures in their historical and geographical contexts.
♦ With the captions covered, show selected pictures from the work to young people and ask them to explain the historical or geographical significance of the scene.
1. Boston (Mass.)—Description and travel—Views.

917.44
Tree, Christina. *The Other Massachusetts, Beyond Boston and Cape Cod*. 1st ed. County Press (0-88150-075-5), 1987. 357p. (Interest level: 6-8).

Tree's book brings into focus many parts of the "other" Massachusetts, very specific regions that cannot be homogenized into one image. The book can serve as a guide for visitors to the two-thirds of the state that lies beyond the Boston and Cape Cod axis.
♦ Using this book as a guide, young people could compile little-known facts, activities, and places to visit in their own state, publish the information and put a copy in their school and/or community library.
1. Massachusetts—Description and travel.

917.44
Westman, Barbara. *A Boston Picture Book*. Houghton Mifflin (0-395-19336-2), 1974. 48p. Color illus. (Interest level: K-4).

A picture book tour of Boston that covers nearly all the sights, this book includes a look at the Public Garden, Charles Street, Beacon Hill, and the picturesque North End. After several more interesting stops, including the waterfront, readers return to the point of departure.
♦ Children can choose an area of Boston that was mentioned in the book and write and illustrate a poem about it.
1. Boston (Mass.)—Description—1951-1980—Views.

917.44
Whitehall, Walter Muir. *Massachusetts: From the Berkshires to the Cape*. Viking Press (0-670-46123-7), 1977. 136p. B/W photos. (Interest level: 5-8).

Through black-and-white photos, the reader is taken on a 190-mile journey across the state, exploring the varied landscape—mountains, farms, cities, and coastal areas—that makes Massachusetts so unique.
♦ Students can choose an area in Massachusetts where they would like to live and write two or three paragraphs explaining why they chose that area.
1. Historical buildings—Massachusetts—Conservation and restoration 2. Massachusetts—Description and travel.

970.004
People of the First Light. (Videocassette). Massachusetts Educational Television and WGBY-TV. 1 videocassette, 7 programs, (30 min. each); teacher's guide. $29.95. (Interest level: 4-8).

This videocassette explores the history, traditions, and cultures of Native Americans living in Massachusetts and other parts of New England.
♦ Viewers can compare various aspects of the lives of local Native Americans with those of the Native Americans of New England.
1. Indians of North America—New England.

973
Massachusetts Department of Public Works. *Massachusetts State Transportation Map*. (Map). Massachusetts Department of Public Works, 1990. Color illus. (Interest level: grade 4-adult).

Enlargements of major cities, including Boston, are featured on this map of Massachusetts. Colorful illustrations accompany lists of historical sites and points of interest.
♦ Young people can point out famous locations, such as Plymouth, Salem, Lexington, Concord, Walden Pond, or Cape Cod National Seashore. Young people can also use the map to trace the route of Paul Revere's famous ride.
1. Massachusetts—Maps.

973
Massachusetts Office of Business Development. *Massachusetts Cities and Towns*. (Pamphlet). Massachusetts Office of Business Development (No ISBN), 1989. 12p. (Interest level: grade 6-adult).

This pamphlet includes information on the state of Massachusetts and each of its cities and towns, including average salaries and population employed in government, agriculture, construction, manufacturing, trade, finance, insurance, real estate, and services. Data are clearly organized by area of the state and individual city or town.

♦ Teachers could assign specific research questions about the state's 10 largest cities, as well as the state as a whole. Answering these questions will give students practice using charts and tables.
1. Massachusetts—Statistics 2. Massachusetts—Economic geography.

973
Office of the Massachusetts Secretary of State. *Massachusetts Facts.* (Pamphlet). Office of the Massachusetts Secretary of State (No ISBN), 1990. 34p. B/W illus. (Interest level: 2-8).

Readers of this pamphlet will find geographical information; the official state flower, bird, song, march, rock, dog, cat, and other miscellaneous facts; as well as a list of Massachusetts "firsts." An excellent historical sketch, ranging from the colonial period to the present, is provided in a short five-page section.
♦ Read the historical sketch aloud and discuss what students have learned. Use the list of "firsts" as an overhead transparency to spark student interest in the state. Younger students can use this pamphlet as a research tool to locate the official Massachusetts bird, song, flower, etc.
1. Massachusetts—History 2. Massachusetts—State symbols 3. Massachusetts—Geography.

973.2
New England and the Middle Colonies. (Sound filmstrip). National Geographic Society, 1990. (Life in Colonial America Series). 2 filmstrips, 2 audiocassettes, (16 min. each); teacher's guide. $45.00. (Interest level: 2-6).

These filmstrips depict daily life and the struggle to survive in early settlements of the colonies.
♦ Working in groups, students can identify and compare the lifestyles of the colonists with their own.
1. United States—History—Colonial period, ca 1600-1776.

973.3
Boston Massacre. (Videocassette). Life Video, 1988. Color, (10 min.). $19.95. (Interest level: 5-8).

Paintings, color illustrations, and sketches are used to dramatize the events in Boston on March 5, 1770.
♦ Class members can do further research on the events that led up to and followed the massacre to determine how it affected the American people's views about revolution.
1. United States—History—Revolution, 1775-1783.

973.33
Colby, Jean Poindexter. *Lexington & Concord, 1775: What Really Happened.* Photos by Barbara Cooney. Hastings (0-8038-4292-9), 1975. 128p. Color illus. (Interest level: 5-8).

Colby examines what happened before, during, and after the first battles of the American Revolution.
♦ Students could construct a topographically correct relief map of the Lexington and Concord area and discuss what geographical features helped or hindered the opposing forces.
1. Lexington, Battle of, 1775 2. Concord, Battle of, 1775 3. United States—History—Revolution, 1775-1783.

973.7
History of New England. (Sound filmstrip). National Geographic Society, 1990. (History of the United States: A Regional Portrait Series). 3 filmstrips, 3 audiocassettes, (16 min. each); teacher's guide. $98.00. (Interest level: 4-8).

These filmstrips present a regional history, beginning with the original inhabitants and moving through exploration, settlement, and development. The filmstrips are sold as a set; one filmstrip covers New England, one covers the Great Lakes states, and one covers the Mid-Atlantic states.
♦ Young people can create a map of the region and identify the location of significant events depicted in the series.
1. New England—History 2. Mid-Atlantic States—History 3. Great Lakes—History.

973.744
Cox, Clinton. *Undying Glory.* Scholastic (0-590-44170-1), 1991. 167p. B/W illus. (Interest level: 5-8).

Cox describes the formation of the all-black 54th Massachusetts Regiment and its valiant battle history from 1863 to 1865.
♦ Children can draw a map depicting the battles the 54th Regiment took part in during the Civil War.
1. United States. Army. Infantry Regiment, 54th (1863-1865)—History 2. United States—History—Civil War, 1861-1865—Regimental histories 3. Massachusetts—History—Civil War, 1861-1865.

974.4
Anderson, Joan. *The First Thanksgiving Feast.* Clarion Books (0-89919-287-4), 1984. Unpaginated. B/W illus. (Interest level: K-4).

Anderson re-creates the first harvest feast celebrated by the Pilgrims and Native Americans in 1621 using the seventeenth-century setting of Plimoth Plantation, a living history museum in Plymouth, Massachusetts.
♦ For a week before Thanksgiving, children can keep a journal, imagining that they are Pilgrims or Native Americans living in the seventeenth century. In the journal, they can document their

everyday activities as children of this time period. At the end of the week, students and teachers can re-create the first Thanksgiving feast in one or several classrooms, wearing costumes appropriate to the era.

1. Massachusetts—History—New Plymouth, 1620-1691 2. Pilgrims (New Plymouth Colony) 3. Thanksgiving Day.

974.4
Monke, Ingrid. *Boston.* Dillon Press (0-87518-382-4), 1988. 60p. Color illus. (Interest level: K-4).

This work, which explores the city of Boston, both past and present, describes neighborhoods, attractions, festivals, and historic sites.

♦ Children can compare their own town or city to Boston, focusing on such areas as location, population, flag, form of government, cultural makeup, history, fun and entertainment, and noteworthy people.

1. Boston (Mass.).

974.4
Pilgrims and Indians. (Sound filmstrip). National Geographic Society, 1990. (People behind Our Holidays Series). 4 filmstrips, 4 audiocassettes, (16 min. each); teacher's guide. $124.00 for set. (Interest level: K-4).

The filmstrips in this series describe the people and events behind our national holidays. This particular filmstrip provides the background for Thanksgiving.

♦ Students can compare traditions of different cultures on the various holidays.

1. United States—History—Colonial period, ca 1600-1776.

974.4
The Pilgrims of Plimoth. (Videocassette). Weston Woods, 1988. VHS, (26 min.). $30.00. (Interest level: K-3).

The arrival of the Pilgrims to the New World is chronicled in this reenactment of daily activities during those first trying years in the colony they called Plimoth. This is an iconographic video of Marcia Sewell's striking pictures and story.

♦ Viewers can construct a miniature Plimoth village based on Marcia Sewell's illustrations.

1. Pilgrims (New England colonists)—Social life—Fiction.

974.4
Who Were the Pilgrims? (Kit). National Geographic Society, 1989. (Wonders of Learning Kit). 30 booklets; teacher's guide; activity sheets; read-along cassette. $89.95. (Interest level: K-2).

The food the Pilgrims ate, the houses they built, the games they played, and the work and chores required of all ages are described in this kit.

♦ Students can create and play games that the Pilgrim children played.

1. Pilgrims (New England colonists)—Social life.

974.4092
Waters, Kate. *Sarah Morton's Day: A Day in the Life of a Pilgrim Girl.* Photos by Russ Kendall. Scholastic (0-590-42634-6), 1989. 32p. B/W photos. (Interest level: K-3).

Text and photographs of Plymoth Plantation follow a modern-day girl in Pilgrim dress through a typical day as she milks the goats, cooks and serves meals, learns her letters, and adjusts to her new stepfather.

♦ If possible, arrange a field trip to Plymouth Plantation. Some children might want to collaborate and write an account of a day in the life of a twentieth-century child. A videotape of this account would be fun and useful for classmates and future students.

1. Pilgrims (New Plymouth Colony)—Pictorial works 2. Children—Massachusetts—History—17th century 3. Massachusetts—Social life and customs—Colonial period, ca 1600-1775.

974.482
Sewall, Marcia. *The Pilgrims of Plimoth.* Atheneum (0-689-31250-4), 1986. 48p. Color illus. (Interest level: K-4).

Sewell chronicles in text and illustration the day-to-day life of the early Pilgrims in Plymouth Colony. A glossary of terms is included in the book.

♦ Students can list things they use today that did not exist during colonial times and then discuss how the Pilgrims managed without them.

1. Pilgrims (New Plymouth Colony) 2. Massachusetts—Social life and customs—Colonial period, ca 1600-1775.

974.6
Thompson, Kathleen. *Massachusetts.* Raintree (0-86514-435-4), 1986. 47p. Color illus. (Interest level: K-4).

Thompson's work discusses the history, economy, culture, and future of Massachusetts. It also includes a state chronology, pertinent statistics, and maps.

♦ Using this book as a reference, children can draw a large outline of Massachusetts, then fill in the outline with a collage of original drawings, magazine pictures, and other pictorial and historical material depicting different aspects of the state.

1. Massachusetts.

Biography

920
Amory, Cleveland. *The Proper Bostonians.* Parnassus (0-940160-25-0), 1984. 381p. (Interest level: 8).
Amory presents an amusing, lighthearted examination of the Boston culture and traits of Bostonians. This book deals with the attributes of the leading names in Boston history, such as the Adamses, Appletons, Coolidges, Lowells, and Cabots, that reveal Bostonian culture.
♦ Young people can describe traits of the culture of their town or community and include humorous anecdotes.
1. Boston (Mass.)—Biography 2. Boston (Mass.)—Wit and humor.

920
Davis, Burke. *Black Heroes of the American Revolution.* Harcourt Brace & Company (0-15-208561-0), 1992, 1976. 77p. B/W illus. (Interest level: 3-5).
Davis's collective biography looks at the African Americans who performed key roles in the American Revolution. Prints and portraits of the period are included.
♦ Students can create biography blocks by constructing cubes out of construction paper. On one side of the cube, each student can write the subject name, author, title, publisher, and copyright date of one of the biographies they have read. On the other sides, he or she can illustrate the biography and write a short description of the life of the individual.
1. History—Revolution, 1775-1783—African Americans.

92 Adams, Abigail
Akers, Charles W. *Abigail Adams: An American Woman.* HarperCollins (0-673-39318-6), 1987. 207p. (Interest level: 8).
Abigail Adams helped to shape the affairs of state through her extraordinary letters to her husband and other prominent people in London, Paris, and Philadelphia.
♦ After reading this biography, students can write letters to their classmates on current events.
1. Adams, Abigail, 1744-1818 2. United States—History—1783-1865.

92 Adams, Abigail
Osborne, Angela. *Abigail Adams.* Chelsea House (1-555-46635-4), 1989. 111p. (Interest level: 5-8).
Abigail Adams, daughter of a Braintree, Massachusetts, minister, grew up to become a writer, the wife of one of the presidents of the United States, and the mother of another.
♦ If possible, young people can visit the childhood home of Abigail Smith Adams, located in Weymouth, Massachusetts. Students could conduct further research on the life of Abigail Adams and construct a time line of significant events in her life. They may also wish to dramatize scenes from those events.
1. Adams, Abigail, 1744-1818 2. United States—History—Revolution, 1775-1783.

92 Adams, Abigail
Peterson, Helen Stone. *Abigail Adams, "Dear Partner."* Illus. by Betty Fraser. Chelsea House (0-7910-1402-9), 1991, 1967. (Discovery Biographies Series). 80p. (Interest level: 3-5).
Peterson has written a simple account of Abigail's interest in politics, her support for the American Revolution, and the organization of the U.S. government.
♦ Imagining that they are Abigail Adams, children can write historically accurate journal entries.
1. Adams, Abigail, 1744-1818 2. United States—History—Revolution, 1775-1783.

92 Adams, John
Dwyer, Frank. *John Adams.* Chelsea House (1-555-46801-2), 1989. 109p. (Interest level: 5-8).
John Adams, vice president under George Washington and the second president of the United States, is the subject of this biography.
♦ Students can do research to determine what issues were important when John Adams was president and compare them with the issues of today.
1. Adams, John, 1735-1826 2. United States—History—Revolution, 1775-1783.

92 Adams, John
John Adams. (Videocassette). Zenger Video, 1964. VHS, (50 min.); teacher's guide. $49.95. (Interest level: 6-8).
In this video, young Massachusetts lawyer John Adams, one of the Sons of Liberty, represents British soldiers accused of firing into the crowd at the Boston Massacre. Adams insists that the defendants' right to a fair trial is the primary issue in the case.
♦ Viewers can imagine they are Massachusetts citizens attending the trial after the Boston Massacre and write a diary entry describing their feelings toward the accused soldiers and John Adams.
1. Adams, John, 1735-1826 2. United States—History—Revolution, 1775-1783.

92 Adams, John Quincy
Coelho, Tony. *John Quincy Adams.* Chelsea House (1-55546-802-0), 1989. (World Leaders Past and Present). 112p. (Interest level: 4-8).
Coelho presents a biography of John Quincy Adams, an astute diplomat, a vigorous senator, and sixth president of the United States.
♦ Students can visit the home of John Quincy Adams, which is located in Quincy, Massachu-

setts. Or, young people could create a model of his home and write a short description to accompany it. They could display the model in the school library.

1. Adams, John Quincy, 1767-1848 2. United States—History—1783-1865.

92 Adams, Samuel
Fritz, Jean. *Why Don't You Get a Horse, Sam Adams?* Illus. by Trina Shart Hyman. Coward-McCann (0-698-20292-9), 1982. 48p. Color illus. (Interest level: 3-5).

This brief biography of Samuel Adams describes how he stirred up the revolt against the British and how he was finally persuaded to learn to ride a horse.
♦ After reading the selection, children may want to dramatize the story through reader's theater.

1. Adams, Samuel, 1722-1803 2. United States—History—Revolution, 1775-1783.

92 Alcott, Louisa May
Burke, Kathleen. *Louisa May Alcott.* Chelsea House (1-555-46636-0), 1988. 111p. (Interest level: 5-8).

Burke offers a rendering of the life of Louisa May Alcott, American author of books for children.
♦ Young people can visit the home of Louisa May Alcott, which is located in Concord, Massachusetts. They can also visit Fruitlands, a community founded by her father, Amos Bronson Alcott, where Louisa lived as a young girl. Readers could conduct further research on Fruitlands: why was it founded, what was everyday life like in the community, and what effect did this lifestyle have on Louisa? They could report their findings orally to the class.

1. Alcott, Louisa May, 1832-1888 2. Women authors.

92 Barton, Clara
Stevenson, Augusta. *Clara Barton: Founder of the Red Cross.* Illus. by Frank Giacola. Aladdin (0-02-041820-5), 1986. 192p. Color illus. (Interest level: 3-5).

Stevenson tells the story of a courageous woman who devoted her life to others. Colorful illustrations and lively text recount the Massachusetts childhood of Clara Barton, nurse and founder of the American Red Cross.
♦ Students may wish to research the beginning of the American Red Cross.

1. Barton, Clara, 1821-1912 2. American Red Cross 3. Nursing—Careers.

92 Bowditch, Nathaniel
Latham, Jean Lee. *Carry on, Mr. Bowditch.* Illus. by John O'Hara Cosgrave. Houghton Mifflin (0-395-06881-9), 1955. 251p. B/W illus. (Interest level: 5-8).

Nathaniel Bowditch had a troubled family life and grew up in revolutionary times, but he had a thirst for learning mathematics, surveying, navigation, astronomy, and languages. There is some fictionalization of dialogue in this book.
♦ Students can research further Nathaniel's interest in mathematics, surveying, navigation, astronomy, and languages and discuss his influence in each of these areas. Young people could also create models of some of the instruments used by Bowditch and explain how they have changed over the years.

1. Bowditch, Nathaniel, 1773-1838 2. Navigation 3. United States—History—Revolution, 1775-1783.

92 Child, Lydia Maria
Meltzer, Milton. *Tongue of Flame: The Life of Lydia Maria Child.* Crowell (0-690-04903-X), 1991. 224p. (Interest level: 5-8).

Lydia Maria Child, who was born a slave and was later freed, lived in Massachusetts during the time of the American Civil War. She was primarily known for her writings. This work contains good historical accounts of the anti-slavery movement, the Harpers Ferry incident, and the status of African Americans during the Civil War.
♦ On pages 171-73, readers will find Lydia's record of everything she accomplished in one year. Students may wish to prepare a similar list of everything they have accomplished for a selected period of time.

1. Child, Lydia Maria, 1802-1880 2. African Americans—Massachusetts—Biography 3. Women authors.

92 Copley, John
Frankenstein, Alfred. *The World of Copley: 1738-1815.* Time-Life, 1970 (out of print). 192p. (Interest level: 7-8).

This is a biography of one of the foremost artists of the Georgian Age, who became the painter of heroes of the American Revolution. Unable to come to terms with either the Tories or the Whigs, he moved to London. Picture essays support the text.
♦ Children can create picture essays on current events.

1. Copley, John, 1738-1815 2. Artists—Massachusetts 3. United States—History—Colonial period, ca 1600–1775 4. Boston (Mass.)—History.

92 Cuffe, Paul
Diamond, Arthur. *Paul Cuffe: Merchant and Abolitionist.* Chelsea House (1-55546-579-X), 1989. (Black Americans of Achievement). 105p. B/W illus. (Interest level: 5-8).

Paul Cuffe, who was born a slave but was later freed, and who in 1810 proposed the founding of an African colony for African Americans, also lobbied

for a Massachusetts law giving African Americans the right to vote. Detailed illustrations enhance the biography.
♦ Young people may want to discuss laws that they would like to enact or change in order to gain or retain certain rights.
1. Cuffe, Paul, 1759-1817   2. African Americans—Massachusetts—Biography   3. African Americans—Colonization—Sierra Leone.

92 Dickinson, Emily
Barth, Edna. *I'm Nobody: Who Are You? The Story of Emily Dickinson*. Illus. by Richard Cuffari. Clarion Books (0-395-28843-6), 1979. 128p. (Interest level: 4-8).

Barth presents a carefully researched but somewhat fictionalized account of the shy, reclusive life and views of Emily Dickinson. Dickinson's writings are woven into the text.
♦ This well-documented and well-indexed source will be useful for papers and inspiration. Students could read some of Dickinson's works and write an essay about how her life and views are reflected in her writings.
1. Dickinson, Emily, 1830-1886   2. Poets—Massachusetts.

92 Forten, Charlotte
Longsworth, Polly. *I, Charlotte Forten: Black and Free*. Harper, 1970 (out of print). 247p. (Interest level: 5-8).

Longworth's well-documented biography of a teacher who was effective in the abolitionist movement will support multicultural approaches to U.S. history. Sources listed in this book were contemporary in Charlotte Forten's lifetime and include references to her diary.
♦ Young people may choose a local social issue to get involved in and document their progress through a diary.
1. Forten, Charlotte   2. Abolitionists   3. African Americans—Massachusetts—Biography   4. United States—History—Civil War, 1861-1865.

92 Fortune, Amos
Yates, Elizabeth. *Amos Fortune: Free Man*. Illus. by Nora S. Unwin. Dutton (0-525-25570-2), 1967. 181p. B/W illus. (Interest level: 5-8).

A Newbery Medal winner, this is an account of how as a young boy Amos Fortune was enslaved and taken to Massachusetts. Eventually, Amos was able to buy his freedom.
♦ Children could write an essay on freedom and what it means to live in freedom.
1. Fortune, Amos   2. African Americans—Massachusetts—Biography   3. Slavery—United States.

92 Fuller, Margaret
Wilson, Ellen. *Margaret Fuller: Bluestocking, Romantic, Revolutionary*. Farrar, 1977 (out of print). 186p. (Interest level: 5-8).

Margaret Fuller, an articulate author who wrote extensively on women's rights, became liberated early in life. Well educated, Margaret met with the major literary figures of her day. Wilson's biography includes numerous quotes from Fuller's writings and her personal love story, which ended tragically.
♦ Readers may wish to conduct further research on women's rights.
1. Fuller, Margaret, 1810-1850   2. Women's movement   3. Women—Civil rights.

92 Hancock, John
Fowler, William M. *The Baron of Beacon Hill: A Biography of John Hancock*. Houghton Mifflin, 1980 (out of print). 366p. (Interest level: 8).

John Hancock, a "founding father," sacrificed his fortune for Boston and his country. This biography presents a well-documented history of the American Revolution and an up-close view of the man who signed the Declaration of Independence boldly.
♦ Students can investigate further the Continental Congress and Boston's role in the American Revolution. They may also wish to re-enact the signing of the Declaration of Independence.
1. Hancock, John, 1737-1793   2. United States—Declaration of Independence   3. Boston (Mass.)—History.

92 Hancock, John
Fritz, Jean. *Will You Sign Here, John Hancock?* Illus. by Trina Shart Hyman. Coward-McCann (0-698-20308-9), 1982. 48p. Color illus. (Interest level: 3-5).

Fritz's biography of the first signer of the Declaration of Independence outlines what he did for Massachusetts and the new nation.
♦ After examining a copy of the Declaration of Independence, each student can research and write a biographical sketch of the signer of their choice. Also, the class can write its own declaration or compact, and each member of the class can sign it.
1. Hancock, John, 1737-1793   2. History—Revolution, 1775-1783   3. United States—Declaration of Independence.

92 Hawthorne, Nathaniel, and Peabody, Sophia
Gaeddert, LouAnn. *A New England Love Story: Nathaniel Hawthorne and Sophia Peabody*. Dial, 1980 (out of print). 150p. (Interest level: 7-8).

These letters, which led to courtship and marriage, will provide readers with a sense of history and literature and a love story as celebrated as the Brownings'!

♦ Imagining themselves as either Nathaniel Hawthorne or Sophia Peabody, students can write historically accurate journal entries.
1. Hawthorne, Nathaniel, 1804-1864 2. Peabody, Sophia, 1811-1871 3. Authors, American.

92 Holmes, Oliver Wendell
Hoyt, Edwin P. *The Improper Bostonian: Dr. Oliver Wendell Holmes*. Morrow, 1979 (out of print). 319p. (Interest level: 8).

A man of great wit and ability, Oliver Wendell Holmes made significant contributions to literature and medicine during the abolitionist movement and the Civil War.

♦ Young people could choose individuals who made significant contributions on which to conduct further research and then create a documentary on the life of that person. They may also wish to write some "historical" poetry.
1. Holmes, Oliver Wendell, 1809-1894 2. Poets—Massachusetts.

92 Hutchinson, Anne
Faber, Doris. *Anne Hutchinson*. Illus. by Frank Vaughn. Garrard, 1970 (out of print). 64p. Color illus. (Interest level: 3-6).

Faber's biography of Anne Hutchinson relates her quest for religious freedom. That quest took Hutchinson from England to the Massachusetts Bay Colony, where official harassment forced her to continue her flight.

♦ Young people can write an individual or group essay on the topic of individual expression.
1. Hutchinson, Anne, 1591-1643 2. Freedom of expression.

92 Kennedy, John Fitzgerald
Graves, Charles P. *John F. Kennedy: New Frontiersman*. Illus. by Paul Frame. Chelsea House (0-7910-1444-4), 1992. (Discovery Biographies). 80p. (Interest level: 4-8).

This readable biography does not sensationalize any part of Kennedy's life.

♦ Readers can interview parents and grandparents to find out what they were doing when President Kennedy was assassinated and how they felt when they heard the news.
1. Kennedy, John Fitzgerald, 1917-1963 2. Presidents—United States—Biography.

92 Kennedy, John Fitzgerald
Martin, Patricia Miles. *John Fitzgerald Kennedy*. Illus. by Paul Frame. Putnam (No ISBN), 1964 (out of print). (See and Read). 64p. (Interest level: K-2).

A beginning-to-read biography of the 35th president of the United States, this selection acquaints young readers with Kennedy's boyhood, his service in the Navy as skipper of PT 109, as well as his political career.

♦ The teacher can use this biography to help children identify the parts of a biographical sketch. Youngsters can then brainstorm questions they might ask an individual in order to write a biography about that individual.
1. Kennedy, John Fitzgerald, 1917-1963 2. Presidents—United States—Biography.

92 Kennedy, John Fitzgerald
Randall, Marta. *John F. Kennedy*. Chelsea House (0-877-54586-3), 1987. (World Leaders Past and Present Series). 112p. (Interest level: 4-8).

Randall presents an account of the life of John F. Kennedy, congressman from Massachusetts and president of the United States.

♦ Young people can visit the boyhood home of John Fitzgerald Kennedy, which is located in Brookline, Massachusetts. They could also arrange a field trip to the Kennedy Library in Dorchester, Massachusetts. Children outside Massachusetts could interview members of their community about what they were doing when they heard that Kennedy was shot and how it made them feel. Students could report their findings to the class.
1. Kennedy, John Fitzgerald, 1917-1963 2. Presidents—United States—Biography 3. United States—Politics and government.

92 Longfellow, Henry Wadsworth
Holberg, Ruth. *An American Bard: The Story of Henry Wadsworth Longfellow*. Illus. by Aldren A. Watson. Crowell, 1963 (out of print). 168p. (Interest level: 5-8).

Holberg weaves the story of Longfellow's life with his poetry. Longfellow's life greatly influenced his writing.

♦ Students can write poetry based on their life experiences.
1. Longfellow, Henry Wadsworth, 1807-1882 2. Poets—Massachusetts.

92 Mann, Horace
Pierce, Edith. *Horace Mann: Our Nation's First Educator*. Lerner, 1972 (out of print). 55p. (Interest level: 4-8).

Horace Mann was a champion of many causes, including mental patients, children, and free public education. As first secretary of the Massachusetts Board of Education, Mann initiated reforms that influenced education all over the country.

♦ This concise account can be used to initiate a class discussion regarding present-day educational reforms.
1. Mann, Horace, 1796-1859 2. Education—United States—Massachusetts 3. Teachers—Training.

92 Morison, Samuel Eliot
Morison, Samuel Eliot. *One Boy's Boston, 1887-1901*. Northeastern University Press (0-930350-49-9), 1983. 81p. Photos. (Interest level: 5-8).

This is a memoir of the ordinary life of Samuel Morison in late-nineteenth-century Boston and its environs. Photographs support the text.
♦ Children can create a photo essay of everyday life in today's world.
1. Boston (Mass.)—History—1865-1898 2. Morison, Samuel, 1887-1976.

92 Pocahontas
Fritz, Jean. *The Double Life of Pocahontas*. Illus. by Feodor Rojanovsky. Puffin (0-14-032257-4), 1987. 85p. B/W illus. (Interest level: 4-7).

Fritz offers an updated version of the story of the Native American woman who befriended Captain John Smith and the English settlers. A "Clarifying Notes" section, a bibliography, and an index add to this fresh biography.
♦ Class members may want to re-create either the Indian village or the settlers' villages.
1. Pocahontas, ca 1595-1617 2. Smith, John, ca 1580-1631 3. Indians of North America—Massachusetts.

92 Revere, Paul
Forbes, Esther. *America's Paul Revere*. Illus. by Lynd Ward. Houghton Mifflin (0-395-24907-4), 1990, 1946. 46p. illus. (Interest level: 3-5).

Forbes's tribute to Paul Revere's achievements vividly presents excellent information about the American Revolution. Exceptional illustrations complement the text.
♦ This biography can be used to initiate a class discussion on individual accomplishments. Children could choose various aspects of Paul Revere's life and create a video to share with another class.
1. Revere, Paul, 1735–1818 2. Boston—Massachusetts—History 3. United States—History—Revolution, 1775-1783.

92 Revere, Paul
Forbes, Esther. *Paul Revere and the World He Lived In*. Peter Smith (0-8446-6526-6), 1992, 1942. 510p. (Interest level: 5-8).

This engrossing narrative covers the extraordinary life and accomplishments of Paul Revere, the master craftsman, patriot, and family leader.
♦ Students can list the significant contributions Paul Revere made to American history. They could create a time line showing accomplishments and events in his life.
1. Revere, Paul, 1735–1818 2. Boston—Massachusetts—History 3. United States—History—Revolution, 1775-1783.

92 Revere, Paul
Fritz, Jean. *And Then What Happened, Paul Revere?* Illus. by Margot Tomes. Coward, McCann & Geoghegan (0-698-30526-4), 1973. 48p. Color illus. (Interest level: 3-5).

Fritz describes some of the well-known as well as the lesser-known details of Paul Revere's life and exciting ride.
♦ With its humorous descriptions and clever illustrations, this is an excellent read-aloud. A follow-up reading of Henry Wadsworth Longfellow's "Paul Revere's Ride" is suggested.
1. Revere, Paul, 1735-1818 2. United States—History—Revolution, 1775-1783.

92 Sampson, Deborah
McGovern, Ann. *The Secret Soldier: The Story of Deborah Sampson*. Illus. by Ann Grifalconi. Four Winds Press (0-02-765780-9), 1987, 1975. 62p. (Interest level: 3-5).

Disguised as Robert Shurtleff, a brave soldier in the Continental Army, Deborah survived as a soldier until her real identity became known.
♦ This is a useful source to support units on the role of women in society, especially in traditional male bastions. Students could debate or have a panel discussion on women in the military, especially in combat positions.
1. Sampson, Deborah 2. Women—United States 3. United States—History—Revolution, 1773-1783.

92 Squanto
Bulla, Clyde Robert. *Squanto, Friend of the Pilgrims*. Illus. by Peter Burchard. Scholastic (0-590-44055-1), 1990. 112p. B/W illus. (Interest level: 3-5).

This is a biography of the Native American who was captured by some of the first English explorers, taken to London, and sold into slavery in Spain. Squanto finally escaped and returned to America, where he befriended the Pilgrims when they landed.
♦ The class could discuss this story, focusing on the characters and their motives, and how children relate to the experiences, concerns, and interests of Squanto.
1. Squanto, d. 1622 2. Wampanoag Indians 3. Indians of North America—Biography.

92 Squanto
Ziner, Feenie. *Squanto*. Linnet (0-208-02218-X), 1988. 149p. (Interest level: 5-8).

Ziner relates the story of the Wampanoag Indian who became friends with the Pilgrims. Squanto was kidnapped and taken to England, but later returned to America. The text is long but filled with interesting information.

♦ Young people can do further reading to find current information on the Wampanoag tribe, which is still active on Martha's Vineyard.
1. Squanto, d. 1622   2. Wampanoag Indians   3. Indians of North America—Biography.

92 Thoreau, Henry David
Stern, Philip Von Doren. *Henry David Thoreau: Writer and Rebel.* Crowell, 1972 (out of print). 184p. (Interest level: 8).

Henry David Thoreau is remembered best for his solitary life in the cabin on Walden Pond, which led to his writing *Walden* and the essay "Civil Disobedience." He was also a farmer, house painter, schoolmaster, surveyor, carpenter, mason, glass maker, paper maker, pencil maker, and writer.
♦ Use this work to initiate a class discussion on individual resistance to established government.
1. Thoreau, Henry David, 1817-1862   2. Government, Resistance to   3. Passive resistance   4. Authors—Massachusetts.

92 Wheatley, Phillis
Fuller, Miriam Morris. *Phillis Wheatley: America's First Black Poetess.* Illus. by Victor Mays. Garrard, 1971 (out of print). 94p. (Interest level: 5-8).

As a child, Phillis was a slave, but she was well tutored by the Wheatley family. When she began to write poetry, she had great difficulty getting published until colonial and revolutionary leaders interviewed her and came to her support.
♦ Young people can read more of Wheatley's poetry.
1. Wheatley, Phillis, 1753?-1784   2. American poetry—African American authors   3. United States—History—Revolution, 1775-1783—Poetry.

92 Whistler, James Abbott McNeil
Prideaux, Tom and the **Editors of Time-Life Books.** *The World of Whistler 1834-1903.* Time-Life, 1970 (out of print). 192p. (Interest level: 8).

James Whistler was one of Massachusetts's most famous artists, even though his only connection with Massachusetts is the fact that he was born there. A fascinating, flamboyant, and eccentric life is presented in this understated biography of a key figure in modern art.
♦ Class members can put together an art show of Whistler's paintings.
1. Whistler, James Abbott McNeil, 1834-1903   2. Artists—Massachusetts.

92 Whittier, John Greenleaf
Vining, Elizabeth Gray. *Mr. Whittier.* Viking, 1974 (out of print). 169p. (Interest level: 8).

John Greenleaf Whittier made significant contributions to freedom and literature. This is a richly detailed view of the man who became a force for influencing public opinion. Whittier had strong opinions on women's rights and the right to strike.
♦ Students can list social issues that were influenced by John Whittier. They could then choose one of those issues on which to conduct further research. What is the status of that issue today? How did Whittier influence it?
1. Whittier, John Greenleaf, 1807-1892   2. Poets—Massachusetts   3. Abolitionists.

Fiction

Aiken, Joan. *Nightbirds on Nantucket.* Illus. by Robin Jacques. Doubleday (0-84466254-2), 1966. 243p. (Interest level: 5-8).

Dido Twite, an imp of eight or nine, follows young Simon, who lodges with the Twites, when he is shipped off for Holland. The children take to the water; Simon is rescued and believes Dido has drowned. Dido is picked up by a whaling ship (*Nightbirds on Nantucket*) that plays a prominent part in a plot to assassinate King James III.
♦ Readers can find Nantucket on a map, then research whaling and report on how the early colonists depended on the whaling industry for their needs.
1. New England—Fiction.

Alcott, Louisa May. *Little Women.* Illus. by Tasha Tudor. Philomel (0-52900529-8), 1968. 544p. Color illus. (Interest level: 5-8).

Here is the well-known story of the New England home life of the four March sisters: Meg, Jo, Beth, and Amy.
♦ Students can brainstorm the character traits of the four girls, compare similarities and differences, and make a Venn diagram to illustrate the results of their comparison. Children can then write about how members of the same family have similar and dissimilar character traits.
1. Family life—Fiction   2. New England—Fiction   3. United States—History—Civil War, 1861-1865—Fiction   4. Girls—Fiction.

Avi. *Emily Upham's Revenge, or How Deadwood Dick Saved the Banker's Niece: A Massachusetts Adventure.* Illus. by Paul O. Zelinsky. Morrow (0-688-11898-4), 1992. 192p. (Interest level: 3-6).

In this spoof of bandits and bank robbers, Emily has an encounter with real thieves while living with her unscrupulous uncle. The melodramatic plot is set in Massachusetts in 1875.
♦ Students could write an additional adventure for Emily and read it aloud to the class.
1. Banking—Fiction   2. North Brookfield (Mass.)—Fiction   3. Massachusetts—Fiction.

Benchley, Nathaniel. *George, the Drummer Boy.* Illus. by Don Bolognese. HarperCollins (0-06-444106-7), 1987. 64p. (Interest level: K-3).

Told from the young redcoat's point of view, this story focuses on revolutionary events at Concord and Lexington. This is a good starter for a discussion on the many points of view of war.
♦ Consider using this book with Benchley's *Sam the Minuteman* (see following entry). Children can read both books and compare and contrast the two.
1. United States—History—Revolution, 1775-1783—Fiction 2. Massachusetts—History—Fiction.

Benchley, Nathaniel. *Sam the Minuteman.* Illus. by Arnold Lobel. Harper & Row (0-06-020480-X), 1969. 62p. Color illus. (Interest level: K-4).

This is an easy-to-read account of Sam and his father, who fought as Minutemen against the British in the Battle of Lexington.
♦ Since clothing design and materials have changed since colonial times, the class can discuss the methods and materials used to construct a Minuteman's uniform.
1. Lexington, Battle of, 1775—Fiction 2. Minutemen (Militia)—Fiction 3. United States—History—Revolution, 1775-1783—Fiction.

Bond, Nancy. *The Best of Enemies.* Atheneum (0-689-50108-0), 1978. 247p. (Interest level: 5-8).

Anticipating a lonely spring vacation because her parents and grown brothers and sister are preoccupied with their own pursuits, Charlotte becomes involved in Concord's annual Patriots' Day celebration.
♦ Students can plan a Patriots' Day celebration to be held at their school or in their community.
1. Family life—Fiction.

Bond, Nancy. *A Place to Come Back To.* McElderry (0-689-50302-4), 1984. 185p. (Interest level: 4-8).

Bond's description of growing up in Concord, Massachusetts, features well-developed characters. In this story, Charlotte Paige and Oliver Shattuck become very close until Oliver's mother remarries and moves to Washington, DC.
♦ Young people can write a descriptive essay about growing up, friendships, and what it feels like to lose a good friend.
1. Friendship—Fiction 2. Concord (Mass.)—History—Fiction 3. Massachusetts—Fiction.

Bond, Nancy. *The Voyage Begun.* Atheneum (0-689-50402-4), 1981. 319p. (Interest level: 5-8).

Living in the not-so-distant future, when the energy supply has been almost depleted, a teenage boy explores the deserted colonies near his father's Cape Cod research station and begins to understand the long-term effects of recent climate and weather changes and environmental pollution.
♦ Imagining the future, students can discuss how they think the world will function as the energy supply is depleted. They can also create charts and graphs to show the supply of and demand for different types of energy.
1. Ecology—Fiction 2. Pollution—Fiction.

Christian, Mary Blount. *Goody Sherman's Pig.* Illus. by Dirk Zimmer. Macmillan (0-02-718251-7), 1991. 48p. (Interest level: 4-6).

This is a vividly written fictional account of the little-known historical figure Goody Sherman, whose legal battle to replace her pig resulted in the reorganization of the Massachusetts legislature into two separate voting bodies.
♦ Students can use this book to research colonial life and historical fiction. After discussing the characteristics of historical fiction, children can try writing a short story.
1. United States—Politics and government—Fiction 2. Massachusetts—Fiction 3. Pigs—Fiction.

Clapp, Patricia. *Constance: A Story of Early Plymouth.* Illus. by Betty Frazer. Lothrop, Lee & Shepard (0-688-51127-9), 1968. 255p. (Interest level: 5-8).

Clapp's historical novel is based on a journal that records a 15-year-old girl's journey from London and the hardships and stern pleasures of colonial life in Massachusetts.
♦ As they read the story, students can keep their own journals, thinking and writing about how they would have felt journeying to a new country and their experiences as new settlers.
1. Pilgrims (New England colonists)—Fiction 2. Massachusetts—History—Colonial period, ca 1600-1775—Fiction.

Clapp, Patricia. *Witches' Children: A Story of Salem.* Puffin (0-14-032407-0), 1987. 160p. (Interest level: 4-8).

Here is a fictional account of the Salem witch story. The focus of this book is on the feelings and motives of the young girls whose imagination inspired community-wide hysteria.
♦ The class can discuss how hysteria can influence people.
1. Salem (Mass.)—History—Fiction 2. United States—History—Colonial period, ca 1600-1776—Fiction 3. Witchcraft—Fiction.

Clarke, Mary Stetson. *The Limner's Daughter.* Viking, 1967 (out of print). 256p. (Interest level: 5-8).

Set in the early 1800s, this novel is about a young woman who must cope with an endless series of tragedies and adventures. The woman seems to be

haunted by her family's mysterious role in the American Revolution.
- ♦ Young people can write additional adventures for the young woman. They should do research to make sure their story is historically accurate.
1. Woburn (Mass.)—History—Fiction.

Collier, James Lincoln and **Collier, Christopher.** *The Winter Hero.* Scholastic (0-590-42604-4), 1985. 132p. (Interest level: 5-8).

The Colliers' story focuses on a 14-year-old who serves as a spy and joins Shay's band, fighting for a lost cause against unjust taxation by the Massachusetts General Court.
- ♦ Students can research how unjust taxation could be fought today.
1. Shay's Rebellion—Fiction 2. Springfield (Mass.)—History—Fiction.

Cooney, Ellen. *Small Town Girl.* Houghton, 1983 (out of print). 184p. (Interest level: 5-8).

Cooney has written a sensitive story about growing up in central Massachusetts during the 1960s, when social injustice, the threat of nuclear war, and the assassination of President John F. Kennedy preoccupied everyone's thoughts.
- ♦ This novel provides excellent background information on the atmosphere of the time. Students could write an essay supported by research on the issues and events that have characterized the 1990s as this book reflects the 1960s.
1. Massachusetts—Fiction 2. United States—History—1961-1974—Fiction.

Corcoran, Barbara. *The Hideaway.* Macmillan (0-689-31353-5), 1987. 128p. (Interest level: 6-8).

An 18-year-old runaway from a security facility who was involved in a drunk-driving accident eventually finds out who are true friends.
- ♦ This high-interest, low-reading level book can be used to initiate discussions on social issues, such as runaways, homelessness, and drunk driving.
1. Runaways—Fiction 2. Massachusetts—Fiction.

Dalgliesh, Alice. *The Courage of Sarah Noble.* Scribner (0-684-18830-9), 1987, 1954. 64p. (Interest level: 1-5).

Eight-year-old Sarah accompanies her father to look for a new homesite on the Connecticut frontier. After the new home is built, Sarah stays behind with friendly Indians while her father returns to Massachusetts to retrieve the rest of the family.
- ♦ Use this book to initiate a discussion of the rigors of frontier life and the role of women in colonial times.
1. Massachusetts—History—Fiction 2. United States—History—Colonial period, ca 1600-1776—Fiction 3. Frontier life—Fiction.

Dalgliesh, Alice. *The Thanksgiving Story.* Illus. by Helen Sewell. Charles Scribner's Sons (0-684-18999-2), 1988, 1954. 32p. Color illus. (Interest level: K-4).

This work provides a look at the first Thanksgiving. Dalgliesh focuses on the Hopkins family and their reaction to the journey and the settlement.
- ♦ After reading and discussing the story, students can write and perform a play about the first Thanksgiving. They may also want to prepare some of the foods from the first Thanksgiving to use in their play. Or, students can trace the voyage that the Pilgrims took in coming to this land.
1. Holidays—Thanksgiving Day—Fiction 2. Pilgrims (New England colonists)—Fiction.

Devlin, Wendy and **Devlin, Harvey.** *Cranberry Thanksgiving.* (Videocassette or Combined entry). Spoken Arts, n.d. 1 videocassette, VHS; or 1 audiocassette and hardcover book. $44.95 for video; $23.90 for read-along. (12 min.). (Interest level: K-3).

In this mystery story, someone is trying to steal Grandma's secret cranberry-bread recipe. The book can be used in a discussion of Thanksgiving or cranberries, a major Massachusetts crop.
- ♦ Included with the package are cranberry recipes, which students can prepare and share.
1. Cranberries—Fiction 2. Thanksgiving Day—Fiction.

Forbes, Esther. *Johnny Tremain.* Illus. by Lynd Ward. Houghton Mifflin (0-690-82677-X), 1943. 256p. (Interest level: 5-8).

Forbes tells the story of a young Boston apprentice during the exciting time of the Boston Tea Party, culminating in the Battle of Lexington. The book gives a clear, vivid picture of a great period in American history.
- ♦ Children can discuss the reasons behind the Boston Tea Party and then decide on a cause that they think would warrant a "tea party."
1. United States—History—Revolution, 1775-1783—Fiction 2. Boston (Mass.)—Fiction.

Fritz, Jean. *Early Thunder.* Illus. by Lynd Ward. Puffin (0-14-032259-0), 1987. 255p. illus. (Interest level: 5-8).

Fritz deals with the tensions that led up to the Revolutionary War and a 14-year-old's attempt to come to terms with himself and make the decision to support his chosen side. This is a powerful, well-researched story with dramatic drawings.
- ♦ This book provides excellent background information that could support a debate or discussion between students taking on the roles of the Tories and the revolutionaries.

1. Salem (Mass.)—History—Fiction 2. United States—History—Colonial period, ca 1600-1775—Fiction.

Harness, Cheryl. *Three Young Pilgrims.* Bradbury (0-02-742643-2), 1992. 40p. B/W illus. (Interest level: K-5).

Harness's fictional story about three children who sailed on the *Mayflower* reflects on their first year in the colony. Time lines, charts, and a bibliography make this a useful research tool for grades 3-5. This is also a good read-aloud for K-3.
♦ Readers could pretend they are one of these children and keep a journal of their trip. They could also write a letter home to a friend describing their life in the colony.
1. Pilgrims—Fiction 2. Massachusetts—History—New Plymouth, 1620-1691—Fiction 3. Thanksgiving Day—Fiction.

Hayes, Wilma Pitchford. *Pilgrims to the Rescue.* Illus. by Marilyn Miller. Ives Washburn (02-0117355), 1971. 47p. Color illus. (Interest level: K-4).

The passengers of the stranded ship *Hawk* spent their first Christmas on Cape Cod. Later they were rescued by the Plymouth Pilgrims.
♦ After reading this story aloud, students can discuss other Christmas customs, carols, foods, and poems.
1. Cape Cod (Mass.)—History—Fiction 2. Christmas—Fiction

Heidish, Marcy Moran. *Witnesses: A Novel.* Ballantine (0-345-29742-3), 1983. 224p. (Interest level: grade 8-adult).

This is a dramatic novel about religious conflict in the 1630s in the Massachusetts Bay Colony. The focus is on the beliefs and practices of Anne Hutchinson and Goody Benedict, which led to Anne's imprisonment and eventual exile.
♦ Young adults can discuss what happens when individual beliefs conflict with prevailing community beliefs.
1. Massachusetts—History, 1600-1691—Fiction.

Hightower, Florence. *The Secret of the Crazy Quilt.* Illus. by Beth Krush and Joe Krush. Houghton, 1972 (out of print). 160p. (Interest level: 5-8).

By decoding a secret message in an old quilt, 13-year-old Jerusha and her Aunt Edith uncover an old mystery linking illegal acts during Prohibition with Nazi sabotage attempts.
♦ Students can create their own quilt with a message. When completed, the quilt could be displayed in a prominent place in the school so that other students could try to decipher the message.
1. Massachusetts—History—Fiction 2. Mystery and detective stories.

Langton, Jane. *The Diamond in the Window.* Illus. by Erik Blegvad. Peter Smith (0-8446-6414-6), 1962. 242p. (Interest level: 5-8).

Langton's story mixes transcendentalism with humorous fantasy in a mystery that relies on a secret room, a riddle, and a search for lost treasure.
♦ Young people can write their own mystery stories, withholding the endings. Classmates could attempt to solve the mystery using the clues provided in the story.
1. Concord (Mass.)—Fiction 2. Mystery and detective stories 3. Transcendentalism—Fiction.

Langton, Jane. *The Fledgling.* Illus. by Erik Blegvad. Harper & Row (0-06-023678-7), 1980. 182p. (Interest level: 3-6).

Eight-year-old Georgie lives with her mother, stepfather, orphaned cousins, and assorted animals in Concord, Massachusetts, where her stepfather runs the Concord College of Transcendental Knowledge. Georgie is determined to learn to fly despite her family's opposition. Her meeting with a great Canada goose fulfills her wish, but not without danger.
♦ Young people can locate Walden Pond on a map of Massachusetts and find out who Henry Thoreau and Ralph Waldo Emerson were. After discussing their dreams and Georgie's dream, students can write about their own dreams.
1. Canada goose—Fiction 2. Flight—Fiction 3. Fantasy.

Lasky, Kathryn. *Tugboats Never Sleep.* Illus. by Christopher B. Knight. Little, 1977 (out of print). 48p. Illus. (Interest level: K-3).

A young boy, Jason, experiences tugboat life through visits and stories by the crew. Well-done illustrations enhance the text.
♦ Children can write a tugboat adventure, create a model of a tugboat, or illustrate a facet of tugboat life.
1. Boston (Mass.)—Harbor—Fiction 2. Tugboats—Fiction.

Lawrence, Mildred. *Touchmark.* Illus. by Deanne Hollinger. Harcourt Brace Jovanovich, 1975 (out of print). 186p. (Interest level: 5-8).

Abigail, a 14-year-old indentured servant, learns the pewter craft and helps the rebel cause by distracting British soldiers while Paul Revere rows across the river to begin his ride. Designing pewterware becomes her ambition during a time when women were not encouraged to learn a trade.
♦ Students can compare women's roles in society in the 1700s with their roles today, for example, women in politics, women in the military, and women in traditionally male-dominated professions.

1. Massachusetts—History—Fiction 2. United States—History—Revolution, 1775-1783—Fiction 3. Women—Employment—Fiction.

Lowry, Lois. *Taking Care of Terrific.* Houghton Mifflin (0-395-34070-5), 1983. 160p. (Interest level: 4-8).

This is the humorous story of young Enid, who spends a summer baby-sitting a four-year-old, chiefly at Boston's Public Garden. They meet and befriend numerous characters in a story that focuses on human worth.
♦ Lowry's book provides an excellent basis for a discussion of social issues.
1. Massachusetts—Social life and customs—Fiction 2. Boston (Mass.)—Public Garden—Fiction.

McCloskey, Robert. *Make Way for Ducklings.* Illus. by author. Viking Press (0-670451-49-5), 1941. 67p. Color illus. (Interest level: K-4).

Mr. and Mrs. Mallard have a family of eight ducklings and then return to Boston Public Garden.
♦ Children can complete a creative writing activity about some other adventures for the ducklings.
1. Ducks—Fiction 2. Boston (Mass.)—Fiction.

McCloskey, Robert. *Make Way for Ducklings.* (Combined entry). Weston Woods, 1968. 1 audiocassette, (11 min.). $30.00 read-along cassette; $22.95 hardback book; $13.95 paperback book. (Interest level: K-4).

After raising her ducklings on an island in Boston's Charles River, Mrs. Mallard leads her brood to their permanent home in the Boston Public Garden.
♦ Students can research and discuss how different animals protect their young. Compare the dangers ducklings face crossing a large city like Boston with the dangers human children face.
1. Ducks—Fiction 2. Boston (Mass.)—Fiction.

O'Connor, Edwin. *The Last Hurrah.* Little (0-316-62659-7), 1985. 448p. (Interest level: 3-6).

O'Connor's novel chronicles the life of James Michael Curley and his political development and influence among the people of Massachusetts.
♦ Students could discuss political manipulation today. How do politicians and the media manipulate people?
1. Boston (Mass.)—Politicians—Fiction 2. Massachusetts—Politics and government—Fiction.

Ox-Cart Man. (Videocassette). Live Oak Media (0-87499-079-3). VHS, (8 min.). $34.95. (Interest level: K-3).

Lorne Greene relates Donald Hall's account of family life in nineteenth-century New England, and LeVar Burton visits Old Sturbridge Village, Massachusetts, a hands-on living museum of the 1800s. Barbara Cooney's marvelous illustrations enhance the story.
♦ Students can visit a historical museum in their community.
1. United States—History—Colonial period, ca 1600-1776—Fiction.

Paterson, Katherine. *Lyddie.* Lodestar Books (0-525-67338-5), 1991. 182p. (Interest level: 5-8).

Paterson tells the story of Lyddie, a factory worker in the 1840s in Massachusetts.
♦ Readers can make a time line, starting with the 1840s, outlining factory conditions and mill equipment. Discuss how factory conditions have changed today.
1. Self-reliance—Fiction 2. Work—Fiction 3. Factories—Fiction 4. Historical fiction.

Petry, Ann. *Tituba of Salem Village.* Crowell (0-690-82677-X), 1964. 254p. (Interest level: 5-8).

Petry tells the story of a slave, Tituba, and her husband, John Indian, from the day they were sold in Barbados until the tragic Salem witchcraft trials.
♦ Students can conduct further research on the Salem witchcraft trials.
1. Salem (Mass.)—Fiction 2. Witchcraft—Fiction.

PilgrimQuest. (CD-ROM). Decision Development Corporation, 1992. 1 CD-ROM. $129.95 for school version. (Interest level: 3-adult).

This is an interactive simulation game in which players attempt to sustain their colony as they confront situations and choices faced by the original Pilgrims. Players must consider the distribution of wealth, basic needs, nourishment, the perils of travel, government, and trade and production of goods. Some of the skills this game tests are map and graph reading and knowledge of basic physical geography.
♦ Children can play the game and discuss strategies they develop for survival.
1. Pilgrims (New England colonists)—Social life—Fiction.

Rinaldi, Ann. *A Break with Charity: A Story of the Salem Witch Trials.* Harcourt Brace Jovanovich (0-15-200353-3), 1992. 288p. (Interest level: 5-8).

Told from the point of view of an ancestor of Nathaniel Hawthorne, this story gives a plausible explanation for the Salem witch trials. The book is well researched and well written.
♦ Students can conduct further research on the Salem witch trials. The bibliography and notes contained in this book are a good place to start their research.
1. Salem (Mass.)—History—Fiction 2. United States—History, Colonial period, ca 1600-1775—Fiction 3. Witchcraft—Fiction.

Tresselt, Alvin. *Hide and Seek Fog.* Illus. by Roger Duvoisin. Lothrop, Lee & Shepard (0-688-51169-

4), 1965. Unpaginated. Color illus. (Interest level: K-4).

Tresselt's book contains reactions of children and grown-ups to a three-day fog at a seaside village on Cape Cod.
♦ Read the story aloud, and then discuss the combination of weather conditions that must be present in order to have foggy weather.
1. Fog—Fiction   2. Cape Cod (Mass.)—Fiction.

Turkle, Brinton. *The Advent of Obadiah.* Puffin (0-14-050794-9), 1987. Unpaginated. Illus. (Interest level: K-3).

Obadiah is a very imaginative young Quaker boy living on Nantucket Island in colonial days. The illustrations in this book are exceptional.
♦ This is an excellent read-aloud. Students can learn or make up stories to tell to other students. The story also would be a good introduction to a discussion of the difference between lies and creative storytelling.
1. Nantucket Island (Mass.)—History—Fiction
2. Massachusetts—History—Colonial period, ca 1600-1775—Fiction   3. Society of Friends—Fiction.

Turkle, Brinton. *Rachel and Obadiah.* Dutton (0-525-38020-5), 1978. Unpaginated. Illus. (Interest level: K-3).

Rachel competes against her brother, Obadiah, to determine who will be the messenger to report when ships arrive in the harbor. Rachel wins the race and shares the reward. Illustrations reveal Obadiah's changing reactions.
♦ This story is a variation on the tortoise and the hare tale and serves as a basis for discussion.
1. Nantucket Island (Mass.)—History—Fiction
2. Massachusetts—History—Colonial period, ca 1600-1775—Fiction   3. Society of Friends—Fiction.

Turkle, Brinton. *Thy Friend, Obadiah.* Illus. by author. Penguin (0-14-050393-5), 1969. Unpaginated. Color illus. (Interest level: K-3).

Obadiah, a Quaker boy, becomes friends with a seagull who lives on Nantucket Island.
♦ Students can find Nantucket on the map and briefly study Quaker history.
1. Gulls—Fiction   2. Nantucket (Mass.)—Fiction
3. Friends, Society of—Fiction   4. United States—History—Colonial period, ca 1600-1775—Fiction.

Voigt, Cynthia. *The Callender Papers.* Macmillan (0-689-30971-6), 1983. 224p. (Interest level: 5-8).

Voigt's novel is set in the Berkshire region of Massachusetts in 1894. For a summer job, Jean is helping to organize a collection of family papers, which slowly reveal a mystery of death and disappearance.
♦ Students can write their own mystery and detective stories after a discussion of the elements of such stories.
1. Massachusetts—Berkshire Mountains—Fiction
2. Mystery and detective stories.

Wibberley, Leonard. *John Treegate's Musket.* Peter Smith (0-8446-665-6), 1951. 188p. (Interest level: 5-8).

This novel is the fictionalized story of Peter Treegate, son of the famous John Treegate. A powerful series of adventures leads Peter back to Boston to see his father take down his musket to fight against the British.
♦ Wibberley's book provides background information on the events leading up to the Revolutionary War and colonial life and challenges. Students could pretend they are Peter and write a letter to a friend describing their thoughts and feelings about the war and their father's involvement.
1. Massachusetts—History—Fiction   2. United States—History—Colonial period, ca 1600-1775—Fiction.

Professional Materials

973
Giese, James R. and Parisi, Lynn S. *A Humanities Approach to Early National U.S. History: Activities and Resources for the Junior High School Teacher.* Social Science Education Consortium, 1986. ERIC, ED 274 612. 181p. (Interest level: Professional).

This resource uses an integrated humanities perspective for teaching U.S. history. Twenty-eight titles and activities are listed, which relate to topics such as the Boston Massacre, New England daily life, churchyards and gravestones, and architecture.
♦ Students can identify and compare lifestyles, do map reading, and sing songs.
1. United States—History—Colonial period, ca 1600-1775   2. Social history.

New Hampshire

by Linda Mack

Nonfiction

289
Sprigg, June. *Shaker Life, Work and Art.* Photos by Michael Freeman. Stewart, Tabori & Chang (1-55670-011-3), 1987. 272p. B/W and Color photos. (Interest level: 4-8).

All aspects of Shaker life are preserved in this collection of pictures depicting daily routine, history, communal work, and worship in villages from Maine to Kentucky, with numerous references to one of the last remaining Shaker communities in Canterbury, New Hampshire. Large color photographs with captioned explanations make this excellent source of information accessible to even younger readers.
♦ Young people could design and create a replica of a tool, piece of furniture, container, household good or fabric shown in the book.
1. Shakers.

289
Thompson, Nancy M. *Learning about Shakers for Young People.* Illus. by Jane Cowen-Fletcher. Pleasant Grove (No ISBN), 1988. 36p. B/W illus. and maps. (Interest level: 2-6).

The history, education, beliefs, inventions, music, food, architecture, and children of Shaker Village in East Canterbury, New Hampshire, are described from its establishment in 1792. Written from personal experience by a public school teacher residing in the community, this wonderful collection of samples of Shaker life is presented in a clear format accompanied by activity instructions and patterns.
♦ Using the map and building patterns provided in the book, students may work with others to create a model of the Shaker Village in Canterbury as it appears today.
1. Shakers.

289.8
Bollick, Nancy O'Keefe. *Shaker Inventions.* Illus. by Melissa Francisco. Walker and Company (0-8027-6934-9), 1990. 96p. B/W illus. and maps. (Interest level: 4-8).

Inventions inspired by the orderly life of the Shakers in Canterbury, New Hampshire; Pittsfield, Massachusetts; and other communities are described and illustrated. The usefulness of each tool is related to its purpose and place in Shaker life, providing an understanding of the ingenuity of this unique religious sect.
♦ Each student can select one Shaker invention currently in use and describe how it makes daily life easier. Others may wish to invent a simple tool that streamlines daily tasks.
1. Shakers.

289.8
Yolen, Jane. *Simple Gifts: The Story of the Shakers.* Illus. by Betty Fraser. Viking (0-670-64584-2), 1976. 116p. B/W illus. (Interest level: 6-8).

The establishment, existence, and decline of the Shakers to the two remaining communities in Sabbathday Lake, Maine, and Canterbury, New Hampshire, are traced from their immigration from England in 1774. This detailed history provides authentic descriptions of Shaker life, researched and experienced by the author, including rituals, songs, dances, and crafts.
♦ Readers may examine the rise and decline of the Shaker community by creating and illustrating a time line of Shaker history in New England.
1. Shakers.

333.73
Wyzga, Marilyn. *Exploring the Land We Call New Hampshire: An Activity Guide.* Photos by Bill Finney, Alison Forbes, and Ernie Gould. New Hampshire Historical Society and the Society for the Protection of New Hampshire Forests (No ISBN),

1992. 33p. B/W illus., photos, and maps. (Interest level: 4-8).

Wyzga's booklet explores the history of land use in the New Hampshire communities of Portsmouth, Walpole, Manchester, White Mountains, Berlin, and the Weirs and Lake Winnipesaukee using five geographical themes. The heavily illustrated guide, designed to be used in conjunction with a visit to the exhibit at the New Hampshire Historical Society, contains a wealth of information and activities for the study of New Hampshire history and geography by individuals and small and large groups.
♦ Children may choose any one of the activities suggested in the guide.
1. Land use—New Hampshire—History.

342.73
New Hampshire: The State That Made Us a Nation—A Celebration of the Bicentennial of the United States Constitution. Peter E. Randall (0-914339-28-1), 1989. 273p. B/W and Color photos. (Interest level: 7-8).

This publication commemorates New Hampshire's celebration of the 200th anniversary of the ratification of the U.S. Constitution. Written by experts, it examines regional histories of the state and changes after the American Revolution, and describes Bicentennial Commission activities previously held in the state.
♦ Young people might re-create the New Hampshire Convention to ratify the U.S. Constitution that took place in February 1788.
1. United States—Constitutional history 2. New Hampshire—Constitutional history.

398.2
Bruchac, Joseph. *Return of the Sun: Native American Tales from the Northeast Woodlands.* Illus. by Gary Carpenter. Crossing (0-89594-344-1), 1989. 204p. B/W illus. (Interest level: 4-8).

Traditional stories of the Onondaga, Tuscarora, Penobscot, Seneca, Oneida, Mahican, Anishinabe, Abenaki, and Passamaquoddy Indians of the northeast woodlands are retold in this collection of Native American folktales. Short versions of already printed stories convey the spirit and identity of each tribe in large-print format followed by a glossary of terms at the end of the book.
♦ After reading a selection of folktales from the book, each student can choose and practice one story to retell in the oral tradition.
1. Woodland Indians—Legends 2. Indians of North America—Northeast states—Legends.

398.2
Cohlene, Terri. *Little Firefly: An Algonquian Legend.* Illus. by Charles Reasoner. Rourke (0-86593-005-8), 1990. (Native American Legends Series).

48p. B/W and Color illus., photos, and maps. (Interest level: K-4).

The Algonquian Indians lived in the northeast woodlands from the shores of the Great Lakes to the Atlantic Ocean. This retelling of the legend of a young girl who is mistreated by her family and later becomes the bride of a great hunter is followed by a section of factual information on the history, customs, and other aspects of Algonquian life.
♦ Class members may wish to script a play, design scenery, create props, and plan a performance based on this Native American story.
1. Indians of North America—Legends 2. Algonquian Indians—Legends 3. Indians of North America—Social life and customs 4. Algonquian Indians—Social life and customs.

398.8
Hastings, Scott E., Jr., ed. *Miss Mary Mac All Dressed in Black: Tongue Twisters, Jump-Rope Rhymes and Other Children's Lore from New England.* August (0-87483-156-3), 1990. 159p. B/W illus. (Interest level: K-adult).

Collected primarily from teachers and students in Vermont and a few from western New Hampshire on the border of the two states, jump rope rhymes, counting rhymes, tongue twisters, and more make up this book. These entertaining and fun examples, which came from children ages 7-14, provide a unique look at folk culture and oral tradition.
♦ Children can present rhymes from the book orally or teach them to a group.
1. Children—Vermont—Folklore 2. Folklore—Vermont 3. Children—New England—Folklore 4. Jump rope rhymes—Vermont 5. Counting-out rhymes—Vermont.

624
DuPont, Irene E. *Spanning Time: New Hampshire Covered Bridges.* Photos by author. Irene Dupont (No ISBN), 1986. 64p. B/W photos. (Interest level: K-8).

Fifty-three covered bridges in New Hampshire, representative of various early American styles, are presented in large, high-quality photographs. An entry for each includes the bridge number, span type, length, date built, and the specific location or construction history. Readers of all ages will enjoy reading and looking at this tribute to engineering.
♦ Students may build a scale model of one of the covered bridges shown in the book.
1. Bridges—New Hampshire 2. New Hampshire—History, Local.

641.3
The Maple Sugaring Story. (Videocassette). Perceptions, 1989. VHS, (29 min.). $29.95. (Interest level: 2-8).

The history, production, and use of maple syrup are related through pictures, music, and action. Viewers of this award-winning video, which combines legend, science, history, and geography, will gain an appreciation of a regional agricultural tradition.
♦ After finding and collecting recipes, children may plan a maple syrup party for parents, serving dishes they have prepared themselves. A cookbook containing these recipes could then be compiled and printed for distribution.
1. Maple sugar.

641.5
Perl, Lila. *Slumps, Grunts, and Snickerdoodles: What Colonial America Ate and Why.* Illus. by Richard Cuffari. Clarion Books (0-395-28923-8), 1975. 125p. B/W illus. and maps. (Interest level: 4-8).

Foods of New England, the Middle Atlantic colonies, and southern colonies are examined for their cultural and social contributions to colonial America. Thirteen authentic recipes are provided, with fascinating stories of the origins of such traditional dishes as succotash, johnnycake, Indian pudding, red flannel hash, corn oysters, and apple pandowdy.
♦ Each student may choose one of the recipes from the book to prepare and serve.
1. Cookery, American   2. United States—Social life and customs—Colonial period, ca 1600-1775.

680
Wilbur, C. Keith. *Indian Handcrafts: How to Craft Dozens of Practical Objects Using Traditional Indian Techniques.* Illus. by author. Globe Pequot Press (0-87106-496-0), 1990. 144p. B/W illus. (Interest level: grade 2-adult).

Descriptions and illustrated directions for making many different kinds of tools, implements, toys, clothes, ornaments, and other items are provided with great detail and appreciation for the Native American way of life. Collecting and utilizing natural materials to craft these items will appeal to those who enjoy hands-on activities.
♦ Following the instructions provided in the book, young people may craft an Algonquian Indian possession using natural New Hampshire materials.
1. Indians of North America—Industries   2. Handicraft—North America.

727
Hillis, Mary Carroll, comp. *Goffstown's One Room Schoolhouses Remembered.* Goffstown Historical Society (No ISBN), 1989. 57p. B/W photos. (Interest level: 6-8).

Sixteen Goffstown, New Hampshire, schoolhouses in use from 1851 to 1960 are described through excerpts from annual town reports, memories of local residents, and old photographs. Entries for each school contain an annotated chronology, information about the teachers' salaries and performance, number of students attending, ownership of the building, renovations made, and current status.
♦ The class could research and write a detailed history of its own school.
1. School buildings—Goffstown (N.H.)—History
2. Goffstown (N.H.)—History, Local.

811
Sarton, May. *As Does New Hampshire and Other Poems by May Sarton.* William L. Bauhan (0-87233-098-2), 1987. 61p. B/W photos. (Interest level: 7-8).

Reissued after being out of print, these 31 poems by accomplished writer May Sarton commemorate the people, land, and seasonal events of the small New Hampshire village in which she resided. The beauty and serenity of country life are sensitively conveyed through verse and black-and-white photographs.
♦ Each student could write a poem about some aspect of life in New Hampshire and illustrate it.
1. New Hampshire—Poetry   2. American poetry.

811.52
Frost, Robert. *Stopping by Woods on a Snowy Evening.* Illus. by Susan Jeffers. Dutton (0-525-40115-6), 1978. Unpaginated. B/W and Color illus. (Interest level: K-2).

This picture-book version of the familiar poem by one of New Hampshire's well-known poets conveys the magic of a snowy evening in the New England woods. Black-and-white background illustrations with soft touches of color accompany each line of the poem, representing the patterns and feathery textures of a forest at wintry dusk.
♦ Young people may illustrate a wintry New Hampshire scene by sponge painting white tempera onto black construction paper around cutouts of trees, animals, houses, and other objects they have made.
1. Winter—Poetry   2. American poetry.

912
The New Hampshire Atlas & Gazetteer. DeLorme Mapping Company (0-89933-004-5), 1988. 88p. B/W and Color maps. (Interest level: 4-8).

Area maps of the state and city street maps are provided as well as lists and descriptions of recreational areas, the arts and museums, and historic sites. Large-scale maps with easy-to-read detail provide valuable information about where to go and how to get there in New Hampshire.
♦ On a state map of New Hampshire, young people may wish to locate 10 of the museums or historic sites featured in the atlas.

1. New Hampshire—Maps 2. New Hampshire—Description and travel.

917.4
Duggan, Moira. *New England.* Gallery Books (0-8317-8842-9), 1990. Unpaginated. Color photos. (Interest level: 5-8).

Back roads, picturesque scenery, traditional architecture, and historic sites are captured in color pictures of Connecticut, Maine, Massachusetts, Rhode Island, New Hampshire, and Vermont. Brief text and captions describe more than 100 excellent photographs and inform readers about regional history, discovery, and early settlers.
♦ Readers can identify one of the photographs taken in New Hampshire and write a descriptive paragraph about it, indicating its location and possible historical significance.
1. New England.

917.4
Over New England. (Videocassette). KCTS-TV, 1992. VHS, (60 min.). $19.95. (Interest level: 5-8).

Aerial views of landscapes and landmarks of Connecticut, Maine, Massachusetts, New Hampshire, Rhode Island, and Vermont reveal the beauty and character of the six New England states. For each state, the video provides brief narrative passages, references to literature that describe the area, and captions identifying individual towns.
♦ After viewing the video, young people could choose one place of interest and research its history.
1. New England—Description and travel.

917.4
Schuman, Michael A. *New England's Special Places: Easy Outings to Historic Villages, Working Museums, Presidential Homes, Castles, and Other Year-Round Attractions.* Countryman Press (0-88150-152-2), 1990. 215p. B/W photos and maps. (Interest level: 6-8).

The author's visits to 50 destinations in six states are related in this adventure guide to New England, as well as historical and contact information about each site. Each attraction was included for its ability to offer historical insights and quality displays.
♦ Young people may wish to write about their experiences after visiting one of the New Hampshire locations described in the book. Choices include Castle in the Clouds in Moultonboro, New England Ski Museum in Franconia, Currier Gallery of Art in Manchester, Fort No. 4 in Charlestown, Strawberry Banke in Portsmouth, or Shaker Village in Canterbury. Using the book as a model, students outside of New Hampshire may write an entry for a special place in their own state, including a comprehensive description, photograph or drawing, location with directions, cost of admission, hours, and where to write for information.
1. New England—Description and travel—Guidebooks 2. Historic sites—New England—Guidebooks.

917.4
Tree, Christina and **Randall, Peter.** *New Hampshire: An Explorer's Guide.* Countryman Press (0-88150-200-6), 1991. B/W photos and maps. (Interest level: 6-8).

Organized regionally, Tree and Randall's guide to exploring New Hampshire describes the landscape and local history with an emphasis on covered bridges, museums, and historical houses. The authors spent 10 years visiting fairs, restaurants, recreational and educational facilities, and historic sites to produce this comprehensive and useful handbook.
♦ Using this book as a model, students could create and publish an explorer's guide for their own community, including places of interest and historical significance.
1. New Hampshire—Description and travel—Guidebooks.

917.42
Rogers, Barbara Radcliffe. *New Hampshire: Off the Beaten Path.* Globe Pequot Press (1-56440-023-9), 1992. 147p. B/W illus. (Interest level: 6-8).

The seacoast, Merrimack Valley, Monadnock, Cartmouth-Sunapee, Lakes & Foothills, White Mountains, and North Country are described in detail in this travel guide to some of New Hampshire's most interesting and obscure places. Brief histories of the areas are combined with current price and booking information for meals, lodging, and points of interest.
♦ Using this guide, young people may plan a field trip, including a place to eat, lodging, and a visit to a historic site. The plan must include a determination of the best travel route and cost of the trip.
1. New Hampshire—Description and travel—Guidebooks.

917.42
This Is New Hampshire. (Videocassette). Cineworks Productions, 1989. VHS, (30 min.). $19.95. (Interest level: 4-8).

New Hampshire's people and places are depicted through the seasons in this visual documentation of picturesque landscapes from the seacoast to the mountains. Produced with musical accompaniment and no narration, this video gives viewers a brief glimpse of many well-known locations in the state.
♦ As a conclusion to the study of the state history or geography unit, students may enjoy seeing how many of the locations on the video they can

917.78
Mudge, John T. B. *The White Mountains: Names, Places and Legends.* Durand Press (0-9633560-0-3), 1992. 187p. B/W and Color illus. and maps. (Interest level: 7-8).

Painters, photographers, noted personalities, geographical landmarks, towns, and places of interest are featured in this extensive glossary of the White Mountains of New Hampshire. Fairly lengthy entries are interlaced with chronicles, legends, maps, and illustrations, giving a sense of how visitors of the past helped shape the history of the region.
♦ Working in groups, young people can compile an illustrated glossary of interesting, unusual, or historical people and sites in their own community.
1. Names, Geographical—White Mountains (N.H. and Me.) 2. White Mountains (N.H. and Me.)—History, Local.

917.78
Whitehouse, Bion H. *Central Square and Beyond: Historical Images of Keene and Cheshire County.* Historical Society of Cheshire County (No ISBN), 1992. 140p. B/W photos. (Interest level: 5-8).

Keene, New Hampshire, is in a valley noted for its forests, ponds, fishing streams, hills, and Mount Monadnock. Black-and-white captioned photographs featuring the work of resident artist-photographer Bion H. Whitehouse capture the traditions, Yankee ingenuity, and beauty of this region.
♦ Students may wish to learn to use a 35mm camera to take black-and-white photographs for a pictorial essay about their own community.
1. Keene (N.H.)—History 2. Keene (N.H.)—Description 3. Cheshire County (N.H.)—Description.

940.54
Koop, Allen V. *Stark Decency.* University Press of New England (0-87451-458-4), 1988. 136p. B/W photos. (Interest level: 7-8).

The small logging town of Stark, New Hampshire, in the White Mountains hosted a German POW camp during World War II, feeding and clothing the prisoners and helping them acquire skills. This inspiring story reveals the friendships that developed among prisoners, guards, and villagers during the existence of Camp Stark.
♦ After reading the book, young people may evaluate the decision to locate a prisoner-of-war camp in this tiny New Hampshire town, considering the impact on the community and alternative sites for such an institution.
1. World War, 1939-1945—Prisoners and prisons, American 2. Prisoners of war—New Hampshire—Stark 3. Prisoners of war—Germany 4. Stark (N.H.)—History.

970.004
Calloway, Colin G. *The Abenaki.* Chelsea House (1-55546-687-7), 1989. 112p. B/W and Color photos. (Interest level: 5-8).

The history of the native northern New England people of Maine, New Hampshire, and Vermont before and after exposure to European settlers is presented. This comprehensive account describes Native American life in the past and present and focuses on the clash of cultures, the transition, and changes the Abenaki have made to survive.
♦ Readers might write a story describing what life would be like for the Abenaki today if they had remained in their original New Hampshire locations.
1. Abenaki Indians 2. Indians of North America.

971.04
Wartik, Nancy. *The French Canadians.* Chelsea House (0-87754-879-X), 1990. 112p. B/W and Color illus. (Interest level: 6-8).

The experiences of French Canadian immigrants in New England and other regions are examined in detail. Emphasis is on the lives, customs, and traditions of the people of Quebec and the impact of their ethnic contributions on the futures of Canada and the United States.
♦ Students can interview a French Canadian immigrant or a person of French Canadian descent living in their own community.
1. French Canadians.

973.04
Siegel, Beatrice. *Indians of the Northeast Woodlands.* Illus. by William Sauts Bock. Walker (0-8027-8157-8), 1992. 96p. B/W illus. (Interest level: 1-6).

The way of life of the Algonquian Indians of the northeastern United States before and after the arrival of European settlers is explained in a question-and-answer format. Siegel's excellent source is filled with detailed descriptions that will interest younger readers and answer their questions about this Native American culture.
♦ Children could prepare a chart comparing aspects of northeast woodland Indian life before and after the arrival of European settlers.
1. Woodland Indians 2. Algonquian Indians 3. Indians of North America.

973.04
Wilbur, C. Keith. *The New England Indians.* Illus. by author. Globe Pequot Press (0-87106-004-3),

1978. 108p. B/W illus. and maps. (Interest level: grade 3-adult).

Wilbur's book spans 10,000 years of the history of New England Indians. Line drawings with fascinating detail show how the Native Americans of the region dressed, built shelters, grew crops, fished, hunted, cooked, made tools and weapons, treated disease, and traveled.
♦ Each student may choose a tool or implement shown in the book and describe how it solved one of the problems of daily survival for the Native Americans living in New England before European settlement.
1. Indians of North America—New England.

973.5
Sloane, Eric. *Diary of an Early American Boy: Noah Blake, 1805*. Illus. by author. Ballantine (0-345-32100-6), 1965. 108p. B/W illus. (Interest level: 6-8).

Based on the author's findings of a real diary dated 1805, this partially fictitious account describes early American life through the eyes of 15-year-old Noah Blake. Pages of superbly detailed pen-and-ink drawings and diagrams illustrate the tools, buildings, documents, and landscapes of the time.
♦ Young people can create a daily or yearly schedule indicating the activities and chores performed by Noah Blake on his country homestead.
1. United States—Social life and customs—1783-1865.

974
Aylesworth, Thomas G. and Aylesworth, Virginia L. *Northern New England: Maine, New Hampshire, Vermont*. Chelsea House (1-55546-551-X), 1988. 64p. Color photos, illus., and maps. (Interest level: 3-6).

The geography, history, and culture of Maine, Vermont, and New Hampshire are described using text, maps, and illustrated fact spreads. Highlights of the land, history, and people of each state are presented with limited text in a colorful and visually appealing format for young readers.
♦ Children could create and display a graphic aid, such as a poster, diagram, or chart, comparing one aspect of each of the northern New England states of Maine, New Hampshire, and Vermont.
1. New England 2. Maine 3. Vermont 4. New Hampshire.

974.1
Thaxter, Celia. *Celia's Island Journal*. Adapted and illus. by Loretta Krupinski. Little, Brown (0-316-83921-3), 1992. Unpaginated. Color illus. (Interest level: 1-3).

Celia Thaxter, mid-nineteenth century poet and writer, lived on White Island off the coast of New Hampshire for seven years as a child while her father was the lighthouse keeper. Fourteen journal entries and one poem describing her life there and her observations about the plant and animal life of the Isles of Shoals are beautifully illustrated with realistic paintings in this excellent adaptation.
♦ After reading this story, young people will study one of the plants or animals described by Celia Thaxter and write a nonfiction report.
1. Isles of Shoals (Me. and N.H.)—Description and travel. 2. Isles of Shoals (Me. and N.H.)—History 3. Thaxter, Celia, 1835-1894.

974.2
Bardwell, John D. and Bergeron, Ronald P. *The Lakes Region, New Hampshire: A Visual History*. Donning (0-89865-734-2), 1988. 192p. B/W and Color illus., photos, and maps. (Interest level: 7-8).

The complete history of the lakes region of New Hampshire is told from the time of the glacial formation of its natural features, Indians, explorers, and early settlers, to the introduction of railroads and steamboats, to the evolution of the area as a summer resort. Pages and pages of photographs accompany the text, providing extensive visual information about this popular vacation spot.
♦ Using the list of towns and lakes in the book, readers could plan, draw, and label a lakes region tourist map of their own.
1. Lakes—New Hampshire—Pictorial works 2. New Hampshire—Description and travel—Views.

974.2
Bardwell, John D. and Bergeron, Ronald P. *The White Mountains, New Hampshire: A Visual History*. Donning (0-89865-737-7), 1988. 200p. B/W and Color photos. (Interest level: 7-8).

The discovery by European explorers, settlement, and continuing development of the White Mountains region of scenic northern New Hampshire is covered in depth. Hundreds of archival photographs from local sources depict the mountains, notches, and rivers of the area along with outdoor recreational opportunities, industry, and folk heroes.
♦ Students can work in groups to compile an illustrated guidebook of New Hampshire mountains, indicating names, elevations, locations, recreational activities, and other special information.
1. White Mountains (N.H. and Me.)—Description and travel—Views 2. White Mountains (N.H. and Me.)—History—Pictorial works.

974.2
The Best of New Hampshire Crossroads. (Videocassette). New Hampshire Public Television, 1989. VHS, (60 min.). $19.95. (Interest level: 3-8).

This collection of programs from the popular television series features interesting New Hampshire people and places such as the Old Man in the Mountain, Shaker Village in Canterbury, Frye Measure Mill in Wilton, Appalachian Mountain Club hut in the White Mountains, basketmaker Sweetzer, and others. Narrated by Fritz Weatherbee, the video conveys the unique character and spirit of the people of the Granite State through visits and interviews.
♦ Class members may videotape selected individuals or places in their community to produce a local-interest program.
1. New Hampshire—History   2. New Hampshire—Description and travel.

974.2
Blaisdell, Katharine. *Over the River and through the Years for Children: Book One.* Sherwin/Dodge (No ISBN), 1985. 124p. B/W illus., photos, and maps. (Interest level 3-6).
The history of the Upper Connecticut Valley area of New Hampshire and Vermont from the early days to the mid-1800s is presented chronologically, followed by two chapters devoted to Native American neighbors and towns and villages. Photographs of artifacts, anecdotes about real people, and thought-provoking questions make the history of this region interesting and meaningful.
♦ The author invites readers to write her with corrections and suggestions. Children may enjoy writing to Katharine Blaisdell to make recommendations, ask her questions, or share what they like about her book.
1. Connecticut Valley (N.H. and Vt.)—History   2. New Hampshire—History   3. Vermont—History.

974.2
Clements, John. *Flying the Colors: New Hampshire Facts.* Clements Research (ISSN 0895-8114), 1987. 183p. Color illus.; B/W maps. (Interest level: 5-8).
Statistics about New Hampshire colleges, libraries, child care, people, roads, economy, community services, business regulations, major market areas, communication, transportation, chronology, water resources, and much more are furnished in this extensive compilation of data. Clements's comprehensive statistical volume may be useful for those requiring facts and figures about the state.
♦ Students can select significant data about New Hampshire to format and present as a graph.
1. New Hampshire—Statistics.

974.2
Fradin, Dennis B. *The New Hampshire Colony.* Childrens Press (0-516-00388-7), 1988. 144p. B/W illus., photos, and maps. (Interest level: 4-8).
Fradin traces the history of the state from the time of Native American settlements, through colonization by European settlers, to statehood as the ninth state in 1788. Descriptions of Algonquian life, biographical sketches of noted New Hampshire figures, and reproductions of historical documents combine with clear, concise text in a complete and informative account.
♦ The class could create a pictorial time line of early New Hampshire history.
1. New Hampshire—History—Colonial period, ca 1600-1775.

974.2
Fradin, Dennis Brindell. *New Hampshire.* Childrens Press (0-516-03829-X), 1992. 64p. B/W and Color photos and maps. (Interest level: 3-5).
History, geography, industries, sites of interest, and famous people are introduced in this overview of New Hampshire. Useful and accurate facts, although limited in scope, are arranged in an attractive format providing just enough information to make this resource especially appropriate for use with younger readers.
♦ While reading the book, young people can take notes to prepare an outline of information on some aspect of New Hampshire history, which can then be presented as an oral report.
1. New Hampshire.

974.2
Gilmore, Robert and **Ingmire, Bruce E.** *The Seacoast, New Hampshire: A Visual History.* Conning (0-89865-736-9), 1989. 208p. B/W and Color photos. (Interest level: 7-8).
Three and a half centuries of coastal New Hampshire's history from the American Revolution to the coast's recent revitalization are presented. Numerous black-and-white and color photographs provide an in-depth history of seafaring, lumbering, industry, tourism, and the region's scenic beauty.
♦ Students can design picture postcards depicting a natural or manmade landmark of New Hampshire's seacoast. The completed postcards can then be used to create a visual display showing the coast's outstanding features.
1. Atlantic Coast (N.H.)—History, Local—Pictorial works   2. Coasts—New Hampshire—History—Pictorial works   3. New Hampshire— History, Local—Pictorial works.

974.2
Gosselin, Carol A. *Games: A New Hampshire Learning Experience.* Carol A. Gosselin (No ISBN), 1984. 56p. B/W illus., patterns, and maps. (Interest level: 4-6).
Patterns, directions, and information for making hands-on games are provided for New Hampshire cities, counties, people, events, government, maps,

environment, and resources. Locally produced by a classroom teacher, this activity book may prove useful to other educators for its game ideas, fact lists, and handy reproducibles of the state seal, state emblem, outline map, New Hampshire time line, and places to visit.
♦ Following the instructions in the book, children could make and play a game about New Hampshire.
1. New Hampshire.

974.2
The Granite State Sampler. (Laserdisc). SERES, 1989. B/W and Color. $75.00; free to schools in New Hampshire. (Interest level: 4-8).

Billed as a visual archive chronicling New Hampshire state history and government, this laserdisc contains information about people, places, and events in the state. Distributed to each school in the state free of charge to promote the use of technology by Southeastern Regional Education Service Center, it consists of 12,000 still images and 17 motion sequences organized by chapters and accompanied by a guide to frame numbers.
♦ Students can script and tape-record narration to accompany one of the silent sequences on the laserdisc.
1. New Hampshire.

974.2
Heffernan, Nancy Coffey. *New Hampshire: Crosscurrents in Its Development.* Tompson & Rutter (0-936-98812-6), 1986. 216p. B/W illus. and photos. (Interest level: grade 7-adult).

A chronology of the development of New Hampshire's industry and natural resources from 1607 to 1981 is outlined. Chapters detailing the importance of fish, ports, politics, the masting trade, farms, mills, and railroads will provide economic and political knowledge to more advanced history students and professionals requiring background information on this topic.
♦ Based on information provided in the book, young people may make predictions about New Hampshire's economic and political conditions 20 years from now.
1. New Hampshire—History.

974.2
McNair, Sylvia. *America the Beautiful: New Hampshire.* Childrens Press (0-516-00475-1), 1992. 144p. Color photos and maps. (Interest level: 4-8).

The geography, history, economy, people, and sights of New Hampshire are presented through text, maps, and color photographs. Current and complete information about the Granite State is provided, along with a useful "Facts at a Glance" section, which includes topography, product, and population maps; counties; a list of governors; important people; and a time line covering New Hampshire history to 1990.
♦ Young people may choose six facts from the book they consider to be the most significant in shaping New Hampshire's development and prepare an oral presentation supporting their choices.
1. New Hampshire.

974.2
Morely, Linda. *Western Regions, New Hampshire: A Visual History.* Donning (0-89865-734-2), 1989. 224p. B/W and Color photos. (Interest level: 7-8).

Development and progress in parts of New Hampshire bordering the Connecticut River, the Monadnock area, and the Sunapee region are visually documented in this book, written by the state's folklorist. Photographs cover virtually every page of this topically arranged history of the area's prominent and interesting residents.
♦ Readers can select items for a time capsule that they think would give future generations important information about life in New Hampshire in the 1990s.
1. New Hampshire—History, Local—Pictorial works 2. New Hampshire—Description and travel—Views.

974.2
Mount Washington Among the Clouds: An Early History: 1852-1908. (Videocassette). Wheaton A. Holden, 1974. VHS, (30 min.). $19.95. (Interest level: 7-8).

The history and development of Mt. Washington is recounted through interviews, old pictures, early photographs, and excerpts from articles printed in the newspaper *Among the Clouds*, which chronicled these events. This excellent source allows the viewer to experience such happenings as the fire of 1908, the building of the cog railway, the first auto race up the mountain, and much more.
♦ Each student could choose one event from the video about which to write an original newspaper article that could have appeared in *Among the Clouds*. The articles could then be combined to form a class newspaper.
1. New Hampshire—History 2. Mount Washington (N.H.)—History.

974.2
Older, Julia. *Grand Monadnock: Exploring the Most Popular Mountain in America.* Appledore (0-9627162-1-9), 1990. 111p. B/W and Color photos and maps. (Interest level: 6-8).

The birth, evolution, and development of Grand Monadnock in southwestern New Hampshire is traced from its cultural past to its present status as a recreational area for hiking, sightseeing, and winter sports. Beautifully photographed, this volume con-

tains perspectives from individuals who share their recollections and respect for the mountain.
♦ Young people may suggest ways in which such a popular natural area can be preserved and maintained for recreational use by future generations.
1. New Hampshire—Description and travel 2. Monadnock region (N.H.)—Description and travel.

974.2
Pendergast, John. *The Bend in the River.* Merrimac River Press (0-9629338-0-5), 1991. 92p. B/W illus., photos, and maps (Interest level: grade 7-adult).

Pendergast traces the geological formation of the Merrimac Valley and the history of Lowell, Dracut, Dunstable (Nashua, NH), Chelmsford, and Tyngsborough, Massachusetts. Archaeological evidence is presented to document the river's formation, the arrival and settlement of native people, 80 years of European contact, and the extermination of the natives.
♦ Young people may prepare a chart to present six artifacts discovered in the book and demonstrate what they reveal about the life of the Pennacook Indians before contact with the Europeans.
1. United States—History, Local 2. New Hampshire—History 3. Massachusetts—History 4. New England—History.

974.2
Pinette, Richard E. *Northwoods Echoes: A Collection of True Stories and Accounts of the North Country.* Liebt Printing Co. (No ISBN), 1986. 280p. B/W illus and photos. (Interest level: 7-8).

Accounts of famous and unknown people, places, and events are collected in these true short stories of the north country of New Hampshire from Mount Washington to the Canadian border. Written by one who has lived in the area, these entertaining tales reveal the humorous and sometimes touching details of hunting, fishing, and logging adventures during an exciting era.
♦ Students might write short stories about outdoor experiences they have had.
1. New Hampshire—History—Stories 2. New Hampshire—Description—Stories 3. Coos County—Description—Stories.

974.2
Potter, Parker B., Jr., ed. *New Hampshire Historical Markers.* 8th ed. New Hampshire Division of Historical Resources (No ISBN), 1989. 65p. B/W photos and maps. (Interest level: 4-8).

Potter lists 158 important places in New Hampshire's past, grouped regionally. The history of the marker program, how the program works, and succinct descriptions of each location are provided in this well-organized guide.
♦ Following the guidelines in the book, children can write a proposal for the erection of a historical marker in their own area.
1. New Hampshire—History.

974.2
Rosal, Lorenca Consuelo. *The Liberty Key: The Story of the New Hampshire Constitution.* Illus. by R. P. Hale. Equity Publishing (0-685-19456-6), 1987. 300p. B/W photos and illus. (Interest level: 3-6).

Designed for the celebration of the 200th anniversary of New Hampshire's constitution, this publication details information about the state's premier historical document. Field-tested by 20 classroom teachers prior to distribution, these diagrams, photographs, maps, cartoons, and graphics explain the establishment and organization of state government.
♦ Young people may use this book and other resources to plan and stage a mock election, passage of a bill, or legislative session.
1. New Hampshire—Constitutional history.

974.2
Samson, Gary. *The Merrimack Valley, New Hampshire: A Visual History.* Photos by author. Donning (0-89865-735-0), 1989. 208p. B/W and Color photos. (Interest level: 7-8).

The industrial revolution in the Merrimack Valley of New Hampshire is examined through the history of major industries in Manchester, Nashua, and Concord. Samson, an accomplished fine arts photographer and award-winning film producer, emphasizes the impact of people who shaped the region through numerous quality photographs.
♦ Students could collect or take pictures to create a photography album that tells a story about their own community.
1. Merrimack River Valley (N.H. and Mass.)—History—Pictorial works 2. Merrimack River Valley (N.H. and Mass.)—Industries—History—Pictorial works.

974.2
Thompson, Kathleen. *New Hampshire.* Raintree (0-86514-469-9), 1988. (Portrait of America Series). 48p. Color illus., photos, and maps. (Interest level: 3-5).

The history, economy, culture, and future of New Hampshire are briefly discussed and supported by a state chronology, pertinent statistics, and maps. Through interviews of residents, the limited text, which dwells on current conditions, may be useful as an overview or introduction to state history for younger readers.
♦ Readers may compile a list of statements about New Hampshire in this book, classifying them as fact or opinion.
1. New Hampshire.

974.2
Youst, Yvonne and Ackerman, Susan. *All about New Hampshire*. Jupiter Press (0-113-00000-6), 1989. 20p. (Interest level: 4-8).

This brief tribute to New Hampshire is a collection of images of its past and present, a sampling of its beautiful places, and praise for its people and their spirit. Written in prose, poetry, and a question-and-answer format, the booklet may be useful for giving an overview of the Granite State or for selecting topics for students to study further.
♦ Young people can create an illustration for one section of the booklet.
1. New Hampshire.

974.21
Hengen, Elizabeth Durfee. *Village of Penacook, New Hampshire: An Architectural and Historical View*. Heritage Concord (No ISBN), 1991. 60p. B/W photos and maps. (Interest level: grade 6-adult).

Hengen presents an architectural survey of Penacook Village in Concord conducted during the summer of 1990 to record and preserve its pre-1940 buildings. Black-and-white photographs of each structure, identified by architectural style, distinctive characteristics, and location, provide an interesting look at a small community's emergence from farmland into a successful industrial village.
♦ Children may photograph and describe their own homes, indicating the year built, history, architectural style, and occupants.
1. Architecture—New Hampshire—Penacook 2. Penacook (N.H.)—History.

974.4
Cherry, Lynne. *A River Ran Wild*. Illus. by author. Harcourt Brace Jovanovich (0-15-200542-0), 1992. Unpaginated. Color illus. (Interest level: 2-4).

The environmental history of the Nashua River is traced from its discovery by the Indians through its pollution during the Industrial Revolution and eventual cleanup in 1990. Events, people, tools, and machinery of days past are portrayed in outstanding illustrations and exquisitely detailed and labeled border designs.
♦ After reading this account of an ambitious environmental revitalization effort on the part of local citizens, students may select a polluted area in their own community that requires attention and organize a campaign to clean it up.
1. Nashua River (Mass. and N.H.)—History 2. Nashua River Valley (Mass. and N.H.)—History 3. Water quality—Nashua River (Mass. and N.H.)—History 4. Indians of North America—Nashua River (Mass. and N.H.)—History.

974.74
McAdow, Ron. *New England Time Line*. Nutshell Books (1-880644-01-0), 1992. 95p. (Interest level: 4-8).

A brief New England time line by centuries, followed by an annotated chronology and milestone dates by state, provides an overview of the region's history from 1602 to 1992. McAdow's book can be used as a quick reference for New England's important dates and as an aid to appreciating historic sites in Connecticut, Maine, Massachusetts, New Hampshire, Rhode Island, and Vermont.
♦ The class can predict what a time line for New Hampshire will look like for the next 100 years.
1. New England—History.

977.8
Day, Freida C., ed. *Historic Mont Vernon*. Mont Vernon Historical Society (No ISBN), 1990. 94p. B/W photos. (Interest level: 4-8).

The changing character of Mont Vernon is documented in a chronology of the households of the small New Hampshire town. Significant historical and genealogical information about this residential community is arranged by street address and divided into sections—"The Village," "Streets and Roads Leading into the Village," and "Outlying Streets & Roads."
♦ Readers may create a map of one of the streets of Mont Vernon as it was 100 years ago. Students residing in this community may wish to map their own streets.
1. Mont Vernon (N.H.)—Description—Views 2. Mont Vernon (N.H.)—History.

Biography

920
Brereton, Charles. *New Hampshire Notables*. Peter E. Randall (0-914339-11-7), 1986. 213p. B/W photos. (Interest level: 7-8).

Biographical sketches of men and women of New Hampshire in the arts, banking, business, communications, education, environmental protection, government, law, medicine, religion, social services, and other fields are provided with their photographs. Individuals are selected by a nominating committee for inclusion and entries list information such as date of birth, parents' names, community service, spouse, children, and home address based on responses to a questionnaire.
♦ Readers might write a letter to one of the individuals named in the book.
1. New Hampshire—Biography.

92 Blunt, Susan Baker
Blunt, Susan Baker. *Childish Things: The Reminiscence of Susan Baker Blunt*. Tompson & Rutter

(0-936988-14-2), 1988. 88p. B/W illus. and photos. (Interest level: 6-8).

Born in 1828 in the village of Thornton's Ferry in Merrimack, New Hampshire, Susan Baker Blunt describes such historical events as the passing of the last Indians, erection of the Amoskeag Mills, and the introduction of the railroad. Written when she was 85 years old, this anecdotal memoir preserves an informative record of the life of a young girl growing up along the banks of the Merrimack River.

♦ If possible, the class can visit the Manchester Historic Association in Manchester, New Hampshire, to view the original manuscript and other items of historical interest.

1. Blunt, Susan Baker, 1828-1924—Childhood and youth   2. New England—Biography   3. New England—Social life and customs.

92 Fortune, Amos

Amos Fortune, Free Man. (Audiocassette). Random House/Miller Brody (0-394-76925-2), 1970. (22 min.). $12.95. (Interest level: 5-8).

This recording is based on the story of a slave who was captured, sold at auction, and then regained his freedom to live out his life in Jaffrey, New Hampshire. Portions of the Newbery Award–winning book by Elizabeth Yates (*see* following entry) are brought to life in this sensitive reading.

♦ After listening to the audiocassette, students may enjoy reading the book in its original form.

1. Fortune, Amos   2. Newbery Medal Books   3. Slavery—United States.

92 Fortune, Amos

Yates, Elizabeth. *Amos Fortune: Free Man.* Illus. by Nora S. Unwin. Dutton (0-525-25570-2), 1967. 181p. B/W illus. (Interest level: 5-8).

Amos Fortune, who was born the son of a king in Africa in 1710, captured at the age of 15, and sold as a slave, became a free man at the age of 70 and lived out the rest of his life with his wife and adopted daughter in Jaffrey, New Hampshire. This moving biography received the Newbery Award in 1951.

♦ Young people could read additional accounts of slavery in the United States or biographies of other slaves who gained their freedom.

1. Fortune, Amos   2. African Americans—Biography   3. Slavery—United States.

92 Hall, Donald

Hall, Donald. *Here at Eagle Pond.* Illus. by Thomas W. Nason. Ticknor & Fields (0-89919-978-X), 1990. 141p. B/W illus. (Interest level: 7-8).

Donald Hall writes about his experiences on and around Eagle Pond Farm in Wilmot, New Hampshire, the home of his ancestors. A tribute to the beauty of small town life, these essays import a great deal of history with humor and fondness for the people and places of the Granite State.

♦ Students might write letters to Donald Hall, a New Hampshire author, sharing their own remembrances of a memorable experience they have had in the state or their thoughts and feelings about his book.

1. Hall, Donald, 1928- —Homes and haunts—New Hampshire   2. Poets, American—20th century—Biography   3. New Hampshire—Social life and customs   4. Country life—New Hampshire.

92 McAuliffe, Christa

Naden, Corinne J. *Christa McAuliffe: Teacher in Space.* Millbrook Press (1-56294-046-5), 1991. 48p. B/W and Color photos. (Interest level: 3-4).

Concord, New Hampshire, teacher Christa McAuliffe died when the space shuttle *Challenger* exploded shortly after liftoff in 1986. Her life, special interest in the space program, selection for the mission, and training as the first private American citizen chosen to go on a spaceflight are described in this brief biography through photographs and interviews with those who knew her.

♦ Christa McAuliffe had planned to keep a space journal while in orbit. Young people may record one week's worth of entries they imagine she might have written had the mission been successful.

1. McAuliffe, Christa, 1948-1986   2. Challenger (Space shuttle)   3. Astronauts   4. Space shuttles.

92 Stark, John

Richmond, Robert P. *John Stark: Freedom Fighter.* Dale Books (0-686-15641-2), 1988. 82p. (Interest level: 7-8).

The reader is invited to share episodes in the life of New Hampshire Revolutionary War hero John Stark from his capture and holding for ransom by Abenaki Indians in 1752 to his death in 1822 at the age of 94. Extensive use of dialogue and dramatization of real events help make this historical figure come to life.

♦ Readers could compare this enhanced account of John Stark's life to a less fictionalized one such as an encyclopedia entry.

1. Stark, John, 1728-1822   2. New Hampshire—History—Biography   3. United States—History—Revolution.

92 Tudor, Tasha

Tudor, Bethany. *Drawn from New England: Tasha Tudor, a Portrait in Words and Pictures.* Philomel Books (0-399-20835-6), 1979. 96p. B/W and Color illus. and photos. (Interest level: 3-8).

The work and life on a Webster, New Hampshire, farm from 1945 to 1972 of this noted American illustrator are portrayed through text, photographs, snapshots from family albums, book illustrations, and paintings and drawings. Tudor's daughter fondly remembers and describes the strong influ-

ence of Tasha Tudor's New England lifestyle on her art.
♦ Students can read books by Tasha Tudor listed at the beginning of the biography and discuss how her family and life are reflected in her literature.
1. Tudor, Tasha 2. Illustrators—United States—Biography.

Fiction

Alcott, Louisa May. *An Old-Fashioned Thanksgiving.* Illus. by Jody Wheeler. Ideals Children's Books (0-8249-8630-X), 1993. Unpaginated. Color illus. (Interest level: 1-4).

Set in the hills near Mt. Monadnock, this story follows the activities of seven children as they attempt to prepare Thanksgiving dinner after Mother is called away to care for their sick grandmother. A glimpse at the holiday traditions of a nineteenth-century New England family is provided through beautiful watercolor illustrations and a humorous retelling of this classic tale.
♦ Students may plan, prepare, and re-create an authentic nineteenth-century Thanksgiving celebration based on the story which includes food, beverages, and games.
1. Family life—Fiction 2. Thanksgiving Day—Fiction 3. New England—Fiction 4. New Hampshire—Fiction.

Andler, Kenneth. *Mission to Fort No. 4.* Illus. by Max R. Kaufmann. Regional Center for Educational Training (0-915892-04-9), 1975. (Bicentennial Historiette). 64p. B/W illus. and maps. (Interest level: 4-8).

Orphaned in 1775, 15-year-old David Bradford joins his uncle in Bedford and begins a series of adventures, which take him on a surveying expedition through the New Hampshire wilderness and involve him in the Revolutionary War effort. This fictional account of life in the New Hampshire frontier in the 1700s takes the reader through early towns and war events.
♦ Children can enlarge the Vermont/New Hampshire map provided in the book and record an event from the story that occurred in each town.
1. United States—History—Revolution, 1775-1783—Fiction.

Brady, Philip. *Reluctant Hero: A Snowy Road to Salem in 1802.* Walker and Company (0-8027-6974-8), 1990. 159p. B/W map. (Interest level: 5-8).

The 16-day journey from Barnard's Hill in Weare's Town to Salem, Massachusetts, by New Hampshire farmboy Cutting Favour is described in this fictional account. The high-interest plot combined with historically accurate information will motivate young New Hampshire readers to take an interest in their heritage.
♦ Students might design an advertisement for one of the many taverns at which the main character stopped on his journey.
1. New England—Fiction.

Grant, Louise. *The Fort and the Flag: Two Adventures in Old-Time New Hampshire.* Regional Center for Educational Training (0-915892-09-X), 1977. (Bicentennial Historiette). 73p. B/W illus. and maps. (Interest level: 2-4).

A brother and sister experience different events in the Portsmouth, New Hampshire, area as they support the Revolutionary War effort. Written specifically for the U.S. bicentennial celebration, the story attempts to bring history to life for young readers through fictionalized accounts of the period.
♦ Young people may make a replica of the flag made from the main character's dress for the Ranger as they imagine it looked in November of 1777.
1. New Hampshire—History—Revolution, 1775-1783—Fiction 2. United States—History—Revolution, 1775-1783—Fiction.

Hall, Donald. *The Farm Summer 1942.* Illus. by Barry Moser. Dial Books (0-8037-1502-1), 1994. Unpaginated. Color illus. (Interest level: 1-3).

Peter spends the summer of 1942 on his grandparents' farm in Gale, New Hampshire, while his father serves on a destroyer in the Pacific and his mother works on a secret government war project in New York. This young boy's positive experience in rural New England is effectively contrasted with his San Francisco routine through watercolor illustrations and text.
♦ Students may wish to interview a family member, neighbor, or teacher who can provide information about his or her own "summer of 1942."
1. Grandparents—Fiction 2. Farm life—New Hampshire—Fiction 3. World War, 1939-1945—United States—Fiction.

Hall, Donald. *Ox-Cart Man.* Illus. by Barbara Cooney. Viking (0-670-53328-9), 1979. Unpaginated. Color illus. (Interest level: K-3).

An early nineteenth-century farmer journeys to the Portsmouth market to sell his wares and then returns home again. Caldecott-winning illustrations in bold colors describe the daily life of a rural New England family throughout the changing seasons in a delightfully repetitive story that will appeal to young children.
♦ On a road map of New Hampshire, children could determine and trace the best route to travel from their own community to the marketplace in Portsmouth. Those living in Portsmouth may wish to mark the route on a street map of the city.

1. New England—Fiction 2. New Hampshire—Fiction.

Honness, Elizabeth. *The Spy at Tory Hole.* Illus. by Pamela Distler. Regional Center for Educational Training (0-915892-03-0), 1975. (Bicentennial Historiette). 58p. B/W illus. and maps. (Interest level: 4-6).

A 13-year-old Claremont boy and his cousin find themselves unwilling participants in the Revolutionary War in 1776 when they are captured in the woods by Tory spies. Written to help young people appreciate the celebration of the U.S. bicentennial and their national heritage, this fictionalized account of events in a small New Hampshire town in the late 1700s is fast moving and easy to read.
♦ The class can stage a debate between the Tories and Patriots.
1. New Hampshire—History—Revolution, 1775-1783—Fiction 2. United States—History—Revolution, 1775-1783—Fiction.

Jesep, Paul Peter. *Lady-Ghost of the Isles of Shoals.* Illus. by John Bowdren. Seacoast Publications of New England (0-9634360-0-7), 1992. 13p. B/W illus. (Interest level: 1-4).

Nine-year-old Jim and his seven-year-old sister Mary enjoy a bumpy cruise to Appledore Island, where they encounter Celia Thaxter and Blackbeard's bride, the Lady-Ghost, who helps them find their lost cat, No-Taxes. Factual information about the Isles of Shoals is woven into this mild ghost story set off the coast of New Hampshire.
♦ Students may write and tell a ghost story based on the folklore of their own community.
1. Isles of Shoals (Me. and N.H.)—Fiction 2. New Hampshire—Fiction 3. Ghosts—Fiction.

Kinsey-Warnock, Natalie. *The Bear That Heard Crying.* Illus. by Ted Rand. Cobblehill Books (0-525-65103-9), 1993. Unpaginated. Color illus. (Interest level: 1-4).

This is the unbelievable but true story of three-year-old Sarah Witcher, who became lost in the woods near Warren, New Hampshire, in June of 1783 and was protected by a bear for four days until her rescue. The author dramatically retells this story, based on historical accounts of the incident by those involved, about her great-great-great-great-great aunt.
♦ After reading the description of the search, students will use maps of the area to construct diagrams that show where they think Sarah Witcher was lost and found.
1. Lost children—Fiction 2. Survival—Fiction 3. Bears—Fiction 4. New Hampshire—Fiction.

Piper, Doris D. *A Home for Jamie.* Illus. by Heidi S. Wallace. Regional Center for Educational Training (0-915892-08-1), 1976. (Bicentennial Historiette). 58p. B/W illus. and maps. (Interest level: 4-6).

Lake Opechee in Laconia, New Hampshire, is the setting for this story of a young orphan boy displaced from Portsmouth during the Revolutionary War. Written specifically to celebrate the U.S. bicentennial, this fictional look at the daily life of a colonial child gives a sense of what life was like during the late 1700s.
♦ Readers can compare Jamie's preparation for winter with their own seasonal activities and chores.
1. New Hampshire—History—Fiction.

Ray, Mary Lyn. *Angel Baskets: A Little Story about the Shakers.* Illus. by Jean Colquhoun. Martha Weatherbee Books (0-9609384-3-5), 1987. Unpaginated. Color illus. (Interest level: 1-3).

This is the story of an orphan, Cornelia French, brought in 1842 at the age of two to live with the Shakers in Mt. Lebanon, New York, who becomes a basketmaker for the community. Illustrations depicting examples of furniture, storage areas, music, clothing, daily life, work, religion, schooling, and food provide information about Shaker life that is accessible to young readers.
♦ Students may enjoy learning how to weave baskets.
1. Shakers.

Smith, Harry W. *ABCs of New Hampshire.* Illus. by author. Down East Books (0-89272-187-1), 1984. Unpaginated. Color illus. (Interest level: K-1).

Flowers, animals, people, and geographical features of New Hampshire are presented for each letter of the alphabet. An adjective and a noun in bold type describe the illustrations on each double-page spread, with a more detailed description for each at the end of the book.
♦ Young people may wish to use the book as a model to create alphabet books of their own showing other significant features of New Hampshire or their own community. Drawings can be labeled, alphabetized, and compiled into books by individuals or groups.
1. Alphabet books 2. New Hampshire.

Yates, Elizabeth. *We, the People.* Illus. by Nora S. Unwin. Regional Center for Educational Training (0-914378-06-60), 1974. (Bicentennial Historiette). 46p. B/W illus. (Interest level: 4-6).

A young mother cares for her children and manages their farm in Temple, New Hampshire, while her husband fights in the American Revolution at Bunker Hill and Ticonderoga. Written specifically for students in celebration of the U.S. bicentennial,

this brief work of historical fiction gives readers a glimpse of rural life in the late 1700s.
♦ Readers can compile a list of typical household chores on a farm during the time of the Revolutionary War.
1. United States—History—Revolution, 1775-1783—Fiction   2. New Hampshire—History—Fiction.

Professional Materials

289
Thompson, Nancy. *Learning about Shakers for Teachers and Parents.* Illus. by Jane Cowen-Fletcher. Pleasant Grove (No ISBN), 1988. 40p. B/W illus. and maps. (Interest level: Professional).

This booklet describes and explains the history, architecture, inventions, music, beliefs, education, and games of the people of Shaker Village in Canterbury, New Hampshire, one of two remaining Shaker communities. Published as an accompaniment to *Learning about Shakers for Young People* (see p. 100) and written by a teacher, this guide provides background information and activities for educating children about Shaker religion, life, and customs.
♦ Young people may enjoy taking a field trip to Shaker Village in Canterbury, New Hampshire. Students outside of New Hampshire could write letters to the author to ask specific questions or obtain additional information about Shaker life.
1. Shakers.

641.3
Lockhart, Betty Ann C. *The Maple Sugaring Story.* Illus. by Eugenia Bonyun, Susan Clayton, and Betty Ann Lockhart. Perceptions (1-880327-04-X), 1990. 84p. B/W illus. (Interest level: Professional).

The history of maple sugaring in northeastern North America, along with recipes, references, a glossary of terms, and other information about maple sugaring today, is provided in this teaching guide. Published as a complement to the video of the same name (see p. 101), the book contains language arts, music, art, science, math, and social studies activities for grades K-6, arranged by grade level and discipline.
♦ Students can participate in any of the many activities described in this book.
1. Maple sugar.

974.2
Historical New Hampshire. New Hampshire Historical Society (ISSN 0018-2508). Quarterly. B/W illus. and photos. (Interest level: Professional).

The people and events of New Hampshire's past are researched in this quarterly journal of the New Hampshire Historical Society. Published to encourage research and bring fresh and interesting material to the public, it contains articles and book reviews that reflect original research on many aspects of the state's history and culture.
♦ This is a good professional reference.
1. New Hampshire—History—Periodicals.

974.2
Horizons. New Hampshire Council for the Social Studies. Annual. B/W illus. and photos. (Interest level: Professional).

Book reviews, bibliographies, instruction techniques, activities, historical photographs, and lesson plans are presented in this journal of the New Hampshire Council for the Social Studies. Memberships are available for individuals and schools.
♦ This journal will be useful for professional reference.
1. New Hampshire—History—Periodicals.

974.2
New Hampshire Premier. (ISSN 1050-5512). Monthly. B/W and Color illus. and photos. (Interest level: Professional).

What's happening in New Hampshire is well covered in this monthly publication. Articles and regular features about the arts, travel, law, music, history, calendar, economics, business, recreation, and poetry provide interesting reading and a way to keep up-to-date on the people, places, and events of the state.
♦ Students will research and write an article that could be included in an upcoming issue, such as a discussion of a current legislative concern, restaurant review, political commentary, or travel guide. Others may wish to write a letter to the editor or pose legal questions to be answered in the "Legal Briefs" column.
1. New Hampshire—History—Periodicals.

974.2
Rosal, Lorenca Consuelo. *God Save the People: A New Hampshire History, Level II Teacher's Resource Manual.* Illus. by R.P. Hale. Equity (No ISBN), 1988. 189p. B/W illus. (Interest level: Professional).

Developed by the Constitutional Bicentennial Education Commission to help junior high students explore New Hampshire's government and economy, this manual presents the constitutional principles upon which the state and nation were founded. Young people are encouraged to take an active role and accept the responsibilities of citizenship by gaining information about the constitution, economy, taxes, and important people in history.
♦ Class members may conduct one of the simulations suggested in this manual, such as staging a mock town meeting or role-playing a legislative meeting.
1. New Hampshire—History—Study and teaching.

New Jersey

by Amy G. Job

Nonfiction

305.4
Past and Promise: Lives of New Jersey Women. Scarecrow (0-8108-2201-6), 1990. 468p. Illus. (Interest level: grade 7-adult).

This work includes biographies of women who led the fight for women's rights and whose accomplishments were unique for the time period in which they lived. Portraits are included where possible.
♦ Students could research the impact of these women on society and discuss how women's rights were promoted by their accomplishments. They then could compare accomplishments of prominent women of today.
1. Women—New Jersey—History 2. Women—New Jersey—Biography.

305.8
New Jersey Ethnic Life Pamphlet Series. (Pamphlet). 11 vols. New Jersey Historic Commission (No ISBN), 1986. B/W illus. (Interest level: grade 7-adult).

Ten illustrated pamphlets and a teacher's guide dealing with ethnic groups and immigration in New Jersey history make up this series. The text draws heavily on interviews with representatives of the state's ethnic groups. Subjects include reasons for migrating, the journey from home, arrival and settlement in a new place, schooling and education, work, ethnicity, and looking back.
♦ Designed for high school and general readers as well as teachers, these booklets can be used as background references. The illustrations and the texts of some of the interviews can be used in class for lessons.
1. New Jersey—Social life and customs.

320.47 (Reference)
League of Women Voters of New Jersey. New Jersey: Spotlight on Government. 6th ed. Rutgers University Press (0-8135-1843-1), 1992. 390p. B/W illus. (Interest level: grade 6-adult).

A reference guide to New Jersey's government, this source describes departments, services, costs, organization, personnel, and development.
♦ Valuable as a resource book, this work can be used by teachers for background information in preparing instructional units and by students preparing organizational charts and reports on New Jersey government.
1. New Jersey—Politics and government.

325
America: The Dream of My Life. Rutgers University Press (0-8135-1515-7), 1990. 295p. B/W illus. (Interest level: grade 7-adult).

Selections from the approximately 100 interviews conducted between 1939 and 1941 as part of the Ethnological Survey of New Jersey are collected here. Interviewers were fieldworkers from the Federal Writers Project, and the case studies provide important background for studies of immigrant life of the period.
♦ Class members can read excerpts detailing immigrant life. Students could then conduct interviews of their own family members.
1. Immigration and emigration 2. New Jersey—Social life and customs 3. Minorities—New Jersey—History.

328
Buzzing a Bill into Law. (Sound filmstrip). Afton, 1985. Color, (30 min.). $32.95. (Interest level: grade 4-adult).

Using an unusual approach, this filmstrip presents the legislative process by following the true story of a class that successfully fought to name the honeybee the state insect. This would be useful for teaching New Jersey government from the standpoint of social studies and/or New Jersey studies.

♦ Students could choose a topic for which they might need to petition their local government and write letters to elected representatives.
1. Legislation.

331.88
The House on the Green: Botto House. (Videocassette). William Paterson College, 1985. VHS, Color, (20 min.). $19.95. (Interest level: grade 5-adult).

This videorecording is a documentary on the lives of the members of the Botto family and the evolution of the Botto House American Labor Museum in Haledon, New Jersey. During the great 1913 Paterson Silk Strike, Pietro Botto allowed speakers to address strikers in his house. Segments on child labor and immigration are included.
♦ Young people can research how child labor laws developed and present their findings in a paper or a diorama.
1. Labor unions—New Jersey 2. Immigration and emigration 3. Children—Employment—New Jersey.

398.2
Beck, Henry Charlton. *The Roads of Home: Lanes and Legends of New Jersey.* Rutgers University Press (0-8135-1018-X), 1983. 289p. (Interest level: grade 6-adult).

Traveling the Old Mine and the Old York roads, Beck encountered lost towns and diverse characters. This collection of stories centers around these roads. An index of people and places is included.
♦ After reading the stories, children can divide into groups and dramatize them.
1. Folklore—New Jersey.

398.2
Homer, Larona C. *Blackbeard the Pirate and Other Stories of the Pine Barrens.* Middle Atlantic Press (0-912605-04-8), 1985. 96p. Illus. (Interest level: K-5).

These short stories, set in the Pine Barrens, feature both real people and legendary figures who were connected with the area.
♦ Students can stage the stories or use them for read-aloud and storytelling sessions.
1. Folklore—New Jersey.

398.2
The Jersey Devil. (Sound filmstrip). Afton, 1978. (40 min.). (Interest level: grade 4-adult).

Great for Halloween, *The Jersey Devil* explores the legend of the Jersey Devil, who was supposedly born in October. The illustrations and music are vivid and lend a touch of mystery to the story. The reverse side of the tape has a mini-course for teachers.

♦ The filmstrip might motivate viewers to study New Jersey folklore. Each student can identify a New Jersey folktale and retell it to the class.
1. Folklore—New Jersey 2. Jersey Devil.

398.2
McCloy, James F. and **Miller, Ray.** *The Jersey Devil.* Middle Atlantic Press (0-912608-11-0), 1987. 121p. B/W illus. (Interest level: grade 4-adult).

The story of New Jersey's most famous folklore character, this book gives the background for the legend as well as information on modern-day attempts to prove or disprove the mythical being. Fun illustrations enhance the text.
♦ Children could draw their own interpretation of the devil and act out the story.
1. Folklore—New Jersey 2. Jersey Devil.

398.2
McMahon, William. *Pine Barren Legends: Lore and Lies.* Middle Atlantic Press (0-912608-19-6), 1986. 149p. B/W photos and illus. (Interest level: grade 6-adult).

McMahon offers a delightful social history, written in a light vein and illustrated with photographs and sketches. One chapter deals with the language of the Pine Barrens.
♦ Students can find examples of local language quirks or sayings and make a guide to the language of their community.
1. Legends—New Jersey—Pine Barrens 2. Pine Barrens—Social life and customs 3. Folklore—New Jersey.

398.2
A New Jersey Folklore Sampler. (Sound filmstrip). Middle Atlantic Press (0-912608-15-3), 1981. Color, (30 min.). $25.00. (Interest level: 3-6).

Six New Jersey folktales told and sung by Jim Albertson and illustrated by Murray Callhan are featured in this filmstrip. These tales are a combination of tall tales and spooky stories, from the stretched rooster to the Jersey Devil.
♦ Young people could illustrate or tell their own version of the story after viewing the filmstrip.
1. Folklore—New Jersey.

398.2
Stockton, Frank R. *Stories of New Jersey.* Rutgers University Press (0-8135-0369-8), 1984. 263p. (Interest level: grade 4-adult).

Reproduced exactly as they were first printed in 1896, these stories re-create the events and mood of a vanishing New Jersey. They cover the period from the days of the Lenni Lenape Indians and the Dutch colonists to the exploits of New Jerseyans through the the Mexican War.

♦ Since these stories are based on facts, they are a good source of historical information for students. Each student could choose one topic to research further and share his or her findings in a paper or oral presentation.
1. Folklore—New Jersey.

508.74
Till, Tom. *New Jersey: Images of Wilderness.* Westcliffe (0-929969-42-1), 1991. 112p. B/W illus. (Interest level: grade 5-adult).

Till presents a photographic essay on the diversity of nature in New Jersey. This work is divided into the photographer's world of color, form, moment, and place and examines every possible facet of the richness and wildness of the land.
♦ This would be a perfect opportunity for students to compose poems to match the scenes. Particular emphasis could be placed on the photos that represent scenes near their home town. Students could create photoessays of favorite places in their own state or town.
1. New Jersey—Description and travel.

551.6 (Reference)
Ludlum, David M. *The New Jersey Weather Book.* Rutgers University Press (0-8135-0915-7), 1983. 256p. B/W illus. (Interest level: grade 6-adult).

The answers to many questions about New Jersey's weather can be found here. The role of weather in the state's history, statistics about the state's weather, and information on some of the state's most famous weather disasters are included, along with a section for students on how to learn about weather and keep up with current reports.
♦ Young people could use maps and illustrations for recording the weather and comparing it with past trends.
1. Weather.

559
Mammals of New Jersey. (Sound filmstrip). Afton, 1980. 4 filmstrips, 2 cassettes, (30 min.); 10 posters. $105.00. (Interest level: K-adult).

Photographs of animals inhabiting four different New Jersey settings are divided into sections such as animals of the neighborhood, dwellers in the marshes and meadows, animals of the woodland, and hunters on the prowl. Cassettes tell about the animals and reproduce animal sounds. Posters include a photo on the front and text providing details of each animal on the reverse.
♦ This filmstrip set is useful for showing the variety of wildlife in New Jersey and conservation study. Students could report on the animals and find out how many are found in their own community.
1. Mammals—New Jersey.

608.74
Job, Kenneth. *Early Hi-Tech in New Jersey.* In-Education (No ISBN), 1990. 24p. Illus. (Interest level: 4-7).

The four stories in this volume dealing with problem solving and invention or the improvement of inventions will be very useful for New Jersey science, transportation, and reasoning studies. The tales of the work of John Fitch, James Renwick, Robert Stevens, and Samuel Morse illustrate New Jersey's important role in invention and technology. Designed for student use, the work includes a time line and quick quiz questions for reinforcement learning.
♦ Readers can design their own inventions and make models or illustrations to share with the class.
1. Inventions 2. Technology.

629.133
America's First Air Voyage. (Sound filmstrip). Afton, 1989. (15 min.). Poster. (Interest level: 4-6).

In pictures and narration, this filmstrip relates the exciting events of January 9, 1793, when Jean Pierre Blanchard and his dog lifted off in a balloon from Philadelphia and landed in a field in Deptford, New Jersey. A poster accompanies the filmstrip. This is an excellent tool for introducing air travel and integrating New Jersey into the curriculum.
♦ Imagining that they accompanied Blanchard on his adventure, students can write an account of the balloon ride.
1. Balloons 2. Airships.

700.25 (Reference)
Herold, Patricia. *New Jersey Arts.* Rutgers University Press (0-8135-15534-8), 1990. 189p. Illus. (Interest level: grade 6-adult).

Designed to help locate the best art, music, performances, screenings, and poetry readings throughout the state, the entries in this work include addresses, hours, descriptions, special events, and educational programs.
♦ Teachers can use this guide to plan field trips and also as a reference to gain background on the extensive arts program in New Jersey.
1. Arts—New Jersey—Directories.

790.09 (Reference)
Brown, Michael P. *New Jersey Parks, Forests, & Natural Areas: A Guide.* Rutgers University Press (0-8135-1789-3), 1992. 200p. B/W illus. (Interest level: grade 6-adult).

Arranged by region, this book lists some 250 national, state, and county natural areas. Entries include maps, addresses, hours, fees, descriptions, and special features.

♦ This is an excellent guide to sites suitable for field trips for schools and families. Students could write stories about and draw pictures of their trips.
1. Outdoor recreation—New Jersey—Guidebooks 2. Parks—New Jersey—Guidebooks.

796.357
DiClerico, James M. *The Jersey Game: The History of Modern Baseball from Its Birth to the Big Leagues in the Garden State.* Rutgers University Press (0-8135-1652-8), 1991. 279p. Illus. (Interest level: grade 6-adult).

The record of the development of baseball in New Jersey and its role as a crossroad between New York and Pennsylvania are discussed in this book, which will appeal to baseball fans of all ages. Sources for further reading are included.
♦ Young people could research a player from their town or interview little league coaches and write a history of their local baseball teams.
1. Baseball—New Jersey—History.

797.1 (Reference)
Parnes, Robert. *Canoeing the Jersey Pine Barrens.* Globe Pequot Press (0-87106-491-X), 1990. 288p. B/W illus. (Interest level: grade 6-adult).

Even if a canoe trip is not possible, this guide could be useful as a study of the uniqueness of the Pine Barrens region.
♦ Students can write stories depicting what they might see from the rivers.
1. Canoes and canoeing—New Jersey 2. Pine Barrens—Description and travel.

810.9
Estrin, Herman A. *New Jersey's Literary History.* (Poster). Afton, 1979. Color. $5.95. (Interest level: grade 6-adult).

Estrin's poster lists names of New Jersey authors and illustrates scenes from their works. The varied achievements of the better-known authors are discussed.
♦ Students could do in-depth research on the authors listed. They could also read the books described, dramatize them, or write stories from the scenes on the poster.
1. American literature—New Jersey 2. Authors, American—New Jersey.

811
Bluestones and Salt Hay: An Anthology of New Jersey Poets. Rutgers University Press (0-8135-1486-X), 1990. 210p. (Interest level: grade 6-adult).

This is a comprehensive gathering of poems by 28 New Jerseyans reflecting local history, geography, and culture. Original works by famous poets such as Allen Ginsberg are combined with poems by some not-so-well-known poets such as Stephen Dunn.

♦ As various topics are covered in New Jersey studies, teachers can read these poems to the class. Students could illustrate the poems.
1. New Jersey—Poetry.

912.749
New Jersey. (50" × 50" Map). Color. $94.00. (Interest level: grade 4-adult).

With a large map of New Jersey showing counties and major geographical features in the center and smaller maps and charts on the side, this hanging wall chart covers topics such as agriculture, industry, land, transportation, geographical sections and regions, profile, population, and exports.
♦ This map can be used as a database of New Jersey information for comparing maps. Children can compare the information on the side maps and charts with the main map, drawing right on the chart.
1. New Jersey—Maps.

912.749
New Jersey Historic Map Charts Set. (23" × 29" Charts). Afton (0-89359-008-8), 1983. 4 maps, Color; 4 review sheets. (Interest level: grade 5-adult).

This set includes colorful charts incorporating maps, text, and drawings on four different topics: prehistory, Indians, colonial days, and revolution. Use the charts in this set as wall decorations or for bulletin boards during New Jersey studies, and use the information as introductory material or an evaluation tool.
♦ Students can compare one of the historic maps with a modern map of New Jersey, identifying what has changed and what has stayed the same.
1. New Jersey—History—Maps.

912.749
New Jersey Historic Map Portfolio. (Maps). Afton (No ISBN), 1983. 10 maps, Color. $69.95. (Interest level: grade 5-adult).

The maps contained in this portfolio, reproductions of 10 important maps from 1635 to 1923, represent the development of the state, both historical and economic. A description is included.
♦ Class members can compare and contrast the development of population centers, geographic forms, and transportation networks in New Jersey.
1. New Jersey—History—Maps.

912.749
New Jersey Modern Map Chart Set. (23" × 29" Charts). Afton (0-89359-008-8), 1988. 4 charts, Color; 4 review sheets. $29.95. (Interest level: grade 5-adult).

Informational charts that transpose graphics on a map of New Jersey and present information make

up this set. Topics include travel in New Jersey and those products found in New Jersey, grown in New Jersey, and made in New Jersey.
♦ Students can create their own specialized maps of New Jersey, using graphics to portray some aspect of the state. These charts can be hung as wall decorations for special New Jersey study or as a regular classroom display. Teachers can teach from the information on the charts.
1. New Jersey—Maps.

912.749
New Jersey Wall Outline Map. (23" × 35" Map). Afton (No ISBN), 1987. $12.95. (Interest level: grade 3-adult).

County lines are indicated on this black-and-white outline map. Some basic facts about the state, such as area ranks among counties, are included.
♦ This inexpensive map could be used by teachers for lessons or by students giving reports.
1. New Jersey—Maps.

917.3
Tunis, Edwin. *The Tavern at the Ferry.* Crowell (0-690-0099-5), 1973. 109p. B/W illus. (Interest level: 5-8).

Through the history of the Ferry Tavern House on the Delaware River, this juvenile book tells the tale of the Battle of Trenton and related events. The story is nicely illustrated with more than 100 pencil-and-wash drawings.
♦ Some of the chapters are suitable for storytelling or for dramatic presentations. Students can memorize a story to tell for younger students.
1. Trenton, Battle of, 1776   2. New Jersey—History.

917.49
Barrow, Scott. *Extraordinary New Jersey.* Foremost (0-89909-154-7), 1988. 128p. Color photos. (Interest level: 7-8).

Barrow gives readers a full-color photographic look at the wonderful variety of New Jersey. The photographer chose unusual angles and settings to vividly portray the state from wilderness to cities and from people to buildings.
♦ Young people can write poems or prose describing the settings of these photographs. The descriptions could be pulled together to complete a story.
1. New Jersey—Description and travel.

917.49
Bernard, April and **Sante, Luc.** *New Jersey: An American Portrait.* Taylor (0-87833-540-4), 1986. 184p. Color and B/W photos. (Interest level: grade 7-adult).

Bernard and Sante present a portrait of New Jersey, divided into sections on transportation, social life, agriculture, industry, history, and recreation. Many beautiful photographs enhance the text.
♦ Readers could use the book by sections and write stories or poems to match the pictures.
1. New Jersey—Description and travel—Views
2. New Jersey—History—Pictorial works.

917.49
Choroszewski, Walter. *New Jersey: A Scenic Discovery.* Foremost (0-89909-049-4), 1984. 120p. Photos. (Interest level: grade 7-adult).

This beautiful photographic essay includes an introduction and identifying labels. Various aspects of New Jersey life and geography are covered.
♦ Students could use this book to create stories or poems describing the scenes.
1. New Jersey—Description and travel.

917.49
Fradin, Dennis. *New Jersey: In Words and Pictures.* Childrens Press (0-516-43930-8), 1980. 48p. B/W illus. (Interest level: 2-5).

Fradin's illustrated simple history and description of New Jersey includes pronunciation keys for complex words and names. A list of facts about New Jersey and a brief chronology are appended.
♦ Children could write stories about some of the incidents mentioned in the work and provide additional illustrations.
1. New Jersey—Description and travel   2. New Jersey—History.

917.49
Fredeen, Charles. *New Jersey.* Lerner (0-8225-2732-4), 1993. 72p. Color illus. (Hello USA Series). (Interest level: 4-6).

Nicely illustrated, this overview of the state will be useful as an introduction to New Jersey. The book includes a description, history, activities, biographies, a glossary, and an index.
♦ Students can pick a topic from each chapter to write reports.
1. New Jersey—Description and travel   2. New Jersey—History.

917.49 (Reference)
Hudgins, Barbara. *New Jersey Day Trips: A Guide to Outings in New Jersey, New York, Pennsylvania, & Delaware.* 5th ed. Woodmont Press (0-9607762-4-9), 1991. 253p. B/W illus. (Interest level: grade 6-adult).

Hudgins's guidebook offers detailed reviews of popular attractions in New Jersey, New York, Pennsylvania, and Delaware. Arranged by subject, the book also includes a regional index, sorting attractions by county and state. Some entries are illustrated, adding to the value of the guide.
♦ This book is great for teachers and families planning field trips. Students can report on the trips,

including such items as best features and what they learned.
1. New Jersey—Description and travel 2. Field trips—New Jersey.

917.49
Jersey Jeopardy. 3rd ed. (Game). New Jersey Historical Society, 1992. $5.00. (Interest level: grade 3-adult).

Jersey Jeopardy is a game consisting of eight cards with 50 questions at three different levels on each card. The cards are arranged by subject, ranging from potpourri to history to entertainment.
♦ This game is best utilized as a supplement to an existing New Jersey studies curriculum, since the questions are specific and require background knowledge. Students can have a contest to see who can answer the most questions or use the game as a culminating New Jersey studies activity.
1. New Jersey—Questions and answers 2. New Jersey—Study and teaching.

917.49 (Reference)
League of Women Voters. *Know Your Town.* (Pamphlet). League of Women Voters (No ISBN). (Interest level: grade 4-adult).

Found in libraries across the state, this is a series of informational pamphlets on various New Jersey towns. Each contains a brief history of the town or township, governmental structure, and a list of town services. These pamphlets are updated each year.
♦ Wonderful for local town studies, the histories in these pamphlets are usually the most valuable sections, since much of the other information is sometimes dated. Students can use them as points of departure for writing reports to update the information.
1. New Jersey—History, Local 2. New Jersey—Description and travel.

917.49
Lewis, Paul M. *Beauty of New Jersey.* LTA (0-917630-84-X), 1989. 78p. Color photos and illus. (Interest level: grade 4-adult).

Photographs and essays stressing the natural and man-made features of New Jersey make up this work. The illustrations are clear and colorful and the text descriptive of the three major regions of the state.
♦ Young people can tell stories or write poems to express the feelings behind the scenes.
1. New Jersey—Description and travel.

917.49
Magic Carpet Journey. (Kit). Afton, 1983. 1 filmstrip; 1 cassette; script, (30 min.). $36.95. (Interest level: 4-8).

All the settings and instructions for producing this musical play are included in the kit. The filmstrip provides backgrounds and pictures for the journey, the script includes full staging directions, and the cassette consists of music and sound effects, along with an original song, "New Jersey's the Place for Me."
♦ The class can present the play as a conclusion to the New Jersey studies unit.
1. New Jersey—Description and travel 2. New Jersey—History.

917.49
Meet New Jersey. (Sound filmstrip). Afton, 1987. 1 filmstrip, Color; 1 cassette, (30 min.). $32.95. (Interest level: 4-8).

This filmstrip takes viewers on a photographic journey across New Jersey. Geography, communities, economy, people, historical sites, and much more are examined. The filmstrip could be used as an introductory tool to acquaint students with the state or as a review.
♦ After viewing the filmstrip, each student can choose one topic to illustrate with a photograph. These photographs can then be combined to create a photographic essay on the community.
1. New Jersey—Description and travel.

917.49
New Jersey Studies. (Sound filmstrip). Society for Visual Education, 1990. 3 filmstrips, Color; 3 cassettes, (15 min. each); teacher's guide. $39.00 each; $79.00 for the set. (Interest level: 4-6).

A skill booster supplement for the curriculum, these filmstrips provide a geographic, economic, and futuristic look at New Jersey. This is a good introductory set.
♦ Teachers can show the filmstrips with the sound first and then without the sound, allowing viewers to create their own text.
1. New Jersey—Study and teaching.

917.49
New Jersey Trips on Film. (Sound filmstrip). Afton, 1975. 5 filmstrips; 5 cassettes, (30 min. each). $119.95. (Interest level: 4-8).

A combination of photographs and colored drawings illustrate this guide to five trips in the state. They range from Trenton to Morristown, West Orange, and the Pine Barrens and include a summary.
♦ Young people can narrate the filmstrip without the cassette as a review.
1. New Jersey—Description and travel 2. Field trips.

917.49
Ride with Me: New Jersey/Delaware I-95 South. (Audiocassette). RWM (0-94264901-X), 1987. (85 min.). (Interest level: grade 7-adult).

A unique way to study the state, this cassette views New Jersey from the vantage point of the New Jersey Turnpike. The history and importance of each area are related to accompany the traveler on the turnpike.
♦ Students can create their own tape of their town or county by recording their impressions on travels through the area.
1. New Jersey—Description and travel.

917.49 (Reference)
Scheller, William G. *New Jersey: Off the Beaten Path*. Globe Pequot Press (0-87106-233-X), 1991. 144p. (Interest level: grade 6-adult).

Written in a narrative style, this is a guide to various sites, museums, and reserves in New Jersey. The work is divided into five regions, with information and interesting details for each site and, where appropriate, historical background and hours of operation.
♦ New Jersey teachers will find this useful as a guide for field trips within easy reach of a school district. The book could be illustrated by students, following the descriptions provided for each entry (and each field trip).
1. New Jersey—Description and travel—Guidebooks 2. New Jersey—History, Local 3. Folklore—New Jersey.

917.49
Symbols of New Jersey. (19" × 25" Chart). Afton, 1992. Color. (Interest level: K-adult).

This chart depicts the official state symbols, including the state bird, tree, flower, insect, motto, seal, fish, and dinosaur.
♦ Children could prepare reports on the various symbols or write a story tying them all together.
1. New Jersey—Description and travel 2. Signs and symbols, State—New Jersey.

917.49 (Reference)
Tomlinson, Gerald and **Mayer, Ronald A.** *The New Jersey Book of Lists*. Home Run Press (0-917125-01-0), 1992. 192p. B/W illus. (Interest level: grade 4-adult).

Perfect for trivia lovers, this small volume offers the state's most interesting points in a nutshell. Brief entries cover such topics as people, places, events, superlatives, sights, counties, tours, museums, homes, businesses, schools, and sports. Sources and an index of place-names make the information accessible by topic and name.
♦ Students can use this book of lists for suggestions for reports and as a model for compiling their own list of local important places, people, and events.
1. New Jersey—Miscellanea.

917.49
Zatz, Arline. *New Jersey's Special Places: Scenic, Historic, and Cultural Treasures in the Garden State*. Countryman Press (0-88150-161-1), 1990. 213p. Illus. (Interest level: 7-adult).

Zatz provides a listing of 52 unique places in New Jersey to visit, one for each weekend of the year. Each chapter includes details on location, the best season to visit, highlights, admission, hours, facilities, and special notes. All sites are suitable for adults and children.
♦ Using this book, class members could plan a trip. They could trace the route on a map, and, based on information in the book, decide when to go, what to take, and what the cost will be.
1. New Jersey—Description and travel—Guidebooks 2. Field trips.

917.49
Zero in on New Jersey. (Sound filmstrip). Afton, 1973. 5 filmstrips, Color; 5 cassettes, (30 min. each); poster. $31.50 each; $119.95 for the set; $5.95 for the poster. (Interest level: 4-8).

The color filmstrips and cassettes in this set give an overview of New Jersey and are a wonderful way to begin a lesson on the state.
♦ Students could use the set of filmstrips to begin their study of New Jersey. As they view the set, they should look for topics they would like to research further.
1. New Jersey—Description and travel.

974.9
The Afton Portfolio of Indians of the Forest. (14" × 17" charts; 23" × 29" map). Afton, 1975. 6 charts, Color; 1 map, Color. $25.95. (Interest level: 3-8).

These posters provide a wealth of information about the Lenape Indians. The front of each poster is illustrated, and the reverse has descriptive information. Themes of the posters include how and where the Lenape lived, customs of the village, how the Lenape traveled, what they wore, and family. The map, which locates the regions where the Lenape lived, folds around the posters for storage.
♦ Children can use this set to present information on the Lenape or as a guide for developing dioramas.
1. Delaware Indians.

974.9
Bain, Geri. *New Jersey*. Watts (0-531-10389-7), 1987. 93p. Color and B/W illus. (Interest level: 4-8).

Bain surveys the history of New Jersey and describes its geography, natural resources, industry, agriculture, principal cities, and people.
♦ Some social issues are raised in the text, and students can choose issues to explore further in reports.
1. New Jersey.

974.9
Brown, Edward. *Just around the Corner in New Jersey*. Middle Atlantic Press (0-912608-17-X), 1987. 112p. B/W illus. (Interest level: 6-8).

Brown has collected short stories featuring New Jersey. The stories are grouped by topics such as "they took giant steps," "whispers from the woods," and the "sea around them."
♦ Children can act out the stories for other classes. Class discussions could center around the theme for each section.
1. New Jersey—History—Anecdotes   2. New Jersey—Description and travel.

974.9
Carpenter, Allan. *New Jersey*. Childrens Press (0-516-04130-4), 1978. 96p. Color and B/W illus. (Interest level: 4-8).

This book contains a history of the state and a view of its industries and sites of interest today. A handy reference section and numerous short biographical sketches make this a good source for information.
♦ Some chapters have questions for discussion. Students might construct their own questions for other chapters and prepare reports based on the questions.
1. New Jersey—History   2. New Jersey—Description and travel.

974.9
Cunningham, John T. *New Jersey: America's Main Road*. Rev. ed. Afton (0-89359-007-X), 1976. 336p. Illus. (Interest level: 7-8).

Cunningham's illustrated history of the state is highly readable. Chapters on the state's geology, Native Americans, colonial times, the revolution, and detailed nineteenth- and twentieth-century developments are provided. A brief bibliography is included.
♦ Students could use this source as a starting point to gain background information on various topics about New Jersey.
1. New Jersey—History.

974.9
Cunningham, John T. *The New Jersey Sampler: Historic Tales of Old New Jersey*. Afton (0-89359-014-2), 1977. 212p. B/W illus. (Interest level: 4-8).

Illustrated with drawings, the tales in this collection describe 50 New Jersey personalities who made their mark in the state and nation. Included in the work are the sponsors of Labor Day, Thanksgiving, and Standard Time and the inventor of the steamboat. The range of histories will appeal to most students. An index provides entry to names and subjects.
♦ Young people could enact some of the stories.
1. New Jersey—History—Anecdotes   2. New Jersey—Biography   3. Folklore—New Jersey.

974.9
Cunningham, John T. *Newark*. Rev. ed. New Jersey Historical Society (0-911020-18-7), 1988. 384p. B/W illus. (Interest level: 6-8).

A profusely illustrated history of the third oldest major city in the United States and the transportation center of New Jersey, this revised edition includes commentary on the recent renaissance of the city.
♦ Using the facts in this book, readers can create and play a trivia game.
1. Newark (N.J.)—History.

974.9
Cunningham, John T. *This Is New Jersey*. 3rd ed. Rutgers University Press (0-8135-0862-2), 1978. 291p. B/W illus. (Interest level: 6-8).

Heavily illustrated, this county-by-county look at the state includes a brief history of the political situation in each county. An extensive index and a list of books about New Jersey are included.
♦ Students can do research to bring the chapters up to date.
1. New Jersey—History, Local   2. New Jersey—Description and travel.

974.9
Fleming, Thomas. *New Jersey: A History*. Norton (0-393-30180-X), 1984. 214p. B/W illus. (Interest level: grade 6-adult).

Fleming offers a brief, well-written history, especially strong on the political turmoil the state has experienced for three centuries. Also included is a historical guide to museums, historic houses, and historic sites.
♦ Students could use this as a model in preparing a historical guide to museums, houses, or sites in their own community or state.
1. New Jersey—History   2. New Jersey—Politics and government   3. Historic sites—New Jersey.

974.9
Kent, Deborah. *New Jersey*. Childrens Press (0-516-00476-X), 1987. (America the Beautiful Series). 144p. Color and B/W illus. (Interest level: 4-8).

Nicely illustrated, Kent's work introduces the geography, history, government, economy, industry, culture, historic sites, and famous people of New Jersey. Emphasis is placed upon diversity.
♦ This book can lead to ideas for reports and photography jaunts.
1. New Jersey.

974.9
Kraft, Herbert C. *The Lenape or Delaware Indians of New Jersey.* Seton Hall University Museum (No ISBN), 1987. 60p. (Interest level: 3-8).

The approach of this work is archaeological and anthropological, with emphasis on how the Lenape lived in the period just before the first contact with Europeans through the eighteenth century. An excellent introductory book for elementary children, this was developed by the author with the aid of a large group of teachers.
♦ This work can be a sourcebook for children who are preparing reports, constructing dioramas, or preparing classroom Indian villages.
1. Delaware Indians—History.

974.9
Kross, Peter. *New Jersey History.* Middle Atlantic Press (0-912608-45-5), 1987. 121p. B/W illus. (Interest level: 4-8).

The history of New Jersey is told through a collection of stories covering every area of the state. Some tales are illustrated, and the focus is on real people.
♦ A natural for plays for students, this could also be used in art studies where students could illustrate the stories.
1. New Jersey.

974.9
Lenape Indian Teaching Kits. (Kits). Middle Atlantic Press (Kit 1: 0-912608-07-2; Kit 2: 0-912608-08-0; Kit 3: 0-912608-09-9), 1978-79. Kit 1: $22.50; Kit 2: $15.50; Kit 3: $15.50. (Interest level: 3-8).

This is a collection of three teacher-aid kits with maps, diagrams, menus, and other items detailing the study of the Lenape. Topics include numbers and symbols, lore and medicine, food, shelter, clothes, crafts, and weapons.
♦ Students can practice Lenape crafts, prepare food, or replicate a village in the classroom.
1. Delaware Indians.

974.9
Murray, Thomas Christopher. *The Seven Wonders of New Jersey—And Then Some.* Enslow (0-89490-01-X). 130p. Color illus. (Interest level: grade 7-adult).

Murray presents a brief history, description, and other pertinent information about 14 natural and 14 man-made wonders in New Jersey. The sites were selected as a result of a statewide contest. Information, directions, and a photograph are included for each wonder.
♦ Young people could conduct similar contests and create listings for their own community.

1. New Jersey—Miscellanea 2. Curiosities and wonders—New Jersey 3. New Jersey—Description and travel—Guidebooks.

974.9
Pinelands Folklore. Rutgers University Press (0-8135-1189-5), 1987. 234p. Illus. (Interest level: grade 7-adult).

In three illustrated essays, the contributors to this volume portray the richness and diversity of the land, the people, and the technologies of the New Jersey pinelands. This is a useful source of information and illustrations for teachers.
♦ Readers could excerpt some of the stories and facts for reports or pictures, or even dramatic presentations.
1. Pine Barrens—Social life and customs 2. Pine Barrens—Industries 3. Handicraft—New Jersey—Pine Barrens.

974.9
Thompson, Kathleen. *New Jersey.* Raintree (0-96514-438-9), 1986. (Portrait of America Series). 48p. Color and B/W photos. (Interest level: 3-8).

The history, economy, culture, and future of New Jersey are covered in this overview, which also includes a state chronology, pertinent statistics, and maps. The photographs are from the Portrait of America programs.
♦ Students could research each chapter and add facts of their own.
1. New Jersey

974.902
Fradin, Dennis Brindell. *The New Jersey Colony.* Childrens Press (0-516-00395-X), 1991. (The Thirteen Colonies Series). 158p. Color and B/W illus. (Interest level: 4-6).

Fradin examines the history of the New Jersey colony from its beginnings to its achievement of statehood after the Revolutionary War. Profiles of significant individuals such as Lewis Morris, Rev. John Witherspoon, and Molly Pitcher are included.
♦ The biographical sketches could be used as the basis for a play. Each child could choose a person to research further and role-play.
1. New Jersey—History—Colonial period, ca 1600-1775.

974.902
Knight, James E. *The Village: Life in Colonial Times.* Troll (0-89375-728-4), 1982. (Adventures in Colonial America Series). 32p. Illus. (Interest level: 5-8).

Knight describes the lives and occupations during the early eighteenth century of the inhabitants of the village of Glenn Creek, near the Delaware River in New Jersey. Tools, buildings, and skills are illustrated in detail.

♦ This would be a good sourcebook for students preparing for a history fair. The illustrations are clear and can be used as models for construction.
1. New Jersey—Social life and customs.

Biography

92 Barton, Clara
Boylston, Helen D. *Clara Barton: Founder of the American Red Cross.* Random House (0-394-90358-7), 1963. (Landmark Series). 182p. B/W illus. (Interest level: 4-6).

Boylston's biography is an interesting, illustrated story of Clara Barton, the nurse who founded the American Red Cross and established the first public school in Bordentown, New Jersey.
♦ Students could research the Red Cross or prepare a report on education in New Jersey.
1. Barton, Clara, 1821-1912   2. Nurses—Biography   3. American National Red Cross.

92 Barton, Clara
Kent, Zachary. *The Story of Clara Barton.* Childrens Press (0-516-44725-4), 1987. 32p. Color and B/W illus. (Interest level: 3-6).

The life and career of Clara Barton, the nurse who, after fearlessly serving on the battlefields of the Civil War, founded the American Red Cross, are covered in this biography. The book includes her years spent teaching school in Bordentown, New Jersey. This work provides background on the Civil War and the wartime conditions that led to the formation of the Red Cross.
♦ Young people could contact the Red Cross as a follow-up activity and invite a speaker to describe the humanitarian assistance offered by the organization.
1. Barton, Clara, 1821-1912   2. Nurses—Biography   3. American National Red Cross.

92 Barton, Clara
Kraske, Robert. *Clara Barton: The Gentle Warrior.* Harper (0-03-049436-2). 35p. Color illus. (Interest level: 1-2).

Kraske has written a biography of the nurse who served in the Civil War and founded the American Red Cross as well as a boarding school in Bordentown, New Jersey. Written in easy vocabulary, this work can be a good introduction for children to influential women.
♦ Students could research other women who played an important role in the Civil War.
1. Barton, Clara, 1821-1912   2. Nurses—Biography   3. American National Red Cross.

92 Cleveland, Grover
Collins, David R. *Grover Cleveland: 22nd and 24th President of the United States.* Garrett Educational (0-944483-01-1), 1988. 69p. Photos and illus. (Interest level: 5-8).

Born in Caldwell, New Jersey, Grover Cleveland was the only man to serve two nonsequential terms as president of the United States. This biography covers both his personal and political life, placing them in the context of the mid-1800s. A good source of information on Cleveland, this work has some photographs and a bibliography.
♦ Students can debate Cleveland's positions on the issues of his day.
1. Cleveland, Grover, 1837-1908   2. Presidents—United States—Biography.

92 Dix, Dorothea
Melin, Grace H. *Dorothea Dix: Girl Reporter.* Macmillan (0-672-50043-4), 1963. 200p. B/W illus. (Interest level: 3-7).

Dorothea Dix, teacher and crusader, worked to obtain decent living conditions for people with mental disorders. Special mention is made of the favorite hospital she helped build in Trenton, New Jersey, the first entirely new hospital built especially for the care of the insane.
♦ Students can research modern mental hospitals and locate those in New Jersey. They could also research other American women who have achieved prominence as crusaders.
1. Dix, Dorothea Lynde, 1802-1887   2. Mentally ill—Institutional care   3. Reformers   4. Women—Biography.

92 Dodge, Mary Mapes
Mason, Miriam E. *Mary Mapes Dodge: Jolly Girl.* Macmillan (0-672-5013-7), 1949. 199p. B/W illus. (Interest level: 3-7).

This is the life story of Mary Mapes Dodge, the author of *Hans Brinker or the Silver Skates* and editor of *St. Nicholas Magazine* for children. Mary Mapes Dodge spent about half her life in Waverly, New Jersey. In reading this biography, students will gain perspective on life in New Jersey and New York in the mid-1800s.
♦ Young people might also want to follow-up by reading *Hans Brinker or the Silver Skates*.
1. Dodge, Mary Mapes, 1831-1905   2. Skating—Biography.

92 Edison, Thomas Alva
Buranelli, Vincent. *Thomas Alva Edison.* Silver Burdett (0-382-09522-7), 1989. (Pioneers in Change Series). 142p. Color and B/W illus. (Interest level: 5-7).

Thomas Alva Edison changed the world in which he lived with such revolutionary inventions as the phonograph, electric lighting, and motion pictures.
♦ Readers can make models of Edison's inventions and report on the changes in his ideas and how his basic ideas have been expanded today.

1. Edison, Thomas Alva, 1847-1931   2. Inventors—Biography.

92 Edison, Thomas Alva
Kaufmann, Mervyn D. *Thomas Alva Edison: Miracle Worker*. Garrard (0-7910-1426-6), 1962. (Garrard Discovery Series). 59p. Color and B/W illus. (Interest level: 2-5).

Kaufmann tells the story of the life of Thomas Alva Edison, who made more than 1,000 inventions. This work emphasizes Edison's years in New Jersey. The text is clear and the story exciting.
♦ This work would lend itself to a dramatic presentation.
1. Edison, Thomas Alva, 1847-1931   2. Inventors—Biography.

92 Edison, Thomas Alva
Morgan, Nina. *Thomas Edison*. Brookright Press (0-531-18406-4), 1991. (Pioneers of Science). 48p. Illus. (Interest level: 5-8).

Morgan has written an interesting biography of Thomas Alva Edison, the prolific inventor whose creations, including the electric light bulb and the phonograph (invented in New Jersey), have contributed to the comfort, convenience, and entertainment of people all over the world.
♦ The book compares some of Edison's creations with their modern versions; students could continue this process. They could also illustrate the words found in the glossary.
1. Edison, Thomas Alva, 1847-1931   2. Inventors—Biography.

92 Hamilton, Alexander
Crouse, Anna. *Alexander Hamilton and Aaron Burr*. Random House (No ISBN), 1963 (out of print). (Landmark Series). 84p. Illus. (Interest level: 5-8).

Crouse gives readers a vivid, illustrated re-creation of the background for the famous duel fought at Wehawken, New Jersey. This work focuses on the political motives of the two men.
♦ Class members could debate the theory of Hamilton's sacrifice.
1. Hamilton, Alexander, 1757-1804   2. Burr, Aaron, 1757-1836   3. United States—History—1783-1809.

92 Hamilton, Alexander
Higgins, Helen B. *Alex Hamilton: The Little Lion*. Macmillan (0-672-50006-X), 1942. 45p. Illus. (Interest level: 3-7).

Alexander Hamilton, the first secretary of the treasury of the United States, died a tragic death in a duel with Aaron Burr in New Jersey. This biography focuses primarily on his early life and addresses his political career.
♦ Students can research and contrast the lives of Hamilton and Burr.
1. Hamilton, Alexander, 1757-1804   2. Politicians—Biography.

92 Hamilton, Alexander
Keller, Mollie. *Alexander Hamilton*. Franklin Watts (0-531-10214-9), 1986. (Constitution First Books Series). 72p. Color and B/W illus. (Interest level: 4-8).

This is a biography of the man who was killed in a duel with Aaron Burr in New Jersey. Among other achievements, Alexander Hamilton was a Revolutionary War hero, an aide and advisor to George Washington, a framer of the Constitution, and the first secretary of the treasury of the newly formed United States. Keller takes a good look at the constitutional period in U.S. history.
♦ Class members could research when dueling was made illegal and what modern remedies exist to settle disputes peacefully, such as arbitration or intervention. The class could then settle an actual dispute between two class members using a modern reconciliation method.
1. Hamilton, Alexander, 1757-1804   2. Politicians—Biography.

92 Hudson, Henry
Harley, Ruth. *Henry Hudson*. Troll (0-89375-163-4), 1979. 48p. B/W illus. (Interest level: 4-7).

Harley's biography of Henry Hudson, famous explorer who sailed on the *Half Moon* along the shores of New Jersey past Sandy Hook and up the Hudson River, includes information on the Indians of New Jersey he encountered. This is a good reference source for students studying explorers of New Jersey.
♦ Some of the episodes recounted could be reenacted. Or children could plot Hudson's journey on a map.
1. Hudson, Henry, d. 1611   2. Explorers—Biography.

92 Morse, Samuel
Kerby, Mona. *Samuel Morse*. Franklin Watts (0-531-20023-X), 1991. 64p. Illus. (Interest level: 3-5).

Samuel Morse, who spent time in New Jersey developing his telegraphy, is the subject of this biography. The work describes his career as a painter and inventor, and how his development of the Morse Code laid the groundwork for modern telecommunications.
♦ Readers could use the appendix on the Morse Code and the telegraph to build a simple set.
1. Morse, Samuel Finley Breese, 1791-1872   2. Inventors—Biography.

92 Robeson, Paul
Greenfield, Eloise. *Paul Robeson*. Harper (0-690-00660-8), 1975. 40p. Illus. (Interest level: 1-5).

Here is an illustrated biography of Paul Robeson, the black man from Princeton who became a famous singer, actor, and spokesman for equal rights for blacks. This book will provide a good starting point for reports on civil rights.
♦ Students can do further study on the issue of civil rights.
1. Robeson, Paul, 1898-1975   2. Singers, American—Biography   2. African Americans—Biography.

92 Springsteen, Bruce
Bain, Geri. *Picture Life of Bruce Springsteen*. Franklin Watts (0-531-10204-1), 1986. (Picture Life Series). 48p. Illus. (Interest level: 1-6).

Bain examines the life and career of Bruce Springsteen, the popular New Jersey rock performer whose concern for the people and problems of the United States is evident in his music and charity work. This book would have popular appeal for students and could emphasize the humanitarian causes espoused by Springsteen.
♦ Children can report on Springsteen's life and play some of his recordings and videos.
1. Springsteen, Bruce   2. Rock musicians—Biography.

92 Wayne, Anthony
Stevenson, Augusta. *Anthony Wayne: Daring Boy*. Macmillan (0-672-50015-9), 1962. 169p. Illus. (Interest level: 3-7).

This biography captures the childhood of Anthony Wayne, the courageous American officer in the Revolutionary War who was the hero of the recapture of Stony Point. Wayne, New Jersey, was named for him, as he passed often through the state with George Washington.
♦ Students could research the origins of the names of cities, towns, hills, rivers, etc., in New Jersey.
1. Wayne, Anthony, 1745-1796   2. United States—History—1775-1783.

92 Wilson, Woodrow
Leavell, Perry J. *Woodrow Wilson*. Chelsea House (0-87754-557-X), 1987. 112p. Illus. (Interest level: 6-8).

Known as the "peacemaker," Woodrow Wilson was president of Princeton University, governor of New Jersey, and president of the United States. The political setting of the time is emphasized, and quotes from Wilson and others are liberally sprinkled throughout.
♦ Young people could discuss the attributes and activities of Woodrow Wilson that caused him to be known as "the peacemaker."
1. Wilson, Woodrow, 1856-1924   2. Presidents—United States—Biography.

92 Wilson, Woodrow
Monsell, Helen A. *Woodrow Wilson: Boy President*. Macmillan (0-672-50193-7), 1948. 186p. Illus. (Interest level: 3-7).

Monsell's biography focuses primarily upon Woodrow Wilson's early life in Georgia. This work shows his progression from Tommy, young student, to Woodrow, serious student at Princeton, who later became governor of New Jersey and then president of the United States.
♦ Discuss how Wilson's dream of the League of Nations and the United Nations came to fruition. Students could also write a story summary and act out the important parts.
1. Wilson, Woodrow, 1856-1924   2. Presidents—United States—Biography.

Fiction

Avi. *Captain Grey*. Pantheon (0-394-93484-9), 1977. 129p. (Interest level: 6-8).

Following the American Revolution, an 11-year-old boy becomes the captive of a ruthless man who has set up his own "nation," supported by piracy, on a remote part of the New Jersey coast. Students will enjoy this swashbuckling pirate tale.
♦ Young people can illustrate the story and make models of the "nation."
1. Pirates—Fiction   2. New Jersey—History—Revolution, 1775-1783—Fiction.

Avi. *The Fighting Ground*. Harper (006-440185-5), 1987. 139p. (Interest level: 4-8).

Thirteen-year-old Jonathan from Trenton goes off to fight in the Revolutionary War and discovers the real war is being fought within himself.
♦ This is a good starting point for a discussion of war and its effects on civilians and soldiers. Also, the German spoken by the Hessians is translated at the end of the story and could be used to introduce students to other cultures.
1. New Jersey—History—Revolution, 1775-1783—Fiction   2. U.S.—History—Revolution, 1775-1783—Fiction.

Blume, Judy. *Deenie*. Dell (0-440-93259-9), 1991. 144p. (Interest level: 7-8).

This is Blume's portrayal of New Jersey suburban life, where a mother dreams that her 13-year-old daughter will become a famous model. Both her plans and Deenie's, whose only wish is to be exactly like her friends, are dramatically changed when Deenie must put on a heavy brace to straighten her spine. The book is useful for teaching students about scoliosis.
♦ Students can discuss how difficult it is to have a disability. How does Deenie learn to deal with her disability?
1. Physical handicaps—Fiction.

Brady, Esther Wood. *Toliver's Secret.* Crown (0-517-56910-8), 1988. 176p. (Interest level: 3-7).

Since her grandfather is unable to complete his mission, 10-year-old Ellen Toliver needs to disguise herself as a boy and become part of a chain of couriers who will carry an important message to General Washington. Her trip to Elizabethtown, New Jersey, is filled with dangers, forcing Ellen to prove that she has courage, intelligence, and imagination. This is a good story for students to read to learn about part of Washington's campaign in New Jersey during the Revolution.
♦ Readers could map Ellen's trip and explain the significance of her mission.
1. New Jersey—History—Revolution, 1775-1783—Fiction   2. United States—History—Revolution, 1775-1783—Fiction.

Cebulash, Mel. *Ruth Marini: Dodger Ace.* Lerner (0-8225-0726-9), 1983. 137p. (Interest level: 4-8).

Cebulash tells the story of Ruth Marini, New Jersey native and first woman player in professional baseball. Teammate jealousy and romance complicate her life as she competes for a place on the National League All-Star Team.
♦ This might be a starting point for research into the role of women in professional sports and affirmative action in sports.
1. Baseball—Fiction.

Dorian, Edith M. *High-Water Cargo.* Rutgers University Press (0-8135-0473-2), 1965. 224p. Illus. (Interest level: 4-8).

In this novel of the Delaware and Raritan Canal in New Jersey, Dirck Van Arsdale works on the old canal and dreams of attending college at Rutgers so he can become an engineer and build bridges. His hard work on the canal and solving a mystery finally pay off and his dream is realized.
♦ Full of local history and authentic setting, this story could be enacted by students. They could also report on how the canals worked.
1. Delaware and Raritan Canal—Fiction.

Gauch, Patricia Lee. *This Time, Tempe Wick?* Putnam (0-399-21880-7), 1992. 48p. Illus. (Interest level: 1-4).

Based on a true character, this is a juvenile novel of the Revolutionary War adventures of a young girl and her horse near Morristown, New Jersey. When soldiers try to steal her horse, Tempe outwits them in a most unusual manner.
♦ Children will love the delightful drawings and may enjoy illustrating their favorite part of the story.
1. New Jersey—History—Revolution, 1775-1783—Fiction.

Harrington, Mark R. *The Indians of New Jersey: Dickon among the Lenapes.* Rutgers University Press (0-8135-0425-2), 1963. 352p. Illus. (Interest level: 4-6).

This is a reprint of the 1963 story of the Lenape Indians who lived among the hills, barrens, rivers, and forests of New Jersey. The story brings to life the lore and heritage of the Lenape when a shipwrecked English boy, Dickon, becomes their captive and is eventually adopted into the tribe.
♦ Children could act out or draw pictures for each event.
1. Delaware Indians—Fiction.

Homer, Larona C. *The Shore Ghosts and Other Stories of New Jersey.* Middle Atlantic Press (0-912608-145), 1986. 154p. Illus. (Interest level: 4-8).

Ghosts and smugglers at the shore, a brother and sister alone on a terrifying trip to freedom on the Underground Railroad, a courageous boy in a devastating fire, and a horse that spent the night in a guest room—these are but a few of the characters brought to life in this collection of short stories about New Jersey.
♦ Perfect for storytelling or acting, these stories could be adapted very easily for use by students.
1. Folklore—New Jersey   2. Ghosts—Fiction.

Krumgold, Joseph. *Onion John.* Harper (0-690-59957-9), 1987. 248p. (Interest level: 5-8).

This story of the generation gap between father and son and local prejudice is set on a farm in Serenity, New Jersey. Onion John is a friend of Andy Rusch, Jr., and when the town tries to change the way of life of the man who eats onions the way Andy eats apples, all sorts of trouble erupts.
♦ This is an excellent story to discuss, as it deals with values and prejudices.
1. Prejudices—Fiction.

Rinaldi, Ann. *Time Enough for Drums.* Holiday House (0-8234-0603-2), 1986. 249p. (Interest level: 7-8).

Fifteen-year-old Jemima Emerson, sheltered by a loving family, watches in fascination as the colonists' struggle for independence from the British king divides her hometown of Trenton, New Jersey, and her family.
♦ For older readers, this work is useful as a touchstone for discussion on the loyalists and the patriots.
1. Trenton (N.J.)—History—Fiction   2. New Jersey—History—Revolution, 1775-1783—Fiction.

Robertson, Keith. *Henry Reed, Inc.* Viking (0-067-367-96-6), 1958. 239p. (Interest level: 4-6).

This is one of the stories about Henry Harris Reed, who spends his summers with his aunt and uncle in Grovers Corners, New Jersey. Henry is ingenious, and these stories tell of his many adven-

tures in free enterprise, show business, and other activities.
♦ Young people could write stories about their summer activities.
1. Family life—Fiction.

Terhune, Albert Payson. *Lad: A Dog.* Dutton (0-451-16417-2), 1978. 256p. Illus. (Interest level: 6-8).
Lad is one of a series of stories about a collie who lived at Sunnybank in Wayne, New Jersey.
♦ Students could write stories about their own pets.
1. Dogs—Fiction.

Periodicals

574
New Jersey Outdoors. New Jersey Department of Environmental Protection and Energy (ISSN 08625-0402). Bimonthly. (Interest level: grade 6-adult).
Articles in this periodical deal with the environment, biology, and related New Jersey recreational and educational topics.
♦ Readers will find this a good source of current information on New Jersey and environmental issues. Students can carry out suggested experiments and go on field trips.
1. Nature study—New Jersey—Periodicals 2. Outdoor life—Periodicals 3. Ecology—Periodicals.

Professional Materials

016.3
New Jersey Library Association. *New Jersey and the Negro: A Bibliography, 1715-1966.* New Jersey Library Association (No ISBN), 1971. 196p. (Interest level: Professional).
The New Jersey Library Association presents a listing of 1,601 works dealing with African Americans from the early eighteenth century to the mid-1960s. This bibliography has not been superseded by more recent works and remains a useful tool.
♦ Using the bibliography, teachers will find works on black history in New Jersey, which would be especially useful for Black History Month.
1. African Americans—New Jersey—Bibliography.

016.3
Steiner-Scott, Elizabeth and **Wagle, Elizabeth P.** *New Jersey Women, Seventeen Seventy to Nineteen Seventy: A Bibliography.* Fairleigh Dickinson University Press (0-8386-1967-3), 1978. 167p. (Interest level: Professional).
This is a guide to the identification and location of all print works pertaining to New Jersey women from the colonial period to 1970. The entries range from general to specific and are annotated as needed.
♦ The work is useful for teachers preparing material on New Jersey women for New Jersey studies and Women's History Month.
1. Women—New Jersey—History—Bibliography.

016.8
New Jersey State Library. *Fiction Set in New Jersey: A Bibliography of Holdings in the Collections of the New Jersey State Library.* New Jersey State Library (No ISBN), 1990. 62p. (Interest level: Professional).
Readers will find here a listing of primarily adult fiction with a New Jersey setting held by the state library. All types of fiction are included, and the titles are available on interlibrary loan from the New Jersey State Library and many other libraries.
♦ Adults and teachers can use this as a guide for background reading and as a sourcebook for selecting fiction for library collections.
1. New Jersey—Fiction—Bibliography.

300.5
The Docket: Journal of the New Jersey Council for the Social Studies. New Jersey Council for the Social Studies (No ISSN). Quarterly. (Interest level: Professional).
The official journal of the council, this periodical includes practical articles with ideas for teachers, scholarly articles, reviews, informational articles, and letters to the editor.
♦ This periodical will be useful for ideas for teachers, as well as a source for stories and information. Each issue is devoted to a theme and provides valuable references.
1. New Jersey—Study and teaching—Periodicals.

305.896
Wright, Giles R. *Afro-Americans in New Jersey: A Short History.* New Jersey Historical Commission (0-89743-076-1), 1988. 100p. (Interest level: Professional).
Wright offers a concise history of blacks in New Jersey since the seventeenth century. Topics include slavery, the Underground Railroad, segregation, social and business life within the black community, and changes in black life over time.
♦ This resource can be used by teachers to gain information as they research special topics. Some of the text could be adapted for use with advanced students.
1. African Americans—New Jersey 2. History.

307.7 (Reference)
The New Jersey Municipal Data Book. 11th ed. Information Publications (0-911273-15-8), 1991. 608p. (Interest level: Professional).

This work provides an alphabetical locational/subject approach to commonly requested facts and figures about New Jersey municipalities.
♦ With guidance from the teacher or librarian, students can look up data on their own community or a community of their choice and report on expenditures, types of services, etc.
1. Cities and towns—New Jersey.

320.749
Lacetti, Silvio R., ed. *New Jersey Profiles in Public Policy*. Commonwealth Books (0-940390-05-1), 1990. 334p. B/W illus. and maps. (Interest level: Professional).

Twelve essays on the major policy concerns of New Jersey, including the economy, social services, transportation, and environmental issues, are collected here. Where appropriate, charts and maps are included and references are provided for each entry.
♦ A good overview for the teacher and adult, this work could spark debates and reports on the various topics. Students could take a subject and summarize it or apply the issues to their own communities.
1. New Jersey—Politics and government.

342.7 (Reference)
Williams, Robert F. *The New Jersey State Constitution: A Reference Guide*. Greenwood (0-313-26245-4), 1990. 129p. (Interest level: Professional).

Williams's guide to and analysis of the history and current status of the New Jersey constitution provides a clause-by-clause commentary, a bibliography, a table of cases, and an index.
♦ This is valuable as a reference work for the teacher for background on the development of the state's constitution and the current text.
1. New Jersey—Constitutional law 2. New Jersey—Constitution.

349.74
Miller, Melville D. *You and the Law in New Jersey: A Resource Guide*. Rutgers University Press (0-8135-1342-1), 1988. 394p. (Interest level: Professional).

Miller's work, arranged by subject, provides an overview of the laws of New Jersey and the United States. It presents the laws as information sources. This is an excellent reference guide for teachers preparing units on New Jersey law, including personal and education law.
♦ The section on laws and the schools would be of particular use to teachers in New Jersey as general information, not necessarily for New Jersey studies. The section on the environment could be used as a resource for students who are writing reports.
1. Law—New Jersey.

361.6
New Jersey Reporter. Center for Analysis of Public Issues (ISSN 0195-3192). Monthly. (Interest level: Professional).

This is a monthly journal covering political and legal issues of New Jersey. Prominent personages are featured in some issues.
♦ Teachers could use this periodical to obtain current information for government studies. Featured people could bring government close to home for students.
1. New Jersey—Politics and government—Periodicals.

374.0005
NJN Instructional Resources Manual, K-12. New Jersey Network (No ISBN), 1985. (Interest level: Professional).

This resource provides a listing of the educational programs presented on NJN television. The stories are supplemented with instructional objectives and activities. The manual is available in three levels: primary, intermediate, and secondary.
♦ Teachers can use the manual as a guide for incorporating current programs into the New Jersey program.
1. New Jersey—Study and teaching 2. Television in education.

390
Bartis, Peter T. *Folklife Resources in New Jersey*. New Jersey Historical Commission (No ISBN), 1985. 91p. (Interest level: Professional).

Published jointly with the American Folklife Center of the Library of Congress, this survey lists the folk culture collections of 172 institutions in New Jersey. Topics include architecture, art, furniture, tools and equipment, boats, and Indian artifacts.
♦ This guide will provide teachers with information on locating works on the topics mentioned above.
1. Folklore—New Jersey 2. New Jersey—Social life and customs.

390
Cohen, David Steven. *Folklife in New Jersey: An Annotated Bibliography*. New Jersey Historical Commission (0-89743055-9), 1982. 108p. (Interest level: Professional).

Folklorists, teachers, students, and the general public will find this guide useful. Cohen lists 477 published works in 12 categories, including folk narratives, place-names, folk music and folk dance, folk medicine, folk art, proverbs, riddles, and jokes.
♦ Teachers and middle school students can use this bibliography to locate materials for reports and storytelling.
1. Folklore—New Jersey 2. New Jersey—Social life and customs.

390
Cohen, David Steven. *The Folklore and Folklife of New Jersey*. Rutgers University Press (0-8135-0989-0), 1983. 223p. (Interest level: Professional).

A comprehensive view of New Jersey's rich folk culture, this work covers native folklore, folktales, speech, music, song, dance, and medicine. Cohen focuses on the folklife of material folk culture, leisure activities, and symbolic behavior and examines architecture, sculpture, painting, furniture, crafts, and festivals.
♦ This is a good teacher resource. Some of the stories, songs, and pictures can be used as illustrations for lessons. Students could retrieve information for reports on various special topics.
1. Folklore—New Jersey 2. New Jersey—Social life and customs.

398
New Jersey Folklife. Rutgers University Press (ISSN 0887-8048). Annual. (Interest level: Professional).

The annual journal of the New Jersey Folklore Society, this includes stories, pictures, and official records.
♦ Teachers could read excerpts from the stories to students and discuss how folktales reflect the folklife.
1. Folklore—New Jersey.

507 (Reference)
Held, Patricia Contreras. *A Field Guide to New Jersey's Nature Centers*. Rutgers University Press (0-8135-1290-5), 1988. 157p. (Interest level: Professional).

Divided into four sections, this handbook examines the nature centers in the state. Information on location, hours, fees, special programs, and event is included for each center, as well as maps and photographs. A bibliography and index facilitate research.
♦ Useful for environmental studies, this work could also be a guide for field trips and studies of the plants and animals of the different areas of New Jersey. Students can write to the various groups listed in the appendix for further information.
1. Nature study—New Jersey—Guidebooks.

572.97
Cohen, David Steven, comp. *New Jersey Ethnic History: A Bibliography*. New Jersey Historical Commission (0-89743-102-2), 1986. 58p. (Interest level: Professional).

Cohen has compiled a selective bibliography of nonfiction publications about New Jersey ethnic history. Readers can use the guide to identify areas given extensive or limited coverage.
♦ Teachers can use this guide to gather information for themselves or students on specific ethnic groups. Using this book as a model, students can compile their own bibliographies on local areas.
1. Ethnology—New Jersey—Bibliography
2. New Jersey—History—Bibliography.

598.05
New Jersey Audubon. New Jersey Audubon Society (No ISSN). Quarterly. (Interest level: Professional).

Articles in this periodical cover such topics as New Jersey birdlife, book reviews, and poetry.
♦ This periodical is a useful reference tool for teachers. Pictures can be used for displays, and students could use some of the articles to identify birds in their area.
1. Birds—Study and teaching—Periodicals.

790.09 (Reference)
Lippman, Helen and **Reardon, Patricia**. *Enjoying New Jersey Outdoors: A Year-Round Guide to Outdoor Recreation in the Garden State & Nearby*. Rutgers University Press (0-8135-1655-2), 1991. 216p. Color and B/W illus. (Interest level: Professional).

A wide range of outdoor sports and recreational activities available in and around New Jersey are described in this guide, along with places to enjoy them. Divided into types of activities, entries describe activities all can enjoy, including young and old people and people with disabilities.
♦ This will be useful for planning trips. The listing of organizations involved with each type of activity could be used to solicit information on ecology and other outdoor studies.
1. Outdoor recreation—New Jersey 2. New Jersey—Description and travel.

917.49 (Reference)
Dann, Kevin. *Twenty-Five Walks in New Jersey*. Rutgers University Press (0-8135-1010-4), 1988. 193p. Color and B/W illus. and maps. (Interest level: Professional).

Half- and full-day walks in the various natural areas and regions of New Jersey are outlined in this guide. Plant guides, markers, and courtesy reminders are indicated, along with some illustrations and maps of each area.
♦ Adults or teachers can use this guide to plan field walks to introduce children to resource conservation and teach them how to protect the environment.
1. Hiking—New Jersey 2. Parks—New Jersey
3. New Jersey—Description and travel.

917.49
New Jersey Monthly. Tomlinson Enterprises (ISSN 0273-270X). Monthly. (Interest level: Professional).

New Jersey Monthly is an illustrated journal of current news topics on New Jersey life. Special

department columns and feature articles are included.
♦ This journal could be used for all aspects of New Jersey study. The pictures would be good for displays and the articles for current information for teachers and advanced students.
1. New Jersey—Periodicals.

917.49 (Reference)
Westergaard, Barbara. *New Jersey: A Guide to the State.* Rutgers University Press (0-8135-1242-5), 1987. 400p. B/W illus. and maps. (Interest level: Professional).

Alphabetically arranged by cities, towns, and areas in New Jersey, this work delves into the history, culture, technology, industry, and topology of 215 of the state's communities. The offerings range from local legends to museum operating hours and park descriptions. Entries include maps.
♦ A good resource for teachers and parents, this guide can be used for field trips and area studies.
1. New Jersey—Description and travel—Guidebooks.

917.49 (Reference)
Works Progress Administration. *New Jersey: A Guide to Its Present & Past.* Omnigraphics (1-55888-380-0), 1992, 1939. 349p. B/W illus. (Interest level: Professional).

A three-part guide to New Jersey, this work provides short essays covering its history, economy, social life, ethnic groups, art, and recreation; describes the state's most noteworthy cities and towns; and details road tours of the state. This is a wonderful resource book with essays by such writers as William Carlos Williams, Lewis Mumford, and Edmund Wilson.
♦ Readers could bring the entries up to date.
1. New Jersey—Description and travel.

970.449
Weslager, C. A. *The Delaware Indians.* Rutgers University Press (0-8135-1494-0), 1989. 576p. (Interest level: Professional).

Weslager offers a comprehensive tribal history with an update on what happened to the main body of the Delaware Nation over the past three centuries.
♦ Teachers will find this source useful for supplementing the juvenile books on the Delaware Indians.
1. Delaware Indians.

974.9
Bill, Alfred Hoyt. *New Jersey and the Revolutionary War.* Rutgers University Press (0-8135-0642-5), 1970, 1964. 117p. B/W illus. (Interest level: Professional).

A complete account of New Jersey's important role in the Revolutionary War, this work contains a survey of the major military developments as well as the social and economic effects of the war on the state. Bill describes the people who were responsible for the surrender of Cornwallis and who helped win the war and shape the United States.
♦ This is useful as a teacher reference, and excerpts could be used for students in seventh and eighth grades for studying economic forces.
1. New Jersey—History—Revolution, 1775-1783
2. United States—History—Revolution, 1775-1783.

974.9
Jannuzzelli, Diane C. *Creating New Jersey Learning Centers: An Exciting Multi-Disciplinary Approach to Teaching New Jersey Studies in the Elementary Grades.* Afton (089-359-0053), 1981. 64p. B/W illus. (Interest level: Professional).

Thirty-two different learning stations, complete with purposes, directions, follow-up, and evaluation make up this resource. Each idea is illustrated, and, where appropriate, answers are provided.
♦ Teachers and librarians can incorporate these ideas into units on New Jersey. Clear directions enhance the book's value.
1. New Jersey—Study and teaching.

974.9
Kraft, Herbert C. *The Lenape: Archaeology, History, and Ethnology.* New Jersey Historical Society (0-911020-20-9), 1987. 300p. (Interest level: Professional).

Kraft's study focuses on the Lenape or Delaware Indians, their Munsee-speaking kinsmen, and the prehistoric forebears of both. The tribes are traced from their beginnings to the present in Oklahoma, other western states, and Canada. Maps and photographs of artifacts are included.
♦ Although this is a resource book for teachers, students can use the illustrations in presentations to the class. Students could also discover the functions of the artifacts.
1. Delaware Indians—History.

974.9
McCormick, Richard Patrick. *New Jersey from Colony to State, 1609-1789.* Rev. ed. New Jersey Historical Society (0-911020-02-0), 1981. 191p. B/W illus. (Interest level: Professional).

McCormick's book is a classic study of a specific time period in New Jersey's history. Illustrations and a chronology enhance the text. This work is useful as a reference source for the teacher in understanding the important role of the state in the formation of the nation.
♦ Students could prepare a time line highlighting the important events leading to New Jersey statehood. They could prepare one for their own state as well and do a comparison.

1. New Jersey—History—Colonial period, ca 1600-1775 2. New Jersey—History—Revolution, 1775-1783.

974.9
Mellick, Andrew D. *The Story of an Old Farm: Or Life in New Jersey in the 18th Century: With A Genealogical Appendix.* Higginson Book Company (0-8328-2248-5), 1991, 1889. 724p. (Interest level: Professional).

Centered around the theme of a German middle-class family's migration to the United States and the three generations of people who lived in their farmhouse, this work presents New Jersey history from the human rather than civic side. An index provides entry to family names and some subjects.
♦ Portions of the work could be presented to students who could then trace their own family's settlement.
1. New Jersey—History 2. Genealogy.

974.9
New Jersey History. New Jersey Historical Society (ISSN 0028-5757). Quarterly. (Interest level: Professional).

Issued quarterly by the New Jersey Historical Society, this journal is a scholarly treatment of history and contemporary problems in New Jersey. Reviews of current books in the area are also included.
♦ This is an excellent background reference for teachers, who can extract facts to use in teaching. In some cases, portions of entire articles could be used as motivational tools (e.g., articles on sports in New Jersey).
1. New Jersey—History—Periodicals.

974.9
New Jersey History Series. New Jersey Historical Commission, 1991. (Interest level: Professional).

This series of topical histories is designed primarily for adult use. Titles include *One State in Arms*, *The Use of Abundance*, and *The Indians of New Jersey*.
♦ Some sections could be condensed for young children. Bibliographies lead to further research.
1. New Jersey—History.

New York

by Mary R. Lenart

Nonfiction

333.912
Ancona, George. *Riverkeeper.* Macmillan (0-02-700911-14), 1990. Unpaginated. B/W photos. (Interest level: 4-6).

Some of the many duties of John Cronin, riverkeeper of the Hudson River, include helping to keep the river clean and catching polluters. The photos and the text accurately describe the many facets of this important position.
♦ If a large body of water exists nearby, have the students make up and conduct interviews with the riverkeeper or caretaker of the waterway. The students could then list ways that they could help keep the rivers, lakes, and streams clean and pollution-free.
1. Stream conservation—Hudson River (N.Y. and N.J.) 2. Water—Pollution—Environmental aspects—Hudson River (N.Y. and N.J.) 3. Riverkeepers—Hudson River (N.Y. and N.J.) 4. Conservation of natural resources.

381.415
Horwitz, Joshua. *Night Markets: Bringing Food to a City.* Thomas Y. Crowell (0-690-04379-1), 1984. 90p. B/W photos. (Interest level: 3-7).

The various means of transporting food and flowers into New York City are presented. Informative text and pictures relay this interesting story.
♦ If you are near a local food or produce distributor, invite a speaker from that company to discuss food transportation with the class. Perhaps a representative of a trucking firm could also speak.
1. Produce trade—New York (N.Y.) 2. New York (N.Y.)—Markets 3. Wholesale trade—New York (N.Y.) 4. Food supply— New York (N.Y.).

386
Garrity, Richard. *Canal Boatman: My Life on Upstate Waterways.* Syracuse University Press (0-8156-0139-5), 1977. 222p. B/W photos and illus. (Interest level: 7-8).

Garrity's interesting account of a life spent on the Erie Canal is rich with history, humor, and factual information. The author, a canaller himself, shares anecdotes that bring both the era and the area alive for the reader.
♦ Students could make a comparison chart for the old Erie Canal and the newer Barge Canal, indicating differences in uses, equipment, etc.
1. Garrity, Richard G. 2. Boatmen—New York (State)—Biography 3. Canals—New York (State)—History.

394.2
Munro, Roxie. *Christmastime in New York City.* Illus. by author. Dodd, Mead (0-396-08909-7), 1987. Unpaginated. Color illus. (Interest level: K-adult).

This collection of illustrations covers many events and scenes that are a part of New York City during the Christmas season. Munro's big, bold illustrations are colorful and so realistic that they make the reader feel part of the scene.
♦ In groups of two, students can prepare audiotapes describing the places found in the book. Young people may do research in the library to find several additional facts about these places. Each group may then share the audiotape it has made with the class.
1. Christmas—New York (N.Y.)—Pictorial works 2. Christmas decorations—New York (N.Y.)—Pictorial works 3. New York (N.Y.)—Social life and customs—Pictorial works.

398.2
Bierhorst, John, ed. *The Naked Bear: Folktales of the Iroquois.* Illus. by Dirk Zimmer. William Morrow (0-688-06422-1), 1987. 123p. B/W illus. (Interest level: grade 3-adult).

For young and old alike, this is a collection of stories told by the Iroquois. Many of the stories feature animals and fierce creatures.
♦ In groups, students can narrate a story on audiotape. Then the groups should prepare presentations for the class using pictures they have drawn or found in the library. If the pictures are prepared on giant poster board, group members can hold up each picture as the story is played on the tape.
1. Iroquois Indians—Legends   2. Indians of North America—Legends.

398.2
Bruchac, Joseph. *Iroquois Stories: Heroes and Heroines, Monsters and Magic.* Illus. by Daniel Burgevin. The Crossing Press (0-89594-167-8), 1985. 202p. B/W illus. (Interest level: 5-8).

Based on original stories told by the Iroquois centuries ago, these tales focus primarily on the interactions of animals and humans. The author accurately retells the stories and helps to explain the habits, customs, and characteristics of the Iroquois world.
♦ Several of the stories are short. In a storytelling unit, older students could learn and tell one of the stories either to the class or to groups of younger children. Students could also illustrate the stories. An extended unit might include the making of storyboards and eventually slide/tape programs.
1. Iroquois Indians—Legends   2. Indians of North America—Legends.

398.2
DuMond, Frank L. *Tall Tales of the Catskills.* Frank L. DuMond (No ISBN), 1968. 179p. (Interest level: 5-8).

DuMond has collected tall tales, mostly involving animal-like creatures, which evolved in the area of the Catskill Mountains in New York State. The tall tales presented are both amusing and interesting.
♦ Studying tall tales can be such fun, because it gives the children a chance to use their imagination. For each story presented, students could draw a picture of what they think the "animal" looks like. They might draw the pictures as the story is read.
1. Tall tales   2. Legends—New York (State).

398.2
Legend of Firefly Marsh. (Videocassette). Phoenix Films, 1987. Color, (28 min.). (Interest level: 5-8).

Appealing to the story-lover in all of us, this wonderful film combines tall tales, ghost stories, and believe-it-or-not creatures. The story also focuses on courage, compassion, and deep beliefs.
♦ Young people may write a tall tale or ghost story based on something that relates to their life, such as a dream, a favorite animal, or something they have seen.
1. Tall tales   2. Legends—New York (State).

398.2
Thompson, Harold W. *Body, Boots, and Britches: Folktales, Ballads, and Speech from Country New York.* Syracuse University Press (0-8156-2218-X), 1979. 538p. (Interest level: grade 7-adult).

Thompson's marvelous collection of legends and ballads from the state of New York (outside of New York City) includes stories about Indians, pirates, animals, lumbermen, murderers, and many others. Perhaps most appealing are the ballads, retold, for the most part, in original dialects. An index is included.
♦ Children can choose the chapter they would most like to learn more about. For each story in the chapter, they should label a map with some marking indicating where the story originated or took place. Then they can examine the complete map. A question for discussion might be why certain types of stories originated in certain places.
1. Folklore—New York (State)   2. New York (State)—Social life and customs   3. Legends—New York (State)   4. Folk songs, American—New York (State)—History and criticism   5. Ballads, American—New York (State)—History and criticism.

398.23
Jagendorf, M. A. *The Ghost of Peg-Leg Peter, and Other Stories of Old New York.* Illus. by Lino S. Lipinski. Vanguard Press (0-8149-0327-4), n.d. 125p. B/W illus. (Interest level: 5-8).

This unique compilation of folktales, some of which are based on factual accounts, adds a new dimension to the history of New York City. The stories are humorous and enlightening. The book also includes some songs of old New York.
♦ Groups of students can choose stories to learn and act out for the entire class. One of the students in each group may have to serve a narrator. The students may use costuming and scenery props as needed.
1. Tales, American—New York (N.Y.)   2. New York (N.Y.)—History   3. New York (N.Y.)—Folklore.

552
Hiscock, Bruce. *The Big Rock.* Illus by author. Atheneum (0-689-31402-7), 1988. Unpaginated. Color illus. (Interest level: 2-4).

Bright, colorful illustrations help trace the history of a chunk of granite located in the Adirondack Mountains. The author also covers the movement of glaciers.
♦ As part of a unit on fossils, students can bring examples into the classroom to study.
1. Rocks—New York (State)   2. Geology—New York (State).

624.55
St. George, Judith. *The Brooklyn Bridge: They Said It Couldn't Be Built.* G. P. Putnam (0-399-20873-9), 1982. 125p. B/W photos. (Interest level: grade 5-adult).

The challenge that the Roebling family faced in constructing the massive Brooklyn Bridge is explored in this fascinating account. The book's informative tone makes the technical information easy to read.
♦ Young people can develop a time line showing the construction of the Brooklyn Bridge, including disasters, setbacks, and accomplishments. They could also draw a diagram of the bridge and label the diagram with statistics given in the back of the book, such as length of river span, length of land span, and weight of anchorages.

1. Brooklyn Bridge (New York, N.Y.) 2. New York (N.Y.)—Bridges 3. Bridge construction.

636.088
Scott, Elaine. *Safe in the Spotlight: The Dawn Animal Agency and the Sanctuary for Animals.* Photos by Margaret Miller. Morrow Junior Books (0-688-08178-9), 1991. 77p. B/W photos. (Interest level: 4-8).

Scott takes a look at the people and the different animals who make up the Dawn Animal Agency and Sanctuary for Animals in Westtown, New York. The author successfully relays the significance of the work done at the agency.
♦ In a class discussion, students can talk about their favorite exotic animals, then they can do research in the library to find information on the proper care and training of these animals. The class could also write to the agency (the address is listed in the book) to inquire about "adopting" an animal.

1. Animal welfare—New York (State) 2. Working animals—New York (State) 3. Animals in television—New York (State) 4. Animals in motion pictures—New York (State) 5. Dawn Animal Agency 6. Sanctuary for Animals.

690.523
Macaulay, David. *Unbuilding.* Houghton Mifflin (0-395-29457-6), 1980. 80p. B/W illus. (Interest level: 7-8).

This is a fictional account of the demolition of the Empire State Building in New York City. Macaulay's detailed descriptions are a special feature of the book.
♦ Here is an excellent source to use in the study of architecture. Students could identify different architectural styles in other buildings in New York City or in their own community.

1. Wrecking 2. New York (N.Y.)—Empire State Building 3. Skyscrapers.

720.974
Fancher, Pauline. *Chautauqua: Its Architecture and Its People.* Banyan Books (0-916224-32-5), 1978. 120p. B/W photos. (Interest level: grade 7-adult).

Chautauqua, a cultural center located in western New York, is known for its art, architecture, study sessions, and worship services. Fancher focuses on the architecture of the buildings in the institution.
♦ One of the novel characteristics of entries in this book is that they describe each house in Chautauqua and include a history of the ownership of each home. Students can describe their own homes and determine what type of architecture was employed in building the home. Students could also develop a chronological history of the ownership of their homes.

1. Chautauqua, New York (State).

720.974
Nineteenth Century Architecture in New York State. (Slides). New York State Historical Association, 1991. 25 color slides; guide. $11.00. (Interest level: grade 6-adult).

The various styles of architecture used in the state of New York during the nineteenth century are featured in this slide program. The wide variety of architectural styles presented makes this a useful and interesting guide.
♦ Children can attempt to reconstruct or draw the facades of some of the buildings using available materials. The class could also discuss any local buildings that may have been built according to styles of architecture being presented.

1. Architecture, American 2. New York (State)—Description and travel.

730.92
Maestro, Betsy and **Maestro, Giulio.** *The Story of the Statue of Liberty.* Illus. by Giulio Maestro. Lothrop, Lee and Shepard (0-688-05774-8), 1986. 45p. Color illus. (Interest level: 3-5).

The beautiful color illustrations in this book enhance the story of the creation of the Statue of Liberty, from the first sketches by Bartholdi to the present-day restoration movement. Both text and illustrations detail the enormous task of constructing and transporting this monument.
♦ Young people can create a pictorial time line, showing the historical highlights of the building of the Statue of Liberty.

1. Statue of Liberty (New York, N.Y.) 2. Bartholdi, Frédéric-Auguste, 1834-1904 3. New York (N.Y.)—Buildings, structures, etc. 4. National monuments—United States 5. Statues.

784.4
The Erie Canal. Illus. by Peter Spier. Doubleday and Co. (0-385-06777-1), 1970. Unpaginated. Color illus. (Interest level: grade 1-adult).

The well-known illustrator Peter Spier has created beautiful, lively pictures to illustrate the folk song about the Erie Canal; the illustrations also serve to present a view of life on and around the Erie Canal. One of the great aspects of this book is the information about the Erie Canal given in the back.
♦ Children can videotape a program about the Erie Canal. Acting as interviewers and interviewees, and using the information in the back of the book, students could develop an interesting program.
1. Erie Canal—New York (State).

796.357
Editors of Sporting News, comp. *Cooperstown: Baseball's Hall of Fame.* Outlet (0-517-66986-2), 1988. 336p. Color illus. (Interest level: 4-8).

This is a collection of biographical sketches of baseball players whose hard work helped them become a part of our national pastime. The sketches include information on their personal and professional careers.
♦ Students can design or build their own imaginary "dream" team from the sketches presented and illustrate their team in the form of baseball cards. Then students can explain why they chose the baseball players they did.
1. Baseball 2. New York (State)—Description and travel.

796.357
Hahn, James and **Hahn, Lynn.** *Casey! The Sports Career of Charles Stengel.* Crestwood House (0-89686-126-0), 1981. (Sports Legends Series). 47p. B/W photos. (Interest level: 3-6).

The Hahns tell the life story of Charles (Casey) Stengel, a baseball Hall of Fame member, who was the only manager ever to win five World Series in a row with the New York Yankees team. Stengel's love for the game of baseball and skill in managing a major league baseball team are highlighted.
♦ Students can research the Yankees baseball team and make a list of the players on the team during Stengel's fifth World Series championship. Many students enjoy collecting baseball cards. If any students have cards for baseball players who were or are members of any of the teams that Stengel managed during his career, they could show them to the class.
1. Stengel, Charles (Casey) 2. Baseball managers—United States—Biography 3. New York (N.Y.)—Baseball club (American League).

917.3
Tinseltown and the Big Apple. (Videocassette). Films for the Humanities, 1988. Color, (24 min.). $79.00. (Interest level: 5-8).

Often a city that is exciting to an adult is completely foreign to a child. This video looks at Los Angeles and New York City with a "child's eye," focusing on sites and attractions that would appeal to a young tourist.
♦ In two groups, class members can develop pamphlets of materials that a tour guide might use to promote tourism in Los Angeles or New York.
1. Los Angeles (Calif.)—Description 2. New York City (N.Y.)—Description.

917.47
Bertinetti, Marcello and **White, Angela.** *New York.* Photos by authors. W. H. Smith Publishers (0-8317-6352-3), 1984. 123p. Color photos. (Interest level: grade 5-adult).

These scenes of New York City include everything from the homeless to the Statue of Liberty. Together they give a beautiful and complete view of a great cultural center.
♦ Young people can write creative essays about one or more of the pictures in the book and illustrate their essays.
1. New York (N.Y.)—Pictorial works.

917.47
Ehling, William P. *Canoeing Central New York.* Backcountry Publications (0-942440-01-3), 1982. 176p. B/W photos and illus. (Interest level: grade 6-adult).

Similar to Ehling's guidebook of western New York trails (*see* following entry), this book highlights the many diverse waterways of central New York. Information includes a summary of each stream's trip, the trip's length, the skill level required, principal access spots, an introduction to the stream, features of the trip, and alternate canoe trips in the area.
♦ Students can write essays on the importance of waterways to this area throughout history, beginning with how the rivers were used by the Indians of the area and concluding with how the rivers are used today.
1. Canoes and canoeing—New York (State)—Guidebooks 2. Outdoor recreation—New York (State)—Guidebooks 3. Family recreation—New York (State)—Guidebooks 4. New York (State)—Description and travel—Guidebooks.

917.47
Ehling, William P. *Fifty Hikes in Western New York: Walks and Day Hikes from the Cattaraugus Hills to the Genesee Valley.* Backcountry Publications (0-88150-164-6), 1990. 256p. B/W maps and illus. (Interest level: grade 7-adult).

Capitalizing on two of western New York's most important natural resources, its forests and its natural wildlife, the author presents a guidebook to the area's state forest trails. Information includes loca-

tion, hiking distance and time, vertical rise, and the names of the topographic maps of the area.
♦ For students living in the area, a day field trip to any of the 50 trails may prove to be interesting and could be integrated with the science curriculum. Students not within traveling distance to this area could read the entries and draw a map of a trail or write a description of western New York, emphasizing the importance of the forestry and wildlife.
1. Hiking—New York (State)—Guidebooks
2. New York (State)—Description and travel—Guidebooks.

917.47
The Empire State—New York. (Puzzle). Illus. by Denise Cessna. Globe Pequot Press, 1988. 100 pieces. $9.95. (Interest level: 4-8).

This brightly colored puzzle provides a wealth of information about the state of New York. Each county is highlighted with many different attractions, and the borders of the puzzle include such elusive information as the state fossil and the state gem.
♦ Each student can research the attraction on a piece of the puzzle. Then, when the puzzle is put together, students could present short commercials promoting the attractions that they researched.
1. New York (State)—Description and travel—Games.

917.47
Fein, Cheri. *New York: Open to the Public: A Comprehensive Guide to Museums, Collections, Exhibition Spaces, Historic Houses, Botanical Gardens and Zoos.* Photos by Joseph Kugielski. Stewart, Tabori & Chang (0-941434-00-1), 1982. 221p. Color photos. (Interest level: grade 6-adult).

Beautiful photographs are the soul of this guide to cultural attractions in New York City. Information includes addresses, descriptions, hours, admissions, rules/regulations, access routes, and features, which are represented with pictorial symbols.
♦ Readers can develop a database of favorite attractions to visit in New York City, using any computerized database program. The database fields could include short descriptions of the attractions they have chosen, giving students practice in summarizing information.
1. New York (N.Y.)—Description—Guidebooks
2. Museums—New York (N.Y.)—Guidebooks
3. Botanical gardens—New York (N.Y.)—Guidebooks 4. Exhibition buildings—New York (N.Y.)—Guidebooks 5. Historic buildings—New York (N.Y.)—Guidebooks 6. Zoological gardens—New York (N.Y.)—Guidebooks.

917.47
Webster, Harriet. *Favorite Short Trips in New York State.* Yankee Publishing (0-89909-090-7), 1986. 176p. B/W photos. (Interest level: grade 6-adult).

After casing the state of New York, the author has selected not-so-famous places that are a real pleasure to visit. Areas such as Watkins Glen, Corning, and Saratoga Springs are a few of the places mentioned.
♦ Using the beginning line "I've Never Heard of...," each student can write an essay on one of the areas in this book. They must include maps of how to get to the places they have chosen and describe what they would see and do if they traveled there.
1. New York (State)—Description and travel.

917.471
Appleberg, Marilyn J. *I Love New York Guide.* 3rd rev. ed. Illus. by Albert Pfeiffer. Collier Macmillan (0-02-097303-9), 1988. 303p. B/W illus. (Interest level: grade 7-adult).

One special section of this guidebook is the chapter "Kids' New York," which includes guides to children's specialty shops and parties for children. Information includes addresses, phone numbers, descriptions, hours, and special attractions. The guide also includes subway information, postal zones, and a street map of the city.
♦ The city of New York is a cultural center that reflects the lives and interests of its residents. Students could plan a real or imaginary trip to New York City that would fit their interests. In scanning the guidebook, students can list places they would like to visit that describe their likes and dislikes. Then each student can exchange papers with another student to see whether the other student can accurately describe some of the attributes of the student who wrote the paper.
1. New York (N.Y.)—Description—Guidebooks.

917.471
Deegan, Paul J. *New York, New York.* Crestwood House (0-89686-467-7), 1989. (See the USA Series). Color photos. (Interest level: 3-6).

Deegan's interesting and informative guide to New York presents an appealing view of this fascinating city. Well illustrated, the book provides facts about the city of New York, area maps, and lists of addresses of places to write for further information.
♦ Using the terms presented in the book, students can draw a map of the city, locate and mark each attraction on the map, and then connect the dots to finish a visual tour of the city.
1. New York (N.Y.)—Description and travel
2. Manhattan (New York, N.Y.)—Description and travel.

917.471
Dreschler-Marx, Carin. *Broadway: From the Battery to the Bronx.* Photos by author. Harry N. Abrams (0-8109-0745-3), 1988. 160p. B/W and Color photos. (Interest level: grade 7-adult).

One of the highlights of this book is the photography. The author and photographer take readers along Broadway, as it crosses each avenue in New York City. The photos accurately depict all aspects of life in the city.
♦ Students can trace the author's route on a city map and highlight some of the major attractions mentioned. The book also features many pictures of the statues in New York City, and readers can create a database of statues in the city, including short biographies of the people the statues represent.
1. Broadway (New York, N.Y.)—Pictorial works
2. Broadway (New York, N.Y.)—Guidebooks
3. New York (N.Y.)—Description—Views 4. New York (N.Y.)—Description—Guidebooks.

917.471
Lovett, Sarah. *Kidding Around New York City: A Young Person's Guide to the City.* Illus. by Sally Blakemore. John Muir Publications (0-945465-33-5), 1989. 64p. Color illus. (Interest level: 3-8).

This fascinating and useful guide for kids includes maps, sightseeing highlights, unique places for young people, restaurants, shops, parks, museums, zoos, and a calendar of special events. The book gives the reader a refreshing look at the special features of New York City.
♦ Older children can plan an itinerary for a trip to New York City, including means of transportation and meals.
1. New York (N.Y.)—Description and travel—Guidebooks 2. Children—Travel—New York (N.Y.)—Guidebooks.

917.471
Munro, Roxie. *The Inside-Outside Book of New York City.* Illus. by author. Dodd, Mead (0-396-08513-X), 1985. Unpaginated. Color illus. (Interest level: K-adult).

Munro's enchanting picture book will delight both children and adults. The book takes readers to 12 different attractions in New York City and gives them a view from the inside looking out and from the outside looking in.
♦ After looking through the book and reading the descriptions in the back of the book, young people can write short paragraphs on which building they would most like to visit and why. A second activity might be to draw what they see around them, and then draw what they think their surroundings would look like from the outside.

1. New York (N.Y.) in art 2. Buildings in art
3. New York (N.Y.)—Buildings, structures, etc.—Pictorial works.

917.471
Thomas, Pamela. *Reflections of New York.* Photos by Karen Kent. Smithmark (0-8317-6321-3), 1991. 176p. Color photos. (Interest level: grade 7-adult).

Readers will enjoy this beautiful tour of New York City, with its historical text and contemporary photographs. The photographs provide a candid view of New York City life.
♦ New York City's buildings are one of the city's major attractions. Students can choose three buildings they would like to visit, and then identify the architect, the location, and the style of architecture. Teachers may also wish to make a list of buildings from which students can choose.
1. New York (N.Y.)—Description—Pictorial works.

970.004
Where Is the Eagle? (Videocassette). Gateway Communications, 1979. VHS, Color, (25 min.). No price available. (Interest level: grade 5-adult).

This video is a study of the Iroquois of New York State. Interviews conducted with a Tuscarora Indian relay the beliefs of the Iroquois, and describe the development of the Iroquois Nation.
♦ Viewers should watch for symbols in the video, and then draw the important symbols/animals of the Iroquois Nation (such as the turtle, the pine tree, and the eagle). They should also write short explanations of the importance of these symbols.
1. Indians of North America—Legends 2. Iroquois Indians.

971.339
Granfield, Linda. *All about Niagara Falls: Fascinating Facts, Dramatic Discoveries.* Morrow Junior Books (0-688-08456-7), 1988. 79p. B/W illus. (Interest level: grade 5-adult).

Granfield's fascinating collection of scientific, geographic, and historic facts about Niagara Falls will give the reader a new perspective on this natural wonder of the world.
♦ The possibilities for activities using this book are endless! Students could build models of the generator/hydroelectric plant/transmission system, develop a database of stuntmen and stuntwomen who crossed the falls, or design a brochure for Niagara Falls.
1. Niagara Falls (N.Y. and Ont.)—Description.

973.3
Boardman, Fon Wyman. *Against the Iroquois: The Sullivan Campaign of 1779 in New York State.* David McKay Co. (0-8098-0014-4), 1978. 112p. B/W illus. (Interest level: 6-8).

Boardman presents a detailed account of the military campaign led by Major General John Sullivan in 1779 against the Iroquois Indians of New York State who were allied with British troops and American Loyalists. The author includes a detailed history of the Six Nations Indian Confederation.
♦ Students could determine Sullivan's objectives in beginning the march against the Iroquois and then list the actual effects of the campaign.
1. Sullivan's Indian Campaign, 1779 2. Sullivan, John, 1740-1795 3. New York (State)—History—Revolution, 1775-1783.

974.7
Aylesworth, Thomas G. and **Aylesworth, Virginia L.** *Let's Discover the States: Upper Atlantic: New Jersey, New York.* Chelsea House (1-55546-553-6), 1987. 64p. Color photos. (Interest level: 5-8).

New York State, nicknamed the "Empire State," boasts a variety of resources and attractions. Using many colorful photographs, this short overview provides a complete look at the geographic, historic, and social makeup of the state.
♦ As either a beginning or culminating activity, readers can choose a photograph in the book and write a short essay on that picture.
1. New York—Description and travel 2. New York—History.

974.7
Beame, Bernard. *The ER-I-E Canal.* (Videocassette). Bailey Films, 1968. VHS, B/W, (17 min.). (Interest level: grade 5-adult).

This video gives an interesting view of the Erie Canal. The filmmaker examines at not only the canal's historical importance as a transportation route but also the canal's current cultural, social, and recreational value.
♦ Students may draw and describe the lock system used on the Erie Canal, labeling some of the locations of locks. As a creative thinking activity, students could brainstorm about how the obsolete canal routes might be used today. They may come up with a better idea than using it for a garbage dump, which is shown in the video.
1. Erie Canal.

974.7
Carmer, Carl. *The Hudson River.* Illus. by Rafaello Busoni. Holt, Rinehart & Winston (0-91293-061-2), 1962. 114p. B/W illus. (Interest level: 6-8).

The history of the Hudson River is really a combination of the histories of many different things—the Algonquian, the whaling trade, the rich manor farms, the brickyards, and the cement work industry. The author blends interesting anecdotes about each history into a compelling story.
♦ Each student can choose one chapter or story in the book and conduct additional research.

1. Hudson River (N.Y. and N.J.)—History 2. Hudson Valley—History 3. New York (State)—History.

974.7
Desens, Joan. *Patterns of Homespun: A Conversation with Henry and Anna.* (Videocassette). New York State Historical Association, 1991. VHS, B/W and Color, (28:38 min.). $40.00. (Interest level: 4-8).

Rural farm life in the 1830s is the subject of this video. An upstate New York farm couple relates the seasonal tasks, the hardships, and the occasional amusements of life on the farm during this time period. The paintings and prints used to illustrate the video were well chosen.
♦ Young people can choose a household or farm task, such as candle making, soap making, or harvesting a crop, and create a storyboard for a program about that task, focusing on the process of the task. The program, which could be a slide show or filmstrip, should include narration.
1. New York (State)—History, 1815-1861—Pictorial works 2. Country life—New York (State).

974.7
Ellis, David M. *New York State: Gateway to America.* Windsor Publications (0-89781-246-8), 1988. 399p. B/W and Color photos. (Interest level: grade 8-adult).

Ellis's detailed history of the state of New York is full of information on all areas of the state. A section on the financial institutions, businesses, and other organizations that have had an effect on the history of New York State is included.
♦ Students can develop a database of New York companies described in the book that still exist. The fields should include a history of the company, its location, major executives, purpose, and current status (future growth or decline).
1. New York (State)—History 2. New York (State)—Description and travel—Views 3. New York (State)—Industries.

974.7
Fradin, Dennis B. *The New York Colony.* Childrens Press (0-516-00389-5), 1988. 160p. B/W illus. (Interest level: 4-8).

Fradin traces the history of the colony of New York from its beginnings as Indian territory until the time it was named the eleventh state. The book also includes several biographical sketches.
♦ Readers could choose one of the biographies in the book and compose an obituary for that person. They may have to look in a local newspaper for a format for the obituary. They may also need to find more information on that individual.

1. New York (State)—History—Colonial period, ca 1600-1775 2. New York (State)—History—Colonial period, ca 1600-1775—Biography 3. New York (State)—History—Revolution, 1775-1783 4. New York (State)—History—Revolution, 1775-1783—Biography 5. New York (State)—Biography.

974.7
Goodnough, David. *The Colony of New York Series: A First Book*. Franklin Watts (0-531-00783-9), 1973. 88p. B/W illus. (Interest level: 5-8).

Each short chapter of this book features a different occurrence in the history of New York State that had an effect on the state's future development. The time periods cover important events from 1609 to 1776.
♦ Using a time line computer program, students can construct a time line of these events in New York State history. They can then illustrate the time line.
1. New York (State)—History—Colonial period, ca 1600–1775.

974.7
Hott, L. R. and **Garey, D.** *The Adirondacks*. (Videocassette). Florentine Films, 1987. VHS, Color, (20 min.). $95.00. (Interest level: grade 6-adult).

Hott and Garey present a fascinating study of the Adirondack region's history and present-day characteristics. In interviews, residents of the region speak about the problems and joys of living in the Adirondacks. Special emphasis is placed on the preservation of this wilderness area.
♦ The video mentions the passage of a wildlife act entitled "Forever Wild," which prohibits the taking of logs in state forests and parks. Class members could discuss the controversy between the logging industry and the environmentalists. Invite speakers into the class to present both perspectives.
1. New York (State)—Description and travel 2. Wilderness areas—New York (State).

974.7
I Love New York. (Videocassette). New York Education Department, 1980. VHS, Color, (28 min.). $60.00. (Interest level: grade 3-adult).

It is quite obvious that this video is a promotional video for the state of New York; however, it does give the audience an overview of the different areas of the state. The video also succeeds in showing the various lifestyles that make up New York.
♦ Students can create a promotional video for their own community following the format of this video.
1. New York (State)—Description and travel.

974.7
Lancaster, Bruce. *Ticonderoga: The Story of a Fort*. Illus. by Victor Mays. Houghton Mifflin (No ISBN), 1959. 181p. Color illus. (Interest level: 4-8).

The history of Fort Ticonderoga, from its discovery by Champlain, has affected the history of the United States. Ticonderoga's importance in defending the colonies from invasion during the French and Indian War and during the American Revolution cannot be ignored. This historical account of the fort also highlights the lives of several important people.
♦ Young people may research Fort Ticonderoga and build a diorama of one of the battles at the fort. Included in the diorama would, of course, be a replica of the fort itself. Students could also develop a biographical chart of the people involved in the history of Fort Ticonderoga, including specific characteristics such as nationality, physical traits, leadership qualities, and accomplishments.
1. Fort Ticonderoga, New York (State) 2. New York (State)—History—Colonial period, ca 1600-1775.

974.7
Lape, Fred. *A Farm and Village Boyhood*. Syracuse University Press (0-8156-0162-X), 1980. 168p. B/W photos. (Interest level: grade 6-adult).

Lape's autobiographical work gives the reader an accurate and detailed description of life in a small rural New York village during the early 1900s. Esperance, New York, the village featured in the book, was also located on Route 20, a major east-west road during that time period.
♦ Much of farm life in the early 1900s depended on the change of seasons. For each season, students could make a chart of activities that were necessary or common during that season, as described in this book.
1. Lape, Fred, 1900- 2. Esperance, New York—Social life and customs 3. Esperance, New York—Biography.

974.7
Lord, Beman. *On the Banks of the Hudson: A View of Its History and Folklore*. Illus. by Rocco Negri. Henry Z. Walck (0-8098-2075-7), 1971. 63p. Color illus. (Interest level: 4-7).

The Hudson River is an important waterway that runs along the eastern border of New York. As the author slowly makes his way along the Hudson River, he describes places along the banks and briefly retells legends about the cities and the people who lived in the area. The history of the Hudson River comes alive in this book.
♦ Students may create slides or filmstrips of the legends with narration.
1. Hudson River (N.Y. and N.J.)—History 2. Folklore—New York (State).

974.7
McClard, Megan. *Hiawatha and the Iroquois League.* Illus. by Frank Riccio. Silver Burdett (0-382-09568-5), 1989. 123p. B/W illus. (Interest level: 4-8).

McClard tells the story of Hiawatha, the Iroquois Indian whose quest for peace, despite personal suffering and hardship, led to the formation of the Iroquois Confederacy. The book also discusses how this governmental body was a forerunner of the U.S. government.

♦ Older students can develop a chart of the similarities between the Iroquois Confederacy and the U.S. democracy. Students could also make a map of the Five Nations, label the locations of the various tribes, and describe how the tribes adopted certain duties, e.g., Fire-Keeper.

1. Hiawatha, 15th century 2. Iroquois Indians—Biography 3. Iroquois Indians—Tribal government 4. Indians of North America—New York (State)—Biography 5. Indians of North America—New York (State)—Tribal government.

974.7
New York in American History. (Sound filmstrip). Society for Visual Education, 1989. 3 filmstrips, Color; 3 cassettes, (14-18 min. each); teacher's guide. (Interest level: 7-8).

Each filmstrip in this interesting series covers a century in the development of New York State, and the series as a whole will serve as a great introduction to a study of the state. The cultural, economic, and geographic history of the state in relation to the growth of the United States is highlighted. The guide includes skill boosters and other suggested activities to aid the teacher in presenting the filmstrips. The vocabulary lists included in each program will also be useful.

♦ Cooperative groups can complete detailed studies of each region. Areas to focus on might be physical and geographic landmarks, famous people, products or resources, and cities in the area. The final product might be a portfolio of the region.

1. New York (State)—History 2. United States—History.

974.7
Portrait of New York State: Discover Corning. (Videocassette). New York Education Department, 1987. VHS, Color, (8 min.). $30.00. (Interest level: grade 4-adult).

One of several videos in this series, this video features the attractions found in the area around Corning. Heavily emphasized is the Corning Glass Museum, which is both a historic and futuristic center.

♦ The making of glass is very important in history and will be important in years to come. Children can draw a diagram or flowchart of the glass-making process, including the materials and tools needed in the process.

1. New York (State)—Description and travel.

974.7
Portrait of New York State: New York State's Seaway Trail. (Videocassette). New York State Education Department, 1987. VHS, Color, (11 min.). $30.00. (Interest level: grade 5-adult).

This video traces the Seaway Trail of New York State. Beginning at Chautauqua Lake, near Lake Erie, the trail basically follows the course of the St. Lawrence Seaway along Lake Ontario to the St. Lawrence River itself.

♦ Students can draw a map of the Seaway Trail, with numbers where the attractions are located. Then the students can develop a matching game to identify the attractions.

1. New York (State)—Description and travel.

974.7
Present Meets Past: Making History and the Mysteries of Town Histories. (Videocassette). New York State Historical Association, 1989. VHS, B/W, (27 min.). $69.00. (Interest level: 4-8).

Based on a young girl's diary, this comparison of a young child's life in the 1850s and today covers school life, play, home life, and child labor. The manual that accompanies the video provides activities and worksheets, which are built around the New York State social studies curriculum.

♦ The class could invite older people into the classroom to describe what life was like when they were growing up. Students could also tape an interview with an older person.

1. New York (State)—History, Local 2. New York (State)—Country life.

974.7
Shapiro, Mary J. *How They Built the Statue of Liberty.* Illus. by Huck Scarry. Random House (0-394-86957-5), 1985. 63p. B/W illus. (Interest level: 7-8).

Shapiro's detailed portrayal of the construction of the Statue of Liberty is a tribute to that important monument, which stands in the New York harbor. Some of the book may prove to be a bit technical for the average junior high reader; however, the diagrams and corresponding captions help make the history of the statue come alive.

♦ Students can find the properties of copper, iron, and steel and tell why these raw materials may present a problem for sculptors. Or, students can make a model (either in clay, with sticks, or on paper) of the Statue of Liberty.

1. Statue of Liberty (New York, N.Y.) 2. National monuments—United States 3. Statues.

974.7
Stein, R. Conrad. *New York.* Childrens Press (0-516-00478-6), 1989. (America the Beautiful). 144p. Color photos and maps. (Interest level: 4-8).

This colorful and interesting book covers all aspects of the state of New York, including its geography, history, and cultural diversity. A complete reference section includes key statistics, important dates, important people, and maps.
♦ To get a better idea of the students' familiarity with the state of New York, make a classroom map of places in New York students have visited or where they have lived. Students can read corresponding sections in the book and report to the class about those areas, incorporating their own experiences. Assign those students who have not visited New York an area that no one in the class has visited. A second activity might be to have students write about one of the important people born in New York listed in the book, including why they chose that individual to research.
1. New York (State) 2. New York (State)—History.

974.71
Statue of Liberty. (Videocassette). Direct Cinema, 1985. VHS, Color, (37 min.). $24.95. (Interest level: 7-8).

This is a fascinating documentary of the history of the Statue of Liberty and its construction. A special focus of the video is Bartholdi's original designs of the statue.
♦ After viewing the video, students can detail two ways in which they would have deviated from Bartholdi's methods or ideas in designing, constructing, and transporting the statue.
1. Statue of Liberty (New York, N.Y.) 2. National monuments 3. Statues.

974.753
Farb, Nathan. *The Adirondacks.* Rizzoli International Publications (0-8478-0583-2), 1985. 183p. Color photos. (Interest level: grade 6-adult).

The pictures and descriptions of this wilderness area in New York State convince the reader that the Adirondacks area ranks as one of the most beautiful in the world.
♦ Using location names found throughout the book, along with the map at the end of the book, children can develop a crossword puzzle of Adirondack place-names. They could also write poetry describing pictures in the book.
1. Adirondack Mountains (N.Y.)—Description and travel—Views.

Biography

920
Quackenbush, Robert. *Watt Got You Started, Mr. Fulton?* Illus. by author. Prentice-Hall (0-13-944397-5), 1982. Color illus. Unpaginated. (Interest level: 1-5).

Robert Fulton's first steamboat, the *Clermont,* ran successfully partly because of his wise use of the Boulton-Watt steam engine, invented by James Watt. Quackenbush's humorous illustrations highlight short biographies of the two men.
♦ Teachers can compile a list of household and/or transportation machinery. Then students can imagine what simple inventions or ideas made it possible to construct the "whole" piece.
1. Watt, James, 1736-1819 2. Fulton, Robert, 1765-1815 3. Inventors—United States—Biography.

920
St. George, Judith. *Dear Dr. Bell—Your Friend, Helen Keller.* Putnam (0-399-22337-1), 1992. 95p. Color illus. (Interest level: 4-6).

Dr. Alexander Graham Bell was instrumental in leading Helen Keller to her teacher, Annie Sullivan, and he continued to support her throughout her life. Both of their lives are portrayed in this unique book.
♦ In cooperative learning groups, children can develop lists of accomplishments of Dr. Bell and Helen Keller. From these lists, they can compile a final listing of accomplishments.
1. Keller, Helen, 1880-1968 2. Bell, Alexander Graham, 1847-1922 3. Blind—United States—Biography 4. Deaf—United States—Biography 5. Physically handicapped—United States—Biography 6. Inventors—United States—Biography.

92 Anthony, Susan B.
Peterson, Helen Stone. *Susan B. Anthony: Pioneer in Women's Rights.* Illus. by Paul Frame. Garrard (0-8116-4570-3), 1971. 96p. B/W and Color illus. (Interest level: 3-5).

Susan B. Anthony dedicated her life to fighting for equality for all people. This account details particularly her work in the anti-slavery movement and in the women's rights movement.
♦ Young people can draw pictures or write short essays describing what they think was the most important right that Susan B. Anthony gained.
1. Anthony, Susan B., 1820-1906 2. Feminists—Biography.

92 Cooper, Peter
Gurko, Miriam. *The Lives and Times of Peter Cooper.* Illus. by Jerome Snyder. Diagrams by Ava Morgan. Thomas Y. Crowell (No ISBN), 1959. 277p. B/W illus. (Interest level: 6-8).

Peter Cooper's interests and achievements encompassed many different areas, including industry, politics, economics, transportation, communication, reform, and education. His many inventions will amaze the reader, as will his spirit of generosity and goodwill.
- Students could create an award for Peter Cooper, noting his achievements and contributions to society.

1. Cooper, Peter, 1791-1883   2. New York (State)—History.

92 De Mille, Agnes
Gherman, Beverly. *Agnes De Mille: Dancing Off the Earth.* Atheneum (0-689-31441-8), 1990. 138p. B/W photos. (Interest level: 7-8).

This is an interesting, dramatic account of how Agnes De Mille overcame her feelings of insecurity and, through hard work and perseverance, became a well-known dancer and choreographer.
- Teachers can show a videocassette of a work choreographed by Agnes De Mille. After viewing the video, students could critique the film and write about how the dancing made them feel.

1. De Mille, Agnes, 1905-   2. Dancers—United States—Biography   3. Choreographers—United States—Biography.

92 Eastman, George
Mitchell, Barbara. *Click!: A Story about George Eastman.* Illus. by Jan Hosking Smith. Carolrhoda Books (0-876-14289-7), 1986. (Carolrhoda Creative Minds). 56p. Color illus. (Interest level: 3-6.)

George Eastman drastically improved the field of photography with his invention of a camera that anyone could use. Mitchell's biography particularly illustrates Eastman's contributions to the world of photography.
- Class members could design a bulletin board of cameras throughout history. Pictures of the earliest cameras and more modern cameras can be obtained at the library.

1. Eastman, George, 1854-1932   2. Inventors—Biography   3. Photography—History.

92 Fillmore, Millard
Casey, Jane Clark. *Millard Fillmore: Thirteenth President of the United States.* Childrens Press (0-516-01353-X), 1988. 100p. B/W illus. and photos. (Interest level: 4-8).

Though many of Millard Fillmore's actions as president were misunderstood, he demonstrated a love for the Union and fought hard to preserve it. Casey's work chronicles Fillmore's life, beginning in western New York and climaxing during his short presidency in 1850.
- Students can compile a list of Fillmore's achievements during his presidency and then discuss whether each achievement was popular or unpopular with his constituency and why.

1. Fillmore, Millard, 1800-1874   2. Presidents—United States—Biography.

92 Fulton, Robert
Hill, Ralph Nading. *Robert Fulton and the Steamboat.* Illus. by Lee J. Ames. Random House (No ISBN), 1954. 181p. Color illus. (Interest level: 4-8).

Hill's interesting book makes it is easy to imagine Robert Fulton's enthusiasm and dedication to his inventions. Fulton, who not only invented the first successful steamboat but also contributed to the invention of the submarine, made a lasting impression on our changing country.
- Readers can devise a time line illustrating the history of the *Clermont,* the first successful steamboat.

1. Fulton, Robert, 1765-1815   2. Inventors—Biography.

92 Heiden, Eric
Aaseng, Nathan. *Eric Heiden: Winner in Gold.* Lerner (0-8225-0481-2), 1980. (The Achievers Series). 56p. Color photos. (Interest level: 3-6).

This informative biography details the Olympic career of Eric Heiden, a speed skater who won five gold medals in the 1980 Lake Placid winter Olympics. The biography includes information about his sister, also a speed skater.
- Using the "Record Breaking Times" listed in the back of the book, children can research other Olympics to see if those records have been broken. Students can write to the Lake Placid Chamber of Commerce requesting a map of the Olympic Village of the 1980 Olympics. They could also inquire as to how the buildings which were built for the Olympics are being used today.

1. Heiden, Eric   2. Skaters—United States—Biography   3. Speed skating   4. Olympic Games (Winter)—Lake Placid (N.Y.).

92 Hiawatha
Fradin, Dennis Brindell. *Hiawatha: Messenger of Peace.* Macmillan (0-689-50519-1), 1992. 40p. B/W and Color photos and map. (Interest level: 3-6).

The real Hiawatha, an Iroquois Indian who lived about 500 years ago, overcame personal tragedy to become a major "peace-maker" and founder of the Iroquois Federation. The author does an outstanding job in using photographs of Indian artifacts and paintings to illustrate the life and world of the Iroquois.
- The photos in the book are very well chosen and detailed. Students can choose two photos and write a description of how they feel or what they think of when they look at the pictures. They might also state how the pictures relate to their own life or beliefs.

1. Hiawatha, 15th century   2. Iroquois Indians—Biography.

92 Irving, Washington
Washington Irving's New York. (Videocassette). Master Teacher, 1987. VHS, Color, (30 min.). $94.50. (Interest level: 5-8).

This is an interesting account of Washington Irving's life and literary contributions. The video includes details about Irving's home on the Hudson, Sunnyside, and discusses his legend of Sleepy Hollow.
♦ Young people can develop a chronological bibliography of Washington Irving's literary works.
1. Irving, Washington, 1783-1859   2. Hudson River (N.Y.).

92 LaGuardia, Fiorello Henry
Kamen, Gloria. *Fiorello: His Honor, the Little Flower.* Illus. by author. Atheneum (0-689-30869-8), 1981. 60p. B/W illus. (Interest level: 3-6).

Young readers of this biography will get an idea of the character and achievements of one of New York City's most important mayors. The book especially notes LaGuardia's fair but firm crusade to reform the city during his time in office.
♦ Comics were used by LaGuardia in his work as mayor. Students can create their own "funnies" about an event or many events in Fiorello LaGuardia's life.
1. LaGuardia, Fiorello Henry, 1882-1947   2. New York (N.Y.)—Politics and government—1898-1951   3. New York (N.Y.)—Mayors—Biography.

92 Lazarus, Emma
Levinson, Nancy Smiler. *I Lift My Lamp: Emma Lazarus and the Statue of Liberty.* Dutton (0-525-67180-3), 1989. 104p. (Interest level: 6-8).

Levinson tells the story of a quiet, introverted poet whose work with the Jewish immigrants and whose poem "The New Colossus" have inspired many. The author presents an informative and enjoyable biography.
♦ There are several passages of Emma Lazarus's poems in the book. Each student can choose one passage and tell whether or not the title of the poem is appropriate (in his or her opinion) and why.
1. Lazarus, Emma, 1849-1887   2. Statue of Liberty (New York, N.Y.)   3. Poets, American—19th century—Biography   4. Jews—New York (N.Y.)—Biography.

92 Moses, Grandma
Moses, Grandma. *Grandma Moses: My Life's History.* Harper & Brothers (No ISBN), 1952. 140p. B/W and Color illus. (Interest level: 5-8).

Fans of Grandma Moses's paintings will realize that her paintings reflect the life she lived. Her account of both her northern and southern life on the farm is refreshing.
♦ Each anecdote in Grandma Moses's autobiography seems to "paint a picture" in the reader's mind. Young people can choose stories from the book and illustrate the scenes as they imagine them.
1. Moses, Grandma, 1860-1961   2. Painters—United States—Biography.

92 Oppenheimer, Robert
Driemen, J. E. *Atomic Dawn: A Biography of Robert Oppenheimer.* Dillon (0-87518-397-2), 1989. 160p. B/W photos. (Interest level: 6-8).

Driemen covers Robert Oppenheimer's life as he progressed from overachiever as a student to a leader of a team of scientists developing the first atomic bomb. The author does a good job describing the political atmosphere of the country during and after this trying period in U.S. history.
♦ Students can do more research into the Manhattan Project and then create a newspaper with articles on this project and other events of the day.
1. Oppenheimer, J. Robert, 1904-1967   2. Atomic bomb—United States—History   3. Physicists—United States—Biography.

92 Roosevelt, Eleanor
Freedman, Russell. *Eleanor Roosevelt: A Life of Discovery.* Clarion Books (0-89919-862-7), 1993. 198p. B/W photos. (Interest level: 4-8).

Eleanor Roosevelt was one of the first first ladies to maintain a public life and a career of her own. Freedman's fascinating biography includes photos and interesting anecdotes about the life of this stately woman.
♦ Students can choose three to five first ladies since Eleanor Roosevelt and write short summaries of their accomplishments during their spouse's term of office.
1. Roosevelt, Eleanor, 1884-1962   2. Presidents—United States—Wives—Biography   3. First ladies—United States.

92 Roosevelt, Franklin Delano
Freedman, Russell. *Franklin Delano Roosevelt.* Clarion (0-89919-379-X), 1990. 200p. B/W photos. (Interest level: 4-8).

One of the greatest presidents in U.S. history is the subject of this interesting and enjoyable work. Freedman's biography is easy to read and describes the president's personal and political life during a time of great social, economic, and political conflict.
♦ As part of Roosevelt's New Deal, many government programs and agencies were developed. Students can list at least five of these programs and explain how they helped the economy.
1. Roosevelt, Franklin D., 1882-1945   2. Presidents—United States—Biography.

92 Roosevelt, Theodore
Fritz, Jean. *Bully for You, Teddy Roosevelt.* Putnam (0-399-21769-X), 1991. 128p. (Interest level: 5-8).

Teddy Roosevelt, who once served as governor of New York State, went on to become one of the presidents of the United States. This excellent biography, which includes quotes from letters and speeches, details his personal and political life.
- What are some of Teddy Roosevelt's accomplishments that had a direct impact on the history of the state of New York? Young people can construct a time line of these accomplishments and discuss why they may have led Teddy to the presidency.

1. Roosevelt, Theodore, 1858-1919   2. Presidents—United States.

92 Roosevelt, Theodore
Quackenbush, Robert. *Don't You Dare Shoot That Bear!: A Story of Theodore Roosevelt.* Prentice Hall (0-13-218496-6), 1984. 36p. Color illus. (Interest level: 1-5).

Younger students may be interested to learn how the teddy bear got its name. This story about the life of one of our most colorful and interesting presidents will be a pleasant surprise.
- Readers of this book will learn that Teddy Roosevelt did many things in his life. After reading or listening to the book, children can draw pictures of the events in Roosevelt's life that they enjoyed the most.

1. Roosevelt, Theodore, 1858-1919   2. Presidents—United States—Biography.

92 Salk, Jonas
Sherrow, Victoria. *Jonas Salk.* Facts on File (0-8160-2805-2), 1993. 134p. B/W photos. (Interest level: 6-8).

Sherrow presents an interesting biographical portrait of the medical scientist who was instrumental in discovering an effective vaccine for polio. This book, which focuses on the polio epidemic of the 1940s and 1950s, also emphasizes Salk's continuing medical research at the Salk Institute.
- Students can interview nurses, doctors, parents, and teachers about the polio epidemic scare of the 1950s. They also may want to find out more about immunization schedules for children then and now.

1. Salk, Jonas, 1914-   2. Virologists—United States—Biography 3. Poliomyelitis vaccine.

92 Stanton, Elizabeth Cady
Cullen-DuPont, Kathryn. *Elizabeth Cady Stanton and Women's Liberty.* Facts on File (0-8160-2413-8), 1992. (Makers of America Series). 133p. B/W illus. (Interest level: 5-8).

This complete biography of Elizabeth Cady Stanton includes excerpts from her speeches and essays that were key in the fight for women's rights. Photos of Stanton and other important figures who played a part in the passing of the Nineteenth Amendment are also included.
- Students can list the primary sources found in the book that describe Stanton's life and work. The class might discuss the importance of these sources.

1. Stanton, Elizabeth Cady, 1815-1902   2. Feminists—United States—Biography   3. Women's rights—History.

92 Steinmetz, Charles P.
Guy, Anne Welsh. *Steinmetz: Wizard of Light.* Illus. by Leonard Rosoman. Alfred A. Knopf (No ISBN), 1965. B/W illus. (Interest level: 4-8).

Charles P. Steinmetz's contributions to the world of electricity are outstanding, although his name is seldom heard. This heartwarming story tells of a physically disabled individual whose mathematical and electrical genius quietly changed our country's electrical future.
- Students can research Steinmetz's law of hysteresis or magnetism and prepare short descriptions and simple illustrative diagrams of the law.

1. Steinmetz, Charles P., 1866-1923   2. Electricity—Biography.

92 Truth, Sojourner
Bernard, Jacqueline. *Journey toward Freedom: The Story of Sojourner Truth.* Feminist Press (1-55861-024-3), 1990. 272p. B/W illus. (Interest level: 7-8).

The story of Sojourner Truth is fascinating, especially when one considers the perseverance she showed in fighting for the rights of all people. Her faith and dedication to her cause was unparalleled, as portrayed in this biography.
- Sojourner Truth is similar to Harriet Tubman in many ways. Students can prepare charts noting similarities and differences between the two women.

1. Truth, Sojourner, 1797?-1883   2. African Americans—Biography   3. Slavery—Biography.

92 Truth, Sojourner
McKissack, Pat. *Sojourner Truth: Ain't I a Woman?* Scholastic (0-590-44690-8), 1992. 186p. Color illus. (Interest level: 5-8).

McKissack's biography of a former slave illustrates the dedication and perseverance she demonstrated in her fight for the rights of all people. The book focuses on her work both as an abolitionist and as a champion of women's rights.
- Young people can write essays about the causes that are important to them and how they might work for these causes.

1. Truth, Sojourner, 1797?-1883   2. African Americans—Biography   3. Abolitionists—United States—Biography   4. Social reformers—United States—Biography.

92 Tubman, Harriet

Sterling, Dorothy. *Freedom Train: The Story of Harriet Tubman.* Illus. by Ernest Crichlow. Doubleday (0-590-43628-7), 1987, 1954. 192p. B/W illus. (Interest level: 5-8).

Known as "Moses" to her people, Harriet Tubman helped over 300 people escape the slavery of the South to find freedom in the northern states and Canada. This biography tells the story of her courageous life of service in times of war and unrest.

♦ Students can develop a list of other people mentioned in the book who were involved with the Underground Railroad. Then each student can choose two or three of these people to research further.

1. Tubman, Harriet, 1820?-1913   2. African Americans—Biography   3. Slavery—Biography   4. Underground Railroad—Biography.

92 Two Trees, Joe

Kazimiroff, Theodore L. *The Last Algonquin.* Walker (0-8027-0698-3), 1982. 197p. (Interest level: 6-8).

Joe Two Trees, the last surviving member of the Turtle Clan of the Algonquian Indians, encounters love, hate, life, and death in his journey through the white man's world. This is a heartwarming story of an American Indian's struggle to survive in a land populated by strangers.

♦ Students might list the practices or habits of Joe Two Trees that we might benefit from adopting today.

1. Two Trees, Joe   2. Algonquian Indians—Biography.

92 Van Buren, Martin

Ellis, Rafaela. *Martin Van Buren: Eighth President of the United States.* Garrett Educational Corp. (0-944483-12-7), 1989. (Presidents of the United States Series). 120p. B/W illus. (Interest level: 6-8).

Martin Van Buren is certainly not as well known as some of our other presidents, but he did bring about many changes to the American government. Ellis provides a clear account of his life.

♦ Many of our presidents started to climb the political ladder of success at a young age. Using a "ladder" diagram, young people can outline each of Van Buren's positions and appointments. They can also find out how many other presidents were originally from New York State and where they were born.

1. Van Buren, Martin, 1782-1862   2. Presidents—United States—Biography.

92 Washington, George, and Washington, Martha

Siegel, Beatrice. *George and Martha Washington at Home in New York.* Illus. by Frank Aloise. Four Winds Press (0-02-782721-6), 1989. 74p. B/W illus. (Interest level: 4-6).

George and Martha Washington's stay in our first nation's capital, New York City, was filled with enjoyment and apprehension. It was a time of optimism in the new nation, but our founding fathers still had many problems to face. Young readers of this book will get a sense of the atmosphere of the times.

♦ Discuss with students the importance of writing a list of things to do when beginning a new job or project. Students can list problems that George Washington had to face as the first president, and then list possible solutions to the problems.

1. Washington, George, 1732-1799   2. Washington, Martha, 1731-1802   3. New York (N.Y)—History, 1775-1865   4. Washington, George, 1732-1799—Inauguration, 1789.

92 Westinghouse, George

Levine, I. E. *Inventive Wizard: George Westinghouse.* Messner (No ISBN), 1962. 190p. (Interest level: 6-8).

The many inventions of George Westinghouse include railroad air brakes, automobile shock absorbers, and the means to harness water power. More important, however, was his desire to invent things that would bring safety and comfort to others. In this interesting biography, the author portrays the man and the importance of this era in American history.

♦ Students can research the Westinghouse Company; find, if possible, the trademarks of the company; and perhaps survey parents and older members of the community, listing the Westinghouse appliances they remember.

1. Westinghouse, George, 1846-1914   2. Westinghouse Electric Company—History.

92 Zenger, Peter

Galt, Tom. *Peter Zenger: Fighter for Freedom.* Illus. by Ralph Ray. Thomas Y. Crowell (No ISBN), 1951. 242p. B/W illus. (Interest level: 4-8).

This is the fascinating story of Peter Zenger's life as a printer and the trial that ensued when he openly protested the colonial Governor Cosby. Zenger's stubborn fight for what he believed was right makes readers realize the importance of our right to freedom of the press.

♦ Young people can create their own newspaper, which should include headlines and articles about events that happened before and during Zenger's trial.

1. Zenger, Peter, 1697-1746   2. New York (N.Y.)—History—Colonial period, ca 1600-1775.

Fiction

Baker, Betty. *Little Runner of the Longhouse*. Illus. by Arnold Lobel. Harper & Row (0-06-020341-2), 1962. 64p. Color illus. (Interest level: K-2).

Through this "I Can Read" book, young children will learn about Iroquois customs and ceremonies used to celebrate the New Year. Children will also discover that Little Runner's motives may be similar to those of small boys and girls everywhere.

♦ This story could be read around maple-sugaring time, when a visit to a maple syrup farm could be arranged. After they've tasted maple candy, younger children can tell how they might try to convince their mothers to get them candy. The story could also be connected to an Indian mask-making activity.

1. Indians of North America—Stories.

Burchard, Peter. *Digger*. G. P. Putnam's Sons (0-399-20717-1), 1980. 154p. (Interest level: 5-8).

Digger, a top-notch newsboy in New York City during the 1860s, investigates the cause of a fatal fire and unwillingly becomes a player in a game that leads to the deaths of some of his closest friends. The arsonist, it is discovered, once had connections with Boss Tweed, but has become his bitter enemy. This is an accurate depiction of life on the streets of New York City during this time period.

♦ Young people can watch "Newsies," a Disney movie (1992), and compare portrayals of the New York City newsboys in this movie and in *Digger*. A second activity may be to make a "WANTED" poster for Boss Tweed.

1. Newsboys—Fiction   2. New York (N.Y.)—History, 1863-1898—Fiction.

Carr, Harriett. *Valley of Defiance*. Macmillan (No ISBN available), 1957. 178p. (Interest level: 5-8).

Walter finds himself torn between joining his father's nonviolent political strategy and joining his brother's active and potentially violent tactics in their revolt against the unjust patroon system. This system of farm rentals was in place in the Hudson Valley in the mid-1800s. Walter eventually chooses his own path in life and helps his family beat the patroon system.

♦ Students can pick out the names of some of the landowners and politicians mentioned in the book and research the people to find out whether they actually existed. Another activity might be to identify the counties mentioned in the story on a map of New York State and list what resources are available from these counties.

1. Patroons—Stories   2. New York (State)—History—Fiction.

Coatsworth, Elizabeth. *The Peddler's Cart*. Illus. by Zhenya Gay. Macmillan (No ISBN), 1956. 151p. B/W illus. (Interest level: 4-8).

George has the opportunity to travel with his father as he takes his peddler's cart throughout western New York. The experiences George has and the people he meets present the reader with an excellent cross section of the activities and concerns of the time period.

♦ Readers can locate George's hometown on a map and reconstruct the path George and his father followed in their travels. Or, recalling the story of the three crows found in the book, young people can find five other Indian folk beliefs.

1. New York (State)—Stories   2. Peddlers—Stories.

Collier, James Lincoln and **Collier, Christopher**. *War Comes to Willy Freeman*. Delacorte (0-440-09642-1), 1983. 178p. (Interest level: 5-8).

After she watches her Pa die in the battle of Fort Griswold and her mother is taken prisoner by the British, Willy finds her way to New York City. She begins working at the Sam Fraunces Tavern, with the ultimate goal of finding her mother.

♦ Young people may research and make replicas of either Fort Griswold or Canvas Town, or they may write a short history on the famous Sam Fraunces Tavern.

1. United States—History—Revolution, 1775-1783—Fiction   2. African Americans—Fiction   3. Slavery—Fiction.

Collier, James Lincoln and **Collier, Christopher**. *Who Is Carrie?* Delacorte (0-385-29295-3), 1984. 158p. (Interest level: 5-8).

Carrie enjoys her job at the Sam Fraunces Tavern in New York City, and she feels especially lucky to be able to work at the presidential mansion, but she lives with the constant fear of being kidnapped into slavery and a nagging uncertainty about her ancestry. The authors succeed in portraying the fears of African Americans soon after the American Revolution.

♦ Students may devise a map of New York City that identifies, in chronological order, the highlights of President Washington's terms and the locations of the presidential mansions. Students can also write an essay on New York City's role in the history of the U.S. government.

1. United States—History, 1789-1797—Fiction   2. New York (N.Y.)—History—Fiction   3. Slavery—Fiction   4. African Americans—Fiction.

Danziger, Paula. *Remember Me to Harold Square*. Delacorte (0-385-29610-X), 1987. 145p. (Interest level: 6-8).

What better way to explore the city of New York than on a scavenger hunt? Kendra's parents devise the "hunt" to help Kendra, her brother, and a visiting friend enjoy a summer in the city. Paula Danziger's unique treatment of subject matter in this book is refreshing.
♦ Students can brainstorm to devise a scavenger hunt for their community or town, similar to the hunt in the book.
1. Friendship—Fiction 2. New York (N.Y.)—Description and travel—Fiction.

Davis, Burke. *Mr. Lincoln's Whiskers.* Illus. by Douglas Gorsline. Coward, McCann & Geoghegan (0-698-20455-7), 1978. 40p. B/W illus. (Interest level: grade 2-adult).

The truly great, humorous, and humble character of Abraham Lincoln is portrayed in this book. The story focuses on a young western New York girl's suggestion that Lincoln grow a beard.
♦ Older students can trace Mr. Lincoln's journey from Springfield, Illinois, to Washington, DC, through the town of Westfield, New York. Students can also write to the Historical Society in Westfield, New York, to find out whether more information is available on Grace Bedell Billings.
1. Lincoln, Abraham, 1809-1865—Fiction.

Davis, Lavina R. *Island City: Adventures in Old New York.* Illus. by Peter Spier. Doubleday (No ISBN), 1961. 256p. B/W illus. and maps. (Interest level: 6-8).

Davis's collection of five different stories focuses on the activity and excitement inherent in the development of a major port city. This is a tool that will aid in teaching the history of New York City during the 1600s and 1700s.
♦ Students can write stories that have the same themes as the stories in this book but focus on events in New York City in a more recent time period. Using the maps in the book, students can also retrace and relabel the map with today's place-names.
1. Dutch in the United States—Stories.

Foreman, Michael. *Cat and Canary.* E. P. Dutton (0-8037-0137-3), 1985. Unpaginated. Color illus. (Interest level: K-3).

The illustrations in this book truly enhance the story of a cat whose dream of flying above the streets of New York City comes true. Several key attractions in New York City are included in the story of the cat's special journey.
♦ While reading the story, ask older children to identify the buildings as they appear in the pictures. Young people can also draw their own pictures of the buildings in the book.
1. Children's stories 2. Cats—Fiction 3. Birds—Fiction 4. Flight—Fiction.

Fox, Paula. *Monkey Island.* Orchard (0-531-08562-7), 1991. 151p. (Interest level: 6-8).

Clay Garrity, abandoned by his father and later by his expectant mother, finds himself sleeping in a New York City park with several other homeless people. The author portrays the homeless as people who have a desire to help themselves and to escape life on the streets.
♦ Invite speakers from local social agencies to speak to the class on homelessness in the community.
1. Homeless persons—Fiction 2. New York (N.Y.)—Fiction.

Clyne, Patricia Edwards. *The Corduroy Road.* Illus. by Louis F. Cary. Dodd, Mead (0-396-06815-4), 1973. 93p. B/W illus. (Interest level: 3-4).

After learning that his mean uncle is a Tory, young Tiberius Wade Jr., or Tib, decides that he must leave his uncle's farm immediately. Before Tib's father died, he told Tib to follow the Corduroy Road to his aunt's home. How Tib finds the Corduroy Road and eventually travels over it is an adventure worth reading.
♦ Children can construct a model of the Corduroy Road.
1. New York (State)—History—Revolution, 1775-1783—Fiction.

George, Jean Craighead. *My Side of the Mountain.* Illus. by author. E. P. Dutton (0-525-35530-8), 1959. 178p. B/W illus. (Interest level: 4-8).

Young Sam Gribley discovers the hardships, the fears, and the joys of surviving in the wilderness when he hikes into the Catskill Mountains of New York State. His confidence in his ability to live comfortably in the wild is inspiring and informative.
♦ Students can create models of Sam's traps, utensils, musical instruments, and tools.
1. Catskill Mountains, New York (State)—Fiction 2. Wilderness survival—Fiction.

Holman, Felice. *Slake's Limbo.* Scribner's (0-684-13926-X), 1974. (Interest level: 5-7).

Artemis Slake finds that he can escape from the world in the tiny "room" he discovers in a subway tunnel. In his struggle to survive, he gains confidence and the courage to face and appreciate the outside world he once feared.
♦ Students can discuss why some people have difficulty functioning in today's world. They can also make a list of the people Artemis may have called "friends" at the conclusion of the story and why.
1. Runaways—Fiction 2. Subways—Fiction.

Jones, Hettie. *Longhouse Winter.* Illus. by Nicholas Gaetano. Holt, Rinehart & Winston (0-03-086745-

2), 1972. Unpaginated. Color illus. (Interest level: K-adult).

This is a beautifully illustrated collection of Iroquois legends about humans transforming into animals. The stories were originally published in the book *Iroquois' Myths and Legends by Ya-ie-wa-noh* (University of the State of New York, 1974) by Harriet Maxwell Converse, an adopted Seneca of the Iroquois Nation.

♦ While listening to the stories, young children can guess what animals the humans were transformed into. After the stories, children could draw their own illustrations.

1. Iroquois Indians—Legends   2. Indians of North America—Legends.

Konigsburg, E. L. *From the Mixed-Up Files of Mrs. Basil E. Frankweiler.* Illus. by author. Atheneum (0-689-20586-4), 1967. 162p. B/W illus. (Interest level: 5-8).

Runaways Claudia and Jamie Kincaid find the New York Metropolitan Museum of Art a perfect shelter, but Claudia discovers that her best-made plans do not lead to the exact results she had hoped for. This is an amusing and interesting story of a young girl's search for the secrets of life.

♦ In her notes to Mr. Saxonberg, Mrs. Frankweiler often gives advice, such as "the search proves more profitable than the goal." Teachers could devise a list of clichés that correspond to those passages and then have students match the clichés with the passages.

1. New York (N.Y.)—Metropolitan Museum of Art—Fiction   2. Runaways—Fiction.

Kovalski, Maryann. *Jingle Bells.* Little, Brown (0-316-50258-8), 1988. Unpaginated. Color illus. (Interest level: K-2).

Jenny and Joanna's grandmother takes them on a carriage ride through Central Park in New York City during the Christmas holiday season. The amusing illustrations accurately depict the city of New York.

♦ Choose several strategic pictures in the book and ask children what in the pictures makes them think of a city (or New York City).

1. Christmas stories.

Kroll, Steven. *The Hokey-Pokey Man.* Illus. by Deborah Kogan Ray. Holiday House (0-8234-0728-4), 1989. Unpaginated. Color illus. (Interest level: K-3).

Ben and Sarah's friend Joe, a peddler in the New York City streets, tells them the story of how the ice cream cone was invented at the St. Louis World's Fair. His secret story inevitably slips out and creates quite a disruption in the neighborhood. This book also gives readers a funny view of the consequences of telling secrets.

♦ After talking about the pushcarts in the New York City streets, students could plan a "Fair Day" and design a pushcart with goods they would like to sell.

1. Ice cream, ices, etc.—Fiction   2. New York (N.Y.)—Fiction.

Lipsyte, Robert. *The Brave.* HarperCollins (0-06-023915-8), 1991. 195p. (Interest level: 7-8).

The anger some young adults feel is often difficult to understand and control, as witnessed in this story of an Indian boxer from a reservation in New York. In this sequel to *The Contender* (Harper & Row, 1967), Sonny discovers that running away to New York City doesn't answer any questions either, until he runs into an ex-boxer who helps him discover his own strengths.

♦ In this book, Sonny finds that many people support him in his journey to become a champion boxer. Readers can list the people in the book who supported Sonny, explain their relationships to him, and then rank those people according to their influence on Sonny's life. Young people should include reasons for their choices.

1. Indians of North America—Fiction   2. Boxing—Fiction   3. New York (N.Y.)—Fiction.

Mayerson, Evelyn Wilde. *The Cat Who Escaped from Steerage: A Bubbemeiser.* Charles Scribner's Sons (0-684-19209-8), 1990. 66p. (Interest level: 4-8).

Chanah, a young Polish immigrant, finds that she must hide many things, including her cat, on her passage to America in the steerage section of the ship. Mayerson's story will give the reader an idea of the hardships faced by many European immigrants who came to the United States during the early 1900s.

♦ Have students draw a diagram, using either research materials on ships or information from the story itself, to show where the steerage section of ships is located. Then discuss what life must have been like for immigrants arriving at that time. Teachers may also want to discuss the prejudices against immigrants with disabilities.

1. Emigration and immigration—Fiction   2. Cats—Fiction   3. Ships—Fiction.

Mazer, Harry. *Snow Bound.* Delacorte (0-440-96134-3), 1973. 146p. (Interest level: 7-8).

Two teenagers find themselves fighting for survival when they become stranded in a snowstorm in upstate New York. The author's realistic portrayal of the maturity process reveals his knowledge of adolescent emotion.

♦ Because of the size and importance of New York City, people are often surprised to realize that there are still some areas of true wilderness in the state. Students can identify some of these areas.

They may also want to look at maps of state parks or forests and try to identify the state park in which the main characters stayed, if it exists.
1. Survival—Fiction   2. Wilderness areas—New York (State)—Fiction.

Myers, Walter Dean. *Hoops.* Delacorte (0-440-03707-7), 1981. 183p. (Interest level: 7-8).

This story, which portrays life in a Harlem ghetto, is set in the world of sports, which will interest young people. Lonnie and his coach, Cal, find that they must make some tough decisions that will directly affect their futures.
♦ Young people can write essays about the struggles or hardships that Lonnie must overcome to realize his dreams. Or, they may write a personal essay about obstacles that they will have to overcome to reach their dreams.
1. Basketball—Fiction   2. New York (N.Y.)—Fiction.

O'Dell, Scott. *Sarah Bishop.* Houghton Mifflin (0-395-29185-2), 1980. 184p. (Interest level: 5-8).

Being an outsider seems to be a way of life for Sarah Bishop. As a young girl she is part of a family of Tories in a community of Patriots, but Sarah loses her family when both her father and brother are killed in the War for Independence. In trying to rebuild a life for herself in the wilderness, Sarah learns to survive despite conflicts with nature and civilization itself.
♦ O'Dell writes books with strong female characters; often, it is the experiences that these girls and women have that help to build their strong characters. Students can write essays relating at least three events in the book that helped shape Sarah's personality.
1. United States—History—Revolution, 1775-1783—Fiction   2. American Loyalists—Fiction   3. Survival—Fiction.

Orton, Helen Fuller. *The Treasure in the Little Trunk.* Niagara County Historical Society and Lockport Public Library (1-878233-00-9), 1932. 200p. B/W illus. (Interest level: 3-8).

Patty Armstrong and her family find many hardships on their move from Vermont to western New York during the 1850s. The author's stories are enjoyable to read and describe the realities of rural life during this time period.
♦ Identify "Genesee Country" on a large map. Students can then make a large wall map of their own, label the important towns and cities in the area, and identify the rivers, important roads, and natural resources in this area. They can also list reasons why people might want to move to the area.
1. New York (State)—History—Fiction.

Peck, Richard. *Voices after Midnight.* Delacorte (0-385-29779-3), 1989. 181p. (Interest level: 5-7).

When Chad, Luke, and Heidi move into the old house in New York City, they begin to hear voices late at night that cannot be explained. They eventually learn that the great blizzard of 1888 left some haunting mysteries to be solved. This is an excellent time-travel mystery.
♦ Imagining themselves to be living during the blizzard of 1888, students may write a story about time traveling from that point back to another blizzard. Their research on the blizzards should be accurate.
1. Time travel—Fiction   2. Brothers and sisters—Fiction   3. New York (N.Y.)—Fiction.

Pinkwater, Jill. *Tails of the Bronx: A Tale of the Bronx.* Macmillan (0-02-774652-6), 1991. 208p. (Interest level: 6-8).

A lively group of neighborhood children sets out to solve the mystery of the missing cats and winds up helping a homeless family. The author has done an excellent job of showing how residents in the Bronx are rebuilding their neighborhoods and how the plight of homeless people in the city affects everyone.
♦ Class members could brainstorm the hardships that homeless people face and discuss what can be done by individuals, communities, and governments to assist the homeless.
1. Bronx (New York, N.Y.)—Fiction   2. Neighborhood—Fiction   3. Homeless persons—Fiction.

Rockwell, Anne. *The Dancing Stars: An Iroquois Legend.* Thomas Y. Crowell (0-690-23176-8), 1972. Unpaginated. Color illus. (Interest level: 1-7).

This is an Iroquois legend describing the creation of the stars commonly called the Pleiades. The author's rendition of the story gives us a better understanding of the relationship between the Iroquois and their world.
♦ It is important for students to understand how the Iroquois used legends to explain their world. Younger children might draw pictures of some of the constellations and then fill in the shapes they see. This activity would integrate nicely with a science unit. Older children may illustrate the story with storyboard drawings.
1. Iroquois Indians—Legends   2. Indians of North America—Legends.

Rounds, Glen. *Mr. Yowder and the Steamboat.* Illus. by author. Holiday House (0-8234-0294-0), 1977. Unpaginated. B/W illus. (Interest level: 2-6).

Mr. Yowder, a sign painter by trade, finds himself in New York City one year with a desire to go fishing. How he comes back with a large steamboat by way of Broadway is a humorous and enjoyable story.

♦ The teacher may want to list events and occurrences in the story and then have children explain whether these events are fact or fiction.
1. Boats and boating—Fiction   2. Humorous stories.

St. George, Judith. *By George, Bloomers!* Illus. by Margot Tomes. Coward, McCann & Geoghegan (0-698-30601-5), 1976. 48p. Color illus. (Interest level: 2-5).

Hannah would love to be able to wear bloomers so that she could easily climb or skate, but her mother forbids these unladylike outfits. Then, one day, Hannah shows her mother how practical bloomers can be! This is an interesting view of the beginning of the women's movement.
♦ Young children can pick out bloomers from several pictures of period costumes and draw a picture of Hannah with bloomers. Older students can research the leaders of the Women's Rights Convention in Seneca Falls, New York, and find out how many of these leaders were originally from New York State.
1. Women's rights—Fiction   2. Sex roles—Fiction.

Selden, George. *Chester Cricket's Pigeon Ride.* Illus. by Garth Williams. Farrar, Straus, Giroux (0-374-31239-7), 1981. Unpaginated. B/W illus. (Interest level: 1-5).

Chester Cricket likes his new friends in New York City, but he misses the country fields and ponds. Then he meets a special friend, Lulu the pigeon, and she takes him on a flight over the beautiful city of New York. The illustrations are well done, and the text explores many different emotions with sensitivity.
♦ The illustrations in the book concentrate on the view of the city both above and below human eye level. Explain the meaning of the word *perspective* and relate it to the characters' views of the city and country. Students can then draw pictures of scenes from different perspectives.
1. Crickets—Fiction   2. Pigeons—Fiction   3. New York (N.Y.)—Fiction.

Selden, George. *The Genie of Sutton Place.* Farrar, Straus, Giroux (0-374-32527-8), 1973. 175p. (Interest level: 4-8).

This blend of reality and fairy tale will warm the heart of any reader. Tim Farr, in looking through his archaeologist father's diary, discovers how to use museum tapestries to release a genie from his bondage. Their adventures are amusing and somewhat "magical"!
♦ Tapestries are art forms and are historically significant. Students can find examples of tapestries and discuss the stories woven into the fabric. Teachers may also draw in the study of Indian wampum as tapestries of life, which could also lead to a discussion of the value of historical records.
1. Magic—Stories   2. New York (N.Y.)—Fiction.

Selden, George. *Harry Kitten and Tucker Mouse.* Illus. by Garth Williams. Farrar, Straus, Giroux (0-374-32860-9), 1986. 79p. B/W illus. (Interest level: 1-5).

Harry Kitten and Tucker Mouse surprisingly become good friends and together they explore the city of New York looking for the perfect home. A good theme of the book is recognizing and respecting personal differences.
♦ Each person (or, in this case, animal) sees something different in everything he or she encounters. Students can write one thing about each place that Harry Kitten and Tucker Mouse visited that they would have liked and then share these with the rest of the class.
1. Mice—Stories   2. Cats—Stories   3. New York (N.Y.)—Fiction.

Sharmat, Marjorie Weinman. *Gila Monsters Meet You at the Airport.* Illus. by Byron Barton. Macmillan (0-02-782450-0), 1980. Unpaginated. Color illus. (Interest level: K-3).

Moving is scary for anyone, especially moving from a big city in the east to "the West," as this boy is doing. He just knows that everything will be different. This is a great affirmation book, which tells children that everyone has the same feelings about some things.
♦ Children can describe what they think life in a major city (one different from their own) is like. The teacher may wish to make a list of these descriptions and then show a video about the city, so that children can see what the city is really like.
1. The West—Fiction   2. New York—Fiction.

Shyer, Marlene Fanta. *Ruby, the Red-Hot Witch at Bloomingdales.* Viking (0-670-83473-4), 1991. 151p. (Interest level: 6-8).

When Petra and Thomas witness Ruby's success at stopping Thomas's hiccups, they begin to believe in the Bloomingdales witch's magic. Is it possible that Ruby's magic could bring Petra's parents together again? Some critics might warn against this story's "happy ending," but, in a world where so many stories have bad endings, it is nice to read an optimistic book.
♦ The importance of the famous department stores of New York City cannot be overlooked in a study of the city's growth as a major financial center. Students can research the histories of the famous department stores of New York City. Then they can write essays about what "magic" the department stores have.

1. Department stores—New York (N.Y.)
2. Bloomingdales—New York (N.Y.).

Skolsky, Mindy Warshaw. *The Whistling Teakettle and Other Stories about Hannah.* Illus. by Karen Ann Weinhaus. Harper & Row (0-06-025689-3), 1977. 70p. B/W illus. (Interest level: 2-5).

These short stories describe the life of a young Polish girl living just outside of New York City. The author recognizes the beauty of both the country life (near the Hudson River) and the city life (the Bronx) in the state of New York.
♦ Both Hannah and her grandmother had special places where they enjoyed being alone. Children can write a description of the special place where they go to be alone. Emphasize that they do not need to tell where the place is but they should describe the place or how they feel when they are there. One of the places mentioned in the book is the George Washington Bridge; children can trace on a map the route that Hannah took to visit her grandmother.
1. New York (N.Y.)—Fiction   2. City and town life—Fiction   3. Humorous stories.

Swift, Hildegarde. *The Little Red Lighthouse and the Great Gray Bridge.* Harcourt, Brace & World (0-15-247040-9), 1942. Unpaginated. Color illus. (Interest level: K-3).

The little red lighthouse, which actually exists on the Hudson River near the George Washington Bridge, slowly realizes that its job as a river beacon is and always will be important. The story also conveys the role of the river in the transportation of goods and services
♦ Children can discuss the importance of a lighthouse. They can then draw the lighthouse and the bridge from the story.
1. George Washington Bridge—Fiction   2. Lighthouses—Fiction.

Talbot, Charlene Joy. *An Orphan for Nebraska.* Atheneum (0-689-30698-9), 1979. 208p. (Interest level: 5-8).

Kevin finds that his job as a newsboy in New York City is tolerable, but when the Children's Aid Society offers him a chance to go West, he readily accepts. The story also takes place in nineteenth-century Nebraska, giving the reader a view of life in each place.
♦ Students can research the Children's Aid Society. They can also draw or develop a flowchart diagramming the process of printing a newspaper in the 1800s. A visit to a local newspaper printer might also be arranged.
1. Orphans—Fiction   2. Frontier and pioneer life—Fiction   3. Nebraska—Fiction   4. New York (N.Y.)—Fiction.

Tolles, Martha. *Darci and the Dance Contest.* E. P. Dutton (0-525-67166-8), 1985. 100p. (Interest level: 4-7).

Darci, like any teenager who has moved to a new school, finds it hard to adjust to life in New York City. She would like to make some friends, but she finds that the price of making certain friends is more than she should pay. Peer pressure is realistically portrayed in this story.
♦ This novel could be used to initiate a discussion of the trials people face in coming to a new country. One of the problems Darci faced was peer pressure, along with loneliness. Students could also discuss ways in which they could make new students welcome in their school, perhaps making a handbook for new students.
1. Schools—Fiction   2. Moving, Household—Fiction   3. Friendship—Fiction.

Van Leeuwen, Jean. *The Great Christmas Kidnapping Caper.* Illus. by Steven Kellogg. Dial Press (0-8037-5416-7), 1975. 133p. B/W illus. (Interest level: 3-5).

Children who enjoy animal adventures will delight in this story of three mice—Marvin, Fats, and Raymond—who find a home and a Christmas friend at Macy's. The story will give children an idea of what can be found at Macy's.
♦ Younger children may wish to imagine that they could live in a department store, like the mice. They could write about which department of the store they would most like to live in. Students could also draw a floor plan of Macy's.
1. Mice—Fiction   2. Christmas stories.

Waber, Bernard. *The House on East 88th Street.* Houghton Mifflin (0-395-18157-7), 1962. 48p. Color illus. (Interest level: K-3).

What a surprise it was to the Primm family to find Lyle the Crocodile living in their new home on East 88th Street in New York City! The Primms easily got to know Lyle, however, and readily welcomed him into the family.
♦ Children can make a list of the chores that Lyle does throughout the book and then discuss what chores they do at home.
1. Crocodiles—Fiction   2. New York (N.Y.)—Fiction.

Waber, Bernard. *Lyle and the Birthday Party.* Houghton Mifflin (0-395-15085-X), 1966. 48p. Color illus. (Interest level: K-3).

It's hard to believe that lovable Lyle could be jealous, but when Joshua plans his birthday party, Lyle becomes upset because he can't have a birthday party. When someone in the class celebrates a birthday, this book would make an excellent read-aloud.
♦ After reading the book, students can discuss how they feel when someone else has a birthday. They

could also draw birthday cards for local hospital patients or senior citizens.
1. Crocodiles—Fiction   2. New York (N.Y.)—Fiction.

Waber, Bernard. *Lyle, Lyle Crocodile.* Houghton Mifflin (0-395-16995-X), 1965. 48p. Color illus. (Interest level: K-3).

Lyle the crocodile enjoys life on East 88th Street, but his neighbor, Mr. Brumps, dislikes Lyle and finally manages to have Lyle put into the zoo. Will Lyle spend his life behind bars?

♦ Lyle the crocodile is the Primms' pet, just as the students have pets. Young people can draw pictures of their pets and the things their pets do.
1. Crocodiles—Fiction   2. New York (N.Y.)—Fiction.

Wilder, Laura Ingalls. *Farmer Boy.* Illus. by Garth Williams. Harper & Row (0-06-026425-X), 1933. 372p. B/W illus. (Interest level: 4-8).

Everyone familiar with the Little House series will enjoy this story of Almanzo's childhood in upstate New York. Each chapter focuses on a different custom of farming life during the end of the nineteenth century.

♦ After reading this book, students can choose one custom (such as harvesting ice, sheep shearing, going to the county fair) that they would like to research. A variety of products that are grown or raised in New York State are presented in this book. Students can do research to determine whether these are still products of the state.
1. Country life—Stories   2. New York (State)—Fiction.

Winter, Jeanette. *Follow the Drinking Gourd.* Illus. by author. Alfred A. Knopf (0-394-99694-1), 1988. Unpaginated. Color illus. (Interest level: 1-5).

A legendary leader of the Underground Railroad, Peg-Leg Joe, teaches slaves a nonsense song called "Follow the Drinking Gourd," which actually gives the directions the slaves must take to escape to freedom in Canada. This is a wonderfully original book on the Underground Railroad.

♦ Using the words to the song, children can draw a map showing the route the slaves took when they "followed the drinking gourd" to freedom. Also, children can create their own songs, with directions to a famous location in their community. As they perform the song before the class, the other students in the class can try to guess where the song leads.
1. Fugitive slaves—Fiction   2. Slavery—Fiction   3. Underground Railroad—Fiction.

Wojciechowski, Susan. *And the Other, Gold.* Orchard Books (0-531-05702-X), 1987. 151p. (Interest level: 6-8).

Patty discovers two important things during her eighth-grade year at St. Ignatius Catholic school: the excitement of first love and the value of friendship. This is a heartwarming story of friendship.

♦ Often, religious schools are stereotyped and students in public schools have a distorted view of life in religious schools. Students can compare their school activities with Patty's and Tracy's activities. Students in public schools might also want to arrange an exchange with a group of students from a religious school.
1. Schools—Fiction   2. Friendship—Fiction.

Yashima, Taro. *Umbrella.* Illus. by author. Viking (0-670-73858-1), 1958. 35p. Color illus. (Interest level: K-1).

Momo, a young Japanese girl living in New York City, can't wait to use her new umbrella and red rubber boots. When a rainy day finally does come, she wears her new things and discovers a new world. An important theme in this book is independence.

♦ Using enlarged versions of the Japanese symbols in the book, teachers can reproduce the symbols in outline form and have the children color them. Students can discuss how the Japanese language is based on pictures of what words mean; then they can draw a picture of the meaning of a word, such as *spring, rain,* or *peach.*
1. Umbrellas and parasols—Stories   2. New York (N.Y.)—Fiction.

Yorinks, Arthur. *Oh, Brother.* Illus. by Richard Egielski. Farrar, Straus, Giroux (0-374-35599-1), 1989. Unpaginated. Color illus. (Interest level: K-3).

Morris and Milton, two orphaned boys from New York City, find themselves facing many hardships. Then a kind tailor named Nathan takes them in and teaches them to love.

♦ The two brothers, Morris and Milton, are shown doing many different things together. Ask children to tell, either in writing or orally, which picture of Morris and Milton is their favorite and why.
1. Twins—Fiction   2. New York (N.Y.)—Fiction.

Zindel, Paul. *A Begonia for Miss Applebaum.* Harper & Row (0-06-026877-8), 1989. 180p. (Interest level: 6-8).

Henry and Zelda find that it is life, not death, that ultimately triumphs when they come to terms with their teacher's struggle against cancer. Miss Applebaum teaches them, through thoughtful deeds and actions, to laugh, love, learn, and enjoy life.

♦ Students can discuss Miss Applebaum's legacy and explain how her life touched others.
1. Teacher-student relationships—Fiction   2. Death—Fiction   3. New York (N.Y.)—Fiction.

Periodicals

333.7
The Conservationist. New York State Department of Environmental Conservation (ISSN 0010-650X), 1992. Bimonthly. (Interest level: grade 5-adult).

Bright, colorful illustrations enhance this bimonthly publication, which includes articles about the environment of New York State. The timely features cover a wide range of relevant topics.
♦ Each student can read one article from an issue of this magazine and submit a summary of the article or a copy of the article with the main ideas highlighted. Then students can write editorials or draw editorial cartoons about the article.
1. Environment—Government policy—New York (State)—Periodicals 2. New York (State)—Description and travel—Periodicals.

333.7
New York Alive. Chase Communications Group (ISSN 0734-0265). Quarterly. (Interest level: grade 6-adult).

The articles in this periodical focus on current issues concerning New York State. The magazine gives comprehensive coverage of events in the state.
♦ Students could conduct further research on topics covered in the articles in a particular issue.
1. New York (State)—Description and travel—Periodicals.

333.7
WaterWays: New York's Waterfront News. Morgan Brown (No ISSN). Monthly. (Interest level: grade 7-adult).

This monthly newspaper focuses on the environmental conditions, attractions, and significance of New York's waterways. One highlight is the "news brief" section, which looks at what is happening around waterways throughout the state. A timely resource, this paper is also useful, considering the multitude of waterways in New York.
♦ Students can choose an article in any issue that elicits a strong personal reaction and then write an editorial about the article to send to the publisher.
1. Water conservation—New York (State).

Professional Materials

371.3
Issues and Images: New Yorkers during the Thirties: Teachers' Guide to Using Historical Documents. (Combined entry). New York State Education Department (No ISBN), 1985. 22 documents; teacher's guide. B/W photos. (Interest level: Professional).

This unique packet of teaching materials includes historical documents and explains how to use them. In education today, historical documents are often not used because necessary materials are not available. The documents included in this packet are varied and provide a comprehensive view of life during the thirties.
♦ After a discussion of primary and secondary sources, young people can construct a bulletin-board display identifying these sources. Teachers could also have the students choose a document from the packet and list what they have learned about that document.
1. New York (State)—History, 1930s 2. New York (State)—Study and teaching.

371.3
New York Is Reading Country Manual: The 1992 New York Summer Reading Program. Created by Sandra Stoner Sivulich and Randall Enos. Canterbury Press and Liverpool Litho, Ltd. (No ISBN), n.d. Unpaginated. (Interest level: Professional).

For public librarians, this informative and useful manual was developed to help in implementing active summer reading programs with the theme "New York is Reading Country." Included are bibliographies, fresh ideas for projects, worksheets, etc.
♦ Activities for using this resource are included in the resource itself. Perhaps students could construct their own manual of additional activities using the same theme.
1. New York (State)—Study and teaching.

Pennsylvania

by Margaret Jetter

Nonfiction

271.8
Alderfer, E. Gordon. *The Ephrata Commune: An Early American Counterculture*. University of Pittsburgh Press (0-8229-5801-5), 1985. 273p. B/W illus. and photos. (Interest level: grade 6-adult).

Ephrata, a mystical religious community in eastern Pennsylvania, flourished in the eighteenth century and produced exquisitely decorated manuscripts in its printing center. The commune's surviving buildings are administered by the Pennsylvania Historical and Museum Commission as the Ephrata Cloisters Park.
♦ Young people can find examples of the type of manuscripts published at Ephrata and compare them with other illuminated manuscripts.
1. Ephrata Community—History

289.7
Ammon, Richard. *Growing Up Amish*. Atheneum (0-689-31387-X), 1989. 102p. B/W illus., photos, and maps. (Interest level: 4-8).

Anna, daughter of an Amish farmer, is the focus of this illustrated study, which reveals the homes, work, education, and recreation of the Pennsylvania Dutch community. A bibliography, maps, and an index complete the book.
♦ Class members could learn some of the songs, games, and poems that are included in this book, or prepare one of the recipes included.
1. Amish—Pennsylvania—Social life and customs.

289.7
Faber, Doris. *The Amish*. Illus. by Michael E. Erkel. Doubleday (0-385-26130-6), 1991. 45p. Color illus. (Interest level: 3-7).

This book provides detailed information on the history, culture, daily lifestyle, and future of the Amish people in Pennsylvania. Contemporary experiences, such as the silent protest by a group of Amish farmers against a proposed highway cutting through their land, are described. Faber explores the reasons that Amish communities are growing.
♦ Children can research the recent Amish protest more thoroughly.
1. Amish—Pennsylvania.

289.7
Fisher, Sara and **Stahl, Rachel K.** *The Amish School*. Good Books (0-934672-17-2), 1986. 96p. B/W photos. (Interest level: 2-8).

One of the authors of this authoritative book on Amish education was an Amish teacher in Pennsylvania; the other has completed extensive research on the subject. The book answers many questions children have about Amish education, such as why do the Amish have separate schools, what do the Amish children study, who are the teachers, and what role do parents have in their children's education?
♦ After brainstorming a list of questions about the Amish school system, the class can invite an Amish teacher to visit and answer their questions, or students can conduct further research to find the answers.
1. Amish—Pennsylvania.

289.7
Foster, Sally. *Where Time Stands Still*. Illus. by author. Dodd, Mead (0-396-09090-7), 1987. Unpaginated. B/W photos. (Interest level: 3-7).

A year's seasonal activities for children living in an Amish farming community in Lancaster, Pennsylvania, are presented via photographs and simple narrative. Amish customs and traditions are reflected in the activities.
♦ Readers could compare farming methods on an Amish farm with those on a mechanized farm.
1. Amish—Pennsylvania—Social life and customs
2. Farm life—Pennsylvania 3. Pennsylvania—Social life and customs.

289.7
Good, Merle. *Who Are the Amish?* Good Books (0-934672-26-1), 1985. 128p. Color photos. (Interest level: 2-8).

Traditional Amish culture is presented in 12 categories, including Amish school, tradition and history, interaction with the larger world, and sources of energy, via photographs and informative text. The author lives in Lancaster, Pennsylvania, and has researched and written about the Amish and Mennonites for many years.
♦ Students could create a model of an Amish school or a diorama reflecting the lifestyle, culture, or traditions of the Amish.
1. Amish—Pennsylvania 2. Mennonites—Pennsylvania.

289.7
Good, Merle and Good, Phyllis. *Twenty Most Asked Questions about the Amish and Mennonites.* Good Books (0-934672-00-8), 1979. 96p. B/W photos. (Interest level: 4-8).

The authors of this book are Lancaster natives, Mennonites, and co-directors of the People's Place, an arts and crafts educational center. In answering common questions about the Amish and Mennonite cultures, this book resolves misconceptions about these people and their beliefs.
♦ The book could be used as a starting point for a discussion about various religious sects.
1. Amish—Pennsylvania 2. Mennonites—Pennsylvania.

289.7
Hostetler, John. *Amish Society.* 3rd ed. Johns Hopkins University Press (0-801-23343-X), 1983. 414p. B/W photos. (Interest level: 5-8).

The author, born and reared in an Amish community in Pennsylvania, takes the reader inside Amish culture and explains the nature of Amish religious beliefs and ceremonies, community and family life, separation, mutual-aid practices, temptations and tensions with worldly values, and interactions with outsiders. The expanded third edition of this definitive work reflects recent research and current developments within the Amish community.
♦ Young people could research an area of Amish life that they find interesting and prepare an oral presentation for the class.
1. Amish—Social life and customs.

289.7
Kraybill, Donald B. *The Riddle of the Amish Culture.* Johns Hopkins University Press (0-8018-3682-4), 1989. 304p. B/W photos. (Interest level: grade 5-adult).

The 300th anniversary of Amish society in America was in 1993, and Kraybill investigates the culture of the traditional Amish community in juxtaposition with modern industrialization. He shows how some puzzling aspects of contemporary Amish life are reasonable solutions to the merger of tradition with modernization. A bibliography and index complete this book.
♦ Students could identify current Amish practices that are different from the traditional lifestyle of the past.
1. Amish—Pennsylvania.

289.7
Meyer, Carolyn. *Amish People: Plain Living in a Complex World.* Photos by author. Atheneum (0-689-50041-6), 1976. 138p. B/W photos. (Interest level: 5-8).

The Amish insistence on a simple lifestyle, despite the pressures of the surrounding technological world, are revealed through this study of a hypothetical, but typical family in Lancaster County, Pennsylvania. Through details of work, customs, and beliefs, the reader will gain a genuine understanding of what it means to be Amish.
♦ In a creative writing assignment, young people can explore what it would be like to be Amish.
1. Amish—Pennsylvania—Social life and customs.

289.7
Naylor, Phyllis Reynolds. *An Amish Family.* Illus. by George Armstrong. Lamplight Publishing (0-87955-809-1), 1974. 181p. B/W illus. (Interest level: 4-8).

Focusing on the Stoltzfus family of Lancaster County, Pennsylvania, this book reports on the traditional lifestyle of the Amish community: work habits, religious practices, education, recreation, and history. A bibliography and index are included.
♦ Classes in Pennsylvania can arrange a field trip to Lancaster County. Other students may choose a particular facet of Amish life to research further and present to the class.
1. Amish—Pennsylvania—Social life and customs.

289.7
Scott, Stephen. *Why Do They Dress That Way?* Illus. by author. Good Books (0-934672-18-0), 1986. 160p. B/W illus. and photos. (Interest level: 3-8).

Scott examines several groups, such as the Pennsylvania Dutch, Amish, Mennonite, and Shakers, whose dress sets them apart. The author, a member of the Old Order River Brethren of Lancaster, Pennsylvania, who has researched plain dress for over 20 years, interprets clothing as indicative of identity and image. Charts and drawings illustrate differences and similarities among the dress of the several groups.

♦ Children can design costumes for a school dramatic presentation that will show the contrasting culture of several Pennsylvania ethnic groups.
1. Clothing and dress.

289.7
Smith, Elmer L. *The Amish*. Photos. by Mel Horst. Applied Arts Publishers (0-911410-14-7), 1989. 34p. B/W photos. (Interest level: 4-8).

This photographic essay focuses on the communal lifestyle of the Amish people. Topics covered include church, marriage and family, work, education, and mutual support, including care of the aged. Photographs were taken in several locations in eastern Pennsylvania.
♦ Students can illustrate some aspect of Amish life.
1. Amish—Pennsylvania—Social life and customs.

289.7
Stone, Erika and **Good, Merle**. *Nicole Visits an Amish Farm*. Photos by Erika Stone. Walker Publishing (0-8027-6444-4), 1982. 48p. B/W photos. (Interest level: 1-5).

Nicole, a girl from New York City, visits an Amish farm in Lancaster, Pennsylvania, for a two-week vacation. Although homesick for her family, Nicole learns to enjoy the lifestyle of her host family. Stone and Good present additional information about the Amish culture and the Fresh Air Fund, which supports the vacation program, in an endnote.
♦ As a class, students can write and film a news documentary on Amish life.
1. Amish—Pennsylvania—Social life and customs 2. Farm life—Pennsylvania 3. Pennsylvania—Social life and customs.

289.7
Wasilchick, John V. *Amish Life: A Portrait of Plain Living*. Photos by Jerry Irwin. Crescent Books (0-517-06584-3), 1991. 157p. Color photos. (Interest level: 3-8).

In words and photographs, this book examines the history, customs, and practices of the Plain People (Amish, Old Order Mennonites, and Hutterites). This portrait looks beyond the distinctive outer symbols (clothing, horse and buggy) and into the rich and complex way of life of the communities. The pictures were taken in rural farm areas and at historic sites in Pennsylvania.
♦ Young people could create a slide or videotape show about Amish life.
1. Amish—Pennsylvania 2. Farm life—Pennsylvania 3. Mennonites—Pennsylvania.

307.3
The Spirit of Pittsburgh. (Videocassette). WQED, 1989. VHS, Color and B/W, (40 min.). $19.95. (Interest level: grade 4-adult).

This film, winner of the 1989 Silver Screen Award, documents the renaissance of Pittsburgh, Pennsylvania. During the past 40 years, the people of Pittsburgh transformed their city from one of industrial pollution to "America's most livable city." The film highlights a variety of cultural elements that reflect the changing life of the city.
♦ Viewers can document the Pittsburgh renaissance by locating before and after pictures of Pittsburgh. Students can also conduct interviews of people who lived through the change.
1. Urban renewal—Pittsburgh (Pa.) 2. City planning 3. Community development.

331.7
Brestensky, Dennis; **Hovanec, Evelyn A.**; and **Skomra, Albert N.** *Patch Work Voices*. University of Pittsburgh Press (0-8229-5460-5), 1991. 83p. B/W photos. (Interest level: 5-8).

In their own words, the people who settled and labored in southwestern Pennsylvania tell of their daily lives at work in the coal mines and at home in the nearby mining town (known as a patch). With pride, these people talk about the hardships of the workplace and the gardens, baseball teams, and social events that filled their lives.
♦ Students can write a letter to relatives back home (identify the country) describing their life as a coal miner in a coal-mining town.
1. Coal miners—Pennsylvania—History.

331.89
Demarest, David P., ed. *The River Ran Red*. University of Pittsburgh Press (0-8229-5478-8), 1992. 232p. B/W photos, reproductions. (Interest level: 7-8).

The violence that erupted at Carnegie Steel's giant Homestead Mill near Pittsburgh, Pennsylvania, on July 6, 1892, resulted in a congressional investigation and changed the course of the American Labor Movement. The book, which commemorates the 100th anniversary of the Homestead Strike, is composed of contemporary newspaper and magazine accounts, passages from congressional records, firsthand accounts of participants and observers, and reproductions of on-the-scene photographs and sketches.
♦ Students can develop a time line of the major events of the Homestead Strike.
1. Homestead Strike, 1892 2. Steel industry and trade—Pennsylvania—History—19th century.

342.73
Fritz, Jean. *Shh! We're Writing the Constitution*. Illus. by Tomie De Paola. G. P. Putnam's Sons (0-399-21403-8), 1987. 64p. B/W and Color illus. (Interest level: 2-5).

Fritz presents the unique personalities of the delegates who gathered in Philadelphia in 1786 to

write the Constitution. She details the physical discomforts they endured, their disagreements, and their compromises. Notes, which expand on some of the historical events and decisions, and a copy of the Constitution enhance the text.
♦ Children can choose one of the delegates to research further. Then the class can reenact the writing of the Constitution.
1. United States—Constitutional Convention (1787) 2. United States—Constitution 3. Philadelphia (Pa.)—History.

388.1
Cupper, Dan. *The Pennsylvania Turnpike: A History.* Applied Arts Publishers (0-911410-90-1), 1990. 48p. B/W and Color photos. (Interest level: 5-8).

This history of the Pennsylvania Turnpike, America's first superhighway, which opened on October 1, 1940, traces the planning, construction, and 50 years of service provided by the road. Preservation of and improvements to the turnpike are discussed, as is its influence on the design of superhighways in other states.
♦ Young people could write about experiences they have had on the Pennsylvania turnpike or another major highway. They may also invite a speaker from their local department of transportation to speak to the class.
1. Express highways—Pennsylvania 2. Pennsylvania Turnpike.

394.2
A Child's Christmas in Pittsburgh. (Videocassette). WQED, 1990. VHS, Color and B/W, (60 min.). $19.95. (Interest level: grade 1-adult).

Photographic tours of popular Pittsburgh Christmas attractions and celebrations, such as a miniature railroad at Buhl Science Center, candlelight services at Heinz chapel, and animated window displays downtown, are interspersed with musical performances and visits to selected private homes to share pre-Christmas activities. Adult/children interactions are highlighted.
♦ Pennsylvania viewers can visit one or more of the sites shown in the film. Others can film their own favorite Christmas sites and experiences.
1. Christmas 2. Christmas—Songs and music.

398.2
Fins, Furs, and Feathers: Animal Tales from the Pennsylvania Mountains. (Audiocassette). Groundhog Press, 1990. (45 min.). $10.00. (Interest level: K-4).

Robin Moore, author and storyteller, recounts six traditional animal tales from the Pennsylvania mountain culture. Several of the stories are based on anecdotes recalled from Moore's childhood experiences with his grandfather and other relatives during his summer vacations at Silver Lake. Stories include how a trout was trained to live on land, how the groundhog became the official "awakener," and how an eagle was taught to fly.
♦ Students could learn one of these stories to tell to other children in the school.
1. Tall tales—Pennsylvania 2. Folklore—Pennsylvania 3. Animals—Fiction.

398.2
Glimm, James York. *Flatlanders and Ridgerunners.* University of Pittsburgh Press (0-8229-5345-5), 1983. 199p. (Interest level: 7-8).

James Glimm, a flatlander newcomer to the mountain area of northern Pennsylvania, has collected a rich array of tall tales, superstitions, hunting yarns, anecdotes, cures, history, and personal vignettes that reveal the culture of the native ridgerunners. The stories are organized into categories and documented with source notes.
♦ Each student can write a tall tale, and then all of the stories can be bound into a book to be placed in the school library.
1. Tall tales—Pennsylvania 2. Manners and customs 3. Folklore—Pennsylvania 4. Pennsylvania—Social life and customs.

398.2
Glimm, James York. *Snakebite: Lives and Legends of Central Pennsylvania.* University of Pittsburgh Press (0-8229-5444-3), 1991. 208p. Silhouettes. (Interest level: 4-8).

This collection of orally transmitted folktales, true stories, anecdotes, and tall tales reflects the unique flavor of central Pennsylvania's people and life. Stories are organized by subject, and sources are identified.
♦ The class can plan a storytelling program for the school using stories from this collection or stories students have heard at home or have written themselves.
1. Tall tales—Pennsylvania 2. Folklore—Pennsylvania.

398.2
Shapiro, Irwin. *Joe Magarac and His USA Citizen Papers.* Illus. by James Daugherty. University of Pittsburgh Press (0-8229-5305-3), 1979. 58p. B/W illus. (Interest level: 4-8).

Hungarian-born Joe Magarac comes to Braddock, Pennsylvania, to make steel and to become a citizen of the United States. Accidentally, Joe becomes part of a Washington, DC, building where he is recognized by the president.
♦ Students could illustrate their favorite Joe Magarac adventure.
1. Magarac, Joe (Legendary character) 2. Tall tales—Pennsylvania 3. Folklore—Pennsylvania.

398.2
When the Moon Is Full: Supernatural Stories from the Pennsylvania Mountains. (Audiocassette). Groundhog Press, 1991. (45 min.). $10.00. (Interest level: 2-8).

Author and storyteller Robin Moore presents five chilling traditional and original tales from the Pennsylvania mountain culture. Vocal and instrumental music and wolf howls provide an eerie background. Stories include Uncle Bill's dream of being turned into a donkey by a witchy woman, how Spearfinger was defeated, and how Dark Catrina and Fiddling Jack disappeared with the wolves.
♦ Young people could prepare a ghost story or other scary story to tell to other class members.
1. Tall tales—Pennsylvania 2. Folklore—Pennsylvania 3. Supernatural—Fiction.

551.48
Dolson, Hildegarde. *Disaster at Johnstown.* Illus. by Joseph Cellini. Random House, 1965. 174p. B/W illus. (Interest level: 4-8).

As the Memorial Day Parade in 1889 was marching through Johnstown, Pennsylvania, the South Fork Dam burst sending 20 million tons of water toward the city. Dolson's account of the flood focuses on the victims, the people responsible, and the people who helped to restore the city.
♦ Students could write a script for a TV news report of the flood.
1. Floods—Johnstown (Pa.).

551.48
The Johnstown Flood. (Videocassette). Guggenheim Productions, 1989. VHS, B/W, (26 min.). $24.95. (Interest level: grade 4-adult).

Using archival photographs, creative dramatizations, and special effects, this film, winner of the 1989 Academy Award for best documentary, re-creates the events of one of the most shocking disasters in America: the bursting of a private dam in 1889, which allowed a wall of water to sweep away the city of Johnstown, Pennsylvania, killing 2,200 persons. Almost immediately, volunteers from across the United States and local survivors began the task of rebuilding lives and the city.
♦ Children can write a letter home, as a volunteer, that describes their work in rebuilding Johnstown, or they can research later floods (such as the floods in 1937 and 1977) and compare them with the one in 1889.
1. Floods—Johnstown (Pa.).

551.48
McCullough, David G. *The Johnstown Flood.* Simon and Schuster (0-671-20714-8), 1968. 302p. B/W illus. and photos. (Interest level: 6-8).

Based on diaries, letters, interviews with survivors, and the transcript of a private investigation conducted by the Pennsylvania railroad, this history of the 1889 Johnstown flood graphically details the events leading to the catastrophe, the flood itself, and the aftermath for the town and its people. A list of victims, a bibliography, and index complete this book.
♦ Young people could write, in diary form, their impressions of the flood from the perspective of a survivor.
1. Floods—Johnstown (Pa.).

553.2
Born in Freedom: The Story of Colonel Drake. (16mm film). American Petroleum Industry, 1954. Color, (28 min.). Free loan through intermediate unit film libraries. (Interest level: 4-8).

This historical documentary film reports the birth of the petroleum industry with the drilling of the first commercial oil well at Titusville, Pennsylvania, in 1859. Vincent Price portrays Colonel Edwin Drake.
♦ Classes in Pennsylvania can arrange a field trip to the Drake Well Museum at Titusville. If a field trip is not possible, students can research the early development of the oil industry.
1. Drake, Edwin Laurentine, 1819-1880 2. Smith, William (Uncle Billy) 3. Oil well drilling 4. Petroleum.

553.2
Dolson, Hildegarde. *The Great Oildorado.* Random House, 1959. 300p. (Interest level: 6-8).

In recounting the events of the first oil rush in Venango County from 1859 to 1880, the author, a native of Franklin, Pennsylvania, enlivens the history with humor, pathos, catastrophe, and a sense of the turbulence that colored the events and the people. A bibliography suggests further reading.
♦ Students may create models of early and present-day oil well structures. They might also schedule a field trip to a local oil refinery.
1. Oil well drilling 2. Petroleum.

553.2
Pennsylvania Crude. (Videocassette). Venango Museum Productions, 1993. Color, VHS, (30 min.). $29.95. (Interest level: 4-8).

This documentary film opens with "Colonel" Edwin L. Drake's success in drilling an oil well in Titusville, Pennsylvania; historical sites in Oil City, Franklin, Emlenton, and Titusville reveal the continuing development of the petroleum industry in northwest Pennsylvania. Local historians, geologists, and industrialists provide information about the social, cultural, and business activities in the region.
♦ If possible, students can visit the Drake Well Memorial Park in Titusville, Pennsylvania. Located on the site of the original well, the museum

and library preserve historic artifacts of the early oil industry.
1. Oil well drilling   2. Petroleum.

567.9
McGinnis, Helen J. *Carnegie's Dinosaurs.* Illus. by Vincent J. Abromitis. Carnegie Museum (0-911239-00-6), 1982. 120p. Color photos. (Interest level: 3-8).

Carnegie Museum in Pittsburgh houses one of the world's outstanding collections of Mesozoic reptiles; this guidebook describes each of the specimens in the collection. The book also discusses excavation of famous dinosaur sites, dinosaur ways of life and death, and the installation of the skeletons in the museum's Dinosaur Hall.
♦ Classes in Pennsylvania can arrange a field trip to Dinosaur Hall, and students can prepare a list of questions to ask the curator. Students could create their own dinosaur museum and invite other classes to visit.
1. Dinosaurs   2. Dinosaurs—Museums.

598
Wakeley, James S. and **Wakeley, Lillian D.** *Birds of Pennsylvania: Natural History and Conservation.* Illus. by George Lavanish. Pennsylvania Game Commission (No ISBN), 1989. 214p. B/W illus. and photos; Color photos. (Interest level: 3-8).

The Wakeleys summarize many aspects of the natural history, conservation, and enjoyment of birds in Pennsylvania, including origins and adaptations for flight, migration, benefits and detriments, how to attract birds, and bird observation. A detailed analysis of six types of habitats and the birds living in them is included, and a checklist of Pennsylvania birds and an index facilitate research.
♦ Children can record the number and kind of birds in their community.
1. Birds—Pennsylvania.

599.09
Merritt, Joseph F. *Guide to the Mammals of Pennsylvania.* Illus. by Hal S. Korber. University of Pittsburgh Press (0-8229-5393-5), 1987. 408p. B/W illus. and photos. (Interest level: grade 4-adult).

Pennsylvania is endowed with a fascinating variety of mammals, and this guidebook discusses 63 wild mammals known to live in the state today. The accounts are organized by order, family, genus, and species; information for each mammal includes description, ecology, behavior, reproduction and development, and status for endangered species. A glossary, appendix, bibliography, and index are included.
♦ Students can identify mammals that live in their area and prepare a slide show or videotape about them.
1. Mammals—Pennsylvania—Identification.

622
Poliniak, Louis. *When Coal Was King: Mining Pennsylvania's Anthracite.* Applied Arts Publishers (0-911410-26-0), 1989. 32p. B/W photos. (Interest level: 4-8).

In the late eighteenth century, anthracite or "hard" coal began to be mined in eastern Pennsylvania. Poliniak traces the history of the industry: technology, danger and disasters, transportation in and from the mines, living conditions, strikes, and labor disputes.
♦ Young people can research the differences between bituminous and anthracite coal. They can also research the living conditions of families in the mine "patches" (small mining communities).
1. Coal mines and mining—Pennsylvania
2. Mines and mineral resources—Pennsylvania.

624.20
Shank, William H. *Historic Bridges of Pennsylvania.* American Canal and Transportation Center (0-933788-33-9), 1986. 70p. B/W photos. (Interest level: 3-8).

This report reveals that early bridge designers in Pennsylvania (1800s and onward) attempted radically new designs, which eventually revolutionized bridge building. Information about the designers and their bridges is arranged chronologically.
♦ Students can compare bridges in their community with the bridges shown in this book, or they can build models of bridges.
1. Bridges—Pennsylvania.

624.37
Evans, Benjamin and **Evans, June R.** *Pennsylvania's Covered Bridges: A Complete Guide.* Photos by Benjamin Evans. University of Pittsburgh Press (0-8229-5504-0), 1993. 255p. B/W photos. (Interest level: 4-8).

First designed to protect wooden floor surfaces against the weather, covered bridges have become a rare artifact of America's past. This guide identifies all remaining covered bridges in Pennsylvania, with descriptions, locations, and photographs. The information is arranged alphabetically by county, and an index identifies the bridges by name. An introductory chapter discusses the history and structure of Pennsylvania's covered bridges.
♦ Readers can construct a model, using one or several of the truss structures described in the introduction of this book.
1. Bridges—Pennsylvania.

624.37
Flying Off the Bridge to Nowhere. (Videocassette). WQED, 1993. Color, VHS, (60 min.). $19.95 (Interest level: 4-8).

Pittsburgh is the site for many outstanding bridges with innovative and beautiful designs,

which accommodate the hilly terrain and three major rivers. This video presents details of the construction, maintenance, design, and history of the city's bridges. Anecdotal stories of persons and events relating to bridges are included, such as the title story and the story of the "recycled" bridge to Neville Island near Corapolis.
♦ Using resources in the school library, students can investigate the designs of some of the types of bridges shown in the video, such as the tied arch, truss, suspension, girder, or cable. Young people can then examine the bridges in their town or community.
1. Pittsburgh (Pa.)—Description and travel 2. Bridges—Pittsburgh.

624.37
Zacher, Susan M. *The Covered Bridges of Pennsylvania.* Rev. ed. Pennsylvania Historical and Museum Commission (0-89271-019-5), 1982. 141p. B/W photos and illus. (Interest level: 5-8).

This survey provides location and historical information for Pennsylvania's remaining 221 covered bridges, arranged by geographic region. An introductory chapter outlines the types of bridges described in the guide, and an index lists the bridges alphabetically by county.
♦ Students could prepare a slide show or a videotape of covered bridges.
1. Bridges—Pennsylvania.

664
Grist Mills of Early America and Today. Rev. ed. Applied Arts Publishers (0-911410-45-7), 1987. 32p. B/W illus. and photos. (Interest level: 4-8).

This history of grist mills in America explains their many designs, sources of power, and importance in rural settlements; several Pennsylvania mills are pictured and discussed. Folklore and legends associated with grain mills and an array of recipes using mill products are included.
♦ Readers can prepare recipes included in the book or conduct further research on the sources of power for operating the grist mills.
1. Flour mills.

724.9
The House on the Waterfall. (Videocassette). WQED, 1989. VHS, Color and B/W, (30 min.). $19.95. (Interest level: grade 5-adult).

One of the world's greatest architectural wonders, Fallingwater, a private home designed by Frank Lloyd Wright, is the subject of this documentary. Edgar Kaufmann, Jr., discusses his family's decisions to build the house near Pittsburgh, Pennsylvania, in 1936 and then give it to the Western Pennsylvania Conservancy in 1963. Attention is focused on the alliance between natural setting and architectural design.
♦ If possible, arrange a field trip to Fallingwater. Young people can design a house that illustrates the relationship between the natural setting and the architectural design.
1. Fallingwater 2. Wright, Frank Lloyd, 1869-1959 3. Architecture, American.

726
Holy Pittsburgh. (Videocassette). WQED. 1990. VHS, Color, (60 min.). $19.95. (Interest level: grade 5-adult).

A tour of 20 historic Pittsburgh churches, synagogues, and temples traces the needs and customs of the immigrant groups who founded them; present-day members continue the practices to preserve ethnic traditions. Unique architectural designs are related to religious characters.
♦ Students can research design and construction of stained glass windows, statues, or other decorative church elements.
1. Church architecture 2. Churches 3. Tiffany, Louis Comfort, 1848-1933.

745.4
Lichten, Frances. *Authentic Pennsylvania Dutch Designs.* Illus. by author. Dover Publications (0-486-23303-0), 1976. 71p. B/W and Color illus. (Interest level: K-8).

Lichten explains the significance of individual motifs, such as the tulip, urn, bird, pomegranate, and heart, in Pennsylvania Dutch folk art and discusses the ways the art forms were used on furniture, quilts, and buildings. Patterns and suggestions for transferring design and color are included.
♦ Children can design greeting cards using Pennsylvania Dutch motifs to represent a personal message to the recipient of the card.
1. Decorative arts—Pennsylvania 2. Pennsylvania Dutch.

791.106
Kennywood Memories. (Videocassette). WQED, 1990. VHS, B/W and Color, (60 min.). $19.95. (Interest level: grade 4-adult).

This documentary traces the history of Pittsburgh's Kennywood Park, which opened in 1899 and was named a National Historic Landmark in 1987. Vintage attractions, such as wooden roller coasters, make Kennywood a family recreation center.
♦ Students can compare Kennywood Park with an amusement park that they have visited.
1. Amusement parks 2. Kennywood Park (Pa).

796
The Greatest Moments in Western Pennsylvania Sports History. (Videocassette). Ross Sports Productions, 1991. VHS, B/W and Color, (58 min.). $19.95. (Interest level: grade 2-adult).

From Pittsburgh's 1937 Rose Bowl victory to the Penguins' 1991 Stanley Cup, this video highlights more than 50 years of dramatic moments in western Pennsylvania sports history. Famous sports heros appear and discuss the role of sports in their lives and that of the viewers. Scenes from boxing, football, golf, hockey, and baseball games are featured.
♦ Viewers can prepare a set of questions to use in interviewing a sports personality and then divide into two groups and role-play the interview.
1. Sports   2. Professional sports.

818.5
Dillard, Annie. *An American Childhood.* Harper & Row (0-06-015805-0), 1987. 255p. (Interest level: grade 6-adult).

Dillard recounts her childhood in Pittsburgh, Pennsylvania, in the 1950s; readers will gain an understanding of the special sense of neighborhood in the city and its impact on residents. The history of the area is interwoven with personal reminiscences.
♦ Students can interview senior citizens in their community to find out how the community has changed over the years and then prepare a documentary.
1. Pittsburgh (Pa.)—Social life and customs.

909.08
Foster, Genevieve. *The World of William Penn.* Illus. by author. Scribner (0-684-13188-9), 1973. 192p. B/W illus. and maps. (Interest level: 4-8).

Using a "horizontal" approach to world history, Foster describes the whole world as it existed in the time of William Penn and shows how persons and events in Europe, Asia, and America affected the direction of Penn's life, including how the war between France and England in 1688 affected Penn's role in the Pennsylvania colony.
♦ Students can research persons discussed in the book to determine more about their encounters with Penn; for example, students might imagine the conversation between Penn and Peter the Great, tsar of Russia, when he visited with Penn in 1698.
1. Seventeenth century   2. World history.

912.74 (Reference)
Cuff, David, ed. *The Atlas of Pennsylvania.* Temple University Press (0-87722-618-0), 1989. 289p. Color maps, charts, and photos. (Interest level: 4-8).

A cooperative project of Temple University, the University of Pittsburgh, and Pennsylvania State University, this Pennsylvania atlas contains four major topical sections: the land and its resources, its history, its human patterns, and its economic activity. Information from hundreds of sources is organized in a visually inviting and readily accessible format.

♦ Students can use the atlas in researching various aspects of Pennsylvania and preparing maps for reports and presentations.
1. Pennsylvania—Economic conditions—Maps
2. Pennsylvania—Maps   3. Pennsylvania—Social conditions—Maps   4. Pennsylvania—History.

917.48
Beyer, George R. *Guide to the State Historical Markers of Pennsylvania.* Pennsylvania Historical and Museum Commission (0-89271-040-3), 1991. 211p. B/W photos and maps. (Interest level: 4-8).

Famous people, places, and events in Pennsylvania history are identified in this guidebook. The entries are grouped in regions with counties listed alphabetically; the exact location, date of the marker dedication, and text of each marker are included.
♦ Young people can create a video of historical locations in their community.
1. Pennsylvania—Description—Guidebooks
2. Pennsylvania—History.

917.48
Harris, Bill. *Pennsylvania: A Photographic Journey.* Crescent Books (0-517-00175-6), 1989. 128p. Color photos. (Interest level: 4-8).

An introductory essay discusses the unique aspects of Pennsylvania's history and people. Annotated photographs, in historic order with geographic subheadings, reinforce and interpret the state's places, people, buildings, and events. An index facilitates use.
♦ Students can create a photographic essay of their community.
1. Pennsylvania—Description   2. Pennsylvania—History.

917.48
Llewellyn, Robert. *Pennsylvania: A Scenic Discovery.* Photos by author. Foremost Publishers (0-89909-129-6), 1987. 128p. Color photos. (Interest level: K-8).

Following a brief historical introduction to Pennsylvania by Douglas Day, a photographic essay explores the state through changing seasons, showing historic sites, tranquil wilderness, and people in their day-to-day lives. The site for each photograph is identified.
♦ Children can draw or photograph a site in their community showing the changing seasons.
1. Pennsylvania—Description.

917.48
McCaig, Barb and **Boyce, Chris.** *Pennsylvania Parks Guide.* Affordable Adventures (0-935201-37-8), 1988. 104p. B/W maps and photos. (Interest level: 3-8).

This guidebook provides detailed information about Pennsylvania's major state parks, arranged in alphabetical order. Site maps and recreational activities are explained.

♦ Students in Pennsylvania could plan a trip to a state park using this guide. Students in other states could create guides to the parks in their area.

1. Parks—Pennsylvania.

917.48
Marion, John Francis. *Walking Tours of Historic Philadelphia.* Camino Books (0-940159-05-8), 1989. 214p. B/W photos. (Interest level: 3-8).

Twelve fully illustrated walking tours bring alive the history and architecture, famous persons and legends, and fascinating manners and customs of Philadelphia, Pennsylvania. Places and events of the contemporary city are related to the richness of the past. An index facilitates research.

♦ Students can create a travel brochure describing and illustrating their community.

1. Philadelphia (Pa.)—Description 2. Historical buildings—Philadelphia (Pa.)—Guidebooks 3. Architecture—Philadelphia (Pa.)—Guidebooks.

917.48
The Mon, the Al and the O. (Videocassette). WQED, 1993. Color, VHS, (60 min.). $19.95. (Interest level: 4-8).

Pittsburgh, Pennsylvania, is located at the confluence of the Monongahela, the Allegheny, and the Ohio Rivers. This video introduces persons who work and play on the rivers (using towboats, packet boats, barges, and pleasure craft) and examines the history of the locks and dams along the rivers and their value for local business and industry. The program also details the clearing of water pollution and reveals the various uses of the water.

♦ Viewers can draw a diagram or map of the Pittsburgh area showing the paths of the three rivers in western Pennsylvania.

1. Pittsburgh (Pa.)—Description and travel 2. Rivers.

917.48
Murphy, E. Raymond and **Murphy, Marian F.** *Pennsylvania Landscapes: A Geography of the Commonwealth.* Penns Valley (0-931992-19-2), 1974. 298p. B/W photos and illus. (Interest level: 5-8).

An introductory chapter describing the physical features of Pennsylvania is followed by 10 chapters that focus on 10 regions of the state. Agriculture, industry, natural resources, and city development are among the topics discussed in each chapter.

♦ Students can write a geographic description of their community.

1. Pennsylvania—Geography.

917.48
Pennsylvania Gazetteer. American Historical Publications (0-937862-81-9), 1989. 431p. B/W illus. (Interest level: 3-8).

This historic gazetteer of Pennsylvania identifies geographic sites in the state and provides information such as population, area and zip codes, agriculture/industry, elevation, founding dates, and points of interest. People and events important to the founding and development of each area are discussed. A biography index provides access to persons who have influenced state history.

♦ Readers can research geographic sites to determine persons and events important to the historical development of that area.

1. Pennsylvania—Gazetteers.

917.48
The Pennsylvania Road Show, First Trip. (Videocassette). WQED, 1992. VHS, Color, (60 min.). $19.95. (Interest level: 2-8).

This televised travelogue takes the viewer along a variety of Pennsylvania highways, ranging from the turnpike to an almost hidden country road leading to the Tom Mix Birthplace Park. Featured roads were chosen because of their location and destinations, buildings or sites along them, persons conducting unique businesses along them or curious activities associated with them.

♦ In groups, students can prepare a travelogue about a road or highway in their community.

1. Pennsylvania—Description.

917.48
Peterson, Edwin L. *Penn's Woods West.* Photos by Thomas M. Jarrett. University of Pittsburgh Press, 1958. 247p. B/W and Color photos. (Interest level: grade 6-adult).

Peterson's photographic study reports seasonal aspects of the land, creatures, and environment of western Pennsylvania. The author recounts his experiences with and feelings about many familiar sites.

♦ Young people can create a photographic study of their community.

1. Pennsylvania—Description.

917.48
Pitzer, Sara. *Pennsylvania: Off the Beaten Path.* 2nd ed. Illus. by Carole Drong. Globe Pequot Press (0-87106-160-0), 1991. B/W illus. (Interest level: 4-8).

Dividing the state into seven geographic regions, this guidebook provides maps, detailed descriptions, and pertinent information for travelers who want to explore little-known places in Pennsylvania. Historic, geographic, and contemporary sites are interwoven in an interesting study of the state.

♦ Students can create a travel brochure of sites that would be of interest to travelers.
1. Pennsylvania—Description.

917.48
Seitz, Ruth Hoover. *Pennsylvania's Historic Places.* Illus. by Blair Seitz. Good Books/Pennsylvania Historical and Museum Commission (0934672-75-X), 1989. 176p. B/W photos. (Interest level: 3-8).

Following a brief historical introduction to Pennsylvania, 31 historic sites and museums, including Valley Forge, Railroad Museum of Pennsylvania, Drake's Well, and Ephrata Cloister, are presented in photographs and descriptions. Suggestions for visiting each site are accompanied by a map and address/telephone list.
♦ Readers can choose one of the historical sites discussed in this book for further research. Using the information they have discovered in their research, class members can then create their own book of historic places.
1. Historic sites—Pennsylvania—Guidebooks
2. Historic museums—Pennsylvania—Guidebooks
3. Pennsylvania—Description.

917.48
Shangle, Robert D. *Images of Pennsylvania.* Illus. by James Blank. LTA Publishing (1-55988-219-0), 1990. Unpaginated. Color photos. (Interest level: K-8).

This collection of photographs reveals a wide range of Pennsylvania places, buildings, and natural phenomena. The site for each photograph is identified.
♦ Children can create a series of drawings of a site in their community that focuses on the unique aspects of that place.
1. Pennsylvania—Description 2. Pennsylvania—Pictorial works.

917.48
Smith, Helen and **Swetnam, George.** *Guidebook to Historic Western Pennsylvania.* Rev. ed. Illus. by authors. University of Pittsburgh Press (0-8229-3630-5), 1991. 410p. B/W photos. (Interest level: 3-8).

Historic sites in each of Pennsylvania's counties are described through text and photography. Chapters begin with a map and a capsule history of the county. Discussions include history, past and present use, location, and hours for public-access sites. General and site indexes permit ready-reference use of the guidebook.
♦ Students can create an illustrated guide to a historic site in their community.
1. Pennsylvania—Description—Guidebooks
2. Historic sites—Pennsylvania—Guidebooks.

917.48
Toker, Franklin. *Pittsburgh, an Urban Portrait.* Illus. by Marlene Boyle. Pennsylvania State University Press (0-271-00415-0), 1986. 351p. B/W maps and photos. (Interest level: 4-8).

Over 750 Pittsburgh buildings, grouped in geographic neighborhoods, are presented in photographs and informed historic discussion. Economic, social, and intellectual aspects of the city's development are incorporated into the text. An events calendar, directory of resources, bibliography, and index complete the book.
♦ Young people can develop a similar guide to their community, using a map, photographs, and written description.
1. Pittsburgh (Pa.)—Description and travel—Tours
2. Pittsburgh (Pa.)—Buildings, structures, etc.—Guidebooks 3. Architecture—Pennsylvania.

917.48
The WPA Guide to Philadelphia. University of Pennsylvania Press (0-8122-1270-3), 1988. (American Guide Series). 704p. B/W illus., maps, and photos. (Interest level: 4-8).

Originally published in 1937, this book depicts the society, politics, economy, and culture of Philadelphia, Pennsylvania, 50 years ago. Focus is on the lifestyle, the significance of places, and the development of neighborhoods in the city. Suggested tours reveal how much of the 1930s city has survived.
♦ Students can research the Federal Writers' Project of the WPA (Works Progress Administration) to learn more about the origin of the American Guide Series.
1. Philadelphia (Pa.)—Description—Guidebooks.

970.1
Wallace, Paul A. W. *Indian Paths of Pennsylvania.* Pennsylvania Historical and Museum Commission (0-911124-39-9), 1987. 227p. B/W maps. (Interest level: 4-8).

Using historic maps, travelers' journals, archaeologists' findings, reminiscences of old timers, place-names, land surveys, and personal research, the author traces Indian paths across the state of Pennsylvania. The book is intended as a field guide, with directions for locating each named path.
♦ Readers can attempt to locate Indian paths in their area and determine whether these paths have influenced the development of roads.
1. Roads—Pennsylvania 2. Indians of North America—Pennsylvania.

970.4
Wallace, Paul A. W. *Indians in Pennsylvania.* Illus. by William Rohrbeck. Pennsylvania Historical and Museum Commission (0-892710-17-9), 1991. 200p. B/W illus. and maps. (Interest level: 5-8).

This study investigates the history and customs of four distinct Indian peoples living in Pennsylvania at the beginning of the seventeenth century. The findings of modern scholars are used to update and correct earlier accounts of the first inhabitants of the state.
♦ Students can conduct further research on the Indians of Pennsylvania to determine their impact on the development of the state.
1. Indians of North America—History   2. Indians of North America—Pennsylvania.

973.3
Mason, F. Van Wyck. *The Winter at Valley Forge.* Illus. by Harper Johnson. Random House, 1953. 180p. B/W/Blue drawings. (Interest level: 4-6).

Mason's narrative details the six-month ordeal of Washington's army at Valley Forge, Pennsylvania, during the winter of 1777-78. Drama and suspense bring life to the persons and events.
♦ Class members could dramatize Washington's winter at Valley Forge and the crossing of the Delaware.
1. United States—History—Revolution, 1775-1783   2. Valley Forge (Pa.).

973.3
Phelan, Mary Kay. *Four Days in Philadelphia.* Illus. by Charles Walker. Crowell, 1967. 189p. B/W illus. (Interest level: 5-8).

Drawing on contemporary accounts—memories, letters, diaries of participants—the author recounts the events of the first four days of July 1776, when the gentlemen of the Second Continental Congress gathered in Philadelphia to determine whether they should declare independence for the 13 original colonies. Debate among the statesmen and the editing of Thomas Jefferson's statement of independence are highlighted.
♦ Students could role-play the debate and Thomas Jefferson's speech.
1. Pennsylvania—History—Revolution, 1775-1783   2. Philadelphia (Pa.)—History.

973.7
Johnson, Neil. *Battle of Gettysburg.* Maps by Andrew Mudryk; photos by author. Four Winds Press (0-02-747831-9), 1989. 56p. B/W maps and photos. (Interest level: 3-8).

Johnson recounts the day-to-day events of the historic Civil War battle at Gettysburg, Pennsylvania. The accompanying photographs were taken during a reenactment of the encounter performed in 1988 in honor of the 125th anniversary. Maps show the positions of Union and Confederate forces for each day.
♦ Young people can create a diorama of the Battle of Gettysburg along with an audiotape describing the events.

1. Gettysburg (Pa.), Battle of, 1863   2. Pennsylvania—History—Civil War, 1861-1865.

973.7
Kantor, MacKinlay. *Gettysburg.* Illus. by Donald McKay. Random House (0-394-90323-4), 1963, 1952. 189p. B/W/Blue illus. (Interest level: 4-8).

This account of the battle at Gettysburg, Pennsylvania, in July 1863, the bloodiest engagement of the Civil War, reveals not only the advances and retreats, defeats and victories of the opposing armies, but also the effect of the three days of fighting on the men and women who lived in the town. An index is included.
♦ Students can draw a map of the Gettysburg battlefield.
1. Gettysburg (Pa.), Battle of, 1863   2. Pennsylvania—History—Civil War, 1861-1865.

973.7
Murphy, Jim. *The Long Road to Gettysburg.* Illus. by Henry Groskinsky. Clarion Books (0-395-55965-0), 1992. 128p. Sepia photos, reproductions. (Interest level: 6-8).

The story of the Battle of Gettysburg is told from the perspective of two participants—19-year-old Lieutenant John Dooley, CSA, and 17-year-old Union army Corporal Thomas Galway. Alternating narratives detail the march to the battlefield and the troop movements during the battle. The book concludes with Lincoln's delivery of the Gettysburg Address. Quotes from the young men's journals and an epilogue about their postwar lives focus on the personal nature of the historical account.
♦ Students can imagine they are participants in the war and write a letter to family or friends back home describing their thoughts and feelings and the events of the war.
1. Gettysburg (Pa.), Battle of, 1863   2. Pennsylvania—History—Civil War, 1861-1865.

974.8
Balcer, Bernadette and **O'Byrne-Pelham, Fran.** *Philadelphia: A Downtown America Book.* Dillon Press (0-87518-388-3), 1989. 60p. Color photos and maps. (Interest level: 2-6).

Photographs and simple text describe the past and present of Philadelphia, Pennsylvania. Neighborhoods, historic sites, festivals, and activities are highlighted. A chronology, an index, and a "Places to Visit" listing complete the book.
♦ Children can create a similar work about their own community.
1. Philadelphia (Pa.)—History   2. Philadelphia (Pa.)—Description.

974.8
Civil War. (Sound filmstrip). CC Audio-Visual and Publishing, 1989. (Pennsylvania History Series). 1

filmstrip, Color; 1 audiocassette, (16 min.). Sold only as a set with five other filmstrips in the series: $145.00. (Interest level: 3-8).

This program details the development of water and land transportation systems in Pennsylvania before the Civil War and other issues associated with the war: anti-slavery attitudes, the rise of the Republican Party, raising and training troops, and significant battle sites (including Gettysburg).
♦ Students can investigate the major battles of the Civil War fought in Pennsylvania and analyze how the transportation systems affected each of the battles.
1. Pennsylvania—History—Civil War, 1861-1865 2. Gettysburg (Pa.), Battle of, 1863.

974.8
Clements, John. *Flying the Colors: Pennsylvania Facts*. Clements Research (ISSN 0894-3850), 1987. 423p. Maps, charts, and Color photos. (Interest level: grade 4-adult).

This comprehensive collection of information about Pennsylvania includes a county-by-county examination of history, government, community services, people, transportation, and resources. The organization of data, alphabetical by county, facilitates location of specific facts.
♦ Students may compile information about the counties in their state or do additional research to update the information in the book.
1. Pennsylvania—Description 2. Pennsylvania—History.

974.8
Cornell, William A. and Altland, Millard. *Our Pennsylvania Heritage*. Penns Valley Publishers (0-931992-44-3), 1990. 398p. B/W photos and maps. (Interest level: 6-8).

Beginning with an overview of the current status of Pennsylvania (geography, population, transportation, economy), the authors trace the history and development of the state from the early Indian culture to the present time. Several chapters explore community life in Pennsylvania today, stressing government functions and citizen responsibilities.
♦ Using information in this book, students can analyze the nature of the governmental structure in their community.
1. Pennsylvania—History 2. Pennsylvania—Politics and government.

974.8
Couch, Ernie and Couch, Jill. *Pennsylvania Trivia*. Rutledge Hill Press (0-934395-72-1), 1988. 191p. (Interest level: grade 3-adult).

This collection of miscellaneous information about Pennsylvania groups questions and answers in six categories: geography, entertainment, history, arts and literature, sports and leisure, and science and nature.
♦ Children can develop a set of trivia questions for use in the classroom.
1. Pennsylvania—Miscellanea 2. Questions and answers.

974.8
Gille, Frank H., ed. *The Encyclopedia of Pennsylvania*. Somerset (0-403-09977-3), 1983. 764p. B/W illus., maps, and photos. (Interest level: 3-8).

Extending the Federal Writers' Project state guidebooks, this general reference focuses on the history, chronology, geography, persons, and places of Pennsylvania. The information is organized in broad topics, and an index aids in the location of specific facts. The text of the state constitution and a bibliography complete the book.
♦ Students could research one of the persons or places in their area.
1. Pennsylvania—Description 2. Pennsylvania—History.

974.8
Gutkind, Lee. *The People of Penn's Woods West*. University of Pittsburgh Press (0-8229-5360-9), 1984. 137p. (Interest level: 6-8).

The uniqueness of rural western Pennsylvania is revealed through the experiences of its people, including a librarian turned restaurateur, hunters, a blacksmith, and an innkeeper. The author met most of his informants accidentally, learned their stories casually, and recognized how their special traits related to their area of the state.
♦ Young people can interview various individuals in their community who they think have some special qualities.
1. Pennsylvania—Description 2. Pennsylvania—Personal narratives.

974.8
Harrisburg, Our State Capital. (Sound filmstrip). CC Audio-Visual and Publishing, 1986. 1 filmstrip, Color; 1 audiocassette, (19 min.). $30.00. (Interest level: 3-8).

This narrated tour focuses on the state capitol building in Harrisburg, Pennsylvania, and the legislative chambers, showing architectural and artistic details. Other sites in the state capital, such as the State Museum of Pennsylvania, the Museum of Scientific Discovery, and John Harris's home and burial site, are shown.
♦ Students could conduct further research into the capitol to determine who painted the murals in the building and what historic events are depicted in the paintings.
1. Pennsylvania—History 2. Harrisburg (Pa.)—Public buildings.

974.8
Historic Old Economy Village. (Sound filmstrip). CC Audio-Visual and Publishing, 1986. 1 filmstrip, Color; 1 audiocassette, (19 min.). $30.00. (Interest level: 3-8).

Old Economy Village, the home of one of Pennsylvania's (and America's) most successful communal societies, now restored and maintained by the Pennsylvania Historical and Museum Commission, is the subject of this filmstrip. Pictures show buildings on the site: homes, workplaces, and community meeting rooms. The narrative, which presents an overview of the society's history, covers religious principles, activities to sustain the community, contact with the outside world, farm work, printing operation, and products for society use and for sale.
♦ Young people can conduct further research into communal societies and theorize as to why some failed and this one succeeded. If possible, the class can plan a field trip to Old Economy Village, located near Ambridge, Pennsylvania.
1. Pennsylvania—History.

974.8
Historic Pennsylvania. (Pamphlet). Pennsylvania Historical and Museum Commission, 1976. A series of 40 four-page leaflets. B/W illus., maps, and photos. (Interest level: 4-8).

This series of 40 four-page leaflets introduces persons, places, and events important to the historic development of Pennsylvania, including Pennsylvania canals, Stephen Foster, the Liberty Bell, and the Battle of Brandywine. There are 41 titles in the series.
♦ Students could choose one of the topics of the leaflets to research further.
1. Pennsylvania—History.

974.8
Independence. (Sound filmstrip). CC Audio-Visual and Publishing, 1989. (Pennsylvania History Series). 1 filmstrip, Color; 1 audiocassette (15 min.). Sold only as a set with five other filmstrips in the series: $145.00. (Interest level: 3-8).

The breadth and purposes of European settlement in Pennsylvania, the attempts of Britain to control the settlement via treaty and war, and the imposition of taxes on the colonists to pay for wars such as the French and Indian War led to the movements for resistance, independence, and revolution by the American patriots.
♦ Young people could draw a plan for one of the important Pennsylvania forts of the late eighteenth century: Le Boeuf, Duquesne, Necessity, or Pitt.
1. Pennsylvania—History—French and Indian War, 1775-1763.

974.8
Independence National Historical Park. (Sound filmstrip). CC Audio-Visual and Publishing, 1986. 1 filmstrip, Color; 1 audiocassette, (17 min.). $30.00. (Interest level: 3-8).

This narrated tour identifies sites in Philadelphia, Pennsylvania, that played an important role in the independence movement. These sites, including Independence Hall, Congress Hall, the Liberty Bell Pavilion, Old City Hall, Carpenters' Hall, and Franklin Court, have been restored for visitors and historians. Architectural details and the original use of each site are emphasized.
♦ Readers can further research the historic sites discussed in this book.
1. Philadelphia (Pa.)—Description 2. Philadelphia (Pa.)—History 3. Historic sites—Philadelphia (Pa.).

974.8
Knight, James E. *The Farm: Life in Colonial Pennsylvania.* Illus. by Karen Milone. Troll Associates (0-89375-730-6), 1982. 32p. B/W illus. (Interest level: 2-5).

Thomas Ellison, an indentured servant, recalls his five years of service on the farm of a Pennsylvania German family in the 1760s and looks forward to establishing his own home on nearby land. Narrative and illustrations provide details of farm life in the eighteenth century.
♦ Students can research all aspects of colonial farm life.
1. Farm life—Pennsylvania 2. Indentured servants 3. Pennsylvania—Social life and customs—Colonial period, ca 1600-1775.

974.8
McGough, Michael R. *Pennsylvania from Wilderness Colony to National Leader.* Thomas Publications (0-939631-15-6), 1989. 44p. B/W photos and illus. (Interest level: 3-7).

McGough's brief overview of Pennsylvania history traces the impact of the state's development on the emerging new nation. Incorporated into the chronology of historical events are biographical sketches of persons who provided leadership to the state and the country.
♦ Children can research one of the Pennsylvania leaders introduced in this book to learn more about his or her life and contributions to the state.
1. Pennsylvania—History.

974.8
Mitchell, Barbara. *Tomahawks and Trombones.* Illus. by George Overlie. Carolrhoda (0-87614-191-2), 1982. Color illus. (Interest level: 1-3).

Based on an event recorded in the diary of a Moravian sister, this book tells how Moravian settlers in Bethlehem, Pennsylvania, convinced Dela-

ware Indians not to attack on Christmas day in 1755 by playing trombone music.
♦ Students could research the ways Moravians celebrated religious holidays.
1. Moravians—Pennsylvania 2. Bethlehem (Pa.)—Seige, 1755 2. Delaware Indians—Wars, 1750-1815.

974.8
Modernization. (Sound filmstrip). CC Audio-Visual and Publishing, 1989. 1 filmstrip, Color; 1 audiocassette, (16 min.). (Pennsylvania History Series). Sold only as a set with five other filmstrips in the series: $145.00. (Interest level: 3-8).

Developments in all aspects of post–Civil War Pennsylvania are detailed: transportation, industry, education, communication, medicine, growth of cities, and public and private building.
♦ Young people could investigate an aspect of modernization in their community that has contributed to its development.
1. Pennsylvania—Industries 2. Pennsylvania—Transportation 3. Pennsylvania—Cities and towns—Growth 4. Pennsylvania—Public buildings 5. Pennsylvania—History—20th century.

974.8
The Pennsylvania Trail of History. (Brochure). Pennsylvania Historical and Museum Commission, 1992. (Interest level: K-adult).

This brochure provides a seasonal, locational guide to 47 historic sites and museums in Pennsylvania that are available for visits. Photographs, descriptions, and phone numbers are included, and the location of each site is shown on a map.
♦ Students in Pennsylvania could plan a field trip to the historic sites in the area. Other students could create a similar brochure for historic sites in their community or state.
1. Pennsylvania—Historic sites.

974.8
Pennsylvania's Landmarks. 3rd ed. Applied Arts Publishers (0-911410-31-7), 1987. 48p. B/W photos and map. (Interest level: 2-8).

Pennsylvania possesses many historic sites and museums that have been restored and are maintained by the Pennsylvania Historical and Museum Commission and by the National Park Service. This guidebook presents 37 of the sites with their history and current status. A map for locating each site is included.
♦ Class members could prepare a slide show or videotape of the most famous Pennsylvania landmarks and one of the least famous.
1. Pennsylvania—History.

974.8
Pennsylvania's Trail of History—Eastern. (Sound filmstrip). CC Audio-Visual and Publishing, 1986. 1 filmstrip, Color; 1 audiocassette, (21 min.). $30.00. (Interest level: 3-8).

Important historic sites in eastern Pennsylvania, such as Daniel Boone Homestead, Scranton Anthracite Museum, Edkley Miner Village, Ashland Anthracite Museum, Brandywine Battlefield, Pottsgrove Manor, Morton Homestead/Printz Park, Old Chester Courthouse, Hope Lodge/Mather Mill, Graeme Park, Washington Crossing Park, and Pennsburg Manor. Historic details and current status for visits are provided.
♦ Students can choose one of the sites discussed in this filmstrip and conduct further research for an oral presentation to the class.
1. Historic sites—Pennsylvania 2. Pennsylvania—History.

974.8
Pennsylvania's Trail of History—Western and Central. (Sound filmstrip). CC Audio-Visual and Publishing, 1986. 1 filmstrip, Color; 1 audiocassette, (25 min.). $30.00. (Interest level: 3-8).

Important historic sites in western and central Pennsylvania, such as Drake Well, Flagship Niagara, Old Economy Village, Fort Pitt Museum, Joseph Priestly Home, State Museum of Pennsylvania, Cornwall Iron Furnace, Weiser Homestead, Ephrata Cloister, Pennsylvania Farm Museum, Pennsylvania Railroad Museum, and Pennsylvania Lumber Museum, are covered in this filmstrip. Historic details and current status for visits are provided.
♦ Students can write a historical fiction piece set in one of the places in the filmstrip.
1. Historic sites—Pennsylvania 2. Pennsylvania—History.

974.8
Prehistoric Days. (Sound filmstrip). CC Audio-Visual and Publishing, 1989. (Pennsylvania History Series). 1 filmstrip, Color; 1 audiocassette, (13 min.). Sold only as a set with five other filmstrips in the series: $145.00. (Interest level: 3-8).

This program opens with the effects of glacial drift on the natural formation of Pennsylvania and introduces the physical regions of the state: Lake Erie Plain, Allegheny Plateau, Ridge and Valley Region, Piedmont, and Atlantic Coastal Plain. The lifestyle of the earliest (prehistoric) Indian inhabitants is revealed via artifacts located during archeological digs.
♦ Class members can design an Indian village using ideas from this program and from other resources.
1. Pennsylvania—Antiquities 2. Archaeology—Pennsylvania 3. Indians of North America—Pennsylvania—Social life and customs.

974.8
Settlement. (Sound filmstrip). CC Audio-Visual and Publishing, 1989. (Pennsylvania History Series). 1 filmstrip, B/W and Color; 1 audiocassette, (16 min.). Sold only as a set with five other filmstrips in the series: $145.00. (Interest level: 3-8).

Settlement focuses on the various groups of people who settled and developed Pennsylvania: Indian hunters and farmers, explorers, people who immigrated to Pennsylvania from European nations, and religious groups seeking a better life. The differing lifestyles of the settlers are revealed and historic sites of today are presented.
♦ Young people could investigate the role of the settlers from their area of Pennsylvania.
1. Pennsylvania—History—Colonial period, 1600-1775   2. Pennsylvania—Land settlement.

974.8
Smith, Arthur G. *Pittsburgh Then and Now.* Illus. by author. University of Pittsburgh Press (0-8229-3830-8), 1990. 325p. B/W photos. (Interest level: 4-8).

In a series of 161 pairs of photographs of Pittsburgh, Pennsylvania, including historic photographs and rephotographed views replicating exact camera positions, Smith reveals how much and how little the city has changed. Brief commentaries cite changes and similarities.
♦ Young people could locate old photographs of their community or school and create a photographic essay contrasting the old with the new.
1. Pittsburgh (Pa.)—History—Pictorical works
2. Pittsburgh (Pa.)—Description—Views.

974.8
Statehood. (Sound filmstrip). CC Audio-Visual and Publishing, 1989. (Pennsylvania History Series). 1 filmstrip, Color; 1 audiocassette, (16 min.). Sold only as a set with five other filmstrips in the series: $145.00. (Interest level: 3-8).

This program covers the events of the Revolutionary War in Pennsylvania: Washington's crossing of the Delaware, the Battle of Brandywine, the encampment at Valley Forge, the designing of the first American flag, the writing of the U.S. Constitution, and Pennsylvania's role as the second state to approve the Constitution. The restoration of Revolutionary sites is noted in the narrative.
♦ Students could imagine they are members of George Washington's army and record in a diary or letter the events of the crossing of the Delaware, the encampment at Valley Forge, or another episode of the Revolutionary War, including their opinion of George Washington.
1. Pennsylvania—History—Revolution, 1775-1783.

974.8
Things That Aren't There Anymore. (Videocassette). WQED, 1990. 1 videocassette, B/W and Color, (60 min.). $19.95. (Interest level: grade 7-adult).

A nostalgic tour of great buildings, entertainment centers, and landmarks of Pittsburgh, Pennsylvania, that no longer exist reveals the culture of the recent past. City residents recall their favorite memories of places and events. Music of the 1940s through the 1970s enhances the film.
♦ Class members can interview senior citizens about places they used for entertainment and activities they enjoyed.
1. Pittsburgh (Pa.)—History   2. Pittsburgh (Pa.)—Description.

974.8
Wright, J. E. and **Corbett, Doris S.** *Pioneer Life in Western Pennsylvania.* Illus. by Clarence McWilliams. University of Pittsburgh Press (0-8229-6004-3), 1940. 251p. B/W illus. (Interest level: 4-8).

The daily lives of settlers in western Pennsylvania are presented in careful detail; individual chapters deal with housing, food, work, church, recreation, justice, relationships with Indians, and farming. Accurate drawings of artifacts and a glossary explain no-longer-used objects.
♦ Readers could begin a diary in which they describe day-to-day activities in a Pennsylvania pioneer home.
1. Pennsylvania—History—Colonial period, ca 1600-1775   2. Frontier and pioneer life—Pennsylvania.

974.89
Tunis, Edwin. *The Tavern at the Ferry.* Illus. by author. Crowell (0-690-00099-5), 1973. 109p. B/W illus. (Interest level: 3-8).

Tunis describes the development of settlements, ferry crossings, and taverns along the shores of the Delaware River in Pennsylvania and New Jersey during colonial times. He bases his history on the experiences of Quaker Henry Baker, his family, and his descendants. Tunis's drawings provide authoritative information about clothing, weapons, buildings, vehicles, and other artifacts and lifestyles. An index completes the book.
♦ Readers might research Washington's crossing of the Delaware or the Battle of Trenton, events that affected the ferry crossing. If possible, arrange a visit to one of the tavern/ferry crossings discussed in the book. Other students may dramatize Washington's crossing of the Delaware, perhaps dramatizing what would have happened had he crossed earlier or later.
1. Pennsylvania—Social life and customs
2. Pennsylvania—History—Colonial period, ca 1600-1775.

Biography

920 (Reference)
Pennsylvania Biographical Dictionary. American Historical Publications (0-403-09897-1), 1989. 446p. (Interest level: 3-8).

Persons who have contributed to the development of Pennsylvania from Columbian times to the present are identified and discussed in this biographical dictionary. Included are politicians, explorers, artists, authors, musicians, industrialists, and sportsmen. An index to places facilitates research on a geographic basis.
♦ Students can read brief biographical entries in this dictionary before choosing an individual to research further.
1. Biography—Dictionaries   2. Pennsylvania—Biography—Dictionaries.

92 Alcott, Louisa May
Johnston, Norma. *Louisa May: The World and Works of Louisa May Alcott.* Four Winds Press (0-02-747705-3), 1991. 239p. B/W photos. (Interest level: 6-8).

Using recent research regarding Pennsylvania-born Louisa May Alcott's life, including information on her relationship with her mother and her own creative development, biographer Johnston presents a complex person whose persona and work appeal to today's young readers. A bibliography and index are provided.
♦ Students could read one of Alcott's books to document evidence of the autobiographical details in her stories.
1. Alcott, Louisa May, 1832-1888.

92 Anderson, Marian
Tobias, Tobi. *Marian Anderson.* Illus. by Symeon Shimin. Crowell (0-690-51846-3), 1972. 40p. B/W and Color illus. (Interest level: 1-5).

Philadelphia native Marian Anderson began singing in her church choir, studied with vocal coaches in the United States and Europe, and became a successful solo performer in several countries. She gave concerts in the United States but often faced racial discrimination. She was the first black singer to appear with the Metropolitan Opera Company in New York. The text and illustrations convey Anderson's character and personality.
♦ The class could listen to recordings of Anderson's concerts and investigate Eleanor Roosevelt's reaction to the Daughters of the American Revolution's discrimination against Anderson.
1. Anderson, Marian   2. Singers—Biography   3. African Americans—Biography.

92 Appleseed, Johnny
Aliki. *The Story of Johnny Appleseed.* Illus. by author. Prentice-Hall (0-13-850800-3), 1963. Unpaginated. B/W and Color illus. (Interest level: K-3).

This picture-biography portrays the gentle traveler John Chapman, who walked through Pennsylvania and Ohio planting apple seeds, helping pioneer families settle their land, and reading and telling stories to children.
♦ Children can write and present a skit about the life of Johnny Appleseed.
1. Appleseed, Johnny, 1774-1845   2. Frontier and pioneer life—Biography   3. Chapman, John, 1774-1845   4. Apple growers.

92 Appleseed, Johnny
Johnny Appleseed: Gentle Hero. (Audiocassette). August House (0-87483-176-8), 1991. (45 min.). $10.00. (Interest level: 1-3).

Storyteller Marc Joel Levitt presents the life of John Chapman in dramatic fashion, emphasizing his concern for pioneers, their children, and their Indian neighbors. Using survival skills he learned from the Seneca Indians, Johnny walked through Pennsylvania and Ohio, planting his apple orchards and telling tales about his travels.
♦ Students might learn the "Apple Song," which is sung several times on the tape. They could also prepare some apple recipes.
1. Appleseed, Johnny, 1774-1845   2. Frontier and pioneer life—Biography   3. Chapman, John, 1774-1845   4. Apple growers.

92 Appleseed, Johnny
Kellogg, Steven. *Johnny Appleseed.* Illus. by author. Morrow (0-688-06417-5), 1988. Unpaginated. Color illus. (Interest level: 3-6).

Detailed paintings enhance the story of John Chapman, who walked through Pennsylvania, Ohio, and Indiana, planting apple orchards and befriending both American Indians and pioneers who were settling the wilderness. His love of storytelling led to a body of folklore about his own achievements as he traveled west and survived in the wilderness by getting along with people and animals.
♦ The class can prepare a program about Johnny Appleseed using events from his travels to reveal his life.
1. Appleseed, Johnny, 1774-1845   2. Frontier and pioneer life—Biography   3. Chapman, John, 1774-1845   4. Apple growers.

92 Bly, Nellie
Ehrlich, Elizabeth. *Nellie Bly.* Chelsea House (1-55546-643-5), 1989. (American Women of Achievement Series). 111p. B/W illus. and photos. (Interest level: 4-8).

Ehrlich traces the life and career of Elizabeth Cochrane, who wrote under the pseudonym Nellie Bly and began her work as a journalist at the Pittsburgh *Dispatch*. A humanist, Bly gained interna-

tional acclaim for her vigorous support of social causes.
♦ Young people can investigate the life of Nellie Bly further, determine what causes she fought for, and suggest several current causes that might attract her support.
1. Cochrane, Elizabeth, 1867-1922   2. Journalists—United States—Biography.

92 Bly, Nellie
Emerson, Kathy Lynn. *Making Headlines: A Biography of Nellie Bly.* Dillon Press (0-87518-406-5), 1989. (A People in Focus Book). 111p. B/W illus., maps, and photos. (Interest level: 2-5).

Because she began her career in journalism as a reporter for the Pittsburgh *Dispatch* at a time when the position was considered inappropriate for women, Elizabeth Cochrane adopted the name Nellie Bly from a Stephen Foster song. This biography traces her life and international career, focusing on her concerns for the plight of people and social causes.
♦ Pretending that they are Nellie Bly, children can write a news story in support of a social cause in their school or community.
1. Cochrane, Elizabeth, 1867-1922   2. Journalists—United States—Biography.

92 Boone, Daniel
Wallace, Paul. *Daniel Boone in Pennsylvania.* Pennsylvania Historical and Museum Commission (0-911124-56-X), 1987. 21p. B/W photos. (Interest level: 5-8).

Daniel Boone was born in Berks County, Pennsylvania, one of 11 children in a Quaker family. His early upbringing in the Society of Friends tradition and in the practicalities of life in rural Pennsylvania prepared him for his later pioneer life in Kentucky. Historians can document three return visits Boone made to Pennsylvania. The Boone Homestead near Reading is a historic site restored and maintained by the Pennsylvania Historical and Museum Commission.
♦ Young people might dramatize important events in the life of Daniel Boone.
1. Boone, Daniel, 1734-1820.

92 Calder, Alexander
Lipman, Jean. *Alexander Calder and His Magic Mobiles.* Illus. by Alexander Calder. Hudson Hills Press (0-933920-17-2), 1981. 96p. B/W and Color photos. (Interest level: 3-7).

Following a brief biography of Alexander Calder, an engineer, artist, and sculptor born in Lawnton, Pennsylvania, this book examines and illustrates his work in several categories: sketches and drawings, paintings, sculptures, mobiles, stabiles, and jewelry. One of his most famous works is a 55-piece performing circus, which he demonstrated in museums and galleries throughout the United States and Europe.
♦ Following Calder's pattern, students can design a mobile for the classroom.
1. Calder, Alexander, 1898-1976   2. Artists—United States—Biography.

92 Carnegie, Andrew
Shippen, Katherine. *Andrew Carnegie and the Age of Steel.* Illus. by Ernie Barth. Random House (No ISBN), 1958. B/W illus. and photos. (Interest level: 4-6).

This biography focuses on Carnegie's struggle to achieve success in the competitive steel industry and stresses the importance of steel in the economy of Pennsylvania. An index enhances the text.
♦ Children can further investigate Carnegie's humanitarian contributions to society and determine whether he contributed to the local community in any way. Non-Pennsylvania students could research philanthropists from their state and the contributions they have made.
1. Carnegie, Andrew, 1835-1919   2. Steel industry.

92 Carson, Rachel
Harlan, Judith. *Sounding the Alarm: A Biography of Rachel Carson.* Dillon Press (0-87518-407-3), 1989. 128p. B/W illus. (Interest level: 5-8).

Harlan focuses on Pennsylvania native Rachel Carson's determination to effect change through her dual career interests in biology and writing. Harlan's portrait of the founder of the modern ecology movement reveals the early influence of her family and educational experiences, her concern with the natural world, and her commitment to restricting the use of pesticides and to deterring toxic waste pollution.
♦ Young people might read Carson's *Silent Spring* to learn about her concerns regarding potential pollution problems.
1. Carson, Rachel, 1907-1964   2. Conservationists—Biography   3. Biologists—Biography.

92 Carson, Rachel
Jezer, Marty. *Rachel Carson.* Chelsea House (1-55546-646-X), 1988. (American Women of Achievement Series). 111p. B/W photos. (Interest level: 3-7).

Born in Springdale, Pennsylvania, and educated at the Pennsylvania College for Women (now Chatham College) in Pittsburgh, Rachel Carson became a marine biologist and author whose writing stressed the interrelationship of all living things and the dependence of human welfare on natural processes. Her determined advocacy of ecological principles stirred controversy but led to legislation and a revolution in public attitudes toward the environment.
♦ Class members might investigate evidence of pollution and environmental dangers in their

community and identify potential pollution problems.
1. Carson, Rachel, 1907-1964 2. Conservationists—Biography 3. Biologists—Biography.

92 Carson, Rachel
Kudlinski, Kathleen V. *Rachel Carson: Pioneer of Ecology*. Illus. by Ted Lewin. Viking Kestrel (0-670-81488-1), 1988. 55p. B/W illus. (Interest level: 2-5).

Rachel Carson, born on a farm in Springdale, Pennsylvania, in 1907, was fascinated by the ocean she had never seen. Her early interest in science and her natural ability as a writer led to a career in ecology.
♦ Investigate Carson's influence on current ecological practices.
1. Carson, Rachel, 1907-1964 2. Conservationists—Biography 3. Biologists—Biography 4. Ecology.

92 Cassatt, Mary
McKown, Robin. *The World of Mary Cassatt*. Crowell (0-690-90274-3), 1972. (Women of America Series). 253p. B/W photos. (Interest level: 6-8).

Mary Cassatt, a native of Pittsburgh and Philadelphia who was termed "America's First Lady of Art," lived most of her adult life in France, where she studied and painted. Influenced by such artists as Manet, Renoir, Monet, Pissarro, and Degas, she encouraged wealthy American collectors to purchase her friends' works. Her major art works featured mothers and children, although she never married or had children.
♦ Readers could examine Cassatt's paintings to determine her style and the influences on her work.
1. Cassatt, Mary, 1844-1926 2. Painters—Biography 3. Women artists.

92 Cassatt, Mary
Mary Cassatt. (Videocassette). WNET/13, 1975. (Portrait of an Artist Series). VHS, Color, (30 min.). $19.95. (Interest level: grade 7-adult).

Mary Cassatt, born in Pittsburgh, Pennsylvania, in 1844 and reared in Philadelphia, became the only American painter invited to exhibit with the Impressionists in Paris. This documentary film traces Cassatt's career using still photographs of her paintings, critical commentary from contemporary artists, biographical details from family members, and personal responses from Cassatt. She is best known for her mother-and-child paintings.
♦ Using books and prints from the library and/or art department, students could create a gallery of Cassatt's paintings.
1. Cassatt, Mary, 1844-1926 2. Painters—Biography 3. Women artists.

92 Cassatt, Mary
Meyer, Susan E. *Mary Cassatt*. Harry N. Abrams (0-8109-3154-0), 1990. 92p. B/W and Color illus. (Interest level: 3-8).

Despite the objections of her Victorian father, Pennsylvania native Mary Cassatt was determined to study painting in France. She became a friend of the leading French Impressionist artists, Degas, Manet, Monet, Renoir, and Pissarro, and exhibited with them. She urged her wealthy family and friends to buy Impressionist paintings for pleasure and investment.
♦ Each student can choose one of Cassatt's paintings and write an essay describing what Cassatt intended the painting to depict.
1. Cassatt, Mary, 1844-1926 2. Painters—Biography 3. Women artists.

92 Cosby, Bill
Kettelkamp, Larry. *Bill Cosby, Family Funny Man*. Messner (0-671-62382-6), 1987. 117p. B/W photos. (Interest level: 4-7).

Kettelkamp traces Bill Cosby's life from his childhood in Philadelphia and year as a high school dropout through his Navy and college career to his success as a comedian and actor. The focus of the book is on Cosby's concern with family values and educational achievement.
♦ Students can prepare a set of interview questions that they would like to ask Cosby and then mail the questions to him for answers.
1. Cosby, Bill, 1937- 2. Comedians—Biography 3. Entertainers—Biography.

92 Foster, Stephen
Peare, Catherine Owens. *Stephen Foster: His Life*. Illus. by Margaret Ayer. Holt (No ISBN), 1952. 87p. B/W illus. (Interest level: 3-5).

Born on the fourth of July in Pittsburgh, Pennsylvania, Stephen Foster found his greatest joy as a child and as an adult in playing and composing music. Although he had extraordinary musical talent, he was not a good businessman and died impoverished.
♦ Children could learn several of Foster's songs to present to the class. If feasible, a visit could be arranged to the Foster memorial in the Oakland area of Pittsburgh.
1. Foster, Stephen Collins, 1826-1864 2. Composers—Biography.

92 Franklin, Benjamin
Aliki. *The Many Lives of Benjamin Franklin*. Illus. by author. Prentice-Hall (0-13-556019-5), 1977. Unpaginated. Color illus. (Interest level: 1-3).

Aliki's informative text, supplemented with captioned cartoons, reveals Benjamin Franklin's varied contributions to his country as a writer, printer, inventor, politician, and diplomat. The author cap-

tures the fascinating life of this beloved Founding Father who lived in Philadelphia.
♦ Readers can conduct further research on an aspect of Franklin's life and prepare an oral presentation.
1. Franklin, Benjamin, 1706-1790.

92 Franklin, Benjamin
d'Aulaire, Ingri and **d'Aulaire, Edgar Parin.** *Benjamin Franklin.* Illus. by authors. Doubleday (0-385-07219-8), 1950. 48p. Color illus. (Interest level: 2-5).

This picture biography of Benjamin Franklin emphasizes incidents that have special appeal for young children. Marginal drawings add details of eighteenth-century life in Philadelphia and other sites pertaining to the diplomat and politician.
♦ Children might make a booklet of Franklin's favorite sayings.
1. Franklin, Benjamin, 1706-1790.

92 Franklin, Benjamin
Fritz, Jean. *What's the Big Idea, Ben Franklin?* Illus. by Margot Tomes. Coward, McCann & Geoghegan (0-698-20365-8), 1976. 48p. B/W and Color illus. (Interest level: 2-5).

Fritz's brief biography of Pennsylvanian Benjamin Franklin focuses on his many original ideas that resulted in new ways of doing things and in new products. Notes at the end of the book expand on some of the information in the main text.
♦ Young people might make a model of one of Franklin's inventions.
1. Franklin, Benjamin, 1706-1790.

92 Franklin, Benjamin
Meltzer, Milton. *Benjamin Franklin: The New American.* Franklin Watts (0-531-10582-2), 1988. 288p. B/W photos and illus. (Interest level: 4-8).

Benjamin Franklin, resident of Philadelphia and a multitalented Founding Father, is presented as an agreeable and approachable person who excelled in business, writing, science, politics, and diplomacy. However, he had his own prejudices and weaknesses, which led to occasional misjudgments. His ideas and leadership influenced the writing of the Declaration of Independence, the success of the American Revolution, and the writing of the U.S. Constitution.
♦ Each student can choose one event of Franklin's life and present a dramatization of it to the class.
1. Franklin, Benjamin, 1706-1790   2. Statesmen—United States.

92 Fulton, Robert
Landau, Elaine. *Robert Fulton.* Franklin Watts (0-531-20016-7), 1991. 62p. Color illus. and photos. (Interest level: 2-5).

Landau describes the life and work of this talented inventor and resourceful businessman, with special emphasis on his development of the steamboat. His family's home in Little Britain Township, Pennsylvania, is open to the public as a museum. A glossary, bibliography, and index complete the book.
♦ Students could draw or create a model of Fulton's steamboat and write a short narrative explaining why this invention was important for Pennsylvania.
1. Fulton, Robert, 1765-1815   2. Inventors—Biography   3. Steamboats—History—19th century.

92 Hershey, Milton
Malone, Mary. *Milton Hershey: Chocolate King.* Illus. by William Hutchinson. Garrard (0-816-4565-7), 1971. 95p. B/W illus. and photos. (Interest level: 4-8).

Milton Hershey, born in 1857 in a Mennonite Community in the Lebanon Valley of Pennsylvania, prepared for his career in the candy business by running a retail shop and making caramels before he opened his chocolate factory in Hershey.
♦ The teacher could arrange a field trip to Hershey, Pennsylvania, where students could tour Chocolate World to see how chocolate is made. If this is not possible, students could research how chocolate is made and make chocolate in the classroom.
1. Hershey, Milton, 1857-1945   2. Chocolate.

92 Jemison, Mary
Lenski, Lois. *Indian Captive: The Story of Mary Jemison.* Illus. by author. Lippincott (0-397-30072-7), 1941. 270p. B/W illus. (Interest level: 4-8).

Mary Jemison, a child of Scotch-Irish parentage, was captured by Indians in 1758 and taken from her Pennsylvania home to a Seneca village. This biography focuses on the early years of her captivity and provides excellent details of Indian life and culture. At the end of the French and Indian War, she was offered an opportunity to return to her own people but stayed with her Indian family and friends.
♦ Writing as young "Molly" Jemison, students can tell friends at home about life in the Seneca village. Children could also read more about Mary Jemison's adult life as a landowner and cattle rancher in the Indian community.
1. Jemison, Mary, 1743-1833   2. Indians of North America—Captivities.

92 Jones, Mary Harris
Werstein, Irving. *Labor's Defiant Lady: The Story of Mother Jones.* Crowell (No ISBN), 1969. 146p. (Interest level: 5-8).

Mary Harris (Mother) Jones was one of the most dedicated and fearless labor union organizers of the nineteenth and early twentieth centuries. She led workers' wives against scabs during a mine strike; helped to organize the United Mine Workers; and worked to end child labor, demonstrating its evils

by leading a children's crusade of injured and ill Pennsylvania millworkers from Philadelphia to the home of President Theodore Roosevelt in New York. This biography presents a thoughtful, balanced portrayal of Jones's life and activities.
♦ Readers could trace the path of Mother Jones's travels across the United States as she worked to solve labor problems throughout the nation.
1. Jones, Mary Harris, 1830-1930 2. Labor unions.

92 Namath, Joe
Kipman, David. *Joe Namath: A Football Legend.* Putnam (0-399-60317-4), 1968. 194p. (Interest level: 3-8).

A native of Beaver Falls, Pennsylvania, Joe Namath became a star quarterback at the University of Alabama and with the New York Jets. Details of his high school, college, and professional football career are given here.
♦ Young people can read more about Namath's life after football, especially his work with young people.
1. Namath, Joe, 1938- 2. Football—Biography.

92 Peary, Robert E.
Kent, Zachary. *The Story of Admiral Peary at the North Pole.* Childrens Press (0-516-04738-8), 1988. 32p. B/W and Color photos. (Interest level: 3-6).

Robert Edwin Peary, a native of Cresson, Pennsylvania, and a U.S. Navy engineer, was the first person to reach the North Pole on April 6, 1909. His achievement was challenged by Dr. Frederick Cook, but the National Geographic Society accepted Peary's evidence. Kent's biography details the grueling events of Peary's expedition across the frozen Arctic.
♦ Children might develop a time line of Peary's several preparatory trips to Greenland before his eighth polar expedition in 1908–09. They could also trace on a map Peary's expedition from New York City to the North Pole (July 6, 1908 to April 6, 1909).
1. Peary, Robert E., 1856-1920 2. Explorers—Biography 3. North Pole.

92 Penn, William
Aliki. *The Story of William Penn.* Illus. by author. Simon & Schuster (0-671-88558-8), 1994. Unpaginated. B/W and Color illus. (Interest level: 1-3).

This simplified biography of William Penn reveals the gentle, loving nature of the man who opened the New World (Pennsylvania Colony) to British citizens seeking a place where they would be free to think and speak as they pleased.
♦ Children could investigate what conditions existed in Britain that kept citizens from speaking freely and why they were seeking a better life.
1. Penn, William, 1644-1718.

92 Penn, William
Dolson, Hildegarde. *William Penn, Quaker Hero.* Illus. by Leonard Everett Fisher. Random House (No ISBN), 1961. 186p. B/W and Color illus. (Interest level: 4-7).

Contrasting Penn's lifestyles in Britain and Europe with his lifestyle in the Pennsylvania colony he founded, Dolson presents a stimulating recounting of events in the New World. A bibliography and index complete the biography.
♦ Imagining they are members of Penn's colony, students can write a letter home describing conditions in the New World.
1. Penn, William, 1644-1718.

92 Penn, William
Syme, Ronald. *William Penn: Founder of Pennsylvania.* Illus. by William Stobbs. Morrow, 1966. 95p. B/W illus. (Interest level: 3-6).

William Penn, a young aristocrat of London and Paris, emerged as the idealistic proprietor of the New World province named for him. Penn's decision to join the Society of Friends changed his life and affected the course of U.S. history as he developed his new settlement in the wilderness of Pennsylvania.
♦ Readers could select details of Penn's life in Europe and America that show most clearly his leadership qualities and prepare a biographical sketch of him for classmates.
1. Penn, William, 1644-1718.

92 Penn, William
Vining, Elizabeth Gray. *Penn.* Illus. by George Gillett Whitney. Philadelphia Yearly Meeting (0-941308-06-5), 1986, 1938. 298p. B/W illus. (Interest level: 4-8).

Son of a wealthy and worldly British family, William Penn converted to Quakerism and sought justice for all. Penn's activities in England led to frequent imprisonment, so he and his Friends of Truth sought freedom and liberty in America. The constitution he wrote for his Pennsylvania colony served as a model for the Constitution of the United States. A listing of authorities consulted and an index are appended.
♦ Students could research Quaker religious practices today and write a report comparing and contrasting the religious practices of today and yesterday.
1. Penn, William, 1644-1718.

92 Pitcher, Molly
Gleiter, Jan and **Thompson, Kathleen**. *Molly Pitcher.* Illus. by Charles Shaw. Steck-Vaughn (0-8172-2652-4), 1991. 32p. Color illus. (Interest level: 2-5).

Like many Pennsylvania wives, Molly Hays followed her husband to military camps during the

Revolutionary War. At the Battle of Monmouth, she delivered water to soldiers who were suffering from the extreme heat (hence her nickname, Molly Pitcher) and took her husband's place on a cannon team when he was overcome by heat exhaustion.
♦ Young people could research the roles of women in past and current wars and also conduct research on the Battle of Monmouth to determine its value to the Revolutionary War effort.
1. Pitcher, Molly, 1754-1832 2. Monmouth, Battle of, 1778 3. United States—History—Revolution, 1775-1783.

92 Pitcher, Molly
Stevenson, Augusta. *Molly Pitcher: Girl Patriot.* Illus. by Sandra James. Macmillan (No ISBN), 1986. 192p. B/W illus. (Interest level: 3-5).

Molly Ludwig's early training on her father's farm prepared her well for her life as the wife of Pennsylvanian John Hays, an artillery gunner in the Revolutionary War army. During the Battle of Monmouth, Molly distributed water to the soldiers who suffered from the heat (they would call for "Molly Pitcher") and replaced her husband at a cannon when he was overcome by heat exhaustion. In 1822, the Pennsylvania legislature honored Molly for her bravery by giving her a military pension.
♦ Children might research Molly's and her husband's life after the revolution. Students could also visit Molly's grave in Carlisle, Pennsylvania, if feasible.
1. Pitcher, Molly, 1754-1832 2. Monmouth, Battle of, 1778 3. United States—History—Revolution, 1775-1783.

92 Salomon, Haym
Fast, Howard. *Haym Salomon: Son of Liberty.* Illus. by Eric M. Simon. Messner (No ISBN), 1941. 243p. B/W illus. (Interest level: 4-8).

Imprisoned by the British in New York City before the Revolutionary War for his support of the American cause, Haym Salomon escaped to Philadelphia, Pennsylvania, where he became a success in banking and business. He made his fortune available to those who planned and supported the war effort and was recognized as a great patriot. The biography reveals the human behaviors of persons—diplomats, military personnel, business leaders, spies, and pirates—who affected war operations.
♦ Readers could investigate further the contribution of business leaders to the conduct of the war. Pennsylvania students could also visit the cemetery of the Mikveh Israel Congregation where Haym Salomon is buried.
1. Salomon, Haym, 1740-1785.

92 Stevens, Thaddeus
Meltzer, Milton. *Thaddeus Stevens and the Fight for Negro Rights.* Crowell (No ISBN), 1967. 231p. (Interest level: 4-8).

Pennsylvania lawyer and member of the U.S. Congress, Thaddeus Stevens is often portrayed as a fanatic who sought to destroy the South. In this biography, Meltzer reveals Stevens's dedication to humanitarian causes: free public schools, defense for fugitive slaves in the court system, the right of free speech for dissenters, racial equality for Indians and blacks, and civil rights for minorities. U.S. history is presented from the viewpoint of an individual struggling to reshape his own time.
♦ Students could research the role of the Quakers in the abolition and Underground Railroad movements with which Stevens was involved.
1. Stevens, Thaddeus, 1792-1868 2. Abolitionists—Biography.

92 Tarbell, Ida
Conn, Frances G. *Ida Tarbell, Muckraker.* Thomas Nelson (0-8407-6220-8), 1972. 160p. (Interest level: 4-7).

Born and raised in Pennsylvania's oil country (as was biographer Conn), Ida Tarbell gained fame as a journalist and social reformer, but she considered herself a historian. Her early interest in women's rights and her view that education led to freedom influenced her other activities, which included lecturing, teaching, and serving on government advisory boards. Her most famous and influential work is her *History of the Standard Oil Company,* which led to antitrust laws and a Supreme Court decision that forced Standard Oil to divide into smaller companies.
♦ Readers might suggest current issues, industrial or political, that might interest Ida Tarbell if she were living today and explain why.
1. Tarbell, Ida, 1857-1944 2. Journalists—United States—Biography.

92 Tarbell, Ida
Fleming, Alice. *Ida Tarbell: First of the Muckrakers.* Crowell (0-690-42881-2), 1971. (Women of America Series). 170p. B/W illus. (Interest level: 4-8).

Ida Tarbell, who spent her childhood in Titusville, Pennsylvania, became an investigative reporter and one of the most influential women of her time. Her history of the Standard Oil Company, her biography of Abraham Lincoln, and her report from France during World War I earned her worldwide recognition. As one of the militant journalists called "muckrakers" by Theodore Roosevelt, she opened America's eyes to the corrupt business practices of the time.
♦ Students could identify journalists who might be called "muckrakers" today and conduct research

on these individuals, comparing their work with that of Ida Tarbell.
1. Tarbell, Ida, 1857-1944   2. Journalists—United States—Biography.

92 Thorpe, Jim
Santrey, Laurence. *Jim Thorpe: Young Athlete*. Illus. by George Ulrich. Troll (0-89375-845-0), 1983. 48p. B/W illus. (Interest level: 4-6).

Strong ties to his deceased twin brother and to his Indian culture made it difficult for Jim Thorpe to adjust to life in several boarding schools. When he became involved in sports at the Carlisle Institute in Pennsylvania, however, he and coach Glen "Pop" Warner discovered his superior athletic ability. Termed "the greatest athlete in the world" by King Gustav of Sweden, who presented him with his two gold medals at the 1912 Olympics, Thorpe followed his collegiate athletic achievements with professional careers in both baseball and football.
♦ Children could conduct further research into Thorpe's life to identify problems that plagued his sports career.
1. Thorpe, Jim, 1888-1953   2. Athletes—Biography   3. Native Americans—Biography.

92 Thorpe, Jim
Schoor, Gene. *The Jim Thorpe Story: America's Greatest Athlete*. Messner (0-671-32525-6), 1951. 186p. B/W photos. (Interest level: 4-8).

Reared on an Indian reservation in Oklahoma, Jim Thorpe played football, baseball, and track and field at the Carlisle Indian School in Pennsylvania and led his teams to victory over such colleges as West Point, Harvard, and Lehigh. He won gold medals in the 1912 Olympics for the pentathlon and decathlon events. Hardships in his early life gave Thorpe the skills to succeed as an athlete and to cope with problems in his adult life.
♦ Young people may chart Thorpe's athletic achievements.
1. Thorpe, Jim, 1888-1953   2. Athletes—Biography   3. Native Americans—Biography.

92 West, Benjamin
Henry, Marguerite. *Benjamin West and His Cat Grimalkin*. Illus. by Dennis Wesley. Bobbs-Merrill (No ISBN), 1947. 147p. B/W illus. (Interest level: 4-8).

Born in Springfield, Pennsylvania, Benjamin West convinced the elders of his Quaker community that his painting was a way to preserve history. He fashioned his first brush with hairs from his cat Grimalkin and devised his paints from earth and plants. After studying and painting in Philadelphia, Pennsylvania, West moved to England where he became president of the Royal Academy and court painter for George III.
♦ Students could study prints of West's works and choose one on which to write a creative essay.
1. West, Benjamin, 1738-1820.

92 Woolworth, Frank Winfield
Baker, Nina Brown. *Nickels and Dimes*. Illus. by Douglas Gorsline. Harcourt Brace (No ISBN), 1954. 134p. B/W illus. (Interest level: 4-8).

Frank Woolworth opened his first successful five-and-ten store in Lancaster, Pennsylvania, in 1879. This biography traces his early struggles to his eventual ownership of a chain of stores from coast to coast. His devotion to his family and to those who helped him in his business ventures is emphasized; he always recognized the needs of people in his business decisions.
♦ Class members could create a model of Woolworth's first store or research other five-and-ten store owners and compare and contrast their success with that of Woolworth.
1. Woolworth, Frank Winfield, 1852-1919.

92 Wyeth, Andrew
Meryman, Richard. *Andrew Wyeth*. Harry N. Abrams (0-8109-3956-8), 1991. (An Abrams First Impressions Book). 92p. B/W illus. and photos; Color illus. (Interest level: 4-8).

This biography of artist Andrew Wyeth details the influences on his art career, of his childhood experiences with family and friends in Chadds Ford, Pennsylvania, and his painting classes with N. C. Wyeth, his father. Reproductions of his paintings illustrate the effects of certain events, decisions, and friendships on his life and creative work. Paintings by Andrew and N. C. Wyeth and Howard Pyle (N. C. Wyeth's teacher) are exhibited in the Gristmill Art Museum in Chadds Ford.
♦ Students could visit local art galleries to view paintings by Andrew Wyeth, or create their own gallery using books and art prints from the library or art department. They also could choose one of Wyeth's paintings on which to write a creative essay.
1. Wyeth, Andrew, 1917-   2. Artists—Biography
2. Painting, American.

Fiction

Avi. *Encounter at Easton*. Pantheon (0-394-84342-8), 1980. 138p. (Interest level: 5-7).

An unlikely assortment of persons in eighteenth-century Easton, Pennsylvania, is brought together by the flight of two young indentured servants from their cruel master.
♦ Young people may research the laws regarding indentured servants in colonial America.
1. Pennsylvania—History—Fiction   2. Contract labor—Fiction.

Avi. *Night Journeys.* Pantheon (0-394-84116-6), 1979. 143p. (Interest level: 5-7).

In 1767, orphaned Peter York is taken in by a Quaker, Everett Shinn, a farmer who serves as justice of the peace for his community (Easton, Pennsylvania). Peter joins Shinn and other townspeople in a search for two escaped indentured servants. When he encounters one of them, 11-year-old Elizabeth, Peter is determined to help them escape.
♦ Young readers will enjoy reading the sequel to this book, *Encounter at Easton* (*see* preceding entry), to discover the fate of Elizabeth and Robert.
1. Pennsylvania—History—Fiction   2. Society of Friends—Fiction   3. Contract labor—Fiction.

Aylesworth, Jim. *The Folks in the Valley.* Illus. by Stefano Vitale. HarperCollins (0-06-021672-7), 1992. Unpaginated. Color illus. (Interest level: K-3).

A rhyming alphabet book presents the people and activities of a Pennsylvania Dutch settlement in a rural valley. The illustrations reflect the folkways and motifs of the Pennsylvania Dutch, and the text introduces the letters of the alphabet via the daily work and play activities of farm people.
♦ Children can, using scenes from the community, create an alphabet book.
1. Pennsylvania Dutch—Fiction   2. Alphabet books.

Beatty, Patricia. *Who Comes with Cannons?* Morrow (0-688-11028-2), 1992. 185p. (Interest level: 4-8).

Twelve-year-old Truth Hopkins, a Quaker, is sent to live on her uncle's farm in the early months of the Civil War. She becomes involved in his activities with the Underground Railroad and helps to gain the release of her cousin Robert, who was captured at the Battle of Gettysburg in Pennsylvania. Although the characters live in North Carolina, the ideals of the American Quaker society, which originated in Pennsylvania, are a focus of the novel.
♦ Students could research the role of women in Quaker society or conduct further research into the activities of the Quaker society in the Underground Railroad.
1. Society of Friends—Fiction   2. Slavery—United States—Fiction   3. Underground Railroad—Fiction.

Bell, Frederic. *Jenny's Corner.* Illus. by Zenowij Onyshkewych. Random House (0-394-82741-4), 1974. 58p. B/W illus. (Interest level: K-8).

Nine-year-old Jenny Drury moves in 1856 with her family to a mountain valley in Bucks County (eastern Pennsylvania), where she first discovers and grows to love the deer who drinks at the pond near her home. Jenny's love and her deep despair at the killing of deer lead to a promise by neighbors that no more hunting will be permitted in "Jenny's Corner."
♦ Discuss the values and shortcomings of conservation of deer and other wildlife.
1. Wildlife conservation—Fiction   2. Deer—Fiction   3. Pennsylvania—Fiction.

Brancato, Robin. *Don't Sit under the Apple Tree.* Knopf (0-394-93034-7), 1975. 163p. (Interest level: 5-7).

Ellis Capenter relates events of the summer of 1945 in Wissining, Pennsylvania, as World War II nears an end. Ellis wins a citizenship award, copes with the deaths of her grandmother and a young serviceman, and forges new relationships with old and new friends.
♦ Young people could discuss the effects of World War II on life at home with family members or friends who experienced it and present their information to the class.
1. Pennsylvania—History—Fiction   2. World War, 1939-1945—Fiction.

Brecht, Edith. *Ada and the Wild Duck.* Illus. by Charlotte Erickson. Viking (No ISBN), 1964. 63p. B/W illus. (Interest level: 2-5).

Eight-year-old Ada befriends a wild duck, whom she names Clyde. As Ada confides her secrets to Clyde, the reader learns the customs and traditions of the Mennonite people of eastern Pennsylvania. Ada learns the bittersweet aspects of love as Clyde seeks a mate in the wilds.
♦ Children may illustrate the story with pictures of their own.
1. Mennonites—Fiction.

Collier, James Lincoln and **Collier, Christopher.** *The Bloody Country.* Four Winds Press (0-590-07411-3), 1976. 183p. (Interest level: 4-8).

The Buck family moves from Connecticut to the Wyoming Valley of Pennsylvania and builds a mill on the Susquehanna River. Their right to the land is questioned by the Pennamites, a group of Pennsylvanians who settled in the area earlier. Conflicts with Indians, floods, and local warfare increase the hardships faced by the Connecticut immigrants.
♦ Students can investigate the activities of the Pennamites during the American Revolution and determine how they were driven away by the U.S. Army. Students could also investigate the escape of Connecticut women and children from the Wyoming Valley.
1. Pennsylvania—History—Fiction   2. Frontier and pioneer life—Fiction.

Colver, Anne. *Bread-and-Butter Indian.* Illus. by Garth Williams. Holt (0-03-089735-1), 1964. 96p. B/W illus. (Interest level: 3-6).

Barbara Baum, the eight-year-old daughter of German settlers in western Pennsylvania in 1783, longs for a best friend, and one day she gives her "treat," a piece of bread, butter, and sugar, to an Indian. Later, the Indian rescues Barbara when she is taken captive by the tribe. This story is based on the life of a member of the author's family.
♦ Class members can research what American Indian tribes were located in Pennsylvania in colonial times and what tribes continue to live in Pennsylvania.
1. Pennsylvania—History—1783-1809—Fiction.

Colver, Anne. *Bread-and-Butter Journey*. Illus. by Garth Williams. Holt, Rinehart and Winston (0-03-072220-9), 1970. 101p. B/W illus. (Interest level: 3-6).

Shortly after Barbara Baum becomes friends with Tess and Trudy Donner in the settlement of Burnt Cabins, Pennsylvania, their families decide to move further west. Using journals of a family ancestor, the author recounts the 1784 journey, by foot and pack horses, to Mead's Landing (present-day Meadville, Pennsylvania), telling of illness and other tragedies, help from strangers, and quiet joy in reaching their destination.
♦ Trace the journey on a map from Burnt Cabins to Mead's Crossing. Class members could identify what they would pack if they were facing the kind of journey described in the story.
1. Pennsylvania—History—1783-1809—Fiction.

Curry, Jane Louise. *What the Dickens!* Macmillan (0-689-50524-8), 1991. 153p. B/W map. (Interest level: 4-8).

Based on one of Charles Dickens's visits to Pennsylvania in 1842, this novel focuses on 11-year-old Cherry Dobbs and her twin Sam, whose father operates a freight boat on the Juniata Canal. Their mother often reads them Dickens's books. When Cherry stumbles on a Harrisburg bookseller's plan to steal Dickens's new manuscript, she determines to foil his plan. Authentic detail, surprise, comedy, and danger add to this action-packed story.
♦ Young people may begin keeping their own journal of the events of their lives. They could also research Dickens's visits to the United States.
1. Canals—Pennsylvania—Fiction   2. Dickens, Charles, 1812-1870—Fiction.

Dahlstedt, Marden. *The Terrible Wave*. Illus. by Charles Robinson. Coward, McCann & Geohegan (TR-698-20188-4), 1972. 125p. B/W illus. (Interest level: 4-7).

On May 31, 1889, South Fork Dam burst and flooded Johnstown, Pennsylvania. Megan Maxwell survives by riding out the flood on a raft with Brian, a delivery boy; Septimus, an elderly watchmaker; and Tom and Daisy, traveling actors. Her experiences with these companions and with Clara Barton, the nurse who established medical care for flood survivors, give her a direction for her future life and future career.
♦ Students could imagine they are volunteer workers and write letters home describing the rebuilding of Johnstown.
1. Floods—Johnstown (Pa.)—Fiction.

Dalgliesh, Alice. *The Bears on Hemlock Mountain*. Illus. by Helen Sewell. Scribner (0-684-12654-0), 1952. Unpaginated. B/W illus. (Interest level: K-3).

This tall tale of a boy, a bear, and an iron pot is a favorite of Pennsylvania storytellers.
♦ Children might locate other tall tales and learn them to tell to the class.
1. Bears—Fiction   2. Pennsylvania—Tall tales.

De Angeli, Marguerite. *Henner's Lydia*. Illus. by author. Doubleday (No ISBN), 1936. 76p. B/W and Color illus. (Interest level: 3-6).

DeAngeli's novel reveals the day-to-day life of a Pennsylvania Dutch farm family through the eyes of Lydia. Readers will learn about food, school, music, farming, household tasks, recreation, and the excitement of a trip to the Lancaster market.
♦ Young people might make a hooked rug like the one Lydia was trying to make for market.
1. Amish—Pennsylvania—Fiction.

De Angeli, Marguerite. *Skippack School*. Illus. by author. Doubleday (No ISBN), 1961. 92p. B/W and Color illus. (Interest level: 3-6).

Eli Shrawder moves in 1750 with his family to Skippack Village, Pennsylvania, where he attends a school run by Christopher Dock and befriends an Indian boy, White Eagle. Information about Pennsylvania Dutch arts and crafts such as printing are incorporated into the story.
♦ Class members can make one of the Pennsylvania Dutch crafts.
1. Mennonites—Pennsylvania—Fiction.

De Angeli, Marguerite. *Yonie Wondernose*. Illus. by author. Doubleday (0-385-07573-1), 1944. Unpaginated. B/W and Color illus. (Interest level: 2-4).

Seven-year-old Yonie, son of a Pennsylvania Dutch farmer, wants to prove he is old enough to be trusted like a man, but his curiosity often distracts him. When the barn catches on fire, he responds properly and promptly.
♦ The class could discuss ways in which young people today try to prove that they are grown up.
1. Pennsylvania Dutch—Fiction   2. Farm life—Fiction.

DeFord, Deborah H. and **Stout, Harry S.** *An Enemy among Them*. Houghton Mifflin (0-395-44239-7), 1987. 203p. B/W map. (Interest level: 4-8).

In 1776, Margaret Volpert, daughter of a German immigrant family living in Reading, Pennsylvania, meets a young Hessian mercenary, Christian Molitar, when he is held prisoner in her home. The two young people must confront questions of loyalty to one's country, family, and long-held ideals.
♦ Students can research the role of mercenary soldiers in the American Revolution.
1. Pennsylvania—History—Fiction 2. German Americans—Fiction 3. United States—History—Revolution, 1775-1783—Fiction.

Finlayson, Ann. *Greenhorn on the Frontier.* Illus. by W. T. Mars. Warne (No ISBN), 1974. 209p. B/W illus. (Interest level: 5-8).
Nineteen-year-old Harry Warrilow and his sister Sukey move their possessions by handcart from eastern Pennsylvania to the frontier near Fort Pitt to begin their own farm in pre-Revolutionary days. Land ownership, slavery issues, and preparations for war affect their lives.
♦ Readers could investigate problems faced by pioneers in claiming land in the American frontier and the role of Pennsylvania forts in the lives of frontier farm families.
1. Pennsylvania—History—1755-1763—Fiction 2. Frontier and pioneer life—Pennsylvania—Fiction.

Finlayson, Ann. *Rebecca's War.* Illus. by Sherry Streeter. Warne (0-723-26090-7), 1972. 280p. B/W illus. and maps. (Interest level: 5-8).
Philadelphia, Pennsylvania, in 1775, under British occupation, becomes a challenging and often dangerous place for 14-year-old Rebecca Ransome. While her privateer father and older brothers are gone, she has to care for a younger brother and sister and protect the hiding places for family and government monies, all under the scrutiny of British officers billeted in the family home.
♦ Students could research the topic of billeting members of the American and German armies in private homes in various European countries during World War II.
1. Pennsylvania—History—Revolution, 1775-1783—Fiction 2. Philadelphia (Pa.)—Fiction.

Fritz, Jean. *Brady.* Illus. by Lynd Ward. Coward-McCann (0-698-20014-4), 1960. 223p. B/W illus. (Interest level: 4-8).
Brady Minton's ordered life on a farm in pre-Civil War nineteenth-century Washington County, Pennsylvania, becomes confused by conflicting attitudes among neighbors about the emancipation of slaves. When he affirms his decision regarding slavery, he can say with pride: "On this day Brady Minton did a man's work."
♦ Young people could investigate the Underground Railroad during the Civil War.
1. Underground Railroad—Fiction 2. Pennsylvania—History—1815-1861—Fiction.

Fritz, Jean. *Cabin Faced West.* Illus. by Feodor Rojankovsky. Coward-McCann/Puffin (0-698-20016-0), 1958. 124p. B/W illus. (Interest level: 4-6).
Ten-year-old Ann Hamilton is lonely and unhappy in western Pennsylvania, as she misses her friends and life in Gettysburg. An unexpected visit from General George Washington and the opportunity to use the treasured linen tablecloth and lavender flower dishes enable Ann to appreciate the opportunities available in Washington County. Ann Hamilton was the great-great-grandmother of author Jean Fritz.
♦ Children might plan what personal items they would take if they were forced to move as Ann was. They might also enjoy keeping diaries to record the important events in their lives.
1. Frontier and pioneer life—Fiction 2. Pennsylvania—History—Fiction 3. Washington, George, 1732-1799—Fiction.

Fritz, Jean. *Homesick: My Own Story.* Illus. by Margot Tomes. Dell/Yearling (0-44-043683-4), 1982. 163p. B/W illus. and photos. (Interest level: 4-8).
In this fictionalized biography, Jean Fritz tells about her childhood in China but emphasizes her belief that she "belonged on the other side of the world" in Pennsylvania with her grandmother and other relatives. The final two chapters detail Jean's arrival in Washington, Pennsylvania, and her first day in an American school.
♦ Young people can read *China Homecoming*, the sequel to *Homesick*.
1. China—Fiction 2. Fritz, Jean, 1915-.

Gauch, Patricia Lee. *Thunder at Gettysburg.* Illus. by Stephen Gammell. Putnam (0-399-22201-4), 1990. 48p. B/W illus. and map. (Interest level: 2-6).
Based on a book published in 1889 by Tillie Pierce Alleman, this novel tells of three days in the life of 14-year-old Tillie, who is sent away from her home in Gettysburg, Pennsylvania, to Weikert farm, where her family thinks she will be safe from the war. Instead, she is drawn helplessly into the battle.
♦ Children can write a letter home as Tillie, describing life on the Weikert farm.
1. Gettysburg, Battle of, 1863—Fiction 2. United States—History—Civil War, 1861-1865—Campaigns—Fiction.

Graybill, Kathryn. *Cassie and the General.* Illus. by Kurt Werth. Thomas Nelson (No ISBN), 1962. 95p. B/W illus. (Interest level: 2-5).
General Lafayette came to Lancaster, Pennsylvania, on July 28, 1825, to meet with his U.S. Army

colleagues. When eight-year-old Cassie is unable to sing for the general during the public reception, she earns a second opportunity to greet the French hero in a special way.
♦ To determine why the Marquis de Lafayette returned to the United States after the Revolution, students can read more about him.
1. Lafayette, Marquis de, 1757-1834—Fiction 2. Pennsylvania—History—1783-1865—Fiction.

Gross, Virginia T. *The Day It Rained Forever: A Story of the Johnstown Flood.* Illus. by Ronald Himler. Viking (0-670-83552-8), 1991. 127p. B/W illus. (Interest level: 3-5).

On Memorial Day in 1889, the privately owned dam on Lake Conemaugh broke, causing a devastating flood in Johnstown, Pennsylvania. This story reveals the impact of the flood on one family.
♦ Students could write newspaper accounts of the Johnstown flood, or other floods, focusing on the people affected by the flood.
1. Floods—Johnstown (Pa.)—Fiction.

Jensen, Dorothea. *The Riddle of Penncroft Farm.* Harcourt Brace Jovanovich (0-15-200574-9), 1989. 180p. (Interest level: 4-6).

After Lars Olafson moves with his family to Aunt Cass's farm near Valley Forge, Pennsylvania, he meets the ghost of an eighteenth-century boy who tells him exciting tales of Revolutionary War events. A glossary of eighteenth-century terms and a bibliography complete this book.
♦ Class members can prepare a dramatization of one of the adventures in the book.
1. Pennsylvania—History—Revolution, 1775-1783—Fiction 2. Ghosts—Fiction.

Jordan, Mildred. *Proud to Be Amish.* Illus. by W. T. Mars. Crown (No ISBN), 1968. B/W illus. (Interest level: 4-8).

Katie Zook is proud of her Old Order Amish heritage, but she is tempted by worldly possessions and activities. Details of Amish farm life and customs in eastern Pennsylvania contrast with "English" lifestyle. A glossary defines idioms used in the story.
♦ In essays or a class discussion, students can compare and contrast their lifestyle with that of the Amish.
1. Amish—Pennsylvania—Fiction.

Jordan, Mildred. *Shoo-Fly Pie.* Illus. by Henry C. Pitz. Knopf (No ISBN), 1953. 118p. B/W and Color illus. (Interest level: 3-6).

The everyday events of life on a farm in Reading, Pennsylvania, are revealed as Debbie Weissfinger tries to participate in grown-up activities. A glossary of Pennsylvania Dutch terms is included.

♦ Using the recipe in the book, children may make a shoo-fly pie.
1. Pennsylvania Dutch—Fiction.

Keehn, Sally M. *I Am Regina.* Philomel (0-399-21797-5), 1991. 240p. B/W illus. (Interest level: 4-8).

Based on the true story of Regina Leininger, who was captured by Allegheny Indians from her farm home in Selinsgrove, Pennsylvania, in 1755, this fictionalized account tells of her life with the Indians and her neverending hope to return to her mother. Her tombstone, with a notation about her three-and-one-half years of captivity, can be seen in Christ's Church cemetery, Stouchsburg, Pennsylvania.
♦ Readers might write journal entries describing life in an Indian village.
1. Indians of North America—Pennsylvania—Captives 2. Pennsylvania—History, 1775-1763.

Lawson, Robert. *Ben and Me.* Illus. by author. Dell (0-440-42038-5), 1976. 114p. B/W illus. (Interest level: 3-5).

Benjamin Franklin's closest friend and advisor, Amos, reveals his role in the great man's inventions, discoveries, and successes. Readers will learn much about Franklin's activities in Pennsylvania and France through the eyes of the mouse who shared his fur cap.
♦ Children can illustrate a favorite adventure of Amos and Franklin.
1. Franklin, Benjamin, 1706-1790—Fiction 2. Mice—Fiction.

Meadowcroft, Enid LaMonte. *Silver for General Washington.* Illus. by Lee Ames. Crowell (No ISBN), 1957. 247p. B/W illus. (Interest level: 4-8).

After burying the family silverware in the cellar of their Philadelphia, Pennsylvania, home, Gilbert and Jennifer Emmet go to their aunt and uncle's Valley Forge home, where their father thinks they will be safe from the Revolutionary War. When they visit the army encampment of General Washington and see the need for money and supplies, Gilbert decides to return home to get the silverware. Other experiences of the Emmets—capturing a spy and sewing with Martha Washington—give readers a sense of civilian life at Valley Forge in 1777-78.
♦ Writing as Gilbert or Jennifer, students can record in a diary or journal the important events of their life in Valley Forge.
1. Valley Forge (Pa.)—Fiction.

Meigs, Cornelia. *Wind in the Chimney.* Illus. by Louise Mansfield. Macmillan (No ISBN), 1960. 144p. B/W and Color illus. (Interest level: 4-7).

Widowed Elizabeth Moreland brings her three children to America, where they find a home in the country west of Philadelphia, Pennsylvania. Each

family member finds a way to contribute to the new lifestyle, and their experiences culminate in their attending a wedding at which President Washington is an honored guest.
♦ Writing as one of the Moreland children, Richard, Ann, or Debbie, young people could prepare a letter for a friend back home in England telling of the new experiences they have enjoyed in America.
1. Pennsylvania—History, 1783-1809—Fiction 2. Philadelphia (Pa.)—Fiction.

Milhous, Katherine. *Appolonia's Valentine.* Illus. by author. Scribner (No ISBN), 1954. Unpaginated. Color illus. (Interest level: 2-5).

Appolonia and Dan attend a one-room school in rural Pennsylvania. One year the children learn to make valentines using traditional Pennsylvania Dutch designs. Appolonia sends her valentine to Jean-Jacques, a friend in Brittany, France.
♦ Children could make cards for friends and family using the Pennsylvania Dutch designs in the book.
1. Pennsylvania Dutch—Fiction 2. Valentine's Day—Fiction.

Milhous, Katherine. *The Egg Tree.* Illus. by author. Scribner (0-684-12716-4), 1950. Unpaginated. Color illus. (Interest level: 1-5).

Cousins celebrating a Pennsylvania Dutch Easter learn how to decorate eggs for an Easter egg tree. Detailed illustrations will enable readers to follow traditional designs in decorating their own eggs.
♦ Students can make an egg tree for the classroom or for their home.
1. Pennsylvania Dutch—Fiction 2. Easter—Fiction 3. Egg decoration—Fiction.

Moore, Robin. *Bread Sister of Sinking Creek.* HarperCollins (0-397-32418-9), 1984. 154p. (Interest level: 4-7).

Maggie Callahan travels from Philadelphia to Penns Valley in the western Pennsylvania frontier in 1776 to live with her aunt Franny, but Aunt Franny has moved further west. Maggie's special talent for making bread ensures her a place in the valley until she too is ready to move on. To discover what happens next, young readers can read *Maggie among the Seneca* (see following entry), the sequel to this book. Author Robin Moore has adapted and recorded his story of Maggie Callahan for presentation on the radio. Children could listen to the cassettes alone, or teachers could play the cassettes for storytime in the classroom.
♦ Students could make sourdough bread, following the recipe on pages 147-54.
1. Bread—Fiction 2. Frontier and pioneer life—Pennsylvania—Fiction 3. Pennsylvania—History—Fiction.

Moore, Robin. *Maggie among the Seneca.* Illus. by William Sauts Bock. HarperCollins (0-9613433-3-8), 1987. 136p. B/W illus. (Interest level: 4-7).

Based on the lives of Mary Jemison and other frontier women taken captive by Indians during the Revolutionary War, this sequel to *Bread Sister of Sinking Creek* (see preceding entry) recounts what happens to Maggie Callahan when she leaves Penns Valley in western Pennsylvania to catch up with Aunt Franny. Maggie is taken by Seneca Indians and lives with them for several years before her search for her aunt is successful. While living with the Senecas, Maggie experiences first love.
♦ The Senecas chose a special name for Maggie. Students could choose names for themselves and their classmates based on their special qualities.
1. Indians of North America—Pennsylvania—Fiction 2. Pennsylvania—History—Fiction.

Moore, Robin. *Up the Frozen River.* Illus. by William Sauts Bock. Groundhog Press (No ISBN), 1993. 164p. B/W illus. (Interest level: 4-7).

In the final volume of the Maggie Callahan trilogy, Maggie and mountain man Jake Logan leave Aunt Franny's tavern in Kittanning and travel north to Seneca Indian country to find her child, Hoot Owl, who was rescued by a witch woman called Ragpicker when the colonial army destroyed the Indian village several months earlier. The two survive severe weather, wild animal attacks, and the death of a friend in their search for the child.
♦ Using a contour map, students may trace the route Maggie and Jake follow from Kittanning to the Seneca Indian country. They may also investigate the use of herbs for food and medicine to determine whether Ragpicker's methods for saving Hoot Owl and herself are plausible.
1. Frontier and pioneer life—Pennsylvania—Fiction 2. Indians of North America—Pennsylvania—Fiction 3. Pennsylvania—History—Fiction.

Perez, Norah A. *Breaker.* Houghton Mifflin (0-395-45537-5), 1988. 207p. (Interest level: 6-8).

After his father dies in an underground accident in 1902, 14-year-old Pat takes a job in the breaker where coal is sorted at the mine in Scatter Patch, Pennsylvania. Union activities and a workers' strike dominate life in the patch, and Pat's family and friends face changes at home and at work.
♦ Students could research life in the patch: company stores, recreation, or the role of child labor in the mining industry.
1. Coal mines and mining—Fiction 2. Strikes and lockouts—Fiction 3. Pennsylvania—History—1865—Fiction.

Polacco, Patricia. *Just Plain Fancy.* Illus. by author. Bantam (0-553-05884-3), 1990. Unpaginated. (Interest level: 2-5).

Naomi and Ruth, Amish sisters who take care of the chickens on the family farm, watch over a "fancy" egg and chick. On the day of the Community Working Bee, Fancy is revealed as a peacock, and Naomi earns her organdy cap.
♦ Children could conduct further research on the Amish way of life and report on an aspect of their life and culture.
1. Amish—Fiction   2. Peacocks—Fiction.

Rappaport, Doreen. *Trouble at the Mines.* Illus. by Joan Sandin. Thomas Y. Crowell (0-690-04445-3), 1987. 85p. B/W illus. (Interest level: 3-7).
Rosie and her family are caught up in a Pennsylvania mining strike in 1899. The role of the union organizer Mary Harris (Mother) Jones is emphasized in this episode of U.S. industrial history.
♦ Young people may research the life of miners in late nineteenth-century.
1. Strikes and lockouts—Fiction   2. Jones, Mary Harris, 1830-1930—Fiction   3. Coal mines and mining.

Reilly, Robert T. *Rebels in the Shadows.* University of Pittsburgh Press (0-8229-5304-5), 1979. 180p. (Interest level: 6-8).
In Pottsville, in 1870, the men in the Flannery family are employed in the anthracite coal mines. Uncle Niall joins the Molly Maguires, a secret society of miners who protest the dangerous working conditions. When Red McKenna, a boarder in the Flannery home, joins the Molly Maguires, trouble erupts for the family.
♦ Students could write an account of the trial from the point of view of Sean, Kitty, or Captain Mike. They could also research the history of the Molly Maguires.
1. Coal mines and mining—Fiction   2. Molly Maguires—Fiction   3. Pennsylvania—History—1865—Fiction.

Richter, Conrad. *Light in the Forest.* Illus. by Warren Chappell. Knopf (0-394-81404-5), 1966. 176p. B/W illus. (Interest level: 6-8).
Kidnapped as a child by the Delaware Indians, True Son at age 15 is returned to his family at Fort Pitt, Pennsylvania. Unable to adjust to white civilization, he returns to the Delawares, but his loyalty is tested by Indian/white conflict.
♦ Young people might write essays about how they would feel and what they would do in True Son's situation.
1. Indians of North America—Fiction   2. Pennsylvania—History—Fiction.

Richter, Conrad. *Over the Blue Mountains.* Illus. by Herbert Danska. Knopf (No ISBN), 1967. 81p. B/W illus. (Interest level: 3-5).

Abie and Henner misunderstand the Pennsylvania Dutch legend that says 40 days of rain would follow Mary's crossing the mountain on a rainy day. When they follow neighbor Mary Heim, they have unexpected adventures.
♦ Readers can investigate other Pennsylvania Dutch legends.
1. Pennsylvania Dutch—Fiction.

Robinson, Tom. *Trigger John's Son.* Illus. by Robert McCloskey. Viking (No ISBN), 1949. 284p. B/W illus. (Interest level: 4-8).
Orphaned Trigger from Maine slips into Beechwood, Pennsylvania, where he was sent to live with adoptive parents, the Smiths. He joins the Goosetown Gang and stays with blind Mr. England, but when he meets the Smiths, he decides to follow the original plan.
♦ Students can write essays explaining what they like about their community.
1. Pennsylvania—History—1919-1933—Fiction   2. Adoption—Fiction.

Singmaster, Elsie. *I Heard of a River.* Illus. by Henry C. Pitz. John C. Winston (No ISBN), 1948. 209p. B/W illus. (Interest level: 5-8).
Hannes Berg, a 17-year-old German gunsmith, immigrates to Pennsylvania in the early eighteenth century, seeking a better lifestyle and religious freedom. It is only after he sees the great Susquehanna River that he understood his father's dying words about the special rifle design he taught Hannes.
♦ Students could compare the lifestyles in Germany during this time period with the lifestyles in America.
1. Mennonites—Pennsylvania—Fiction   2. Rifles—Fiction.

Skurzynski, Gloria. *Good-bye, Billy Radish.* Bradbury (0-02-782921-9), 1992. 138p. B/W photos. (Interest level: 4-7).
Best friends Hank Kerner and Bazyli Radichevvych (Billy Radish) experience changes in the mill town of Canaan, Pennsylvania, during the First World War. This book centers around one of the families in *The Tempering* (see following entry), a 1983 book written by the same author.
♦ Young people might read more about the development of the steel industry in Pennsylvania and report on how it affected the economic development of the state. Students may also wish to research industries that have affected the economic development of their state.
1. World War, 1914-1918—United States—Fiction   2. Friendship—Fiction.

Skurzynski, Gloria. *The Tempering.* Clarion Books (0-89919-152-5), 1983. 178p. (Interest level: 6-8).

In 1912 three young men prepare for adult life in a Pennsylvania steel town and lose jobs, fall in love, and test their friendships. Poverty and hardships affect the behavior of characters at all levels of the social structure, and rich detail enhances the several layers of plot development.
♦ Readers can investigate the development of the steel industry in Pittsburgh, Duquesne, and Braddock, major industrial centers in western Pennsylvania.
1. Steel industry and trade—Fiction 2. Pennsylvania—History—Fiction.

Sorenson, Virginia. *Plain Girl.* Illus. by Charles Geer. Harcourt, Brace and World (0-15-262437-6), 1955. 151p. B/W illus. (Interest level: 4-8).
Esther is 10 years old when she first attends a public school. Through her friendship with Mary, the prettiest girl in school, she learns about customs outside the Amish community. Her brother Dan helps her come to terms with Amish ways. Sorenson presents details of Amish life in an interesting and authentic way.
♦ Students can read more about the Amish way of life and create a slide/tape show to share with the class.
1. Amish—Fiction 2. Pennsylvania—Fiction.

Vining, Elizabeth Gray. *The Taken Girl.* Viking (0-670-69099-6), 1972. 190p. (Interest level: 4-8).
Orphaned Veer Schuyler leaves the Phoebe Moon Home to become a servant girl in the Underwood home, where she is constantly reminded to learn "her place." Rescued by a Philadelphia Quaker family, she becomes an integral part of the Healy family, which operates a boarding house. Veer meets John Greenleaf Whittier and becomes aware of the slavery and abolitionist issues that pervade pre–Civil War Pennsylvania.
♦ Young people may research abolition in pre–Civil War history.
1. Society of Friends—Fiction 2. Slavery—United States—Fiction 3. Abolitionists—Fiction.

Wallower, Lucille. *Roll of Drums.* Illus. by author. Whitman (No ISBN), 1945. 111p. Color illus. (Interest level: 5-7).
The brothers of Ephrata Cloister in southeastern Pennsylvania care for wounded soldiers during the Revolutionary War. Stephens's life is changed as a result of his experiences with members of the community.
♦ Children can read more about the activities of the Seventh Day Baptists who founded the Ephrata Cloister and compare and contrast the activities and customs of this sect with other religious groups.
1. Pennsylvania—History—Revolution, 1775-1783.

Welch, Catherine A. *Danger at the Breaker.* Illus. by Andrea Shine. Carolrhoda (0-87614-693-0), 1992. 48p. Color illus. (Interest level: 2-5).
Eight-year-old Andrew leaves school in 1885 to work as a "breaker boy" in the sorting chutes of a Pennsylvania coal mine. An underground explosion threatens his life and that of his miner father.
♦ Students could read more about the work of "breaker boys" in nineteenth-century coal mine operations.
1. Coal mines and mining—Fiction.

Periodicals

974.8
Pennsylvania Heritage. Pennsylvania Historical and Museum Commission (ISSN 0270-7500). Quarterly. (Interest level: grade 4-adult).
This journal exists to "introduce readers to Pennsylvania's rich culture and historic legacy, to educate and sensitize them to the value of preserving that legacy, and to entertain and involve them in such a way as to ensure that Pennsylvania's past has a future."
♦ Young people may read one of the feature articles on a historic topic from this periodical and prepare an oral report for the class.
1. Pennsylvania—Description 2. Pennsylvania—History.

974.8
Pennsylvania Magazine. Pennsylvania Magazine Company (No ISSN available). Bi-monthly. (Interest level: grade 4-adult).
Pennsylvania Magazine presents articles of current interest on all aspects of Pennsylvania history and culture, arts and sciences, business and economy, and people and places. Suggestions for travel and recreation are included.
♦ Students can read several articles in the magazine and choose one to share with the class.
1. Pennsylvania—Description 2. Pennsylvania—History.

Professional Materials

331.89
Krause, Paul. *The Battle for Homestead, 1880-1892: Politics, Culture and Steel.* University of Pittsburgh Press (0-8229-5466-4), 1992. 548p. B/W photos, reproductions. (Interest level: Professional).
As part of the centennial observance of the Homestead Strike of 1892, historian Paul Krause documents one of the most famous industrial conflicts in U.S. history by focusing on the owners, managers, workers, scientists, and engineers in-

volved. Twelve appendixes, detailed notes, a bibliography, and an index complete the book.
♦ Students could compare the contemporary news reports in *The River Ran Red* (*see* p. 156) with the factual presentation of this book.
1. Homestead Strike, 1892 2. Steel industry and trade—Pennsylvania—History—19th century.

974.8
Harpster, John W., ed. *Crossroads, Descriptions of Western Pennsylvania, 1720-1829*. University of Pittsburgh Press (0-8229-6088-5), 1986. 337p. B/W illus. (Interest level: Professional).

Crossroads is a collection of 37 written impressions of western Pennsylvania in journal and letter format by early travelers and settlers. Traders, surveyors, soldiers, preachers, and immigrants tell of the loneliness, terror, and beauty of the frontier. A selective bibliography and index are provided.
♦ Students could compare and contrast these personal impressions of Pennsylvania with accounts in other resources.

1. Pennsylvania—Description 2. Pennsylvania—History—Colonial period, ca 1600-1775 3. Pennsylvania—History—1775-1865.

Demarest, David P., Jr., ed. *From These Hills, from These Valleys*. University of Pittsburgh Press (0-8229-1123-X), 1976. 240p. B/W photos. (Interest level: Professional).

Short fiction pieces by such authors as Taylor Caldwell, Conrad Richter, O. Henry, Mary Roberts Rinehart, Agnes Sligh Turnbull, John Dos Passos, Willa Cather, and Marcia Davenport commemorate life in western Pennsylvania from 1763 to 1970 and celebrate the future. Each fiction selection is introduced with a discussion of the setting and the author's ties to Pennsylvania. Pennsylvania readers will recognize some of the settings, such as Pithole, site of Drake's Well; Kennywood Park; the Pittsburgh steel mills; and Pittsburgh's Carnegie Museum.
♦ Students could write a personal memoir of an experience told to them by a senior citizen.
1. American fiction—Pennsylvania 2. Pennsylvania—History—Fiction.

Rhode Island

by Gloria Schmidt

Nonfiction

387.1
Gibbons, Gail. *Beacons of Light: Lighthouses.* Morrow (0-688-07379-4), 1990. Unpaginated. Color illus. (Interest level: K-3).

Gibbons's beautiful picture book surveys the history of lighthouses and contains interesting diagrams, facts, and examples, including a mention of Newport lighthouse keeper Ida Lewis. The clear, easy-to-understand illustrations and text are ideal for younger students.
♦ A great variety of historic lighthouses are included, and children can use any of them to create a model or draw an illustration. They could then write a short descriptive paragraph about the lighthouse they depicted.
1. Lighthouses—United States.

387.2
Wilbur, C. Keith. *Tall Ships of the World.* Globe Pequot Press (087106-898-2), 1986. 87p. B/W illus. (Interest level: grade 4-adult).

Included in this illustrated encyclopedia of the history of tall ships are chapters on racing and sail training out of Rhode Island harbors. Wilbur offers a wealth of facts on navigation, trade routes, sailing history, ship identification, and other maritime topics, along with simple illustrations.
♦ The maps of trade routes, trade winds, and calms can be used to practice simple geography skills. Students can follow one of the trade or training routes and overlay the trade winds and calms map on a clear slide to understand what conditions for sailing would be encountered.
1. Sailing ships 2. Seafaring life.

398.2
Cabral, Len. *Nho Lobo and Other Stories.* (Sound recording). Story Sound Productions, 1980. (45 min.). $10.00. (Interest level: 2-8).

Storyteller Len Cabral provides a taste of Cape Verdean folklore, music, dialect, and even some history with the humorous tale of Nho Lobo and how he was tricked into coming to America. The other stories on this audiocassette are from the African American traditions, but all of the tales are enjoyable and representative of Rhode Island ethnic groups.
♦ Cabral ends the story of Nho Lobo with sightings of him in America. Young people might continue the story with their own versions of how the lazy Nho Lobo would take to life in Rhode Island.
1. Folklore—Cape Verde 2. Folklore—African.

398.2
Cohlene, Terri. *Little Firefly: An Algonquian Legend.* Illus. by Charles Reasoner. Rourke (0-86593-005-8), 1990. (Native American Legends Series). 48p. B/W and Color illus. (Interest level: K-4).

In this Native American Cinderella story, a mistreated younger sister trades her rags for birch bark garments and wins the heart of The Invisible One. The beautiful tale from the language traditions of Rhode Island tribes is simply illustrated and includes excellent explanations of Algonquian lands, tribes, food, clothing, and life today.
♦ Children can compare and contrast this story with the traditional French Cinderella story.
1. Indians of North America—Legends 2. Algonquian Indians—Legends 3. Indians of North America—Social life and customs 4. Algonquian Indians—Social life and customs.

398.2
Levitt, Marc Joel. *Tales of an October Moon.* (Sound recording). North Star Stories, 1989. (60 min.). $9.98. (Interest level: 4-8).

A Rhode Island storyteller shares four haunting stories from New England, including one based on the flooding of seven towns to make the Scituate, Rhode Island, reservoir and a tale about the stone

walls so common locally. These ghost stories are scary enough to be enjoyed by intermediate audiences, but they also comment on sacrificing the old ways for modern improvements.
♦ The two stories described above can be a vehicle for discussions of how things have changed locally. Old photographs, and town maps can be used to research the changes, and students can develop their own ghost stories based on local history.
1. Folklore—New England 2. Ghosts—Fiction.

398.2
Princess Red Wing. *What Cheer Netop, "Greeting Friends", History, Culture & Legends of American Indians of the Northeast.* (Sound recording). Mary Benjamin, 1986. (60 min.). $9.00. (Interest level: grade 1-adult).

Princess Red Wing, a Wampanoag and Narragansett, recorded these stories and traditions of her people when she was 90 years old. All ages will enjoy the brief, simple way she tells of the five Thanksgivings, creation myths, animal legends, and especially how "Rock a Bye Baby" was borrowed from Wampanoag songs.
♦ Princess Red Wing shares wonderful chants, songs, and poems that could be learned by even the youngest children and used during Earth Day or Thanksgiving celebrations.
1. Indians of North America—Legends 2. Wampanoag Indians—Legends.

398.2
Simmons, William. *Spirit of the New England Tribes.* University Press of New England (0-87451-372-3), 1986. 331p. (Interest level: grade 3-adult).

Simmons's sourcebook of folklore from the southern New England tribes includes creation stories, legends, ghost stories and giant tales recorded from colonial times to the present. Although this is not a reference students can use on their own, wonderful stories such as Wampanoag legends about giant Maushop and Narragansett tales of John Onion and the devil can be gleaned from the book and told to eager listeners.
♦ This book offers wonderful opportunities to understand the evolution of folktales because the versions of the stories are presented chronologically. Readers can follow the different variations of how Sakonnet Point in Rhode Island was formed with recorded texts in 1817, 1830, 1900, 1904, 1915, and 1934.
1. Indians of North America—New England—Folklore 2. Legends—New England 3. New England—History, Local.

497
Davis, Hadassah. *What Cheer, Netop! Selections from "A Key into the Language of America" by Roger Williams.* Haffenreffer Museum/Brown University (0-912089-03-2), 1986. 62p. B/W illus. (Interest level: grade 4-adult).

Translated into modern English, this selection from Robert Williams's dictionary of Narragansett words includes interesting comments and gives readers a glimpse of native culture when the English arrived. Because it is an understandable primary source full of information that children will enjoy reading, this is an excellent resource.
♦ Class members can make a visual dictionary of Narragansett words by making drawings and labeling them with words from this source. Examples of entries could include dugout, canoes, foods, animals, stars, and numbers.
1. Dictionaries—Narraganset.

574.974
Hansen, Judith. *Seashells in My Pocket: A Child's Guide to Exploring the Atlantic Coast.* Illus. by Donna Sabaka. Appalachian Mountain Club Books (1-878239-15-5), 1992. 160p. B/W illus. (Interest level: K-8).

Hansen's simple guidebook to Atlantic coastal plants and animals offers suggestions of what to wear, what to take, safety rules, and rules to protect the environment when visiting the Atlantic Coast. It also lists recommended places to observe and explore in Rhode Island. Compact but filled with simple drawings and descriptions, this is a reference that even the youngest children can enjoy with help and that older explorers can use to observe on their own.
♦ Field trips to any of the recommended Rhode Island sites could focus on a scavenger hunt to find sea creatures, insects, birds, shells, and plants from the checklist in the appendix. Students from other states might visit a local stream, river, or park to study the flora and fauna; after their visit, they may prepare their own guide to the area.
1. Seashore fauna—Atlantic Coast 2. Seashore flora—Atlantic Coast.

595.3
Pallotta, Jerry. *Going Lobstering.* Illus. by Rob Bolster. Charlesbridge (0-88106-475-0), 1990. Unpaginated. Color illus. (Interest level: K-3).

In this richly illustrated picture book, two children spend a day aboard a lobster boat learning about and catching lobsters. Although the setting is unspecified, this book depicts one of Rhode Island's major industries in an appealing, realistic and informative way that young children will enjoy.
♦ After sharing the book aloud, children can draw their own pictures of lobstering. The illustrations of lobster pots, buoys, flounders, crabs, boats, and sharks can guide them in their designs.
1. Lobsters.

599.32
McNulty, Faith. *Orphan: The Story of a Baby Woodchuck.* Illus. by Darby Morrell. Scholastic (0-590-43838-7), 1992. 48p. B/W illus. (Interest level: 3-8).

A Rhode Island farm is the setting for this true story about an orphan woodchuck, its rescue, nurturence in captivity, and return to the wild. The charm of the book is that it makes us aware of the wildlife around us and how the animal world and human world are interrelated.
♦ When she needed to know more about the life of wild woodchucks, the author did research at the library. Students can choose one of the local animals (deer, rabbits, skunks, raccoons, possums, etc.) and do research to create a poster about how that animal lives in the wild. Another good project would be to find out about local organizations and agencies that help protect and care for wildlife.
1. Woodchucks 2. Wildlife rescue.

628.4
Landfilled: The Trash Crises in Rhode Island. (Videocassette). Geoff Adams for the Rhode Island Solid Waste Management Corporation, 1987. VHS, Color, (25 min.). Available on free loan from Rhode Island College Film and Video Library. (Interest level: grade 5-adult).

Three short segments cover the economics of the Rhode Island trash problem, recycling efforts, and possible solutions through resource recovery systems. Short and informative, this film is especially effective in illustrating how much waste each individual and family generates daily.
♦ One segment shows how much trash is generated by the cooking of one meal. This would be an easy experiment to re-create at home. Class members could keep track of the cans, bottles, plastics, and other recyclable items that end up as trash from a single meal at home and then combine their data into charts to make comparisons.
1. Refuse and refuse disposal.

639.2
Carrick, Carol. *Whaling Days.* Illus. by David Frampton. Clarion (0-395-50948-3), 1993. 40p. Color illus. (Interest level: 3-6).

The history of whaling (including participation by Rhode Island ports), the excitement of the chase and the drudgery of life aboard a whaler are depicted in Carrick's detailed book. The information is outstanding, and the original woodcuts convey the awesome power of the whales and the difficulty of whaling.
♦ After reading this book, children will have plenty of information to write a fictitious journal of a whaling voyage. The glossary, cross section of a whaling boat, and vivid descriptions give readers a good model of terms and ship locations.
1. Whaling.

641.4
Dyer, Ceil. *The Newport Cookbook.* Weathervane Books (0-89909-056-7), 1972. B/W illus. (Interest level: grade 4-adult).

Not just a cookbook, this is a culinary history of Rhode Island foods, including Roger Williams's first meal with the Indians, colonial foods, the battle over johnnycake recipes, clambakes, and the cuisine at the mansions. Dyer offers an excellent source of recipes, historical menus, descriptions of dining experiences, and anything else you might want to know about typical state foods.
♦ Students can use the recipes, narratives, and menu reproductions to prepare their own menus for different historical periods. They might also test out the various johnnycake recipes and vote on which regional version they like best.
1. Cookery.

641.59
Bisignano, Alphonse. *Cooking the Italian Way.* Lerner (0-8225-0906-7), 1982. (Easy Menu Ethnic Cookbooks Series). 47p. Color photos and illus. (Interest level: 4-8).

The Italian community is one of the largest ethnic groups in Rhode Island, and this cookbook provides a sample of markets, customs, and cooking typical in Italian neighborhoods. The book is a great source of menus and dining traditions that highlight Italian heritage celebrations.
♦ Markets in Italian neighborhoods provide some specialty items, but Italian foods have become part of everyone's diet. Looking at the special-ingredients chapter, students can check off pastas, cheeses, and other items that are used in their own homes.
1. Cookery, Italian.

641.59
Henry, Edna (Blue Star Woman). *Native American Cookbook.* Messner (0-671-41896-3), 1983. 96p. B/W illus. (Interest level: 4-8).

Included in this collection of authentic recipes are dishes from the Narragansett and Nipmuc tribes native to Rhode Island. The author weaves in chants, tribal lore, and native culture to provide background for the recipes and gives a table of substitutes for native foods.
♦ Cooking cattail biscuits Narragansett style or Nipmuc stews will give young people insight into how local tribes lived off the land. Recipes for snacks and desserts are easy and fun to make.
1. Cookery 2. Indians of North America.

641.59
Nguyen, Chi. *Cooking the Vietnamese Way.* Lerner (0-8225-0914-8), 1985. (Easy Menu Ethnic Cookbooks Series). 47p. B/W and Color photos and illus. (Interest level: 4-8).

Although this is a cookbook, chapters on Vietnamese culture, history, and traditions help readers get to know Rhode Island's newest immigrants. Nguyen's cookbook is easy to read and use and even includes instructions on how to use chopsticks.
♦ Cooking often reflects culture and it is interesting for students to note the foreign influence in Vietnamese cooking. The class could discuss what influences various ethnic groups have had on cuisine.
1. Cookery, Vietnamese.

677.009
Macaulay, David. *Mill.* Houghton Mifflin (0-395-34830-7), 1983. 128p. B/W illus. (Interest level: grade 6-adult).

Macaulay's richly illustrated book follows the history of an imaginary mill community in Rhode Island from planning to construction and operation. The magnificent drawings and interesting story give an informative, detailed, and technical look at all aspects of the mills, which have been a fixture in Rhode Island life for two centuries.
♦ Macaulay uses fictionalized diary excerpts to give a taste of mill life. Assuming the role of mill workers, mechanics, or owners, young people can write their own diary entries based on research from this and other sources on mill life.
1. Textile factories—Rhode Island—History.

680
Wilbur, C. Keith. *Indian Handcrafts: How to Craft Dozens of Practical Objects Using Traditional Indian Techniques.* Illus. by author. Globe Pequot Press (0-87106-496-0), 1990. 144p. B/W illus. (Interest level: grade 2-adult).

Reproducing King Philip's fingerwoven belt, playing a native dice game described by Roger Williams, and making wampum Narragansett style are just a few of the New England native crafts described step-by-step in this well-illustrated book. Packed with interesting information, this resource provides examples of crafts that will interest children of all ages.
♦ Making any of the Algonquian crafts described would be an excellent way to involve students in a hands-on activity characteristic of the Rhode Island tribes.
1. Indians of North America—Industries 2. Handicraft—North America.

720.9
A Sense of Place. (Videocassette). WJAR Channel 10 and Fleet National Bank, 1989. VHS, Color, (55 min.). No price available. (Interest level: grade 5-adult).

Noted author and illustrator David Macaulay takes us on a cross-state tour of the various styles of architecture that give Rhode Island a special character. The video tour stresses the heritage of design to be preserved but also illustrates Rhode Island's history
♦ Students can explore the architectural treasures in their own area by visiting old homes and buildings, photographing them, identifying the styles, and researching their history.
1. Architecture, American 2. Architecture—Conservation and restoration.

741.5
Bousquet, Don. *The Quahog Stops Here.* Covered Bridge Press (0-924771-38-0), 1992. Unpaginated. B/W illus. (Interest level: grade 5-adult).

Bousquet's collection of cartoons pokes fun at the peculiarities of the life in Rhode Island by highlighting its people's heritage, dialect, diet, character flaws, and politics. This volume, as well as his earlier Quahog books, is useful in the classroom because it quickly and graphically illustrates topics of concern in the state.
♦ After students brainstorm about what is funny about Rhode Island, they can create their own cartoons and possibly submit them to local publications.
1. Rhode Island—Cartoons and caricatures.

910.45
McCall, Edith. *Pirates and Privateers.* Childrens Press (0-516-03360-3), 1980, 1963. 128p. B/W illus. (Interest level: 3-6).

Among the pirates and privateers who sailed in Rhode Island waters were Captain Kidd and Silas Talbot, whose stories are featured in this collection of adventures. Talbot's story is exciting to read aloud because it illustrates the ingenuity of Rhode Islanders during the Revolutionary War.
♦ Using a Rhode Island or Narragansett Bay map, readers can trace Talbot's route in capturing the *Pigot.* They can research other naval skirmishes in the area and mark them on the map as well.
1. Pirates—United States.

912
Olsen, Stephen. *An Interpretive Atlas of Narragansett Bay.* University of Rhode Island (No ISBN), 1980. 82p. B/W photos; Color illus. (Interest level: grade 6-adult).

Everything students might want to know about Narragansett Bay landforms, storms, ecology, fisheries, shipping, recreation, military functions, and pollution is covered briefly and graphically. The excellent maps and charts present information in an efficient and appealing manner.

♦ The abundance and clarity of graphs in this book provide an excellent introduction to different methods of presenting information. Logarithmic plots, polar plots, hurricane tracking charts, bar charts, cross sections, seasonal variation charts, and all kinds of special maps can be used by the students to gather information.
1. Atlases—Narragansett Bay (R.I.)   2. Atlases—Rhode Island.

912
Rhode Island Puzzle. (Game). Austin Pierce (0-87106-487-1), 1989. Available from Globe Pequot Press. $9.95. (Interest level: 2-4).

This puzzle is a 20-by-13-inch map of Rhode Island, complete with color-coded counties, history, and points of interest, as well as the official state motto, flag, bird, etc. The pieces are large enough to make it easy to put together, and the added information makes the puzzle a high-interest way to learn state geography.
♦ Having students put the puzzle together and read it as they work is a visual and hands-on way learn about the state.
1. Rhode Island—Maps.

912
Tyce, Robert. *The Depths of Narragansett Bay.* (18" × 24" poster). Rhode Island Sea Grant, n.d. $2.50. (Interest level: grade 4-adult).

A computer-generated image, this poster presents the contours of Rhode Island's Narragansett Bay seafloor with colors representing depths. The extraordinary poster introduces students to new methods of mapping and graphically illustrates topographical information.
♦ Students can compare this type of map with traditional navigational maps to determine the kind of information each can give about the bay.
1. Rhode Island—Maps.

912
Wright, Marion. *The Rhode Island Atlas.* R. I. Publications Society (0-917012-19-4), 1982. 239p. B/W photos; Color illus. (Interest level: grade 6-adult).

Wright presents a comprehensive collection of maps and information pertaining to all aspects of Rhode Island: climate, resources, geography, demographics, economy, commerce, agriculture, transportation, history, and recreation. Most of the material is presented visually in thematic maps, charts, and graphs that are easy to understand.
♦ Young people may use the maps and charts from the "Places and Names" chapter to delve into the origin of the place-names in their area. There are charts and maps of Indian names and their meanings, derivations of city and town names, names honoring prominent people, and names derived from natural features.
1. Atlases—Rhode Island.

917.45
Hale, Stuart. *Narragansett Bay: A Friend's Perspective.* URI Sea Grant (0-938412-19-1), 1980. 122p. B/W illus. (Interest level: grade 7-adult).

Narragansett Bay's topography, geology, history, and recreational uses, such as resorts, beaches, parks, and shore dinner halls, are all described in Hale's informative book. Well illustrated with interesting historical photographs, the book conveys the many dimensions of Rhode Island's most prominent physical feature.
♦ The book concludes with questions about the future of the bay. Readers can list all the recreational activities on the bay and write about what could happen to them if measures are not taken to save the bay.
1. Narragansett Bay (R.I.).

917.45
Newport and the Rhode Island Coast. (Videocassette). SITE Productions, 1992. VHS, Color, (45 min.). $19.95. (Interest level: grade 5-adult).

Divided into short segments on Newport colonial history, the Gilded Age, and coastal Rhode Island towns and beaches, this is a video tour of many important historical and recreational sights in the area. Authoritative narration by local historians, preservation specialists, curators, and local residents adds to the authentic flavor of the tour.
♦ Part of the film takes viewers on the walking tour given by the Newport Historical Society, highlighting architecture from the seventeenth century to the present. Imagining themselves living in one of the colonial homes, a mansion, or even a Block Island lighthouse, students could write a description of a tour through their house.
1. Newport (R.I.)—Description and travel   2. Rhode Island—Description and travel.

917.45
Progue, Pamela. *Public Access to the Rhode Island Coast.* University of Rhode Island (0-938412-32-9), 1993. 74p. Color photos and illus. (Interest level: grade 5-adult).

Progue has written a selective guide to public parks, wildlife refuges, beaches, fishing sites, boat ramps, pathways, and views along the 400 miles of Rhode Island coastline. This is an excellent source of detailed local maps and current information that could be used to research possible field trips for bird watching, nature walks, habitat studies, or visits to historical sites.
♦ The class could participate in the "Adopt a Spot" program mentioned in the guide and take a special interest in maintaining and protecting a local pub-

lic access site. Students could keep the area clean and create posters stressing safety tips as well as the public access code of conduct.
1. Rhode Island—Description—Guidebooks.

917.45
Rhode Island: A Picture Book to Remember Her By. Crescent (0-517-62596-2), 1987. Unpaginated. Color photos. (Interest level: 2-6).

Mansion interiors, city scenes, beaches, and sailboats in the harbor are all captured in this slender book of photographs illustrating typical state views. A useful addition to a classroom or library, this expensive publication depicts historical sites, styles of architecture, state attractions, and industries.
◆ Children can cooperatively create their own picture book of Rhode Island by putting together postcards and pictures from brochures.
1. Rhode Island—Pictorial works.

917.45
Smith, Clyde. *Coastal Rhode Island.* Foremost Publications (0-89909-127X), 1987. 128p. Color photos. (Interest level: grade 1-adult).

Rhode Island lighthouses, stone walls, mansions, rocky shorelines, farms, picturesque harbors, and tall ships are some of the highlights featured in this beautiful collection of photographs. The pictures superbly depict the natural features and traditional industries that have shaped the Rhode Island character.
◆ Photographs from this book can be used in illustrating a great number of topics—maritime industries, mills, farm life, stone walls, and architecture. Young people can make a list of local scenes they would photograph if they were trying to portray what was special about their area.
1. Rhode Island—Pictorial works.

917.45
Weber, Ken. *More Walks and Rambles in Rhode Island.* Backcountry Publications (0-88150-224-3), 1992. 175p. B/W illus. (Interest level: grade 4-adult).

Opportunities to experience the Rhode Island of 200 years ago, explore Revolutionary fortifications, walk along an old canal, stroll along a beach, or take a historic city tour are covered in the 40 suggested walks and rambles in the Ocean State. Both this work and the original *Walks and Rambles in Rhode Island* are excellent tools for planning field trips because they specify the best hikes for children and provide clear maps and descriptions of interesting places to ramble for nature and history.
◆ Students may map out and write a description of a good local walking spot. Coastal, rural, and city walks are all modeled in the book.

1. Walking—Rhode Island—Guidebooks
2. Rhode Island—Description and travel.

917.45
Welch, Wally. *Lighthouses of Rhode Island.* Lighthouse Press (0-9618410-0-1), 1987. 34p. Color photos and map. (Interest level: grade 4-adult).

The 24 current lighthouses in the state are portrayed with impressive photographs and brief historical descriptions. Visually pleasing, this book also has a good map of lighthouse locations and the addresses of preservation groups working to safeguard the lighthouses.
◆ Children in Rhode Island can make posters urging the preservation of some of the lighthouses nearby and send them to the group working for that lighthouse. Other children may create models of famous lighthouses and write short narratives to display with their models.
1. Lighthouses—Rhode Island.

952.025
Blumberg, Rhoda. *Commodore Perry in the Land of the Shogun.* Lothrop (0-688-03723-2), 1985. 144p. B/W illus. (Interest level: 4-8).

The focus of Blumberg's history is Newporter Mathew Perry's "Black Ships" voyage in 1853 to open Japanese ports to trade, but the book also provides a wealth of information on the feudal society he encountered. The exquisite illustrations, mostly from Japanese woodcuts done at the time, help convey the cultural shock that resulted from this curious meeting between an isolated people and a modern steamer.
◆ An appendix contains a list of presents for the Japanese that Perry had very carefully selected as representative of U.S. culture. Students can make up a list of presents they would send to Shimodo, Newport's sister city, if they were to select what is typical of our modern culture.
1. United States Naval Expedition to Japan (1852-1954)   2. Perry, Mathew Calbraith, 1794-1858.

970.004
Quiri, Patricia. *The Algonquians.* Franklin Watts (0-531-15633-8), 1992. (A First Book Series). 63p. Color photos and illus. (Interest level: 3-6).

The Rhode Island tribes belong to the larger Algonquian group, and Quiri's brief description focuses on their civilization before contact with whites. This is a good early research book for intermediate readers because it is easy to read and well indexed, has a wonderful glossary, and provides helpful illustrations.
◆ Readers can focus on how much historical paintings and artifacts help us to understand a culture. They can look at the well-chosen illustrations and describe what they think the illustration reveals

about Algonquian culture. They can then read the text to see whether their observations are correct.
1. Algonquian Indians   2. Indians of North America.

973
People of the First Light: Part I, Indians of Southern New England. (Videocassette). WGBH, 1985. VHS, Color, (29 min.). Available on free loan from Rhode Island College Film and Video Library. (Interest level: 3-8).

This overview of modern life for tribes around Rhode Island features Narragansett wampum making, a Wampanoag clambake and pow-wow, Pequot maple syrup gathering, and Micmac basket making. An appealing portrait of a people trying to maintain their culture, the video will generate interest in viewing more in-depth studies with Part 3 (Narragansetts) and Part 7 (Wampanoags).
♦ The Mohegans were the only tribe portrayed that had no tribal land. Class members can discuss how this makes it harder for them to retain their culture.
1. Indians of North America.

973
Sewall, Marcia. *People of the Breaking Day.* Atheneum (0-689-31407-8), 1990. 48p. Color illus. (Interest level: 1-6).

Sewall's wonderfully illustrated picture book gives cultural information on one of Rhode Island's dominant tribes, the Wampanoag. Tribal history, culture, games, traditions, food gathering, and family life are portrayed in a simple and sensitive way.
♦ The dictionary of Wampanoag/Narragansett words provides an excellent basis for a seasonal mural of Native American life. The seasons could be labeled with the Wampanoag/Narragansett words and the students could draw the activities the tribe would have done during that season.
1. Wampanoag Indians   2. Indians of North America.

973.04
Siegel, Beatrice. *Indians of the Northeast Woodlands.* Illus. by William Sauts Bock. Walker (0-8027-8157-8), 1992. 96p. B/W illus. (Interest level: 1-6).

Arranged in simple question-and-answer style, this book explains how Northeast Woodland Indians dressed, farmed, hunted, built villages, and communicated. Here is an excellent introduction to the life of Rhode Island tribes and Siegel gives readers fascinating facts such as how to make wampum or speak a few words in Narragansett.
♦ The chapter "Why Did They Paint Their Faces and Bodies?" includes a chart of the special significance of each color of paint. Even the youngest students would have a great time painting their own faces with symbolic designs.
1. Woodland Indians   2. Algonquian Indians.

973.04
Simmons, William. *The Narragansett.* Chelsea House (1-55546-718-0), 1989. (Indians of North America Series). 111p. B/W and Color photos, illus., and maps. (Interest level: 5-8).

Beginning with tribal origins and ending with life today, this book relates the history of the Narragansett, the dominant tribe of western Rhode Island. Beautifully illustrated, the book contains examples of Narragansett beadwork, interesting items such as the marks of the chiefs, maps and photographs, a chart of Narragansett place-names, a glossary of native words, and bits and pieces of Narrangansett stories.
♦ Writing stories similar to the Narrangansett stories and illustrating them with artwork typical of Narrangansett designs would be an excellent project for older children to make and share with younger children.
1. Narragansett Indians   2. Indians of North America.

973.04
Wilbur, C. Keith. *The New England Indians.* Illus. by author. Globe Pequot Press (0-87106-004-3), 1978. 104p. B/W illus. (Interest level: grade 3-adult).

Detailed drawings of artifacts such as arrowheads, bowls, tools, beads, baskets, decorations, weapons, and clothing make this a sourcebook of information on the everyday life of the indigenous tribes of Rhode Island. This well-illustrated and rich source of facts is fascinating reading on almost any topic from the spirit world to spoons.
♦ To illustrate tribal organization, a class can be grouped into clans with a chief sachem, tribal council, and shaman or medicine man. Class members can design a totem or pendants for their clan based on designs in the book.
1. Indians of North America—New England.

973.3
Wilbur, C. Keith. *Pirates and Patriots of the Revolution.* Globe Pequot Press (0-87106-866-4), 1984. 96p. B/W illus. (Interest level: grade 3-adult).

Wilbur tells how the privateers like Rhode Islander Captain Abraham Whipple became a civilian navy during the Revolutionary War and plundered for patriotism and profit. Well illustrated and filled with fascinating details of seamanship, this is a superb source of information on rigging, shipbuilding, crews, battle strategy, and anything else concerning life at sea.
♦ *Ditty bags, fathoms, quarterdeck, halyards, block and tackle,* and many other terms can be defined and illustrated in a "seafaring dictionary."

1. United States—History—Revolution, 1775-1783—Naval operations 2. Privateering—History—18th century.

974.004
Weinstein-Farson, Laurie. *The Wampanoag.* Chelsea House (1-55546-733-4), 1988. (Indians of North America Series). 96p. B/W and Color photos and illus. (Interest level: 5-8).

The history of the Wampanoag of eastern Rhode Island, including early life, food gathering, family, religion, and struggles for survival, and life for the modern Wampanoag are all covered in this interesting cultural history. One of the book's best features is a craft section that illustrates a rich tradition in pottery design, beadwork, and basket weaving.
♦ The craft section can provide examples for young people to create their own designs in Wampanoag style.
1. Wampanoag Indians—Social life and customs
2. Indians of North America—Wampanoags.

974.4
Peters, Russell. *Clambake—A Wampanoag Tradition.* Lerner (0-8225-2651-4), 1992. (We Are Still Here Series). 48p. Color photos. (Interest level: 4-8).

A 12-year-old Wampanoag learns from his grandfather how to prepare the appanaug (clambake), a ceremony rich in symbolism. Because Wampanoag land stretched to Rhode Island, the history, spirituality, and customs the grandfather shares are part of the state's heritage and give new meaning to a favorite state meal.
♦ One Wampanoag belief the elder shared is that each generation is responsible for keeping the land clean and safe for the next seven generations. The class can create a bulletin board with ideas on how to protect the air, water, and land so that future generations can enjoy the tradition of the appanaug.
1. Wampanoag Indians—Rites and ceremonies
2. Clambakes.

974.5
Aubin, Albert. *The French in Rhode Island.* (Pamphlet). Rhode Island Publications Society (0-917012-97-6), 1988. (Rhode Island Ethnic Heritage Pamphlet Series). 45p. B/W photos. (Interest level: grade 7-adult).

The struggle of the French to preserve their religion, culture, and language rather than be assimilated into Rhode Island society is the subject of this brief history. Their insistence on bilingual education and their clashes with other national groups parallel current issues and make this story all the more relevant and interesting.
♦ Bilingual picture books in French/English would be appropriate to read together because French schools taught subjects in both languages. It might be interesting to see how many students are bilingual or have relatives who are bilingual.
1. Rhode Island—Ethnic groups.

974.5
The Best Place to Live. (Videocassette). Produced for Rhode Island Committee for the Humanities, 1982. VHS, Color, (55 min.). Available on free loan from Rhode Island College Film and Video Library. (Interest level: grade 7-adult).

This film portrays the struggle of Providence's Hmong community to retain its culture despite the trauma of war, misunderstanding of neighbors, poverty, and lack of a written language. The film is graphic in its portrayal of ritual animal sacrifices, but such realism and the words of the Hmong themselves serve to illustrate the conflicts of cultures.
♦ Hmong weddings, birth ceremonies, and funerals are all depicted in the film. Viewers can compare their customs with those of this refugee group.
1. Rhode Island—Ethnic groups.

974.5
Carpenter, Allan. *Rhode Island.* Childrens Press (0-516-04139-8), 1978. (New Enchantment of America Series). 96p. Color photos and illus. (Interest level: 4-8).

Carpenter offers a good general introduction to Rhode Island, with information on early history, industry, natural resources and cultural topics. The chapter on "Creative Rhode Islanders" which details their creations and accomplishments, is especially good for biographical research.
♦ The "Creative Rhode Islanders" chapter might inspire students to design a bulletin board display of famous Rhode Islanders and their accomplishments. Young people can match Rhode Islanders with their creations and achievements.
1. Rhode Island.

974.5
Conley, Patrick. *An Album of Rhode Island History, 1636-1986.* Rhode Island Publications Society (0-898655-513-7), 1986. B/W photos, illus., and maps. (Interest level: grade 7-adult).

A wealth of photographs, maps, facsimiles of documents, old advertisements, and drawings makes this pictorial history a visual source of information on all aspects of Rhode Island history. This browsing book invites the student to study the pictures and read the lengthy captions for information on important Rhode Islanders who may not be well known.
♦ Using any one of the historic photos, young people might make up a story about what was happening or what life was like or research events that led up to and followed the photo.
1. Rhode Island—History—Pictorial works.

974.5
Conley, Patrick. *The Irish in Rhode Island.* (Pamphlet). Rhode Island Publications (0-917012-83-6), 1986. (Rhode Island Ethnic Heritage Pamphlet Series). 46p. B/W photos. (Interest level: grade 7-adult).

This pamphlet chronicles how the Irish came to Rhode Island in flight from famine, the discrimination they faced, and how they strived for political power and financial security. Filled with information on noted Irish Rhode Islanders, the work helps us to understand the struggles of the Irish and the contributions they have made to the state.
♦ Students can use the names and dates listed to make a time line of famous Irish Americans and their contributions. It would be especially interesting to note how long it takes from the famine migrations to when the Irish hold places of importance in politics, economics, and culture.
1. Rhode Island—Ethnic groups.

974.5
Conley, Patrick. *Rhode Island Profile.* Rhode Island Publications Society (0-917012-40-2), 1982. 60p. B/W maps. (Interest level: grade 7-adult).

This slender reference source supplies quick information on a variety of Rhode Island topics. Conley has compiled an excellent source of data on cities, towns, and villages in Rhode Island.
♦ Students can work cooperatively to create their own gazetteer of Rhode Island by using the chart on towns, cities, and places, which includes information on original names, boundaries, size, history, etc. The gazetteer could be in booklet form with five teams of students working on the five Rhode Island counties.
1. Rhode Island—History.

974.5
Conley, Patrick. *Rhode Island's Road to Liberty.* Rhode Island Publications Society (0-917012-85-2), 1991. Unpaginated. B/W photos. (Interest level: grade 7-adult).

Eleven documents important to Rhode Island history, including the original Patent, Royal Charter, and Emancipation of Rhode Island Slaves, are presented in facsimile form. This is a valuable collection of primary sources, and the brief commentaries included are helpful in understanding the documents' impact on Rhode Island history.
♦ Discrimination in Rhode Island is an interesting issue to explore and debate using the documents as a source of information. Students can use the documents to make a time line of when Catholics, Jews, Blacks, and the poorer classes were given citizenship rights.
1. Rhode Island—History.

974.5
Cunha, M. Rachel. *The Portuguese in Rhode Island.* (Pamphlet). Rhode Island Publications Society (0-17012-72-0), 1985. (Rhode Island Ethnic Heritage Pamphlet Series). 33p. B/W photos. (Interest level: grade 7-adult).

Portuguese explorers in Rhode Island, colonial Sephardic Jews in Newport, and especially the lives of today's hardworking immigrants are covered in this brief pamphlet. The well-written pamphlet is especially sensitive to the Portuguese focus on extended family and how that has had an impact on immigration and life in Rhode Island.
♦ The Portuguese community's focus on family, illustrated in this pamphlet, can lead to some discussions with children of what a family is and the importance of extended family in our society.
1. Rhode Island—Ethnic groups.

974.5
Davis, Hadassah. *History You Can See.* Rhode Island Publications Society (0-917012-81-X), 1985. 184p. B/W photos and illus. (Interest level: grade 6-adult).

Focusing on nineteenth-century Rhode Island life, this book gives background to historic sites to visit in Providence, Slatersville, Pawtucket, Bristol, Foster, Peace Dale, east Greenwich, Woonsocket, Cumberland, Warwick, and Newport. The book encourages students to visit the places discussed and it provides a wealth of material to make the visit a meaningful experience.
♦ Visiting one of the sites covered is the recommended use of this book. Students may create their own book of historical places in their town or state using the format of this book as a guide.
1. Rhode Island—History.

974.5
Dearden, Paul. *The Rhode Island Campaign of 1778.* Rhode Island Publications Society (0-917012-17-8), 1980. 169p. B/W illus. (Interest level: grade 7-adult).

Serious research into the Revolutionary War in Rhode Island is aided by this detailed account of the British occupation of Newport culminating in the Battle of Rhode Island. Primary source material from diaries and letters and vivid battle descriptions make this period of history come alive for researchers.
♦ This source is best used as a reference and research tool for students studying the Revolutionary period, the "Black Regiment," and military leaders such as Greene, Lafayette, and d'Estaing.
1. Rhode Island—History—Revolution, 1775-1783.

974.5
Foster, Geraldine. *The Jews in Rhode Island.* (Pamphlet). Rhode Island Publications Society (0-917012-80-1), 1985. (Rhode Island Ethnic Heritage Pamphlet Series). 48p. B/W photos. (Interest level: grade 7-adult).

Beginning with the first Jewish settlers in 1658, this work traces the history of the Jewish community in Rhode Island and its new growth during the twentieth century. Filled with anecdotes of Jewish life in the state, this pamphlet is enjoyable to read as well as informative.
♦ The recollections of the sights and sounds of a Jewish neighborhood around 1900 are an excellent example of the value of recording the memories of our older citizens. Grandparents, senior citizens' groups, and town elders can be interviewed on tape to record what life was like in Rhode Island neighborhoods when they were growing up.
1. Rhode Island—Ethnic groups.

974.5
Fradin, Dennis. *The Rhode Island Colony.* Childrens Press (0-516-00391-7), 1989. 160p. B/W illus. (Interest level: 4-8).

Fradin traces the history of Rhode Island from exploration to statehood and covers interesting topics such as pirates, the slave and triangle trade, and constitutional debates. Excellent biographical sketches of famous Rhode Islanders Roger Williams, Anne Hutchinson, Stephen and Esek Hopkins, King Philip, and Abraham Whipple make this one of the best reference sources on colonial times and influential people.
♦ The reproductions of Rhode Island documents such as indenture papers and the king's proclamation on the burning of the Gaspee can be used to introduce young people to primary documents.
1. Rhode Island—History—Colonial period, ca 1600-1755.

974.5
Fradin, Dennis. *Rhode Island in Words and Pictures.* Childrens Press (0-516-03939-3), 1981. 47p. Color photos. (Interest level: 2-4).

Information on Rhode Island history, geography, towns, and famous citizens is included in this brief and easy-to-read book. Clear maps, easy time lines and fact sheets make this a good reference source for beginning readers.
♦ Young students can make an easy trivia game from information given in the "Facts about Rhode Island" section. It lists such interesting facts as the coldest temperature, highest point, and greatest distance east to west and north to south.
1. Rhode Island.

974.5
Heinrichs, Ann. *Rhode Island.* Childrens Press (0-516-00485-9), 1990. (America the Beautiful Series). 144p. Color photos and illus. (Interest level: 4-8).

Heinrichs presents an excellent overview of the state covering geography, history, government, economy, culture, historic sites, and famous people. The "Facts at a Glance" feature provides quick access to interesting information and the "A Tour of the Ocean State" chapter is a wonderful guide to places of interest.
♦ Travel brochures for each of the interesting places listed in "A Tour of the Ocean State" could be produced by students working cooperatively. The students could also plan field trips to Rhode Island sites, listing how to get there, what they would see, and how the places could tie into what they have been studying in class.
1. Rhode Island.

974.5
Lind, Louise. *The Southeast Asians in Rhode Island.* (Pamphlet). Rhode Island Publications (0-917012-86-0), 1989. (Rhode Island Ethnic Heritage Pamphlet Series). 37p. B/W photos. (Interest level: grade 5-adult).

This pamphlet is an introduction to the Vietnamese, Cambodian, Hmong, and Laotian refugees in the state and their hardships—the trauma of war memories, language barriers, cultural misunderstandings, and poverty. Lind's is a particularly sensitive portrait of the people with practical details on customs that greatly add to understanding their cultures.
♦ The custom of the Hmong pan dau is an example of a project children could design and make on paper or cloth.
1. Rhode Island—Ethnic groups.

974.5
A Lively Experiment. (Videocassette). Rhode Island Committee for the Humanities, 1986. VHS, Color, (50 min.). Available on free loan from Rhode Island College Film and Video Library. (Interest level: 4-8).

Short segments featuring historical figures such as Roger Williams and landmarks such as Slater's Mill are loosely woven together to present an overview of Rhode Island history. The brevity of the segments and the "you are there" feel of the production make this interesting and informative for intermediate students.
♦ Imitating the style of this video, young people can assume the character of historical figures they have researched and tell the story of what went on in Rhode Island during their time period. The various skits can be videotaped or presented in play form.
1. Rhode Island—History.

974.5
McLoughlin, William. *Rhode Island: A History.* Norton (0-393-30271-7), 1986. 240p. B/W photos and illus. (Interest level: grade 7-adult).

McLoughlin's authoritative and comprehensive survey of the history of the state includes a brief guide to historical locations. The book is well indexed, interesting to read, and filled with insights into the development of the "Rhode Island" qualities of individualism, resilience, and ingenuity.
- ♦ Because this source has a little information on a variety of topics, students can use it to provide background for their research and to gain a general understanding of what was happening during a particular era.

1. Rhode Island—History.

974.5
Millar, John. *Rhode Island: Forgotten Leader of the Revolutionary Era.* Providence Journal (No ISBN), 1975. 64p. B/W illus. (Interest level: 3-6).

Rhode Island's pre-Revolutionary cultural leadership, first moves toward rebellion, and fight for independence are covered in this picture book with simple line drawings and short explanations. The variety of topics, characters, and incidents covered and the wonderful illustrations make this a great source for intermediate students.
- ♦ A list of more than 50 Rhode Islanders prominent in the Revolution suggests that readers find out more about one or more of them. There is also a terrific list of important dates that could form the basis of a Revolutionary War time line.

1. Rhode Island—History—Revolution, 1775-1783.

974.5
Narragansett Bay. (Videocassette). Save the Bay (No ISBN), 1986. VHS, Color, (45 min.). Available on free loan from Rhode Island College Film and Video Library. (Interest level: 5-8).

The importance of the bay to the state's history, economy, and recreation from Indian times to the present is stressed in this documentary. In an interesting and factual manner, it conveys the unique qualities of the bay and encourages efforts to preserve it for future generations.
- ♦ After viewing this film, children can discuss what they can do to contribute to the "Save the Bay" effort. Writing slogans for posters, collecting litter along the shoreline, and other class activities might come out of this discussion. Students could also create a campaign for conservation or against pollution in their community and publicize their efforts through the local news media.

1. Narragansett Bay.

974.5
Ramus, Daniel. *Connecticut and Rhode Island Trivia.* Rutledge Hill (1-555853-067-3), 1990. 191p. (Interest level: grade 4-adult).

Rhode Island trivia and Connecticut trivia are mixed and topically arranged in chapters about geography, history, the arts, sports, and science. It is a little tedious to identify the Rhode Island questions, but the questions are interesting and will entice students to research the answers.
- ♦ Weekly Rhode Island trivia contests can reward children who figure out the answers and verify their sources. The trivia could be part of regular bulletin board displays. With the variety of topics covered in this book, an end of the year activity could be a game of Rhode Island Jeopardy.

1. Rhode Island—Miscellanea 2. Connecticut—Miscellanea.

974.5
Santoro, Carmela. *The Italians in Rhode Island.* (Pamphlet). Rhode Island Publications Society (0-917012-92-5), 1990. (Rhode Island Ethnic Heritage Pamphlet Series). 53p. B/W photos and illus. (Interest level: grade 7-adult).

Although this story begins with Verrazano's explorations in 1524, most of the pamphlet is concerned with twentieth-century Italian settlements, churches, social groups, and contributions to Rhode Island society. Here is an interesting look at the importance of support groups, such as ethnic parishes, neighborhoods, and cultural societies, in helping Italians rise to prominence in the state.
- ♦ In the style of Italian feasts, students can observe an Italian heritage day with the music, foods, dances, and games that are part of this ethnic tradition.

1. Rhode Island—Ethnic groups.

974.5
Schroder, Walter. *Defenses of Narrangansett Bay in World War II.* Rhode Island Bicentennial Foundation (0-917012-22-4), 1980. 131p. B/W photos. (Interest level: grade 6-adult).

Rhode Island's special role in World War II, the production of PT boats, the ingenuity of the Quonset Hut, the battle against German U-boats, and top secret missions with German POWs are all chronicled in this history of the military facilities in the state. Filled with photographs and based on first-hand accounts, the book gives students a unique sense of the war at home.
- ♦ How close did the battle get to Rhode Island shores? Readers can use the listing of sunken merchant ships and the accounts of undersea warfare to plot the sightings of U-boats.

1. Rhode Island—History—World War, 1939-1945.

974.5
Thompson, Kathleen. *Rhode Island*. Raintree (0-86514-457-5), 1987. (Portrait of America Series). 48p. B/W and Color photos and illus. (Interest level: 3-6).

"Rhode Island" qualities such as creativity, solidarity, and preservation, along with the darker aspects of Rhode Island history such as slavery, discrimination, and corruption, are the focus of this slender volume. Quotes from Rhode Islanders about their own lives help make this book a balanced and contemporary view of the state.
♦ Students can cooperatively create a time line of special moments in Rhode Island history using the chart "Important Historical Events in Rhode Island," found at the back of the book. Pairs of students can research events such as the "Dorr War" and the "Bloodless Rebellion" to explore why these were turning points in developing the "Rhode Island" character.
1. Rhode Island.

974.5
Warner, J. F. *Rhode Island*. Lerner (0-8225-2731-6), 1993. (Hello USA Series). 72p. B/W and Color photos. (Interest level: 3-6).

Warner's introduction to Rhode Island for the intermediate reader presents current information on the state's geography, history, economy, social conditions, and environment. Visually attractive to young readers, the book is up-to-date and includes "hot topics" such as efforts to protect the environment.
♦ Young people can use the excellent listings of Rhode Island endangered species to begin research on local plants and animals in need of protection in their own community or state. Data can be presented in poster or booklet form.
1. Rhode Island—History   2. Rhode Island—Social life and customs.

974.52
Conley, Patrick. *Providence, a Pictorial History*. Donning (0-89865-128-X), 1982. 247p. B/W photos, illus., and maps. (Interest level: grade 7-adult).

Richly illustrated with photographs, maps, and drawings, this history focuses on the city founded by Roger Williams, expanded by colonial merchants, and transformed by the Industrial Revolution, now struggling to meet the needs of its multicultural population. Providence's history mirrors that of the state, and this book is an excellent visual presentation and reference source of people and places important to Rhode Island.
♦ Browsing through the pictures, students can create a history of transportation in the state featuring clipper ships, steamboats, ox-carts, buggies, railroads, and trolleys.
1. Providence (R.I.)—Description—Views
2. Providence (R.I.)—History—Pictorial works.

974.56
Jefferys, C. P. D. *Newport: A Short History*. Newport Historical Society (0-9633200-0-9), 1992. 101p. B/W photos and illus. (Interest level: grade 6-adult).

Newport, the colonial seaport, the queen of resorts, and the jewel of the preservation movement, is described in this historical overview. Anecdotes, interesting illustrations, and an informal writing style make this an engaging case history of a Rhode Island city that has changed with the times but preserved its heritage.
♦ Preserving its architectural treasures has become a Newport tradition. Using the illustrations in this book and descriptions of architectural styles, readers can identify the styles of historic city buildings.
1. Newport (R.I.)—History.

974.56
Warburton, Eileen. *In Living Memory: A Chronicle of Newport, Rhode Island, 1888-1988*. Newport Savings and Loan (0-917012-89-5), 1988. 177p. B/W photos. (Interest level: grade 6-adult).

Warburton's browsing book, with a detailed narrative and over 100 historical photographs, traces the history of Newport from the Gilded Age to the present. Because it is one of the few histories that focuses on the modern period, this book is an excellent study of the Rhode Island experience of boom and depression, devastating hurricanes, the war effort, and preservation of the past.
♦ Young people can compare some of the photographs of the same locations over time, such as the King's Park area in 1905 and in 1988, and decide what has changed and what the pictures reveal about those periods in history.
1. Newport (R.I.)—History.

Biography

920
Fontaine, Marie. *Puritans, Pioneers and Pacesetters: Eight People Who Shaped Rhode Island*. Illus. by Bill Morrison. Old Stone Bank (No ISBN), 1986. 48p. Color illus. (Interest level: 1-4).

Brief biographies of explorer Verrazano, founder Roger Williams, founder Anne Hutchinson, governor Samuel Cranston, artist Edward Bannister, lighthouse keeper Ida Lewis, singer Sussieretta Jones, and storyteller Princess Red Wing are featured. The short, factual, and interesting chapters have just enough information to capture the attention of younger readers and listeners.
♦ Older students could use the biographies as the basis for skits on famous Rhode Islanders. The book is also appropriate as read-aloud material for units on Rhode Island history, because it in-

cludes noteworthy people from all eras of Rhode Island's history.
1. Rhode Island—Biography.

92 Hutchinson, Anne
Fradin, Dennis. *Anne Hutchinson: Fighter for Religious Freedom.* Enslow (0-89490-229-6), 1990. 48p. B/W photos. (Interest level: 2-4).

Fradin has written a simple introduction to one of Rhode Island's founders, Anne Hutchinson, covering her life in England and Boston and her banishment to Portsmouth, Rhode Island, in 1638. An excellent introduction to the concept of religious freedom, this book also provides a glossary with easy-to-understand definitions of words associated with early founders such as the Pilgrims, Puritans, and Separatists.
♦ The glossary is an excellent vocabulary lesson, and children can match the groups of early settlers who came for religious reasons with terms that would describe them.
1. Hutchinson, Anne, 1591-1643 2. Puritans—Biography.

92 Hutchinson, Anne
IlgenFritz, Elizabeth. *Anne Hutchinson.* Chelsea House (1-55546-660-5), 1991. (American Women of Achievement Series). 110p. B/W illus. (Interest level: grade 7-adult).

Anne Hutchinson and her followers were founders of the Rhode Island colony, and this biography provides the background to why these early settlers sought refuge in the area. Hutchinson's religious views and those of the Puritan ministers she opposed are difficult to understand, but this book offers excellent explanations of their differences and why she was banished.
♦ Young people can debate whether Anne Hutchinson was banished for her religious beliefs or for being an outspoken woman, using the portions of trial transcripts to argue either side of the debate.
1. Hutchinson, Anne, 1591-1643.

92 Philip, Sachem of the Wampanoags
Cwikik, Robert. *King Philip and the War with the Colonists.* Silver Burdett (0-382-09573-1), 1989. (Alvin Josephy Biography of American Indian Series). 132p. B/W photos and illus. (Interest level: 5-8).

Cwikik tells the story of Philip, a Wampanoag leader, and the tragic tale of how cultural conflicts led to one of the bloodiest episodes in Rhode Island history—King Philip's War. Although the account of Philip's childhood is fictionalized, this book's strength is that it provides a Native American view of the early dealings with white people and the misunderstandings that arose.
♦ Readers could compare the traditional Thanksgiving accounts from the Pilgrims' perspective with that of Native Americans. Half of the students could write journal accounts as if they were Pilgrims and the others as if they were Wampanoags.
1. Philip, Sachem of the Wampanoags, 1639?-1676 2. Wampanoag Indians—Biography 3. King Philip's War.

92 Philip, Sachem of the Wampanoags
Fradin, Dennis B. *King Philip: Indian Leader.* Enslow (0-89490-231-8), 1990. (Colonial Profile Series). 48p. B/W illus. and maps. (Interest level: 3-6).

This easy-to-read biography of Metacomet (Philip) includes a short history of the Wampanoag and their dealings with the Pilgrims until the end of King Philip's War. The author tries to represent both Pilgrim and Native American views in the disputes and is partially successful.
♦ There are excellent maps illustrating Wampanoag, Narragansett, Sakonnet, and Poccaset lands in Rhode Island. By taking an outline map of Rhode Island or New England and shading in tribal lands, students will gain a better understanding of where the tribes were located.
1. Philip, Sachem of the Wampanoags, 1639?-1676 2. Wampanoag Indians—Biography 3. King Philip's War, 1675-1676.

92 Philip, Sachem of the Wampanoags
Roman, Joseph. *King Philip.* Chelsea House (0-7910-1704-4), 1992. (North American Indians of Achievement Series). 112p. B/W illus. (Interest level: 6-8).

King Philip's leadership is the focus of this biography and extensive account of the battles between settlers and tribes that came to be called King Philip's War. The author presents young adult readers with a well written and fairly balanced view of a bloody, controversial period in Rhode Island history.
♦ Young people can compare the ways Rhode Island and Massachusetts colonists related to native tribes.They could debate whether King Philip's War would have occurred if Rhode Isand's peace initiatives had been successful.
1. Philip, Sachem of the Wampanoags, 1639?-1676 2. King Philip's War, 1675-1676 3. Wampanoag Indians—Biography.

92 Slater, Samuel
Simonds, Christopher. *Samuel Slater's Mill and the Industrial Revolution.* Silver Burdett (0-382-09951-6), 1990. (Turning Points in American History Series). 64p. B/W and Color photos and illus. (Interest level: 4-8).

When Samuel Slater emigrated to Rhode Island in 1789, he carried in his head the blueprints for machines that would bring the Industrial Revolution

to the United States. In a clear and concise way, this biography chronicles Slater's role in U.S. urbanization, the impact of the factory system on workers, and the growth of U.S. manufacturing.
♦ Slater began his mill with nine children. Students can research the following questions: What was life like for children in the mills? How did child labor impact families? How good are child labor laws today?
1. Slater, Samuel, 1768-1835   2. Industrialists—Biography.

Fiction

Avi. *The Man Who Was Poe*. Avon Books (0-380-71192-3), 1989. 213p. (Interest level: 5-8).

A frail boy named Edmund roams the streets of Providence in 1848 looking for his missing twin sister when a mysterious stranger who calls himself Auguste Dupin offers to help. Readers are treated to a mix of historical fact and fiction in this curious story based on Edgar Allan Poe's visit to Providence the year before he died.
♦ After reading this book, young people can do their own research into Poe's life and visit to Rhode Island. They can use this biographical research to write a short story based on historical fact.
1. Poe, Edgar Allan—Fiction.

Avi. *Something Upstairs: A Tale of Ghosts*. Orchard Books (0-531-05782-8), 1988. 120p. (Interest level: 4-7).

When Kenny moves into an old Providence house, he is lured into a quest for the killer of a teenage slave who died 100 years earlier. This thrilling story, a combination of mystery, historical fiction, and ghost story, takes the reader back to a time of slavery and militant abolitionists.
♦ Students can use the names and events mentioned in the novel as a starting point for research on Rhode Island's role in the slave trade and the work of abolitionists like Moses Brown. Students will begin to understand how much research is involved in writing historical fiction.
1. Ghosts—Fiction   2. Slavery—Fiction   3. Space and time—Fiction.

Avi. *The True Confessions of Charlotte Doyle*. Orchard Books (0-531-08493-0), 1990. 215p. (Interest level: 5-8).

Thirteen-year-old Charlotte is the only passenger sailing aboard the *Seahawk* to Providence in 1832, and the journey suddenly becomes perilous when the crew mutinies against a ruthless captain. This is an exciting story to read aloud because Charlotte's descriptions of her hardships and adventures make the voyage come alive.
♦ At the back of the book are a diagram of a brig such as the *Seahawk* and an explanation of ship's time. Readers can make enlarged posters of the ship and watch schedules and follow the diagram as the story is read aloud.
1. Sea stories.

Fleischman, Paul. *Saturnalia*. Harper (0-06-021913-0), 1990. 113p. (Interest level: 6-8).

Captured from his Rhode Island home six years before, 14-year-old apprentice William roams the streets of Boston searching for members of his Narragansett family. This story presents a vivid account of life for apprentices and those in colonial trades such as printers, wigmakers, lens grinders, and carvers.
♦ William decides to be a rememberer, a preserver of his Narragansett heritage. Children can gather local traditions and lore to make a remembering and preserving book to share with others.
1. Narragansett Indians—Fiction   2. Apprentices—Fiction.

Jennings, Paulla. *Strawberry Thanksgiving*. Illus. by Ramona Peters. Modern Curriculum Press (0-8136-2287-5), 1992. 23p. Color photos and illus. (Interest level: K-3).

When young Adam and his sister scuffle while getting ready for the tribal feast of Strawberry Thanksgiving, their grandmother shares a traditional Narragansett/Wampanoag story that reminds them that this festival is a time for forgiveness. The Native American author and illustrator have produced a beautiful picture book, which gives a glimpse of modern tribal life while providing a poignant lesson in family relationships.
♦ Children could paint a smooth rock like the one Adam gave to his sister as a peace offering.
1. Indians of North America—Fiction.

McNulty, Faith. *Hurricane*. Illus. by Gail Ownes. Harper (0-06-024143-8), 1983. 45p. B/W illus. (Interest level: 3-6).

Rhode Island author McNulty chronicles a common experience for many state families—surviving a hurricane. This fictional account will bring back memories of making preparations, losing power, worrying about safety, and coping with destruction.
♦ Because hurricanes are such a typical experience in the state, this is an excellent topic for oral history. Students can tape-record older family members' recollections of the Great Hurricane of 1938, and students themselves can relate what happened to their own property and families during Hurricane Bob.
1. Hurricanes—Fiction.

Manes, Stephen. *Some of the Adventures of Rhode Island Red*. Illus. by William Joyce. Harper (0-397-

32347-6), 1990. 117p. B/W illus. (Interest level: 4-8).

Raised in a hen house, egg-sized Rhode Island Red stands up for the rights of his fowl friends and rescues them from tyrannical farmers, crafty foxes, and shifty politicians. Perfect for reading aloud, this tongue-in-cheek story will delight listeners and readers with a tall-tale hero well suited for the smallest state.
♦ Further adventures of Rhode Island Red can be written by young people with the exaggeration, setting, and superhuman qualities typical of tall tales. (The author even suggests that Red whipped Paul Bunyan, John Henry, and Pecos Bill all at once.)
1. Chickens—Fiction 2. Rhode Island—Fiction.

Monjo, F. N. *Slater's Mill.* Simon (0-671-61578-1), 1973 (out of print). 78p. B/W illus. (Interest level: 4-8).

Samuel Slater immigrated to Rhode Island in 1789 with a knowledge of textile machines and with his partner Moses Brown. Slater launched the state and the nation into the Industrial Revolution. This fictionalized account is filled with good information on state history, the Brown family, inventions, and textile manufacturers.
♦ Slater's success was based on his knowledge of the new inventions of his day. Pairs of students can research the inventors and inventions mentioned in the book and cooperatively make a flowchart of how these innovations were related.
1. Slater, Samuel, 1768-1835—Fiction.

Rand, Gloria. *Salty Dog.* Illus. by Ted Rand. Holt (0-8050-0837-3), 1989. Unpaginated. Color illus. (Interest level: K-2).

Rands's picture book follows the adventures of a puppy as he grows up in a boat yard, travels by ferry, and prepares to sail around the world with his master. The setting is not specified, but realistic illustrations give young students a good look at the traditional Rhode Island craft of boat building, and the book gives a brief introduction to sailing vocabulary.
♦ Sailing words (ferry, life vest, charts, and compass) can be used as vocabulary words. The story ends with Salty Dog and his owner Zack setting out to sail around the world. Students can use the vocabulary in stories they write about Salty's adventures at sea.
1. Dogs—Fiction 2. Boats and boating—Fiction 3. Sailboats—Fiction.

Rodgers, Richard and **Hammerstein, Oscar.** *A Real Nice Clambake.* Illus. by Nadine Westcott. Little, Brown (0-316-75422-6), 1992. 32p. Color illus. (Interest level: K-2).

Based on a song from the musical "Carousel," this lively picture book presents the sights and sounds of a Rhode Island tradition—the clambake. Young children will be delighted by the brightly colored illustrations bordered by clambake ingredients and the words that mimic the Yankee dialect of days gone by.
♦ The music is included in the book, and students can learn to sing the song. They could also draw their own pictures depicting a clambake they have attended or a picnic on the beach.
1. Songs and music—United States 2. New England—Songs and music 3. Beaches—Songs and music.

Weller, Frances. *Matthew Wheelock's Wall.* Illus. by Ted Lewin. Macmillan (0-20-792612-5), 1992. Unpaginated. Color illus. (Interest level: K-3).

Matthew Wheelock lovingly prepares the ground, drags the rock, and builds a stone wall that will be his monument and his gift to future generations. Walls like his are fixtures in the Rhode Island countryside, and this realistically illustrated picture book will help children understand the continuity with past generations.
♦ Children can draw a stone wall with one side of the wall depicting the countryside in Matthew's day and the other a modern scene.
1. New England—Fiction.

Zolotown, Charlotte. *The Seashore Book.* Illus. by Wendell Minor. Harper (0-06-020213-0), 1992. Unpaginated. Color illus. (Interest level: K-2).

In this beautiful picture book a mother helps her son imagine what it is like at the seashore. The setting is indefinite, but the realism of the illustrations and the eloquence of the prose reflect the sights, sounds, tastes, and smells of a day on the Rhode Island shore.
♦ Students can imagine spending a day at their favorite seashore. They could write and illustrate what they imagine, using the descriptive language of this book as an example.
1. Seashore—Fiction 2. Imagination—Fiction 3. Mothers and sons—Fiction.

Periodicals

317.3
Journal-Bulletin Rhode Island Almanac. Providence Journal Bulletin (ISSN 0731-5511), 1993. Annual. (Interest level: grade 6-adult).

This is the best source for current Rhode Island information and statistics on government, towns, laws and regulations, population, economics, employment, libraries, education, weather, sports, social organizations, and more. Well indexed and easy

to use, the almanac can provide facts for almost any Rhode Island topic.
♦ Students can use the addresses and descriptions of community and government organizations as part of letter writing projects. They could write to professional organizations for information on careers or request pamphlets from service or health organizations.
1. Rhode Island—Almanacs.

974.5
Old Rhode Island. Nostalgia Publishing (No ISSN). Monthly. B/W and Color illus. (Interest level: grade 5-adult).

Each issue is filled with Rhode Island historical sketches, anecdotes, poems, recipes, photographs, trivia, and other items of local interest. Well written and reseached by some of the best Rhode Island authors, this is a treasure trove of information presented in a manner students will enjoy.
♦ After browsing through several issues of the magazine, young people could get ideas for their own Rhode Island poems, artwork, local trivia, and recipes to submit for publication.
1. Rhode Island.

974.5
Rhode Island Monthly. Narragansett Media (ISSN 1041-1380). Monthly. Color illus. (Interest level: grade 5-adult).

Current Rhode Island people, politics, places, entertainment, and special events are highlighted in this attractive magazine. Outstanding photographs of state scenery and monthly features such as the "Almanac," "Rhode Island Scene" (trivia), and "Neighbors" (biographical sketches of Rhode Islanders) make this a useful classroom resource.
♦ The "Best of Rhode Island" is a popular yearly feature which judges the best aspects of the state, from beaches to bookstores. Students can use this as a model for the "best" in their community. Students could also write a letter to the editor of the magazine and possibly have it published.
1. Rhode Island.

Vermont

by Helene W. Lang

Nonfiction

371.8
Montgomery, Constance. *Vermont School Bus Ride*. Crossroads Press (No ISBN), 1974. 32p. B/W photos. (Interest level: K-2).

An easy reader, this book describes school bus travel in rural Vermont in all types of weather. Useful and appropriate for children in rural areas who ride school buses, this is a fun and familiar book.
♦ Young people could write about or orally describe their own school bus ride.
1. Vermont   2. School buses.

508.743
Rood, Ronald. *Vermont: A Nature Guide*. New England Press (0-933050-56-9), 1988. 215p. B/W illus. (Interest level: 4-8).

With knowledge, wit, and a practiced eye, Rood takes the reader on a hike with this field guide to the natural world. A naturalist and a teacher, the author brings his expertise in both areas to this guide.
♦ Students can take a nature hike in their own community and observe and record nature.
1. Natural history—Vermont—Guidebooks.

508.743
Rood, Ronald. *Vermont Life Book of Nature*. Stephen Press, 1967. 188p. B/W photos and illus. (Interest level: K-8).

This book, which features special animals, seasons, and locations in Vermont, presents facts and principles of nature in an interesting style. Visuals and text are well balanced in a very thorough and comprehensive resource.
♦ Children might choose one of the animals or locations presented in this book and conduct further research for an oral report to the class.
1. Nature   2. Vermont.

574.1
Rood, Ronald. *Who Wakes the Ground Hog?* Norton (0-393-08524-4), 1973. 206p. B/W illus. (Interest level: 4-8).

On an extensive field trip from a Vermont spring to a Vermont winter, Rood explains how every living thing encountered is at the right place at the right time, and how each fits into the great scheme of things. Information is presented with humor, so the reader learns a most pleasant lesson without realizing it.
♦ Each student can select one bird, bug, animal, or plant and study it over time, observing seasonal changes.
1. Nature   2. Vermont.

591.92
Arnosky, Jim. *Otters under Water*. Putnam (0-399-22339-8), 1992. 24p. Color illus. (Interest level: K-2).

True-to-life glimpses of two young otters swimming, playing, and feeding in a sunlit pond under the watchful eye of their mother are provided. Children enjoy learning about wildlife when the animal's lives are paralleled with their own.
♦ Students might enjoy reading other books in this series, including books about deer, muskrats, raccoons, and foxes.
1. Otters.

599
Arnosky, Jim. *Crinkleroot's Book of Animal Tracking*. Bradbury Press (0-02-705851-4), 1979. 48p. B/W and Color illus. (Interest level: 3-5).

Arnosky explains how to find and understand the signs made by animals around water, in the woods, and in the snow. Clear drawings allow accurate identification.
♦ Young people could observe animal signs in nature and make drawings of different animal signs to share with the class.
1. Animal tracks   2. Tracking and trailing.

599
Arnosky, Jim. *Crinkleroot's Book of Animal Tracks and Wildlife Signs.* Longman (0-399-20663-9), 1979. 48p. Color illus. (Interest level: 3-5).

Crinkleroot gives a folksy introduction to the habits, habitats, and hoof, paw, and claw prints of a variety of wild critters. Children's curiosity about the natural world will be well satisfied.
♦ Take a nature walk so that young people can identify animal tracks in nature.
1. Animal tracks.

630
Gibbons, Gail. *Farming.* Holiday House (0-8234-0682-2), 1988. 32p. Color illus. (Interest level: K-2).

With simple text and illustrations, the book introduces farming and the work done on a farm throughout the seasons. The subject of this book may be especially familiar to Vermont children but is appropriate for all children.
♦ Students can select one of the seasons and research more fully the activities that occur on a farm during that season.
1. Agriculture   2. Farm life   3. Farms.

630
Graff, Nancy Price. *The Strength of the Hills: A Portrait of a Family Farm.* Little, Brown (0-316-32277-6), 1989. 80p. (Interest level: 4-7).

This is the story of life on the Nelson farm, and of the kinds of work it takes to tend and hold on to one small piece of the earth, generation after generation. Graff offers an honest portrayal of the hardships and rewards of working on a farm.
♦ Class members can study further the demise of the family farm and conduct a panel discussion on the topic.
1. Family farm—Vermont   2. Farm life.

630
Montgomery, Constance and **Montgomery, Raymond.** *Vermont Farm and the Sun.* Vermont Crossroads Press (0-915248-01-8), 1975. 32p. B/W photos. (Interest level: K-1).

This photo essay, with a brief text for beginning readers, uses the farm to introduce the concept of energy. Large, realistic photographs enhance a very easy beginner book.
♦ Students can conduct further science experiments about energy, perhaps using the energy of sunlight to grow seeds.
1. Farming   2. Energy.

636.089
Jaspersohn, William. *A Day in the Life of a Veterinarian.* Little, Brown (0-316-45810-4), 1978. B/W photos. (Interest level: 3-6).

Jaspersohn follows a Morrisville, Vermont, veterinarian as he treats patients in his clinic and operating room, makes farm visits, and takes emergency calls. The subject of this book, a real veterinarian who is much respected by his community, radiates the same caring personality toward animals and their owners.
♦ Invite a local veterinarian to speak to the class about his or her work. Students could prepare a list of questions to ask.
1. Veterinary medicine.

636.1
Mellin, Jeanne. *The Morgan Horse.* Rev. ed. Viking (0-8289-0590-8), 1986. 288p. B/W photos and illus. (Interest level: 4-8).

A complete account of the great Justin Morgan and his stock, this book reveals why the Morgan horse, which originated in Vermont, is the first American breed of horse. Although most appropriate for the horse-loving reader, this history is both informative and inspirational.
♦ After doing more research on the Morgan horse, young people can present an illustrated oral report to the class.
1. Morgan horses.

637
Carrick, Daniel. *Milk.* Greenwillow (0-688-04822-6), 1985. 24p. Color illus. (Interest level: K-1).

The story of milk, from cow to carton, is simply told and beautifully illustrated in this book. Carrick gives a perfect answer to the familiar question "Where does it come from?" The illustrations make readers feel as though they are participants in the story.
♦ Students could visit a local dairy farm and/or invite a dairy farmer to speak to the class.
1. Milk   2. Dairying.

637
Gibbons, Gail. *The Milk Makers.* Macmillan (0-02-736640-5), 1985. 32p. Color illus. (Interest level: K-2).

Bold illustrations tell how milk gets from the cow to the table, including actual milking, processing, cooling, and transporting. The clear, bold graphic design presents the information well.
♦ Children can draw charts illustrating the dairy process.
1. Dairying   2. Dairy cattle   3. Milk   4. Cows.

637
Jaspersohn, William. *Ice Cream.* Macmillan (0-02-747821-1), 1988. 44p. B/W photos. (Interest level: 3-7).

The author takes the reader on a tour of Ben and Jerry's ice cream plant to explain where ice cream comes from and how it is made. This story about Vermont's foremost company and number-one tour-

ist attraction enables the reader to experience the tour vicariously.
- Invite a representative from a local ice cream maker to talk to the class about how ice cream is made. Young people might compare the information they get from the speaker with the information about Ben and Jerry's ice cream presented in this book.
1. Ice cream   2. Ice cream industry.

664
Burns, Diane. *Sugaring Season: Making Maple Syrup.* Photos by Cheryl Walsh Belville. Carolrhoda (0-87614-422-9), 1990. 48p. Color photos. (Interest level: 2-6).

A concise text describes maple sugaring today. Sections tell how to identify the sugar maple tree, describe the sugaring process step-by-step, and discuss ecological concerns about the future of the trees. In a long line of books about sugaring in Vermont, this book holds its own with photographs and simple text.
- Students can compare sugaring methods of today and yesterday. They could also make a flowchart illustrating the process.
1. Maple syrup.

808.81
Tudor, Tasha, ed. *Wings from the Wind.* Illus. by author. Lippincott, 1964. 119p. B/W illus. (Interest level: K-8).

Poems for fun, for beauty, and for pleasure have been collected here and enhanced by Vermont artist Tasha Tudor's superb illustrations of country life. This book is a must for classroom and home, where poetry may be a lesser-used genre.
- Students can illustrate their favorite poems.
1. Poetry.

974.3
Allen, Richard. *The Vermont Geography Book.* Northern Cartographic (0-317-53895-0), 1986. 44p. B/W illus. (Interest level: 3-8).

This book includes maps, graphs, and activities to teach students about the geography of Vermont. Allen provides the perfect nonfiction companion to the study of the state. Knowing the facts about Vermont increases both understanding and appreciation.
- Children can gather information about their own community, focusing on areas such as population, geology, and natural resources.
1. Vermont   2. Geography   3. Maps.

974.3
Bailey, Bernadine. *Picture Book of Vermont.* Whitman, 1965. 32p. Color illus. (Interest level: K-3).

Bailey covers interesting facts about Vermont, from people, places, and events to history, government, and commerce. Brief and somewhat dated, this small book is selective in scope.
- Students can gather trivia about Vermont and then play a trivia game with their classmates.
1. Vermont.

974.3
Bishop, Alice R. *My Little Vermont Book.* Alice R. Bishop, 1966. 70p. B/W illus. (Interest level: 1-4).

This work contains a short history of the state of Vermont, from the time before the white settlers to the 1960s. A period piece about Vermont, the book enhances the reader's understanding about earlier times, but the time period and format may not "speak" to contemporary youngsters.
- Readers could update this book by writing the history of Vermont from 1960 to the present day.
1. Geography—Vermont   2. History—Vermont.

974.3
Brown, Jane Clark. *The Second Vermont Fun Book.* Jane Clark Brown, 1971. 32p. B/W illus. (Interest level: 3-6).

Brown's work contains Vermont-related games, puzzles, stories, and crafts. Interactive activities encourage reader involvement. This would be a good supplement to classroom study or a useful book for a long automobile ride.
- Young people could create their own Vermont fun books.
1. Vermont   2. Puzzles, games.

974.3
Carpenter, Allan. *Vermont.* Childrens Press (0-516-04145-2), 1979. 96p. B/W and Color illus. (Interest level: 3-7).

Carpenter tells the story of Vermont, from its glorious past to its present. This is a fairly well-balanced portrayal, which describes the physical qualities of Vermont and the human qualities of its people.
- Class members can dramatize aspects of the history of Vermont such as its founding or a particularly important event in its history.
1. Vermont.

974.3
Cheney, Cora. *Vermont: The State with the Storybook Past.* New England Press (0-8289-0283-6), 1986. 239p. B/W illus. (Interest level: 4-8).

Cheney highlights and provides details of the Green Mountain State's adventurous past, from prehistoric times to the late twentieth century. Teachers, students, and adults with an interest in Vermont will find this thoroughly researched, authentic, and accurate presentation of Vermont worthwhile.
- Students could prepare a time line depicting Vermont's history.
1. Vermont—History.

974.3
Cooley, Oscar. *When Grandpa Was a Boy*. Vermont Historical Society (0-934720-29-0), 1985. 32p. B/W illus. (Interest level: 3-6).

This work follows a Vermont farm family of the early 1900s through a typical year and shows how each season demands new activities and responsibilities. Cooley has captured a true view of a Vermont farm experience in the 1900s, which is important because farming has changed and continues to change.
♦ Each child can choose a farm activity to research and then write an in-depth report about it.
1. Farm life—Vermont—History—20th century 2. Vermont—Social life and customs.

974.3
Dodge, Bertha. *Tales of Vermont Ways and People*. Stakepole Books (0-8117-1722-4), 1977. 192p. B/W illus. (Interest level: 4-8).

The tales in this book come from real people whose traditions, outlook on life, and sturdy independence are spiced with humor and enchantment. Through these stories readers will meet real Vermonters and gain insight into the Vermont experience and the character of Vermont.
♦ After interviewing people in their own community, students can create a book of tales of their own.
1. Vermont—History 2. Vermont—Social life and customs.

974.3
Dodge, Bertha S. *Vermont by Choice*. New England Press (0-933050-50-X), 1987. 148p. (Interest level: 4-8).

Dodge investigated grant documents and contracts, correspondence, and town histories of a century ago to write this book. Topics covered include growing crops, building a dam, and building sawmills and gristmills. This cultural history, well researched and presented in an interesting and appealing way, would be appropriate for the designated reading levels but equally appropriate for interested adults.
♦ Young people might illustrate a typical gristmill, sawmill, or dam as described in the book. They could also research further the topic of land grants and how they helped or hindered the development of Vermont.
1. Land grants—History—Vermont.

974.3
Guyette, Elise A. *Vermont: A Cultural Patchwork*. Cobblestone Publishing (0-9607638-5-6), 1986. 123p. B/W photos. (Interest level: 4-8).

Guyette's historical narrative is accompanied by a collection of stories, games, activities, and recipes. This book, by an experienced and creative teacher, features exceptional research and presentation. People in a variety of endeavors will find this a most useful and enjoyable resource.
♦ Students can make one of the recipes in this book or play one or more of the games.
1. Vermont.

974.3
Herdan-Zuckmayer, Alice. *The Farm in the Green Mountains*. New England Press (0-933050-46-1), 1968. 216p. (Interest level: 4-8).

Life at a Vermont farm in Barnard, Vermont, is described by the author and her husband, both of whom fled Nazi Germany. Animals, a chicken farm, telephone party lines, and unusual Vermont characters are some of the topics covered in this book. The personal account, which celebrates the rural Vermont way of life, portrays a time period in the history of Vermont and the importance of family life.
♦ Students can interview senior citizens in their community and put together a book about life in earlier times.
1. Vermont—World War, 1939-1945—History.

974.3
Hill, Ralph Nading. *The Voyages of Brian Seaworthy*. Vermont Life Magazine (No ISBN), 1971. 151p. B/W illus. (Interest level: 3-8).

This book, which describes steamboat travel on Lake Champlain and the Hudson River a century ago, conveys facts and the spirit of the times. An exceptional historian and writer, Hill involves readers so thoroughly that they feel as if they are participants in the adventure.
♦ Readers can create a model of a steamboat that traveled on Lake Champlain.
1. History 2. Steamboats.

974.3
Jennison, Keith. *Green Mountains and Rock Ribs*. Stephen Greene Press, 1954. 88p. Photos. (Interest level: 3-8).

Vermont humor and stories, along with appropriate photographs, depict life in rural Vermont. Jennison introduces readers to the unique country humor in all its delightful, taciturn wit.
♦ Young people could photograph life in their community and write accompanying text.
1. Humor—Vermont.

974.3
Jennison, Keith. *Vermont Is Where You Find It*. Stephen Greene Press, 1954. 118p. B/W photos. (Interest level: 3-8).

Vermont stories and sayings are kept alive through this book, which depicts Vermonters and their view of their world. The fun collection reflects human foibles.

♦ The class members can collect stories and sayings from people in their community and create their own book. They could place a copy in their school library.
1. Humor—Vermont   2. Idiomatic expressions.

974.3
Kjellerup, Hope R., ed. *Vermont, Our Own State.* Teachers of East Orange School District, 1967. 90p. B/W photos and illus. (Interest level: 4-8).

A useful classroom learning tool designed by teachers, this activity textbook covers the history, geography, employment, heroes, and resources of Vermont. The facts in this book may need an update, and teachers may come up with more contemporary ideas for activities.
♦ Young people may chart the various kinds of employment in their community.
1. Vermont.

974.3
Mussey, June Barrows. *Vermont Heritage.* Stephen Greene Press (0-8289-0241-0), 1975. 71p. illus. (Interest level: 3-8).

This reprint of a work originally published in 1947 is a mini-history of Vermont, illustrated with over 170 woodcut-style engravings. The medium of the woodcuts is especially appropriate for an early view of Vermont, providing aesthetics along with information.
♦ Students could create a time line depicting Vermont's history and development to present day.
1. Vermont—History.

974.3
Needham, Walter and **Mussey, June Barrows**. *A Book of Country Things.* Alan C. Hood & Co. (0-911469-09-5), 1992, 1965. 176p. B/W illus. (Interest level: 4-8).

The simplicity of country things and country ways, which faded away in the dazzle of chrome and neon, is conveyed in this book, which links the reader to early America. The past is precious, so young people should learn, honor, and revere a way of life long gone.
♦ This book can be used in conjunction with fiction books, such as the books by Laura Ingalls Wilder, and, if possible, a visit to Shelburne Museum. Students can interview senior citizens in their community to discover how they lived and worked with limited resources.
1. Early Americana.

974.3
St. John, Gregory and **St. John, Helen**. *Willie in Early Vermont.* John and Helen St. John, 1959. 51p. B/W illus. (Interest level: 2-7).

Stories of traditional Vermont activities such as cutting ice and maple sugaring make up the St. Johns' work. This is one of many books that lend a personal touch to the activities of a particular time and place.
♦ The class could participate in an old-fashioned project such as making candles or soap or dying cloth.
1. Vermont.

974.3
Shaver, Lula A. *The Molly Stark Trail.* Lula Shaver, 1961. 32p. B/W illus. (Interest level: 2-4).

Carl and Nancy, while touring the state of Vermont with their parents along the Molly Stark Trail, learn about the past as well as the present. The location and information in this book are authentic, but Carl and Nancy are now in their mid-forties, so an update is called for.
♦ Young people might research the local history of their own community and conduct interviews with local senior citizens. They could then create a documentary of the growth and development of their community.
1. Vermont.

Biography

92 Allen, Ethan
Brown, Slater. *Ethan Allen and the Green Mountain Boys.* Random, 1956. 184p. B/W illus. (Interest level: 3-8).

Ethan Allen and his boys led the struggle for ownership of the Grants in 1765. This biography of Vermont's well-known swashbuckling hero is dated but still useful because it gives readers a different perspective on Ethan Allen.
♦ After reading more about Ethan Allen and his brother Ira, students could dramatize events in their lives.
1. Allen, Ethan, 1738-1789   2. History—Vermont.

92 Allen, Ethan
Holbrook, Stewart. *America's Ethan Allen.* Illus. by Lynd Ward. Houghton Mifflin, 1949. B/W and Color illus. (Interest level: 3-8).

Ethan Allen forged the state of Vermont out of the "Hampshire Grants" almost single-handedly. It was his cry of "wolf hunt" that brought the men of the Green Mountains by the hundreds to defend their homes and lands against the tyranny of a distant king. The story is told here with vivid simplicity and illustrated with beautiful full color pictures.
♦ Students can research the founding of their state or community and the individuals who played a prominent role in its growth and development.
1. Allen, Ethan, 1738-1789   2. United States—History—Vermont   3. Vermont—History.

92 Allen, Ethan
Pell, John. *Ethan Allen: A Definitive Portrait of an American Patriot.* Ayer Co. (0-8369-6919-7), 1972, 1929. (Select Bibliographies Reprint Series). 331p. (Interest level: 4-8).

The Battle of Fort Ticonderoga is one of the most colorful episodes in the history of the Revolution. Ethan Allen led the Green Mountain Boys in this battle, demanding that the British surrender "in the name of the Great Jehovah and the Continental Congress." His capture and his imprisonment in England for two years only served to enhance his diplomatic role as he preached American independence to his fellow prisoners. This is one of the most scholarly biographies about Ethan Allen.
♦ Readers can compare the leadership styles of Champlain and Allen.
1. Allen, Ethan, 1738-1789   2. United States—History.

92 Allen, Ethan
Ripley, Sheldon. *Ethan Allen: Green Mountain Hero.* Houghton Mifflin, 1961. 191p. Maps. (Interest level: 3-8).

Ripley's easy-to-read story about Vermont's famous hero begins with Ethan Allen's boyhood on the Connecticut frontier. Stories of his speed as a runner, his strength, his experience chewing nails, and his bravery are told in a direct, easy-to-understand manner. Young people will be in awe of Allen after reading about how he caught deer by running them down.
♦ Young people can trace Ethan Allen's journeys using the maps in the book. They could also plan a field day of races and tests of strength and endurance.
1. Allen, Ethan, 1738-1789   2. United States—History.

92 Allen, Ethan
Winders, Gertrude Hecker. *Ethan Allen: Green Mountain Boy.* Bobbs-Merrill, 1962. 200p. Green/Black sketches. (Interest level: 3-8).

Winders has written a narrative that is both engaging and historically accurate. As a boy, Allen, who attended a frontier school for boys, which was held in a barn, was quick and eager to learn and was looked upon as a leader.
♦ Readers can write about adventures in which Ethan and his classmates might have participated.
1. Allen, Ethan, 1738-1789.

92 Champlain, Samuel de
Edwards, Cecile Pepin. *Champlain, Father of New France.* Abingdon Press, 1955. 128p. B/W illus. (Interest level: 3-8).

This is a biography of a brave French explorer who made his first sea voyage when he was still a boy. Champlain met with all kinds of dangers and difficulties: long cold winters, the search for a northwest passage to China, Indian wars, and treachery. He was successful in starting and governing the first American colony for France.
♦ Students could compare and contrast the colony Champlain established with other American colonies.
1. Champlain, Samuel de, ca 1567-1635   2. Explorers.

92 Champlain, Samuel de
Jacobs, William Jay. *Samuel de Champlain.* Franklin Watts (0-531-01275-1), 1974. 64p. B/W illus. and maps. (Interest level: 3-6).

For 32 years, Champlain, the father of New France, was closely identified with the exploration and settlement of Canada; now his life is inextricably intertwined with this period in the continent's development. Jacobs concentrates on Champlain's personal qualities, such as his fairness, stamina, and increasing piety, as well as the disheartening indifference of his patrons back in France. Champlain's explorations and the hardships he experienced are stirringly recounted.
♦ Children can use maps to trace Champlain's explorations and research more thoroughly the places he visited.
1. Champlain, Samuel de, ca 1567-1635   2. Explorers.

92 Champlain, Samuel de
Syme, Ronald. *Champlain of the St. Lawrence.* William Morrow, 1968. 189p. B/W illus. (Interest level: 6-8).

When young Samuel de Champlain first left France in the year 1582 to sail across the North Atlantic in a small, ill-provisioned schooner, he hoped he might see the newly discovered great river beyond the Newfoundland fishing banks, but it was not until 1603 that he got his chance. The broad, majestic St. Lawrence, gateway to a new continent, was Champlain's road to adventure. It was only after long years of struggle against the brutal northern winter, the Iroquois, and the inertia of his own countrymen that Champlain really established New France and opened up the vast interior of North America to Europe.
♦ Readers could research the St. Lawrence today to determine how its role has changed since the 1600s.
1. Champlain, Samuel de, ca 1567-1635   2. Explorers.

92 Champlain, Samuel de
Tharp, Louise Hall. *Champlain Northwest Voyager.* Little, Brown, 1944. 250p. (Interest level: 3-8).

As royal geographer to the king of France, Champlain set sail for what would become New

France in 1603. From then until his death in Quebec, he was constantly exploring, writing down his impressions, and making maps and vivid sketches of the wonders he saw. As a colonist and leader of men at Saint Croix Island, Port Royal, and Quebec, Champlain had to deal with all types of people. This is a warmly personal biography as well as an exciting adventure story.

♦ After listing the qualities that make one a leader, students can compare those qualities with Champlain's qualities. Young people may also wish to conduct further research on those areas that Champlain explored.

1. Champlain, Samuel de, ca 1567-1635 2. Explorers.

92 Coolidge, Calvin
Webb, Kenneth. *From Plymouth Notch to President: The Farm Boyhood of Calvin Coolidge.* Countryman Press (0-914378-44-9), 1978. 100p. B/W illus. (Interest level: 4-8).

Webb dramatizes Coolidge's youthful experiences, observations, escapes, family sorrows, and studies. Events such as the future president's meeting with President Harrison at the dedication of the Battle of Bennington Monument in 1891 are presented in historical context.

♦ Students in Vermont can visit the Coolidge farmhouse in Plymouth, Vermont. Others can get copies of the quotes from Calvin Coolidge that are painted on the walls of the state house and compare the quotes with those of other presidents.

1. Coolidge, Calvin, 1872-1933 2. Presidents—United States.

92 Frost, Robert
Bober, Natalie S. *A Restless Spirit: The Story of Robert Frost.* Holt (08050-1672-4), 1991. 197p. (Interest level: 6-8).

Bober's excellent book relates the dramatic story of Frost's life: his early childhood in San Francisco, the abrupt changes in his family life when his father died, the time spent with his grandparents in New England, his struggles throughout most of his adult life to write poetry and still be able to support his family, and the personal tragedy that marred his great success in later life. Frost was a shy little boy who did not read a book by himself until he was 14, but, when he was 15, he wrote and published his first poem.

♦ Young people could read more of Frost's poetry and write creative essays on the thoughts and feelings evoked by particular poems.

1. Frost, Robert, 1874-1963 2. Poets—United States.

92 Trapp Family
Wilhelm, Hans. *The Trapp Family Book*. William Heinemann, 1983. 88p. B/W and Color illus. (Interest level: K-8).

Here, in pictures, words, and songs, is the story made famous by *The Sound of Music*, of Maria, who won the hearts of Baron von Trapp and his seven children. The book describes how Maria taught the von Trapps to sing, how the family choir became famous, and how the family escaped from Nazi-occupied Austria and made a new life in the United States in Stowe, Vermont. This is a story of timeless appeal, freshly told and illustrated with delightfully humorous and warm-hearted pictures, accompanied by 15 songs.

♦ Class members can write to the Trapp Lodge in Stowe for information. They could also learn some of the songs in the book and present a musical for other students.

1. Trapp Family.

Fiction

Allen, Merrit P. *The Flicker's Feather*. Longmans, 1953. 220p. (Interest level 4-6).

The deep antagonism between the British regulars and the American backwoodsmen in this story is prophetic of the great fight to come. Duff meets adventure and grave danger with John Stark and Robert Rogers. This militaristic story has human and humane characteristics.

♦ Readers can explain what the flicker's feather and other symbols used in the military represent.

1. Revolution, 1775-1783—Fiction 2. French-Canadians—Fiction.

Andler, Kenneth. *Mission to Fort No. 4.* Illus. by Max R. Kaufmann. Regional Center for Educational Training (0-915892-04-9), 1975. (Bicentennial Historiette). 64p. B/W illus. and maps. (Interest level: 4-8).

Fifteen-year-old David Bradford is caught up in the events of the Revolution when he goes to live with his uncle in New Hampshire. This adventure story of the eighteenth-century frontier includes important information about early history, geography, and borders.

♦ Pretending they are David Bradford, students can write letters home describing their experiences.

1. United States—History—Revolution, 1775-1783—Fiction.

Arnosky, Jim. *Mud Time and More: Nathaniel Stories.* Addison Wesley (0-201-00-173-X), 1979. 44p. B/W illus. (Interest level: K-adult).

In this wordless book, illustrations show the adventures of Nathaniel, a Vermonter, as he solves four perplexing problems: getting out of the mud, mounting a weather vane, gathering eggs, and picking apples. A superb illustrator who really knows Vermont and Vermonters has created a useful and entertaining wordless book.

♦ Children could write different endings for each of the Nathaniel stories.
1. Stories without words 2. Vermont—Fiction.

Arnosky, Jim. *Nathaniel.* Addison Wesley (0-201-00171-3), 1978. 44p. B/W illus. (Interest level: K-adult).

Three picture stories present the humorous aspects of a man's reclusive life in the country, where human company is scarce during the long winter. This book, which takes a close look at cabin fever, lends itself to writing activities and discussion.
♦ After logging their day-to-day activities, students can make the ordinary into the unusual by using their imagination.
1. Stories without words 2. Humorous stories 3. Country life—Fiction.

Ashley, Robert P. *Rebel Raiders: A Story of the St. Albans Raid.* Illus. by Floyd J. Torbert. Winston, 1956. 176p. B/W illus. (Interest level: 4-8).

On October 19, 1864, in a small Vermont village near the Canadian border, a daring engagement of the War between the States took place. Twenty-one soldiers of the Confederate Army stormed the town, robbing its banks and creating panic among its citizens. After reading this story, which brings home a major conflict of the Civil War, present-day Vermont youngsters will no longer say "nothing ever happened here."
♦ Young people could create short stories describing an unusual and surprising event that might take place in their town.
1. Civil War, 1861-1865—Fiction 2. Vermont—Fiction.

Avery, Kay. *All for a Horse.* Crowell, 1956. 165p. B/W illus. (Interest level: 4-6).

Tom decides to try for a job at the local store to earn money to buy a horse, but his rival Andy seems to have the edge. This story of Vermont maple sugaring, country school life, races, and surprises combines mystery and laughter.
♦ Children can write essays describing similar experiences of their own.
1. Horses—Fiction 2. Vermont—Fiction.

Azarian, Mary. *A Farmer's Alphabet.* Godine (0-87923-394-X), 1981. 32p. B/W illus. (Interest level: K-adult).

Handsome woodcuts of the letters of the alphabet and rural themes inspired by the illustrator's Vermont experience depict scenes students will find familiar. Size, clarity, and theme are all perfect. This superb book can be used at home and at school.
♦ Students can choose one or more of the letters and write a creative essay about the illustration for that letter. Young people may also enjoy creating their own block-print letters.

1. Alphabet books.

Bacon, Katharine Jay. *Pip and Emma.* Atheneum (0-689-50385-7), 1986. 130p. (Interest level: 3-5).

Twelve-year-old Pip and his younger sister Emma share both pleasant and unpleasant experiences and adventures while spending the summer with their grandmother in Vermont. This story reflects a recurring theme in Vermont fiction: the main characters are "visiting" Vermont but are not really from Vermont. Vermont influences the characters, however, and helps them grow.
♦ Pretending they are either Pip or Emma, students can write letters home describing their experiences.
1. Brothers and sisters—Fiction 2. Grandmothers—Fiction 3. Vermont—Fiction.

Bacon, Katharine Jay. *Shadow and Light.* McElderry (0-689-050431-4), 1987. 197p. (Interest level: 7-8).

Fifteen-year-old Emma, who is looking forward to spending the summer on her beloved grandmother's Vermont farm, is devastated to learn that her grandmother is terminally ill and wants Emma to help her live her last months in peace and dignity. Emma, who also appears in *Pip and Emma* (see preceding entry), must deal with the difficult issues of aging and death.
♦ Young people could write essays describing how they would feel if they were in Emma's situation.
1. Grandmothers—Fiction 2. Death—Fiction.

Bryan, Frank and **Mares, Bill.** *OUT! A Vermont Secession Book.* Illus. by Jeff Danziger. New England Press (0-933050-52-6), 1986. 167p. B/W illus. (Interest level: 7-8).

Following TUGWOS (The Ultimate Great War of Secession) and its aftermath, Vermont is an idyllic place where maple syrup can be used to buy anything and town meetings rule. Children can use this excellent resource to learn about history, political science, and the unique Vermont point of view.
♦ If possible, students can attend a local town meeting or a council meeting.
1. Vermont—Fiction 2. Government—Fiction.

Budbill, David. *Christmas Tree Farm.* Macmillan (0-02-715330-4), 1974. 32p. Color illus. (Interest level: 4-6).

Budbill presents factual information about Christmas trees, including how the trees get their start and how they are planted, pruned, and finally wrapped for transporting. The author, who knows Vermont, conveys mood and tone as well as facts.
♦ Class members can visit a tree farm or invite a forester into the class.
1. Christmas trees—Fiction 2. Tree farms—Vermont.

Butler, Cynthia. *Michael Hendee.* Regional Center for Educational Training (0-915892-03-7), 1976. 51p. B/W illus. (Interest level: 2-4).

This book is based on the true story of seven-year-old Michael Hendee, who was captured by Indians and whose bravery and determination helped him cope with the situation. Authentic experiences make this story especially interesting.
♦ The class can dramatize the action of the story.
1. Vermont—Fiction   2. Indians of North America—Fiction.

Cheney, Cora. *The Doll of Lilac Valley.* Illus. by Carol Beech. Knopf, 1959. 112p. B/W illus. (Interest level: 2-5).

Nine-year-old "fresh air child" Laurie spends a whole summer in Vermont enjoying adventures. The Fresh Air Children program is still in operation, but, 35 years later, the children's interests have changed.
♦ Readers can investigate the Fresh Air Children program and interview families in their community who have hosted children.
1. Vermont—Fiction   2. Dolls—Fiction.

Cheney, Cora. *The Mystery of the Disappearing Cars.* Knopf, 1964. 146p. B/W illus. (Interest level: 4-8).

Sam and Windy, both candidates for a scholarship to a New England college, work during the summer in the Vermont hotel of the eccentric scholarship donor. Mysteriously, antique automobiles disappear. This is a mild mystery by contemporary standards.
♦ Readers can identify the clues given in the story that lead to its resolution and then write their own mystery stories.
1. Mystery and detective stories   2. Antique automobiles—Fiction.

Clayton, Barbara. *Halfway Hannah.* Funk Wagnalls, 1964. 184p. (Interest level: 4-6).

Sensitive Southern girl Hannah-Jo Hanson must adjust to Alpine Junction, Vermont, where her outspoken father has accepted a teaching position, and, in the process, she learns to stand up for her convictions. This story involves economic disaster, community involvement, and mystery. Adjusting to a move is often difficult, and adolescence only adds to the difficulties in this heartwarming novel.
♦ After investigating problems in their community, class members can use panel-discussion techniques to attempt to arrive at solutions.
1. Growing-up—Fiction   2. Vermont—Fiction.

Coblentz, Catherine C. *The Blue Cat of Castle Town.* Illus. by Janice Holland. Countryman Press (0-914378-05-8), 1987, 1974. 136p. B/W illus. (Interest level: 4-8).

Coblentz's story of intrigue and beauty involves a Vermont town during the Revolutionary War, a cat, an artist, and the lyrical sound made by a river. Many levels exist in this story of classical dimensions. Coblentz has written a challenging book of great depth, well worth reading aloud to a class.
♦ After a discussion of plot versus theme, each student can pick a book and write a short description of the book's plot and theme to share with the class.
1. Vermont—Fiction   2. Art and architecture—Fiction.

Cooney, Caroline B. *Family Reunion.* Bantam (0-553-05836-3), 1989. 169p. B/W photos. (Interest level: 6-8).

At a family reunion, Shelley comes to terms with her parents' divorce, her mother's absence, her new stepmother, and being the "stable" member of her colorful family. Cooney, who captures the authentic voice of young people, handles this contemporary family situation extremely well.
♦ After reading the book, young people might discuss the stepfather/stepmother experience.
1. Family life—Fiction.

Crompton, Anne Eliot. *Deer Country.* Little, Brown (0-316-16141-1), 1973. 122p. B/W illus. (Interest level: 4-6).

Human and animal relationships are interwoven as two men and a boy sight the same huge buck; each goes after it with his own private dream. To understand Vermont, one must understand deer hunting, and this book helps.
♦ Students can choose one of the characters and illustrate his dream.
1. Deer—Fiction   2. Hunting stories.

Danziger, Jeff. *The Champlain Monster.* Lanser Press (0-09603900-7-3), 1981. 92p. Color illus. (Interest level: 4-8).

From a chance discovery on an ice-fishing line to the story's startling climax, Tracy and her brother have one surprise after another. The Lake Champlain monster is as important to Vermont as the Loch Ness monster is to Scotland; children and adults have unflagging interest in this phenomenon.
♦ Young people will enjoy investigating the Lake Champlain monster and separating fact from fiction.
1. Monsters—Fiction   2. Lake Champlain—Fiction.

Fairless, Caroline. *Hambone.* Tundra Books (0-912766-97-2), 1980. 48p. B/W illus. (Interest level: 2-4).

While dealing with his mother's abandonment and his pet pig's death, a farm boy works his way through the pain to an affirmation of life. Realistic

and readable, this story appeals to children, perhaps due to their love of Wilbur in *Charlotte's Web*.
♦ Readers can design a memorial for Hambone.
1. Farm life—Fiction   2. Death—Fiction.

Farrow, Rachi. *Charlie's Dream*. Pantheon (0-394-83595-6), 1978. 32p. B/W and Color illus. (Interest level: 1-3).

Charlie Ram becomes discontented with his life on a Vermont farm where the work never ends as he listens to his friend Robin talk about her winters in Florida, where days are bright and warm. This children's story about Vermonters' perennial desire to escape the hard, cold winter hits just the right note.
♦ After collecting travel information about Florida and Vermont, students can make some comparisons.
1. Farm life—Vermont—Fiction   2. Animals—Fiction.

Fisher, Dorothy Canfield. *Understood Betsy*. Holt (0-03-086639-1), 1981. 211p. B/W illus. (Interest level: 4-6).

This tale of the transformation of a pale, timid nine-year-old into healthy, self-reliant Betsy illustrates the way of life in Putney, Vermont. A classic, this book is still relevant today. Dorothy Canfield Fisher is a preeminent writer for children and adults.
♦ Readers might write essays describing aspects of country life that led Betsy to health and confidence.
1. Family relationships—Fiction.

Fleischman, Sid. *The Hey Hey Man*. Atlantic Little (0-316-26001-0), 1979. 34p. Color illus. (Interest level: 3-6).

In this original folktale, set in Vermont, a thief steals a farmer's gold but is outwitted by a mischievous wood spirit—the Hey Hey Man. This modern tale is true to the genre and told with humor and wit.
♦ Students can write different endings for the story.
1. Robbers and outlaws—Fiction.

Frost, Frances. *Maple Sugar for Windy Foot*. McGraw, 1950. 184p. B/W illus. (Interest level: 4-6).

Windy Foot, Toby Clark's Shetland pony, helps with maple sugaring and with the havoc of a rising river. A horse (pony) story always appeals to children, and this one, told with warmth, does not fail.
♦ Children could write about their own experiences with ponies, maple sugaring, and floods or exciting or fearful adventures.
1. Vermont—Fiction   2. Ponies—Fiction   3. Maple sugaring—Fiction.

Frost, Frances. *Sleigh Bells for Windy Foot*. McGraw, 1948. 184p. B/W illus. (Interest level: 4-6).

Tish and Toby Clark are back, and the Burnhams are visiting the Clark farm for Christmas. Holiday fun is interrupted by a rampaging bear and a skiing accident. This is another book that features Windy Foot, this time with holiday cheer and adventure.
♦ Readers can create their own adventure story about skiing.
1. Vermont—Fiction   2. Winter—Fiction.

Frost, Frances. *Windy Foot at the County Fair*. McGraw, 1947. 153p. B/W illus. (Interest level: 4-6).

All the excitement of a country fair—horse races, farm animals, contests, and food exhibits—is described in this book. The first of the Windy Foot books involves the reader in Vermontiana.
♦ Children might illustrate Windy Foot's pony race.
1. Vermont—Fiction   2. Country fair—Fiction.

Gauch, Patricia Lee. *Aaron and the Green Mountain Boy*. Coward (GB-698-30423-3), 1972. 62p. B/W illus. (Interest level: 1-4).

In this easy reader, based on a real incident, Aaron dreams about helping the Green Mountain Boys fight but has to be content with helping to bake bread to feed them. An important event in Vermont history is now available to younger readers.
♦ Students can discuss how Aaron feels and how they felt when they were too young to help with a particular situation or problem.
1. Revolution, 1775-1783—Fiction.

Gibbons, Gail. *The Missing Maple Syrup Sap Mystery*. Illus. by author. Frederick Warne (0-7232-6167-9), 1979. 32p. Color illus. (Interest level: K-5).

Mr. and Mrs. Mapleworth trudge up the snowy hill, hanging buckets from spouts in the maple trees, but when they check the buckets the next day, they are empty. The Mapleworths are determined to find out who is stealing their sap. Gail Gibbons's illustrations accurately convey the sugaring process and enhance the story, motivating the young reader to continue reading this "chapter book."
♦ Readers could make predictions about who is stealing the sap, or they could write another ending to the story with someone else stealing the sap.
1. Maple sugaring—Fiction.

Harris, Kathleen McKinley. *The Wonderful Hay Tumble*. Illus. by Dick Gackenbach. Morrow Junior Books (0-688-07152-X), 1988. 32p. Color illus. (Interest level: K-2).

High on Vermont's highest mountain, a young farmer looks at his woeful farm, a pile of rocks. In this tall tale, a huge rolling pile of hay does all of the farmer's chores for him. Based on a tale the author heard as a child, this story is sheer joy in both text and illustration.

♦ After discussing the elements of tall tales, young people can write their own tall tales, using the characters in this tale or their own characters.
1. Farm life—Fiction 2. Vermont—Fiction.

Henry, Marguerite. *Justin Morgan Had a Horse.* Illus. by Wesley Dennis. Aladdin (0-689-71534-X), 1991, 1945. 176p. B/W illus. (Interest level: 3-6).

Justin Morgan, a schoolmaster, had a pint-sized colt that became the progenitor of the first breed of American horses. President James Monroe rode a Morgan horse in a military parade at the close of the War of 1812. This story, told by the consummate writer of horse stories, is a classic. This is the very best book for young readers about the Morgan horse.
♦ If possible students can visit the Morgan Horse Farm museum, or they can write to the museum for more information about Morgan horses.
1. Morgan horses—Fiction 2. Horses—Fiction 3. Vermont—Fiction.

Huntington, Lee Pennock. *Brothers in Arms.* Countryman Press (0-914378-18X), 1976. 63p. B/W illus. (Interest level: 3-6).

Huntington presents her own family history in this fictionalized account of the Pennock brothers, eight of whom were Loyalists, and one of whom was a Patriot. In this book, a fine writer combines accurate history with personal insight.
♦ Class members could participate in a panel discussion about families divided by their beliefs.
1. Vermont—Fiction 2. Revolution, 1775-1783—Fiction.

Hurwitz, Johanna. *Yellow Blue Jay.* Morrow (0-688-06078-1), 1986. 112p. B/W illus. (Interest level: 3-5).

Happy to spend his summer vacation at home in the city, eight-year-old Jay is horrified by his parents' plan to spend two weeks in the Vermont woods sharing a house with another family. In this very readable story, a popular children's author presents an engaging view of Vermont and of children's feelings.
♦ Children can write essays describing how Jay feels about his parents' decision.
1. Country life—Fiction 2. Vermont—Fiction 3. Friendship—Fiction.

Jackson, Edgar N. *Green Mountain Hero.* New England Press (0-933050-61-5), 1988. 192p. (Interest level: 3-6).

Based on the lives of Ann Story and her son Solomon, this book describes how the Storys settled in Vermont and became involved with the Green Mountain Boys, and how Ann became known as "the Mother of the Green Mountain Boys." This recent version of an old story is much needed to supplement the study of Vermont history.
♦ Students could research more about the Green Mountain Boys and then write a journal entry as one of them, describing their experiences.
1. Vermont—History—Revolution, 1775-1783.

Kelley, Shirley. *Little Settlers of Vermont: A True Story of the Journey of a Pioneer Family through New England.* Equity Publishing (0-685-43894-5), 1987. 104p. B/W illus. (Interest level: 3-7).

In 1786, Polly Davis and her family moved from Charlton, Massachusetts, to Montpelier, Vermont. Accounts of the Deerfield Raid and the Westminster Massacre are softened by descriptions of happier times, such as sugar-on-snow parties. This much-loved story, so personal to Vermont children, is very readable.
♦ Using a map, readers can plot the Davis family's journey from Massachusetts to Vermont.
1. Vermont—History.

Kent, Louise. *He Went with Champlain.* Houghton, 1959. 259p. B/W illus. (Interest level: 6-8).

Samuel de Champlain, cartographer and geographer, and his companion and interpreter, 12-year-old Tome Lee, journey to Canada in 1604. With this historically accurate story, a well-known Vermont adult writer does a fine job writing for a younger audience.
♦ Young people might draw a map of Lake Champlain and research its importance today.
1. Vermont—History.

Kinsey-Warnock, Natalie. *Canada Geese Quilt.* Dutton (0-525-65004-0), 1989. 60p. B/W illus. (Interest level: 3-5).

An intergenerational story set in Vermont in 1940, this book looks at family life and love and the changing seasons. The grandmother creates quilts by hand from original designs. This is a warm family story told by a real Vermonter, whose writing style charms children and adults.
♦ Students can make a class quilt.
1. Quilts 2. Grandmothers 3. Artists.

Kirkpatrick, Doris. *Honey in the Rock.* Elsevier/Nelson (0-525-66643-5), 1979. 218p. (Interest level: 7-8).

During the autumn of 1936, a 16-year-old girl begins to see signs that life in her small village in Vermont is drastically changing because of the construction of a dam. Environmental concerns, so near the heart of all Vermonters, are well presented in this fictional story.

♦ The class could study changes in its own community and determine the causes of the changes.
1. Vermont—Fiction.

Kivlin, Barbara. *ABC's of Vermont.* Barbren Publications, 1987. 26p. B/W illus. (Interest level: K-3).

This is an educational coloring book about the Green Mountain State, from *A* for *autumn* to *Z* for *zip through the snow*. Kivlin's book is less elegant than Mary Azarian's alphabet book, yet useful.
♦ The class can create its own alphabet book about Vermont or some other state, with each student illustrating one letter of the alphabet.
1. Alphabet books   2. Vermont.

Kjellerup, Hope. *Molly the Mule.* Vantage Press (533-04776-5), 1981. 82p. B/W illus. (Interest level: K-3).

Molly and Ward are two mules through whose eyes readers view Vermont. Animal stories always seem to be popular and this one with a Vermont setting is appealing.
♦ Young people can write stories of their own, told from the point of view of an animal.
1. Animals—Fiction   2. Vermont—Fiction.

Kull, Nell. *Over the Mountain.* Nell Kull, 1973. 77p. (Interest level: 4-6).

Set in 1795-1800, this is a fictionalized account of the Daniel Rice family of Somerset, who moved to Dover, Vermont. This story of local people in a historical context is accurate.
♦ Students could write fictionalized accounts of their own families.
1. Family life—Fiction   2. Vermont—Fiction.

Lenski, Lois. *Deer Valley Girl.* Lippincott, 1968. 145p. B/W illus. (Interest level: 4-6).

Lenski's story about 12-year-old Abby is set against the Vermont background of a small dairy farm in a valley named for the white-tailed deer that live there. The author's regional stories lend themselves to social studies teaching, and this one describes Vermont well.
♦ Children can read other regional stories by Lois Lenski, such as *Strawberry Girl*, and compare them with this story.
1. Vermont—Fiction   2. Animals—Fiction.

Mendoza, George. *The Crack in the Wall & Other Terribly Weird Tales.* Dial, 1968. 34p. B/W illus. (Interest level: 2-6).

The eerie stories in this book are not quite ghost stories or horror stories; they are stories of things that could almost happen. The deserted quarry in Vermont with a crack in the wall is scary to encounter but tantalizing to read about. Engaging children in a very popular genre that just happens to have a Vermont setting is easy with this book.
♦ If possible, the class can visit the Barre Granite quarries or any type of geological formation nearby.
1. Vermont—Fiction.

Muller, Charles G. *Hero of Champlain.* John Day, 1961. 192p. (Interest level: 4-8).

In October of 1812, Lieutenant Thomas Macdonough comes to Burlington, Vermont, as naval commander of Lake Champlain, giving Gid an opportunity to fight for his country. For the military-minded, this is a good story set in Vermont.
♦ Readers can investigate further naval history on Lake Champlain, researching the ships, the routes used, and the battles fought.
1. War of 1812—Fiction.

Murrow, Liza Ketchum. *Fire in the Heart.* Holiday House (0-8234-0750-0), 1989. 255p. (Interest level: 5-8).

Fourteen-year-old Vermonter Molly O'Connor tries to uncover the mystery surrounding her mother's death 10 years earlier in California. Seeking the true image of her mother, she is able to reunite a family torn apart by bitter memories. Murrow, a popular writer whose stories readers enjoy, weaves a story that is memorable.
♦ Each student can collect photographs, letters, and stories about his or her own family and create a family scrapbook.
1. Mystery and detective stories   2. Family life—Fiction.

Paterson, Katherine. *Lyddie.* Lodestar Books (0-525-67338-5), 1991. 182p. (Interest level: 5-8).

Impoverished Vermont farm girl Lyddie Worthen is determined to gain her independence by becoming a factory worker in Lowell, Massachusetts, in the 1840s. Vermonters' favorite writer has told a story so real, so convincing, so well researched, and so readable that it is an instant classic.
♦ Discuss why Lyddie wanted her independence and how young people today gain their independence.
1. Self-reliance—Fiction   2. Work—Fiction
3. Factories—Fiction   4. Historical fiction.

Pearson, Tracey Campbell. *The Storekeeper.* Dial (0-8637-0370-8), 1988. 32p. Color illus. (Interest level: K-1).

Based on the general store in Jericho, Vermont, the store in this story is part grocery store, part hardware store, part gift shop, part gas station, part bakery, and part post office. The store has every-

thing one needs, and the helpful storekeeper knows everyone in town. Delightful illustrations show neighbors and friends enjoying a Vermont institution, the general store.
♦ Students can visit a country story and discuss the differences between this store and a grocery store, along with the advantages and disadvantages of both kinds of stores.
1. Stores, Retail—Fiction.

Peck, Robert Newton. *A Day No Pigs Would Die.* Knopf (0-394-48235-2), 1972. 150p. (Interest level: 8).

A Shaker boy learns what adulthood is all about by observing birth and slaughter on a Vermont farm. Peck's extremely readable and emotionally moving story has enticed reluctant readers to read.
♦ Readers can investigate all aspects of Shaker life. They also could design furniture, learn Shaker songs, or study herbs used in cooking.
1. Shakers—Fiction 2. Pigs—Fiction.

Piper, Roberta. *Little Red.* Scribner, 1963. 156p. B/W illus. (Interest level: 4-8).

Little Red, a chestnut pony, was first seen at the fair, and now Nan's grandfather has given the pony to her as a present. Nan's experiences while learning to ride, jump, and drive a pony cart are only part of this story about ponies and people. The book is sure to please the reader who loves horses and may help satisfy the desire to own one.
♦ Class members can investigate the care and feeding of ponies and then invite a local pony expert into the class to answer their questions.
1. Ponies—Fiction.

Pitkin, Dorothy. *The Grass Was That High.* Pantheon, 1959. 192p. B/W illus. (Interest level: 6-8).

Kit's first summer in Vermont away from Old Greenwich and her sailboat seems boring until she learns about farm life and raising a bull for the fair. This interesting story shows how lifestyles are related to geographic limitations.
♦ Students can investigate how animals are prepared for showing at a fair and what characteristics judges of these animals look for. Invite a 4-H representative to speak to the class.
1. Animals—Fiction 2. Growing up—Fiction.

Pitkin, Dorothy. *Wiser than Winter.* Pantheon, 1960. 317p. (Interest level: 6-8).

Kit returns to Vermont and finds the local high school to be very different from the school she attended in the city. Pitkin has written a grown-up city mouse–country mouse story set in high school.
♦ The class could organize a student exchange program with students from urban and rural schools.
1. High school—Fiction 2. Vermont—Fiction.

Purdy, Carol. *Least of All.* Macmillan (0-689-50404-7), 1987. 32p. Color illus. (Interest level: K-2).

A little girl in a big farm family teaches herself to read using the Bible and shares her knowledge with her brothers, parents, and grandmother during a long, cold Vermont winter. The time frame of this story may not "speak" to today's readers. Learning to read is an important theme of the book.
♦ Students could write about their first reading experience. They may also interview others about their reading experiences.
1. Farm life—Fiction 2. Reading—Fiction.

Raftery, Gerald. *City Dog.* Morrow, 1953. 216p. B/W illus. (Interest level: 4-6).

Rod, the handsome, well-groomed collie, has been an old lady's expensive pampered ornament all his life, but all this changes when Rod is sent to live with the lady's nephew in Vermont. This is a good dog story but somewhat dated.
♦ Young people might write descriptive essays comparing and contrasting city and country life.
1. Animals—Fiction 2. Cities and towns—Fiction.

Raftery, Gerald. *Slave's Gold.* T. Vanguard, 1967. 184p. (Interest level: 4-6).

In the hills of Vermont, spurred by the thrill of hidden treasure and haunted houses, children set out to discover whether their Grampa's stories are true. This is a good story with an air of mystery as well as family history.
♦ Readers can create their own coded messages and maps for hidden treasures.
1. Mystery and detective stories 2. Vermont—Fiction.

Roach, Marilynne K. *Encounters with the Invisible World.* Crowell (0-690-01277-2), 1977. 131p. B/W illus. (Interest level: 3-6).

Roach's work, which includes 10 tales of ghosts, witches, and the devil himself, takes place in New England. One of the tales is set in Vermont. This is an ever popular genre with the middle-school population.
♦ Children will enjoy writing their own stories of ghosts and witches.
1. Ghost stories.

Shyer, Marlene Fanta. *Blood in the Snow.* Houghton (0-395-21929-9), 1975. 124p. B/W illus. (Interest level: 4-6).

Max must make some difficult decisions regarding the relative values of a gun, a flute, and an injured silver fox. An understanding father helps Max appreciate their differences.
♦ This story may lead to a good discussion about values or about guns and gun control. Or in essays students can describe a time in their lives when they had to make a difficult decision and how they handled it.
1. Wildlife conservation—Fiction.

Speare, Elizabeth. *Calico Captive.* Illus. by Witold T. Mars. Houghton (0-395-07112-7), 1957. 280p. B/W illus. (Interest level: 3-8).

Speare tells the story of Miriam Willard, who was captured by Indians in 1754, sold to the French for ransom, and later returned to her Vermont home. An excellent writer and storyteller weaves history and personal development into a good story.
♦ Young people can write essays describing how they would feel about having to live in another culture. Perhaps this could contribute to a discussion of different cultures and how it feels to be a minority.
1. French and Indian Wars—Fiction 2. Indians of North America—Fiction.

Stolz, Mary. *Ferris Wheel.* Harper & Row (0-06-025859-4), 1977. 133p. (Interest level: 4-6).

When her best friend moves to California, 10-year-old Polly makes friends with her younger brother and a new girl in town in a Vermont farming community. Friendship and separation are the themes in this good story set in Vermont.
♦ Students could write a letter to a friend or pen pal describing daily life at home and school.
1. Vermont—Fiction 2. Family life—Fiction.

Thompson, Mary Wolfe. *Green Threshold.* Longmans, 1954. 176p. (Interest level: 4-8).

Hal and Ginger have lost their parents, and Ginger feels so responsible for Hal's future that she stands in his way. Hal's interest in architecture is realized when they buy a house in Vermont. Sibling support in times of hardship leads to understanding and success.
♦ Class members can discuss the response to disabilities in this 1954 book and today.
1. Siblings—Fiction 2. Architecture—Fiction.

Thompson, Mary Wolfe. *Wilderness Wedding.* McKay, 1970. 118p. (Interest level: 4-6).

In the 1770s, 15-year-old Tabby and 18-year-old Nathan of neighboring families in the Vermont wilderness marry and establish a home of their own. This sequel tells what happens to Tabby and Nathan following *Wilderness Winter* (*see* following entry).
♦ Historic wedding customs, food, and homemaking are all topics that students could investigate and present to the class. Children could also create a model of Tabby and Nathan's house or cook a wilderness meal.
1. History—Fiction 2. Vermont—Fiction.

Thompson, Mary Wolfe. *Wilderness Winter.* McKay, 1968. 89p. B/W illus. (Interest level: 4-6).

Thompson's book describes the seasonal changes a young family experiences while living in the family cabin on a Vermont holding, and she predicts the beginning of a community. This warm family story, set in a time when daily living was often a hardship, is reminiscent of Laura Ingalls Wilder's books.
♦ Readers could investigate how their town began and complete a time line of events.
1. Wilderness living—Fiction 2. Vermont—Fiction.

Towne, Mary. *Wanda the Worrywart.* Atheneum (0-689-31511-2), 1989. 138p. (Interest level: 3-6).

Wanda's worries become even greater than usual during her family's vacation at a Vermont lodge when her divorced stepgrandmother develops an interest in a prospective husband. This combination of a very contemporary theme and a Vermont setting helps to offset many earlier books about Vermont.
♦ Wanda's obsession was "be prepared." Students can write about their obsessions.
1. Vacations—Fiction 2. Grandmothers—Fiction.

Trask, Margaret P. *At the Sign of the Rocking Horse.* Crowell, 1964. 178p. B/W illus. (Interest level: 4-6).

Two young friends, Cassie and Fergus, have a wonderful summer in Vermont solving a mystery involving Aunt Emerald's antique shop, the annual church bazaar, and a country supper. This story of young friends sharing typical Vermont experiences describes the rituals of rural living.
♦ Young people might write their own mystery stories, based on events in their own town. They could also collect recipes of foods that might be served at a church bazaar, put them into a book, and hold their own bazaar.
1. Mystery and detective stories 2. Country life—Fiction.

Trask, Margaret P. *Three for the Treasure.* Crowell, 1962. 115p. B/W illus. (Interest level: 4-6).

Summer vacation at their grandparents' farm, High Over farm in Vermont, provides fun, mystery, and adventure for Lissa and Danny. The story involves clue maps and buried treasure in the

garden. An adventure coupled with mystery provides a satisfying story for readers at this grade level.
♦ Children can design their own clue maps and have a treasure hunt.
1. Farm life—Fiction.

Viereck, Philip. *Independence Must Be Won.* Day, 1964. 158p. B/W illus. (Interest level: 7-8).

Lake Champlain, Fort Ticonderoga, and Mount Independence are the settings for this Revolutionary War story, which is told through the eyes of fictional Nathan Robinson. All facts ring true and are well documented. The author knows young readers and Vermont very well, and his book addresses both with forthright honesty and pleasure.
♦ If possible, students can visit Mount Independence and Fort Ticonderoga. Or, they can write for information about these two historic places.
1. Revolution, 1775-1783—Vermont—Fiction.

Wallace-Brodeur, Ruth. *The Godmother Tree.* HarperCollins (0-06-022458-4), 1992. 128p. B/W illus. (Interest level: 3-6).

Resigned to her family's move to yet another farm in Vermont, 10-year-old Laura discovers something very special about the new place and comes to realize that home is a feeling you carry inside you. Realistic children in a realistic setting yield a warm and engaging story.
♦ This book could stimulate a discussion of things we carry inside of ourselves regardless of where we are living.
1. Farm life—Fiction   2. Family life—Fiction   3. Migrant labor—Fiction   4. Moving, Household—Fiction.

Wallace-Brodeur, Ruth. *The Kenton Year.* Atheneum (0-689-50186-2), 1980. 93p. (Interest level: 4-6).

In this warm story about facing change, nine-year-old Mandy and her mother move to Kenton, Vermont, after the accidental death of Mandy's father. New friends and a job on the local newspaper help to make this new home acceptable after a year of adjustment. This fine writer faces issues head-on and honestly.
♦ Discuss the changes that take place when a loved one dies. Students can write about difficult experiences they have had and how they have dealt with them.
1. Moving, Household—Fiction   2. Death—Fiction   3. Mothers and daughters—Fiction.

Watson, Nancy D. *Sugar on Snow.* Viking, 1964. 44p. Color illus. (Interest level: 3-6).

The children work hard to boil sap until they have syrup for a sugar-on-snow birthday party. But will there be snow? This is a clear demonstration of one of Vermont's special treats and a harbinger of springtime, sugar-on-snow.
♦ If possible, students could plan a sugar-on-snow birthday party and invite another class to share it. Or, they could select a local food specialty and prepare it for a party.
1. Maple syrup—Fiction.

Wilson, Charles M. *The Green Mountain Toymakers.* Washburn, 1975. 149p. (Interest level: 4-6).

Set in Vermont in the year 1845, this story of a toy company in Thetford, Vermont, is a historical novel about fun and profit. Interestingly, toys are still made in Thetford, Vermont.
♦ If possible, a trip to the toy collection at Shelburne Museum would be fun. Or, children could build some simple early toys or some futuristic toys.
1. Toy making—Fiction.

Wilson, Charles Morrow. *Crown Point and the Destiny Road.* McKay, 1965. 191p. (Interest level: 4-6).

Wilson relates the story of the building of the Crown Point Road through Vermont in 1758 and the parts played by an American Indian boy and an English settler boy. This realistic story of an earlier time is told with honesty from the perspective of boys who are around the same age as the reader.
♦ Class members can interview a logger and a road construction engineer and then plan the construction of a road.
1. History—Vermont—Fiction.

Wriston, Hildreth T. *Andy and the Red Canoe.* Farrar, 1960. 149p. B/W illus. (Interest level: 4-6).

While spending his summer vacation in northern Vermont near the Canadian border, 14-year-old Andy wants to take the canoe and follow the river to its source. The author's familiarity with every aspect of the lake and the region shows in her writing, which makes readers feel as if they are sharing the experience.
♦ Class members can write about their own camping or canoeing experiences. Or, invite a canoeing enthusiast from the community to speak to the class.
1. Adventure—Fiction.

Wriston, Hildreth T. *Show Lamb.* Abingdon, 1953. 191p. B/W illus. (Interest level: 4-6).

A Vermont farm boy in the 1850s raises a pet lamb to take to the Tunbridge Fair. Fairs are still common in Vermont today and are just as important as in 1850.
♦ Readers could visit a fairground at the end of summer to compare today's blue-ribbon winners or invite the fair organizer to speak to the class. Also, students could hold a class or school fair.
1. Sheep—Fiction.

Directory of Publishers and Vendors

Abingdon
P.O. Box 801
201 Eighth Avenue South
Nashville, TN 37202

Harry N. Abrams, Inc.
100 Fifth Avenue
New York, NY 10011

Acadia Publishing Company
P.O. Box 170
Bar Harbor, ME 04609

Acropolis Books
2400 17th Street, NW
Washington, DC 20009-9964

Addison Wesley
One Jacob Way
Reading, MA 01867

Affordable Adventures, Inc.
6330 W. North Avenue
Milwaukee, WI 53213

Afton Publishing Company
P.O. Box 1399
Andover, NJ 07821

Aladdin
P.O. Box 364
Palmer, AK 99645

American & World Geographic Publishing
P.O. Box 5630
Helena, MT 59604

American Association of University Women
2401 Virginia Avenue, NW
Washington, DC 20037

American Canal & Transportation Center
809 Rathan Road
York, PA 17403

American Friends Service Committee
Maine Indian Program
P.O. Box 1096
Bath, ME 04530

American Historical Publications, Inc.
725 Market Street
Wilmington, DE 19801

American People's Historical Society
P.O. Box 25
Burlington, VT 05402

American School Publishers
P.O. Box 4520, 155 N. Wacker Drive
Chicago, IL 60680-4520

Americana Press
520 Commonwealth Avenue
Boston, MA 02215-2605

Andrews and McMeel
4900 Main Street
Kansas City, MO 64112

Appalachian Mountain Club Books
5 Joy Street
Boston, MA 02108

Appledore Books
Hancock, NH 03449

Applied Arts Publishers
Box 479
Lebanon, PA 17042

Art Calendar
Box 1040
Great Falls, VA 22066

Atheneum
866 Third Avenue
New York, NY 10022

Atlantic
34 Beacon Street
Boston, MA 02106

Atlas Video, Inc.
4915 St. Elmo Avenue, Suite 305
Bethesda, MD 20814

August House
P.O. Box 3223
Little Rock, AR 72203-3223

Avon Books
105 Madison Avenue
New York, NY 10016

Ayer Co., Publishers, Inc.
Box 958
Salem, NH 03079

Backcountry Publications
P.O. Box 175
Woodstock, VT 05091

Bailey Films
Phoenix Learning Resources
10 N. Main Street
Yardley, PA 19067

Ballantine Books, Inc.
201 E. 50th Street
New York, NY 10022

Bantam Books
666 Fifth Avenue
New York, NY 10103

Banyan Books
P.O. Box 431160
Miami, FL 33243

Barbren Publications
(Out of business)

Bardwell/Thompson
Little River Design Group
P.O. Box 324
York, ME 03909

A. S. Barnes
c/o Oak Tree Publications, Inc.
P.O. Box 119
Stamford, CT 06904-0119

William L. Bauhan Publishers, Inc.
P.O. Box 443, Old County Road
Dublin, NH 03444

Beachcomber Press
Box 500, Belgrade Road
Oakland, ME 04963

Beautiful American Publishing
P.O. Box 646
Wilsonville, OR 97070

Beckley Films
Box 28
Brandenton, FL 33506

Beech Tree
c/o William Morrow & Co.
1350 Avenue of the Americas
New York, NY 10014

Beech Tree Press
P.O. Box 15669
Long Beach, CA 90815

Mary Benjamin
P.O. Box 154
South Casco, ME 04077

Alice R. Bishop
(Out of business)

Black Ice Publishers
100 Prescott Street
Worcester, MA 01605

Katherine Blaisdell
Box 250
North Haverhill, NH 03774

Bobbs-Merrill
866 Third Avenue
New York, NY 10022

Bond Wheelwright
(Out of business)

Bookright Press
Division of Franklin Watts, Inc.
95 Madison Avenue
New York, NY 10016

Botto House
83 Norwood Avenue
Haledon, NJ 07508

Bowerbank Publishing
Box 2361
New Sharon, ME 04955

Bradbury Press/Macmillan
866 Third Avenue
New York, NY 10022

Carol A. Brosselin
Auburn Village School
Auburn, NH 03032

Jane Clark Brown
(Now defunct)

Buccaneer Books
P.O. Box 168
Cutchogue, NY 11935

C C Audiovisual and Publishing
P.O. Box 923
Seymour, IN 47274

Camino Books
Box 59026
Philadelphia, PA 19102

Canterbury Press
2054 University Avenue, Suite 100
Berkeley, CA 94704

Canterbury Shaker Village
288 Shaker Road
Canterbury, NH 03224

Cape Cod Chamber of Commerce
Mid Cape Highway
Hyannis, MA 02601

Carnegie Museum
4400 Forbes Avenue
Pittsburgh, PA 15213

Carolrhoda Books
241 First Avenue North
Minneapolis, MN 55401

Center for Analysis of Public Issues
16 Vandeventer Avenue
Princeton, NJ 08542

Charlesbridge Publishing
85 Main Street
Watertown, MA 02172

Chartwell Books
110 Enterprise Avenue
Secaucus, NJ 07094

Chase Communications, Inc.
1776 Nancy Creek Bluff, NW
Atlanta, GA 30377

Chelsea House
95 Madison Avenue
New York, NY 10016

Chesapeake Bay Foundation
Save the Bay Shop
188 Main Street
Annapolis, MD 21401

Childrens Press
5440 N. Cumberland Avenue
Chicago, IL 60656-1494

Chilton
Chilton Way
Radnor, PA 19089

Chronicle Books
275 Fifth Street
San Francisco, CA 94103

Cineworks Productions
Great Bay Road
Greenland, NH 03301

Clarion Books
215 Park Avenue South
New York, NY 10003

Clarkson Potter
c/o Crown Publishing Company
201 E. 50th Street
New York, NY 10022

Clements Research, Inc.
16850-A Dallas Parkway
Dallas, TX 75248-1999

Coastwire Press
434 Main Street
Rockland, ME 04841

Cobblestone Books/Dutton
See Dutton Children's Books

Cobblestone Publishing
7 School Street
Peterborough, NH 03458-1454

Robert Cole Films
1139 Cumberstone Road
Harwood, MD 20776
Distributed by:
  PBS Video
  1320 Braddock Place
  Alexandria, VA 22314

Collier Macmillan
866 Third Avenue, 25th floor
New York, NY 10022

Colonial Dames of America
See National Society of Colonial Dames of America

Columbia Books, Inc.
1212 New York Avenue, NW, Suite 330
Washington, DC 20037

Commonwealth Books, Inc.
P.O. Box 66
Palisades Park, NJ 07650

Commonwealth of Pennsylvania
Department of General Services
Bureau of Publications and Paperwork
  Management
P.O. Box 1365
Harrisburg, PA 17105

Congressional Quarterly, Inc.
1414 22nd Street, NW
Washington, DC 20037

Connecticut Botanical Society
Yale University Herbarium
Osborn Memorial Laboratory
Yale University
New Haven, CT 06511

Connecticut College Aboretum
Box 5511
270 Mohegan Avenue
New London, CT 06320

Connecticut Department of Environmental Protection
P.O. Box 1550
Burlington, CT 06013

Connecticut Department of Transportation
2800 Berlin Turnpike
Newington, CT 06111

Connecticut Heritage
234 Chestnut Tree Road
Oxford, CT 06483

Connecticut Historical Commission
State Historical Preservation Office
59 Prospect Street
Hartford, CT 06106

Connecticut Historical Society Education Department
One Elizabeth Street
Hartford, CT 06105

Connecticut Humanities Council
195 Church Street
Wesleyan Station
Middletown, CT 06457

Connecticut Magazine
789 Reservoir Avenue
Bridgeport, CT 06606

Connecticut Sea Grant College Program
University of Connecticut
Marine Sciences Institute
1084 Shennecossett Road
Groton, CT 06340-6097

Connecticut Secretary of State
State Capitol, Room 104
30 Trinity Street
Hartford, CT 06106

Connecticut Waste Management Service
179 Allyn Street
Hartford, CT 06103

Corner House
1321 Green River Road
Williamstown, MA 01267

Country Press
P.O. Box 7652, Route One
Henderson, NY 13650

Countryman Press, Inc.
P.O. Box 175
Woodstock, VT 05091-0175

Covered Bridge Press
7 Adamsdale Road
North Attleboro, MA 02760

Coward, McCann & Geoghegan
Putnam Publishing Group
200 Madison Avenue
New York, NY 10016

George F. Cram Co., Inc.
P.O. Box 426
Indianapolis, IN 46206

Creative Classrooms
81 Chester Road
Raymond, NH 03077

Creative Education, Inc.
Box 227
123 S. Broad Street
Mankato, MN 56001

Creek Books House
P.O. Box 793
Ojai, CA 93023

Crestwood House
866 Third Avenue
New York, NY 10022

The Crossing Press
P.O. Box 1048, 22D Roache Road
Freedom, CA 95019

Thomas Y. Crowell
10 E. 53rd Street
New York, NY 10022

Crowell-Collier
See Macmillan Publishing Co., Inc.

Crown Publishing Co., Inc.
P.O. Box 4397
Glendale, CA 91222-0397

Curbstone Press
321 Jackson Street
Willimantic, CT 06226

Dale Books
51 Springdale Avenue
Waterbury, CT 06708

J. B. Day
(Out of business)

Decision Development Corporation
2680 Bishop Drive, Suite 122
San Ramon, CA 94583

Delacorte Press
666 Fifth Avenue
New York, NY 10103

Delapeake Publishing
301 N. Walnut Street
Wilmington, DE 19801-3974

Delaware American Revolution Bicentennial Commission
(Now defunct)

Dell Young Yearling
Dell Publishing
666 Fifth Avenue
New York, NY 10103

DeLorme Mapping Company
Box 298
Freeport, ME 04032

Dial Press
375 Hudson Street
New York, NY 10014

Dillon Press, Inc.
866 Third Avenue, 24th Floor
New York, NY 10022

District of Columbia Offices of Policy and Program Evaluation
District Building
13 G Street, NW
Washington, DC 20001

District of Columbia Statehood Commission
415 12th Street, NW, Room 226
Washington, DC 20014

Dodd Mead & Co.
71 Fifth Avenue
New York, NY 10003

Dodge Printers
Refer orders to:
Katherine Blaisdell
Box 250
North Haverhill, NH 03774

The Donning Company
5659 Virginia Beach Road
Norfolk, VA 23502

Doubleday
666 Fifth Avenue
New York, NY 10103

Dover Post Company
P.O. Box 664
Dover, DE 19903

Dover Publications, Inc.
31 E. Second Street
Mineola, NY 11501

Down East Books
Box 679
Camden, ME 04843

Frank L. Dumond
See Atheneum

Irene E. DuPont
116 Gilford Street
Manchester, NH 03102

Durand Press
374 Dogford Road
Etna, NH 03750

Dutton Children's Books
375 Hudson Street
New York, NY 10014

Elsevier/Nelson
See Lodestar Books

EMSPAC
530 Silas Deane Highway
Wethersfield, CT 06109

Encyclopaedia Britannica Educational Corporation
310 S. Michigan Avenue
Chicago, IL 60604

Enjoy Communications, Inc.
P.O. Box 444
Mechanicsville, MD 20659

Enslow Publishers, Inc.
Box 777, Bloy Street and Ramsey Avenue
Hillside, NJ 07205

Equity Publishing Company
Main Street, R.R. 1, Box 3
Oxford, NH 03777

Eye Gate Media
Division of Carnation Co.
3333 Elston Avenue
Chicago, IL 60618

Facts on File, Inc.
460 Park Avenue South
New York, NY 10016

Fairleigh Dickinson University Press
Affiliate of Associated University Press
c/o Associated University Press
440 Forsgate Drive
Cranbury, NJ 08512

Farragut Press
5448 E. View Park
Chicago, IL 60615

Farragut Publishing
2033 M Street, NW, Suite 640
Washington, DC 20036

Farrar, Straus, & Giroux, Inc.
19 Union Square West
New York, NY 10003

Feminist Press at the City University of New York
311 E. 94th Street
New York, NY 10128

Filmic Archives
600 Main Street
The Cinema Center
Botsford, CT 06404-0386

Finley Holiday
12607 E. Philadelphia Street
Whittier, CA 90601

Fleet National Bank
111 Westminster Street
Providence, RI 02902

Foremost Books
142 Ferry Road, Suite 16
Old Saybrook, CT 06475

Foremost Publishers, Inc.
Yankee Publishing, Inc.
Dublin, NH 03444

Four Winds Press
866 Third Avenue
New York, NY 10022

Funk & Wagnalls
One International Boulevard, Suite 444
Mahwah, NJ 07495-0017

Gallery Books
112 Madison Avenue
New York, NY 10016

Gallopade Publishing Group
235 E. Ponce de Leon Avenue, Suite 100
Decatur, GA 30030

Gannett Books
P.O. Box 1460B
Portland, ME 04101

Gareth Stevens, Inc.
River Center Building, Suite 201
1555 N. River Center Drive
Milwaukee, WI 53212

Garrard
1607 N. Market Street
Champaign, IL 61820

Garrett Educational Corp.
Box 1588, 130 E. 13th Street
Ada, OK 74820

Gateway Communications
One Bala Plaza, Suite 237
Bala Cynwyd, PA 19004

Georgetown University Learning Resource Center
Georgetown University
37th and O Streets, NW
Washington, DC 20057

Georgetown University Press
37th and O Streets, NW
Washington, DC 20057

German Information Center
410 Park Avenue
New York, NY 10022

Globe Pequot Press
138 W. Main Street
Chester, CT 06412

Glove Compartment Books
P.O. Box 1602
Portsmouth, NH 03801

David R. Godine, Publisher, Inc.
Horticultural Hall
300 Massachusetts Avenue
Boston, MA 02115

Goffstown Historical Society
Goffstown, NH 03045

Golden Press
850 Third Avenue
New York, NY 10022

Good Books
People's Place
P.O. Box 419
Intercourse, PA 17534

GPN/Nebraska ETV Network
P.O. Box 80669
Lincoln, NE 68501-0669

Graphics Communications, Inc.
Scarborough, ME

Greater Portland Landmarks, Inc.
165 State Street
Portland, ME 04101

Green Acres School
11701 Danville Drive
Rockville, MD 20852

Stephen Green Press
Rutland, VT 05701

Greenfield Review Press
2 Middle Grove Road
Greenfield Center
New York, NY 12833

Greenwillow Books
1350 Avenue of the Americas
New York, NY 10019

Greenwood Publishing Group, Inc.
Box 5007, 88 Post Road West
Westport, CT 06881

Grey Gull Publications
HC 61, Box 069
Damriscotta, ME 04593

Grossett & Dunlap Publishers
200 Madison Avenue
New York, NY 10016

Groundhog Press
Box 181
Springhouse, PA 19477

Gruber Almanack Company
P.O. Box 609, 1120 Professional Court
Hagerstown, MD 21741-0609

Guggenheim Production, Inc.
(Available from University of Pittsburgh Press)

Haffenreffer Museum of Anthropology
Brown University
Mt. Hope Grant
Bristol, RI 02809

Hambleton Company, Inc.
309 Greenbrier Avenue
Ronceverte, WV 24970

Harcourt Brace Jovanovich, Inc.
6277 Sea Harbor Drive
Orlando, FL 32887

Harper & Row
10 E. 53rd Street
New York, NY 10022

HarperCollins Publishers, Inc.
10 E. 53rd Street
New York, NY 10022

Harpswell Press
132 Water Street
Gardiner, ME 04345

Hasting House Book Publishers
141 Halstead Avenue
Mamaronick, NY 74110

Hawthorn Books, Inc.
P.O. Box 225
Spring Valley, NY 10977

Heritage Books
1540 E. Pointer Ridge Place
Bowie, MD 20716

Heritage Concord, Inc.
Kimball Jenkins Estate
266 N. Main Street
Concord, NH 03301

Higginson Book Company
14 Derby Square
Salem, MA 01970

Hippocrene Books
171 Madison Avenue
New York, NY 10016

Historical Society of Cheshire County
P.O. Box 803
Keene, NH 03431

Historical Society of Delaware
505 N. Market Street
Wilmington, DE 19801

Holiday House, Inc.
425 Madison Avenue
New York, NY 10017

Holt, Rinehart and Winston, Inc.
6277 Sea Harbor Drive
Orlando, FL 32887

Home Run Press
P.O. Box 432A, R. D. #1
Lake Hopatcong, NJ 07849

Alan C. Hood & Company
28 Birge Street
Brattleboro, VT 05301

Houghton Mifflin
One Beacon Street
Boston, MA 02108

Howell Press
700 Harris Street, Suite B
Charlottesville, VA 22901

Hudson Hills Press, Inc.
30 Rockefeller Plaza, Suite 4323
New York, NY 10112

In-Education
Valley Forge Towers West, Suite 624
King of Prussia, PA 19406

Information Publications
3790 El Camino Real, Suite 162
Palo Alto, CA 94306

International Video Network
2242 Camino Ramon
San Ramon, CA 94583

Ives Washburn, Inc.
750 Fifth Avenue
New York, NY 10017

Jared Company
510 Philadelphia Pike
Wilmington, DE 19801

Johns Hopkins University Press
701 W. 40th Street
Baltimore, MD 21211

Jupiter Press
New Hampton, NH 03256

Kalmar Nyckel Foundation
1124 E. Seventh Street
Wilmington, DE 19801

KCTS-TV
401 Mercer Street
Seattle, WA 98109

Kennebec River Press
36 Old Mill Road
Falmouth, ME 04105-1637

Kinderatlas
Thomas E. Sherer
31 Sulgrave Road
West Hartford, CT 06107

Alfred A. Knopf, Inc.
201 E. 50th Street
New York, NY 10022

Dave Krysty
P.O. Box 91222
Pittsburgh, PA 15221

Nell M. Kull
(Out of business)

Lamplight Publishing
P.O. Box 1307
Denedin, FL 34697

Lanser Press
P.O. Box 38
Plainfield, VT 05667

Lerner Publications
241 First Avenue North
Minneapolis, MN 55401

Library of Congress
First and Independence Avenue, SE
Washington, DC 20540

Liebt Printing Company
East Colebrook, NH 03576

Life Video
Time Life Broadcast, Inc.
9 Rockefeller Plaza
New York, NY 10020

Lighthouse Press
50 Evans Road
Marblehead, MA 01945

J. B. Lippincott
227 E. Washington Square
Philadelphia, PA 19106

Little, Brown & Co.
34 Beacon Street
Boston, MA 02106

Liveright Publishing Corporation
500 Fifth Avenue
New York, NY 10110

Lockport Public Library
23 East Avenue
Lockport, NY 14094

Lodestar Books
2 Park Avenue
New York, NY 10016

Long Island Soundkeepers Fund
P.O. Box 4058
Norwalk, CT 06855

Lothrop, Lee & Shepard Books
1350 Avenue of the Americas
New York, NY 10019

Louisiana State University Press
Highland Road
Baton Rouge, LA 70893

LTA Publishing Co.
2735 S.E. Raymond Street
Portland, OR 97202

Lyman Orchards
Rt. 147 & 157
Middlefield, CT 06455

Lyons and Burford Publications, Inc.
31 W. 21st Street
New York, NY 10010

Margaret K. McElderry
Macmillan Publishing Co.
866 Third Avenue
New York, NY 10022

McGraw-Hill, Inc.
1221 Avenue of the Americas
New York, NY 10020

David McKay Company, Inc.
201 E. 50th Street
Brooklyn, NY 11229

Macmillan Educational Distribution Center
Front and Brown Streets
Riverside, NJ 08370

Maine Historic Preservation Commission
55 Capital Street Station, No. 65
Augusta, ME 04330

Maine Historical Society
485 Congress Street
Portland, ME 04101

Maine Maritime Museum
963 Washington Street
Bath, ME 04530

Maryland Historical Press
9205 Tuckerman Street
Lanham, MD 20706

Maryland Historical Society
201 W. Monument Street
Baltimore, MD 21201

Maryland Instructional Television
Maryland State Department of Education
1767 Bonita Avenue
Owings Mills, MD 21117

Maryland Sea Grant Publications
P.O. Box 456
Centreville, MD 21617

Maryland State Archives
Hall of Records
350 Rowe Boulevard
Annapolis, MD 21401

Maryland State Archives Publications
P.O. Box 456
Centreville, MD 21617

Massachusetts Business Development Corp.
One Liberty Square
Boston, MA 02128

Massachusetts Department of Public Works
10 Park Plaza
Boston, MA 02128

Massachusetts Educational Television & WGBY-TV
1385 Hancock Street
Quincy, MA 02169

Massachusetts Office of Business Development
Research Office
100 Cambridge Street
Boston, MA 02128

Massachusetts Water Resources Authority
100 First Avenue
Charlestown, MA 02129

Media Basics Video
1200 Post Road
Guilford, CT 06437

Merrimac River Press
P.O. Box 245
Tyngsborough, MA 01879

Julian Messner
Prentice Hall Building
Rte. 9W
Englewood Cliffs, NJ 07632

Middle Atlantic Press
P.O. Box 945
Wilmington, DE 19899

Millbrook Press
2 Old New Milford Road, Box 335
Brookfield, CT 06804-0335

Miller-Brody
  See American School Publishers

Mino Publications
9009 Paddock Lane
Potomac, MD 20854

Modern Curriculum Press
13900 Prospect Road
Cleveland, OH 44136

Mont Vernon Historical Society
Mont Vernon, NH 03057

Morgan Brown
132 Grand Street
Croton-on-Hudson, NY 10520-9918

Morrow Junior Books
105 Madison Avenue
New York, NY 10016

William Morrow & Company, Inc.
1350 Avenue of the Americas
New York, NY 10019

Mountain Press Publishing Co.
P.O. Box 2399
Missoula, MT 59806

Mountaineers Books
1011 South Klickitat Way, Suite 107
Seattle, WA 98134

John Muir Publications
P.O. Box 613
Santa Fe, NM 87504-0613

Mustang Publishing
P.O. Box 9327
New Haven, CT 06533

Mystic Seaport Museum
75 Greenmanville Avenue
Mystic, CT 06355

Narragansett Media
18 Imperial Place
Providence, RI 02903

National Audiovisual Center
National Archives and Records Administration
8700 Edgewood Drive
Capitol Heights, MD 20743

National Geographic Society
1145 17th Street, NW
Washington, DC 20036

National Park Service
Harpers Ferry Center
Harpers Ferry, WV 25425

National Society of Colonial Dames of America
Delaware Chapter
P.O. Box 4026
Greenville, DE 19807

Naval Institute Press
118 Maryland Avenue
Annapolis, MD 21402

Thomas Nelson, Inc.
Nelson Place at Elm Hill Pike
Nashville, TN 37214

New England Press
P.O. Box 575
Shelburne, VT 05482

New Hampshire Council for Social Studies
P.O. Box 475
Concord, NH 03301-0475

New Hampshire Division of Historical Resources
P.O. Box 2043
Concord, NH 03302-2043

New Hampshire Historical Society
30 Park Street
Concord, NH 03301

New Hampshire Movies
124 Great Bay Road
Greenland, NH 03840

New Hampshire Premier
20 Ladd Street
Portsmouth, NH 03801

New Hampshire Public Television
Box 1100
Durham, NH 03824

New Hampshire Publishing Company
P.O. Box 70
Somersworth, NH 03878

New Hampshire Society for the Protection of New Hampshire Forests
30 Park Street
Concord, NH 03301

New Jersey Audubon Society
590 Ewing Avenue
Franklin Lakes, NJ 07417

New Jersey Council for the Social Studies
75 Cedar Bridge Road
Manahawkin, NJ 08050

New Jersey Department of Environmental Protection and Energy
401 E. State Street CN402
Trenton, NJ 08625

New Jersey Historical Commission/Society
230 Broadway
Newark, NJ 07104

New Jersey League of Women Voters
204 W. State Street
Trenton, NJ 08625

New Jersey Library Association
P.O. Box 1534
Trenton, NJ 08607

New Jersey Network
1573 Parkside Avenue CN 777
Trenton, NJ 08625

New Jersey State Library
185 W. State Street
Trenton, NJ 08625

Newport Historical Society
82 Touro Street
Newport, RI 02840

Newport Savings & Loan/Island Trust
100-122 Bellevue Avenue
Newport, RI 02840

New York Broadcasting Corporation
State Education Department
State Education Building
89 Washington Avenue
Albany, NY 12234

New York Department of Commerce
200 Madison Avenue
New York, NY 10016

New York State Board of Education
State Education Department
State Education Building
89 Washington Avenue
Albany, NY 12234

New York State Committee on the Bicentennial
State Education Department
State Education Building
89 Washington Avenue
Albany, NY 12234

New York State Department of Environmental Conservation
50 Wolf Road
Albany, NY 12233

New York State Education Department
State University of New York
State Education Building
89 Washington Avenue
Albany, NY 12234

New York State Historical Association/Society
170 Central Park West
New York, NY 10024

Niagara County Historical Society
The Bond House
143 Ontario Avenue
Lockport, NY 14904

Nimbus
c/o Chelsea Green Publishing Company
P.O. Box 130, Route 113
Port Mills, VT 05058

North Country Press
3934 Plymouth Circle
Madison, WI 53705

North Light Studio
1507 Dana Avenue
Cincinnati, OH 45207

North Star Stories
116 Chestnut Street
Providence, RI 02903

Northeast Archives of Folklore and Oral History
Northeast Historic Films
Blue Hill Falls, ME 04615

Northern Cartographic, Inc.
P.O. Box 133
Burlington, VT 05402

Jeffrey Norton Publishers, Inc.
On-the-Green
Guilford, CT 06437

Nostalgia Publishing
P.O. Box 999
Davisville Branch
North Kingston, RI 02854

Nutshell Books
6 Wood Street
Southborough, MA 01772

Office of the Massachusetts Secretary of State
Citizens Information Service
One Ashburton Place
Boston, MA 02128

Offices of Policy and Program Evaluation
See District of Columbia Offices of Policy and Program Evaluation

Old Brandywine Village, Inc.
(Now defunct)

Old Rhode Island
P.O. Box 999
Davisville, RI 02854

Old Stone Bank
150 South Street
Providence, RI 02906
(Now closed and is being reorganized)

Old Sturbridge Village
One Old Sturbridge Village Road
Sturbridge, MA 01566

Omnigraphics, Inc.
2400 Penobscot Building
Detroit, MI 48226

Orchard Books
387 Park Avenue South
New York, NY 10003

Pantheon Books
201 E. 50th Street
New York, NY 10022

Parnassus Press
Box 335, 21 Canal Road
Orleans, MA 02653

Passport Books
4255 W. Touhy Avenue
Lincoln Wood, IL 60646-1975

PBS Video
1320 Braddock Place
Alexandria, VA 22314-1698

Pen Mor Printers
280 Park Street
Lewiston, ME 04240

Penguin Books
375 Hudson Street
New York, NY 10014

Penns Valley Publishers
154 E. Main Street
Lansdale, PA 19446

Pennsylvania Game Commission
2001 Elmerton Avenue
Harrisburg, PA 17110-9797

Pennsylvania Historic Association/Commission
See Pennsylvania Historical and Museum Commission

Pennsylvania Historical and Museum Commission
P.O. Box 11466
Harrisburg, PA 17108-1460

Pennsylvania Magazine Company
P.O. Box 576
Camp Hill, PA 17001-0576

Pennsylvania Newspaper Publishers Association
c/o Pennsylvania Humanities Council
320 Walnut Street, Suite 305
Philadelphia, PA 19106-3829

Pennsylvania State University Press
215 Wagner Building
University Park, PA 16802

Perceptions, Inc.
Box 250, Rural Route 1
Charlotte, VT 05445

Peregrine Press
24 Gregory Street
Marblehead, MA 01945

Peregrine Smith Books
P.O. Box 667
Layton, VT 84041

Philomel Books
200 Madison Avenue
New York, NY 10016

Pleasant Grove Publishing Company
(Available from Canterbury Shaker Village or from Nancy Thompson)

Prentice-Hall Press
15 Columbus Circle
New York, NY 10023

Project Oceanology
Avery Point
Groton, CT 06340

Providence Journal Bulletin
75 Fountain Street
Providence, RI 02902

Puffin Books
375 Hudson Street
New York, NY 10014

Putnam
200 Madison Avenue
New York, NY 10016

G. P. Putnam's Sons
200 Madison Avenue
New York, NY 10016

Queen Anne Press
P.O. Box 456
Centreville, MD 21617

Rainbow Educational Video, Inc.
170 Keyland Court
Bohemia, NY 11716

Rainbow Press
Gene Billings
28 Sunset Ridge
Norfolk, CT 06058

Raintree Publishers
Raintree/Steck-Vaughn Publishers
310 W. Wisconsin Avenue
Milwaukee, WI 53203

Peter E. Randall Publisher
P.O. Box 4726, Nobles Island Market Street
Portsmouth, NH 03801

Random House, Inc.
201 E. 50th Street
New York, NY 10022

RB Books
Seitz & Seitz, Inc.
1006 N. Second Street, Suite 1-A
Harrisburg, PA 17102-3121

Regional Center for Educational Training
(Available from Creative Classrooms)

Reprint Services Corp.
3972 Barranca Parkway, Suite J412
Irvine, CA 92714

Research and Reference Publications, Inc.
P.O. Box 901
Adelphi, MD 20783

Rhode Island College Film and Video Library
600 Mount Pleasant Avenue
Providence, RI 02908

Rhode Island Monthly
Narragansett Media, Inc.
18 Imperial Place
Providence, RI 02903

Rhode Island Publications Society
1445 Wampanoag Trail
East Providence, RI 02915

Rhode Island Sea Grant
University of Rhode Island
Narragansett, RI 02882

R.I. Bicentennial Foundation
c/o Rhode Island Publications Society
1445 Wampanoag Trail
East Providence, RI 02915

Rizzoli International Publications
300 Park Avenue South, 12th Floor
New York, NY 10010

Ross Sports Publications
(Available from University of Pittsburgh Press)

Rourke Corporation
P.O. Box 3328
Vero Beach, FL 32964

Rutgers University Press
109 Church Street
New Brunswick, NJ 08901

Rutledge Hill Press
513 Third Avenue
Nashville, TN 37210

RWM Assoc. Audio
P.O. Box 1324
Bethesda, MD 10817

Scarecrow Press, Inc.
52 Liberty Street
Metuchen, NJ 08840

Schneidereith and Sons
2905 Whittington Avenue
Baltimore, MD 21230

Scholastic, Inc.
730 Broadway
New York, NY 10003

Schooner, Inc.
60 Water Street
New Haven, CT 06106

Scribner Book Companies
866 Third Avenue
New York, NY 10022

Charles Scribner's Sons
866 Third Avenue
New York, NY 10022

Seabury Press
Icehouse 1-401
151 Union Street
San Francisco, CA 94111

SERESC, Inc.
(Southeastern Regional Education Service Center, Inc.)
111 Peabody Road
Derry, NH 03038

Seton Hall University Press
South Orange Avenue
South Orange, NJ 07079

Sherwin/Dodge Printers
See Dodge Printers

Silver Burdett & Ginn
250 James Street
Morristown, NJ 07960

Silverleaf Press
Box 884
Green Farms, CT 06436

Simon & Schuster
The Simon & Schuster Building
Avenue of the Americas
New York, NY 10020

SITE Productions
P.O. Box 937
Brookline, MA 02146

W. H. Smith Publishers, Inc.
112 Madison Avenue
New York, NY 10016

Smithmark
16 E. 32nd Street
New York, NY 10016

Smithsonian Institution Press
470 L'Enfant Plaza, Suite 7100
Washington, DC 20560

SNET
227 Church Street
New Haven, CT 06506

Society for Visual Education, Inc.
1345 Diversey Parkway
Chicago, IL 60614

Somerset Publishing
P.O. Box 4386
Troy, MI 48099

Spoken Arts, Inc.
10100 SBF Drive
Pinellas Park, FL 34666

Stackpole Books
P.O. Box 1831
Cameron & Kelker Streets
Harrisburg, PA 17105

Starboard Cove Publishing
HCR 70, Box 442
Bucks Harbor, ME 04618

State Geological and Natural History Survey of Connecticut
165 Capital Avenue, Room 553
Hartford, CT 06106

Steck-Vaughn Company
P.O. Box 26015
Austin, TX 78755

Stemmer House Publishers, Inc.
2627 Caves Road
Owings Mills, MD 21117

Stewart, Tabori & Chang
740 Broadway
New York, NY 10003

Story Sound Productions, Inc.
30 Marcy Street
Cranston, RI 02905

Syracuse University Press
1600 Janesville Avenue
Syracuse, NY 13244-5160

Taylor Publishing Company
P.O. Box 597, 1550 W. Mockingbird Lane
Dallas, TX 75221

Teachers of East Orange School District
East Orange, VT 05670

Temple University Press
Broad and Oxford Streets
University Services Building, Room 305B
Philadelphia, PA 19122

Thomas Publications
P.O. Box 3031
Gettysburg, PA 17325

Nancy M. Thompson
RFD #2, Box 70
Warner, NH 03278

Thorndike Press
P.O. Box 159
Thorndike, ME 04986

Ticknor & Fields
215 Park Avenue South
New York, NY 10003

Tide Grass Press
Peak's Island, ME 04108

Tidewater Publishers
P.O. Box 456, 306 E. Water Street
Centreville, MD 21617

Tillbury House
132 Water Street
Gardiner, ME 04345

Tomlinson Enterprises
P.O. Box 920
Morristown, NJ 07963-0920

Tompson & Rutter, Inc.
P.O. Box 297
Grantham, NH 03753

Top Ten Software
Advanced Ideas, Inc.
2902 San Pablo Avenue
Berkeley, CA 94702

Troll Associates
100 Corporate Drive
Mahwah, NJ 07430

Trumpet Club
3920 South King's Avenue
Brandon, FL 33511

Tundra Books
P.O. Box 1030
Plattsburgh, NY 12901

Turner Broadcasting Systems
Box 105366, One CNN Center
Atlanta, GA 30348

Twin City Printery
Box 890
Lewiston, ME 04240

United States Capitol Historical Society
200 Maryland Avenue, NE
Washington, DC 20002

United States Department of the Interior
See U.S. Government Printing Office

United Way of Connecticut
900 Asylum Street
Hartford, CT 06105

University of Delaware
c/o Associated University Presses, Inc.
440 Forsgate Drive
Cranbury, NJ 08512

University of Maine Press
PICS Building
Orono, ME 04469

University of Massachusetts Press
Box 429
Amherst, MA 01004

University of Pennsylvania Press
418 Service Drive
Blockley Hall, 13th Floor
Philadelphia, PA 19104-6097

University of Pittsburgh Press
127 N. Bellefield Avenue
Pittsburgh, PA 15260

University of Rhode Island
Narragansett, RI 02882-1197

University of South Carolina Press
1716 College Street
Columbia, SC 29208

University Press of New England
23 S. Main Street
Hanover, NH 03755

U.S. Government Printing Office
Superintendent of Documents
Washington, DC 20401

U.S. History Society, Inc.
25 E. Main Street
Richmond, VA 23219

Van Nostrand Reinhold
115 Fifth Avenue
New York, NY 10003

Vandamere Press
P.O. Box 5243
Arlington, VA 22205

Vanguard Press
424 Madison Avenue
New York, NY 10017

Vantage Press
516 W. 34th Street
New York, NY 10001

Vermont Crossroads Press
(Out of business)

Vermont Historical Society
109 State Street
Montpelier, VT 05602

Vermont Life Magazine
61 Elm Street
Montpelier, VT 05602

Vermont Migrant Education Program
South Burlington School
South Burlington, VT 05403

Video Tours
300 Winding Brook Drive
Glastonbury, CT 06033

Viking Kestrel
40 W. 23rd Street
New York, NY 10010

Wabank Bilingual Education Program
1501 Cherry Street
Philadelphia, PA 19102

Henry Z. Walck
201 E. 50th Street
New York, NY 10022-7703

Walker Publishing Co./Walker & Co.
720 Fifth Avenue
New York, NY 10019

Frederick Warne
Division of Penguin USA
40 W. 23rd Street
New York, NY 10010

Washburn
(Out of business)

Washington Book Trading Company
P.O. Box 1676
Arlington, VA 22210

Washington Opera/John F. Kennedy Center for the Performing Arts
Washington, DC 20566

Watermill
4 Crescent Drive
Albertson, NY 11507

Franklin Watts
387 Park Avenue South
New York, NY 10016

Martha Weatherbee Books
Star Route, Box 35
Sanbornton, NH 03269

Weathervane Books
Distributed by Crown Publishers
419 Park Avenue South
New York, NY 10016

Westcliffe Publications, Inc.
1441 Avocado #408
Newport Beach, CA 92660

Westcliffe Publishers, Inc.
P.O. Box 1261
Englewood, CO 80150

Sheldon Weiss Productions
(Available from University of Maine)

Western New York Public Broadcasting
Box 1263, 184 Barton Street
Buffalo, NY 14213

Weston Woods
389 Newton Turnpike
Weston, CT 06883

WETA-TV 26-Radio FM 91
P.O. Box 2626
Washington, DC 20013

Wheaton A. Holden Production
Refer orders to:
NH Movies
Great Bay Road
Greenland, NH 03840

Whitehouse Historical Association
740 Jackson Place, NW
Washington, DC 20503

Albert Whitman Company
5747 W. Howard Street
Niles, IL 60648

William Paterson College
300 Pompton Road
Wayne, NJ 07470

Windsor Publications
P.O. Box 2500, 9121 Oakdale Avenue
Chatsworth, CA 91313

Windswept House
P.O. Box 159
Mount Desert, ME 04660

John C. Winston
1006-1020 Arch Street
Philadelphia, PA 19106-3829

WJAR-TV
23 Kenney Drive
Cranston, RI 02920

WNET
(Available from University of Pittsburgh Press)

Woodmont Press
P.O. Box 108
Green Village, NJ 07935

World Education Project
School of Education
University of Connecticut
Storrs, CT 06268

WQED
Box INFO
Pittsburgh, PA 15213

Yankee Publishing, Inc.
P.O. Box 520
Main Street
Dublin, NH 03444

Zenger Video
P.O. Box 802, 1200 Jefferson Boulevard, Room 40
Culver City, CA 90232-0802

Author Index

Aaseng, Nathan, 77, 142
Ackerman, Susan, 109
Adler, David, 44
Agger, Lee, 56
Aiken, Joan, 94
Aikman, Lonnelle, 27
Akers, Charles W., 89
Albert, Burton, 24
Alcott, Louisa May, 94, 111
Alderfer, E. Gordon, 154
Aldred, Lisa, 77
Aldridge, Josephine, 57
Aliki, 169, 171, 173
Allen, Merrit P., 206
Allen, Richard, 202
Alter, Judith, 13
Altland, Millard, 165
Ammon, Richard, 154
Amory, Cleveland, 89
Amsel, Sheri, 19
Ancona, George, 132
Anderson, Elizabeth B., 70
Anderson, Joan, 87
Andler, Kenneth, 111, 206
Apicerno, William, 5
Appleberg, Marilyn J., 136
Applegate, Katherine, 39
Arden, Lorraine, 47
Ardizzone, Edward, 57
Arnosky, Jim, 20, 200, 201, 206, 207
Ashabranner, Brent K., 32
Ashley, Robert P., 207
Askins, Robert A., 5
Atkin, John, 4
Aubin, Albert, 191
Avery, Kay, 207
Avi, 14, 94, 125, 175, 176, 197
Ayer, Eleanor, 32
Aylesworth, Jim, 176
Aylesworth, Thomas G., 53, 105
Aylesworth, Virginia L., 53, 105, 138
Azarian, Mary, 207

Bacon, Katharine Jay, 207
Bailey, Bernadine, 202
Bain, Geri, 120, 125

Baker, Betty, 146
Baker, Marybeth, 57, 58
Baker, Nina Brown, 175
Balano, James W., 53
Balcer, Bernadette, 164
Baldwin, Sidney, 58
Banks, Ronald R., 53
Bardwell, John D., 49, 50, 105
Barrow, Scott, 118
Barth, Edna, 91
Bartis, Peter T., 128
Beame, Bernard, 138
Beatty, Patricia, 176
Beck, Henry Charlton, 115
Beck, Horace, 2
Bell, Frederic, 176
Bell, Michael, 3
Benchley, Nathaniel, 95
Bennett, Dean B., 53
Bergeron, Ronald P., 105
Berman, Eleanor, 27
Bernard, April, 118
Bernard, Jacqueline, 144
Bernier, Evariste, 58
Bertinetti, Marcello, 135
Beyer, George R., 161
Bigler, Philip, 33
Bill, Alfred Hoyt, 130
Billings, Gene, 5
Bishop, Alice R., 202
Bisignano, Alphonse, 186
Blair, Anne Denton, 45
Blaisdell, Katharine, 106
Blos, Joan, 24
Blumberg, Rhoda, 189
Blume, Judy, 125
Blunt, Susan Baker, 109
Bober, Natalie S., 206
Bock, William Sauts Netamuxwe, 21
Boehm, Bruce, 14
Bollick, Nancy O'Keefe, 100
Bond, Nancy, 95
Bosco, Peter I., 72
Bourne, Miriam, 32
Bousquet, Don, 187
Boyce-Ballweber, Hettie, 73
Boylston, Helen D., 123

Brady, Esther Wood, 38, 126
Brady, Philip, 111
Brancato, Robin, 176
Brandt, Keith, 77
Brecht, Edith, 176
Brereton, Charles, 109
Brestensky, Dennis, 156
Bridner, E. L., Jr., 75
Brown, Edward, 121
Brown, Ellen, 27
Brown, Jane Clark, 202
Brown, Michael P., 116
Brown, Slater, 204
Bruce, Preston, 33
Bruchac, Joseph, 49, 101, 133
Bryan, Frank, 207
Budbill, David, 207
Bulla, Clyde Robert, 93
Bunting, Eve, 45
Buranelli, Vincent, 123
Burchard, Peter, 14, 146
Burdett, Harold, 75
Burke, Kathleen, 90
Burney, Eugenia, 23
Burns, Diane, 202
Butler, Brian, 47
Butler, Cynthia, 208

Cabral, Len, 184
Callahan, North, 10
Calloway, Colin G., 8, 104
Calvert, Mary, 51
Carey, George, G., 67
Carmer, Carl, 138
Carpenter, Allan, 20, 33, 54, 121, 191, 202
Carpenter, John Allan, 73
Carpenter, Mimi Gregoire, 58
Carr, Harriett, 146
Carr, Lois Green, 73
Carrick, Carol, 186
Carrick, Daniel, 201
Casey, Jane Clark, 142
Cebulash, Mel, 126
Cheney, Cora, 202, 208
Cherry, Lynne, 109
Chesler, Bernice, 85
Choroszewski, Walter, 118

Choukas, Bradley, 27
Christensen, Gardell Dano, 23
Christian, Mary Blount, 95
Church, Thomas, 54
Churchman, Deborah, 27
Clapp, Patricia, 95
Clark, Diane, 28
Clarke, Mary Stetson, 95
Clayton, Barbara, 208
Cleere, Gail S., 33
Clements, John, 6, 106, 165
Clifford, Harold, 58
Climo, Shirley, 28
Clouette, Bruce, 5
Coatsworth, Elizabeth, 24, 146
Coblentz, Catherine C., 208
Coelho, Tony, 89
Cohen, David Steven, 128, 129
Cohlene, Terri, 101, 184
Colbert, Judy, 28
Colby, Barnard, 11
Colby, Jean Poindexter, 87
Coldrey, Jennifer, 68
Collier, Bonnie B., 17
Collier, Christopher, 14, 17, 96, 146, 176
Collier, James Lincoln, 14, 42, 96, 146, 176
Collins, David R., 123
Colver, Anne, 176
Comegys, Fred, 21
Conley, Kevin, 41
Conley, Patrick, 191, 192, 195
Conn, Frances G., 174
Converse, Harriet Maxwell, 148
Cooke, John C., 4
Cooley, Oscar, 203
Cooney, Barbara, 58, 59
Cooney, Caroline B., 208
Cooney, Ellen, 96
Coope, Peter M., 6
Corbett, Doris S., 168
Corcoran, Barbara, 96
Cornell, William A., 165
Couch, Ernie, 165
Couch, Jill, 165
Cox, Clinton, 87
Crompton, Anne, 49
Crompton, Anne Eliot, 208
Crouse, Anna, 124
Crouthamel, James L., 53
Cuff, David, ed., 161
Cummings, Priscilla, 78, 79
Cunha, M. Rachel, 192
Cunningham, Janice, 1
Cunningham, John T., 121
Cupper, Dan, 157
Curran, Polly, 24
Curry, Jane Louise, 177
Cutler, Carl C., 11

Cwikik, Robert, 196
Czarra, Fred, 83

D'Amato, Alex, 85
D'Amato, Janet, 85
d'Aulaire, Edgar Parin, 172
Dahlstedt, Marden, 177
Dalgliesh, Alice, 14, 96, 177
Dann, Kevin, 129
Danziger, Jeff, 208
Davidson, Margaret, 76
Davis, Burke, 89, 147
Davis, Hadassah, 185, 192
Davis, Lavina R., 147
Davis, Marion, 59
Day, Freida C., 109
Day, Michael, 53, 54
de Angeli, Marguerite, 24, 177
Deans, Sis Boulas, 59
Dearden, Paul, 192
Decker, Robert Owen, 11
Deegan, Paul J., 136
DeFord, Deborah H., 177
DeGering, Etta, 42
Demarest, David P., 156
Desens, Joan, 138
Devlin, Harvey, 96
Devlin, Wendy, 96
Diamond, Arthur, 90
Dibner, Martin, 54
Dickerson, Paul, 28
DiClerico, James M., 117
Dietz, Lew, 59
Dillard, Annie, 161
Dingwall, Laima, 20
Dodd, Anne Wescott, 59
Dodge, Bertha, 203
Dodge, Mary Mapes, 123
Dolson, Hildegarde, 158, 173
Dorian, Edith M., 126
Dorsey, Michael, 3, 17
Douglas, Evelyn E., 28
Dowell, Susan Stiles, 69
Dreschler-Marx, Carin, 137
Dreyer, Glenn D., 9
Driemen, J. E., 143
Dubowski, Cathy East, 76
Duffield, Judy, 28
Duggan, Moira, 103
DuMond, Frank L., 133
Dunn, Wendy, 40
DuPont, Irene E., 101
Dwyer, Frank, 89
Dyer, Ceil, 186

Eager, Edward, 15
Editors of Time-Life Books, 94
Edwards, Cecile Pepin, 205
Egan, Joseph B., 54
Ehling, William P., 135

Ehrlich, Elizabeth, 169
Eichelberger, Rosa Kohler, 79
Eisenberg, Lisa, 78
Ellis, David M., 138
Ellis, Rafaela, 145
Emerson, Kathy Lynn, 170
Engfer, LeeAnne, 54
Epstein, Beryl, 20, 34
Epstein, Sam, 20, 34, 78
Estes, Eleanor, 15
Estrin, Herman A., 117
Ewin, Gail, 21

Faber, Doris, 92, 154
Fairless, Caroline, 208
Fancher, Pauline, 134
Farb, Nathan, 141
Farrow, Rachi, 209
Fast, Howard, 174
Faude, Wilson H., 9
Fein, Cheri, 136
Fendler, Donn, 54
Fennelly, Catherine, 10
Fennimore, Harvey Curtis, Jr., 22
Ferris, Jean, 13
Ferris, Jeri, 76, 77, 78
Field, Rachel, 59
Finlayson, Ann, 178
Fisher, Dorothy Canfield, 209
Fisher, Leonard, 34
Fisher, Sara, 154
Fitzpatrick, Sandra, 28
Fleischman, Paul, 197
Fleischman, Sid, 209
Fleming, Alice, 174
Fleming, Thomas, 121
Fletcher, Marvin E., 41
Fogle, Jeanne, 34
Fontaine, Marie, 195
Forbes, Esther, 93, 96
Foreman, Michael, 147
Foster, Genevieve, 161
Foster, Geraldine, 193
Foster, Sally, 154
Fowler, William M., 91
Fox, Paula, 147
Fradin, Dennis, 9, 12, 21, 29, 54, 73, 106, 118, 122, 138, 193, 196
Fradin, Morris, 79
Francek, Thomas, 34
Frank, William P., 24
Frankenstein, Alfred, 90
Frankl, Ron, 42
Fredeen, Charles, 118
Freedman, Russell, 143
Freeman, Melville, 54
Friedland, Joan W., 9
Fritz, Jean, 90, 91, 93, 96, 144, 156, 172, 178

Frost, Ed, 51
Frost, Frances, 209
Frost, Robert, 102
Frost, Roon, 51
Fuller, Miriam Morris, 94

Gaeddert, LouAnn, 91
Gallagher, Trish, 68
Galt, Tom, 145, 147
Gauch, Patricia Lee, 126, 178, 209
Geer, Jack, 82
Gelman, Amy, 9
George, Jean Craighead, 147
Gherman, Beverly, 142
Gibbons, Gail, 49, 51, 184, 201, 209
Gibbs, Carroll R., 35
Gibbs, Valerie, 35
Giblin, James Cross, 44
Giese, James R., 99
Gille, Frank H., 165
Gilmore, Robert, 106
Gjelfriend, George E., 59
Gleason, David King, 86
Glimm, James York, 157
Good, Merle, 155, 156
Good, Phyllis, 155
Goodnough, David, 139
Goodwin, Maria R., 28
Goodwin, Richard H., 4
Gore, Doris, 60
Gosselin, Carol A., 106
Gottlief, Steven, 29
Goudey, Alice, 60
Graff, Nancy Price, 55, 201
Granfield, Linda, 137
Grant, Louise, 111
Grant, Marion Hepburn, 7
Graves, Charles P., 92
Graybill, Kathryn, 178
Greene, Carol, 13, 43, 77
Greene, Ellin, 19
Greenfield, Eloise, 125
Greer, Jack, 82
Grierson, Ruth Gortner, 51
Gross, Virginia T., 179
Gurko, Miriam, 141
Gutkind, Lee, 165
Guy, Anne Welsh, 144
Guyette, Elise A., 203

Hahn, James, 135
Hahn, Lynn, 135
Hahn, Mary Downing, 79
Hale, Stuart, 188
Hall, Clayton Colman, 73
Hall, Donald, 110, 111
Hammerstein, Oscar, 198
Hansen, Judith, 19, 185

Hansen, Robert, 70
Harlan, Judith, 170
Harley, Ruth, 124
Harness, Cheryl, 97
Harpster, John W., 183
Harriman, Edward, 60
Harrington, Mark R., 126
Harrington, Ty, 55
Harris, Bill, 161
Harris, Kathleen McKinley, 209
Haskell, Bess C., 60
Haskins, James, 40, 43
Hassett, Ann, 60
Hassett, John, 60
Hastings, Scott E., Jr., 101
Hayes, Wilma Pitchford, 97
Heffernan, Nancy Coffey, 107
Heidish, Marcy Moran, 97
Heinrichs, Ann, 193
Held, Patricia Contreras, 129
Hengen, Elizabeth Durfee, 109
Henry, Edna (Blue Star Woman), 186
Henry, Marguerite, 175, 210
Herdan-Zuckmayer, Alice, 203
Herold, Patricia, 116
Herzig, Alison, 15
Higgins, Helen B., 124
Hightower, Florence, 97
Hill, Ralph Nading, 142, 203
Hillis, Mary Carroll, 102
Hiscock, Bruce, 133
Hofer, Evelyn, 38
Hoffecker, Carol E., 22
Hoig, Stan, 34
Holbrook, Stewart, 204
Holman, Felice, 147
Holmes, Edward M., 51
Homer, Larona C., 115, 126
Honness, Elizabeth, 112
Hornor, Edith R., 84
Horwitz, Joshua, 132
Hostetler, John, 155
Hott, L. R., 139
Hovanec, Evelyn A., 156
Howard, Elizabeth Fitzgerald, 79, 80
Hoyt, Edwin P., 92
Hubbard, Jim, 26
Hudgins, Barbara, 118
Huntington, Lee Pennock, 210
Hurwitz, Johanna, 210

Igus, Toyomi, 40
IlgenFritz, Elizabeth, 196
Ingmire, Bruce E., 106
Inshaw, Norman, 6
Ipcar, Dahlov, 60

Jackson, Edgar N., 210

Jacobs, William Jay, 205
Jacobus, Melanchthon W., 2
Jacoby, Mark E., 68
Jagendorf, M. A., 133
Jakoubek, Robert, 13, 43
Jane, Mary Childs, 60
Jannuzzelli, Diane C., 130
Jaspersohn, William, 201
Jefferys, C. P. D., 195
Jennings, Paulla, 197
Jennison, Keith, 203
Jensen, Ann, 67
Jensen, Dorothea, 179
Jewett, Sarah Orne, 61
Jezer, Marty, 170
Johnson, Neil, 164
Johnson, Sylvia A., 68
Johnston, Norma, 169
Jones, Hettie, 147
Jones, Rebecca C., 80
Jordan, Mildred, 179
Junior League of Washington, 35

Kaessman, Beta Ennis, 74
Kallgren, Beverly H., 53
Kamen, Gloria, 143
Kane, Robert S., 29
Kantor, MacKinlay, 164
Katakis, Michael, 35
Kaufmann, Mervyn D., 124
Keehn, Sally M., 179
Keiper, Ronald P., 69
Keller, Mollie, 124
Kelley, Shirley, 210
Kellogg, Steven, 169
Kent, Deborah, 7, 22, 35, 71, 121
Kent, Louise, 210
Kent, Zachary, 123, 173
Kerby, Mona, 124
Kerr, Mary Brandt, 6
Kettelkamp, Larry, 171
Key, Francis Scott, 69
Keyarts, Eugene, 10
Keyworth, Cynthia, 57
Kimber, Robert, 50
King, B. A., 51
Kingsley, Gretchen H., 3
Kinsey-Warnock, Natalie, 112, 210
Kipman, David, 173
Kirkpatrick, Doris, 210
Kittredge, Mary, 43
Kivlin, Barbara, 211
Kjellerup, Hope, 204, 211
Klemens, Michael W., 5
Knight, James E., 122, 166
Konigsburg, E. L., 15, 148
Koop, Allen V., 104
Kopper, Philip, 47
Kovalski, Maryann, 148

Kraft, Herbert C., 130
Kramer, William, 28
Krause, Paul, 182
Kraybill, Donald B., 155
Krementz, Jill, 30
Kroll, Steven, 148
Kross, Peter, 122
Krumgold, Joseph, 126
Kudlinski, Kathleen V., 171
Kull, Nell, 211
Kuller, Alison Murray, 50

Lacetti, Silvio R., 128
Ladd, Elizabeth, 61
Lancaster, Bruce, 139
Landau, Elaine, 172
Langley, Virginia, 61
Langton, Jane, 97
Lape, Fred, 139
Lapp, Eleanor, 61
Larkin, Alice True, 61
Lasky, Kathryn, 62, 97
Latham, Jean Lee, 13, 90
Lawrence, Mildred, 97
Lawson, Robert, 179
League of Women Voters, 119
League of Women Voters of New Jersey, 114
Leavell, Perry J., 125
Lenski, Lois, 172, 211
Lesko, Kathleen, 35
Levin, Betty, 62
Levine, I. E., 145
Levinson, Nancy Smiler, 80, 143
Levitt, Marc Joel, 184
Lewis, Cynthia C, 6
Lewis, David L., 35
Lewis, Paul M., 119
Lewis, Thomas J., 6
Lind, Louise, 193
Lindbergh, Anne, 45
Lipfert, Nathan R., 55
Lipman, Jean, 170
Lippson, Alice Jane, 66
Lipsyte, Robert, 148
Llewellyn, Robert, 30, 161
Lockhardt, Barbara M., 80
Lockhart, Betty Ann C., 113
Lockhart, Lynne, 80
Loewen, Nancy, 35
Longsworth, Polly, 91
Lord, Beman, 20, 139
Lovett, Sarah, 137
Lowry, Lois, 98
Lumley, Catherine Wentzel, 36
Lunt, Dudley Cammett, 22
Lyman, Nancy A., 22

McAdow, Ron, 109
McArdie, Dana, 3

Macaulay, David, 134, 187
McCaig, Barb, 161
McCall, Edith, 187
McClard, Megan, 140
McCloskey, Robert, 61, 62, 98
McCloy, James F., 115
McCormick, Richard Patrick, 130
McCullough, David G., 158
MacDonald, Amy, 62
McEwing, Barbara, 23
McGee, Harold, 53
McGinnis, Helen J., 159
McGough, Michael R., 166
McGovern, Ann, 93
McGraw, Ryder, 36
McKissack, Frederick, 76
McKown, Robin, 171
McLoughlin, William, 194
McMahon, William, 115
McMillan, Bruce, 49, 63
McNair, Sylvia, 107
McNulty, Faith, 186, 197
MacPherson, Mary, 20
Maestro, Betsy, 15, 134
Maestro, Giulio, 134
Mahone-Lonesome, Robyn, 41
Malone, Mary, 172
Manakee, Harold, 74
Manes, Stephen, 197
Mares, Bill, 207
Marion, John Francis, 162
Marrin, Albert, 72
Marsh, Carole, 7, 8, 12
Martin, Charles, 63
Martin, Kenneth R., 55
Martin, Patricia Miles, 92
Martin, Rafe, 2
Mason, F. Van Wyck, 164
Mason, Miriam E., 123
Massachusetts Department of Public Works, 86
Mayer, Ronald A., 120
Mayerson, Evelyn Wilde, 148
Mazer, Harry, 148
Meacham, Margaret, 80
Meadowcroft, Enid LaMonte, 179
Meanley, Brooke, 68
Meg, Elizabeth, 24
Meigs, Cornelia, 179
Melin, Grace H., 123
Mellick, Andrew D., 131
Mellin, Jeanne, 201
Meltzer, Ida, 84
Meltzer, Milton, 44, 90, 172, 174
Menard, Russell R., 73
Mendoza, George, 211
Merritt, Joseph F., 159
Meryman, Richard, 175
Meyer, Carolyn, 155

Meyer, Susan E., 171
Miers, Earl Schenck, 36
Milhous, Katherine, 180
Millar, John, 194
Miller, Douglas, 76
Miller, Melville D., 128
Miller, Natalie, 70
Miller, Ray, 115
Miller, William J., Jr., 19
Mitchell, Barbara, 25, 166
Mitchell, Lewis, 49
Monjo, F. N., 198
Monke, Ingrid, 88
Monsell, Helen A., 125
Montgomery, Constance, 200, 201
Montgomery, Raymond, 201
Moore, Robin, 180
Morely, Linda, 107
Morey, Janet Nomuira, 40
Morgan, Nina, 124
Morgan, Patricia Griffith, 52
Morison, Samuel Eliot, 93
Morris, Gerald E., 51
Morrison, Russell, 70
Moulton, Deborah, 63
Mudge, John T. B., 104
Muller, Charles G., 211
Munro, Roxie, 36, 132, 137
Murphy, Jim, 164
Murray, Michele, 15
Murray, Thomas Christopher, 122
Murrow, Liza Ketchum, 211
Mussey, June Barrows, 204
Myers, Walter Dean, 149

Naden, Corinne J., 110
National Gallery of Art, 27
Naylor, Phyllis Reynolds, 155
Needham, Walter, 204
Neimark, Anne E., 12
Nevison, Henry, 50
New Jersey Library Association, 127
New Jersey State Library, 127
Nguyen, Chi, 187
Niering, William, 4
Niss, Bob, 56
Nyiri, Alan, 52

O'Brien, Alice Rowan, 25
O'Byrne-Pelham, Fran, 164
O'Connor, Edwin, 98
O'Dell, Scott, 149
Oatway, Pete, 63
Older, Julia, 107
Olsen, Stephen, 187
Oman, Anne H., 27
Orton, Helen Fuller, 149
Osborne, Angela, 89

Pallotta, Jerry, 185
Papenfuse, Edward, 66
Parisi, Lynn S., 99
Parnall, Peter, 63
Parnes, Robert, 117
Paterson, Katherine, 80, 81, 98, 211
Peare, Catherine Owens, 171
Pearson, Tracey Campbell, 211
Peck, Richard, 149
Peck, Robert Newton, 212
Peddicord, Louis, 73
Peffer, Randall S., 72
Pell, John, 205
Pelta, Kathy, 41
Pendergast, John, 108
Penn, William, 22
Perez, Norah A., 180
Perl, Lila, 102
Perry, Estelle H., 54
Perry, Rae, 57
Peters, Russell, 191
Peters, Samuel, 16
Peterson, Edwin L., 162
Peterson, Helen Stone, 89, 141
Peterson, William N., 6
Petry, Ann, 98
Phelan, Mary Kay, 164
Philips, David E., 2
Pierce, Edith, 92
Pinette, Richard E., 108
Pinkwater, Jill, 149
Piper, Doris D., 112
Piper, Roberta, 212
Pitch, Anthony S., 36
Pitkin, Dorothy, 212
Pitzer, Sara, 162
Pohl, William L., 56
Polacco, Patricia, 180
Poliniak, Louis, 159
Potter, Parker B., Jr., 108
Price, Robert L., 30
Prideaux, Tom, 94
Princess Red Wing, 185
Prinz, Lucie, 39
Progue, Pamela, 188
Purdy, Carol, 212
Pyle, Katharine, 22

Quackenbush, Robert, 44, 144
Quiri, Patricia, 189

Raftery, Gerald, 212
Rambeck, Richard, 70
Ramus, Daniel, 194
Rand, Gloria, 198
Randall, Harold, 74
Randall, Marta, 92
Randall, Peter, 103

Rappaport, Doreen, 181
Ray, Mary Lyn, 112
Reardon, Patricia, 129
Reber, James Q., 32
Reed, Clay, 23
Reef, Catherine, 37, 41, 71
Reef, Pat Davidson, 57
Reilly, Robert T., 181
Reps, John William, 30
Reynolds, Michael M., 82
Rich, Louise Dickinson, 52, 55
Richmond, Robert P., 110
Richter, Conrad, 181
Rinaldi, Ann, 98, 126
Ripley, Sheldon, 205
Ritchie, David, 8
Ritchie, Deborah, 8
Roach, Marilynne K., 212
Robertson, Keith, 126
Robinson, Jane W., 63
Robinson, Tom, 181
Roche, A. K., 15
Rockwell, Anne, 149
Rodowsky, Colby, 81
Rogers, Barbara Radcliffe, 103
Rolde, Neil, 55
Rollo, Vera Foster, 67, 71, 75, 77
Roman, Joseph, 12, 196
Rood, Ronald, 200
Roop, Connie, 56
Roop, Peter, 56
Rosal, Lorenca Consuelo, 108, 113
Ross, Betty, 30
Roth, David M., 17
Roth, Matthew, 5
Rounds, Glen, 149
Rowe, William Hutchinson, 55
Rowinski, Kate, 64
Ruskin, Thelma G., 72
Russell, John, 47

Samson, Gary, 108
Sanger, David, 55
Sante, Luc, 118
Santoro, Carmela, 194
Santrey, Laurence, 175
Sargent, Ruth, 57, 64
Sarton, May, 102
Saures, J. C., 37
Sawin, Nancy, 23
Sawyer, Kate, 17
Scheid, Margaret, 52
Scheller, William G., 120
Scherer, Thomas E., 10
Schoor, Gene, 175
Schroder, Walter, 194
Schuan, Virginia, 75
Schuman, Michael A., 103
Scott, Donnie Porter, 64

Scott, Elaine, 134
Scott, Stephen, 155
Seabrook, Brenda, 81
Seale, William, 48
Searles, James W., 56
Seitz, Ruth Hoover, 163
Selden, Bernice, 84
Selden, George, 150
Sewall, Marcia, 87, 190
Shain, Charles, 56
Shain, Samuella, 56
Shangle, Robert D., 163
Shank, William H., 159
Shapiro, Irwin, 157
Shapiro, Mary J., 140
Sharmat, Marjorie Weinman, 150
Sharpe, Susan, 81
Shaver, Lula A., 204
Shaw, Ray, 31
Sheppard, Cynthia, 28
Sherrow, Victoria, 144
Shippen, Katherine, 170
Shyer, Marlene Fanta, 150, 212
Siegel, Beatrice, 104, 145, 190
Silliker, Ruth L., 57
Simmons, Amelia, 6
Simmons, William, 185, 190
Simonds, Christopher, 196
Singmaster, Elsie, 181
Skolnick, Arnold, 50
Skolsky, Mindy Warshaw, 151
Skurzynski, Gloria, 181
Sloane, Eric, 105
Smith, Catherine Schneider, 37
Smith, Clyde, 189
Smith, Elmer L, 156
Smith, Harry W., 64, 112
Smith, Helen, 163
Snediker, Quentin, 67
Sorenson, Virginia, 182
Speare, Elizabeth George, 16, 64, 213
Sprigg, June, 100
St. George, Judith, 37, 134, 150
St. John, Gregory, 204
St. John, Helen, 204
Stahl, Rachel K., 154
Stapler, Sarah, 64
Starkey, Marion, 84
Stave, Bruce, 17
Stein, R. Conrad, 37, 141
Steiner-Scott, Elizabeth, 127
Stephen, R. J., 1
Sterling, Dorothy, 145
Stern, Jane, 6
Stern, Michael, 6
Stern, Philip Von Doren, 94
Stevenson, Augusta, 90, 125, 174
Sticles, Frances Copeland, 77
Stockton, Frank R., 115

Stolz, Mary, 213
Stone, Erika, 156
Stone, James, 5
Stout, Harry S., 177
Sullivan, George, 38
Sutherland, John F., 17
Swann, Don, 69
Swanson, June, 12
Swetnam, George, 163
Swift, Hildegarde, 151
Syme, Ronald, 173, 205

Tager, Jack, 85
Talbot, Charlene Joy, 151
Taylor, John, 1
Taylor, John W., 69
Taylor, Sally L., 4, 5
Terhune, Albert Payson, 127
Tharp, Louise Hall, 205
Thaxter, Celia, 105
Thomas, Pamela, 137
Thompson, Harold W., 133
Thompson, Kathleen, 23, 75, 88, 108, 173, 195
Thompson, Mary Wolfe, 213
Thompson, Nancy, 100, 113
Thompson, William O., 50
Thoreau, Henry David, 94
Thurston, Doris, 64
Till, Tom, 116
Tilp, Fay, 76
Tilp, Fred, 76
Titherington, Jeanne, 64
Titus, Charles, 75
Tobias, Tobi, 169
Tobin, Michael F., 17
Toker, Franklin, 163
Tolles, Martha, 151
Tomlinson, Gerald, 120
Towne, Mary, 213
Townsend, George Alfred, 81
Trask, Margaret P., 213
Trecker, Janice Law, 10
Tree, Christina, 86, 103
Tresselt, Alvin, 98
Trueworthy, Nance, 52
Tucker, Louis Leonard, 11
Tuckerman, Stephen, 8
Tudor, Bethany, 110
Tudor, Tasha, 202
Tunis, Edwin, 118, 168
Turck, Mary, 31
Turkle, Brinton, 99

Turner, Gregg M., 2
Twain, Mark, 16
Tyce, Robert, 188

Underwood, Betty, 16
United States Department of the Interior, 66
United States National Planning Commission, 46
Unl, Michael, 52

Van Leeuwen, Jean, 151
VanRynbach, Iris, 2
Verrier, Suzy, 65
Viereck, Philip, 214
Villalard, Martine, 5
Villalard-Bohnsack, Martine, 4
Villani, Robert, 52
Vining, Elizabeth Gray, 94, 182
Vining, Elizabeth Janet, 173
Voigt, Cynthia, 16, 82, 99

Waber, Bernard, 151 - 152
Wagle, Elizabeth P., 127
Wahle, Lisa, 4
Wakeley, James S., 159
Wakeley, Lillian D., 159
Wallace, Paul A. W., 163, 170
Wallace-Brodeur, Ruth, 214
Wallower, Lucille, 182
Walton, William, 38
Warburton, Eileen, 195
Warner, J. F., 195
Warner, William W., 69
Warren, R. Scott, 4
Wartik, Nancy, 104
Wasilchick, John V., 156
Waters, Kate, 39, 88
Watson, Nancy D., 214
Webb, Kenneth, 206
Weber, Ken, 189
Webster, Harriet, 136
Weibust, Patricia, 10
Weinstein-Farson, Laurie, 191
Weiss, Howard M., 3, 17
Welch, Catherine A., 182
Welch, Wally, 189
Weller, Frances, 198
Werstein, Irving, 172
Weslager, C. A., 23, 130
Westergaard, Barbara, 130
Westman, Barbara, 86
Wheeler, Joseph L., 74

White, Angela, 135
White, Christopher P., 68
White, David O., 11
White House Historical Association, 47
White, Sylvia, 65
Whitehall, Walter Muir, 86
Whitehead, Ruth Holmes, 53
Whitehouse, Bion H., 104
Whitmore, Carol, 54
Whitney, Phyllis A., 16
Wibberley, Leonard, 99
Wilbur, C. Keith, 50, 102, 104, 184, 187, 190
Wilder, Laura Ingalls, 152
Wilhelm, Hans, 206
Wilke, Richard W., 85
Wilkinson, Brenda, 43
Williams, Harold A., 75
Williams, Robert F., 128
Wilroy, Mary Edith, 39
Wilson, Charles M., 214
Wilson, Ellen, 91
Wilson, Richard, 75
Wilson, W. Emerson, 23
Winders, Gertrude Hecker, 205
Winter, Jeanette, 152
Wojciechowski, Susan, 152
Wolfe, Rinna Evelyn, 42
Wood, James Playsted, 31
Works Progress Administration, 130
Wright, Giles R., 127
Wright, J. E., 168
Wright, Marion, 188
Wriston, Hildreth T., 214
Wroten, William, 72
Wyler, Rose, 20
Wyzga, Marilyn, 100

Yashima, Taro, 152
Yates, Elizabeth, 91, 110, 112
Yolen, Jane, 100
Yorinks, Arthur, 152
Youst, Yvonne, 109

Zacher, Susan M., 160
Zatz, Arline, 120
Ziner, Feenie, 93
Zolotown, Charlotte, 198

Title Index

Aaron and the Green Mountain Boy, 209
Abbie Burgess, Lighthouse Heroine, 56
ABC's of Maine, 64
ABCs of New Hampshire, 112
ABC's of Vermont, 211
The Abenaki, 104
Abigail Adams, 89
Abigail Adams: An American Woman, 89
Abigail Adams, "Dear Partner," 89
Ada and the Wild Duck, 176
The Adirondacks (Farb), 141
The Adirondacks (Hott/Garey), 139
The Advent of Obadiah, 99
The Adventures of Maynard . . . a Maine Moose, 57
Afro-Americans in New Jersey: A Short History, 127
The Afton Portfolio of Indians of the Forest, 21, 120
Against the Iroquois: The Sullivan Campaign of 1779 in New York State, 137
Agnes De Mille: Dancing Off the Earth, 142
Airports: A Community Need, 67
An Album of Rhode Island History, 1636–1986, 191
Alex Hamilton: The Little Lion, 124
Alexander Calder and His Magic Mobiles, 170
Alexander Graham Bell, 41
Alexander Hamilton, 124
Alexander Hamilton and Aaron Burr, 124
The Algonquians, 189
All about New Hampshire, 109
All about Niagara Falls: Fascinating Facts, Dramatic Discoveries, 137
All for a Horse, 207

Always Nine Years Old: Sarah Orne Jewett's Childhood, 57
Always to Remember: The Story of the Vietnam Veterans Memorial, 32
America: A Regional Cookbook, 6
America: The Dream of My Life, 114
America the Beautiful. Delaware, 22
America the Beautiful: New Hampshire, 107
America the Beautiful: New York, 141
An American Bard: The Story of Henry Wadsworth Longfellow, 92
An American Childhood, 161
American Cooking, 6
The American Oyster, 82
America's Ethan Allen, 204
America's First Air Voyage, 116
America's First Black General: Benjamin O. Davis, Sr., 1880-1970, 41
America's National Gallery: A Gift to the Nation, 47
America's Paul Revere, 93
The Amish (Faber), 154
The Amish (Smith), 156
An Amish Family, 155
Amish Life: A Portrait of Plain Living, 156
Amish People: Plain Living in a Complex World, 155
The Amish School, 154
Amish Society, 155
Among the Clouds, 107
Amos Fortune: Free Man, 91, 110
Amos Fortune, Free Man (audiocassette), 110
And the Other, Gold, 152
And Then What Happened, Paul Revere?, 93
Andre, 59

Andrew Carnegie and the Age of Steel, 170
Andrew Wyeth, 175
Andy and the Red Canoe, 214
Angel Baskets: A Little Story about the Shakers, 112
Annapolis: A Walk through History, 70
Annapolis and Maryland State Symbols, 70
Anne Hutchinson (Faber), 92
Anne Hutchinson (IlgenFritz), 196
Anne Hutchinson: Fighter for Religious Freedom, 196
Anthony Wayne: Daring Boy, 125
Appalachian Mountain Club River Guide, 8
Appolonia's Valentine, 180
Arctic Explorer: The Story of Matthew Henson, 77
Arthur, the White House Mouse, 45
As Does New Hampshire and Other Poems by May Sarton, 102
Assateague, 72
The Assateague Ponies, 69
At the Sign of the Rocking Horse, 213
Atlas of National Wetlands Inventory Maps of the Chesapeake Bay, 66
The Atlas of Pennsylvania, 161
Atomic Dawn: A Biography of Robert Oppenheimer, 143
Audubon Wildlife Adventure: Whales, 85
Aunt Flossie's Hats (and Crab Cakes Later), 79
Authentic Pennsylvania Dutch Designs, 160

Babes in the Woods, 61
Baltimore, 71
Baltimore Afire, 75
Baltimore Harbor and Skyline, 70

Baltimore Orioles, 70
The Baron of Beacon Hill: A Biography of John Hancock, 91
The Battle for Homestead, 1880-1892: Politics, Culture and Steel, 182
Battle of Gettysburg, 164
Baxter Bear and Moses Moose, 58
Bayside Guide to Weather on the Chesapeake, 68
Beacons of Light: Lighthouses, 184
The Bear That Heard Crying, 112
The Bears on Hemlock Mountain, 177
Beautiful Delaware, 20
Beautiful Swimmers: Watermen, Crabs and the Chesapeake Bay, 69
Beauty of New Jersey, 119
A Begonia for Miss Applebaum, 152
Beloved Brick House, 64
Ben and Me, 179
The Bend in the River, 108
Benjamin Banneker, 41
Benjamin Davis, Jr., 41
Benjamin Franklin, 172
Benjamin Franklin: The New American, 172
Benjamin West and His Cat Grimalkin, 175
Bernard Langlais, Sculptor, 57
Berry Ripe Moon, 53
Best Hikes with Children in Connecticut, Massachusetts, & Rhode Island, 6
The Best of Enemies, 95
The Best of New Hampshire Crossroads, 105
The Best of Washington, D.C., 27
The Best Place to Live, 191
Between Boston and New York, 8
Big Fire in Baltimore, 79
The Big Green Umbrella, 24
The Big Rock, 133
The Biggest (and Best) Flag That Ever Flew, 80
Bill Cosby, Family Funny Man, 171
Birds and Marshes of the Chesapeake Bay Country, 68
Birds of Connecticut Salt Marshes, 5
Birds of Pennsylvania: Natural History and Conservation, 159

Birds of Prey in Connecticut, 5
Birds of the Chesapeake Bay, 69
Birds of the Connecticut College Arboretum, 5
BirdWatch, 20
Black American Heroes, 11
Black Georgetown Remembered (videocassette), 33
Black Georgetown Remembered: A History of Its Black Community from the Founding of the Town of George in 1751 to the Present Day, 35
Black Heroes of the American Revolution, 89
Blackbeard the Pirate and Other Stories of the Pine Barrens, 115
Blazing Bear, 59
Blood in the Snow, 212
The Bloody Country, 14, 176
The Blue Cat of Castle Town, 208
Blueberries for Sal, 61, 62, 63
Blueberry Bears, 61
Bluestones and Salt Hay: An Anthology of New Jersey Poets, 117
Body, Boots, and Britches: Folktales, Ballads, and Speech from Country New York, 133
A Book of Country Things, 204
Born in Freedom: The Story of Colonel Drake, 158
Boston, 88
Boston Massacre, 87
A Boston Picture Book, 86
Boy Who Saved the Town, 81
Brady, 178
Brandywine Village, the Story of a Milling Community, 22
The Brave, 148
Bread Sister of Sinking Creek, 180
Bread-and-Butter Indian, 176
Bread-and-Butter Journey, 177
A Break with Charity: A Story of the Salem Witch Trials, 98
Breaker, 180
Broadway: From the Battery to the Bronx, 137
The Brooklyn Bridge: They Said It Couldn't Be Built, 134
Brother Moose, 62
Brothers in Arms, 210
Brown Cow Farm, 60
Bully for You, Teddy Roosevelt, 144
Burt Dow, Deep Water Man, 62, 63
Buzzing a Bill into Law, 114

By George, Bloomers!, 150

Cabin Faced West, 178
Caesar Rodney Patriot, Delaware's Hero for All Times and All Seasons, 24
Calico Bush, 59
Calico Captive, 213
The Call of the Running Tide, a Portrait of an Island Family, 55
The Callender Papers, 99
Canada Geese Quilt, 210
Canal Boatman: My Life on Upstate Waterways, 132
Canoeing Central New York, 135
Canoeing the Jersey Pine Barrens, 117
Cape Cod: Sands of Time, 85
A Capital for the Nation, 34
The Capitol and Our Lawmakers, 36
Captain Grey, 125
Carnegie's Dinosaurs, 159
Carry on, Mr. Bowditch, 90
Casey! The Sports Career of Charles Stengel, 135
Cassie and the General, 178
Cat and Canary, 147
The Cat Who Escaped from Steerage: A Bubbemeiser, 148
Celia's Island Journal, 105
Central Square and Beyond: Historical Images of Keene and Cheshire County, 104
Chadwick and the Garplegrungen, 78
Chadwick the Crab, 78
Chadwick's Wedding, 78
Champlain, Father of New France, 205
The Champlain Monster, 208
Champlain Northwest Voyager, 205
Champlain of the St. Lawrence, 205
A Changing Connecticut, 1
Charles Drew, 41
Charles Richard Drew, M.D., 42
Charlie's Dream, 209
Charlotte's Web, 209
The Charter of Maryland, 66
Charting the Chesapeake, 70
Chautauqua: Its Architecture and Its People, 134
Checklist of the Amphibians and Reptiles of Connecticut, 5

Chesapeake: Fact, Fiction and Fun: Pungoteague, St. Clement, Patapsco . . ., 76
Chesapeake Bay: Nature of the Estuary, a Field Guide, 68
The Chesapeake Bay in Maryland: An Atlas of Natural Resources, 66
Chesapeake Bay Schooners, 67
Chester Cricket's Pigeon Ride, 150
The Chester Town Tea Party, 81
Childish Things: The Reminiscence of Susan Baker Blunt, 109
A Child's Christmas in Pittsburgh, 157
Chita's Christmas Tree, 79
Christa McAuliffe: Teacher in Space, 110
Christmas Tree Farm, 207
Christmastime in New York City, 132
City! Washington, D.C., 28
City Dog, 212
City of Trees: The Complete Field Guide to the Trees of Washington, D.C., 27
The City of Washington, 35
The City of Washington: An Illustrated History, 34
City out of Wilderness: Washington, 33
City Paper, 46
Civil War, 164
Clambake—A Wampanoag Tradition, 191
Clara and the Bookwagon, 80
Clara Barton: Founder of the American Red Cross, 123
Clara Barton: Founder of the Red Cross, 90
Clara Barton: Healing the Wounds, 76
Clara Barton: The Gentle Warrior, 123
Clear Sailing: How an Augusta Boy Becomes a Monhegan Fisherman, 58
Click!: A Story about George Eastman, 142
The Clock, 14
Coastal Rhode Island, 189
Colonial and Historic Homes of Maryland, 69
Colonial Crafts for You to Make, 85
The Colony of Delaware, 22
The Colony of New York Series: A First Book, 139

A Coloring Book of the First Americans, Lenape Indian Drawings, 21
Come Out, Muskrats, 20
Commodore Perry in the Land of the Shogun, 189
Common Mushrooms of New England, 4
Connecticut (Gelman), 9
Connecticut (Kent), 7
Connecticut: A Picture Book to Remember Her by, 7
Connecticut: The Early Years, 8
Connecticut and Rhode Island Trivia, 194
The Connecticut Atlas, 10
Connecticut Audubon News, 16
The Connecticut Colony, 9
Connecticut Facts/Rhode Island Facts, 6
Connecticut Field Trip Guide Book, 17
Connecticut Firsts, 9
Connecticut History and Culture: An Historical Overview and Resource Guide for Teachers, 17
Connecticut in the Civil War, 9
Connecticut in the Revolution, 9
Connecticut Jeopardy, 7
Connecticut Law, 14
Connecticut Magazine, 17
The Connecticut Media Book: A Surprising Guide to the Amazing Print, Broadcast, and Online Media of Our State for Students, Teachers, Writers, and Publishers, 7
Connecticut off the Beaten Path, 8
Connecticut Originals, 11
Connecticut Railroads: An Illustrated History, 2
Connecticut Revolutionary War Leaders, 10
Connecticut State Greats, 12
Connecticut State Register and Manual, 1
Connecticut Wildlife, 16
Connecticut Women in the Revolutionary Era, 10
A Connecticut Yankee in King Arthur's Court, 16
Connecticut's Black Soldiers, 11
Connecticut's First, 7
Connecticut's Historic Highway Bridges, 5

Connecticut's Most (Devasting) Disasters and Most (Calamitous) Calamities, 8
Connecticut's Notable Trees, 9
Connecticut's Seminary of Sedition: Yale College, 11
The Conservationist, 153
Constance: A Story of Early Plymouth, 95
Cooking the Italian Way, 186
Cooking the Vietnamese Way, 187
Cooperstown: Baseball's Hall of Fame, 135
The Corduroy Road, 147
Cornstalks and Cannonballs, 25
The Country of the Pointed Firs, 61
The Courage of Sarah Noble, 14, 96
The Covered Bridges of Pennsylvania, 160
Crabs, 68
The Crack in the Wall & Other Terribly Weird Tales, 211
Cranberry Thanksgiving, 96
Creating New Jersey Learning Centers: An Exciting Multi-Disciplinary Approach to Teaching New Jersey Studies in the Elementary Grades, 130
Crinkleroot's Book of Animal Tracking, 200
Crinkleroot's Book of Animal Tracks and Wildlife Signs, 201
Crossroads, Descriptions of Western Pennsylvania, 1720-1829, 183
A Crown for Henrietta Maria: Maryland's Namesake Queen, 77
Crown Point and the Destiny Road, 214
Crystal Nights, 15

The Dancing Stars: An Iroquois Legend, 149
Danger at the Breaker, 182
Daniel Boone in Pennsylvania, 170
Darci and the Dance Contest, 151
David Bushnell and His Turtle: The Story of America's First Submarine, 12
A Day in the Life of a Veterinarian, 201

The Day It Rained Forever: A Story of the Johnstown Flood, 179
A Day No Pigs Would Die, 212
D.C. for Free: Hundreds of Free Things to Do in Washington, D.C., 47
A Deaf Child Listened, 12, 42
Dear Dr. Bell—Your Friend, Helen Keller, 141
"Dear Friend, Anna": The Civil War Letters of a Common Soldier from Maine, 53
Decision Making, the Chesapeake Bay: An Interdisciplinary Environmental Education Curriculum Unit, 82
A Declaration of Maryland, 66
Deenie, 125
Deer Country, 208
Deer Valley Girl, 211
Defenses of Narrangansett Bay in World War II, 194
Delaware (Christensen/Burney), 23
Delaware (Thompson), 23
Delaware, Close to Home, 21
Delaware Colony, 23
Delaware in Words and Pictures, 21
The Delaware Indians, 130
The Depths of Narragansett Bay, 188
The Diamond in the Window, 97
Diaries of Phoebe George Bradford, 1832-1839, 24
Diary of an Early American Boy: Noah Blake, 1805, 105
Dicey's Song, 82
Digger, 146
Disaster at Johnstown, 158
Discovering Acadia, a Guide for Young Naturalists, 52
Discovering Maine's Archeological Heritage, 55
District of Columbia: A Bicentennial History, 35
District of Columbia: From Its Glorious Past to the Present, 33
District of Columbia in Words and Pictures, 36
The Docket: Journal of the New Jersey Council for the Social Studies, 127
The Doll of Lilac Valley, 208
Don't Sit under the Apple Tree, 176

Don't You Dare Shoot That Bear!: A Story of Theodore Roosevelt, 144
Dorothea Dix: Girl Reporter, 123
The Double Life of Pocahontas, 93
Drawn from New England: Tasha Tudor, a Portrait in Words and Pictures, 110
Duke Ellington (Collier), 42
Duke Ellington (Frankl), 42

Early Connecticut Houses, 6
Early Hi-Tech in New Jersey, 116
Early Thunder, 96
The Eastern Shore of Maryland: An Annotated Bibliography, 83
Ecology of the Bay, 68
The Egg Tree, 180
1812: The War Nobody Won, 72
Eleanor Roosevelt: A Life of Discovery, 143
Eli Whitney, 13
Eli Whitney: Great Inventor, 13
Elin's Amerika, 24
Elizabeth Cady Stanton and Women's Liberty, 144
Emily Upham's Revenge, or How Deadwood Dick Saved the Banker's Niece: A Massachusetts Adventure, 94
The Empire State—New York, 136
Enchantment of America—Delaware from Its Glorious Past to the Present, 20
Encounter at Easton, 175, 176
Encounters with the Invisible World, 212
The Encyclopedia of Pennsylvania, 165
An Enemy among Them, 177
Enjoying New Jersey Outdoors: A Year-Round Guide to Outdoor Recreation in the Garden State & Nearby, 129
The Ephrata Commune: An Early American Counterculture, 154
Eric Heiden: Winner in Gold, 142
The Erie Canal, 135
The ER-I-E Canal, 138
Ethan Allen: A Definitive Portrait of an American Patriot, 205
Ethan Allen: Green Mountain Boy, 205
Ethan Allen: Green Mountain Hero, 205

Ethan Allen and the Green Mountain Boys, 204
Everyday Life in Colonial Maryland, 75
Everything from a Nail to a Coffin, 2
The Evidence of Washington, 38
Exclusively Washington Trivia, 36
Exploring Maine on Country Roads and Byways, 52
Exploring the Land We Call New Hampshire: An Activity Guide, 100
Exploring the Maine Coast, 52
Extraordinary New Jersey, 118

The Face of Connecticut: The People, Geology and the Land, 3
Faces of Maine, 56
The Faithful Hunter: Abenaki Stories, 49
Family Reunion, 208
Famous Asian Americans, 40
The Farm: Life in Colonial Pennsylvania, 166
A Farm and Village Boyhood, 139
The Farm in the Green Mountains, 203
The Farm Summer 1942, 111
Farmer Boy, 152
A Farmer's Alphabet, 207
Farming, 201
Favorite Short Trips in New York State, 136
Ferris Wheel, 213
A Ferry Tale, Crossing the Delaware on the Cape May-Lewes Ferry, 19
Ferryboat, 15
Fiction Set in New Jersey: A Bibliography of Holdings in the Collections of the New Jersey State Library, 127
A Field Guide to New Jersey's Nature Centers, 129
Fifty Hikes in Western New York: Walks and Day Hikes from the Cattaraugus Hills to the Genessee Valley, 135
The Fighting Ground, 125
Finestkind O'Day, Lobstering in Maine, 63
Fins, Furs, and Feathers: Animal Tales from the Pennsylvania Mountains, 157
Fiorello: His Honor, the Little Flower, 143
Fire in the Heart, 211

The First Americans, Lenape Indian Drawings, 21
The First People of Maryland, 73
The First Thanksgiving Feast, 87
Flatlanders and Ridgerunners, 157
The Fledgling, 97
The Flicker's Feathers, 206
Flying Off the Bridge to Nowhere, 159
Flying the Colors: New Hampshire Facts, 106
Flying the Colors: Pennsylvania Facts, 165
Folklife in New Jersey: An Annotated Bibliography, 128
Folklife Resources in New Jersey, 128
The Folklore and Folklife of New Jersey, 129
Folklore and the Sea, 2
The Folks in the Valley, 176
Follow the Drinking Gourd, 152
Food Webs in an Estuary (A Marine Science Education Workbook), 82
Footprints and Shadows, 59
Forever Wild, Maine's Magnificent Baxter State Park, 52
The Fort and the Flag: Two Adventures in Old-Time New Hampshire, 111
Fort Delaware, 23
Four Days in Philadelphia, 164
Franklin Delano Roosevelt, 143
Frederick Douglass: An American Life, 76
Frederick Douglass: Leader against Slavery, 76
Frederick Douglass and the Fight for Freedom, 76
Frederick Douglass Fights for Freedom, 76
Free Men: The Amistad Revolt and the American Anti-Slavery Movement, 17
Freedom Train: The Story of Harriet Tubman, 145
The French Canadians, 104
The French in Rhode Island, 191
From Plymouth Notch to President: The Farm Boyhood of Calvin Coolidge, 206
From Stump to Ship, a 1930 Logging Film, 50
From the Door of the White House, 33
From the Mixed-Up Files of Mrs. Basil E. Frankweiler, 15, 148

From These Hills, from These Valleys, 183
Frommer's Budget Travel Guide: Washington, D.C. '92-'93 on $40 a Day, 47
Frommer's Family Travel Guide: Washington, D.C. with Kids, 29

Gallaudet: Friend of the Deaf, 42
Games: A New Hampshire Learning Experience, 106
A Gathering of Days, 24
General History of Connecticut, 16
The Genie of Sutton Place, 150
A Geography of Maryland: Ask Me! (about Maryland), 71
George and Martha Washington at Home in New York, 145
George, the Drummer Boy, 95
George Washington: A Picture Book Bibliography, 44
George Washington: Father of Our Country, 44
George Washington and the Birth of our Nation, 44
Getting to Know Robert McCloskey, 63
Gettysburg, 164
The Ghost of Peg-Leg Peter, and Other Stories of Old New York, 133
Ghosts and Haunted Houses of Maryland, 68
Gila Monsters Meet You at the Airport, 150
Ginger Pye, 15
Go Free or Die: A Story about Harriet Tubman, 78
God Save the People: A New Hampshire History, Level II Teacher's Resource Manual, 113
The Godmother Tree, 214
Goffstown's One Room Schoolhouses Remembered, 102
Going Lobstering, 185
Going on a Whale Watch, 49
Going Places with Children in Washington, D.C., 29
Goldstein's Maryland, 71
Good-bye, Billy Radish, 181
Goody Sherman's Pig, 95
Grand Monadnock: Exploring the Most Popular Mountain in America, 107
Grandma Moses: My Life's History, 143
The Granite State Sampler, 107

The Grass Was That High, 212
The Great Christmas Kidnapping Caper, 151
Great Houses of Maryland, 69
The Great Hurricane of 1938, 3
Great Leaders from Connecticut, 12
The Great Oildorado, 158
Great Women in the Struggle, an Introduction for Young Readers, 40
The Greatest Moments in Western Pennsylvania Sports History, 160
Green Mountain Hero, 210
The Green Mountain Toymakers, 214
Green Mountains and Rock Ribs, 203
Green Threshold, 213
Greenhorn on the Frontier, 178
Grist Mills of Early America and Today, 160
Grover Cleveland: 22nd and 24th President of the United States, 123
Growing Up Amish, 154
Growing Up in Maine, Recollections of Childhood from the 1780's to the 1920's, 56
The Guide to Black Washington: Places and Events of Historical and Cultural Significance in the Nation's Capital, 28
A Guide to Government Records at the Maryland State Archives: A Comprehensive List by Agency and Record Sites, 82
Guide to the Mammals of Pennsylvania, 159
Guide to the State Historical Markers of Pennsylvania, 161
Guidebook to Historic Western Pennsylvania, 163

H. My Name Is Henley, 81
Hagerstown Town and Country Almanack, 66
Halfway Hannah, 208
Hambone, 208
Hans Brinker or the Silver Skates, 123
The Hard-to-Believe-but-True! Book of Connecticut History, Mystery, Trivia, Legend, Lore, Humor, & More, 8

Harriet Beecher Stowe (Jakoubek), 13
Harriet Beecher Stowe (sound filmstrip), 13
Harriet Tubman: Guide to Freedom, 78
Harrisburg, Our State Capital, 165
Harry Kitten and Tucker Mouse, 150
Haym Salomon: Son of Liberty, 174
He Went with Champlain, 210
Helen Hayes, 43
Henner's Lydia, 177
Henry David Thoreau: Writer and Rebel, 94
Henry Harford: Last Proprietor of Maryland, 77
Henry Hudson, 124
Henry Reed, Inc., 126
Here and There in Maryland: Field Trips, 74
Here at Eagle Pond, 110
Hero of Champlain, 211
The Hey Hey Man, 209
Hey-Ey-Ey, Lock: Adventures on the Chesapeake and Ohio Canal, 79
Hiawatha: Messenger of Peace, 142
Hiawatha and the Iroquois League, 140
Hide and Seek Fog, 98
The Hideaway, 96
High Island Treasure, 59
High-Water Cargo, 126
Historic Bridges of Pennsylvania, 159
Historic Buildings at Mystic Seaport Museum, 6
Historic Mont Vernon, 109
Historic Old Economy Village, 166
Historic Pennsylvania, 166
Historic Preservation in Connecticut, 1
The Historical Atlas of Massachusetts, 85
An Historical List of Public Officials of Maryland: Governors, Legislators, and Other Principal Officers of Government, 1632 to 1990, 72
Historical New Hampshire, 113
History of New England, 87
The History of Philip's War, 1675-1676, 54

History of the Standard Oil Company, 174
A History of Washington, D.C., 34
History You Can See, 192
The Hokey-Pokey Man, 148
Holy Pittsburgh, 160
A Home for Jamie, 112
Home Is Best, 65
Homecoming, 16, 82
Homesick: My Own Story, 178
Honey in the Rock, 210
Hoops, 149
Horace Mann: Our Nation's First Educator, 92
Horizons, 113
The House on East 88th Street, 151
The House on Observatory Hill: Home of the Vice President of the United States, 33
The House on the Green: Botto House, 115
The House on the Waterfall, 160
Houses from the Sea, 60
How the White House Really Works, 38
How They Built the Statue of Liberty, 140
The Hudson River, 138
A Humanities Approach to Early National U.S. History: Activities and Resources for the Junior High School Teacher, 99
The Hunky Dory, 60
The Hunky-Dory Dairy, 45
The Hunting Camp, 63
Hurray for Christopher! The Story of a Maine Coon Cat, 61
Hurricane, 197

I Am Regina, 179
I Am Somebody: A Biography of Jesse Jackson, 43
I, Charlotte Forten: Black and Free, 91
I Did It with My Hatchet, 44
I Heard of a River, 181
I Lift My Lamp: Emma Lazarus and the Statue of Liberty, 143
I Love New York, 139
I Love New York Guide, 136
Ice Cream, 201
Ida Tarbell: First of the Muckrakers, 174
Ida Tarbell, Muckraker, 174

An Illustrated Treasury of Songs, 27
I'm Nobody: Who Are You? The Story of Emily Dickinson, 91
Images of Pennsylvania, 163
Immigrants from the North: Franco Americans Recall the Settlement of their Canadian Families in the Mill Towns of New England, 56
The Improper Bostonian: Dr. Oliver Wendell Holmes, 92
In and about Hartford: Its People and Places, 7
In and out of Boston with (or without) Children, 85
In Living Memory: A Chronicle of Newport, Rhode Island, 1888-1988, 195
Independence, 166
Independence Must Be Won, 214
Independence National Historical Park, 166
Indian Captive: The Story of Mary Jemison, 172
Indian Handcrafts: How to Craft Dozens of Practical Objects Using Traditional Indian Techniques, 50, 102, 187
Indian Paths of Pennsylvania, 163
Indians in Pennsylvania, 163
Indians of Early Maryland: A Book on Maryland Life, 74
The Indians of New Jersey, 131
The Indians of New Jersey: Dickon among the Lenapes, 126
Indians of the Northeast, 8
Indians of the Northeast Woodlands, 104, 190
Indians of the Tidewater Country of Maryland, Virginia, North Carolina, and Delaware, 73
INDICES: A Statistical Index to District of Columbia Services, 46
Inland Wetland Plants of Connecticut, 4
Inside Blair House, 39
The Inside-Outside Book of New York City, 137
The Inside-Outside Book of Washington, D.C., 36
An Interpretive Atlas of Narragansett Bay, 187
Inventive Wizard: George Westinghouse, 145

Investigating the Marine Environment: A Sourcebook. Vol. 1: Field Studies, 3
Investigating the Marine Environment: A Sourcebook. Vol. 2: Lab Studies, 3
Investigating the Marine Environment: A Sourcebook. Vol. 3: Teacher Manual, 17
The Irish in Rhode Island, 192
Iroquois' Myths and Legends by Ya-ie-wa-noh, 148
Iroquois Stories: Heroes and Heroines, Monsters and Magic, 133
Island Boy, 58
Island City: Adventures in Old New York, 147
Island Rescue, 63
Island Winter, 63
Issues and Images: New Yorkers during the Thirties: Teachers' Guide to Using Historical Documents, 153
The Italians in Rhode Island, 194
The Italians in Their Homeland, in America, in Connecticut, 10

Jacob Have I Loved, 80
Jacob Have I Loved (audiocassette), 81
Jacob Have I Loved (videocassette), 81
Jelly Fish Season, 79
Jem's Island, 62
Jenny's Corner, 176
The Jersey Devil, 115
The Jersey Devil (sound filmstrip), 115
The Jersey Game: The History of Modern Baseball from Its Birth to the Big Leagues in the Garden State, 117
Jersey Jeopardy, 119
Jesse Jackson, 43
Jesse Jackson: Civil Rights Leader and Politician, 43
Jesse Jackson: Still Fighting for the Dream, 43
The Jews in Rhode Island, 193
Jim Henson: Muppet Master, 77
Jim Thorpe: Young Athlete, 175
The Jim Thorpe Story: America's Greatest Athlete, 175
Jingle Bells, 148
Joe Magarac and His USA Citizen Papers, 157
Joe Namath: A Football Legend, 173

John Adams, 89
John Adams (videocassette), 89
John F. Kennedy, 92
John F. Kennedy: New Frontiersman, 92
John Fitzgerald Kennedy, 92
John Paul Jones: Hero of the Seas, 77
John Philip Sousa: The March King, 43
John Quincy Adams, 89
John Stark: Freedom Fighter, 110
John Treegate's Musket, 99
Johnny Appleseed, 169
Johnny Appleseed: Gentle Hero, 169
Johnny Tremain, 96
The Johnstown Flood (McCullough), 158
The Johnstown Flood (videocassette), 158
Jonas Salk, 144
Journal-Bulletin Rhode Island Almanac, 198
Journey toward Freedom: The Story of Sojourner Truth, 144
Just around the Corner in New Jersey, 121
Just for Kids, the New England Guide and Activity Book, 51
Just Plain Fancy, 180
Justin Morgan Had a Horse, 210

Katy of Catoctin: Or Chair Breakers, 81
Keep the Lights Burning, Abbie, 56
The Kennebec River, 55
Kennywood Memories, 160
The Kenton Year, 214
Kidding Around New York City: A Young Person's Guide to the City, 137
A Kid's Guide to Washington, D.C., 28
King Philip, 12, 196
King Philip: Indian Leader, 12, 196
King Philip and the War with the Colonists, 196
Know Your Town, 119

L.L. Bear's Island Adventure, 64
Labor's Defiant Lady: The Story of Mother Jones, 172
Lad: A Dog, 127
Lady-Ghost of the Isles of Shoals, 112

The Lakes Region, New Hampshire: A Visual History, 105
Landfilled: The Trash Crises in Rhode Island, 186
Landmarks and Legends, 35
The Last Algonquin, 145
The Last Hurrah, 98
Learning about Shakers for Teachers and Parents, 113
Learning about Shakers for Young People, 100, 113
Least of All, 212
Legend of Firefly Marsh, 133
The Legend of the Cranberry, 19
Legendary Connecticut, 2
The Lenape: Archaeology, History, and Ethnology, 130
Lenape Indian Teaching Kits, 122
Lenape Lore—Clothing, Shelter, Crafts, Weapons, Tools, Specialties, 21
Lenape Lore—Foods and Medicines, 21
The Lenape or Delaware Indians of New Jersey, 122
Lentil, 63
Leroy the Lobster and Crabby Crab, 60
Let's Discover the States: Upper Atlantic: New Jersey, New York, 138
Lexington & Concord, 1775,: What Really Happened, 87
The Liberty Key: The Story of the New Hampshire Constitution, 108
Light in the Forest, 181
Lighthouses of Rhode Island, 189
The Limner's Daughter, 95
Links of Life: The Housatonic and You, 3
Links to Learning, 11
The Literature of Connecticut History, 17
Little Beaver and the Echo, 62
Little Firefly: An Algonquian Legend, 101, 184
Little Red, 212
The Little Red Lighthouse and the Great Gray Bridge, 151
Little Runner of the Longhouse, 146
Little Settlers of Vermont: A True Story of the Journey of a Pioneer Family through New England, 210
Little Women, 94
The Littlest Lighthouse, 64
A Lively Experiment, 193

The Lives and Times of Peter Cooper, 141
Lobstering and the Maine Coast, 55
The Log of the Skipper's Wife, 53
The Long Road to Gettysburg, 164
Longhouse Winter, 147
Lost on a Mountain in Maine, 54
Louisa May: The World and Works of Louisa May Alcott, 169
Louisa May Alcott, 90
Low-Level Radioactive Waste Management Plan, 1993, 2
Lucy Peale, 81
Lyddie, 98, 211
Lyle and the Birthday Party, 151
Lyle, Lyle Crocodile, 152

Maggie Among the Seneca, 180
Magic Carpet Journey, 119
Magic or Not, 15
Maine Becomes a State, 53
The Maine Bicentennial Atlas, an Historical Survey, 51
Maine, Captured in Color, 51
Maine Dirigo, "I Lead," 53
Maine Folk History in Story, Legend and Myth, 54
Maine Forts, the Eastern Frontier, 49
Maine Historic Bridges, a Vanishing Treasure, 50
Maine in Four Seasons, 52
Maine in Words and Pictures, 54
Maine Lighthouses, the Last Watch, 50
Maine (Engfer), 54
Maine (Harrington), 55
Maine, a Narrative History, 55
Maine, Captured in Color, 51
Make Way for Ducklings, 63, 98
Make Way for Ducklings (combined entry), 98
Making Headlines: A Biography of Nellie Bly, 170
Mammals of New Jersey, 116
A Man and His Ship: Peter Minuit and the Kalmar Nyckel, 23
The Man Who Was Poe, 197
The Many Lives of Benjamin Franklin, 171
Maple Sugar for Windy Foot, 209
The Maple Sugaring Story, 113
The Maple Sugaring Story (videocassette), 101
The March on Washington, 40

Margaret Fuller: Bluestocking, Romantic, Revolutionary, 91
Marian Anderson, 169
The Maritime History of Maine: Three Centuries of Shipbuilding and Seafaring, 55
Marjorie of Monhegan, a Year in a Girl's Life on a Maine Coast Island, 58
Mark Twain: Author of Tom Sawyer, 13
Martin Van Buren: Eighth President of the United States, 145
Mary Cassatt, 171
Mary Cassatt (videocassette), 171
Mary Mapes Dodge: Jolly Girl, 123
Maryland (Carpenter), 73
Maryland (Kent), 71
Maryland (Thompson), 75
Maryland: A Guide to Information and Reference Sources, 82
Maryland: A Regional Study, 74
Maryland: In Words and Pictures, 73
Maryland: Its Past and Present, 75
Maryland A to Z: A Topographical Dictionary, 71
Maryland . . . At the Beginning, 73
The Maryland Colony, 73
Maryland Day, March 25th, 67
Maryland Folklore, 67
Maryland History Resource Guide, 83
Maryland Manual, 71
Maryland's Government, 67
Massachusetts, 88
Massachusetts: From the Berkshires to the Cape, 86
Massachusetts Cities and Towns, 86
Massachusetts Facts, 87
Massachusetts Gazetteer, 85
Massachusetts Municipal Profiles, 1990-91, 84
Massachusetts State Transportation Map, 86
Master Smart Woman, a Portrait of Sarah Orne Jewett, 57
Matthew Wheelock's Wall, 198
Mayflower, 97
Maynard's Allagash Friends, 58
Meet New Jersey, 119
Meg of Heron's Neck, 61
Mermaid in a Tidal Pool, 58

The Merrimack Valley, New Hampshire: A Visual History, 108
Michael and the Mary Day, 64
Michael Hendee, 208
The Micmac, How Their Ancestors Lived Five Hundred Years Ago, 53
Mike and Marnie Learn about Delaware's Indians, 22
Mike and Marnie Learn about Delaware's Symbols, Slogan, Name, and Nicknames, 22
Milk, 201
The Milk Makers, 201
Mill, 187
The Mill Girls: Lucy Larcom, Harriet Hanson Robinson, Sarah G. Bagley, 84
Millard Fillmore: Thirteenth President of the United States, 142
Milton Hershey: Chocolate King, 172
Miracle at Egg Rock, a Puffin's Story, 60
Miss Mary Mac All Dressed in Black: Tongue Twisters, Jump-Rope Rhymes and Other Children's Lore from New England, 101
Miss Rumphius, 59
The Missing Maple Syrup Sap Mystery, 209
Mission to Fort No. 4, 111, 206
Modernization, 167
The Moffat Museum, 15
Molly Pitcher, 173
Molly Pitcher: Girl Patriot, 174
The Molly Stark Trail, 204
Molly the Mule, 211
The Mon, the Al and the O, 162
Monkey Island, 147
Moose on the Loose, 60
More Colonial Crafts for You to Make, 85
More Walks and Rambles in Rhode Island, 189
The Morgan Horse, 201
Mount Washington among the Clouds: An Early History: 1852-1908, 107
A Mountain Adventure, 52
Mr. Lincoln's Whiskers, 147
Mr. Whittier, 94
Mr. Yowder and the Steamboat, 149
Mud Time and More: Nathaniel Stories, 206

A Museum Guide to Washington, D.C., 30
My Brother Sam Is Dead, 14
My Brother Sam Is Dead (sound filmstrip), 14
My Island Grandma, 62
My Little Vermont Book, 202
My Maine Thing, 51
My Maryland: Her Story for Boys and Girls, 74
My Side of the Mountain, 147
Mystery at Pemaquid Point, 60
Mystery in Longfellow Square, 60
The Mystery of Illiard's Castle, 59
Mystery of the Angry Idol, 16
The Mystery of the Disappearing Cars, 208
Mystic: The Story of a Small New England Seaport, 11

The Naked Bear: Folktales of the Iroquois, 132
The Narragansett, 190
Narragansett Bay, 194
Narragansett Bay: A Friend's Perspective, 188
Narratives of Early Maryland, 1633-1684, 73
Nathaniel, 207
Native American Cookbook, 186
Nature Diary of Mt. Desert Island, 51
Nature's Children—Muskrats, 20
Nellie Bly, 169
Neptune's Car, 56
New ABC's of Maine, 64
New Columbia: State of the Union, 36
The New Enchantment of America: Maine, 54
New England, 103
New England (videocassette), 85
New England and the Middle Colonies, 87
The New England Indians, 104, 190
A New England Love Story: Nathaniel Hawthorne and Sophia Peabody, 91
New England Time Line, 109
New England's Special Places: Easy Outings to Historic Villages, Working Museums, Presidential Homes, Castles, and Other Year-Round Attractions, 103
New Hampshire (Fradin), 106
New Hampshire (Thompson), 108

New Hampshire: An Explorer's Guide, 103
New Hampshire: Crosscurrents in Its Development, 107
New Hampshire: Off the Beaten Path, 103
New Hampshire: The State That Made Us a Nation—A Celebration of the Bicentennial of the United States Constitution, 101
The New Hampshire Atlas & Gazetteer, 102
The New Hampshire Colony, 106
New Hampshire Historical Markers, 108
New Hampshire Notables, 109
New Hampshire Premier, 113
New Jersey (Bain), 120
New Jersey (Carpenter), 121
New Jersey (Fredeen), 118
New Jersey (Kent), 121
New Jersey (map), 117
New Jersey (Thompson), 122
New Jersey: A Guide to Its Present & Past, 130
New Jersey: A Guide to the State, 130
New Jersey: A History, 121
New Jersey: A Scenic Discovery, 118
New Jersey: America's Main Road, 121
New Jersey: An American Portrait, 118
New Jersey: Images of Wilderness, 116
New Jersey: In Words and Pictures, 118
New Jersey: Off the Beaten Path, 120
New Jersey: Spotlight on Government, 114
New Jersey and the Negro: A Bibliography, 1715-1966, 127
New Jersey and the Revolutionary War, 130
New Jersey Arts, 116
New Jersey Audubon, 129
The New Jersey Book of Lists, 120
The New Jersey Colony, 122
New Jersey Day Trips: A Guide to Outings in New Jersey, New York, Pennsylvania, & Delaware, 118
New Jersey Ethnic History: A Bibliography, 129

New Jersey Ethnic Life Pamphlet Series, 114
New Jersey Folklife, 129
A New Jersey Folklore Sampler, 115
New Jersey from Colony to State, 1609-1789, 130
New Jersey Historic Map Charts Set, 117
New Jersey Historic Map Portfolio, 117
New Jersey History, 131
New Jersey History (Kross), 122
New Jersey History Series, 131
New Jersey Modern Map Chart Set, 117
New Jersey Monthly, 129
The New Jersey Municipal Data Book, 127
New Jersey Outdoors, 127
New Jersey Parks, Forests, & Natural Areas: A Guide, 116
New Jersey Profiles in Public Policy, 128
New Jersey Reporter, 128
The New Jersey Sampler: Historic Tales of Old New Jersey, 121
The New Jersey State Constitution: A Reference Guide, 128
New Jersey Studies, 119
New Jersey Trips on Film, 119
New Jersey Wall Outline Map, 118
The New Jersey Weather Book, 116
New Jersey Women, Seventeen Seventy to Nineteen Seventy: A Bibliography, 127
New Jersey's Literary History, 117
New Jersey's Special Places: Scenic, Historic, and Cultural Treasures in the Garden State, 120
New Sweden on the Delaware: 1638-1655, 23
New York (Bertinetti/White), 135
New York (Stein), 141
New York: Open to the Public: A Comprehensive Guide to Museums, Collections, Exhibition Spaces, Historic Houses, Botanical Gardens and Zoos, 136
New York Alive, 153
The New York Colony, 138
New York in American History, 140

New York Is Reading Country Manual: The 1992 New York Summer Reading Program, 153
New York, New York, 136
New York State: Gateway to America, 138
Newark, 121
Newport: A Short History, 195
Newport and the Rhode Island Coast, 188
The Newport Cookbook, 186
Nho Lobo and Other Stories, 184
Nickels and Dimes, 175
Nicole Visits an Amish Farm, 156
Night Journeys, 176
Night Markets: Bringing Food to a City, 132
Nightbirds on Nantucket, 94
Nineteenth Century Architecture in New York State, 134
NJN Instructional Resources Manual, K-12, 128
North from Wilmington by Oulde Roades and Turnpikes, including Brandywine and Christina Hundreds, Delaware; and Adjacent Areas of Pennsbury and Bethel Townships, Pennsylvania, 24
Northern New England: Maine, New Hampshire, Vermont, 53, 105
Northwoods Echoes: A Collection of True Stories and Accounts of the North Country, 108

Of Monuments and Myths, 36
Oh, Brother, 152
The Old Line State—A History of Maryland, 74
The Old Line State: Her Heritage, 75
Old Rhode Island, 199
Old Sturbridge Village, 84
An Old-Fashioned Thanksgiving, 111
On the Banks of the Delaware, a View of Its History and Folklore, 20
On the Banks of the Hudson: A View of Its History and Folklore, 139
On This Spot: Pinpointing the Past in Washington, D.C., 28
Once a Pony Time at Chincoteague, 80

Once upon a Time in Connecticut: How the Early Settlers Lived, 1635-1800, 10
Once upon a Time in Delaware, 22
One Boy's Boston, 1887-1901, 93
One More River to Cross, 40
One Morning in Maine, 62
Onion John, 126
Orphan: The Story of a Baby Woodchuck, 186
An Orphan for Nebraska, 151
Oswald and the Timberdoodles, 78
The Other Massachusetts, Beyond Boston and Cape Cod, 86
Otters under Water, 200
Our Federal Government: The Legislative Branch, 26
Our Federal Government: The Presidency, 26
Our Federal Government: The Supreme Court, 26
Our National Monuments, 32
Our Pennsylvania Heritage, 165
OUT! A Vermont Secession Book, 207
An Outward Bound School, 50
Over Boston, 86
Over New England, 103
Over the Blue Mountains, 181
Over the Mountain, 211
Over the River and through the Years for Children: Book One, 106
Ox-Cart Man, 111
Ox-Cart Man (videocassette), 98

Packet Alley, a Magic Story of Now and Long Ago, 24
Paintings of Maine, 50
A Part of the Main: Short Stories of the Maine Coast, 51
Passamaquoddi Legends: When Koluskap Left the Earth, 49
Past and Promise: Lives of New Jersey Women, 114
Patch Work Voices, 156
Patterns of Homespun: A Conversation with Henry and Anna, 138
Paul Cuffe: Merchant and Abolitionist, 90
Paul Revere and the World He Lived In, 93
Paul Robeson, 125
Pea Patch Island, 24
The Peddler's Cart, 146
Penn, 173

Penn's Woods West, 162
Pennsylvania: A Photographic Journey, 161
Pennsylvania: A Scenic Discovery, 161
Pennsylvania: Off the Beaten Path, 162
Pennsylvania Biographical Dictionary, 169
Pennsylvania Crude, 158
Pennsylvania from Wilderness Colony to National Leader, 166
Pennsylvania Gazetteer, 162
Pennsylvania Heritage, 182
Pennsylvania Landscapes: A Geography of the Commonwealth, 162
Pennsylvania Magazine, 182
Pennsylvania Parks Guide, 161
The Pennsylvania Road Show, First Trip, 162
The Pennsylvania Trail of History, 167
Pennsylvania Trivia, 165
The Pennsylvania Turnpike: A History, 157
Pennsylvania's Covered Bridges: A Complete Guide, 159
Pennsylvania's Historic Places, 163
Pennsylvania's Landmarks, 167
Pennsylvania's Trail of History—Eastern, 167
Pennsylvania's Trail of History—Western and Central, 167
A Penny and a Periwinkle, 57
People in Pineapple Place, 45
The People of Penn's Woods West, 165
People of the Breaking Day, 190
People of the First Light, 86
People of the First Light: Part I, Indians of Southern New England, 190
People Who Made America Pictorial Encyclopedia, 84
Peter Zenger: Fighter for Freedom, 145
Philadelphia: A Downtown America Book, 164
Phillis Wheatley: America's First Black Poetess, 94
A Picture Book of George Washington, 44
Picture Book of Submarines, 1
Picture Book of Vermont, 202
Picture Life of Bruce Springsteen, 125
PilgrimQuest, 98

Pilgrims and Indians, 88
The Pilgrims of Plimoth, 88
Pilgrims to the Rescue, 97
Pine Barren Legends: Lore and Lies, 115
Pinelands Folklore, 122
Pioneer Life in Western Pennsylvania, 168
Pip and Emma, 207
Pirates and Patriots of the Revolution, 190
Pirates and Privateers, 187
Piscataway Indians of Maryland, 72
Pittsburgh, an Urban Portrait, 163
Pittsburgh Then and Now, 168
A Place to Come Back To, 95
Places to Go with Children in the Delaware Valley, 25
Places to Go with Children in Washington, D.C., 28
Plain Girl, 182
Plants and Animals of the Estuary, 4
Plants and Animals of the Long Island Sound, 4
Plimoth Plantation, 84
Portland, 54
Portrait of America: Maryland, 74
Portrait of New York State: Discover Corning, 140
Portrait of New York State: New York State's Seaway Trail, 140
The Portuguese in Rhode Island, 192
Potomac: American Reflections, 32, 33
Potomac Portrait, 32
Preachers, Rebels, and Traders—Connecticut, 1818-1865, 10
Prehistoric Days, 167
Present Meets Past: Making History and the Mysteries of Town Histories, 140
The President's House: A History, 48
Project Soundwise, 3
The Proper Bostonians, 89
Proud to be Amish, 179
Providence, a Pictorial History, 195
Public Access to the Rhode Island Coast, 188
The Pumpkin Heads, 15
Pumpkin Pumpkin, 64

Puritans, Pioneers and Pacesetters: Eight People Who Shaped Rhode Island, 195

The Quahog Stops Here, 187

Rachel and Obadiah, 99
Rachel Carson, 170
Rachel Carson: Pioneer of Ecology, 171
The Raft, 60
Rambling Raft, 80
A Real Nice Clambake, 198
Rebecca's War, 178
Rebel Raiders: A Story of the St. Albans Raid, 207
The Rebel Yell and the Yankee Hurrah, the Civil War Journal of a Maine Volunteer, 57
Rebels in the Shadows, 181
Reflections of New York, 137
Reflections of Washington, D.C., 27
Reflections on the Wall, the Vietnam Veterans Memorial, 37
Reluctant Hero: A Snowy Road to Salem in 1802, 111
Remember Me to Harold Square, 146
A Restless Spirit: The Story of Robert Frost, 206
Return of the Sun: Native American Tales from the Northeast Woodlands, 101
Rhode Island (Carpenter), 19
Rhode Island (Heinrichs), 193
Rhode Island (Thompson), 195
Rhode Island (Warner), 195
Rhode Island: A History, 194
Rhode Island: A Picture Book to Remember Her By, 189
Rhode Island: Forgotten Leader of the Revolutionary Era, 194
The Rhode Island Atlas, 188
The Rhode Island Campaign of 1778, 192
The Rhode Island Colony, 193
Rhode Island in Words and Pictures, 193
Rhode Island Monthly, 199
Rhode Island Profile, 192
Rhode Island Puzzle, 188
Rhode Island's Road to Liberty, 192
Ride with Me: New Jersey/Delaware I95 South, 119
The Riddle of Penncroft Farm, 179

The Riddle of the Amish Culture, 155
A River Adventure, 52
The River Ran Red, 156, 183
A River Ran Wild, 109
Riverkeeper, 132
The Roads of Home: Lanes and Legends of New Jersey, 115
Robert Fulton, 172
Robert Fulton and the Steamboat, 142
Robert McCloskey Library, 63
Roll of Drums, 182
The Rough-Face Girl, 2
Ruby, the Red-Hot Witch at Bloomingdales, 150
Ruth Marini: Dodger Ace, 126

Safe in the Spotlight: The Dawn Animal Agency and the Sanctuary for Animals, 134
Salt Marsh Plants of Connecticut, 4
Salty Dog, 198
Sam Predicts a Storm, 59
Sam the Minuteman, 95
Samuel de Champlain, 205
Samuel Morse, 124
Samuel Slater's Mill and the Industrial Revolution, 196
Sarah Bishop, 149
Sarah Morton's Day: A Day in the Life of a Pilgrim Girl, 88
Saturday's Child: Family Activities in Metropolitan Washington, 27
Saturnalia, 197
Sea Horse, 58
Sea Mouse, 61
The Seacoast, New Hampshire: A Visual History, 106
Seashells in My Pocket, 19
Seashells in My Pocket: A Child's Guide to Exploring the Atlantic Coast, 185
The Seashore Book, 198
Seashore Surprises, 20
Seaweeds of the Connecticut Shore: A Waders Guide, 5
The Second Vermont Fun Book, 202
The Secret of Heron Creek, 80
The Secret of the Crazy Quilt, 97
The Secret Soldier: The Story of Deborah Sampson, 93
A Sense of Place, 187
Settlement, 168
The Seven Wonders of New Jersey—And Then Some, 122
Shadow and Light, 207

Shaker Inventions, 100
Shaker Life, Work and Art, 100
Sharks, 49
Shh! We're Writing the Constitution, 156
Shoo-Fly Pie, 179
Shooting Back: A Photographic View of Life by Homeless Children, 26
The Shore Ghosts and Other Stories of New Jersey, 126
Show Lamb, 214
Sid and Sal's Famous Channel Marker Diner, 79
The Sign of the Beaver, 64
Silent Spring, 170
Silver for General Washington, 179
Simple Gifts: The Story of the Shakers, 100
Sixty Selected Nature Walks in Connecticut, 10
Skippack School, 177
Slake's Limbo, 147
Slater's Mill, 198
Slave's Gold, 212
Sleigh Bells for Windy Foot, 209
Slumps, Grunts, and Snickerdoodles: What Colonial America Ate and Why, 102
Small Town Girl, 96
Snakebite: Lives and Legends of Central Pennsylvania, 157
Snow Bound, 148
Sojourner Truth: Ain't I a Woman?, 144
Some of the Adventures of Rhode Island Red, 197
Something Upstairs: A Tale of Ghosts, 197
The Sound of Music, 206
The Soundbook, 4
Sounding the Alarm: A Biography of Rachel Carson, 170
The Southeast Asians in Rhode Island, 193
Spanning Time: New Hampshire Covered Bridges, 101
The Spirit of Pittsburgh, 156
Spirit of the New England Tribes, 185
Spruce the Moose Cuts Loose, 64
The Spy at Tory Hole, 112
Squanto, 93
Squanto, Friend of the Pilgrims, 93
St. Nicholas Magazine, 123
Stark Decency, 104
Star-Spangled Banner, 69
State O'Maine, 52

Statehood, 168
Statue of Liberty, 141
Steinmetz: Wizard of Light, 144
Stephen Foster: His Life, 171
Stopping by Woods on a Snowy Evening, 102
The Storekeeper, 211
Stories of New Jersey, 115
The Story of Admiral Peary at the North Pole, 173
The Story of an Old Farm: Or Life in New Jersey in the 18th Century: With a Genealogical Appendix, 131
Story of Babe Ruth: Baseball's Greatest Legend, 78
The Story of Clara Barton, 123
The Story of Johnny Appleseed, 169
The Story of Maine for Young Readers, 54
The Story of the Burning of Washington, 37
The Story of the Star Spangled Banner, 70
The Story of the Statue of Liberty, 134
The Story of the White House, 39
The Story of Two American Generals, Benjamin O. Davis, Jr. and Colin L. Powell, 39
The Story of William Penn, 173
Strawberry Thanksgiving, 197
The Strength of the Hills: A Portrait of a Family Farm, 201
Sugar on Snow, 214
Sugaring Season: Making Maple Syrup, 202
Summer Girl, 63
Surrounded by Sea, Life on a New England Fishing Island, 51
Susan B. Anthony: Pioneer in Women's Rights, 141
Symbols of New Jersey, 120

Tails of the Bronx: A Tale of the Bronx, 149
The Taken Girl, 182
Taking Care of Terrific, 98
Tales of an October Moon, 184
Tales of Vermont Ways and People, 203
Talking about Connecticut: Oral History in the Nutmeg State, 17
Tall Ships of the World, 184
Tall Tales of the Catskills, 133
Tallahassee Higgins, 79
The Tamarack Tree, 16

A Taste of America, 6
The Tavern at the Ferry, 168
Taylor's Gut, 22
The Tempering, 181
The Ten Speed Babysitter, 15
The Terrible Wave, 177
Thaddeus Stevens and the Fight for Negro Rights, 174
The Thanksgiving Story, 96
Thar She Blows, a Whale of a Vacation Surprise, 61
Things That Aren't There Anymore, 168
This Is New Hampshire, 103
This Is New Jersey, 121
This Is Washington, D.C., 30
This Time, Tempe Wick?, 126
Thomas Alva Edison, 123
Thomas Alva Edison: Miracle Worker, 124
Thomas Edison, 124
Three for the Treasure, 213
Three Young Pilgrims, 97
Thunder at Gettysburg, 178
Thurgood Marshall, 77
Thurgood Marshall: First Black Supreme Court Justice, 77
Thy Friend, Obadiah, 99
Ticonderoga: The Story of a Fort, 139
Tim to the Lighthouse, 57
Time Enough for Drums, 126
Time of Wonder, 62
Tinseltown and the Big Apple, 135
Titanic, 8
Tituba of Salem Village, 98
Titus Tidewater, 65
To Market! To Market!, 19
Toliver's Secret, 126
Tomahawks and Trombones, 166
Tongue of Flame: The Life of Lydia Maria Child, 90
Touchmark, 97
Train to Lulu's, 80
The Trapp Family Book, 206
The Treasure in the Little Trunk, 149
Trigger John's Son, 181
Trouble at the Mines, 181
The True Confessions of Charlotte Doyle, 197
Tugboats Never Sleep, 97
Twenty Most Asked Questions about the Amish and Mennonites, 155
Twenty-Five Walks in New Jersey, 129

250th Anniversary Cookbook and Recipe Collection: Cooking from a Connecticut Farm, 5
Two Hundred Years: Stories of the Nation's Capital, 34

Umbrella, 152
Unbuilding, 134
Uncle Tom's Cabin, 13
Understood Betsy, 209
Undying Glory, 87
United States Naval Academy, 67
Up the Frozen River, 180
Up the Spine and Down the Creek, a Pictorial History from Queen Christina to William Penn, 23
UpCountry: Reflections from a Rural Life, 50
The Use of Abundance, 131

Valley of Defiance, 146
Vermont, 202
Vermont: A Cultural Patchwork, 203
Vermont: A Nature Guide, 200
Vermont: The State with the Storybook Past, 202
Vermont by Choice, 203
Vermont Farm and the Sun, 201
The Vermont Geography Book, 202
Vermont Heritage, 204
Vermont Is Where You Find It, 203
Vermont Life Book of Nature, 200
Vermont School Bus Ride, 200
Vermont, Our Own State, 204
Vietnam Memorial, 32, 38
The Vietnam Veterans Memorial, 35
The Village: Life in Colonial Times, 122
Village of Penacook, New Hampshire: An Architectural and Historical View, 109
The Visionary Girls: Witchcraft in Salem Village, 84
A Visit to Washington, D.C., 30
The Voice of Maine, Interviews with 31 Outspoken Maine People, 56
Voices after Midnight, 149
The Voyage Begun, 95
The Voyages of Brian Seaworthy, 203

The Wabanakis of Maine and the Maritimes: A Resource Book about Penobscot, Passamaquoddy, Maliseet, Micmac and Abenaki Indians, 65
Walden, 94
Walking Tours of Historic Philadelphia, 162
The Wall, 45
The Wampanoag, 191
Wanda the Worrywart, 213
War Comes to Willy Freeman, 146
The War of 1812, 72
Washington: Portraits of a City, 29
Washington: The District and Beyond, 30
Washington Art: A Guide to Galleries, Art Consultants, and Museums, 47
Washington at Home: An Illustrated History, 37
The Washington Capital Spotlight, 46
The Washington Cookbook: A Tasteful Tour of the Nation's Capital, 26
Washington, D.C. (Fradin), 29
Washington, D.C. (Kent), 35
Washington, D.C. (Loewen), 35
Washington, D.C. (Reef), 37
Washington, D.C. (Saures), 37
Washington, D.C. (Turck), 31
Washington, D.C. (videocassette, Encyclopedia Brittanica), 38
Washington, D.C. (videocassette, Finley Holiday), 39
Washington, D.C. (videocassette, National Geographic), 38
Washington, D.C. (Wood), 31
Washington, D.C.: A Capital Adventure, 38
Washington, D.C.: A Picture Book to Remember Her By, 31
Washington, DC: A Traveler's Guide to the District of Columbia and Nearby Attractions, 31
Washington D.C.: The Complete Guide, 28
Washington, DC: The Nation's Capital (Epstein/Epstein), 34
Washington, D.C.: The Nation's Capital (sound filmstrip), 39
Washington, D.C. at Its Best, 29

Washington, D.C., Fancy Free, 31
Washington, D.C. Today, 39
Washington for Children, 31
Washington in Focus, 33
Washington Information Directory, 1991-92, 48
Washington Irving's New York, 143
The Washington Monthly, 46
Washington Monuments, 39
Washington, '91. A Comprehensive Directory of the Key Institutions and Leaders of the National Capital Area, 47
Washington on View: The Nation's Capital since 1790, 30
The Washington Post Guide to Washington, 30
Washingtoniana Photographs: Collections in the Prints and Photographs Division of the Library of Congress, 46
The Watergate Scandal: People, Power, and Politics, 32
Waterman's Boy, 81
Watermen, 72
Watermen and Lighthouses of the Chesapeake Bay, 69
WaterWays: New York's Waterfront News, 153
Watt Got You Started, Mr. Fulton?, 141
We, the People, 112
We the People, the Story of the United States Capitol, 27
Western Regions, New Hampshire: A Visual History, 107
Wetland Protection in Connecticut, 4
A Wetland Walk, 19
The Whale in Lowell's Cove, 63
Whaleboat Raid, 14
Whaling Captains of New London County, Connecticut: For Oil and Buggy Whips, 11
The Whaling City: A History of New London, 11
Whaling Days, 186
What Are You Figuring Now? A Story of Benjamin Banneker, 76
What Cheer Netop, "Greeting Friends", History, Culture & Legends of American Indians of the Northeast, 185

What Cheer, Netop! Selections from "A Key into the Language of America" by Roger Williams, 185
What Do You Mean? A Story about Noah Webster, 13
What the Dickens!, 177
What the Sea Left Behind, 58
What's for Lunch? The Eating Habits of Seashore Creatures, 20
What's the Big Idea, Ben Franklin?, 172
When Coal Was King: Mining Pennsylvania's Anthracite, 159
When Grandpa Was a Boy, 203
When the Moon Is Full: Supernatural Stories from the Pennsylvania Mountains, 158
Where Does the Trail Lead, 24
Where Is the Eagle?, 137
Where Time Stands Still, 154
Where's Rachel?, 45
The Whistling Teakettle and Other Stories about Hannah, 151
A White Heron, 61
The White House, 34
The White House: An Historic Guide, 47
The White House: Cornerstone of a Nation, 37
The White House and the Presidency, 36
White House Children, 32
The White Mountains: Names, Places and Legends, 104
The White Mountains, New Hampshire: A Visual History, 105
Who Are the Amish?, 155
Who Comes with Cannons?, 176
Who Is Carrie?, 146
Who Wakes the Ground Hog?, 200
Who Were the Pilgrims?, 88
Why Do They Dress That Way?, 155
Why Don't You Get a Horse Sam Adams?, 90
Wild Friends: A True Story of Life with Animal Orphans, 57
Wilderness Wedding, 213
Wilderness Winter, 213
Will You Sign Here, John Hancock?, 91
William Penn: Founder of Pennsylvania, 173
William Penn's Own Account of the Lenni Lenape or Delaware Indians, 22
William Penn, Quaker Hero, 173
Willie in Early Vermont, 204
Wind in the Chimney, 179
Windcatcher, 14
Windy Foot at the County Fair, 209
Wings from the Wind, 202
The Winter at Valley Forge, 164
Winter Barn, 63
The Winter Hero, 96
The Winter Wife: An Abenaki Tale, 49
Wiser than Winter, 212
A Wish on Capitol Hill, 38, 45
The Witch of Blackbird Pond, 16
The Witchcraft Delusion in Colonial Connecticut, 1640-1747, 1
Witches' Children: A Story of Salem, 95
Witnesses: A Novel, 97
Women of Maine, 56
The Wonderful Hay Tumble, 209
Woodrow Wilson, 125
Woodrow Wilson: Boy President, 125
Woodsmen and River Drivers, Another Day, Another Era, 50
The World of Copley: 1738-1815, 90
The World of Crabs, 68
The World of Mary Cassatt, 171
The World of Whistler 1834-1903, 94
The World of William Penn, 161
Worthy of the Nation: The History of Planning for the National Capital, 46
The WPA Guide to Philadelphia, 163

Yellow Blue Jay, 210
Yesteryear in Annapolis, 75
Yonie Wondernose, 177
You and the Law in New Jersey: A Resource Guide, 128
Your Maryland, 75

Zachary Goes Groundfishing on the Trawler Lucille B., 61
Zero in on New Jersey, 120

Subject Index

by Janet Perlman

Abenaki Indians, 49, 65, 101, 104, 110
Abolitionists
  Anthony, Susan B., 141
  Child, Lydia Maria, 90
  Douglass, Frederick, 76–77
  Forten, Charlotte, 91
  Stevens, Thaddeus, 174
  Stowe, Harriet Beecher, 13
  Truth, Sojourner, 144–45
  Tubman, Harriet, 78, 145
Acadia National Park (Maine), 51, 52
Actresses, Hayes, Helen, 43
Adams, John, 89
Adams, John Quincy, 89–90
Adams, Samuel, 90
Adirondak Mountains (N.Y.), 133, 139, 141
African Americans
  Anderson, Marian, 169
  Attucks, Crispus, 40
  Bannecker, Benjamin, 41, 76
  biographies, 11, 39–40, 41
  Bunche, Ralph, 40
  Child, Lydia Maria, 90
  Chisolm, Shirley, 40
  civil rights movement, 40, 43
  Civil War, 87, 90–91
  Connecticut, 11, 12, 16
  Coppin, Fannie Jackson, 40
  Cuffe, Paul, 90
  Davis, Benjamin O., 39–40, 41
  District of Columbia, 28–29, 33, 35, 39–40, 41, 42, 43, 46
  Douglass, Frederick, 76–77
  Drew, Charles Richard, 40, 41–42
  Ellington, Duke, 42
  Farmer, James, 40
  fiction, 146

  folklore, 184
  Forten, Charlotte, 91
  Fortune, Amos, 91, 110
  Henson, Matthew, 40, 77
  Jackson, Jesse, 43
  King, Martin Luther, Jr., 40
  Lewis, John, 40
  McNair, Ronald, 40
  Marshall, Thurgood, 77–78
  Maryland, 76
  Massachusetts, 87, 90–91
  in military service, 11, 39–40, 41, 87, 89
  New Jersey, 127
  Norton, Eleanor Holmes, 40
  Powell, Colin L., 39–40
  Randolph, A. Philip, 40
  Revolutionary War, 89
  Robeson, Paul, 125
  Robinson, Jackie, 12
  Rustin, Bayard, 40
  Truth, Sojourner, 144–45
  Tubman, Harriet, 78, 145
  Walker, Madame C. J., 40
  Waters, Maxine, 40
  Wheatley, Phillis, 94
  Wilkins, Roy, 40
  Winfrey, Oprah, 40
  Young, Whitney, 40
Airports, 67
Airships, 116
Alcott, Louisa May, 90, 94, 111, 169
Algonquin Indians, 138, 145, 189–90
  legends, 2–3, 101, 104, 106, 184
Allagash River (Maine), 52
Allegheny River (Pa.), 162
Allen, Ethan, 10, 205
Almanac, 66

Alphabet books, 64, 76, 112, 176, 207, 211
American Indian legends
  Abenaki, 49, 101
  Algonquin, 2–3, 101, 104, 106, 184
  Anishinabe, 101
  Delaware, 19
  Iroquois, 133, 148
  Mohican, 101
  Narragansett, 185
  Oneida, 101
  Onondata, 101
  Passamaquoddi, 49, 101
  Penobscot, 101
  Seneca, 101
  Tuscarora, 101
  Wampanoag, 185
American Indians, 8, 86
  Abenaki, 49, 65, 101, 104, 110
  Algonquin, 3, 101, 104, 106, 138, 145, 189–90
  Anishinabe, 101
  Connecticut, 2, 8, 10, 12–13
  cookery, 186
  Delaware, 19, 20–21, 22, 72–73, 122, 129
  fiction, 14–15, 126, 148, 197
  handicrafts, 50, 102, 187, 190
  history, 8, 12–13, 93–94, 104–05
  Iroquois, 133, 137–38, 140, 142–43, 146, 148
  Johnny Appleseed, 169
  King Philip, 12, 193, 196
  King Philip's War, 8–9, 12–13, 54
  Lenape, 21–22, 120, 122, 130
  Maine, 49, 53, 54, 65, 104
  Maliseet, 65
  Maryland, 72–73, 74, 79

Massachusetts, 12–13, 86, 93
Massasoit, 12
Metacomet, 12
Micmac, 53, 65, 190
Mohican, 101
Narragansett, 185, 186, 190
New Hampshire, 104–05, 110
New Jersey, 120, 121, 122, 129
New York, 130, 132–33, 138, 140, 146, 148
Nipmuc, 186
Oneida, 101
Onondaga, 101
Passamaquoddi, 49, 65, 101
Pennsylvania, 12–13, 163–64, 167
Penobscot, 53, 65, 101
Piscataway, 72
Pocahontas, 93
Rhode Island, 184–85, 186, 189–90, 191, 196
Seneca, 101
Squanto, 93–94
Thorpe, Jim, 175
Tuscarora, 101
Vermont, 104
Wampanoag, 12–13, 93–94, 185, 190, 191, 196
American Red Cross, Barton, Clara, 76, 90, 123
American Revolution. *See* Revolutionary War
American Sign Language, 12, 42, 43
Amish, 154, 155, 156
  fiction, 177, 179, 180–81, 182
Ancient civilizations. *See* Archaeology
Anderson, Marian, 169
Animal welfare, 134
Animals
  amphibians, 5
  Chesapeake Bay, 68–69
  Connecticut, 3, 4, 16
  Delaware, 19, 20
  estuary, 4
  food habits, 20
  Long Island Sound, 4
  Maine, 51, 52, 57
  mammals, 116, 161
  Maryland, 68–79
  New Jersey, 116
  orphans, 57, 186
  Pennsylvania, 159, 161
  reptiles, 5
  Rhode Island, 185, 186
  tracks, 200, 201
  use in entertainment, 134
  Vermont, 200–01
  See also Birds; Individual animals; Marine animals
Anishinabe Indians, legends, 101
Annapolis (Md.), 67, 70, 75–76
Anthony, Susan B., 141
Appleseed, Johnny, 169
Archaeology
  Maine, 55–56
  Maryland, 73
  New Hampshire, 108
  New Jersey, 122, 130
  Pennsylvania, 167
Architecture
  Connecticut, 6
  Empire State Building, 134
  Maryland, 50, 56, 57, 69, 74–75
  New England, 103
  New Hampshire, 109
  New York, 134
  Rhode Island, 187
  Wright, Frank Lloyd, 160
Arctic exploration
  Henson, Matthew, 77
  Peary, Robert, 56, 173
Arnold, Benedict, 9, 10, 12
Artists
  Calder, Alexander, 170
  Cassatt, Mary, 171
  Copley, John, 90
  Langlais, Bernard, 57
  West, Benjamin, 175
  Whistler, James, 94
  Wyeth, Andrew, 50, 175
Asian Americans, 40–41
Assateague (Md.), 72, 80
Assateague National Seashore (Md.), 69
Astronauts, McAuliffe, Christa, 110
Athletes
  Heiden, Eric, 142
  Namath, Joe, 173
  Pennsylvania, 161
  Robinson, Jackie, 12
  Ruth, Babe, 78
  Thorpe, Jim, 175
Atlas
  Chesapeake Bay, 66, 70
  Connecticut, 10
  historical, 85, 117
  Maine, 51
  Maryland, 66
  Narragansett Bay (R.I.), 187–88
  New Hampshire, 102–03
  New Jersey, 117–18
  Pennsylvania, 161
Atom bomb, Oppenheimer, Robert, 143
Attucks, Crispus, 40
Authors
  Alcott, Louisa May, 90, 94, 111, 169
  Blunt, Susan Baker, 109–10
  Bly, Nellie, 169–70
  Dodge, Mary Mapes, 123
  Fuller, Margaret, 91
  Hall, Donald, 110
  Hawthorne, Nathaniel, 91–92
  Irving, Washington, 143
  Jewett, Sarah Orne, 57
  New Jersey, 117
  Thaxter, Celia, 105, 112
  Thoreau, Henry David, 94
  Tudor, Tasha, 110–11

Bagley, Sarah G., 84
Balloons (airships), 116
Baltimore (Md.), 70–71, 75, 79
Baltimore (Md.) fire, 75, 79
Baltimore Orioles (baseball), 70
Bannecker, Benjamin, 41, 76
Barton, Clara, 76, 90, 123
Baseball
  Baltimore Orioles, 70
  New Jersey, 117
  New York, 135
  Robinson, Jackie, 12
  Ruth, Babe, 78
  Stengel, Charles, 135
Basketball, fiction, 149
Baxter State Park (Maine), 52
Bears, fiction, 58, 61, 62, 64, 112, 177
Beavers, fiction, 62–63
Bell, Alexander Graham, 41, 141
Bethlehem (Pa.), 166–67
Bigotry. *See* Prejudice
Birds
  Chesapeake Bay, 68–69
  Connecticut, 5, 16
  Delaware, 20
  fiction, 60, 61, 78–79, 97–98, 147, 150
  Maine, 51
  New Jersey, 129
  Pennsylvania, 159
Birds of prey, Connecticut, 5
Blacks. *See* African Americans
Blair House (Washington, DC), 39
Blanchard, Jean Pierre, 166
Blizzards, 8
Blume, Judy, 125

Blunt, Susan Baker, 109–10
Bly, Nellie, 169–70
Boatman, 132
Bookmobiles, 80
Boone, Daniel, 170
Boston (Mass.), 85–86, 88, 89, 93
Boston Massacre, 87
Botany. See Plants; Trees
Botto, Pietro, 115
Bowditch, Nathaniel, 90
Bradford, Phoebe George, 24
Bridges
　Brooklyn Bridge, 134
　covered bridges, 101, 160
　historic bridges, 5, 50, 101, 159
　Pennsylvania, 159–60
　Pittsburgh(Pa.), 159–60
Broadway (N.Y.), 137
Brooklyn Bridge (N.Y.), 134
Buell, Abell, 12
Buildings, historic. See Historic buildings
Bunche, Ralph, 40
Burgess, Abbie, 56
Burr, Aaron, 123
Bushnell, David, 12

Calder, Alexander, 170
Cambodian Americans, 193
Camera, Eastman, George, 142
Camping, fiction, 62
Canals
　boatman, 132
　Eric Canal, 135, 138
　fiction, 79
Canoeing
　Connecticut, 8
　Maine, 52
　New Jersey, 117
　New York, 135
Cape Cod (Mass.), 85, 98–99
Cape May–Lewes Ferry, 19
Capitol Building (Washington, DC), 27, 33, 39
Carnegie, Andrew, 170
Carnegie Museum (Pittsburgh), 159
Carson, Rachel, 170–71
Cassatt, Mary, 171
Cats, fiction, 59, 60, 61, 78–79, 97–98, 147, 148, 150, 208
Catskill Mountains (N.Y.), 133, 147
Champlain, Samuel de, 205–06, 210
Chapman, John, 169
Charter Oak, legend, 8–9
Chautauqua (N.Y.), 134

Chesapeake Bay
　ecology, 67, 82
　fiction, 78, 80, 81
　flora and fauna, 68–69
　food chain, 82
　schooners, 67
　weather, 67
　wetlands, atlas, 66
Child, Lydia Maria, 90
Chisolm, Shirley, 40
Choreographers, DeMille, Agnes, 142
Christmas, 132, 148, 157, 207
Civil rights movement, 40
　Jackson, Jesse, 43
　March on Washington, 40
Civil War
　African Americans, 87, 90–91
　Barton, Clara, 76, 90, 123
　Connecticut, 9
　fiction, 81–82, 178
　Fort Delaware, 23
　Gettysburg, Battle of, 164–65
　Maine, 53, 57, 58
　Massachusetts, 87
　Pennsylvania, 164–65
　Vermont, 207
Clermont (ship), 141
Cleveland, Grover, 123
Coal mining, 156, 159
　fiction, 180, 181, 182
Coast. See Seashore
Cochrane, Elizabeth, 169–70
Colonial history
　Connecticut, 8–9
　Delaware, 22, 23, 24
　Hancock, John, 91
　Maryland, 66, 67, 73–74, 77
　Massachusetts, 87, 88, 89–90
　New Hampshire, 106
　New Jersey, 121, 122
　New York, 138–39
　Pennsylvania, 161, 164, 168
　Pilgrims, 87, 88
　Rhode Island, 188, 193
　Zenger, Peter, 145
Colonial life
　Connecticut, 10
　Copley, John, 90
　crafts, 85
　fiction, 81, 95, 96, 99, 178
　foods, 102, 186
　Hutchinson, Anne, 92, 193
　Maryland, 75
　Massachusetts, 84, 85, 98
　New Hampshire, 111, 112–13
　New Jersey, 122–23

Old Sturbridge Village, 84
　Pennsylvania, 166
　religious freedom, 92, 97
　Thanksgiving, 87–88
Coloring books, 21
Colt, Samuel, 12
Communes
　Ephrata (Pa.), 154, 182
　Old Economy Village (Pa.), 166
Composers, Sousa, John Philip, 43–44
Connecticut, ix, 1–18
　African Americans, 11, 12, 16
　animals, 3, 4, 5, 16
　biographies, 10, 11–13
　economy, 7, 8
　fiction, 14–16
　geography, 7
　geology, 3
　government, 1, 6
　history, 1, 2, 7, 8–9, 10, 11, 12, 15–16, 17–18, 109
　immigrants, 10
　Indians, 2, 8, 10, 12–13
　legends, 2–3
　maps, 10
　multiethnic culture, 8
　plants, 4–5, 9
　statistics, 6
Connecticut Yankee in King Arthur's Court, 16
Conservation. See Environmental protection; Wildlife conservation
Constitution (U.S.), 156–57, 164, 168, 173
Cookbooks
　American Indian, 186
　colonial, 102
　Connecticut, 5–6
　District of Columbia, 26–27
　Rhode Island, 186
　Vietnamese, 187
Coolidge, Calvin, 206
Cooper, Peter, 141–42
Copley, John, 90
Coppin, Fannie Jackson, 40
Cormorants, 51
Corning (N.Y.), 136, 140
Cosby, Bill, 171
Counting rhymes, 101
Country life, 50
　fiction, 60, 152
　Hall, Donald, 110
　Thoreau, Henry David, 94
Covered bridges, 101, 160
Crabs, 20, 68, 69, 78
Crafts. See Handicrafts

Cranberries, legends, 19
Cuffe, Paul, 90

Dairying, 201
Dancers, DeMille, Agnes, 142
Davis, Benjamin O., 39–40, 41
Deafness, Gallaudet, Thomas Hopkins, 12, 42–43
Declaration of Independence, 24
  Hancock, John, 91
Deer, fiction, 176, 208
Delaware, ix, 19–25
  animals, 19, 20
  biographies, 23, 24
  economy, 20–21, 22
  fiction, 24–25
  geography, 20–21, 22
  history, ix, 20–21, 22–23, 25
  immigrants, 23
  Indians, 19, 20–21, 22, 72–73
  legends, 19, 20, 24
  maps, 23
Delaware Indians, 129, 166–67
  fiction, 126
  folklore, 19
Delaware River, folklore, 20
DeMille, Agnes, 142
Depression (history), 15
Dickens, Charles, fiction, 177
Dickinson, Emily, 91
Dictionaries
  Narragansett, 185
  Webster, Noah, 13
Dinosaurs, 159
Disasters
  Baltimore (Md.) fire, 75, 79
  Connecticut, 3–4, 8
  Pennsylvania, 158
  Rhode Island, 197
District of Columbia, ix, 26–48
  African Americans, 28–29, 33, 35, 39–40, 41, 42, 43, 46
  biographies, 39–45
  economy, 47
  fiction, 45–46
  government, 26, 30, 36, 39
  history, 28, 29, 30, 32, 33, 34, 35, 37–38, 46
  maps, 35–36
  statehood movement, 36
  statistics, 46–47
  trees, 27
Dix, Dorothea, 123
Dodge, Mary Mapes, 123
Dogs, fiction, 127, 198, 212
Douglass, Frederick, 76–77
Drake, Colonel (Edwin), 158

Drew, Charles Richard, 40, 41–42
Ducks, fiction, 98, 176

Eastman, George, 142
Ecology
  Carson, Rachel, 170–71
  Chesapeake Bay, 68, 69, 82
  Connecticut, 3, 4, 17
  Delaware, 19
  fiction, 78, 81, 95
  Maryland, 68, 69, 72
  New Jersey, 127
Edison, Thomas Alva, 123–24
Education
  Amish schools, 154, 155, 180
  historic schoolhouses, 102
  Mann, Horace, 92
Ellington, Duke, 42
Empire State Building (N.Y.), 134
Endangered species, 16
Environmental history, New Hampshire, 109
Environmental policy, Connecticut, 9
Environmental protection
  Carson, Rachel, 170–71
  Connecticut, 3
  New Jersey, 127, 128
Ephrata Commune (Pa.), 154, 182
Erie Canal (N.Y.), 135, 138
Estuaries
  Chesapeake Bay, 68, 82
  Connecticut, 4
  flora and fauna, 4
Exploration
  New Hampshire, 105
  New Jersey, 124
Explorers
  Champlain, Samuel de, 205–06, 210
  Henson, Matthew, 77
  Hudson, Henry, 124
  Peary, Robert, 56, 173
  Verrazano, 195–96

Fallingwater (home), 160
Farm life, 110–11
  Amish, 179
  fiction, 60, 64, 111, 112, 177, 179, 213–14
  New Jersey, 131
  New York, 138
  Pennsylvania, 154, 166, 179
  Vermont, 200, 203, 209, 212

Farmer, James, 40
Federal government, 26, 30, 36, 39, 48
Ferry Tavern House (N.J.), 118
Ferryboats, 15, 19, 168
Field trips
  Connecticut, 17
  Maryland, 74
  New Jersey, 129
Fillmore, Millard, 142
Fires, Baltimore (Md.), 75, 79
Fishing, 72
  Chesapeake Bay, 50, 56, 57, 69
  fiction, 57, 61–62
  Maine, 51, 55
Fitch, John, 116
Floods
  Connecticut, 8
  fiction, 14, 177
  Pennsylvania, 158
Flour mills, 160
Folk crafts. See Handicrafts
Folk songs. See Music
Folklore. See Legends
Foods, 5–6, 26–27, 102, 113, 186, 187
  maple sugar, 101–02, 113, 202
Football, Namath, Joe, 173
Fort Delaware (Del.), 23
Fort McClary (Maine), 49–50
Fort Sullivan (Maine), 49–50
Fort Ticonderoga, Battle of, 205
Fort Ticonderoga (N.Y.), 139
Forten, Charlotte, 91
Fortune, Amos, 91, 110
Foster, Stephen, 171
Franklin, Benjamin, 171–72, 179
French and Indian Wars
  Fort Ticonderoga, 139
  King Philip's War, 8–9, 12–13, 54
  Pennsylvania, 166
French Canadians, 56, 104, 191, 206
Frontier life
  Boone, Daniel, 170
  fiction, 59, 62, 96, 176, 178, 180
  Johnny Appleseed, 169
  New Hampshire, 111
Frost, Robert, 102, 206
Fuller, Margaret, 91
Fulton, Robert, 141, 142, 172

Gallaudet, Thomas Hopkins, 12, 42–43
Gallaudet University (Washington, DC), 42

Games, 7, 98, 106–07, 119, 202, 203
Geese, fiction, 65
Geology, Connecticut, 3
Georgetown (Washington, DC), 33, 35
German Americans, 131, 178, 181
Gettysburg (Pa.), 164
Ghosts, 68, 126, 133, 179, 184–85, 197, 212
Ginsberg, Allen, 117
Government. *See* Federal government
Grandma Moses, 143
Ground hog, 200
Gulls, 20

Hagerstown (Md.), 66
Hale, Nathan, 9, 12
Haley, John West, 57
Half Moon (ship), 124
Hall, Donald, 110
Hamilton, Alexander, 124
Hancock, John, 91
Handicrafts
  American Indian, 50, 102, 187, 190
  New Jersey, 128, 129
  Pennsylvania Dutch, 260
  Rhode Island, 190
Hans Brinker, 123
Harford, Henry, 77
Harrisburg (Pa.), 165
Hartford (Conn.), 7
Hawthorne, Nathaniel, 91–92
Hayes, Helen, 43
Hearing impaired, Gallaudet, Thomas Hopkins, 42–43
Heiden, Eric, 142
Henrietta Maria, Queen, 77
Henson, Jim, 77
Henson, Matthew, 40
Herons, fiction, 78–79
Hershey, Milton, 172
Hiawatha, 140, 142–43
Hiking
  Connecticut, 6–7, 10
  Maine, 52
  Massachusetts, 6–7
  New Jersey, 129
  New York, 135
  Rhode Island, 6–7
Historic bridges
  Connecticut, 5
  Maine, 50
  New Hampshire, 101
  Pennsylvania, 159
Historic buildings

Capitol (Washington, DC), 27, 33, 39
Connecticut, 1–2, 5, 6, 7
Delaware, 23–24
District of Columbia, 27, 28–29, 32, 33, 34–35, 36, 38, 39, 47, 48
Empire State Building, 134
Maryland, 69
Massachusetts, 85
New England, 103
New Hampshire, 109
New Jersey, 121
New York, 134, 136
Pennsylvania, 23–24, 162, 163
Philadelphia (Pa.), 162
  vice president's home, 34–35
White House, 32, 33, 34, 36, 37, 38, 39, 47, 48
Hmong people, Rhode Island, 191, 193
Holmes, Oliver Wendell, 92
Homelessness, 26, 147, 149
Homestead Strike, 182–83
Horses, 201
  Assateague ponies, 69, 80
  fiction, 207, 210, 212
Housatonic River (Conn.), canoeing, 8
Hudson, Henry, 124
Hudson River (N.Y./N.J.), 124, 132, 138, 139
  fiction, 151
Hunting, fiction, 63
Hurricane
  Connecticut (1938), 3–4, 8
  fiction, 62
  Rhode Island, 197
Hutchinson, Anne, 92, 97, 193, 196

Ice cream, 201–202
Ice skating, Heiden, Eric, 142
Indians of North America. *See* American Indians
Inventors
  Bell, Alexander Graham, 41, 141
  Bushnell, David, 12
  Eastman, George, 142
  Edison, Thomas Alva, 123–24
  Fitch, John, 116
  Franklin, Benjamin, 171–72
  Fulton, Robert, 141, 142, 172
  Morse, Samuel, 116, 124
  Renwick, James, 116
  Slater, Samuel, 196–97

Stevens, Robert, 116
Westinghouse, George, 145
Whitney, Eli, 12, 13
Irish Americans, Rhode Island, 192
Iroquois Indians, 137, 146
  Hiawatha, 140, 142–43
  legends, 133, 148
Irving, Washington, 143
Isles of Shoals (Maine/N.Y.), 105, 112
Italian Americans, 10, 186, 194

Jackson, Jesse, 43
Japanese Americans, fiction, 152
Jazz, Ellington, Duke, 42
Jefferson Memorial (Washington, DC), 39
Jellyfish, 20
Jemison, Mary, 172
Jersey Devil, 115
Jewett, Sarah Orne, 57
Jews, Rhode Island, 192, 193
Johnny Appleseed, 169
Johnny Tremain, 96
Johnstown (Pa.) flood, 158, 177, 179
Jones, John Paul, 77
Jones, Mary Harris (Mother), 172–73
Journalists
  Bly, Nellie, 169–70
  Tarbell, Ida, 174–75
Jump rope rhymes, 101
Justices, Marshall, Thurgood, 77–78

Kayaking, fiction, 62
Keene (N.H.), 104
Keller, Helen, 141
Kennebec River (Maine), 55
Kennedy, John F., 92
Kennywood Park (Pittsburgh), 160
Kidd, Captain, 187
King Arthur, fiction, 16
King, Martin Luther, Jr., 40
King Philip, 12, 193, 196
King Philip's War, 8–9, 12–13, 54

Labor unions, 115, 156
  fiction, 180, 181
  Homestead Strike, 182–83
  Mother Jones, 172–73
LaGuardia, Fiorello, 143
Lancaster County (Pa.), 154, 155, 156

Lancaster (Pa.), 175
Langlais, Bernard, 57
Laotian Americans, 193
Larcom, Lucy, 84
Lazarus, Emma, 143
Legends
  American Indian, 2–3, 19, 49, 101, 104, 106, 132–33, 148, 184–85
  animal tales, 157
  Connecticut, 2–3, 8
  cranberries, 19
  Delaware, 19, 20, 24
  Maine, 49, 54
  Maryland, 67, 68
  New Hampshire, 101
  New Jersey, 116–17, 122, 129
  New York, 132–33
  Pennsylvania, 157, 158
  Rhode Island, 184–85
  sea, 2
Lenape Indians, 21–22, 120, 122, 126, 130
Lewis, John, 40
Libraries, 80
Lighthouses, 50, 56, 57, 69, 105, 151, 184, 189
Little Women, 94
Lobstering, 55, 185
  fiction, 63, 65
Long Island Sound (Conn/R.I./N.Y.), 3, 4, 14, 17
Longfellow, Henry Wadsworth, 56, 92
Lowell (Mass.), 84, 108
Lumbering, 50, 106

McAuliffe, Christa, 110
McNair, Ronald, 40
Maine, ix–x, 49–65
  ancient cultures, 55–56
  animals, 51, 52, 57
  archaeology, 55–56
  biographies, 56–57
  fiction, 51, 57–65
  geography, 53, 54, 55, 105
  history, 50, 52, 53–54, 55, 105, 109
  immigrants, 56
  Indians, 49, 53, 54, 65, 104
  legends, 49, 54
  maps, 51
  plants, 52
Maliseet Indians, 65
Manchester (N.H.), 108
Mann, Horace, 92
Maple sugar, 101–02, 113, 202

fiction, 207, 209, 214
Maps
  Chesapeake Bay, 66, 70
  Connecticut, 10
  Delaware, 23
  District of Columbia, 35–36
  Maine, 51
  Maryland, 66, 70, 71
  Massachusetts, 85, 86
  Narragansett Bay, 187–88
  New Hampshire, 102–03, 108–09
  New Jersey, 117–18
  Pennsylvania, 161
  Rhode Island, 187–88
  Vermont, 202
Marine animals
  Chesapeake Bay, 68–69, 82
  Connecticut, 4, 5, 17
  Delaware, 19–20
  eating habits, 20
  Maine, 51, 52
  Rhode Island, 185
Marine plants, 4, 5
  Chesapeake Bay, 68–69, 82
  Delaware, 19–20
  Maine, 52
  Rhode Island, 185
Marshall, Thurgood, 77–78
Marshes. *See* Wetlands
Maryland, x, 66–83
  African Americans, 76
  animals, 68–69, 82
  archaeology, 73
  biographies, 76–78
  economy, 71, 73, 75
  fiction, 78–82
  geography, 71, 73, 74, 75
  government, 67, 71, 72, 82
  history, 66, 67, 71–72, 73–74, 75, 76, 77, 78, 83, 109
  Indians, 72–73, 74, 79
  legends, 67, 68
  maps, 66, 70, 71
  plants, 68–69
  state capital, 70
Massachusetts, x, 84–99
  African Americans, 87, 90–91
  biographies, 84, 89–94
  economy, 85, 86–87, 88
  fiction, 94–99
  geography, 87
  history, 84, 85, 87–88, 89, 90, 91, 94, 99
  Indians, 12–13, 86, 93
  maps, 85, 86
  statistics, 86–87

Massasoit Indians, 12
Mennonites, 155, 176, 181
Mentally ill, Dix, Dorothea, 123
Merrimac Valley (N.H./Mass.), 108
Merrimack River (Connecticut), canoeing, 8
Metacomet Indians, 12
Mice, fiction, 151
Micmac Indians, 53, 65, 190
Military figures
  African American, 11, 39–40, 41, 87, 89
  Davis, Benjamin O., 39–40, 41
  Powell, Colin L., 39–40
  Sampson, Deborah, 93
Military history
  King Philip's War, 8–9, 12–13
  Pequot War, 8–9
  See also Civil War; French and Indian Wars; Revolutionary War
Milk, 201
Millay, Edna St. Vincent, 56
Milling, 84, 187
  Delaware, 22
  fiction, 14, 180, 181, 182
  Maine, 56
  Pennsylvania, 160
  Slater, Samuel, 196–97, 198
Mining, 156, 159
Minuit, Peter, 23
Mohican Indians, legends, 101
Monadnock region (N.H.), 107–08
Monarchy, Henrietta Maria, Queen, 77
Monongahela River (Pa.), 162
Moose, fiction, 57–58, 60, 64
Morgan horse, 201
  fiction, 210
Morison, Samuel Eliot, 93
Morris, Lewis, 122
Morse, Samuel, 116, 124
Moses, Grandma, 143
Mount Katahdin (Maine), 52, 54
Mount Monadnock (N.H.), 107–08, 111
Mount Vernon (N.H.), 109
Mount Washington (N.H.), 107
Mushrooms, 4–5
Music, 27
  Anderson, Marian, 169
  Foster, Stephen, 171
  New Jersey, 128, 129
  New York, 133
  Robeson, Paul, 125
  Sousa, John Philip, 43–44
  Springsteen, Bruce, 125

Star Spangled Banner, 70
Trapp family, 206
Musicians, Ellington, Duke, 42
Muskrats, 20
Mystic Seaport (Conn.), 6

Namath, Joe, 173
Narragansett Bay (R.I.), 187–88, 194
Narragansett Indians, 185, 186, 190
Nashua (N.H.), 108
Nashua River (N.H.), 109
National monuments, Vietnam Veterans (Washington, DC), 32, 33, 35, 37, 38
National parks
  Acadia National Park (Maine), 51, 52
  Assateague National Seashore (Md.), 69
  Cape Cod National Seashore (Mass.), 85
  Independence National Historical Park (Pa.), 166
  Maine, 51, 52
  Maryland, 69
  New Jersey, 116–17
  Pennsylvania, 166
Native Americans. *See* American Indians
Navigation, Bowditch, Nathaniel, 90
New Castle (Del.), 19
New Hampshire, x, 100–13
  archaeology, 108
  biographies, 109–11
  economy, 106, 107, 108, 113
  exploration, 105
  fiction, 111–13
  geography, 53, 103–05, 106, 107–08
  geology, 108
  government, 107, 113
  history, 53, 101, 105, 106, 107, 108, 113
  Indians, 101, 104–05, 110
  legends, 101
  maps, 102–03, 108–09
  statistics, 106
New Haven (Conn.), 15–16
New Jersey, x, 114–31
  African Americans, 127
  agriculture, 119, 120
  animals, 116, 129
  archaeology, 122, 130
  biographies, 115, 123–25

economy, 118, 120, 121, 122, 128, 129, 130
exploration, 124
fiction, 125–27
geography, 117, 119, 120, 121
geology, 121
history, 117, 118, 119, 121, 122, 123, 124, 125, 129, 130
immigrants, 115, 131
Indians, 120, 121, 122, 129, 130
legends, 116–17, 122, 129
maps, 117–18
multiethnic culture, 115, 129, 131
statistics, 127–28
New London (Conn.), 11
New York, x–xi, 132–53
  biographies, 141–45
  exploration, 124
  fiction, 146–52
  geography, 141
  geology, 133
  history, 132, 138–39, 140, 141, 145, 153
  immigrants, 142, 148
  Indians, 132–33, 138, 140, 148
  legends, 132–33, 139
  multiethnic culture, 141
New York City, 132, 134, 135, 136, 137
  fiction, 147, 151–52
Newark (N.J.), 121
Newport (R.I.), 195
Niagara Falls (N.Y.), 137
Nipmuc Indians, 186
North Carolina, Indians, 72–73
Norton, Eleanor Holmes, 40
Nuclear weapons, Oppenheimer, Robert, 143
Nursery rhymes, 19
Nurses, Barton, Clara, 76, 90, 123

Ohio River (Pa.), 162
Oil industry, 158–59
Old Economy Village (Pa.), 166
Old Sturbridge Village (Mass.), 84, 98
Olympic athletes, Heiden, Eric, 142
Oneida Indians, legends, 101
Onondaga Indians, legends, 101
Oppenheimer, Robert, 143
Oral history, 17–18
Organized labor, 115
  fiction, 180, 181
  Homestead Strike, 182–83

Mother Jones, 172–73
Ospreys, fiction, 78–79
Otters, 200
Outward Bound School (Maine), 50–51
Oysters, 69, 72, 82

Painters, 50
  Cassatt, Mary, 171
  Grandma Moses, 143
Passamaquoddi Indians, 49, 65, 101
Peabody, Sophia, 91–92
Peary, Robert, 56, 173
Penacook Village (N.H.), 109
Penn, William, 173
Pennsylvania, xi, 154–83
  agriculture, 162
  animals, 159
  archaeology, 167
  biographies, 169–75
  economy, 156, 158–59, 162, 163, 170, 182
  exploration, 168
  fiction, 175–82, 183
  geography, 165
  government, 165
  history, 161, 162, 163, 164, 165, 166, 167, 173, 182, 183
  immigrants, 168, 183
  Indians, 12–13, 163–64, 167, 168, 172
  legends, 157, 158
  maps, 161, 162, 163
  multiethnic culture, 165
  state capital, 165
  statistics, 162
Pennsylvania Dutch, 154, 179
  fiction, 176, 177, 179, 180–81, 182
  folk art, 160
  See also Amish
Pennsylvania Turnpike, 157
Penobscot Indians, 53, 65, 101
Pequot War, 8–9
Perry, Mathew, 189
Petroleum industry, 158–59
Philadelphia (Pa.), 162, 163, 164, 166
Philip, Sachem of the Wampanoag. *See* King Philip
Photography, Eastman, George, 142
Physical fitness, Outward Bound, 50–51
Physicians, Drew, Charles, 40, 41–42
Pigs, fiction, 212

Pilgrims, 84
  fiction, 95, 97
  Massachusetts, 84, 87, 88
  Thanksgiving, 87–88
Pine Barrens (N.J.), 115, 117, 119, 122
Pioneer life
  Boone, Daniel, 170
  fiction, 14, 59, 62, 176, 178, 180
  Johnny Appleseed, 169
  Pennsylvania, 168
  Vermont, 210
Pirates, 125, 187
Piscataway Indians, 72
Pitcher, Molly, 122, 173–74
Pittsburgh (Pa.), 156, 157, 168
Plants
  Chesapeake Bay, 68–69
  Connecticut, 4–5
  Delaware, 20
  District of Columbia, 27
  estuary, 4
  Rhode Island, 185
  wetland, 4
Plimoth Plantation (Mass.), 84, 87–88
Plymouth (Mass.), 85, 87–88
Pocahontas, 93
Poets
  Dickinson, Emily, 91
  Frost, Robert, 102, 206
  Holmes, Oliver Wendell, 92
  Lazarus, Emma, 143
  Longfellow, Henry Wadsworth, 56, 92
  Millay, Edna St. Vincent, 56
  New Jersey, 117
  Sarton, May, 102
  Thaxter, Celia, 105
  Wheatley, Phillis, 94
  Whittier, John Greenleaf, 94
Polio vaccine, 144
Ponies
  Assateague ponies, 69, 80
  fiction, 58, 212
Portland (Maine), 54
Portuguese Americans, Rhode Island, 192
Potomac River, 32–33
Powell, Colin L., 39–40
Prejudice, 16, 62, 126
Presidents (U.S.), 33, 36, 37, 48
  Adams, John, 89
  Adams, John Quincy, 89–90
  Cleveland, Grover, 123
  Coolidge, Calvin, 206
  Fillmore, Millard, 142

Kennedy, John F., 92
Roosevelt, Franklin Delano, 143
Roosevelt, Theodore, 144
Van Buren, Martin, 145
Washington, George, 44, 45, 145
Wilson, Woodrow, 125
Princeton University (N.J.), 125
Providence (R.I.), 195, 197
Puffins, fiction, 60
Putnam, Israel, 9, 10
Putnam, Rufus, 10
Puzzles, 188, 202, 203

Quakers, fiction, 99, 176, 182

Radioactive waste disposal, 2
Railroads
  Connecticut, 2
  fiction, 80
  New Hampshire, 107
Randolph, A. Philip, 40
Recycling, 9, 186
Religious freedom, 92
  Hutchinson, Anne, 97, 193, 196
Renwick, James, 116
Revere, Paul, 93
Revolutionary War
  African Americans, 89
  Allen, Ethan, 205
  Connecticut, 9, 10
  Copley, John, 90
  Delaware, 22, 24
  fiction, 14, 81, 95, 96–98, 99, 111, 112–13, 125, 126, 146, 149, 206, 210, 214
  Fort Ticonderoga, Battle of, 205
  Hamilton, Alexander, 124
  Hancock, John, 91
  Massachusetts, 87, 89–90, 91, 93
  New Jersey, 118, 121, 122, 130
  Pennsylvania, 168
  Pitcher, Molly, 122, 173–74
  Revere, Paul, 93
  Rhode Island, 192, 194
  Sampson, Deborah, 93
  Stark, John, 110
  Trenton, Battle of, 118
  Valley Forge (Pa.), 164, 168
  Wayne, Anthony, 125
Rhode Island, xi, 184–99
  agriculture, 188
  animals, 185, 186
  biographies, 195–97

economy, 188, 193, 195, 198–99
exploration, 195–96
fiction, 197–98
geography, 188, 193, 195
geology, 188
government, 193, 198–199
history, 19, 109, 187, 188, 190, 191, 192, 193, 194, 195, 196, 199
immigrants, 186, 187, 191, 192
Indians, 184–85, 186, 189–90, 191, 196
legends, 184–85
maps, 187–88
multiethnic culture, 191, 192, 193
plants, 185
statistics, 6, 198–99
Rhymes, 101
Riverkeeper, 132
Robeson, Paul, 125
Robinson, Harriet Hanson, 84
Robinson, Jackie, 12
Rock music, Springsteen, Bruce, 125
Rodney, Caesar, 24
Roosevelt, Eleanor, 143
Roosevelt, Franklin Delano, 143
Roosevelt, Theodore, 144
Rustin, Bayard, 40
Ruth, Babe, 78

Sailing, 14, 64, 184
St. Albans Raid, 207
Salem (Mass.), 84, 95, 98
Salk, Jonas, 144
Salomon, Haym, 174
Sample, Tim, 50
Sampson, Deborah, 93
Saratoga Springs (N.Y.), 136
Sarton, May, 102
Schooners, 67
Scientists
  Bannecker, Benjamin, 41, 76
  Edison, Thomas Alva, 123–24
  Oppenheimer, Robert, 143
  Salk, Jonas, 144
Scoliosis, 125
Sculptor, Langlais, Bernard, 57
Sea animals. *See* Marine animals
Seafaring life, 53, 55
  fiction, 14, 58, 197
  folklore, 2
Seagulls, 20
Seals, 51, 59, 64
Seashells, 19, 60
Seashore

Assateague (Md.), 72, 80
Cape Cod (Mass.), 85
Connecticut, 3, 4, 5
Delaware, 19, 20
  fiction, 24, 98–99
Maine, 50, 51, 52–53
Maryland, 80, 83
New Hampshire, 106
Rhode Island, 185, 188, 189, 198
Seaway Trail (N.Y.), 140
Seaweed, 5
Seneca Indians, legends, 101
Shakers, 100, 113
  fiction, 112, 212
Shipbuilding, 11, 55
Ships, 67, 184
Sign language, 12, 42–43
Singers
  Anderson, Marian, 169
  Robeson, Paul, 125
Slater, Samuel, 196–97, 198
Slavery, 11, 17
  Anthony, Susan B., 141
  Child, Lydia Maria, 90
  Cuffe, Paul, 90
  Douglass, Frederick, 76–77
  fiction, 98
  Forten, Charlotte, 91
  Fortune, Amos, 91, 110
  Truth, Sojourner, 144–45
  Tubman, Harriet, 78, 145
  Underground Railroad, 78, 145, 152, 176
  Wheatley, Phillis, 94
  See also Abolitionists
Smith, John, 93
Society of Friends, fiction, 99, 176, 182
Soldiers, African American, 11
Sousa, John Philip, 43–44
Speed skating, Heiden, Eric, 142
Sports. *See* Athletes; Individual sports
Springsteen, Bruce, 125
Squanto, 93–94
Stagg, Amos, 12
Stamp Act, 9
Stanton, Elizabeth Cady, 144
Star Spangled Banner, 70
Stark, John, 110
Stark (N.H.), 104
State parks
  Maine, 52
  New Jersey, 116–17
  Pennsylvania, 161–62
Statue of Liberty, 134, 140, 141, 143

Steamboats, 141, 142, 172, 203
  fiction, 149–50
Steel industry, 156
  Carnegie, Andrew, 170
  fiction, 182
  Homestead Strike, 182–83
Stengel, Charles, 135
Stevens, Robert, 116
Stevens, Thaddeus, 174
Stiles, Ezra, 11
Stowe, Harriet Beecher, 12, 13
Sturbridge (Mass.), 84, 98
Submarines, Connecticut, 1, 12
Subways, fiction, 147
Sullivan, Major General John, 138
Supreme Court, 26
  Marshall, Thurgood, 77–78
Surgeons, Drew, Charles Richard, 40, 41–42
Survival stories, 16, 54, 82
  computer game, 98
  fiction, 147, 148–49
Swan Island (Maine), 55
Swedish Americans, 23, 24

Talbot, Silas, 187
Tarbell, Ida, 174–75
Taylor's Gut (Del.), 22
Tea tax, 9
Telegraphy, 124
Thanksgiving, 87–88
  fiction, 96, 97, 111, 197
Thaxter, Celia, 105, 112
Theater, Hayes, Helen, 43
Thoreau, Henry David, 94
Thorpe, Jim, 175
Tidal marshes. *See* Wetlands
Titusville (Pa.), 158–59
Tongue twisters, 101
Trains. *See* Railroads
Trapp family, 206
Trees, District of Columbia, 27
Trenton, (N.J.), 123
Trivia, 36–37, 76, 119, 165, 194
Truth, Sojourner, 144–45
Tubman, Harriet, 78, 145
Tudor, Tasha, 110–11
Tuscarora Indians, legends, 101
Twain, Mark, 12, 13
Two Trees, Joe, 145

Uncle Tom's Cabin, 13
Underground Railroad, 78, 145, 152, 176
U.S. Naval Academy (Md.), 67

Valley Forge (Pa.), 164, 168, 179

Van Buren, Martin, 145
Vermont, xi, 200–14
  biographies, 204–06
  exploration, 205–06
  fiction, 206–14
  geography, 53, 105, 202, 204
  history, 53, 105, 106, 109, 202, 203, 204, 205, 207
  Indians, 104
  maps, 202
Veterinary medicine, 201
Vietnam Veterans Memorial (Washington, DC), 32, 33, 35, 37, 38, 45
Vietnamese Americans, 187, 193
Virginia, Indians, 72–73

Walker, Madame C. J., 40
Wampanoag Indians, 12–13, 93–94, 190, 191, 196
  legends, 185
War of 1812, 25, 38, 70, 72
  fiction, 45, 80, 81
Washington, DC. *See* District of Columbia
Washington, George, 44–45, 145
  fiction, 179–80
Waste management
  Connecticut, 2, 9
  Rhode Island, 186
Water pollution, 78, 81, 95, 132
Watergate scandal, 32
Watermen, 69, 72, 81
Waters, Maxine, 40
Watkins Glen (N.Y.), 136
Wayne, Anthony, 125
Webster, Noah, 12
West, Benjamin, 175
Westinghouse, George, 145
Wetlands
  birds, 5
  Connecticut, 3, 4, 5
  Delaware, 19
  Maryland, 66
Whales, fiction, 62, 63
Whaling
  Connecticut, 11
  Hudson River, 138
  Maine, 49
  New Bedford (Mass.), 85
  Rhode Island, 186
Wheatley, Phillis, 94
Whistler, James, 94
White House (Washington, DC), 32, 33, 34, 36, 37, 38, 39, 47, 48
  fiction, 45

White Mountains (N.H.), 104, 105
Whitney, Eli, 12, 13
Whittier, John Greenleaf, 94
Wilderness survival, 54
  fiction, 147, 148–49
Wildlife conservation, fiction, 60, 176
Wilkins, Roy, 40
Williams, Roger, 195–96
Wilmington (Del.), 22
Wilson, Woodrow, 125
Winfrey, Oprah, 40
Witchcraft
  Connecticut, 1
  fiction, 16, 95, 98
  Salem (Mass.), 84
Witherspoon, John, 122
Women
  Adams, Abigail, 89
  African American, 40
  Alcott, Louisa May, 90, 94, 111, 169
  Anderson, Marian, 169
  Anthony, Susan B., 141
  Bagley, Sarah G., 84
  Barton, Clara, 76, 90, 123
  Blunt, Susan Baker, 109–10
  Bly, Nellie, 169–70
  Burgess, Abbie, 56
  Carson, Rachel, 170–71
  Cassatt, Mary, 171
  Child, Lydia Maria, 90
  Chung, Connie, 40–41
  Coppin, Fannie Jackson, 40
  DeMille, Agnes, 142
  diaries, 24, 53
  Dickinson, Emily, 91
  District of Columbia, 40
  Dix, Dorothea, 123
  Dodge, Mary Mapes, 123
  fiction, 61, 97–98, 126, 150
  Forten, Charlotte, 91
  Fuller, Margaret, 91
  Grandma Moses, 143
  Hayes, Helen, 43
  Hutchinson, Anne, 92, 97, 193, 196
  Jemison, Mary, 172
  Jewett, Sarah Orne, 57
  Jones, Mary Harris (Mother), 172–73
  Larcom, Lucy, 84
  McAuliffe, Christa, 110
  Maine, 56, 57
  New Jersey, 115, 127
  Norton, Eleanor Holmes, 40
  Peabody, Sophia, 91–92
  Pitcher, Molly, 122
  Pocahontas, 93
  Robinson, Harriet Hanson, 84
  Roosevelt, Eleanor, 143
  Sampson, Deborah, 93
  Sarton, May, 102
  Stanton, Elizabeth Cady, 144
  Tarbell, Ida, 174–75
  Truth, Sojourner, 144–45
  Tubman, Harriet, 78, 145
  Tudor, Tasha, 110–11
  Walker, Madame C. J., 40
  Waters, Maxine, 40
  Wheatley, Phillis, 94
  Winfrey, Oprah, 40
Women's rights
  Anthony, Susan B., 141
  fiction, 150
  Fuller, Margaret, 91
  New Jersey, 115
  Stanton, Elizabeth Cady, 144
Woodchucks, 186
Woolworth, Frank, 175
Wooster, David, 10
Wright, Frank Lloyd, 160
Wyeth, Andrew, 50, 175

Yale University (Conn.), 9, 11
Young, Whitney, 40

Zenger, Peter, 145
Zoology. *See* Animals

www.ingramcontent.com/pod-product-compliance
Lightning Source LLC
Chambersburg PA
CBHW080536300426
44111CB00017B/2751